HISTORY
OF
CLAY
COUNTY
MISSOURI

WRITTEN AND COMPILED

FROM THE MOST AUTHENTIC OFFICIAL AND PRIVATE SOURCES,

INCLUDING A HISTORY OF

TOWNSHIPS, TOWNS AND VILLAGES

ST. LOUIS:
NATIONAL HISTORICAL COMPANY.
1885.

Reprinted 2016

ii

CONTENTS.

HISTORY OF MISSOURI.

CHAPTER I.

LOUISIANA PURCHASE.

Brief Historical Sketch 1–7

CHAPTER II.

DESCRIPTIVE AND GEOGRAPHICAL.

Name — Extent — Surface — Rivers — Timber — Climate — Prairies — Soils — Population by Counties 7–13

CHAPTER III.

GEOLOGY OF MISSOURI.

Classification of Rocks — Quatenary Formation — Tertiary — Cretacious — Carboniferous — Devonian — Silurian — Azoic — Economic Geology — Coal — Iron — Lead — Copper — Zinc — Building Stone — Marble — Gypsum — Lime — Clays — Paints — Springs — Water Power 13–21

CHAPTER IV.

TITLE AND EARLY SETTLEMENTS.

Title to Missouri Lands — Right of Discovery — Title of France and Spain — Cession to the United States — Territorial Changes — Treaties with Indians — First Settlement — Ste. Genevieve and New Bourbon — St. Louis — When Incorporated — Potosi — St. Charles — Portage des Sioux — New Madrid — St. Francois County — Perry — Mississippi — Loutre Island — " Boone's Lick " — Cote Sans Dessein — Howard County — Some First Things — Counties — When Organized . 21–27

CHAPTER V.

TERRITORIAL ORGANIZATION.

Organization 1812 — Council — House of Representatives — William Clark First Territorial Governor — Edward Hempstead First Delegate — Spanish Grants — First General Assembly — Proceedings — Second Assembly — Proceedings — Population of Territory — Vote of Territory — Rufus Easton — Absent Members — Third Assembly — Proceedings — Application for Admission 27–31

CHAPTER VI.

Application of Missouri to be Admitted into the Union — Agitation of the Slavery Question — "Missouri Compromise" — Constitutional Convention of 1820 — Constitution Presented to Congress — Further Resistance to Admission — Mr. Clay and his Committee make Report — Second Compromise — Missouri Admitted   31–37

CHAPTER VII.

MISSOURI AS A STATE.

First Election for Governor and other State Officers — Senators and Representatives to General Assembly — Sheriffs and Coroners — U. S. Senators — Representatives in Congress — Supreme Court Judges — Counties Organized — Capital Moved to St. Charles — Official Record of Territorial and State Officers   .   .   .   37–43

CHAPTER VIII.

CIVIL WAR IN MISSOURI.

Fort Sumpter Fired Upon — Call for 75,000 Men — Gov. Jackson Refuses to Furnish a Man — U. S. Arsenal at Liberty, Mo., Seized — Proclamation of Gov. Jackson — General Order No. 7 — Legislature Convenes — Camp Jackson Organized — Sterling Price Appointed Major-General — Frost's Letter to Lyon — Lyon's Letter to Frost — Surrender of Camp Jackson — Proclamation of Gen. Harney — Conference between Price and Harney — Harney Superseded by Lyon — Second Conference — Gov. Jackson Burns the Bridges behind Him — Proclamation of Gov. Jackson — Gen. Blair Takes Possession of Jefferson City — Proclamation of Lyon — Lyon at Springfield — State Offices Declared Vacant — Gen. Fremont Assumes Command — Proclamation of Lieut.-Gov. Reynolds — Proclamation of Jeff. Thompson and Gov. Jackson — Death of Gen. Lyon — Succeeded by Sturgis — Proclamation of McCulloch and Gamble — Martial Law Declared — Second Proclamation of Jeff. Thompson — President Modifies Fremon't Order — Fremont Relieved by Hunter — Proclamation of Price — Hunter's Order of Assessment — Hunter Declares Martial Law — Order Relating to Newspapers — Halleck Succeeds Hunter — Halleck's Order No. 18 — Similar Order by Halleck — Boone County *Standard* Confiscated — Execution of Prisoners at Macon and Palmyra — Gen. Ewing's Order No. 11 — Gen. Rosecrans Takes Command — Massacre at Centralia — Death of Bill Anderson — Gen. Dodge Succeeds Gen. Rosecrans — List of Battles   .   .   43–53

CHAPTER IX.

EARLY MILITARY RECORD.

Black Hawk War — Mormon Difficulties — Florida War — Mexican War   .   53–59

CHAPTER X.

AGRICULTURE AND MATERIAL WEALTH.

Missouri as an Agricultural State — The Different Crops — Live Stock — Horses — Mules — Milch Cows — Oxen and Other Cattle — Sheep — Hogs — Comparisons — Missouri Adapted to Live Stock — Cotton — Broom Corn and Other Products — Fruits — Berries — Grapes — Railroads — First Neigh of the " Iron Horse " in Missouri — Names of Railroads — Manufactures — Great Bridge at St. Louis   59–65

iv

CHAPTER XI.

EDUCATION.

Public School System — Public School System of Missouri — Lincoln Institute — Officers of Public School System — Certificates of Teachers — University of Missouri — Schools — Colleges — Institutions of Learning — Location — Libraries — Newspapers and Periodicals — No. of School Children — Amount Expended — Value of Grounds and Buildings — "The Press" 65–73

CHAPTER XII.

RELIGIOUS DENOMINATIONS.

Baptist Church — Its History — Congregational — When Founded — Its History — Christian Church — Its History — Cumberland Presbyterian Church — Its History — Methodist Episcopal Church — Its History — Presbyterian Church — Its History — Protestant Episcopal Church — Its History — United Presbyterian Church — Its History — Unitarian Church — Its History — Roman Catholic Church — Its History 73–79

CHAPTER XIII.

ADMINISTRATION OF GOVERNOR CRITTENDEN.

Nomination and Election of Thomas T. Crittenden — Personal Mention — Marmaduke's Candidacy — Stirring Events — Hannibal and St. Joseph Railroad — Death of Jesse James — The Fords — Pardon of the Gamblers 79–85

HISTORY OF CLAY COUNTY, MISSOURI.

CHAPTER I.

EARLY HISTORY TO THE ORGANIZATION OF THE COUNTY.

The Indians — The French and Spanish — First Exploration and Settlement by Americans — The First American Settlers in Clay — An Indian Fight — Organization of Clay County 87–100

CHAPTER II.

HISTORY OF THE COUNTY FROM 1822 TO 1830.

General Historical Sketch from 1822 to 1830 — First County Courts — First Circuit Courts — Three Indian Horse Thieves — First Murder Case — Execution of the Murderess — The County in 1822 as Described by Dr. Beck — Martin Palmer, the "Ring-Tailed Painter" — Miscellaneous Items — Liberty Township — Roads and Ferries — Important County Court Proceedings in 1826 — Miscellaneous — Valuation of Property in 1829 — The Indian Alarm of 1828 — The Expedition into the Platte Country 100–118

v

CHAPTER III.

HISTORY OF THE COUNTY FROM 1830 TO 1840.

General Sketch of the County from 1830 to 1840 — Early Days in Clay County — The Deep Snow of 1830 — Building the First Court House — The First Jail — During the Black Hawk War — Origin of the Platte Purchase — The "Hetherly War" — Clay County in 1836 — The Mormon War 118–136

CHAPTER IV.

HISTORY OF THE COUNTY FROM 1840 TO 1850.

The Political Canvass of 1840 and 1844 — Elections of 1846 — The Great Flood of 1844 — Miscellaneous — Negro Killing — Tom Haggerty's Case — Clay County in the Mexican War — List of Capt. Moss's Company, and Sketch of its Services — The Political Canvass of 1848 — The Jackson Resolutions — Benton's Appeal — His Meeting at Liberty 136–152

CHAPTER V.

FROM 1850 TO THE TROUBLES IN KANSAS.

The California Gold Fever — The Political Canvass of 1850 — The Attempted Murde of Mrs. Dinah Allen — Lynching of Her Would-be Assassins — The Cholera — Elections of 1852, 1854, 1856 and 1858 — The Know Nothings — Tragedies — The Great Smithville Melee and Mob in 1854 — Murder of Wm. O. Russell, Esq., by "Pete" Lightburne — Lynching of "Pete." 152–168

CHAPTER VI.

DURING THE KANSAS TROUBLES UP TO 1861.

The Kansas Troubles — Clay County's Interest in Kansas Affairs — Sketch of the Situation in Kansas Territory Upon its Organization — The Election in 1854 — Clay Furnishes Her Quota of Voters — The "Sons of the South" — Election in the Spring of 1855 — The Parkville Mob Indorsed — The "Wakarusa War" — Seizure of the Liberty Arsenal by the Clay County Volunteers — Maj. Leonard's Report — The Arms Returned *Minus* What Were Retained — County Seat Fight in Kansas — Emigrants to Kansas Turned Back — End of the Fight — The Free Soilers Win — Explanation of the Course of Clay County. *Up to 1861* — Census — Miscellaneous — The Present Court-House — The Kansas City and Cameron Railroad — The Presidential and Gubernatorial Campaigns of 1860 — After the Election — Trouble Brewing 168–190

CHAPTER VII.

HISTORY OF THE COUNTY DURING 1861.

The Legislature of 1861 — Election of Delegates to the State Convention — The Work of the Convention — After Fort Sumpter — Capture of the Liberty Arsenal — Maj. Grant's Reports — After the Arsenal's Seizure — Preparing for War in Earnest — Organization of Military Companies — Gen. Doniphan Declines a Military Appointment — Departure of the Secession Companies for the War — The First Federal Troops — Events of the Summer and Early Fall of 1861 — Proclamation of Gen.

Stein — Rallying to His Standard — The Battle of Blue Mills — The Killed and Wounded — Reports of the Leaders — Col. Saunders, Hon. D. R. Atchison, Col. Scott — List of Killed and Wounded in the Third Iowa — War Incidents of the Fall and Winter of 1861 — The Neosho Secession Ordinance . . . 190-222

CHAPTER VIII.

DURING THE YEAR 1862.

The "Gamble Oath" — It is Taken by a Majority of the County Officials — Miscellaneous — Parker's Raid on Liberty — The Reign of Penick — Organization of the Enrolled Militia — Miscellaneous Military Matters — Nov. Election, 1862   224-234

CHAPTER IX.

DURING THE YEAR 1863.

Miscellaneous War Items of the Early Spring — The Raid on Missouri City and Killing of Capt. Sessions — Other War Incidents — After the Lawrence Raid — Threatened Invasion from Kansas Prevented — The "Paw Paw Militia," and Certain Military Incidents in This County During 1862 and 1863 — Interesting Testimony of Col. J. H. Moss — November Election — Sons of Malta — Military Murders. . 234-246

CHAPTER X.

DURING THE YEAR 1864.

Jayhawker raid on Missouri City — The Federal Draft — Bushwhacker's Raid — Fletch Taylors' First Raid, and Murder of Bond and Daily — He Kills the Bigelows — His Letter to Capt. Garth — His Skirmish on Fishing River with Capt. Kemper — Miscellaneous War Items — Ford's and Jennison's Visit which They were not Invited to Repeat — Bill Anderson — Other War Incidents — Census — Presidential Election 246-256

CHAPTER XI.

SOME LEADING INCIDENTS FROM 1865 TO 1885.

Miscellaneous Military Incidents in 1865 — The Last of the Bushwhackers — Surrender of Oll. Shepherd's Band — The Drake Constitution — Robbing of the Clay County Savings Bank — Political Canvasses — The Railroads of Clay County — Hanging of Sam Walker — Census Statistics — The James Brothers. . 256-271

CHAPTER XII.

MISCELLANEOUS.

Clay County Schools — County Teachers' Institute — William Jewell College, etc. 271-279

CHAPTER XIII.

LIBERTY TOWNSHIP.

Position and Description — Early Settlers — Liberty Landing — Country Churches — City of Liberty — First Incorporation — Liberty in 1846 — Churches of Liberty — Secret Societies — Biographical 279-374

CHAPTER XIV.

FISHING RIVER TOWNSHIP.

Position and Description — Early History, First Settlers, etc. — Voters at First Election in Township — Country Churches — Missouri City — Its ___ ler and Subsequent Career — Known formerly as Richfield — Murder of V___ ___ndon — Killing of two men named Titus by G. S. Elgin — Churches and Lodges in Missouri City — History of Excelsior Springs — When Surveyed and Started — Buildings Erected — Its Prosperity during 1881 — Incorporation — The Springs — The Medicinal and Healing Properties which They Possess — Churches at Excelsior Springs — G. A. R. Lodge — Prathersville — Location, etc. — Fishing River Baptist Church — Biographical 374–420

CHAPTER XV.

PLATTE TOWNSHIP.

Position and Description — Early Settlements — Organization — First Justices — First Post-office — Tragedies of the Civil War — Churches in the County — Town of Smithville — "Yankee" Smith and his Eccentric Characteristics — His Death and the Epitaph on his Tombstone — Incorporation — Churches at Smithville — Odd Fellows' Lodge — Gosneyville — Churches — Biographical . . . 420–448

CHAPTER XVI.

KEARNEY TOWNSHIP.

Boundaries, General Surface, etc. — Early Settlements — Tragedies of the Civil War — County Churches — Town of Kearney — Centreville — Location of Kearney and for Whom Named — Incorporation — Ker___ ey's Churches — Holt — Location of this Village — Church and Lodge Records — ___ graphical 448–498

CHAPTER XVII.

WASHINGTON TOWNSHIP.

Location and Physical Features — Hamlets of Greenville and Claysville — Early History — Organization — Mount Vernon Missionary Baptist Church — Biographical 498–507

CHAPTER XVIII.

GALLATIN TOWNSHIP.

Boundary and Physical Features — Villages in this Township — Barry — Harlem — Moscow — Arnold's Station — Minaville — Churches — Biographical . 507–530

viii

HISTORY OF MISSOURI.

CHAPTER I.

LOUISIANA PURCHASE.

BRIEF HISTORICAL SKETCH.

The purchase in 1803 of the vast territory west of the Mississippi River, by the United States, extending through Oregon to the Pacific coast and south to the Dominions of Mexico, constitutes the most important event that ever occurred in the history of the nation.

It gave to our Republic additional room for that expansion and stupendous growth, to which it has since attained, in all that makes it strong and enduring, and forms the seat of an empire, from which will radiate an influence for good unequaled in the annals of time. In 1763, the immense region of country, known at that time as Louisiana, was ceded to Spain by France. By a secret article, in the treaty of St. Ildefonso, concluded in 1800, Spain ceded it back to France. Napoleon, at that time, coveted the island of St. Domingo, not only because of the value of its products, but more especially because its location in the Gulf of Mexico would, in a military point of view, afford him a fine field whence he could the more effectively guard his newly-acquired possessions. Hence he desired this cession by Spain should be kept a profound secret until he succeeded in reducing St. Domingo to submission. In this undertaking, however, his hopes were blasted, and so great was his disappointment that he apparently became indifferent to the advantages to be secured to France from his purchase of Louisiana.

In 1803 he sent out Laussat as prefect of the colony, who gave the people of Louisiana the first intimation they had that they had once more become the subjects of France. This was the occasion of great rejoicing among the inhabitants, who were Frenchmen in their origin, habits, manners, and customs.

Mr. Jefferson, then President of the United States, on being informed of the retrocession, immediately dispatched instructions to Robert Livingston, the American Minister at Paris, to make known to Napoleon that the occupancy of New Orleans, by his government, would not only endanger the friendly relations existing between the two nations, but, perhaps, oblige the United States to make common cause with England, his bitterest and most dreaded enemy; as the possession of the city by France would give her command of the Mississippi, which was the only outlet for the produce of the Western States, and give her also control of the Gulf of Mexico, so necessary to the protection of American commerce. Mr. Jefferson was so fully impressed with the idea that the occupancy of New Orleans, by France, would bring about a conflict of interests between the two nations, which would finally culminate in an open rupture, that he urged Mr. Livingston, to not only insist upon the free navigation of the Mississippi, but to negotiate for the purchase of the city and the surrounding country.

The question of this negotiation was of so grave a character to the United States that the President appointed Mr. Monroe, with full power to act in conjunction with Mr. Livingston. Ever equal to all emergencies, and prompt in the cabinet, as well as in the field, Napoleon came to the conclusion that, as he could not well defend his occupancy of New Orleans, he would dispose of it, on the best terms possible. Before, however, taking final action in the matter, he summoned two of his Ministers, and addressed them follows : —

"I am fully sensible of the value of Louisiana, and it was my wish to repair the error of the French diplomatists who abandoned it in 1763. I have scarcely recovered it before I run the risk of losing it; but if I am obliged to give it up, it shall hereafter cost more to those who force me to part with it, than to those to whom I shall yield it. The English have despoiled France of all her northern possessions in America, and now they covet those of the South. I am determined that they shall not have the Mississippi. Although Louisiana is but a trifle compared to their vast possessions in other parts of the globe, yet, judging from the vexation they have manifested on seeing it return to the power of France, I am certain that

HISTORY OF MISSOURI

their first object will be to gain possession of it. They will probably commence the war in that quarter. They have twenty vessels in the Gulf of Mexico, and our affairs in St. Domingo are daily getting worse since the death of LeClerc. The conquest of Louisiana might be easily made, and I have not a moment to lose in getting out of their reach. I am not sure but that they have already begun an attack upon it. Such a measure would be in accordance with their habits; and in their place I should not wait. I am inclined, in order to deprive them of all prospect of ever possessing it, to cede it to the United States. Indeed, I can hardly say that I cede it, for I do not yet possess it; and if I wait but a short time my enemies may leave me nothing but an empty title to grant to the Republic I wish to conciliate. I consider the whole colony as lost, and I believe that in the hands of this rising power it will be more useful to the political and even commercial interests of France than if I should attempt to retain it. Let me have both your opinions on the subject."

One of his Ministers approved of the contemplated cession, but the other opposed it. The matter was long and earnestly discussed by them, before the conference was ended. The next day, Napoleon sent for the Minister who had agreed with him, and said to him: —

"The season for deliberation is over. I have determined to renounce Louisiana. I shall give up not only New Orleans, but the whole colony, without reservation. That I do not undervalue Louisiana, I have sufficiently proved, as the object of my first treaty with Spain was to recover it. But though I regret parting with it, I am convinced it would be folly to persist in trying to keep it. I commission you, therefore, to negotiate this affair with the envoys of the United States. Do not wait the arrival of Mr. Monroe, but go this very day and confer with Mr. Livingston. Remember, however, that I need ample funds for carrying on the war, and I do not wish to commence it by levying new taxes. For the last century France and Spain have incurred great expense in the improvement of Louisiana, for which her trade has never indemnified them. Large sums have been advanced to different companies, which have never been returned to the treasury. It is fair that I should require repayment for these. Were I to regulate my demands by the importance of this territory to the United States, they would be unbounded; but, being obliged to part with it, I shall be moderate in my terms. Still, remember, I must have fifty millions of francs, and I will not consent to take less.

HISTORY OF MISSOURI

I would rather make some desperate effort to preserve this fine country."

That day the negotiations commenced. Mr. Monroe reached Paris on the 12th of April, 1803, and the two representatives of the United States, after holding a private interview, announced that they were ready to treat for the entire territory. On the 30th of April, the treaty was signed, and on the 21st of October, of the same year, Congress ratified the treaty. The United States were to pay $11,250,000, and her citizens were to be compensated for some illegal captures, to the amount of $3,750,000, making in the aggregate the sum of $15,000,000, while it was agreed that the vessels and merchandise of France and Spain should be admitted into all the ports of Louisiana free of duty for twelve years. Bonaparte stipulated in favor of Louisiana, that it should be, as soon as possible, incorporated into the Union, and that its inhabitants should enjoy the same rights, privileges and immunities as other citizens of the United States, and the clause giving to them these benefits was drawn up by Bonaparte, who presented it to the plenipotentiaries with these words:—

"Make it known to the people of Louisiana, that we regret to part with them; that we have stipulated for all the advantages they could desire; and that France, in giving them up, has insured to them the greatest of all. They could never have prospered under any European government as they will when they become independent. But while they enjoy the privileges of liberty let them remember that they are French, and preserve for their mother country that affection which a common origin inspires."

Complete satisfaction was given to both parties in the terms of the treaty. Mr. Livingston said:—

"I consider that from this day the United States takes rank with the first powers of Europe, and now she has entirely escaped from the power of England," and Bonaparte expressed a similar sentiment when he said: "By this cession of territory I have secured the power of the United States, and given to England a maritime rival, who, at some future time, will humble her pride."

These were prophetic words, for within a few years afterward the British met with a signal defeat, on the plains of the very territory of which the great Corsican had been speaking.

From 1800, the date of the cession made by Spain, to 1803, when it was purchased by the United States, no change had been made by

HISTORY OF MISSOURI

the French authorities in the jurisprudence of the Upper and Lower Louisiana, and during this period the Spanish laws remained in full force, as the laws of the entire province; a fact which is of interest to those who would understand the legal history and some of the present laws of Missouri.

On December 20th, 1803, Gens. Wilkinson and Claiborne, who were jointly commissioned to take possession of the territory for the United States, arrived in the city of New Orleans at the head of the American forces. Laussat, who had taken possession but twenty days previously as the prefect of the colony, gave up his command, and the star-spangled banner supplanted the tri-colored flag of France. The agent of France, to take possession of Upper Louisiana from the Spanish authorities, was Amos Stoddard, captain of artillery in the United States service. He was placed in possession of St. Louis on the 9th of March, 1804, by Charles Dehault Delassus, the Spanish commandant, and on the following day he transferred it to the United States. The authority of the United States in Missouri dates from this day.

From that moment the interests of the people of the Mississippi Valley became identified. They were troubled no more with uncertainties in regard to free navigation. The great river, along whose banks they had planted their towns and villages, now afforded them a safe and easy outlet to the markets of the world. Under the protecting ægis of a government, republican in form, and having free access to an almost boundless domain, embracing in its broad area the diversified climates of the globe, and possessing a soil unsurpassed for fertility, beauty of scenery and wealth of minerals, they had every incentive to push on their enterprises and build up the land wherein their lot had been cast.

In the purchase of Louisiana, it was known that a great empire had been secured as a heritage to the people of our country, for all time to come, but its grandeur, its possibilities, its inexhaustible resources and the important relations it would sustain to the nation and the world were never dreamed of by even Mr. Jefferson and his adroit and accomplished diplomatists.

The most ardent imagination never conceived of the progress which would mark the history of the "Great West." The adventurous pioneer, who fifty years ago pitched his tent upon its broad prairies, or threaded the dark labyrinths of its lonely forests, little thought that a mighty tide of physical and intellectual strength, would so rapidly

HISTORY OF MISSOURI

flow on in his footsteps, to populate, build up and enrich the domain which he had conquered.

Year after year, civilization has advanced further and further, until at length the mountains, the hills and the valleys, and even the rocks and the caverns, resound with the noise and din of busy millions.

> "I beheld the westward marches
> Of the unknown crowded nations.
> All the land was full of people,
> Restless, struggling, toiling, striving,
> Speaking many tongues, yet feeling
> But one heart-beat in their bosoms.
> In the woodlands rang their axes;
> Smoked their towns in all the valleys;
> Over all the lakes and rivers
> Rushed their great canoes of thunder."

In 1804, Congress, by an act passed in April of the same year, divided Louisiana into two parts, the "Territory of Orleans," and the "District of Louisiana," known as "Upper Louisiana." This district included all that portion of the old province, north of "Hope Encampment," on the Lower Mississippi, and embraced the present State of Missouri, and all the western region of country to the Pacific Ocean, and all below the forty-ninth degree of north latitude not claimed by Spain.

As a matter of convenience, on March 26th, 1804, Missouri was placed within the jurisdiction of the government of the Territory of Indiana, and its government put in motion by Gen. William H. Harrison, then governor of Indiana. In this he was assisted by Judges Griffin, Vanderburg and Davis, who established in St. Louis what were called Courts of Common Pleas. The District of Louisiana was regularly organized into the Territory of Louisiana by Congress, March 3, 1805, and President Jefferson appointed Gen. James Wilkinson, Governor, and Frederick Bates, Secretary. The Legislature of the territory was formed by Governor Wilkinson and Judges R. J. Meigs and John B. C. Lucas. In 1807, Governor Wilkinson was succeeded by Captain Meriwether Lewis, who had become famous by reason of his having made the expedition up the Missouri with Clark. Governor Lewis committed suicide in 1809 and President Madison appointed Gen. Benjamin Howard of Lexington, Kentucky, to fill his place. Gen. Howard resigned October 25, 1810, to enter the war of 1812, and died in St. Louis, in 1814. Captain William Clark, of Lewis and Clark's expedition, was appointed Governor in 1810, to succeed Gen.

HISTORY OF MISSOURI

Howard, and remained in office until the admission of the State into the Union, in 1821.

The portions of Missouri which were settled, for the purposes of local government were divided into four districts. Cape Girardeau was the first, and embraced the territory between Tywappity Bottom and Apple Creek. Ste. Genevieve, the second, embraced the territory from Apple Creek to the Meramec River. St. Louis, the third, embraced the territory between the Meramec and Missouri Rivers. St. Charles, the fourth, included the settled territory, between the Missouri and Mississippi Rivers. The total population of these districts at that time, was 8,670, including slaves. The population of the district of Louisiana, when ceded to the United States was 10.120.

CHAPTER II.

DESCRIPTIVE AND GEOGRAPHICAL.

Name — Extent — Surface — Rivers — Timber — Climate — Prairies — Soils — Population by Counties.

NAME.

The name Missouri is derived from the Indian tongue and signifies muddy.

EXTENT.

Missouri is bounded on the north by Iowa (from which it is separated for about thirty miles on the northeast, by the Des Moines River), and on the east by the Mississippi River, which divides it from Illinois, Kentucky and Tennessee, and on the west by the Indian Territory, and the States of Kansas and Nebraska. The State lies (with the exception of a small projection between the St. Francis and the Mississippi Rivers, which extends to 36°), between 36° 30' and 40° 36' north latitude, and between 12° 2' and 18° 51' west longitude from Washington.

The extreme width of the State east and west, is about 348 miles; its width on its northern boundary, measured from its northeast corner along the Iowa line, to its intersection with the Des Moines

HISTORY OF MISSOURI

River, is about 210 miles; its width on its southern boundary is about 288 miles. Its average width is about 235 miles.

The length of the State north and south, not including the narrow strip between the St. Francis and Mississippi Rivers, is about 282 miles. It is about 450 miles from its extreme northwest corner to its southeast corner, and from the northeast corner to the southwest corner, it is about 230 miles. These limits embrace an area of 65,350 square miles, or 41,824,000 acres, being nearly as large as England, and the States of Vermont and New Hampshire.

SURFACE.

North of the Missouri, the State is level or undulating, while the portion south of that river (the larger portion of the State) exhibits a greater variety of surface. In the southeastern part is an extensive marsh, reaching beyond the State into Arkansas. The remainder of this portion between the Mississippi and Osage Rivers is rolling, and gradually rising into a hilly and mountainous district, forming the out-skirts of the Ozark Mountains.

Beyond the Osage River, at some distance, commences a vast ex-panse of prairie land which stretches away towards the Rocky Moun-tains. The ridges forming the Ozark chain extend in a northeast and southwest direction, separating the waters that flow northeast into the Missouri from those that flow southeast into the Mississippi River.

RIVERS.

No State in the Union enjoys better facilities for navigation than Missouri. By means of the Mississippi River, which stretches along her entire eastern boundary, she can hold commercial intercourse with the most northern territory and State in the Union; with the whole valley of the Ohio; with many of the Atlantic States, and with the Gulf of Mexico.

> "Ay, gather Europe's royal rivers all—
> The snow-swelled Neva, with an Empire's weight
> On her broad breast, she yet may overwhelm;
> Dark Danube, hurrying, as by foe pursued,
> Through shaggy forests and by palace walls,
> To hide its terror in a sea of gloom;
> The castled Rhine, whose vine-crowned waters flow,
> The fount of fable and the source of song;
> The rushing Rhone, in whose cerulean depths
> The loving sky seems wedded with the wave;
> The yellow Tiber, chok'd with Roman spoils.

> A dying miser shrinking 'neath his gold;
> The Seine, where fashion glasses the fairest forms;
> The Thames that bears the riches of the world;
> Gather their waters in one ocean mass,
> Our Mississippi rolling proudly on,
> Would sweep them from its path, or swallow up,
> Like Aaron's rod, these streams of fame and song."

By the Missouri River she can extend her commerce to the Rocky Mountains, and receive in return the products which will come in the course of time, by its multitude of tributaries.

The Missouri River coasts the northwest line of the State for about 250 miles, following its windings, and then flows through the State, a little south of east, to its junction with the Mississippi. The Missouri River receives a number of tributaries within the limits of the State, the principal of which are the Nodaway, Platte, Grand and Chariton from the north, and the Blue, Sniabar, Lamine, Osage and Gasconade from the south. The principal tributaries of the Mississippi within the State, are the Salt River, north, and the Meramec River south of the Missouri.

The St. Francis and White Rivers, with their branches, drain the southeastern part of the State, and pass into Arkansas. The Osage is navigable for steamboats for more than 175 miles. There are a vast number of smaller streams, such as creeks, branches and rivers, which water the State in all directions.

Timber. — Not more towering in their sublimity were the cedars of ancient Lebanon, nor more precious in their utility were the almug-trees of Ophir, than the native forests of Missouri. The river bottoms are covered with a luxuriant growth of oak, ash, elm, hickory, cotton-wood, linn, white and black walnut, and in fact, all the varieties found in the Atlantic and Eastern States. In the more barren districts may be seen the white and pin oak, and in many places a dense growth of pine. The crab apple, papaw and persimmon are abundant, as also the hazel and pecan.

Climate. — The climate of Missouri is, in general, pleasant and salubrious. Like that of North America, it is changeable, and subject to sudden and sometimes extreme changes of heat and cold; but it is decidedly milder, taking the whole year through, than that of the same latitudes east of the mountains. While the summers are not more oppressive than they are in the corresponding latitudes on and near the Atlantic coast, the winters are shorter, and very much milder, except during the month of February, which has many days of pleasant sunshine.

Prairies. — Missouri is a prairie State, especially that portion of it north and northwest of the Missouri River. These prairies, along the water courses, abound with the thickest and most luxurious belts of timber, while the " rolling " prairies occupy the higher portions of the country, the descent generally to the forests or bottom lands being over only declivities. Many of these prairies, however, exhibit a gracefully waving surface, swelling and sinking with an easy slope, and a full, rounded outline, equally avoiding the unmeaning horizontal surface and the interruption of abrupt or angular elevations.

These prairies often embrace extensive tracts of land, and in one or two instances they cover an area of fifty thousand acres. During the spring and summer they are carpeted with a velvet of green, and gaily bedecked with flowers of various forms and hues, making a most fascinating panorama of ever-changing color and loveliness. To fully appreciate their great beauty and magnitude, they must be seen.

Soil. — The soil of Missouri is good, and of great agricultural capabilities, but the most fertile portions of the State are the river bottoms, which are a rich alluvium, mixed in many cases with sand, the producing qualities of which are not excelled by the prolific valley of the famous Nile.

South of the Missouri River there is a greater variety of soil, but much of it is fertile, and even in the mountains and mineral districts there are rich valleys, and about the sources of the White, Eleven Points, Current and Big Black Rivers, the soil, though unproductive, furnishes a valuable growth of yellow pine.

The marshy lands in the southeastern part of the State will, by a system of drainage, be one of the most fertile districts in the State.

HISTORY OF MISSOURI

POPULATION BY COUNTIES IN 1870, 1876, AND 1880.

Counties.	1870.	1876.	1880.
Adair	11,449	18,774	15,190
Andrew	15,137	14,992	16,818
Atchison	8,440	10,925	14,565
Audrain	12,307	15,157	19,739
Barry	10,373	11,146	14,424
Barton	5,087	6,900	10,332
Bates	15,960	17,484	25,382
Benton	11,322	11,027	12,398
Bollinger	8,162	8,884	11,132
Boone	20,765	81,923	25,424
Buchanan	85,109	88,165	49,824
Butler	4,298	4,363	6,011
Caldwell	11,390	12,200	13,654
Callaway	19,202	25,257	23,670
Camden	6,108	7,027	7,269
Cape Girardeau	17,558	17,891	20,998
Carroll	17,440	21,498	23,300
Carter	1,440	1,549	2,168
Cass	19,299	18,069	22,431
Cedar	9,471	9,897	10,747
Chariton	19,136	23,294	25,224
Christian	6,707	7,936	9,682
Clark	13,667	14,549	15,631
Clay	15,564	15,320	15,579
Clinton	14,063	18,698	16,073
Cole	10,292	14,122	15,519
Cooper	20,692	21,356	21,622
Crawford	7,982	9,391	10,763
Dade	8,683	11,089	12,557
Dallas	8,383	8,073	9,272
Daviess	14,410	16,557	19,174
DeKalb	9,858	11,159	13,343
Dent	6,357	7,401	10,647
Douglas	8,915	6,461	7,753
Dunklin	5,982	6,255	9,604
Franklin	80,098	26,924	26,536
Gasconade	10,093	11,160	11,153
Gentry	11,607	12,673	17,188
Greene	21,549	24,693	28,817
Grundy	10,567	13,071	15,201
Harrison	14,635	18,530	20,318
Henry	17,401	18,465	23,914
Hickory	6,452	5,870	7,388
Holt	11,652	13,245	15,510
Howard	17,233	17,815	18,428
Howell	4,218	6,756	8,814
Iron	6,278	6,623	8,183
Jackson	55,041	54,045	82,328
Jasper	14,928	29,384	32,021
Jefferson	15,380	16,186	18,736
Johnson	24,648	23,646	28,177
Knox	10,974	12,678	13,047
Laclede	9,380	9,845	11,524
Lafayette	22,624	22,204	25,761
Lawrence	13,067	13,054	17,585
Lewis	15,114	16,360	15,925
Lincoln	15,960	16,858	17,443
Linn	15,906	18,110	20,016
Livingston	16,730	18,074	20,205

HISTORY OF MISSOURI

POPULATION BY COUNTIES — *Continued.*

Counties.	1876.	1876.	1880.
McDonald	5,226	6,072	7,816
Macon	23,230	25,028	26,223
Madison	5,849	8,750	8,866
Maries	5,916	6,481	7,804
Marion	23,780	22,794	24,837
Mercer	11,557	13,393	14,674
Miller	6,616	8,529	9,807
Mississippi	4,982	7,498	9,270
Moniteau	13,875	13,084	14,849
Monroe	17,149	17,751	19,075
Montgomery	10,405	14,418	16,250
Morgan	8,434	9,529	10,134
New Madrid	6,857	6,678	7,694
Newton	12,821	16,875	18,948
Nodaway	14,751	23,196	29,560
Oregon	3,287	4,469	5,791
Osage	10,793	11,200	11,824
Ozark	3,363	4,579	5,618
Pemiscot	2,059	2,578	4,299
Perry	9,877	11,189	11,895
Pettis	18,706	23,167	27,285
Phelps	10,506	9,919	12,565
Pike	23,076	22,828	26,716
Platte	17,352	15,948	17,372
Polk	14,445	13,467	15,745
Pulaski	4,714	6,157	7,250
Putnam	11,217	12,641	13,556
Ralls	10,510	9,997	11,838
Randolph	15,908	19,178	22,751
Ray	18,700	18,894	20,196
Reynolds	3,756	4,716	5,722
Ripley	3,175	3,918	5,877
St. Charles	21,304	21,821	23,060
St. Clair	6,742	11,242	14,126
St. Francois	9,742	11,621	13,822
Ste. Genevieve	8,384	9,409	10,309
St. Louis [1]	351,189	. . .	31,888
Saline	21,672	27,087	29,912
Schuyler	8,820	9,881	10,470
Scotland	10,670	12,030	12,507
Scott	7,317	7,812	8,587
Shannon	2,889	3,236	3,441
Shelby	10,119	13,243	14,024
Stoddard	8,585	10,888	13,432
Stone	3,253	3,544	4,405
Sullivan	11,907	14,039	16,569
Taney	4,407	6,124	5,605
Texas	9,618	10,287	12,207
Vernon	11,247	14,418	19,370
Warren	9,673	10,321	10,806
Washington	11,719	13,100	12,895
Wayne	6,068	7,006	9,097
Webster	10,434	10,684	12,175
Worth	5,004	7,164	8,203
Wright	5,684	6,124	9,733
City of St. Louis	. . .	. . .	350,522
	1,721,295	1,547,080	2,168,804

[1] St. Louis City and County separated in 1877. Population for 1876 not given

SUMMARY.

Males	.	.	.	.	.	.	.	.	.	.	.	.	.	.	.	1,126,424
Females	.	.	.	.	.	.	.	.	.	.	.	.	.	.	.	1,041,380
Native	.	.	.	.	.	.	.	.	.	.	.	.	.	.	.	1,957,564
Foreign	.	.	.	.	.	.	.	.	.	.	.	.	.	.	.	211,240
White	.	.	.	.	.	.	.	.	.	.	.	.	.	.	.	2,023,568
Colored [1]	.	.	.	.	.	.	.	.	.	.	.	.	.	.	.	145,236

CHAPTER III.

GEOLOGY OF MISSOURI.

Classification of Rocks — Quatenary Formation — Tertiary — Cretaceous — Carboniferous — Devonian — Silurian — Azoic — Economic Geology — Coal — Iron — Lead — Copper — Zinc — Building Stone — Marble — Gypsum — Lime — Clays — Paints — Springs — Water Power.

The stratified rocks of Missouri, as classified and treated of by Prof. G. C. Swallow, belong to the following divisions: I. Quatenary; II. Tertiary; III. Cretaceous; IV. Carboniferous; V. Devonian; VI. Silurian; VII. Azoic.

" The Quatenary formations, are the most recent, and the most valuable to man: valuable, because they can be more readily utilized.

The Quatenary formation in Missouri, embraces the Alluvium, 30 feet thick; Bottom Prairie, 30 feet thick; Bluff, 200 feet thick; and Drift, 155 feet thick. The latest deposits are those which constitute the Alluvium, and includes the soils, pebbles and sand, clays, vegetable mould, bog, iron ore, marls, etc.

The Alluvium deposits, cover an area, within the limits of Missouri, of more than four millions acres of land, which are not surpassed for fertility by any region of country on the globe.

The Bluff Prairie formation is confined to the low lands, which are washed by the two great rivers which course our eastern and western boundaries, and while it is only about half as extensive as the Alluvial, it is equally as rich and productive."

" The Bluff formation," says Prof. Swallow, " rests upon the ridges and river bluffs, and descends along their slopes to the lowest valleys, the formation capping all the Bluffs of the Missouri from Fort Union to its mouth, and those of the Mississippi from Dubuque

---

[1] Including 92 Chinese, 2 half Chinese, and 96 Indians and half-breeds.

to the mouth of the Ohio. It forms the upper stratum beneath the soil of all the high lands, both timber and prairies, of all the counties north of the Osage and Missouri, and also St. Louis, and the Mississippi counties on the south.

Its greatest development is in the counties on the Missouri River from the Iowa line to Boonville. In some localities it is 200 feet thick. At St. Joseph it is 140; at Boonville 100; and at St. Louis, in St. George's quarry, and the Big Mound, it is about 50 feet; while its greatest observed thickness in Marion county was only 30 feet."

The Drift formation is that which lies beneath the Bluff formation, having, as Prof. Swallow informs us, three distinct deposits, to wit: "Altered Drift, which are strata of sand and pebbles, seen in the banks of the Missouri, in the northwestern portion of the State.

The Boulder formation is a heterogeneous stratum of sand, gravel and boulder, and water-worn fragments of the older rocks.

Boulder Clay is a bed of bluish or brown sandy clay, through which pebbles are scattered in greater or less abundance. In some localities in northern Missouri, this formation assumes a pure white, pipe-clay color."

The Tertiary formation is made up of clays, shales, iron ores, sandstone, and sands, scattered along the bluffs, and edges of the bottoms, reaching from Commerce, Scott County, to Stoddard, and south to the Chalk Bluffs in Arkansas.

The Cretaceous formation lies beneath the Tertiary, and is composed of variegated sandstone, bluish-brown sandy slate, whitish-brown impure sandstone, fine white clay mingled with spotted flint, purple, red and blue clays, all being in the aggregate, 158 feet in thickness. There are no fossils in these rocks, and nothing by which their age may be told.

The Carboniferous system includes the Upper Carboniferous or coal-measures, and the Lower Carboniferous or Mountain limestone. The coal-measures are made up of numerous strata of sandstones, limestones, shales, clays, marls, spathic iron ores, and coals.

The Carboniferous formation, including coal-measures and the beds of iron, embrace an area in Missouri of 27,000 square miles. The varieties of coal found in the State are the common bituminous and cannel coals, and they exist in quantities inexhaustible. The fact that these coal-measures are full of fossils, which are always confined

HISTORY OF MISSOURI

to the coal measures, enables the geologist to point them out, and the coal beds contained in them.

The rocks of the Lower Carboniferous rormation are varied in color, and are quarried in many different parts of the State, being extensively utilized for building and other purposes.

Among the Lower Carboniferous rocks is found the Upper Archimedes Limestone, 200 feet; Ferruginous Sandstone, 195 feet; Middle Archimedes, 50 feet; St. Louis Limestone, 250 feet; Oölitic Limestone, 25 feet; Lower Archimedes Limestone, 350 feet; and Encrinital Limestone, 500 feet. These limestones generally contain fossils.

The Ferruginous limestone is soft when quarried, but becomes hard and durable after exposure. It contains large quantities of iron, and is found skirting the eastern coal measures from the mouth of the Des Moines to McDonald county.

The St. Louis limestone is of various hues and tints, and very hard. It is found in Clark, Lewis and St. Louis counties.

The Lower Archimedes limestone includes partly the lead bearing rocks of Southwestern Missouri.

The Encrinital limestone is the most extensive of the divisions of Carboniferous limestone, and is made up of brown, buff, gray and white. In these strata are found the remains of corals and mollusks. This formation extends from Marion county to Greene county. The Devonian system contains: Chemung Group, Hamilton Group, Onondaga limestone and Oriskany sandstone. The rocks of the Devonian system are found in Marion, Ralls, Pike, Callaway, Saline and Ste. Genevieve counties.

The Chemung Group has three formations, Chouteau limestone, 85 feet; Vermicular sandstone and shales, 75 feet; Lithographic limestone, 125 feet.

The Chouteau limestone is in two divisions, when fully developed, and when first quarried is soft. It is not only good for building purposes but makes an excellent cement.

The Vermicular sandstone and shales are usually buff or yellowish brown, and perforated with pores.

The Lithographic limestone is a pure, fine, compact, evenly-textured limestone. Its color varies from light drab to buff and blue. It is called "pot metal," because under the hammer it gives a sharp, ringing sound. It has but few fossils.

15

The Hamilton Group is made up of some 40 feet of blue shales, and 170 feet of crystalline limestone.

Onondaga limestone is usually a coarse, gray or buff crystalline, thick-bedded and cherty limestone. No formation in Missouri presents such variable and widely different lithological characters as the Onondaga.

The Oriskany sandstone is a light, gray limestone.

Of the Upper Silurian series there are the following formations: Lower Helderberg, 350 feet; Niagara Group, 200 feet; Cape Girardeau limestone, 60 feet.

The Lower Helderberg is made up of buff, gray, and reddish cherty and argillaceous limestone.

Niagara Group. The Upper part of this group consists of red, yellow and ash-colored shales, with compact limestones, variegated with bands and nodules of chert.

The Cape Girardeau limestone, on the Mississippi River near Cape Girardeau, is a compact, bluish-gray, brittle limestone, with smooth fractures in layers from two to six inches in thickness, with argillaceous partings. These strata contain a great many fossils.

The Lower Silurian has the following ten formations, to wit: Hudson River Group, 220 feet; Trenton limestone, 360 feet; Black River and Bird's Eye limestone, 175 feet; first Magnesian limestone, 200 feet; Saccharoidal sandstone, 125 feet; second Magnesian limestone, 250 feet; second sandstone, 115 feet; third Magnesian limestone, 350 feet; third sandstone, 60 feet; fourth Magnesian limestone, 350 feet.

Hudson River Group: — There are three formations which Prof. Swallow refers to in this group. These formations are found in the bluff above and below Louisiana; on the Grassy a few miles northwest of Louisiana, and in Ralls, Pike, Cape Girardeau and Ste. Genevieve Counties.

Trenton limestone: The upper part of this formation is made up of thick beds of hard, compact, bluish gray and drab limestone, variegated with irregular cavities, filled with greenish materials.

The beds are exposed between Hannibal and New London, north of Salt River, near Glencoe, St. Louis County, and are seventy-five feet thick.

Black River and Bird's Eye limestone the same color as the Trenton limestone.

HISTORY OF MISSOURI

The first Magnesian limestone cap the picturesque oluffs of the Osage in Benton and neighboring counties.

The Saccharoidal sandstone has a wide range in the State. In a bluff about two miles from Warsaw, is a very striking change of thickness of this formation.

Second Magnesian limestone, in lithological character, is like the first.

The second sandstone, usually of yellowish brown, sometimes becomes a pure white, fine-grained, soft sandstone as on Cedar Creek, in Washington and Franklin Counties.

The third Magnesian limestone is exposed in the high and picturesque bluffs of the Niangua, in the neighborhood of Bryce's Spring.

The third sandstone is white and has a formation in moving water.

The fourth Magnesian limestone is seen on the Niangua and Osage Rivers.

The Azoic rocks lie below the Silurian and form a series of silicious and other slates which contain no remains of organic life.

ECONOMIC GEOLOGY.

Coal. — Missouri is particularly rich in minerals. Indeed, no State in the Union, surpasses her in this respect. In some unknown age of the past — long before the existence of man — Nature, by a wise process, made a bountiful provision for the time, when in the order of things, it should be necessary for civilized man to take possession of these broad, rich prairies. As an equivalent for lack of forests, she quietly stored away beneath the soil those wonderful carboniferous treasures for the use of man.

Geological surveys have developed the fact that the coal deposits in the State are almost unnumbered, embracing all varieties of the best bituminous coal. A large portion of the State, has been ascertained to be one continuous coal field, stretching from the mouth of the Des Moines River through Clark, Lewis, Scotland, Adair, Macon, Shelby, Monroe, Audrain, Callaway, Boone, Cooper, Pettis, Benton, Henry, St. Clair, Bates, Vernon, Cedar, Dade, Barton and Jasper, into the Indian Territory, and the counties on the northwest of this line contain more or less coal. Coal rocks exist in Ralls, Montgomery, Warren, St. Charles, Moniteau, Cole, Morgan, Crawford and Lincoln, and during the past few years, all along the lines of all the railroads in North Missouri, and along the western end of the Missouri Pacific, and on the Missouri River, between Kansas City and Sioux

City, has systematic mining, opened up hundreds of mines in different localities. The area of our coal beds, on the line of the southwestern boundary of the State alone, embraces more than 26,000 square miles of regular coal measures. This will give of workable coal, if the average be one foot, 26,800,000,000 tons. The estimates from the developments already made, in the different portions of the State, will give 134,000,000,000 tons.

The economical value of this coal to the State, its influence in domestic life, in navigation, commerce and manufactures, is beyond the imagination of man to conceive. Suffice it to say, that in the possession of her developed and undeveloped coal mines, Missouri has a motive power, which in its influences for good, in the civilization of man, is more potent than the gold of California.

Iron. — Prominent among the minerals, which increase the power and prosperity of a nation, is iron. Of this ore, Missouri has an inexhaustible quantity, and like her coal fields, it has been developed in many portions of the State, and of the best and purest quality. It is found in great abundance in the counties of Cooper, St. Clair, Greene, Henry, Franklin, Benton, Dallas, Camden, Stone, Madison, Iron, Washington, Perry, St. Francois, Reynolds, Stoddard, Scott, Dent and others. The greatest deposit of iron is found in the Iron Mountain, which is two hundred feet high, and covers an area of five hundred acres, and produces a metal, which is shown by analysis, to contain from 65 to 69 per cent of metallic iron.

The ore of Shepherd Mountain contains from 64 to 67 per cent of metallic iron. The ore of Pilot Knob contains from 53 to 60 per cent.

Rich beds of iron are also found at the Big Bogy Mountain, and at Russell Mountain. This ore has, in its nude state, a variety of colors, from the red, dark red, black, brown, to a light bluish gray. The red ores are found in twenty-one or more counties of the State, and are of great commercial value. The brown hematite iron ores extend over a greater range of country than all the others combined, embracing about one hundred counties, and have been ascertained to exist in these in large quantities.

Lead. — Long before any permanent settlements were made in Missouri by the whites, lead was mined within the limits of the State at two or three points on the Mississippi. At this time more than five hundred mines are opened, and many of them are being successfully worked. These deposits of lead cover an area, so far as developed, of more than seven thousand square miles. Mines have been opened in Jefferson, Washington, St. Francois, Madison, Wayne, Carter, Reynolds, Crawford, Ste. Genevieve, Perry, Cole, Cape Girardeau, Camden, Morgan, and many other counties.

Copper and Zinc.—Several varieties of copper ore are found in Missouri. The copper mines of Shannon, Madison and Franklin Counties have been known for years, and some of these have been successfully worked and are now yielding good results.

Deposits of copper have been discovered in Dent, Crawford, Benton, Maries, Green, Lawrence, Dade, Taney, Dallas, Phelps, Reynolds and Wright Counties.

Zinc is abundant in nearly all the lead mines in the southwestern part of the State, and since the completion of the A. & P. R. R. a market has been furnished for this ore, which will be converted into valuable merchandise.

Building Stone and Marble. — There is no scarcity of good building stone in Missouri. Limestone, sandstone and granite exist in all shades of buff, blue, red and brown, and are of great beauty as building material.

There are many marble beds in the State, some of which furnish very beautiful and excellent marble. It is found in Marion, Cooper, St. Louis, and other counties.

One of the most desirable of the Missouri marbles is in the 3rd Magnesian limestone, on the Niangua. It is fine-grained, crystalline, silico-magnesian limestone, light-drab, slightly tinged with peach blossom, and clouded by deep flesh-colored shades. In ornamental architecture it is rarely surpassed.

Gypsum and Lime.—Though no extensive beds of gypsum have been discovered in Missouri, there are vast beds of the pure white crystalline variety on the line of the Kansas Pacific Railroad, on Kansas River, and on Gypsum Creek. It exists also in several other localities accessible by both rail and boat.

All of the limestone formations in the State, from the coal measures to fourth Magnesian, have more or less strata of very nearly pure carbonate of pure lime.

Clays and Paints. — Clays are found in nearly all parts of the State suitable for making bricks. Potters' clay and fire-clay are worked in many localities.

There are several beds of purple shades in the coal measures which possess the properties requisite for paints used in outside work. Yellow and red ochres are found in considerable quantities on the Missouri

River. Some of these paints have been thoroughly tested and found fire-proof and durable.

SPRINGS AND WATER POWER.

No State is, perhaps, better supplied with cold springs of pure water than Missouri. Out of the bottoms, there is scarcely a section of land but has one or more perennial springs of good water. Even where there are no springs, good water can be obtained by digging from twenty to forty feet. Salt springs are abundant in the central part of the State, and discharge their brine in Cooper, Saline, Howard, and adjoining counties. Considerable salt was made in Cooper and Howard Counties at an early day.

Sulphur springs are also numerous throughout the State. The Chouteau Springs in Cooper, the Monagaw Springs in St. Clair, the Elk Springs in Pike, and the Cheltenham Springs in St. Louis County have acquired considerable reputation as salubrious waters, and have become popular places of resort. Many other counties have good sulphur springs.

Among the Chalybeate springs the Sweet Springs on the Blackwater, and the Chalybeate spring in the University *campus* are, perhaps, the most popular of the kind in the State. There are, however, other springs impregnated with some of the salts of iron.

Petroleum springs are found in Carroll, Ray, Randolph, Cass, Lafayette, Bates, Vernon, and other counties. The variety called lubricating oil is the more common.

The water power of the State is excellent. Large springs are particularly abundant on the waters of the Meramec, Gasconade, Bourbeuse, Osage, Niangua, Spring, White, Sugar, and other streams. Besides these, there are hundreds of springs sufficiently large to drive mills and factories, and the day is not far distant when these crystal fountains will be utilized, and a thousand saws will buzz to their dashing music.

CHAPTER IV.

TITLE AND EARLY SETTLEMENTS.

Title to Missouri Lands — Right of Discovery — Title of France and Spain — Cession to the United States — Territorial Changes — Treaties with Indians — First Settlement — Ste. Genevieve and New Bourbon — St. Louis — When Incorporated — Potosi — St. Charles — Portage des Sioux — New Madrid — St. Francois County — Perry — Mississippi — Loutre Island — "Boone's Lick" — Cote Sans Dessein — Howard County — Some First Things — Counties — When Organized.

The title to the soil of Missouri was, of course, primarily vested in the original occupants who inhabited the country prior to its discovery by the whites. But the Indians, being savages, possessed but few rights that civilized nations considered themselves bound to respect; so, therefore, when they found this country in the possession of such a people they claimed it in the name of the King of France, by the *right of discovery*. It remained under the jurisdiction of France until 1763.

Prior to the year 1763, the entire continent of North America was divided between France, England, Spain and Russia. France held all that portion that now constitutes our national domain west of the Mississippi River, except Texas, and the territory which we have obtained from Mexico and Russia. The vast region, while under the jurisdiction of France, was known as the " Province of Louisiana," and embraced the present State of Missouri. At the close of the " Old French War," in 1763, France gave up her share of the continent, and Spain came into the possession of the territory west of the Mississippi River, while Great Britain retained Canada and the regions northward, having obtained that territory by conquest, in the war with France. For thirty-seven years the territory now embraced within the limits of Missouri, remained as a part of the possession of Spain, and then went back to France by the treaty of St. Ildefonso, October 1, 1800. On the 30th of April, 1803, France ceded it to the United States, in consideration of receiving $11,250,000, and the liquidation of certain claims, held by citizens of the United States against France, which amounted to the further sum of $3,750,000, making a total of $15,000,000. It will thus be seen that France has twice, and Spain once, held sovereignty over the territory embracing

Missouri, but the financial needs of Napoleon afforded our Government an opportunity to add another empire to its domain.

On the 31st of October, 1803, an act of Congress was approved, authorizing the President to take possession of the newly acquired territory, and provided for it a temporary government, and another act, approved March 26, 1804, authorized the division of the "Louisiana Purchase," as it was then called, into two separate territories. All that portion south of the 33d parallel of north latitude was called the "Territory of Orleans," and that north of the said parallel was known as the "District of Louisiana," and was placed under the jurisdiction of what was then known as "Indian Territory."

By virtue of an act of Congress, approved March 3, 1805, the "District of Louisiana" was organized as the "Territory of Louisiana," with a territorial government of its own, which went into operation July 4th of the same year, and it so remained till 1812. In this year the "Territory of Orleans" became the State of Louisiana, and the "Territory of Louisiana" was organized as the "Territory of Missouri."

This change took place under an act of Congress, approved June 4, 1812. In 1819, a portion of this territory was organized as "Arkansas Territory," and on August 10, 1821, the State of Missouri was admitted, being a part of the former "Territory of Missouri."

In 1836, the "Platte Purchase," then being a part of the Indian Territory, and now composing the counties of Atchison, Andrew, Buchanan, Holt, Nodaway and Platte, was made by treaty with the Indians, and added to the State. It will be seen, then, that the soil of Missouri belonged:—

1. To France, with other territory.

2. In 1763, with other territory, it was ceded to Spain.

3. October 1, 1800, it was ceded, with other territory from Spain, back to France.

4. April 30, 1803, it was ceded, with other territory, by France to the United States.

5. October 31, 1803, a temporary government was authorized by Congress for the newly acquired territory.

6. October 1, 1804, it was included in the "District of Louisiana" and placed under the territorial government of Indiana.

7. July 4, 1805, it was included as a part of the "Territory of Louisiana," then organized with a separate territorial government.

HISTORY OF MISSOURI

8. June 4, 1812, it was embraced in what was then made the "Territory of Missouri."

9. August 10, 1821, it was admitted into the Union as a State.

10. In 1836, the "Platte Purchase" was made, adding more territory to the State.

The cession by France, April 30, 1803, vested the title in the United States, subject to the claims of the Indians, which it was very justly the policy of the Government to recognize. Before the Government of the United States could vest clear title to the soil in the grantee it was necessary to extinguish the Indian title by purchase. This was done accordingly by treaties made with the Indians at different times.

EARLY SETTLEMENTS.

The name of the first white man who set foot on the territory now embraced in the State of Missouri, is not known, nor is it known at what precise period the first settlements were made. It is, however, generally agreed that they were made at Ste. Genevieve and New Bourbon, tradition fixing the date of the settlements in the autumn of 1735. These towns were settled by the French from Kaskaskia and St. Philip in Illinois.

St. Louis was founded by Pierre Laclede Liguest, on the 15th of February, 1764. He was a native of France, and was one of the members of the company of Laclede Liguest, Antonio Maxant & Co.; to whom a royal charter had been granted, confirming the privilege of an exclusive trade with the Indians of Missouri as far north as St. Peter's River.

While in search of a trading post he ascended the Mississippi as far as the mouth of the Missouri, and finally returned to the present town site of St. Louis. After the village had been laid off he named it St. Louis in honor of Louis XV., of France.

The colony thrived rapidly by accessions from Kaskaskia and other towns on the east side of the Mississippi, and its trade was largely increased by many of the Indian tribes, who removed a portion of their peltry trade from the same towns to St. Louis. It was incorporated as a town on the ninth day of November, 1809, by the Court of Common Pleas of the district of St. Louis; the town trustees being Auguste Chouteau, Edward Hempstead, Jean F. Cabanne, Wm. C. Carr and William Christy, and incorporated as a city December 9, 1822. The selection of the town site on which St. Louis stands was highly judicious, the spot not only being healthful and having the advantages of water transportation unsurpassed, but surrounded by a beautiful region of country, rich in soil and mineral resources. St. Louis has grown to be the fifth city in population in the Union, and is to-day the great center of internal commerce of the Missouri, the Mississippi and their tributaries, and, with its railroad facilities, it is destined to be the greatest inland city of the American continent.

The next settlement was made at Potosi, in Washington County, in 1765, by Francis Breton, who, while chasing a bear, discovered the mine near the present town of Potosi, where he afterward located.

One of the most prominent pioneers who settled at Potosi was Moses Austin, of Virginia, who, in 1795, received by grant from the Spanish government a league of land, now known as the "Austin Survey." The grant was made on condition that Mr. Austin would establish a lead mine at Potosi and work it. He built a palatial residence, for that day, on the brow of the hill in the little village,. which was for many years known as " Durham Hall." At this point the first shot-tower and sheet-lead manufactory were erected.

Five years after the founding of St. Louis the first settlement made in Northern Missouri was made near St. Charles, in St. Charles County, in 1769. The name given to it, and which it retained till 1784, was *Les Petites Cotes*, signifying, Little Hills. The town site was located by Blanchette, a Frenchman, surnamed LeChasseur, who built the first fort in the town and established there a military post.

Soon after the establishment of the military post at St. Charles, the old French village of *Portage des Sioux*, was located on the Mississippi, just below the mouth of the Illinois River, and at about the same time a Kickapoo village was commenced at Clear Weather Lake. The present town site of New Madrid, in New Madrid county, was settled in 1781, by French Canadians, it then being occupied by Delaware Indians. The place now known as Big River Mills, St. Francois county, was settled in 1796, Andrew Baker, John Alley, Francis Starnater and John Andrews, each locating claims. The following year, a settlement was made in the same county, just below the present town of Farmington, by the Rev. William Murphy, a Baptist minister from East Tennessee. In 1796, settlements were made in Perry county by emigrants from Kentucky and Pennsylvania; the latter locating in the rich bottom lands of Bois Brule, the former generally settling in the " Barrens," and along the waters of Saline Creek.

Bird's Point, in Mississippi county, opposite Cairo, Illinois, was settled August 6, 1800, by John Johnson, by virtue of a land-grant

HISTORY OF MISSOURI

from the commandant under the Spanish Government. Norfolk and Charleston, in the same county, were settled respectively in 1800 and 1801. Warren county was settled in 1801. Loutre Island, below the present town of Hermann, in the Missouri River, was settled by a few American families in 1807. This little company of pioneers suffered greatly from the floods, as well as from the incursions of thieving and blood-thirsty Indians, and many incidents of a thrilling character could be related of trials and struggles, had we the time and space.

In 1807, Nathan and Daniel M. Boone, sons of the great hunter and pioneer, in company with three others, went from St. Louis to "Boone's Lick," in Howard county, where they manufactured salt and formed the nucleus of a small settlement.

Cote Sans Dessein, now called Bakersville, on the Missouri River, in Callaway county, was settled by the French in 1801. This little town was considered at that time, as the "Far West" of the new world. During the war of 1812, at this place many hard-fought battles occurred between the whites and Indians, wherein woman's fortitude and courage greatly assisted in the defence of the settlement.

In 1810, a colony of Kentuckians numbering one hundred and fifty families immigrated to Howard county, and settled on the Missouri River in Cooper's Bottom near the present town of Franklin, and opposite Arrow Rock.

Such, in brief, is the history of some of the early settlements of Missouri, covering a period of more than half a century.

These settlements were made on the water courses; usually along the banks of the two great streams, whose navigation afforded them transportation for their marketable commodities, and communication with the civilized portion of the country.

They not only encountered the gloomy forests, settling as they did by the river's brink, but the hostile incursion of savage Indians, by whom they were for many years surrounded.

The expedients of these brave men who first broke ground in the territory, have been succeeded by the permanent and tasteful improvements of their descendants. Upon the spots where they toiled, dared and died, are seen the comfortable farm, the beautiful village, and thrifty city. Churches and school houses greet the eye on every hand; railroads diverge in every direction, and, indeed, all the appliances of a higher civilization are profusely strewn over the smiling surface of the State.

25

Culture's hand
Has scattered verdure o'er the land;
And smiles and fragrance rule serene,
Where barren wild usurped the scene.

SOME FIRST THINGS.

The first marriage that took place in Missouri was April 20, 1766, in St. Louis.

The first baptism was performed in May, 1766, in St. Louis.

The first house of worship, (Catholic) was erected in 1775, at St. Louis.

The first ferry established in 1805, on the Mississippi River, at St. Louis.

The first newspaper established in St. Louis (*Missouri Gazette*), in 1808.

The first postoffice was established in 1804, in St. Louis — Rufus Easton, post-master.

The first Protestant church erected at Ste. Genevieve, in 1806 — Baptist.

The first bank established (Bank of St. Louis), in 1814.

The first market house opened in 1811, in St. Louis.

The first steamboat on the Upper Mississippi was the General Pike, Capt. Jacob Reid; landed at St. Louis 1817.

The first board of trustees for public schools appointed in 1817, St. Louis.

The first college built (St. Louis College), in 1817.

The first steamboat that came up the Missouri River as high as Franklin was the Independence, in May, 1819; Capt. Nelson, master.

The first court house erected in 1823, in St. Louis.

The first cholera appeared in St. Louis in 1832.

The first railroad convention held in St. Louis, April 20, 1836.

The first telegraph lines reached East St. Louis, December 20, 1847.

The first great fire occurred in St. Louis, 1849.

CHAPTER V.

TERRITORIAL ORGANIZATION.

Organization 1812 — Council — House of Representatives — William Clark first Territorial Governor — Edward Hempstead first Delegate — Spanish Grants — First General Assembly — Proceedings — Second Assembly — Proceedings — Population of Territory — Vote of Territory — Rufus Easton — Absent Members — Third Assembly — Proceedings — Application for Admission.

Congress organized Missouri as a Territory, July 4, 1812, with a Governor and General Assembly. The Governor, Legislative Council, and House of Representatives exercised the Legislative power of the Territory, the Governor's vetoing power being absolute.

The Legislative Council was composed of nine members, whose tenure of office lasted five years. Eighteen citizens were nominated by the House of Representatives to the President of the United States, from whom he selected, with the approval of the Senate, nine Councillors, to compose the Legislative Council.

The House of Representatives consisted of members chosen every two years by the people, the basis of representation being one member for every five hundred white males. The first House of Representatives consisted of thirteen members, and, by Act of Congress, the whole number of Representatives could not exceed twenty-five.

The judicial power of the Territory, was vested in the Superior and Inferior Courts, and in the Justices of the Peace; the Superior Court having three judges, whose term of office continued four years, having original and appellate jurisdiction in civil and criminal cases.

The Territory could send one delegate to Congress. Governor Clark issued a proclamation, October 1st, 1812, required by Congress, reorganizing the districts of St. Charles, St. Louis, Ste. Genevieve, Cape Girardeau, and New Madrid, into five counties, and fixed the second Monday in November following, for the election of a delegate to Congress, and the members of the Territorial House of Representatives.

William Clark, of the expedition of Lewis and Clark, was the first Territorial Governor, appointed by the President, who began his duties 1813.

Edward Hempstead, Rufus Easton, Samuel Hammond, and Matthew Lyon were candidates in November for delegates to Congress.

Edward Hempstead was elected, being the first Territorial Delegate to Congress from Missouri. He served one term, declining a second, and was instrumental in having Congress to pass the act of June 13, 1812, which he introduced, confirming the title to lands which were claimed by the people by virtue of Spanish grants. The same act confirmed to the people "for the support of schools," the title to village lots, out-lots or common field lots, which were held and enjoyed by them, at the time of the session in 1803.

Under the act of June 4, 1812, the first General Assembly held its session in the house of Joseph Robidoux, in St. Louis, on the 7th of December, 1812. The names of the members of the House were: —

St. Charles. — John Pitman and Robert Spencer.

St. Louis. — David Music, Bernard G. Farrar, William C. Carr, and Richard Clark.

Ste. Genevieve. — George Bullet, Richard S. Thomas, and Isaac McGready.

Cape Girardeau. — George F. Bollinger, and Spencer Byrd.

New Madrid. — John Shrader and Samuel Phillips.

John B. C. Lucas, one of the Territorial Judges, administered the oath of office. William C. Carr was elected speaker, and Andrew Scott, Clerk.

The House of Representatives proceeded to nominate eighteen persons from whom the President of the United States, with the Senate, was to select nine for the Council. From this number the President chose the following:

St. Charles. — James Flaugherty and Benjamin Emmons.

St. Louis. — Auguste Chouteau, Sr., and Samuel Hammond.

Ste. Genevieve. — John Scott and James Maxwell.

Cape Girardeau. — William Neeley and Joseph Cavenor.

New Madrid. — Joseph Hunter.

The Legislative Council, thus chosen by the President and Senate, was announced by Frederick Bates, Secretary and Acting-Governor of the Territory, by proclamation, June 3, 1813, and fixing the first Monday in July following, as the time for the meeting of the Legislature.

In the meantime the duties of the executive office were assumed by William Clark. The Legislature accordingly met, as required by the Acting-Governor's proclamation, in July, but its proceedings were never officially published. Consequently but little is known in reference to the workings of the first Territorial Legislature in Missouri.

From the imperfect account, published in the Missouri *Gazette*, of that day; a paper which had been in existence since 1808, it is found that laws were passed regulating and establishing weights and measures; creating the office of Sheriff; providing the manner for taking the census; permanently fixing the seats of Justices, and an act to compensate its own members. At this session, laws were also passed defining crimes and penalties; laws in reference to forcible entry and detainer; establishing Courts of Common Pleas; incorporating the Bank of St. Louis; and organizing a part of Ste. Genevieve county into the county of Washington.

The next session of the Legislature convened in St. Louis, December 6, 1813. George Bullet of Ste. Genevieve county, was speaker elect, and Andrew Scott, clerk, and William Sullivan, doorkeeper. Since the adjournment of the former Legislature, several vacancies had occurred, and new members had been elected to fill their places. Among these was Israel McCready, from the county of Washington.

The president of the legislative council was Samuel Hammond. No journal of the council was officially published, but the proceedings of the house are found in the *Gazette*.

At this session of the Legislature many wise and useful laws were passed, having reference to the temporal as well as the moral and spiritual welfare of the people. Laws were enacted for the suppression of vice and immorality on the Sabbath day; for the improvement of public roads and highways; creating the offices of auditor, treasurer and county surveyor; regulating the fiscal affairs of the Territory and fixing the boundary lines of New Madrid, Cape Girardeau, Washington and St. Charles counties. The Legislature adjourned on the 19th of January, 1814, *sine die*.

The population of the Territory as shown by the United States census in 1810, was 20,845. The census taken by the Legislature in 1814 gave the Territory a population of 25,000. This enumeration shows the county of St. Louis contained the greatest number of inhabitants, aud the new county of Arkansas the least — the latter having 827, and the former 3,149.

The candidates for delegate to Congress were Rufus Easton, Samuel Hammond, Alexander McNair and Thomas F. Riddick. Rufus Easton and Samuel Hammond had been candidates at the preceding election. In all the counties, excepting Arkansas, the votes aggregated 2,599, of which number Mr. Easton received 965, Mr. Ham-

HISTORY OF MISSOURI

mond 746, Mr. McNair 853, and Mr. Riddick (who had withdrawn previously to the election) 35. Mr. Easton was elected.

The census of 1814 showing a large increase in the population of the Territory, an appointment was made increasing the number of Representatives in the Territorial Legislature to twenty-two. The General Assembly began its session in St. Louis, December 5, 1814. There were present on the first day twenty Representatives. James Caldwell of Ste. Genevieve county was elected speaker, and Andrew Scott who had been clerk of the preceding assembly, was chosen clerk. The President of the Council was William Neeley, of Cape Girardeau county.

It appeared that James Maxwell, the absent member of the Council, and Seth Emmons, member elect of the House of Representatives, were dead. The county of Lawrence was organized at this session, from the western part of New Madrid county, and the corporate powers of St. Louis were enlarged. In 1815 the Territorial Legislature again began its session. Only a partial report of its proceedings are given in the *Gazette*. The county of Howard was then organized from St. Louis and St. Charles counties, and included all that part of the State lying north of the Osage and south of the dividing ridge between the Mississippi and Missouri Rivers. (For precise boundaries, see Chapter I. of the History of Boone County.)

The next session of the Territorial Legislature commenced its session in December, 1816. During the sitting of this Legislature many important acts were passed. It was then that the " Bank of Missouri " was chartered and went into operation. In the fall of 1817 the " Bank of St. Louis " and the " Bank of Missouri " were issuing bills. An act was passed chartering lottery companies, chartering the academy at Potosi, and incorporating a board of trustees for superintending the schools in the town of St. Louis. Laws were also passed to encourage the " killing of wolves, panthers and wild-cats."

The Territorial Legislature met again in December, 1818, and, among other things, organized the counties of Pike, Cooper, Jefferson, Franklin, Wayne, Lincoln, Madison, Montgomery, and three counties in the Southern part of Arkansas. In 1819 the Territory of Arkansas was formed into a separate government of its own.

The people of the Territory of Missouri had been, for some time, anxious that their Territory should assume the duties and responsibilities of a sovereign State. Since 1812, the date of the organization of the Territory, the population had rapidly increased, many counties had been established, its commerce had grown into importance, its agricultural and mineral resources were being developed, and believing that its admission into the Union as a State would give fresh impetus to all these interests, and hasten its settlement, the Territorial Legislature of 1818–19 accordingly made application to Congress for the passage of an act authorizing the people of Missouri to organize a State government.

CHAPTER VI.

Application of Missouri to be admitted into the Union — Agitation of the Slavery Question — " Missouri Compromise " — Constitutional Convention of 1820 — Constitution presented to Congress — Further Resistance to Admission — Mr. Clay and his Committee make Report — Second Compromise — Missouri Admitted.

With the application of the Territorial Legislature of Missouri for her admission into the Union, commenced the real agitation of the slavery question in the United States.

Not only was our National Legislature the theater of angry discussions, but everywhere throughout the length and breadth of the Republic the " Missouri Question " was the all-absorbing theme. The political skies threatened,

" In forked flashes, a commanding tempest,"

Which was liable to burst upon the nation at any moment. Through such a crisis our country seemed destined to pass. The question as to the admission of Missouri was to be the beginning of this crisis, which distracted the public counsels of the nation for more than forty years afterward.

Missouri asked to be admitted into the great family of States. " Lower Louisiana," her twin sister Territory, had knocked at the door of the Union eight years previously, and was admitted as stipulated by Napoleon, to all the rights, privileges and immunities of a State, and in accordance with the stipulations of the same treaty, Missouri now sought to be clothed with the same rights, privileges and immunities.

As what is known in the history of the United States as the " Missouri Compromise," of 1820, takes rank among the most prominent measures that had up to that day engaged the attention of our National Legislature, we shall enter somewhat into its details, being connected as they are with the annals of the State.

February 15th, 1819. — After the House had resolved itself into a Committee of the Whole on the bill to authorize the admission of Missouri into the Union, and after the question of her admission had been discussed for some time, Mr. Tallmadge, of New York, moved to amend the bill, by adding to it the following proviso : —

"*And Provided*, That the further introduction of slavery or involuntary servitude be prohibited, except for the punishment of crime, whereof the party shall have been duly convicted, and that all children born within the said State, after the admission thereof into the Union, shall be free at the age of twenty-five years."

As might have been expected, this proviso precipitated the angry discussions which lasted nearly three years, finally culminating in the Missouri Compromise. All phases of the slavery question were presented, not in its moral and social aspects, but as a great constitutional question, affecting Missouri and the admission of future States. The proviso, when submitted to a vote, was adopted — 79 to 67, and so reported to the House.

Hon. John Scott, who was at that time a delegate from the Territory of Missouri, was not permitted to vote, but as such delegate he had the privilege of participating in the debates which followed. On the 16th day of February the proviso was taken up and discussed. After several speeches had been made, among them one by Mr. Scott and one by the author of the proviso, Mr. Tallmadge, the amendment, or proviso, was divided into two parts, and voted upon. The first part of it, which included all to the word " convicted," was adopted — 87 to 76. The remaining part was then voted upon, and also adopted, by 82 to 78. By a vote of 97 to 56 the bill was ordered to be engrossed for a third reading.

The Senate Committee, to whom the bill was referred, reported the same to the Senate on the 19th of February, when that body voted first upon a motion to strike out of the proviso all after the word " convicted," which was carried by a vote of 32 to 7. It then voted to strike out the first entire clause, which prevailed — 22 to 16, thereby defeating the proviso.

The House declined to concur in the action of the Senate, and the bill was again returned to that body, which in turn refused to recede from its position. The bill was lost and Congress adjourned. This was most unfortunate for the country. The people having already been wrought up to fever heat over the agitation of the question in the National Councils, now became intensely excited. The press added fuel to the flame, and the progress of events seemed rapidly tending to the downfall of our nationality.

A long interval of nine months was to ensue before the meeting of Congress. The body indicated by its vote upon the "Missouri Question," that the two great sections of the country were politically divided upon the subject of slavery. The restrictive clause, which it was sought to impose upon Missouri as a condition of her admission, would in all probability, be one of the conditions of the admission of the Territory of Arkansas. The public mind was in a state of great doubt and uncertainty up to the meeting of Congress, which took place on the 6th of December, 1819. The memorial of the Legislative Council and House of Representatives of the Missouri Territory, praying for admission into the Union, was presented to the Senate by Mr. Smith, of South Carolina. It was referred to the Judiciary Committee.

Some three weeks having passed without any action thereon by the Senate, the bill was taken up and discussed by the House until the 19th of February, when the bill from the Senate for the admission of Maine was considered. The bill for the admission of Maine included the "Missouri Question," by an amendment which read as follows:

"And be it further enacted, That in all that territory ceded by France to the United States, under the name of Louisiana, which lies north of thirty-six degrees and thirty minutes, north latitude (excepting such part thereof as is) included within the limits of the State, contemplated by this act, slavery and involuntary servitude, otherwise than in the punishment of crimes, whereof the party shall have been convicted, shall be and is hereby forever prohibited; *Provided, always,* That any person escaping into the same from whom labor or service is lawfully claimed, in any State or Territory of the United States, such fugitive may be lawfully reclaimed and conveyed to the person claiming his or her labor or services as aforesaid."

The Senate adopted this amendment, which formed the basis of the "Missouri Compromise," modified afterward by striking out the words, "*excepting only such part thereof.*"

The bill passed the Senate by a vote of 24 to 20. On the 2d day of March the House took up the bill and amendments for consideration, and by a vote of 134 to 42 concurred in the Senate amendment, and

HISTORY OF MISSOURI

the bill being passed by the two Houses, constituted section 8, of "An Act to authorize the people of the Missouri Territory to form a Constitution and State Government, and for the admission of such State into the Union on an equal footing with the original States, and to prohibit slavery in certain territory."

This act was approved March 6, 1820. Missouri then contained fifteen organized counties. By act of Congress the people of said State were authorized to hold an election on the first Monday, and two succeeding days thereafter in May, 1820, to select representatives to a State convention. This convention met in St. Louis on the 12th of June, following the election in May, and concluded its labors on the 19th of July, 1820. David Barton was its President, and Wm. G. Pettis, Secretary. There were forty-one members of this convention, men of ability and statesmanship, as the admirable constitution which they framed amply testifies. Their names and the counties represented by them are as follows:—

Cape Girardeau.—Stephen Byrd, James Evans, Richard S. Thomas, Alexander Buckner and Joseph McFerron.

Cooper.—Robert P. Clark, Robert Wallace, Wm. Lillard.

Franklin.—John G. Heath.

Howard.—Nicholas S. Burkhart, Duff Green, John Ray, Jonathan S. Findley, Benj. H. Reeves.

Jefferson.—Daniel Hammond.

Lincoln.—Malcom Henry.

Montgomery.—Jonathan Ramsey, James Talbott.

Madison.—Nathaniel Cook.

New Madrid.—Robert S. Dawson, Christopher G. Houts.

Pike.—Stephen Cleaver.

St. Charles.—Benjamin Emmons, Nathan Boone, Hiram H. Baber.

Ste. Genevieve.—John D. Cook, Henry Dodge, John Scott, R. T. Brown.

St. Louis.—David Barton, Edward Bates, Alexander McNair, Wm. Rector, John C. Sullivan, Pierre Chouteau, Jr., Bernard Pratte, Thomas F. Riddick.

Washington.—John Rice Jones, Samuel Perry, John Hutchings.

Wayne.—Elijah Bettis.

On the 13th of November, 1820, Congress met again, and on the sixth of the same month Mr. Scott, the delegate from Missouri, presented to the House the Constitution as framed by the convention.

HISTORY OF MISSOURI

The same was referred to a select committee, who made thereon a favorable report.

The admission of the State, however, was resisted, because it was claimed that its constitution sanctioned slavery, and authorized the Legislature to pass laws preventing free negroes and mulattoes from settling in the State. The report of the committee to whom was referred the Constitution of Missouri was accompanied by a preamble and resolutions, offered by Mr. Lowndes, of South Carolina. The preamble and resolutions were stricken out.

The application of the State for admission shared the same fate in the Senate. The question was referred to a select committee, who, on the 29th of November, reported in favor of admitting the State. The debate, which followed, continued for two weeks, and finally Mr. Eaton, of Tennessee, offered an amendment to the resolution as follows : —

" Provided, That nothing herein contained shall be so construed as to give the assent of Congress to any provision in the Constitution of Missouri, if any such there be, which contravenes that clause in the Constitution of the United States, which declares that the citizens of each State shall be entitled to all the privileges and immunities of citizens in the several States."

The resolution, as amended, was adopted. The resolution and proviso were again taken up and discussed at great length, when the committee agreed to report the resolution to the House.

The question on agreeing to the amendment, as reported from the committee of the whole, was lost in the House. A similar resolution afterward passed the Senate, but was again rejected in the House. Then it was that that great statesman and pure patriot, Henry Clay, of Kentucky, feeling that the hour had come when angry discussions should cease,

> " With grave
> Aspect he rose, and in his rising seem'd
> A pillar of state; deep on his front engraver
> Deliberation sat and public care;
> And princely counsel in his face yet shone
> Majestic " * * * * * *

proposed that the question of Missouri's admission be referred to a committee consisting of twenty-three persons (a number equal to the number of States then composing the Union), be appointed to act in conjunction with a committee of the Senate to consider and report whether Missouri should be admitted, etc.

The motion prevailed; the committee was appointed and Mr. Clay made its chairman. The Senate selected seven of its members to act with the committee of twenty-three, and on the 26th of February the following report was made by that committee:—

" Resolved, by the Senate and House of Representatives of the United States of America in Congress assembled: That Missouri shall be admitted into the Union, on an equal footing with the original States, in all respects whatever, upon the fundamental condition that the fourth clause, of the twenty-sixth section of the third article of the Constitution submitted on the part of said State to Congress, shall never be construed to authorize the passage of any law, and that no law shall be passed in conformity thereto, by which any citizen of either of the States in this Union shall be excluded from the enjoyment of any of the privileges and immunities to which such citizen is entitled, under the Constitution of the United States; provided, That the Legislature of said State, by a Solemn Public Act, shall declare the assent of the said State, to the said fundamental condition, and shall transmit to the President of the United States, on or before the fourth Monday in November next, an authentic copy of the said act; upon the receipt whereof, the President, by proclamation, shall announce the fact; whereupon, and without any further proceeding on the part of Congress, the admission of the said State into the Union shall be considered complete."

This resolution, after a brief debate, was adopted in the House, and passed the Senate on the 28th of February, 1821.

At a special session of the Legislature held in St. Charles, in June following, a Solemn Public Act was adopted, giving its assent to the conditions of admission, as expressed in the resolution of Mr. Clay. August 10th, 1821, President Monroe announced by proclamation the admission of Missouri into the Union to be complete.

CHAPTER VII.

MISSOURI AS A STATE.

First Election for Governor and other State Officers — Senators and Representatives to General Assembly — Sheriffs and Coroners — U. S. Senators — Representatives in Congress — Supreme Court Judges — Counties Organized — Capital Moved to St. Charles — Official Record of Territorial and State Officers.

By the Constitution adopted by the Convention on the 19th of July, 1820, the General Assembly was required to meet in St. Louis on the third Monday in September of that year, and an election was ordered to be held on the 28th of August for the election of a Governor and other State officers, Senators and Representatives to the General Assembly, Sheriffs and Coroners, United States Senators and Representatives in Congress.

It will be seen that Missouri had not as yet been admitted as a State, but in anticipation of that event, and according to the provisions of the constitution, the election was held, and the General Assembly convened.

William Clark (who had been Governor of the Territory) and Alexander McNair were the candidates for Governor. McNair received 6,576 votes, Clark 2,556, total vote of the State 9,132. There were three candidates for Lieutenant-Governor, to wit: William H. Ashley, Nathaniel Cook and Henry Elliot. Ashley received 3,907 votes, Cook 3,212, Elliot 931. A Representative was to be elected for the residue of the Sixteenth Congress and one for the Seventeenth. John Scott who was at the time Territorial delegate, was elected to both Congresses without opposition.

The General Assembly elected in August met on the 19th of September, 1820, and organized by electing James Caldwell, of Ste. Genevieve, speaker, and John McArthur clerk; William H. Ashley, Lieutenant-Governor, President of the Senate; Silas Bent, President, *pro tem.*

Mathias McGirk, John D. Cook, and John R. Jones were appointed Supreme Judges, each to hold office until sixty-five years of age.

Joshua Barton was appointed Secretary of State; Peter Didier, State Treasurer; Edward Bates, Attorney-General, and William Christie, Auditor of Public Accounts.

HISTORY OF MISSOURI

David Barton and Thomas H. Benton were elected by the General Assembly to the United States Senate.

At this session of the Legislature the counties of Boone, Callaway, Chariton, Cole, Gasconade, Lillard, Perry, Ralls, Ray and Saline were organized.

We should like to give in details the meetings and proceedings of the different Legislatures which followed; the elections for Governors and other State officers; the elections for Congressmen and United States Senators, but for want of space we can only present in a condensed form the official record of the Territorial and State officers.

OFFICIAL RECORD — TERRITORIAL OFFICERS.

Governors.

Frederick Bates, Secretary and Acting-Governor	1812–18	William Clark	1818–20

OFFICERS OF STATE GOVERNMENT.

Governors.

Alexander McNair	1820–24
Frederick Bates	1824–25
Abraham J. Williams, vice Bates	1825
John Miller, vice Bates	1826–28
John Miller	1828–82
Daniel Dunklin, (1832–86) resigned; appointed Surveyor General of the U. S. Lilburn W. Boggs, vice Dunklin	1886
Lilburn W. Boggs	1886–40
Thomas Reynolds (died 1844),	1840–44
M. M. Marmaduke vice Reynolds — John C. Edwards	1844–48
Austin A. King	1848–52
Sterling Price	1852–56
Trusten Polk (resigned)	1856–57
Hancock Jackson, vice Polk	1857
Robert M. Stewart, vice Polk	1857–60
C. F. Jackson (1860), office vacated by ordinance; Hamilton R. Gamble, vice Jackson; Gov. Gamble died 1864.	
Willard P. Hall, vice Gamble	1864
Thomas C. Fletcher	1864–68
Joseph W. McClurg	1868–70
B. Gratz Brown	1870–72
Silas Woodson	1872–74
Charles H. Hardin	1874–76
John S. Phelps	1876–80
Thomas T. Crittenden (now Governor)	1880

Lieutenant-Governors.

William H. Ashley	1820–24
Benjamin H. Reeves	1824–28
Daniel Dunklin	1828–82
Lilburn W. Boggs	1832–86
Franklin Cannon	1886–40
M. M. Marmaduke	1840–44
James Young	1844–48
Thomas L Rice	1848–52
Wilson Brown	1852–55
Hancock Jackson	1855–56
Thomas C. Reynolds	1860–61
Willard P. Hall	1861–64
George Smith	1864–68
Edwin O. Stanard	1868–70
Joseph J. Gravelly	1870–72
Charles P. Johnson	1872–74
Norman J. Coleman	1874–76
Henry C. Brockmeyer	1876–80
Robert A. Campbell (present incumbent)	1880

Secretaries of State.

Joshua Barton	1820–21
William G. Pettis	1821–24
Hamilton R. Gamble	1824–26
Spencer Pettis	1826–28
P. H. McBride	1829–30
John C. Edwards (term expired 1885, reappointed 1887, resigned 1887)	1830–37
Peter G. Glover	1887–89
James L. Minor	1839–45

38

HISTORY OF MISSOURI

OFFICERS OF STATE GOVERNMENT — Continued.

F. H. Martin	1845–49	*Auditors of Public Accounts.*	
Ephraim B. Ewing	1849–52	William Christie	1820–21
John M. Richardson	1852–56	William V. Rector	1821–23
Benjamin F. Massey (re-elected 1860, for four years)	1856–60	Elias Barcroft	1823–33
		Henry Shurlds	1833–35
Mordecai Oliver	1861–64	Peter G. Glover	1835–37
Francis Rodman (re-elected 1868 for two years)	1864–68	Hiram H. Baber	1837–45
		William Monroe	1845
Eugene F. Weigel, (re-elected 1872, for two years)	1870–72	J. R. McDermon	1845–48
		George W. Miller	1848–49
Michael K. McGrath (present incumbent)	1874	Wilson Brown	1849–52
		William H. Buffington	1852–60
		William S. Moseley	1860–64
State Treasurers.		Alonzo Thompson	1864–68
Peter Didier	1820–21	Daniel M. Draper	1868–72
Nathaniel Simonds	1821–28	George B. Clark	1872–74
James Earickson	1829–33	Thomas Holladay	187 –80
John Walker	1833–38	John Walker (present incumbent)	1880
Abraham McClellan	1838–43		
Peter G. Glover	1843–51	***Judges of Supreme Court.***	
A. W. Morrison	1851–60		
George C. Bingham	1862–64	Matthias McGirk	1822–41
William Bishop	1864–68	John D. Cooke	1822–28
William Q. Dallmeyer	1868–70	John R. Jones	1822–24
Samuel Hays	1872	Rufus Pettibone	1823–25
Harvey W. Salmon	1872–74	Geo. Tompkins	1824–45
Joseph W. Mercer	1874–76	Robert Wash	1825–37
Elijah Gates	1876–80	John C. Edwards	1837–39
Phillip E. Chappell (present incumbent)	1880	Wm. Scott, (appointed 1841 till meeting of General Assembly in place of McGirk, resigned; reappointed	1843
Attorney-Generals.		P. H. McBride	1845
Edward Bates	1820–21	Wm. B. Napton	1849–52
Rufus Easton	1821–26	John F. Ryland	1849–51
Robt. W. Wells	1826–36	John H. Birch	1849–51
William B. Napton	1836–39	Wm. Scott, John F. Ryland, and Hamilton R. Gamble (elected by the people, for six years)	1851
S. M. Bay	1889–45		
B. F. Stringfellow	1845–49		
William A. Robards	1849–51		
James B. Gardenhire	1851–56	Gamble (resigned)	1854
Ephraim W. Ewing	1856–59	Abiel Leonard elected to fill vacancy of Gamble.	
James P. Knott	1859–61		
Aikman Welch	1861–64	Wm. B. Napton (vacated by failure to file oath).	
Thomas T. Crittenden	1864		
Robert F. Wingate	1864–68	Wm. Scott and John C. Richardson (resigned, elected August, for six years)	1857
Horace P. Johnson	1868–70		
A. J. Baker	1870–72		
Henry Clay Ewing	1872–74	E. B. Ewing, (to fill Richardson's resignation)	1859
John A. Hockaday	1874–76		
Jackson L. Smith	1876–80	Barton Bates (appointed)	1862
D. H. McIntire (present incumbent)	1880	W. V. N. Bay (appointed)	1862

HISTORY OF MISSOURI

OFFICERS OF STATE GOVERNMENT — *Continued.*

John D. S. Dryden (appointed)	1862
Barton Bates	1863–65
W. V. N. Bay (elected)	1863
John D. S. Dryden (elected)	1863
David Wagner (appointed)	1865
Wallace L. Lovelace (appointed)	1865
Nathaniel Holmes (appointed)	1865
Thomas J. C. Fagg (appointed)	1866
James Baker (appointed)	1868
David Wagner (elected)	1868–70
Philemon Bliss	1868–70
Warren Currier	1868–71
Washington Adams (appointed to fill Currier's place, who resigned)	1871
Ephraim B. Ewing (elected)	1872
Thomas A. Sherwood (elected)	1872
W. B. Napton (appointed in place of Ewing, deceased)	1873
Edward A. Lewis (appointed, in place of Adams, resigned)	1874
Warwick Hough (elected)	1874
William B. Napton (elected)	1874–80
John W. Henry	1876–86
Robert D. Ray succeeded Wm. B. Napton in	1880
Elijah H. Norton (appointed in 1876), elected	1878
T. A. Sherwood (re-elected)	1882

United States Senators.

T. H. Benton	1820–50
D. Barton	1820–30
Alex. Buckner	1830–33
L. F. Linn	1833–43
D. R. Atchison	1843–55
H. S. Geyer	1851–57
James S. Green	1857–61
T. Polk	1857–63
Waldo P. Johnson	1861
Robert Wilson	1861
B. Gratz Brown (for unexpired term of Johnson)	1863
J. B. Henderson	1863–69
Charles D. Drake	1867–70
Carl Schurz	1869–75
D. F. Jewett (in place of Drake, resigned)	1870
F. P. Blair	1871–77
L. V. Bogy	1873
James Shields (elected for unexpired term of Bogy)	1879

D. H. Armstrong appointed for unexpired term of Bogy.	
F. M. Cockrell (re-elected 1881)	1875–81
George G. Vest	1879

Representatives to Congress.

John Scott	1820–26
Ed. Bates	1826–28
Spencer Pettis	1828–31
William H. Ashley	1831–36
John Bull	1832–34
Albert G. Harrison	1834–39
John Miller	1836–42
John Jameson (re-elected 1846 for two years)	1839–44
John C. Edwards	1840–42
James M. Hughes	1842–44
James H. Relfe	1842–46
James B. Bowlin	1842–50
Gustavus M. Bower	1842–44
Sterling Price	1844–46
William McDaniel	1846
Leonard H. Sims	1844–46
John S. Phelps	1844–60
James S. Green (re-elected 1856, resigned)	1846–50
Willard P. Hall	1846–53
William V. N. Bay	1848–51
John F. Darby	1850–53
Gilchrist Porter	1850–57
John G. Miller	1850–56
Alfred W. Lamb	1852–54
Thomas H. Benton	1852–54
Mordecai Oliver	1852–57
James J. Lindley	1852–56
Samuel Caruthers	1852–53
Thomas P. Akers (to fill unexpired term of J. G. Miller, deceased)	1855
Francis P. Blair, Jr. (re-elected 1860, resigned)	1856
Thomas L. Anderson	1856–60
James Craig	1856–60
Samuel H. Woodson	1856–60
John B. Clark, Sr.	1857–61
J. Richard Barrett	1860
John W. Nool	1858–63
James S. Rollins	1860–64
Elijah H. Norton	1860–63
John W. Reid	1860–61
William A. Hall	1862–64
Thomas L. Price (in place of Reid, expelled)	1862

40

HISTORY OF MISSOURI

OFFICERS OF STATE GOVERNMENT — *Continued.*

Henry T. Blow	1862–66
Sempronius T. Boyd, (elected in 1862, and again in 1868, for two years.)	
Joseph W. McClurg	1862–66
Austin A. King	1862–64
Benjamin F. Loan	1862–69
John G. Scott (in place of Noel, deceased)	1868
John Hogan	1864–66
Thomas F. Noel	1864–67
John R. Kelsoe	1864–66
Robert T. Van Horn	1864–71
John F. Benjamin	1864–71
George W. Anderson	1864–69
William A. Pile	1866–68
C. A. Newcomb	1866–68
Joseph J. Gravelly	1866–68
James R. McCormack	1866–78
John H. Stover (in place of McClurg, resigned)	1867
Erastus Wells	1868–82
G. A. Finklenburg	1868–71
Samuel S. Burdett	1868–71
Joel F. Asper	1868–70
David P. Dyer	1868–70
Harrison E. Havens	1870–75
Isaac G. Parker	1870–75
James G. Blair	1870–72
Andrew King	1870–72
Edwin O. Stanard	1872–74
William H. Stone	1872–78
Robert A. Hatcher (elected)	1872
Richard B. Bland	1872
Thomas T. Crittenden	1872–74
Ira B. Hyde	1872–74
John B. Clark, Jr.	1872–78
John M. Glover	1872

Aylett H. Buckner	1872
Edward C. Kerr	1874–78
Charles H. Morgan	1874
John F. Philips	1874
B. J. Franklin	1874
David Rea	1874
Rezin A. De Bolt	1874
Anthony Ittner	1876
Nathaniel Cole	1876
Robert A. Hatcher	1876–78
R. P. Bland	1876–78
A. H. Buckner	1876–78
J. B. Clark, Jr.	1876–78
T. T. Crittenden	1876–78
B. J. Franklin	1876–78
John M. Glover	1876–78
Robert A. Hatcher	1876–78
Chas. H. Morgan	1876–78
L. S. Metcalf	1876–78
H. M. Pollard	1876–78
David Rea	1876–78
S. L. Sawyer	1878–80
N. Ford	1878–82
G. F. Rothwell	1878–82
John B. Clark, Jr.	1878–82
W. H. Hatch	1878–82
A. H. Buckner	1878–82
M. L. Clardy	1878–82
R. G. Frost	1878–82
L. H. Davis	1878–82
R. P. Bland	1878–82
J. R. Waddell	1878–80
T. Allen	1880–82
R. Hazeltine	1880–82
T. M. Rice	1880–82
R. T. Van Horn	1880–82
Nicholas Ford	1880–82
J. G. Burrows	1880–82

COUNTIES — WHEN ORGANIZED.

Adair	January 29, 1841
Andrew	January 29, 1841
Atchison	January 14, 1845
Audrain	December 17, 1836
Barry	January 5, 1835
Barton	December 12, 1835
Bates	January 29, 1841
Benton	January 8, 1835
Bollinger	March 1, 1851
Boone	November 16, 1820
Buchanan	February 10, 1839

Caldwell	December 26, 1836
Callaway	November 25, 1820
Camden	January 29, 1841
Cape Girardeau	October 1, 1812
Carroll	January 8, 1833
Carter	March 10, 1859
Cass	September 14, 1835
Cedar	February 14, 1845
Chariton	November 16, 1820
Christian	March 8, 1860
Clark	December 15, 1818

HISTORY OF MISSOURI

COUNTIES, WHEN ORGANIZED — Continued.

Butler	February 27, 1849	Monroe	January 6, 1831
Clay	January 2, 1822	Montgomery	December 14, 1818
Clinton	January 15, 1833	Morgan	January 5, 1833
Cole	November 16, 1820	New Madrid	October 1, 1812
Cooper	December 17, 1818	Newton	December 31, 1838
Crawford	January 23, 1829	Nodaway	February 14, 1845
Dade	January 29, 1841	Oregon	February 14, 1845
Dallas	December 10, 1844	Osage	January 29, 1841
Daviess	December 29, 1836	Ozark	January 29, 1841
DeKalb	February 25, 1845	Pemiscot	February 19, 1861
Dent	February 10, 1851	Perry	November 16, 1820
Douglas	October 19, 1857	Pettis	January 26, 1833
Dunklin	February 14, 1845	Phelps	November 13, 1857
Franklin	December 11, 1818	Pike	December 14, 1818
Gasconade	November 25, 1820	Platte	December 31, 1838
Gentry	February 12, 1841	Polk	March 13, 1835
Greene	January 2, 1833	Pulaski	December 15, 1818
Grundy	January 2, 1843	Putnam	February 28, 1845
Harrison	February 14, 1845	Ralls	November 16, 1820
Henry	December 13, 1834	Randolph	January 22, 1829
Hickory	February 14, 1845	Ray	November 16, 1820
Holt	February 15, 1841	Reynolds	February 25, 1845
Howard	January 23, 1816	Ripley	January 5, 1833
Howell	March 2, 1857	St. Charles	October 1, 1812
Iron	February 17, 1857	St. Clair	January 29, 1841
Jackson	December 15, 1826	St. Francois	December 19, 1821
Jasper	January 29, 1841	Ste. Genevieve	October 1, 1812
Jefferson	December 8, 1818	St. Louis	October 1, 1812
Johnson	December 13, 1834	Saline	November 25, 1820
Knox	February 14, 1845	Schuyler	February 14, 1845
Laclede	February 24, 1849	Scotland	January 29, 1841
Lafayette	November 16, 1820	Scott	December 28, 1821
Lawrence	February 25, 1845	Shannon	January 29, 1841
Lewis	January 2, 1833	Shelby	January 2, 1835
Lincoln	December 14, 1818	Stoddard	January 2, 1835
Linn	January 7, 1837	Stone	February 10, 1851
Livingston	January 6, 1837	Sullivan	February 16, 1845
McDonald	March 3, 1849	Taney	January 16, 1837
Macon	January 6, 1837	Texas	February 14, 1835
Madison	December 14, 1818	Vernon	February 17, 1851
Maries	March 2, 1855	Warren	January 5, 1833
Marion	December 23, 1826	Washington	August 21, 1818
Mercer	February 14, 1845	Wayne	December 11, 1818
Miller	February 6, 1837	Webster	March 3, 1855
Mississippi	February 14, 1845	Worth	February 8, 1861
Moniteau	February 14, 1345	Wright	January 29, 1841

CHAPTER VIII.

CIVIL WAR IN MISSOURI.

Fort Sumter fired upon — Call for 75,000 men — Gov. Jackson refuses to furnish a man — U. S. Arsenal at Liberty, Mo., seized — Proclamation of Gov. Jackson — General Order No. 7 — Legislature convenes — Camp Jackson organized — Sterling Price appointed Major-General — Frost's letter to Lyon — Lyon's letter to Frost — Surrender of Camp Jackson — Proclamation of Gen. Harney — Conference between Price and Harney — Harney superseded by Lyon — Second Conference — Gov. Jackson burns the bridges behind him — Proclamation of Gov. Jackson — Gen. Blair takes possession of Jefferson City — Proclamation of Lyon — Lyon at Springfield — State offices declared vacant — Gen. Fremont assumes command — Proclamation of Lieut.-Gov. Reynolds — Proclamation of Jeff. Thompson and Gov. Jackson — Death of Gen. Lyon — Succeeded by Sturgis — Proclamation of McCulloch and Gamble — Martial law declared — Second proclamation of Jeff. Thompson — President modifies Fremont's order — Fremont relieved by Hunter — Proclamation of Price — Hunter's Order of Assessment — Hunter declares Martial Law — Order relating to Newspapers — Halleck succeeds Hunter — Halleck's Order 81 — Similar order by Halleck — Boone County Standard confiscated — Execution of prisoners at Macon and Palmyra — Gen. Ewing's Order No. 11 — Gen. Rosecrans takes command — Massacre at Centralia — Death of Bill Anderson — Gen. Dodge succeeds Gen. Rosecrans — List of Battles.

> " Lastly stood war —
>   With visage grim, stern looks, and blackly hued,
>   *   *   *   *   *   *   *
>   Ah! why will kings forget that they are men?
>   And men that they are brethren? Why delight
>   In human sacrifice? Why burst the ties
>   Of nature, that should knit their souls together
>   In one soft bond of amity and love?"

Fort Sumter was fired upon April 12, 1861. On April 15th, President Lincoln issued a proclamation calling for 75,000 men, from the the militia of the several States, to suppress combinations in the Southern States therein named. Simultaneously therewith, the Secretary of War sent a telegram to all the governors of the States, excepting those mentioned in the proclamation, requesting them to detail a certain number of militia to serve for three months, Missouri's quota being four regiments.

In response to this telegram, Gov. Jackson sent the following answer:

EXECUTIVE DEPARTMENT OF MISSOURI,
    JEFFERSON CITY, April 17, 1861.

To the HON. SIMON CAMERON, *Secretary of War, Washington, D.C.:*
SIR: Your dispatch of the 15th inst., making a call on Missouri for

four regiments of men for immediate service, has been received. There can be, I apprehend, no doubt but these men are intended to form a part of the President's army to make war upon the people of the seceded States. Your requisition, in my judgment, is illegal, unconstitutional, and can not be complied with. Not one man will the State of Missouri furnish to carry on such an unholy war.

C. F. JACKSON,
Governor of Missouri.

April 21, 1861. U. S. Arsenal at Liberty was seized by order of Governor Jackson.

April 22, 1861. Governor Jackson issued a proclamation convening the Legislature of Missouri, on May following, in extra session, to take into consideration the momentous issues which were presented, and the attitude to be assumed by the State in the impending struggle.

On the 22nd of April, 1861, the Adjutant-General of Missouri issued the following military order:

HEADQUARTERS ADJUTANT-GENERAL'S OFFICE, MO.,
JEFFERSON CITY, April 22, 1861.
(*General Orders No. 7.*)

I. To attain a greater degree of efficiency and perfection in organization and discipline, the Commanding Officers of the several Military districts in this State, having four or more legally organized companies therein, whose armories are within fifteen miles of each other, will assemble their respective commands at some place to be by them severally designated, on the 3rd day of May, and to go into an encampment for a period of six days, as provided by law. Captains of companies not organized into battalions will report the strength of their companies immediately to these headquarters, and await further orders.

II. The Quartermaster-General will procure and issue to Quartermasters of Districts, for these commands not now provided for, all necessary tents and camp equipage, to enable the commanding officers thereof to carry the foregoing orders into effect.

III. The Light Battery now attached to the Southwest Battalion, and one company of mounted riflemen, including all officers and soldiers belonging to the First District, will proceed forthwith to St. Louis, and report to Gen. D. M. Frost for duty. The remaining companies of said battalion will be disbanded for the purpose of assisting in the organization of companies upon that frontier. The details in the execution of the foregoing are intrusted to Lieutenant-Colonel John S. Bowen, commanding the Battalion.

IV. The strength, organization, and equipment of the several companies in the District will be reported at once to these Headquarters, and District Inspectors will furnish all information which may be serviceable in ascertaining the condition of the State forces.

By order of the Governor.

WARWICK HOUGH,
Adjutant-General of Missouri.

May 2, 1861. The Legislature convened in extra session. Many acts were passed, among which was one to authorize the Governor to purchase or lease David Ballentine's foundry at Boonville, for the manufacture of arms and munitions of war; to authorize the Governor to appoint one Major-General; to authorize the Governor, when, in his opinion, the security and welfare of the State required it, to take possession of the railroad and telegraph lines of the State; to provide for the organization, government, and support of the military forces; to borrow one million of dollars to arm and equip the militia of the State to repel invasion, and protect the lives and property of the people. An act was also passed creating a "Military Fund," to consist of all the money then in the treasury or that might thereafter be received from the one-tenth of one per cent. on the hundred dollars, levied by act of November, 1857, to complete certain railroads; also the proceeds of a tax of fifteen cents on the hundred dollars of the assessed value of the taxable property of the several counties in the State, and the proceeds of the two-mill tax, which had been theretofore appropriated for educational purposes.

May 3, 1861. "Camp Jackson" was organized.

May 10, 1861. Sterling Price appointed Major-General of State Guard.

May 10, 1861. General Frost, commanding "Camp Jackson," addressed General N. Lyon, as follows:—

HEADQUARTERS CAMP JACKSON, MISSOURI MILITIA, May 10, 1861.
CAPT. N. LYON, *Commanding U. S. Troops in and about St. Louis Arsenal:*

SIR: I am constantly in receipt of information that you contemplate an attack upon my camp, whilst I understand that you are impressed with the idea that an attack upon the Arsenal and United States troops is intended on the part of the Militia of Missouri. I am greatly at a loss to know what could justify you in attacking citizens of the United States, who are in lawful performance of their duties, devolving upon them under the Constitution in organizing and instructing the militia of the State in obedience to her laws, and, therefore, have been disposed to doubt the correctness of the information I have received.

I would be glad to know from you personally whether there is any truth in the statements that are constantly pouring into my ears. So far as regards any hostility being intended toward the United States, or its property or representatives by any portion of my command, or, as far as I can learn (and I think I am fully informed), of any other part of the State forces, I can positively say that the idea has never been entertained. On the contrary, prior to your taking command of the Arsenal, I proffered to Major Bell, then in command of the very few troops constituting its guard, the services of myself and all my command, and, if necessary, the whole power of the State, to protect the United States in the full possession of all her property. Upon General Harney taking command of this department, I made the same proffer of services to him, and authorized his Adjutant-General, Capt. Williams, to communicate the fact that such had been done to the War Department. I have had no occasion since to change any of the views I entertained at the time, neither of my own volition nor through orders of my constitutional commander.

I trust that after this explicit statement that we may be able, by fully understanding each other, to keep far from our borders the misfortunes which so unhappily affect our common country.

This communication will be handed you by Colonel Bowen, my Chief of Staff, who will be able to explain anything not fully set forth in the foregoing.

I am, sir, very respectfully your obedient servant.

BRIGADIER-GENERAL D. M. FROST,
Commanding Camp Jackson, M. V. M.

May 10, 1861. Gen. Lyon sent the following to Gen. Frost:

HEADQUARTERS UNITED STATES TROOPS,
ST. LOUIS, Mo., May 10, 1861.

GEN. D. M. FROST, *Commanding Camp Jackson:*

SIR: Your command is regarded as evidently hostile toward the Government of the United States.

It is, for the most part, made up of those Secessionists who have openly avowed their hostility to the General Government, and have been plotting at the seizure of its property and the overthrow of its authority. You are openly in communication with the so-called Southern Confederacy, which is now at war with the United States, and you are receiving at your camp, from the said Confederacy and under its flag, large supplies of the material of war, most of which is known to be the property of the United States. These extraordinary preparations plainly indicate none other than the well-known purpose of the Governor of this State, under whose orders you are acting, and whose communication to the Legislature has just been responded to by that body in the most unparalleled legislation, having in direct view hostilities to the General Government and co-operation with its enemies.

In view of these considerations, and of your failure to disperse in obedience to the proclamation of the President, and of the imminent necessities of State policy and warfare, and the obligations imposed upon me by instructions from Washington, it is my duty to demand, and I do hereby demand of you an immediate surrender of your command, with no other conditions than that all persons surrendering under this command shall be humanely and kindly treated. Believing myself prepared to enforce this demand, one-half hour's time before doing so will be allowed for your compliance therewith.

Very respectfully, your obedient servant,

N. LYON,
Captain Second Infantry, Commanding Troops.

May 10, 1861. Camp Jackson surrendered and prisoners all released excepting Capt. Emmet McDonald, who refused to subscribe to the parole.

May 12, 1861. Brigadier-General Wm. S. Harney issued a proclamation to the people of Missouri, saying " he would carefully abstain from the exercise of any unnecessary powers," and only use " the military force stationed in this district in the last resort to preserve peace."

May 14, 1861. General Harney issued a second proclamation.

May 21, 1861. General Harney held a conference with General Sterling Price, of the Missouri State Guards.

May 31, 1861. General Harney superseded by General Lyon.

June 11, 1861. A second conference was held between the National and State authorities in St. Louis, which resulted in nothing.

HISTORY OF MISSOURI

June 11, 1861. Gov. Jackson left St. Louis for Jefferson City, burning the railroad bridges behind him, and cutting telegraph wires.

June 12, 1861. Governor Jackson issued a proclamation calling into active service 50,000 militia, "to repel invasion, protect life, property," etc.

June 15, 1861. Col. F. P. Blair took possession of the State Capital, Gov. Jackson, Gen. Price and other officers having left on the 13th of June for Boonville.

June 17, 1861. Battle of Boonville took place between the forces of Gen. Lyon and Col. John S. Marmaduke.

June 18, 1861. General Lyon issued a proclamation to the people of Missouri.

July 5, 1861. Battle at Carthage between the forces of Gen. Sigel and Gov. Jackson.

July 6, 1861. Gen. Lyon reached Springfield.

July 22, 1861. State convention met and declared the offices of Governor, Lieutenant-Governor and Secretary of State vacated.

July 26, 1861. Gen. John C. Fremont assumed command of the Western Department, with headquarters in St. Louis.

July 31, 1861. Lieutenant-Governor Thomas C. Reynolds issued a proclamation at New Madrid.

August 1, 1861. General Jeff. Thompson issued a proclamation at Bloomfield.

August 2, 1861. Battle of Dug Springs, between Captain Steele's forces and General Rains.

August 5, 1861. Governor Jackson issued a proclamation at New Madrid.

August 5, 1861. Battle of Athens.

August 10, 1861. Battle of Wilson's Creek, between the forces under General Lyon and General McCulloch. In this engagement General Lyon was killed. General Sturgis succeeded General Lyon.

August 12, 1861. McCulloch issued a proclamation, and soon left Missouri.

August 20, 1861. General Price issued a proclamation.

August 24, 1861. Governor Gamble issued a proclamation calling for 32,000 men for six months to protect the property and lives of the citizens of the State.

August 30, 1861. General Fremont declared martial law, and declared that the slaves of all persons who should thereafter take an active part with the enemies of the Government should be free.

48

HISTORY OF MISSOURI

September 2, 1861. General Jeff. Thompson issued a proclamation in response to Fremont's proclamation.

September 7, 1861. Battle at Drywood Creek.

September 11, 1861. President Lincoln modified the clause in Gen. Fremont's declaration of martial law, in reference to the confiscation of property and liberation of slaves.

September 12, 1861. General Price begins the attack at Lexington on Colonel Mulligan's forces.

September 20, 1861. Colonel Mulligan with 2,640 men surrendered.

October 25, 1861. Second battle at Springfield.

October 28, 1861. Passage by Governor Jackson's Legislature, at Neosho, of an ordinance of secession.

November 2, 1861. General Fremont succeeded by General David Hunter.

November 7, 1861. General Grant attacked Belmont.

November 9, 1861. General Hunter succeeded by General Halleck, who took command on the 19th of same month, with headquarters in St. Louis.

November 27, 1861. General Price issued proclamation calling for 50,000 men, at Neosho, Missouri.

December 12, 1861. General Hunter issued his order of assessment upon certain wealthy citizens in St. Louis, for feeding and clothing Union refugees.

December 23–25. Declared martial law in St. Louis and the country adjacent, and covering all the railroad lines.

March 6, 1862. Battle at Pea Ridge between the forces under Generals Curtis and Van Dorn.

January 8, 1862. Provost Marshal Farrar, of St. Louis, issued the following order in reference to newspapers:

> OFFICE OF THE PROVOST MARSHAL,
> GENERAL DEPARTMENT OF MISSOURI,
> ST. LOUIS, January 8, 1862.

(General Order No. 10.)

It is hereby ordered that from and after this date the publishers of newspapers in the State of Missouri (St. Louis City papers excepted), furnish to this office, immediately upon publication, one copy of each issue, for inspection. A failure to comply with this order will render the newspaper liable to suppression.

Local Provost Marshals will furnish the proprietors with copies of this order, and attend to its immediate enforcement.

BERNARD G. FARRAR,
Provost Marshal General.

January 26, 1862. General Halleck issued order (No. 18) which forbade, among other things, the display of Secession flags in the hands of women or on carriages, in the vicinity of the military prison in McDowell's College, the carriages to be confiscated and the offending women to be arrested.

February 4, 1862. General Halleck issued another order similar to Order No. 18, to railroad companies and to the professors and directors of the State University at Columbia, forbidding the funds of the institution to be used "to teach treason or to instruct traitors."

February 20, 1862. Special Order No. 120 convened a military commission, which sat in Columbia, March following, and tried Edmund J. Ellis, of Columbia, editor and proprietor of "*The Boone County Standard*," for the publication of information for the benefit of the enemy, and encouraging resistance to the United States Government. Ellis was found guilty, was banished during the war from Missouri, and his printing materials confiscated and sold.

April, 1862. General Halleck left for Corinth, Mississippi, leaving General Schofield in command.

June, 1862. Battle at Cherry Grove between the forces under Colonel Joseph C. Porter and Colonel H. S. Lipscomb.

June, 1862. Battle at Pierce's Mill between the forces under Major John Y. Clopper and Colonel Porter.

July 22, 1862. Battle at Florida.

July 28, 1862. Battle at Moore's Mill.

August 6, 1862. Battle near Kirksville.

August 11, 1862. Battle at Independence.

August 16, 1862. Battle at Lone Jack.

September 13, 1862. Battle at Newtonia.

September 25, 1862. Ten Confederate prisoners were executed at Macon, by order of General Merrill.

October 18, 1862. Ten Confederate prisoners executed at Palmyra, by order of General McNeill.

January 8, 1863. Battle at Springfield between the forces of General Marmaduke and General E. B. Brown.

April 26, 1863. Battle at Cape Girardeau.

August —, 1863. General Jeff. Thompson captured at Pocahontas, Arkansas, with his staff.

August 25, 1863. General Thomas Ewing issued his celebrated Order No. 11, at Kansas City, Missouri, which is as follows: —

. HEADQUARTERS DISTRICT OF THE BORDER,
KANSAS CITY, Mo., August 25, 1863.

(General Order No. 11.)

First. — All persons living in Cass, Jackson and Bates Counties, Missouri, and in that part of Vernon included in this district, except those living within one mile of the limits of Independence, Hickman's Mills, Pleasant Hill and Harrisonville, and except those in that part of Kaw Township, Jackson County, north of Brush Creek and west of the Big Blue, embracing Kansas City and Westport, are hereby ordered to remove from their present places of residence within fifteen days from the date hereof.

Those who, within that time, establish their loyalty to the satisfaction of the commanding officer of the military station nearest their present place of residence, will receive from him certificates stating the fact of their loyalty, and the names of the witnesses by whom it can be shown. All who receive such certificate will be permitted to remove to any military station in this district, or to any part of the State of Kansas, except the counties on the eastern borders of the State. All others shall remove out of this district. Officers commanding companies and detachments serving in the counties named, will see that this paragraph is promptly obeyed.

Second. — All grain and hay in the field, or under shelter, in the district from which the inhabitants are required to remove within reach of military stations, after the 9th day of September next, will be taken to such stations and turned over to the proper officer there, and report of the amount so turned over made to district headquarters, specifying the names of all loyal owners and the amount of such produce taken from them. All grain and hay found in such district after the 9th day of September next, not convenient to such stations, will be destroyed.

Third. — The provisions of General Order No. 10, from these headquarters, will at once be vigorously executed by officers commanding in the parts of the district, and at the stations not subject to the operations of paragraph First of this Order — and especially in the towns of Independence. Westport and Kansas City.

HISTORY OF MISSOURI

Fourth. — Paragraph 3, General Order No. 10, is revoked as to all who have borne arms against the Government in the district since August 20, 1863.

By order of Brigadier-General Ewing:

H. HANNAHS, *Adjutant.*

October 13.   Battle of Marshall.

January, 1864.   General Rosecrans takes command of the Department.

September, 1864.   Battle at Pilot Knob, Harrison and Little Moreau River.

October 5, 1864.   Battle at Prince's Ford and James Gordon's farm.

October 8, 1864.   Battle at Glasgow.

October 20, 1864.   Battle at Little Blue Creek.

September 27, 1864.   Massacre at Centralia, by Captain Bill Anderson.

October 27, 1864.   Captain Bill Anderson killed.

December —, 1864.   General Rosecrans relieved and General Dodge appointed to succeed him.

Nothing occurred specially, of a military character, in the State after December, 1864. We have, in the main, given the facts as they occurred without comment or entering into details. Many of the minor incidents and skirmishes of the war have been omitted because of our limited space.

It is utterly impossible, at this date, to give the names and dates of all the battles fought in Missouri during the Civil War. It will be found, however, that the list given below, which has been arranged for convenience, contains the prominent battles and skirmishes which took place within the State: —

Potosi, May 14, 1861.
Boonville, June 17, 1861.
Carthage, July 5, 1861.
Monroe Station, July 10, 1861.
Overton's Run, July 17, 1861.
Dug Spring, August 2, 1861.
Wilson's Creek, August 10, 1861.
Athens, August 5, 1861.
Moreton, August 20, 1861.
Bennett's Mills, September —, 1861.
Drywood Creek, September 7, 1861.
Norfolk, September 10, 1861.
Lexington, September 12-20, 1861.

Blue Mills Landing, September 17, 1861.
Glasgow Mistake, September 20, 1861.
Osceola, September 25, 1861.
Shanghai, October 13, 1861.
Lebanon, October 13, 1861.
Linn Creek, October 16, 1861.
Big River Bridge, October 15, 1861.
Fredericktown, October 21, 1861.
Springfield, October 25, 1861
Belmont, November 7, 1861.
Piketon, November 8, 1861.
Little Blue, November 10, 1861.
Clark's Station, November 11, 1861.

HISTORY OF MISSOURI

Mt. Zion Church, December 28, 1861.
Silver Creek, January 15, 1862.
New Madrid, February 28, 1862.
Pea Ridge, March 6, 1862.
Neosho, April 22, 1862.
Rose Hill, July 10, 1862.
Chariton River, July 30, 1862.
Cherry Grove, June —, 1862.
Pierce's Mill, June —, 1862.
Florida, July 22, 1862.
Moore's Mill, July 28, 1862.
Kirksville, August 6, 1862.
Compton's Ferry, August 8, 1862.
Yellow Creek, August 13, 1862.
Independence, August 11, 1862.

Lone Jack, August 16, 1862.
Newtonia, September 18, 1862.
Springfield, January 8, 1863.
Cape Girardeau, April 29, 1863.
Marshall, October 13, 1863.
Pilot Knob, September —, 1864.
Harrison, September —, 1864.
Moreau River, October 7, 1864.
Prince's Ford, October 5, 1864.
Glasgow, October 8, 1864.
Little Blue Creek, October 20, 1864.
Albany, October 27, 1864.
Near Rocheport, September 23, 1864.
Centralia, September 27, 1864.

CHAPTER IX.

EARLY MILITARY RECORD.

Black Hawk War — Mormon Difficulties — Florida War — Mexican War.

On the fourteenth day of May, 1832, a bloody engagement took place between the regular forces of the United States, and a part of the Sacs, Foxes, and Winnebago Indians, commanded by Black Hawk and Keokuk, near Dixon's Ferry in Illinois.

The Governor (John Miller) of Missouri, fearing these savages would invade the soil of his State, ordered Major-General Richard Gentry to raise one thousand volunteers for the defence of the frontier. Five companies were at once raised in Boone county, and in Callaway, Montgomery, St. Charles, Lincoln, Pike, Marion, Ralls, Clay and Monroe other companies were raised.

Two of these companies, commanded respectively by Captain John Jamison of Callaway, and Captain David M. Hickman of Boone county, were mustered into service in July for thirty days, and put under command of Major Thomas W. Conyers.

This detachment, accompanied by General Gentry, arrived at Fort Pike on the 15th of July, 1832. Finding that the Indians had not crossed the Mississippi into Missouri, General Gentry returned to Columbia, leaving the fort in charge of Major Conyers. Thirty days having expired, the command under Major Conyers was relieved by two

53

HISTORY OF MISSOURI

other companies under Captains Sinclair Kirtley, of Boone, and Patrick Ewing, of Callaway. This detachment was marched to Fort Pike by Col. Austin A. King, who conducted the two companies under Major Conyers home. Major Conyers was left in charge of the fort, where he remained till September following, at which time the Indian troubles, so far as Missouri was concerned, having all subsided, the frontier forces were mustered out of service.

Black Hawk continued the war in Iowa and Illinois, and was finally defeated and captured in 1833.

MORMON DIFFICULTIES.

In 1832, Joseph Smith, the leader of the Mormons, and the chosen prophet and apostle, as he claimed, of the Most High, came with many followers to Jackson county, Missouri, where they located and entered several thousand acres of land.

The object of his coming so far West — upon the very outskirts of civilization at that time — was to more securely establish his church, and the more effectively to instruct his followers in its peculiar tenets and practices.

Upon the present town site of Independence the Mormons located their "Zion," and gave it the name of "The New Jerusalem." They published here the *Evening Star*, and made themselves generally obnoxious to the Gentiles, who were then in a minority, by their denunciatory articles through their paper, their clannishness and their polygamous practices.

Dreading the demoralizing influence of a paper which seemed to be inspired only with hatred and malice toward them, the Gentiles threw the press and type into the Missouri River, tarred and feathered one of their bishops, and otherwise gave the Mormons and their leaders to understand that they must conduct themselves in an entirely different manner if they wished to be let alone.

After the destruction of their paper and press, they became furiously incensed, and sought many opportunities for retaliation. Matters continued in an uncertain condition until the 31st of October, 1833, when a deadly conflict occurred near Westport, in which two Gentiles and one Mormon were killed.

On the 2d of October following the Mormons were overpowered, and compelled to lay down their arms and agree to leave the county with their families by January 1st on the condition that the owner would be paid for his printing press.

HISTORY OF MISSOURI

Leaving Jackson county, they crossed the Missouri and located in Clay, Carroll; Caldwell and other counties, and selected in Caldwell county a town site, which they called "Far West," and where they entered more land for their future homes.

Through the influence of their missionaries, who were exerting themselves in the East and in different portions of Europe, converts had constantly flocked to their standard, and "Far West," and other Mormon settlements, rapidly prospered.

In 1837 they commenced the erection of a magnificent temple, but never finished it. As their settlements increased in numbers, they became bolder in their practices and deeds of lawlessness.

During the summer of 1838 two of their leaders settled in the town of De Witt, on the Missouri River, having purchased the land from an Illinois merchant. De Witt was in Carroll county, and a good point from which to forward goods and immigrants to their town — Far West.

Upon its being ascertained that these parties were Mormon leaders, the Gentiles called a public meeting, which was addressed by some of the prominent citizens of the county. Nothing, however, was done at this meeting, but at a subsequent meeting, which was held a few days afterward, a committee of citizens was appointed to notify Col. Hinkle (one of the Mormon leaders at De Witt), what they intended to do.

Col. Hinkle upon being notified by this committee became indignant, and threatened extermination to all who should attempt to molest him or the Saints.

In anticipation of trouble, and believing that the Gentiles would attempt to force them from De Witt, Mormon recruits flocked to the town from every direction, and pitched their tents in and around the town in great numbers.

The Gentiles, nothing daunted, planned an attack upon this encampment, to take place on the 21st day of September, 1838, and, accordingly, one hundred and fifty men bivouacked near the town on that day. A conflict ensued, but nothing serious occurred.

The Mormons evacuated their works and fled to some log houses, where they could the more successfully resist the Gentiles, who had in the meantime returned to their camp to await reinforcements. Troops from Saline, Ray and other counties came to their assistance, and increased their number to five hundred men.

Congreve Jackson was chosen Brigadier- General; Ebenezer Price,

HISTORY OF MISSOURI

Colonel; Singleton Vaughan, Lieutenant-Colonel, and Sarshel Woods, Major. After some days of discipline, this brigade prepared for an assault, but before the attack was commenced Judge James Earickson and William F. Dunnica, influential citizens of Howard county, asked permission of General Jackson to let them try and adjust the difficulties without any bloodshed.

It was finally agreed that Judge Earickson should propose to the Mormons, that if they would pay for all the cattle they had killed belonging to the citizens, and load their wagons during the night and be ready to move by ten o'clock next morning, and make no further attempt to settle in Carroll county, the citizens would purchase at first cost their lots in De Witt and one or two adjoining tracts of land.

Col. Hinkle, the leader of the Mormons, at first refused all attempts to settle the difficulties in this way, but finally agreed to the proposition.

In accordance therewith, the Mormons without further delay, loaded up their wagons for the town of Far West, in Caldwell county. Whether the terms of the agreement were ever carried out, on the part of the citizens, is not known.

The Mormons had doubtless suffered much and in many ways — the result of their own acts — but their trials and sufferings were not at an end.

In 1838 the discord between the citizens and Mormons became so great that Governor Boggs issued a proclamation ordering Major-General David R. Atchison to call the militia of his division to enforce the laws. He called out a part of the first brigade of the Missouri State Militia, under command of Gen. A. W. Doniphan, who proceeded to the seat of war. Gen. John B. Clark, of Howard county, was placed in command of the militia.

The Mormon forces numbered about 1,000 men, and were led by G. W. Hinkle. The first engagement occurred at Crooked river, where one Mormon was killed. The principal fight took place at Haughn's Mills, where eighteen Mormons were killed and the balance captured, some of them being killed after they had surrendered. Only one militiaman was wounded.

In the month of October, 1838, Joe Smith surrendered the town of Far West to Gen. Doniphan, agreeing to his conditions, viz.: That they should deliver up their arms, surrender their prominent leaders for trial, and the remainder of the Mormons should, with their

HISTORY OF MISSOURI

families, leave the State. Indictments were found against a number of these leaders, including Joe Smith, who, while being taken to Boone county for trial, made his escape, and was afterward, in 1844, killed at Carthage, Illinois, with his brother Hiram.

FLORIDA WAR.

In September, 1837, the Secretary of War issued a requisition on Governor Boggs, of Missouri, for six hundred volunteers for service in Florida against the Seminole Indians, with whom the Creek nation had made common cause under Osceola.

The first regiment was chiefly raised in Boone county by Colonel Richard Gentry, of which he was elected Colonel; John W. Price, of Howard county, Lieutenant-Colonel; Harrison H. Hughes, also of Howard, Major. Four companies of the second regiment were raised and attached to the first. Two of these companies were composed of Delaware and Osage Indians.

October 6, 1837, Col. Gentry's regiment left Columbia for the seat of war, stopping on the way at Jefferson barracks, where they were mustered into service.

Arriving at Jackson barracks, New Orleans, they were from thence transported in brigs across the Gulf to Tampa Bay, Florida. General Zachary Taylor, who then commanded in Florida, ordered Col. Gentry to march to Okee-cho-bee Lake, one hundred and thirty-five miles inland by the route traveled. Having reached the Kissemmee river, seventy miles distant, a bloody battle ensued, in which Col. Gentry was killed. The Missourians, though losing their gallant leader, continued the fight until the Indians were totally routed, leaving many of their dead and wounded on the field. There being no further service required of the Missourians, they returned to their homes in 1838.

MEXICAN WAR.

Soon after Mexico declared war, against the United States, on the 8th and 9th of May, 1846, the battles of Palo Alto and Resaca de la Palma were fought. Great excitement prevailed throughout the country. In none of her sister States, however, did the fires of patriotism burn more intensely than in Missouri. Not waiting for the call for volunteers, the " St. Louis Legion " hastened to the field of conflict. The " Legion " was commanded by Colonel A. R. Easton. During the month of May, 1846, Governor Edwards, of Missouri, called for volunteers to join the "Army of the West," an expedition to Sante Fe — under command of General Stephen W. Kearney.

Fort Leavenworth was the appointed rendezvous for the volunteers. By the 18th of June, the full complement of companies to compose the first regiment had arrived from Jackson, Lafayette, Clay, Saline, Franklin, Cole, Howard and Callaway counties. Of this regiment, A. W. Doniphan was made Colonel; C. F. Ruff, Lieutenant-Colonel, and Wm. Gilpin, Major. The battalion of light artillery from St. Louis was commanded by Captains R. A. Weightman and A. W. Fischer, with Major M. L. Clark as field officer; battalions of infantry from Platte and Cole counties commanded by Captains Murphy and W. Z. Augney respectively, and the "Laclede Rangers," from St. Louis, by Captain Thomas B. Hudson, aggregating all told, from Missouri, 1,658 men. In the summer of 1846 Hon. Sterling Price resigned his seat in Congress and raised one mounted regiment, one mounted extra battalion, and one extra battalion of Mormon infantry to reinforce the "Army of the West." Mr. Price was made Colonel, and D. D. Mitchell Lieutenant-Colonel.

In August, 1847, Governor Edwards made another requisition for one thousand men, to consist of infantry. The regiment was raised at once. John Dougherty, of Clay county, was chosen Colonel, but before the regiment marched the President countermanded the order.

A company of mounted volunteers was raised in Ralls county, commanded by Captain Wm. T. Lafland. Conspicuous among the engagements in which the Missouri volunteers participated in Mexico were the battles of Bracito, Sacramento, Cañada, El Embudo, Taos and Santa Cruz de Rosales. The forces from Missouri were mustered out in 1848, and will ever be remembered in the history of the Mexican war, for

"A thousand glorious actions that might claim
Triumphant laurels and immortal fame.

CHAPTER X.

AGRICULTURE AND MATERIAL WEALTH.

Missouri as an Agricultural State — The Different Crops — Live Stock — Horses — Mules — Milch Cows — Oxen and other Cattle — Sheep — Hogs — Comparisons — Missouri adapted to Live Stock — Cotton — Broom-Corn and other Products — Fruits — Berries — Grapes — Railroads — First Neigh of the "Iron Horse" in Missouri — Names of Railroads — Manufactures — Great Bridge at St. Louis.

Agriculture is the greatest among all the arts of man, as it is the first in supplying his necessities. It favors and strengthens population; it creates and maintains manufactures; gives employment to navigation and furnishes materials to commerce. It animates every species of industry, and opens to nations the safest channels of wealth. It is the strongest bond of well regulated society, the surest basis of internal peace, and the natural associate of correct morals. Among all the occupations and professions of life, there is none more honorable, none more independent, and none more conducive to health and happiness.

> " In ancient times the sacred plow employ'd
> The kings, and awful fathers of mankind;
> And some, with whom compared your insect tribes
> Are but the beings of a summer's day.
>   Have held the scale of empire, ruled the storm
>   Of mighty war with unwearied hand,
>   Disdaining little delicacies, seized
>   The plow and greatly independent lived."

As an agricultural region, Missouri is not surpassed by any State in the Union. It is indeed the farmer's kingdom, where he always reaps an abundant harvest. The soil, in many portions of the State, has an open, flexible structure, quickly absorbs the most excessive rains, and retains moisture with great tenacity. This being the case, it is not so easily affected by drouth. The prairies are covered with sweet, luxuriant grass, equally good for grazing and hay; grass not surpassed by the Kentucky blue grass — the best of clover and timothy in growing and fattening cattle. This grass is now as full of life-giving nutriment as it was when cropped by the buffalo, the elk, the antelope, and the deer, and costs the herdsman nothing.

59

No State or territory has a more complete and rapid system of natural drainage, or a more abundant supply of pure, fresh water than Missouri. Both man and beast may slake their thirst from a thousand perennial fountains, which gush in limpid streams from the hill-sides, and wend their way through verdant valleys and along smiling prairies, varying in size, as they onward flow, from the diminutive brooklet to the giant river.

Here, nature has generously bestowed her attractions of climate, soil and scenery to please and gratify man while earning his bread in the sweat of his brow. Being thus munificently endowed, Missouri offers superior inducements to the farmer, and bids him enter her broad domain and avail himself of her varied resources.

We present here a table showing the product of each principal crop in Missouri for 1878 : —

Indian Corn	98,062,000 bushels.
Wheat	20,196,000 "
Rye	782,000 "
Oats	19,584,000 "
Buckwheat	46,400 "
Potatoes	5,415,000 "
Tobacco	28,028,000 pounds.
Hay	1,620,000 tons.

There were 3,552,000 acres in corn; wheat, 1,836,000; rye, 48,800; oats, 640,000; buckwheat, 2,900; potatoes, 72,200; tobacco, 29,900; hay, 850,000. Value of each crop: corn, $24,196,-224; wheat, $13,531,320; rye, $300,120; oats, $3,325,120; buckwheat, $24,128; potatoes, $2,057,700; tobacco, $1,151,150; hay, $10,416,600.

Average cash value of crops per acre, $7.69; average yield of corn per acre, 26 bushels; wheat, 11 bushels.

Next in importance to the corn crop in value is live stock. The following table shows the number of horses, mules, and milch cows in the different States for 1879 : —

HISTORY OF MISSOURI

States.	Horses.	Mules.	Milch Cows.
Maine	81,700		196,100
New Hampshire	57,100		98,100
Vermont	77,400		217,800
Massachusetts	131,000		160,700
Rhode Island	16,200		22,000
Connecticut	58,500		116,500
New York	898,900	11,800	1,446,200
New Jersey	114,500	14,400	152,200
Pennsylvania	614,500	24,900	828,400
Delaware	19,900	4,000	28,200
Maryland	108,600	11,800	100,500
Virginia	208,700	80,600	236,200
North Carolina	144,200	74,000	232,300
South Carolina	59,600	51,500	181,800
Georgia	119,200	97,200	278,100
Florida	22,400	11,900	70,000
Alabama	112,800	111,700	215,200
Mississippi	97,200	100,000	188,000
Louisiana	79,800	80,700	110,900
Texas	618,000	180,200	544,500
Arkansas	180,500	89,300	187,700
Tennessee	828,700	99,700	245,700
West Virginia	122,200	2,400	180,500
Kentucky	886,900	117,800	257,200
Ohio	772,700	26,700	714,100
Michigan	833,800	4,300	416,900
Indiana	688,800	61,200	439,200
Illinois	1,100,000	188,000	702,400
Wisconsin	884,400	8,700	477,800
Minnesota	247,800	7,000	278,900
Iowa	770,700	43,400	676,200
MISSOURI	627,300	191,900	516,200
Kansas	275,000	50,000	821,900
Nebraska	157,200	18,600	127,600
California	273,000	25,700	495,600
Oregon	109,700	8,500	112,400
Nevada, Colorado, and Territories	250,000	25,700	423,600

It will be seen from the above table, that Missouri is the *fifth* State in the number of horses; *fifth* in number of milch cows, and the leading State in number of mules, having 11,700 more than Texas, which produces the next largest number. Of oxen and other cattle, Missouri produced in 1879, 1,632,000, which was more than any other State produced excepting Texas, which had 4,800,00. In 1879 Missouri raised 2,817,600 hogs, which was more than any other State produced, excepting Iowa. The number of sheep was 1,296,400. The number of hogs packed in 1879, by the different States, is as follows : —

States.	No.	States.	No.
Ohio	982,878	MISSOURI	965,889
Indiana	622,321	Wisconsin	472,108
Illinois	8,214,896	Kentucky	212,412
Iowa	569,768		

HISTORY OF MISSOURI

AVERAGE WEIGHT PER HEAD FOR EACH STATE.

States.	Pounds.	States.	Pounds.
Ohio	210.47	MISSOURI	211.82
Indiana	198.80	Wisconsin	220.81
Illinois	225.71	Kentucky	210.11
Iowa	211.98		

From the above it will be seen that Missouri annually packs more hogs than any other State excepting Illinois, and that she ranks third in the average weight.

We see no reason why Missouri should not be the foremost stock-raising State of the Union. In addition to the enormous yield of corn and oats upon which the stock is largely dependent, the climate is well adapted to their growth and health. Water is not only inexhaustible, but everywhere convenient. The ranges of stock are boundless, affording for nine months of the year, excellent pasturage of nutritious wild grasses, which grow in great luxuriance upon the thousand prairies.

Cotton is grown successfully in many counties of the southeastern portions of the State, especially in Stoddard, Scott, Pemiscot, Butler, New Madrid, Lawrence and Mississippi.

Sweet potatoes are produced in abundance and are not only sure but profitable.

Broom corn, sorghum, castor beans, white beans, peas, hops, thrive well, and all kinds of garden vegetables, are produced in great abundance and are found in the markets during all seasons of the year. Fruits of every variety, including the apple, pear, peach, cherries, apricots and nectarines, are cultivated with great success, as are also, the strawberry, gooseberry, currant, raspberry and blackberry.

The grape has not been produced with that success that was at first anticipated, yet the yield of wine for the year 1879, was nearly half a million gallons. Grapes do well in Kansas, and we see no reason why they should not be as surely and profitably grown in a similar climate and soil in Missouri, and particularly in many of the counties north and east of the Missouri River.

RAILROADS.

Twenty-nine years ago, the neigh of the "iron horse" was heard for the first time, within the broad domain of Missouri. His coming presaged the dawn of a brighter and grander era in the history of the

State. Her fertile prairies, and more prolific valleys would soon be of easy access to the oncoming tide of immigration, and the ores and minerals of her hills and mountains would be developed, and utilized in her manufacturing and industrial enterprises.

Additional facilities would be opened to the marts of trade and commerce; transportation from the interior of the State would be secured; a fresh impetus would be given to the growth of her towns and cities, and new hopes and inspirations would be imparted to all her people.

Since 1852, the initial period of railroad building in Missouri, between four and five thousand miles of track have been laid; additional roads are now being constructed, and many others in contemplation. The State is already well supplied with railroads which thread her surface in all directions, bringing her remotest districts into close connection with St. Louis, that great center of western railroads and inland commerce. These roads have a capital stock aggregating more than one hundred millions of dollars, and a funded debt of about the same amount.

The lines of roads which are operated in the State are the following: —

Missouri Pacific — chartered May 10th, 1850; The St. Louis, Iron Mountain & Southern Railroad, which is a consolidation of the Arkansas Branch; The Cairo, Arkansas & Texas Railroad; The Cairo & Fulton Railroad; The Wabash, St. Louis & Pacific Railway; St. Louis & San Francisco Railway; The Chicago, Alton & St. Louis Railroad; The Hannibal & St. Joseph Railroad; The Missouri, Kansas & Texas Railroad; The Kansas City, St. Joseph & Council Bluffs Railroad; The Keokuk & Kansas City Railway Company; The St. Louis, Salem & Little Rock Railroad Company; The Missouri & Western; The St. Louis, Keokuk & Northwestern Railroad; The St. Louis, Hannibal & Keokuk Railroad; The Missouri, Iowa & Nebraska Railway; The Quincy, Missouri & Pacific Railroad; The Chicago, Rock Island & Pacific Railway; The Burlington & Southwestern Railroad.

MANUFACTURES.

The natural resources of Missouri especially fit her for a great manufacturing State. She is rich in soil; rich in all the elements which supply the furnace, the machine shop and the planing mill; rich in the multitude and variety of her gigantic forests; rich in her marble, stone and granite quarries; rich in her mines of iron, coal, lead and zinc; rich in strong arms and willing hands to apply the force; rich in water power and river navigation; and rich in her numerous and well-built railroads, whose numberless engines thunder along their multiplied track-ways.

Missouri contains over fourteen thousand manufacturing establishments, 1,965 of which are using steam and give employment to 80,000 hands. The capital employed is about $100,000,000, the material annually used and worked up, amounts to over $150,000,-000, and the value of the products put upon the markets $250,000,000, while the wages paid are more than $40,000,000.

The leading manufacturing counties of the State, are St. Louis, Jackson, Buchanan, St. Charles, Marion, Franklin, Greene, Lafayette, Platte, Cape Girardeau, and Boone. Three-fourths, however, of the manufacturing is done in St. Louis, which is now about the second manufacturing city in the Union. Flouring mills produce annually about $38,194,000; carpentering $18,763,000; meat-packing $16,-769,000; tobacco $12,496,000; iron and castings $12,000,000; liquors $11,245,000; clothing $10,022,000; lumber $8,652,000; bagging and bags $6,914,000, and many other smaller industries in proportion.

REAT BRIDGE AT ST. LOUIS.

Of the many public improvements which do honor to the State and reflect great credit upon the genius of their projectors, we have space only, to mention the great bridge at St. Louis.

This truly wonderful construction is built of tubular steel, total length of which, with its approaches, is 6,277 feet, at a cost of nearly $8,000,000. The bridge spans the Mississippi from the Illinois to the Missouri shore, and has separate railroad tracks, roadways, and foot paths. In durability, architectural beauty and practical utility, there is, perhaps, no similar piece of workmanship that approximates it.

The structure of Darius upon the Bosphorus; of Xerxes upon the Hellespont; of Cæsar upon the Rhine; and Trajan upon the Danube, famous in ancient history, were built for military purposes, that over them might pass invading armies with their munitions of war, to destroy commerce, to lay in waste the provinces, and to slaughter the people.

But the erection of this was for a higher and nobler purpose. Over it are coming the trade and merchandise of the opulent East, and thence are passing the untold riches of the West. Over it are crowd-

HISTORY OF MISSOURI

ing legions of men, armed not with the weapons of war, but with the implements of peace and industry; men who are skilled in all the arts of agriculture, of manufacture and of mining; men who will hasten the day when St. Louis shall rank in population and importance, second to no city on the continent, and when Missouri shall proudly fill the measure of greatness, to which she is naturally so justly entitled.

CHAPTER XI.

EDUCATION.

Public School System — Public School System of Missouri — Lincoln Institute — Officers of Public School System — Certificates of Teachers — University of Missouri—Schools — Colleges — Institutions of Learning — Location — Libraries — Newspapers and Periodicals — No. of School Children — Amount expended — Value of Grounds and Buildings — " The Press."

The first constitution of Missouri provided that " one school or more shall be established in each township, as soon as practicable and necessary, where the poor shall be taught gratis."

It will be seen that even at that early day (1820) the framers of the constitution made provision for at least a primary education for the poorest and the humblest, taking it for granted that those who were able would avail themselves of educational advantages which were not gratuitous.

The establishment of the public-school system, in its essential features, was not perfected until 1839, during the administration of Governor Boggs, and since that period the system has slowly grown into favor, not only in Missouri, but throughout the United States. The idea of a free or public school for all classes was not at first a popular one, especially among those who had the means to patronize private institutions of learning. In upholding and maintaining public schools the opponents of the system felt that they were not only compromising their own standing among their more wealthy neighbors, but that they were, to some extent, bringing opprobrium upon their children. Entertaining such prejudices, they naturally thought that the training received at public schools could not be otherwise than defective; hence many years of probation passed before the popular mind was prepared to appreciate the benefits and blessings which spring from these institutions.

Every year only adds to their popularity, and commends them the more earnestly to the fostering care of our State and National Legislatures, and to the esteem and favor of all classes of our people.

We can hardly conceive of two grander or more potent promoters of civilization than the free school and free press. They would indeed seem to constitute all that was necessary to the attainment of the happiness and intellectual growth of the Republic, and all that was necessary to broaden, to liberalize and instruct.

> "Tis education forms the common mind;
> * * * * * *
> For noble youth there is nothing so meet
> As learning is, to know the good from ill;
> To know the tongues, and perfectly indite,
> And of the laws to have a perfect skill,
> Things to reform as right and justice will;
> For honor is ordained for no cause
> But to see right maintained by the laws."

All the States of the Union have in practical operation the public-school system, governed in the main by similar laws, and not differing materially in the manner and methods by which they are taught; but none have a wiser, a more liberal and comprehensive machinery of instruction than Missouri. Her school laws, since 1839, have undergone many changes, and always for the better, keeping pace with the most enlightened and advanced theories of the most experienced educators in the land. But not until 1875, when the new constitution was adopted, did her present admirable system of public instruction go into effect.

Provisions were made not only for white, but for children of African descent, and are a part of the organic law, not subject to the caprices of unfriendly legislatures, or the whims of political parties. The Lincoln Institute, located at Jefferson City, for the education of colored teachers, receives an annual appropriation from the General Assembly.

For the support of the public schools, in addition to the annual income derived from the public school fund, which is set apart by law, not less than twenty-five per cent. of the State revenue, exclusive of the interest and sinking fund, is annually applied to this purpose.

The officers having in charge the public school interests are the State "Board of Education," the State Superintendent, County Commission-

NORMAL SCHOOL AT CAPE GIRARDEAU.

ers, County Clerk and Treasurer, Board of Directors, City and Town School Board, and Teacher. The State Board of Education is composed of the State Superintendent, the Governor, Secretary of State, and the Attorney-General, the executive officer of this Board being the State Superintendent, who is chosen by the people every four years. His duties are numerous. He renders decisions concerning the local application of school law; keeps a record of the school funds and annually distributes the same to the counties; supervises the work of county school officers; delivers lectures; visits schools; distributes educational information; grants certificates of higher qualifications, and makes an annual report to the General Assembly of the condition of the schools.

The County Commissioners are also elected by the people for two years. Their work is to examine teachers, to distribute blanks, and make reports. County clerks receive estimates from the local directors and extend them upon the tax-books. In addition to this, they keep the general records of the county and township school funds, and return an annual report of the financial condition of the schools of their county to the State Superintendent. School taxes are gathered with other taxes by the county collector. The custodian of the school funds belonging to the schools of the counties is the county treasurer, except in counties adopting the township organization, in which case the township trustee discharges these duties.

Districts organized under the special law for cities and towns are governed by a board of six directors, two of whom are selected annually, on the second Saturday in September, and hold their office for three years.

One director is elected to serve for three years in each school district, at the annual meeting. These directors may levy a tax not exceeding forty cents on the one hundred dollars' valuation, provided such annual rates for school purposes may be increased in districts formed of cities and towns, to an amount not exceeding one dollar on the hundred dollars' valuation, and in other districts to an amount not to exceed sixty-five cents on the one hundred dollars' valuation, on the condition that a majority of the voters who are tax-payers, voting at an election held to decide the question, vote for said increase. For the purpose of erecting public buildings in school districts, the rates of taxation thus limited may be increased when the rate of such increase and the purpose for which it is intended shall have been submitted to a vote of the people, and two-thirds of the

HISTORY OF MISSOURI

qualified voters of such school district voting at such election shall vote therefor.

Local directors may direct the management of the school in respect to the choice of teachers and other details, but in the discharge of all important business, such as the erection of a school house or the extension of a term of school beyond the constitutional period, they simply execute the will of the people. The clerk of this board may be a director. He keeps a record of the names of all the children and youth in the district between the ages of five and twenty-one; records all business proceedings of the district, and reports to the annual meeting, to the County Clerk and County Commissioners.

Teachers must hold a certificate from the State Superintendent or County Commissioner of the county where they teach. State certificates are granted upon personal written examination in the common branches, together with the natural sciences and higher mathematics. The holder of such certificate may teach in any public school of the State without further examination. Certificates granted by County Commissioners are of two classes, with two grades in each class. Those issued for a longer term than one year, belong to the first class and are susceptible of two grades, differing both as to length of time and attainments. Those issued for one year may represent two grades, marked by qualification alone. The township school fund arises from a grant of land by the General Government, consisting of section sixteen in each congressional township. The annual income of the township fund is appropriated to the various townships, according to their respective proprietary claims. The support from the permanent funds is supplemented by direct taxation laid upon the taxable property of each district. The greatest limit of taxation for the current expenses is one per cent; the tax permitted for school house building cannot exceed the same amount.

Among the institutions of learning and ranking, perhaps, the first in importance, is the State University located at Columbia, Boone County. When the State was admitted into the Union, Congress granted to it one entire township of land (46,080 acres) for the support of "A Seminary of Learning." The lands secured for this purpose are among the best and most valuable in the State. These lands were put into the market in 1832 and brought $75,000, which amount was invested in the stock of the old bank of the State of Missouri, where it remained and increased by accumulation to the sum of $100,000. In 1839, by an act of the General Assembly, five commis-

69

sioners were appointed to select a site for the State University, the site to contain at least fifty acres of land in a compact form, within two miles of the county seat of Cole, Cooper, Howard, Boone, Callaway or Saline. Bids were let among the counties named, and the county of Boone having subscribed the sum of $117,921, some $18,000 more than any other county, the State University was located in that county, and on the 4th of July, 1840, the corner-stone was laid with imposing ceremonies.

The present annual income of the University is nearly $65,000. The donations to the institutions connected therewith amount to nearly $400,000. This University with its different departments, is open to both male and female, and both sexes enjoy alike its rights and privileges. Among the professional schools, which form a part of the University, are the Normal, or College of Instruction in Teaching; Agricultural and Mechanical College; the School of Mines and Metallurgy; the College of Law; the Medical College; and the Department of Analytical and Applied Chemistry. Other departments are contemplated and will be added as necessity requires.

The following will show the names and locations of the schools and institutions of the State, as reported by the Commissioner of Education in 1875:—

UNIVERSITIES AND COLLEGES.

Christian University	Canton.
St. Vincent's College	Cape Girardeau,
University of Missouri	Columbia.
Central College	Fayette.
Westminster College	Fulton.
Lewis College	Glasgow.
Pritchett School Institute	Glasgow.
Lincoln College	Greenwood.
Hannibal College	Hannibal.
Woodland College	Independence.
Thayer College	Kidder.
La Grange College	La Grange.
William Jewell College	Liberty.
Baptist College	Louisiana.
St. Joseph College	St. Joseph.
College of Christian Brothers	St. Louis.
St. Louis University	St. Louis.
Washington University	St. Louis.
Drury College	Springfield.
Central Wesleyan College	Warrenton.

FOR SUPERIOR INSTRUCTION OF WOMEN.

St. Joseph Female Seminary	St. Joseph.
Christian College	Columbia.

HISTORY OF MISSOURI

Stephens College...Columbia.
Howard College ....Fayette.
Independence Female College...Independence.
Central Female College...Lexington.
Clay Seminary..Liberty.
Ingleside Female College..Palmyra.
Lindenwood College for Young Ladies...................................St. Charles.
Mary Institute (Washington University)..................................St. Louis.
St. Louis Seminary...St. Louis.
Ursuline Academy..St. Louis.

FOR SECONDARY INSTRUCTION.

Arcadia College..Arcadia.
St. Vincent's Academy..Cape Girardeau.
Chillicothe Academy...Chillicothe.
Grand River College...Edinburgh.
Marionville Collegiate Institute...Marionville.
Palmyra Seminary...Palmyra.
St. Paul's College..Palmyra.
Van Rensselaer Academy ....Rensselaer.
Shelby High School...Shelbyville.
Stewartsville Male and Female Seminary.................................Stewartsville.

SCHOOLS OF SCIENCE.

Missouri Agricultural and Mechanical College (University of Missouri).............Columbia.
Schools of Mines and Metallurgy (University of Missouri)...........................Rolla.
Polytechnic Institute (Washington University)...St. Louis.

SCHOOLS OF THEOLOGY.

St. Vincent's College (Theological Department)........................Cape Girardeau.
Westminster College (Theological School)..............................Fulton.
Vardeman School of Theology (William Jewell College)..............Liberty.
Concordia College..St. Louis.

SCHOOLS OF LAW.

Law School of the University of Missouri................................Columbia.
Law School of the Washington University...............................St. Louis.

SCHOOLS OF MEDICINE.

Medical College, University of Missouri..................................Columbia
College of Physicians and Surgeons......................................St. Joseph.
Kansas City College of Physicians and Surgeons.....................Kansas City.
Hospital Medical College..St. Joseph.
Missouri Medical College...St. Louis.
Northwestern Medical College...St. Joseph.
St. Louis Medical College..St. Louis.
Homeopathic Medical College of Missouri..............................St. Louis.
Missouri School of Midwifery and Diseases of Women and Children.............St. Louis.
Missouri Central College..St. Louis.
St. Louis College of Pharmacy...St. Louis.

HISTORY OF MISSOURI

LARGEST PUBLIC LIBRARIES.

Name.	Location.	Volumes.
St. Vincent's College	Cape Girardeau	5,500
Southeast Missouri State Normal School	Cape Girardeau	1,225
University of Missouri	Columbia	10,000
Athenian Society	Columbia	1,200
Union Literary Society	Columbia	1,200
Law College	Columbia	1,000
Westminster College	Fulton	5,000
Lewis College	Glasgow	8,000
Mercantile Library	Hannibal	2,219
Library Association	Independence	1,100
Fruitland Normal Institute	Jackson	1,000
State Library	Jefferson City	18,000
Fetterman's Circulating Library	Kansas City	1,800
Law Library	Kansas City	8,000
Whittemore's Circulating Library	Kansas City	1,000
North Missouri State Normal School	Kirksville	1,050
William Jewell College	Liberty	4,000
St. Paul's College	Palmyra	2,000
Missouri School of Mines and Metallurgy	Rolla	1,478
St. Charles Catholic Library	St. Charles	1,716
Carl Frielling's Library	St. Joseph	6,000
Law Library	St. Joseph	2,000
Public School Library	St. Joseph	2,500
Walworth & Colt's Circulating Library	St. Joseph	1,500
Academy of Science	St. Louis	2,744
Academy of Visitation	St. Louis	4,000
College of the Christian Brothers	St. Louis	22,000
Deutsche Institute	St. Louis	1,000
German Evangelical Lutheran, Concordia College	St. Louis	4,800
Law Library Association	St. Louis	8,000
Missouri Medical College	St. Louis	1,000
Mrs. Cuthbert's Seminary (Young Ladies)	St. Louis	1,500
Odd Fellow's Library	St. Louis	4,000
Public School Library	St. Louis	40,097
St. Louis Medical College	St. Louis	1,100
St. Louis Mercantile Library	St. Louis	45,000
St. Louis Seminary	St. Louis	2,000
St. Louis Turn Verein	St. Louis	2,000
St. Louis University	St. Louis	17,000
St. Louis University Society Libraries	St. Louis	8,000
Ursuline Academy	St. Louis	2,000
Washington University	St. Louis	4,500
St. Louis Law School	St. Louis	8,000
Young Men's Sodality	St. Louis	1,827
Library Association	Sedalia	1,500
Public School Library	Sedalia	1,015
Drury College	Springfield	2,000

IN 1880.

Newspapers and Periodicals.. 481

CHARITIES.

State Asylum for Deaf and Dumb..Fulton.

St. Bridget's Institution for Deaf and Dumb............................St. Louis.

Institution for the Education of the Blind................................St. Louis.

State Asylum for Insane..Fulton.

State Asylum for the Insane..St. Louis.

HISTORY OF MISSOURI

NORMAL SCHOOLS.

Normal Institute...Bolivar.
Southeast Missouri State Normal School...Cape Girardeau.
Normal School (University of Missouri)...Columbia.
Fruitland Normal Institute...Jackson.
Lincoln Institute (for colored)...Jefferson City.
City Normal School..St. Louis.
Missouri State Normal School...Warrensburg.

IN 1880.

Number of school children.. ———

IN 1878.

Estimated value of school property.. $8,821,899
Total receipts for public schools.. 4,207,617
Total expenditures.. 2,406,189

NUMBER OF TEACHERS.

Male teachers.............................. 6,289; average monthly pay...................... $36.36
Female teachers........................... 5,060; average monthly pay...................... 28.09

The fact that Missouri supports and maintains four hundred and seventy-one newspapers and periodicals, shows that her inhabitants are not only a reading and reflecting people, but that they appreciate "The Press," and its wonderful influence as an educator. The poet has well said : —

> But mightiest of the mighty means,
> On which the arm of progress leans,
> Man's noblest mission to advance,
> His woes assuage, his weal enhance,
> His rights enforce, his wrongs redress —
> Mightiest of mighty 's the Press.

CHAPTER XII.

RELIGIOUS DENOMINATIONS.

Baptist Church — Its History — Congregational — When Founded — Its History — Christian Church — Its History — Cumberland Presbyterian Church — Its History — Methodist Episcopal Church — Its History — Presbyterian Church — Its History — Protestant Episcopal Church — Its History — United Presbyterian Church — Its History — Unitarian Church — Its History — Roman Catholic Church — Its History.

The first representatives of religious thought and training, who penetrated the Missouri and Mississippi Valleys, were Pere Marquette, La Salle, and others of Catholic persuasion, who performed missionary labor among the Indians. A century afterward came the Protestants. At that early period

> " A church in every grove that spread
>   Its living roof above their heads,"

constituted for a time their only house of worship, and yet to them

> " No Temple built with hands could vie
>   In glory with its majesty."

In the course of time, the seeds of Protestantism were scattered along the shores of the two great rivers which form the eastern and western boundaries of the State, and still a little later they were sown upon her hill-sides and broad prairies, where they have since bloomed and blossomed as the rose.

BAPTIST CHURCH.

The earliest anti-Catholic religious denomination, of which there is any record, was organized in Cape Girardeau county in 1806, through the efforts of Rev. David Green, a Baptist, and a native of Virginia. In 1816, the first association of Missouri Baptists was formed, which was composed of seven churches, all of which were located in the southeastern part of the State. In 1817 a second association of churches was formed, called the Missouri Association, the name being afterwards changed to St. Louis Association. In 1834 a general convention of all the churches of this denomination, was held in Howard county, for the purpose of effecting a central organization, at which time was commenced what is now known as the " General Association of Missouri Baptists."

To this body is committed the State mission work, denominational education, foreign missions and the circulation of religious literature. The Baptist Church has under its control a number of schools and colleges, the most important of which is William Jewell College, located at Liberty, Clay county. As shown by the annual report for 1875, there were in Missouri, at that date, sixty-one associations, one thousand four hundred churches, eight hundred and twenty-four ministers and eighty-nine thousand six hundred and fifty church members.

CONGREGATIONAL CHURCH.

The Congregationalists inaugurated their missionary labors in the State in 1814. Rev. Samuel J. Mills, of Torringford, Connecticut, and Rev. Daniel Smith, of Bennington, Vermont, were sent west by the Massachusetts Congregational Home Missionary Society during that year, and in November, 1814, they preached the first regular Protestant sermons in St. Louis. Rev. Samuel Giddings, sent out under the auspices of the Connecticut Congregational Missionary Society, organized the first Protestant church in the city, consisting of ten members, constituted Presbyterian. The churches organized by Mr. Giddings were all Presbyterian in their order.

No exclusively Congregational Church was founded until 1852, when the "First Trinitarian Congregational Church of St. Louis" was organized. The next church of this denomination was organized at Hannibal in 1859. Then followed a Welsh church in New Cambria in 1864, and after the close of the war, fifteen churches of the same order were formed in different parts of the State. In 1866, Pilgrim Church, St. Louis, was organized. The General Conference of Churches of Missouri was formed in 1865, which was changed in 1868, to General Association. In 1866, Hannibal, Kidder, and St. Louis District Associations were formed, and following these were the Kansas City and Springfield District Associations. This denomination in 1875, had 70 churches, 41 ministers, 3,363 church members, and had also several schools and colleges and one monthly newspaper.

CHRISTIAN CHURCH.

The earliest churches of this denomination were organized in Callaway, Boone and Howard Counties, some time previously to 1829. The first church was formed in St. Louis in 1836 by Elder R. B. Fife. The first State Sunday School Convention of the Christian Church, was held in Mexico in 1876. Besides a number of private institutions, this denomination has three State Institutions, all of which have an able corps of professors and have a good attendance of pupils. It has one religious paper published in St. Louis, " *The Christian*," which is a weekly publication and well patronized. The membership of this church now numbers nearly one hundred thousand in the State and is increasing rapidly. It has more than five hundred organized churches, the greater portion of which are north of the Missouri River.

CUMBERLAND PRESBYTERIAN CHURCH.

In the spring of 1820, the first Presbytery of this denomination west of the Mississippi, was organized in Pike County. This Presbytery included all the territory of Missouri, western Illinois and Arkansas and numbered only four ministers, two of whom resided at

HISTORY OF MISSOURI

that time in Missouri. There are now in the State, twelve Presbyteries, three Synods, nearly three hundred ministers and over twenty thousand members. The Board of Missions is located at St. Louis. They have a number of High Schools and two monthly papers published at St. Louis.

METHODIST EPISCOPAL CHURCH.

In 1806, Rev. John Travis, a young Methodist minister, was sent out to the " Western Conference," which then embraced the Mississippi Valley, from Green County, Tennessee. During that year Mr. Travis organized a number of small churches. At the close of his conference year, he reported the result of his labors to the Western Conference, which was held at Chillicothe, Ohio, in 1870, and showed an aggregate of one hundred and six members and two circuits, one called Missouri and the other Meramec. In 1808, two circuits had been formed, and at each succeeding year the number of circuits and members constantly increased, until 1812, when what was called the Western Conference was divided into the Ohio and Tennessee Conferences, Missouri falling into the Tennessee Conference. In 1816, there was another division when the Missouri Annual Conference was formed. In 1810, there were four traveling preachers and in 1820, fifteen travelling preachers, with over 2,000 members. In 1836, the territory of the Missouri Conference was again divided when the Missouri Conference included only the State. In 1840 there were 72 traveling preachers, 177 local ministers and 13,992 church members. Between 1840 and 1850, the church was divided by the organization of the Methodist Episcopal Church South. In 1850, the membership of the M. E. Church was over 25,000, and during the succeeding ten years the church prospered rapidly. In 1875, the M. E. Church reported 274 church edifices and 34,156 members; the M. E. Church South, reported 443 church edifices and 49,588 members. This denomination has under its control several schools and colleges and two weekly newspapers.

PRESBYTERIAN CHURCH.

The Presbyterian Church dates the beginning of its missionary efforts in the State as far back as 1814, but the first Presbyterian Church was not organized until 1816 at Bellevue settlement, eight miles from St. Louis. The next churches were formed in 1816 and 1817 at Bonhomme, Pike County. The First Presbyterian Church was organized in St. Louis in 1817, by Rev. Salmon Gidding. The

HISTORY OF MISSOURI

first Presbytery was organized in 1817 by the Synod of Tennessee with four ministers and four churches. The first Presbyterian house of worship (which was the first Protestant) was commenced in 1819 and completed in 1826. In 1820 a mission was formed among the Osage Indians. In 1831, the Presbytery was divided into three: Missouri, St. Louis, and St. Charles. These were erected with a Synod comprising eighteen ministers and twenty-three churches.

The church was divided in 1838, throughout the United States. In 1860 the rolls of the Old and New School Synod together showed 109 ministers and 146 churches. In 1866 the Old School Synod was divided on political questions springing out of the war—a part forming the Old School, or Independent Synod of Missouri, who are connected with the General Assembly South. In 1870, the Old and New School Presbyterians united, since which time this Synod has steadily increased until it now numbers more than 12,000 members with more than 220 churches and 150 ministers.

This Synod is composed of six Presbyteries and has under its control one or two institutions of learning and one or two newspapers. That part of the original Synod which withdrew from the General Assembly remained an independent body until 1874 when it united with the Southern Presbyterian Church. The Synod in 1875 numbered 80 ministers, 140 churches and 9,000 members. It has under its control several male and female institutions of a high order. The *St. Louis Presbyterian*, a weekly paper, is the recognized organ of the Synod.

PROTESTANT EPISCOPAL CHURCH.

The missionary enterprises of this church began in the State in 1819, when a parish was organized in the City of St. Louis. In 1828, an agent of the Domestic and Foreign Missionary Society, visited the city, who reported the condition of things so favorably that Rev. Thomas Horrell was sent out as a missionary and in 1825, he began his labors in St. Louis. A church edifice was completed in 1830. In 1836, there were five clergymen of this denomination in Missouri, who had organized congregations in Boonville, Fayette, St. Charles, Hannibal, and other places. In 1840, the clergy and laity met in convention, a diocese was formed, a constitution, and canons adopted, and in 1844 a Bishop was chosen, he being the Rev. Cicero S. Hawks. Through the efforts of Bishop Kemper, Kemper College was founded near St. Louis, but was afterward given up on account of

HISTORY OF MISSOURI

pecuniary troubles. In 1847, the Clark Mission began and in 1849 the Orphans' Home, a charitable institution, was founded. In 1865, St. Luke's Hospital was established. In 1875, there were in the city of St. Louis, twelve parishes and missions and twelve clergymen. This denomnation has several schools and colleges, and one newspaper.

UNITED PRESBYTERIAN CHURCH.

This denomination is made up of the members of the Associate and Associate Reformed churches of the Northern States, which two bodies united in 1858, taking the name of the United Presbyterian Church of North America. Its members were generally bitterly opposed to the institution of slavery. The first congregation was organized at Warrensburg, Johnson County, in 1867. It rapidly increased in numbers, and had, in 1875, ten ministers and five hundred members.

UNITARIAN CHURCH.

This church was formed in 1834, by the Rev. W. G. Eliot, in St. Louis. The churches are few in number throughout the State, the membership being probably less than 300, all told. It has a mission house and free school, for poor children, supported by donations.

ROMAN CATHOLIC CHURCH.

The earliest written record of the Catholic Church in Missouri shows that Father Watrin performed ministerial services in Ste. Genevieve, in 1760, and in St. Louis in 1766. In 1770, Father Menrin erected a small log church in St. Louis. In 1818, there were in the State four chapels, and for Upper Louisiana seven priests. A college and seminary were opened in Perry County about this period, for the education of the young, being the first college west of the Mississippi River. In 1824, a college was opened in St. Louis, which is now known as the St. Louis University. In 1826, Father Rosatti was appointed Bishop of St. Louis, and through his instrumentality the Sisters of Charity, Sisters of St. Joseph and of the Visitation were founded, besides other benevolent and charitable institutions. In 1834 he completed the present Cathedral Church. Churches were built in different portions of the State. In 1847 St. Louis was created an arch-diocese, with Bishop Kenrick, Archbishop.

In Kansas City there were five parish churches, a hospital, a convent and several parish schools. In 1868 the northwestern portion of the State was erected into a separate diocese, with its seat at St. Joseph, and Right-Reverend John J. Hogan appointed Bishop. There were, in 1875, in the city of St. Louis, 34 churches, 27 schools, 5 hospitals, 3 colleges, 7 orphan asylums and 3 female protectorates. There were also 105 priests, 7 male and 13 female orders, and 20 conferences of St. Vincent de Paul, numbering 1,100 members. In the diocese, outside of St. Louis, there is a college, a male protectorate, 9 convents, about 120 priests, 150 churches and 30 stations. In the diocese of St. Joseph there were, in 1875, 21 priests, 29 churches, 24 stations, 1 college, 1 monastery, 5 convents and 14 parish schools:

Number of Sunday Schools in 1878	2,067
Number of Teachers in 1878	18,010
Number of Pupils in 1878	139,578

THEOLOGICAL SCHOOLS.

Instruction preparatory to ministerial work is given in connection with collegiate study, or in special theological courses, at:

Central College (M. E. South)	Fayette.
Central Wesleyan College (M. E. Church)	Warrenton.
Christian University (Christian)	Canton.
Concordia College Seminary (Evangelical Lutheran)	St. Louis.
Lewis College (M. E. Church)	Glasgow.
St. Vincent College (Roman Catholic)	Cape Girardeau.
Vardeman School of Theology (Baptist)	Liberty.

The last is connected with William Jewell College.

CHAPTER XIII.

ADMINISTRATION OF GOVERNOR CRITTENDEN.

Nomination and election of Thomas T. Crittenden—Personal Mention—Marmaduke's candidacy—Stirring events—Hannibal and St. Joseph Railroad—Death of Jesse James—The Fords—Pardon of the Gamblers.

It is the purpose in this chapter to outline the more important events of Governor Crittenden's unfinished administration, stating briefly the facts in the case, leaving comment and criticism entirely to the reader, the historian having no judgment to express or prejudice to vent.

Thomas T. Crittenden, of Johnson county, received the Democratic nomination for Governor of Missouri at the convention at Jefferson City, July 22d, 1880. Democratic nomination for a State office in Missouri is always equivalent to election, and the entire State ticket was duly elected in November. Crittenden's competitors before the convention were Gen. John S. Marmaduke, of St. Louis, and John A. Hockaday, of Callaway county. Before the assembling of the convention many persons who favored Marmaduke, both personally and politically, thought the nomination of an ex-Confederate might prejudice the prospects of the National Democracy, and therefore, as a matter of policy, supported Crittenden.

His name, and the fame of his family in Kentucky—Thomas T. being a scion of the Crittendens of that State, caused the Democracy of Missouri to expect great things from their new Governor. This, together with the important events which followed his inauguration, caused some people to overrate him, while it prejudiced others against him. The measures advocated by the Governor in his inaugural address were such as, perhaps, the entire Democracy could endorse, especially that of refunding, at a low interest, all that part of the State debt that can be so refunded; the adoption of measures to relieve the Supreme Court docket; a compromise of the indebtedness of some of the counties, and his views concerning repudiation, which he contemned.

HANNIBAL & ST. JOE RAILROAD CONTROVERSY.

By a series of legislative acts, beginning with the act approved February 22, 1851, and ending with that of March 26, 1881, the State of Missouri aided with great liberality in the construction of a system of railroads in this State.

Among the enterprises thus largely assisted was the Hannibal and St. Joseph Railroad, for the construction of which the bonds of the State, to the amount of $3,000,000, bearing interest at 6 per cent per annum, payable semi-annually, were issued. One half of this amount was issued under the act of 1851, and the remainder under the act of 1855. The bonds issued under the former act were to run twenty years, and those under the latter act were to run thirty years. Some of the bonds have since been funded and renewed. Coupons for the interest of the entire $3,000,000 were executed and made payable in New York. These acts contain numerous provisions intended to secure the State against loss and to require the railroad company to pay the interest and principal at maturity. It was made the duty of the railroad company to save and keep the State from all loss on account of said bonds and coupons. The Treasurer of the State was

HISTORY OF MISSOURI

to be exonerated from any advance of money to meet either principal or interest. The State contracted with the railroad company for complete indemnity. She was required to assign her statutory mortgage lien only upon payment into the treasury of a sum of money equal to all indebtedness due or owing by said company to the State by reason of having issued her bonds and loaned them to the company.

In June, 1881, the railroad, through its attorney, Geo. W. Easley, Esq., paid to Phil. E. Chappell, State Treasurer, the sum of $3,000,-000, and asked for a receipt in 'full of all dues of the road to the State. The Treasurer refused to give such a receipt, but instead gave a receipt for the sum "on account." The debt was not yet due, but the authorities of the road sought to discharge their obligation prematurely, in order to save interest and other expenses. The railroad company then demanded its bonds of the State, which demand the State refused. The company then demanded that the $3,000,000 be paid back, and this demand was also refused.

The railroad company then brought suit in the United States Court for an equitable adjustment of the matters in controversy. The $3,000,000 had been deposited by the State in one of the banks, and was drawing interest only at the rate of one-fourth of one per cent. It was demanded that this sum should be so invested that a larger rate of interest might be obtained, which sum of interest should be allowed to the company as a credit in case any sum should be found due from it to the State. Justice Miller, of the United States Supreme Court, who heard the case upon preliminary injunction in the spring of 1882, decided that the unpaid and unmatured coupons constituted a liability of the State and a debt owing, though not due, and until these were provided for the State was not bound to assign her lien upon the road.

Another question which was mooted, but not decided, was this: That, if any, what account is the State to render for the use of the $3,000,000 paid into the treasury by the complainants on the 20th of June? Can she hold that large sum of money, refusing to make any account of it, and still insist upon full payment by the railroad company of all outstanding coupons?

Upon this subject Mr. Justice Miller, in the course of his opinion, said: "I am of the opinion that the State, having accepted or got this money into her possession, is under a moral obligation (and I do not pretend to commit anybody as to how far its legal obligation goes) to so use that money as, so far as possible, to protect the parties who have paid it against the loss of the interest which it might accumulate,

81

and which would go to extinguish the interest on the State's obligations."

March 26, 1881, the Legislature, in response to a special message of Gov. Crittenden, dated February 25, 1881, in which he informed the Legislature of the purpose of the Hannibal and St. Joseph company to discharge the full amount of what it claims is its present indebtedness as to the State, and advised that provision be made for the " profitable disposal" of the sum when paid, passed an act, the second section of which provided.

" SEC. 2. Whenever there is sufficient money in the sinkiug fund to redeem or purchase one or more of the bonds of the State of Missouri, such sum is hereby appropriated for such purpose, and the Fund Commissioners shall immediately call in for payment a like amount of the option bonds of the State, known as the " 5-20 bonds," provided, that if there are no option bonds which can be called in for payment, they may invest such money in the purchase of any of the bonds of the State, or bonds of the United States, the Hannibal and St. Joseph railroad bonds excepted."

. On the 1st of January, 1882, the regular semi-annual payment of interest on the railroad bonds became due, but the road refused to pay, claiming that it had already discharged the principal, and of course was not liable for the interest. Thereupon, according to the provisions of the aiding act of 1855, Gov. Crittenden advertised the road for sale in default of the payment of interest. The company then brought suit before U. S. Circuit Judge McCrary at Keokuk, Iowa, to enjoin the State from selling the road, and for such other and further relief as the court might see fit and proper to grant. August 8, 1882, Judge McCrary delivered his opinion and judgment, as follows:

"*First.* That the payment by complainants into the treasury of the State of the sum of $3,000,000 on the 26th of June, 1881, did not satisfy the claim of the State in full, nor entitle complainants to an assignment of the State's statutory mortgage.

"*Second.* That the State was bound to invest the principal sum of $3,000,000 so paid by the complainants without unnecessary delay in the securities named in the act of March 26, 1881, or some of them, and so as to save to the State as large a sum as possible, which sum so saved would have constituted as between the State and complainants a credit *pro tanto* upon the unmatured coupons now in controversy.

"*Third*. That the rights and equity of the parties are to be determined upon the foregoing principles, and the State must stand charged with what would have been realized if the act of March, 1881, had been complied with. It only remains to consider what the rights of the parties are upon the principles here stated.

"In order to save the State from loss on account of the default of the railroad company, a further sum must be paid. In order to determine what that further sum is an accounting must be had. The question to be settled by the accounting is, how much would the State have lost if the provisions of the act of March, 1881, had been complied with? * * * * I think a perfectly fair basis of settlement would be to hold the State liable for whatever could have been saved by the prompt execution of said act by taking up such 5-20 option bonds of the State as were subject to call when the money was paid to the State, and investing the remainder of the fund in the bonds of the United States at the market rates.

" Upon this basis a calculation can be made and the exact sum still to be paid by the complainant in order to fully indemnify and protect the State can be ascertained. For the purpose of stating an account upon this basis and of determining the sum to be paid by the complainants to the State, the cause will be referred to John K. Cravens, one of the masters of this court. In determining the time when the investment should have been made under the act of March, 1881, the master will allow a reasonable period for the time of the receipt of the said sum of $3,000,000 by the Treasurer of the State — that is to say, such time as would have been required for that purpose had the officers charged with the duty of making said investment used reasonable diligence in its discharge.

" The Hannibal and St. Joseph railroad is advertised for sale for the amount of the instalment of interest due January 1, 1882, which instalment amounts to less than the sum which the company must pay in order to discharge its liabilities to the State upon the theory of this opinion. The order will, therefore, be that an injunction be granted to enjoin the sale of the road upon the payment of the said instalment of interest due January 1, 1882, and if such payment is made the master will take it into account in making the computation above mentioned."

KILLING OF JESSE JAMES.

The occurrence during the present Governor's administration which did most to place his name in everybody's mouth, and even to herald

HISTORY OF MISSOURI

it abroad, causing the European press to teem with leaders announcing the fact to the continental world, was the "removal" of the famous Missouri brigand, Jesse W. James. The career of the James boys, and the banditti of whom they were the acknowledged leaders, is too well-known and too fully set forth in works of a more sensational character, to deserve further detail in these pages; and the "removal" of Jesse will be dealt with only in its relation to the Governor.

It had been long conceded that neither of the Jameses would ever be taken alive. That experiment had been frequently and vainly tried, to the sorrow of good citizens of this and other States. It seems to have been one of the purposes of Gov. Crittenden to break up this band at any cost, by cutting off its leaders. Soon after the Winston train robbery, on July 15, 1881, the railroads combined in empowering the Governor, by placing the money at his disposal, to offer heavy rewards for the capture of the two James brothers. This was accordingly done by proclamation, and, naturally, many persons were on the lookout to secure the large rewards. Gov. Crittenden worked quietly, but determinedly, after offering the rewards, and by some means learned of the availability of the two Ford boys, young men from Ray county, who had been tutored as juvenile robbers by the skillful Jesse. An understanding was had, when the Fords declared they could find Jesse — that they were to "turn him in." Robert Ford and brother seem to have been thoroughly in the confidence of James, who then (startling as it was to the entire State) resided in the city of St. Joseph, with his wife and two children! The Fords went there, and when the robber's back was turned, Robert *shot him dead in the back of the head!* The Fords told their story to the authorities of the city, who at once arrested them on a charge of murder, and they, when arraigned, *plead guilty to the charge.* Promptly, however, came a full, free and unconditional pardon from Gov. Crittenden, and the Fords were released. In regard to the Governor's course in ridding the State of this notorious outlaw, people were divided in sentiment, some placing him in the category with the Ford boys and bitterly condemning his action, while others — the majority of law-abiding people, indeed, — though deprecating the harsh measures which James' course had rendered necessary, still upheld th Governor for the part he played. As it was, the "Terror of Missouri" was effectually and finally "removed," and people were glad that he was dead. Robert Ford, the pupil of the dead Jesse, had

84

HISTORY OF MISSOURI

been selected, and of all was the most fit tool to use in the extermination of his preceptor in crime.

The killing of James would never have made Crittenden many enemies among the better class of citizens of this State; but, when it came to his

PARDON OF THE GAMBLERS.

The case was different. Under the new law making gaminghouse-keeping a felony, several St. Louis gamblers, with Robert C. Pate at their head, were convicted and sentenced to prison. The Governor, much to the surprise of the more rigid moral element of the State, soon granted the gamblers a pardon. This was followed by other pardons to similar offenders, which began to render the Governor quite unpopular which one element of citizens, and to call forth from some of them the most bitter denunciations. The worst feature of the case, perhaps, is the lack of explanation, or the setting forth of sufficient reasons, as is customary in issuing pardons, This, at least, is the burden of complaint with the faction that opposes him. However, it must be borne in mind that his term of office, at this writing, is but half expired, and that a full record can not, therefore, be given. Like all mere men, Gov. Crittenden has his good and his bad, is liked by some and disliked by others. The purpose of history is to set forth the facts and leave others to sit in judgment; this the historian has tried faithfully to do, leaving all comments to those who may see fit to make them.

HISTORY

OF

CLAY COUNTY, MO.

CHAPTER I.

EARLY HISTORY TO THE ORGANIZATION OF THE COUNTY.

The Indians — The French and Spanish — First Exploration and Settlement by Americans — The First American Settlers in Clay — An Indian Fight — Organization of Clay County.

THE INDIANS.

Prior to about the close of the eighteenth century the country now comprised within the boundaries of Clay county was in undisputed possession of the Missouri tribe of Indians, who fished and trapped in its streams, hunted over its surface, and sang their songs and danced their dances with none to molest them or make them afraid. From about 1680 for a hundred years the Missouris held the north side of the river (to which they gave their name) from a point opposite the mouth of the Gasconade, on the east, out into what is now the State of Kansas. Northward their territory extended to the Des Moines river or until checked by the fierce Dakotas. Occasionally the Missouris crossed the river and went on the war path against the Osages, their long time enemies, whom they had first driven out of this country, and again they would go far north against the tribes along the Upper Des Moines or Upper Missouri. They were warlike and aggressive, although they appeared to greatly enjoy a quiet life, and their forays seem to have been partly for the sake of glory, and partly for recreation, not particularly for conquest.

The name *Missouri* is an old one. Father Marquette, in 1680, called the tribe of Indians in this quarter, "We-Missouret," which

HISTORY OF CLAY COUNTY

Thivenet, his reviser, changed to On-Missouri.[1] The name means *muddy*, or, as is said *dirty*, and doubtless the latter was given to the particular tribe of Indians as indicating their habits and uniform personal condition; though why the term was limited to any particular tribe can not be conjectured. It would seem that a characteristic so generally prevalent among the aborigines of America ought not to have been especially attributed to the tribe that immediately preceded the Anglo-Saxons who first settled Clay county.

But some writers say that the Missouri tribe of Indians took their name from the river, which was called *muddy*, and that the river was named first. To the mind of the writer the testimony is against this theory. Father Marquette called the stream *Pekitanoui* and the tribe *We-Missouret*, and the name Pekitanoui prevailed among Europeans until Marest's time, in 1712. The *Recollects*, the early French monks, called the stream the river of the Osages.[2] Certain Indian tribes called it a name signifying *mad water;* other Indians termed it *Nee-Shuga*, or *smoky water.*[3] But all tribes and every one acquainted with them called the Indians the Missouris, or as it was almost universally pronounced, *Mis-soo-rees* (not "Mizzoorys"). The best testimony is that the French first called the *stream* the Missouri, or as stated by Charlevoix, *La Riviere des Missouris* — the River of the *Missouris*. Evidently the stream was named from the tribe, and not the tribe from the stream.

Upon the appearance of the French in this quarter of the West they almost immediately became on good terms with the Missouris. These friendly relations were never disturbed.

THE FRENCH AND SPANIARDS.

Stoddard's Annals of Louisiana, now a rare but very valuable work, says that the old French colony of Louisiana suffered much from the war which broke out between France and Spain in 1719. Although the contest was chiefly confined to the posts on the Gulf of Mexico, the upper settlements severely felt its injurious effects. Their commerce was interrupted, and the immense expenditures which were necessary to carry on the war impoverished both the company and the colony. The war, however, was not long carried on in a systematic manner, but as the two nations had always been competitors for the

---

[1] Shea's Mississippi Valley, p. 268.

[2] Shea, p. 38.

[3] Wetmore's Gazetteer, p. 33.

88

Indian trade, and as continual disputes arose concerning the rights of territory, they kept up a predatory war for several years.

In 1720 the Spaniards formed a design of destroying the nation of the Missouris, situated on the Missouri river, and of forming a settlement in their country. The object of this was to divert the current of Indian trade, and to confine the settlements of the French to the borders of the Mississippi. The Spaniards believed, that in order to put their colony in safety, it was necessary they should entirely destroy the Missouris, who were the warm and constant friends of the French; but, concluding that it would be impossible to subdue them with their own force alone, they resolved to enter into an alliance with the Osages, a people who were the neighbors of the Missouris, and, at the same time, their most mortal enemies. With these intentions they formed a caravan at Santa Fe, consisting of men, women, and soldiers; having a priest for chaplain, and an engineer captain for their chief conductor, with the horses and cattle necessary for a permanent settlement.

The caravan set out in 1720; but being unacquainted with the country, and not having proper guides, they mistook their way. They wandered about for some time in the wilderness, and at length arrived at the Missouris, whom they supposed to be Osages.[1] Under this impression, the conductor of the caravan, with his interpreter, immediately held a council with the chiefs. He explained to them the object of his visit, telling them that he had come to form an alliance with their tribe, in order to destroy their common enemies, the *Missouris!* The great chief of the Missouris, concealing his thoughts upon this expedition, evinced the greatest joy. He showed the Spaniards every possible attention and promised to act in concert with them. For this purpose he invited them to rest a few days, after their tiresome journey, till he had assembled his warriors and held a council with the old men, to which the Spaniards acceded.

The boldness of the Spaniards, in thus penetrating into a country of which they had no previous knowledge, made the French sensible of their danger and warned them to provide against further encroachment. They suspected the intentions of the Spaniards, and determined to prevent, if possible, their being put into execution. Accordingly, in the summer of 1721 a considerable force was dispatched from

---

[1] This assertion rests upon the authority of several respectable writers, Du Pratz and Charlevoix among them. Maj. Stoddard, however, in his Historical Sketches of Louisiana, states that the Spaniards marched in pursuit of the Pawnee, and not the Osage villages. For the truth of this he refers to the records of Santa Fe.

HISTORY OF CLAY COUNTY

the French posts on Mobile Bay, under M. de Bourgmont, who ascended the Missouri and took possession of an island in the river, about five miles below the mouth of Grand river. On this island a considerable fort was erected which was called Fort Orleans.

A sergeant among the French soldiers, named Dubois, became enamored of a woman of the Missouri tribe of Indians, a large body of whom encamped on the north bank of the river, opposite the fort, and married her. He was afterwards placed in command of the fort.

M. de Bourgmont found the different tribes on and adjacent to the Missouri engaged in a sanguinary warfare, which not only diminished their number but interfered greatly with trade, and rendered all intercourse with them extremely hazardous. Hence it became an object to the French to bring about a general peace. And so in the spring of 1724 Bourgmont ascended the Missouri to the mouth of the "Cansez," or where Kansas City now is, and then went some leagues to the northwest among several Indian tribes. He was accompanied by a few French soldiers and a large party of friendly Indians. His object in visiting the different tribes was to invite their chiefs and head men to a grand peace council, to be held in the early summer. All the tribes received the peacemaker kindly, even joyfully, and promised to send delegates to the council. Bourgmont and his party spent some weeks in this noble endeavor.

July 3, 1724, the council came off. It was held on the Missouri at the "Cansez," then the site of the chief town of the Kansas tribe of Indians, afterward Fort Osage, now Sibley, Jackson county. All the tribes for hundreds of miles to the west, northwest and southwest sent embassadors, and the proceedings were full of interest. Bourgmont made a great speech, and the delegates of the several tribes smoked the pipe of peace, and entered into a treaty of amity and good will between themselves, promising to be always faithful and friendly and to learn war no more. M. de Bourgmont was of course the leading spirit of the council. By his urgent invitation a number of the chiefs and principal men of many of the tribes accompanied him on a visit to France, where they were highly entertained, and their attachment to the French was fully confirmed. Sergeant Dubois and his wife accompanied this excursion party to and from Paris and Versailles, and it was on his return that the sergeant was placed in command of Fort Orleans.

But in the fall of 1725 Fort Orleans was attacked and totally destroyed, and all of its inmates massacred. The town of the Missouris,

HISTORY OF CLAY COUNTY

opposite the fort, was attacked the same time, and 200 or more men and women killed, and the remainder, only a score or less, driven to the other side of the river, and down upon the Little Osage. Though it has never been proved to a certainty who did this bloody work, it is reasonably certain that its authors were those "fierce Huns of the north, the Sacs and Foxes, who swept down from the Des Moines river upon the unsuspecting Missouris and their allies, the French, and annihilated them.

Doubtless M. de Bourgmont and his party, while on their way to invite the Indians to the place of council, in the spring of 1724, were the first whites to visit the soil of what is now Clay county. They made no settlements here, it is true, but they may be said to have discovered the country. Crossing and recrossing the river, they landed upon its southern borders, and when returning passed through it.

After the massacre of the French at Fort Orleans, until the founding of St. Louis, in 1764, there were no Caucasians in this quarter of Missouri. The red Indians held undisputed sway so far as the whites were concerned. But in this year the great province of Louisiana passed from the control and assumed ownership of the French into the hands of the Spaniards. What is now Missouri was then Upper Louisiana, whose capital was St. Louis, and whose first Governor was Don Pedro Piernas. The Spanish Governors (Piernas, from 1764 to 1775; Francisco Cruzat, from 1775 to 1778; Ferdinando Leyba, from 1778 to 1780; Cruzat again from 1780 to 1788; Manuel Perez, from 1788 to 1793, and Zenon Trudeau, from 1793 to 1800) made no especial efforts to extend the settlements until Governor Trudeau came. He encouraged immigration, gave to the fur trade a new impetus and rewarded all projectors of new enterprises according to their own efforts and the merits of their schemes. The fur traders pushed far out into hitherto unexplored regions, and adventurers were frequently setting forth to accomplish enterprises of value and moment. Doubtless some of these traders and trappers visited Clay county in the prosecution of their business.

The days of the Spanish possession were the golden ones in the history of the Upper Mississippi. There was little else but peace and plenty —

"And health and quiet and loving words."

The rulers (except Leyba, who did not last long) were easy, good natured and well disposed; their subjects loyal, obedient, industrious and well behaved. French, English, American and Spanish, though

HISTORY OF CLAY COUNTY

they were by birth, they were each all Spanish in their devotion to Spain and the banner of Castile. Not a man among them but who would have been glad to give his goods and his life *Por el Rey.* The dreamy, sensuous life in the wilderness, amid the glorious forests, by the sweet, clear springs and brooks, and on the flowery prairies, was peculiarly suited to the dreamy, sensuous Dons. The little work done by the colonists in their fields was so easily accomplished and so abundant in its results that it was but pastime to do it.

FIRST EXPLORATIONS AND SETTLEMENTS BY AMERICANS.

In 1803 Missouri Territory underwent an important change. The Indian summer of Spanish possession and occupancy had been succeeded by the stormy winter of French domination, and now there followed the balmy and bustling spring and summer of American rule. From about 1805 to 1812 French voyageurs and American trappers traveled up and down the Missouri Valley, sometimes paddling their way on the river in canoes, sometimes tramping overland. Many of these passed through our county, of course, but none of us can tell how or when. A few actual settlers came up some distance from St. Louis during this period.

The next representatives of the Caucasian race to visit the borders of Clay county, of whom we have definite knowledge, were the members of Lewis and Clark's expedition, sent out by President Jefferson in 1804. Very soon after the acquisition of the Louisiana Territory Mr. Jefferson projected an expedition to explore the newly acquired district from the mouth of the Missouri to its source, and thence across to the Pacific ocean. The President's private secretary, Capt. Merriwether Lewis, then but thirty-one years of age, was given command of the expedition, with Capt. William Clark, of the regular army, as second in command. The company consisted of nine young Kentuckians, fourteen soldiers, two Canadian voyageurs, a hunter, and Capt. Clark's negro servant. In May, 1804, this expedition passed up the Missouri, along the borders of Clay, but from their published journal it does not appear that any particular examination of the country was made. Two years afterward, or in September, 1806, Lewis and Clark passed down the river again, reaching St. Louis and terminating the expedition on the 23d of the month.

From accounts received by Mr. D. C. Allen from early settlers and others, that gentleman felt warranted in stating in *Campbell's Gazetteer* that, without much doubt, the first white settlement within the borders of Clay county was made by a few French families at Ran-

92

dolph Bluff, on the Missouri, three miles northeast of Kansas City, about the year 1800. The heads of these families were trappers, acting probably under the direction of Pierre Chouteau, Sr., of St. Louis. They left scarcely a trace of their occupancy, however, and the compiler has been unable to learn anything definite or explicit about them.

The county was visited in 1808 by Maj. Dougherty, long afterward a resident of the county, where he died December 28, 1860. At the time of his first visit Maj. Dougherty was but 17 years of age, and was on his way to the Rocky Mountains in the employ of the American Fur Company. Other representatives of the fur company passed through here at intervals on their way to and from the waters of the Upper Missouri, but their stay was only temporary.

Some time prior to the War of 1812, one Delancy Bowlin, who had settled a locality in Montgomery county known as the Big Spring, and had given his name to a considerable elevation of land in the neighborhood which is known to this day as Bowlin's Knob, left Loutre Island, with four or five companions, two of whom were John Davis and Lewis Jones, for the mouth of the Kans or Kaw river (now the Kansas). Davis and Jones returned, and old settlers of Montgomery county says that Bowlin and one or two of the others built at least one cabin in what is now Clay county, where they resided some years, engaged in trapping and hunting. What finally become of Bowlin is not known. During the War of 1812 he was in Fort Kincaid, Howard county. Jones and Davis died in the southern part of Montgomery county, where many of their descendants yet reside. The daughter of the man (Jacob Groom) to whom Bowlin sold his claim, yet lives at the Big Spring with her husband, a Mr. Snethen.

In the year 1808 Fort Osage, on the south side of the Missouri, was built by a force of dragoons or mounted rangers, under Capt. James Clemson. The fort was established as a government post or factory, and around it there was laid off a tract of land six miles square, on which a limited number of white settlers were permitted to locate in order to raise supplies for the garrison. The site of Fort Osage is now called Sibley, in honor of Gen. Geo. C. Sibley, who was the government factor and agent at the fort from 1818 until its abandonment in 1825. The locality is about five miles in a straight line southeast of Missouri City, and nearly two miles southeast of the extreme southeast boundary of Clay county.

If there were any American settlers on what is now Clay county soil prior to the breaking out of the War of 1812, it can not at this date

HISTORY OF CLAY COUNTY

be stated who they were and where they located. The war coming on drove all the American settlers who were on the frontiers to the block-houses and forts in Howard county or still further down the Missouri river, and sent the American trappers back to their headquarters and trading posts. The country here belonged to the Indians at that time, and was not open to settlement anyhow, and it can not be proved that there were any *bona fide* settlers in this quarter.

March 9, 1815, a treaty was concluded with the Indians, by which the territory within the following limits were resigned to the whites: " Beginning at the mouth of the Kaw [Kansas] river, thence running north 140 miles, thence east to the waters of the Auhaha [Salt river], which empties into the Mississippi, thence to a point opposite the mouth of the Gasconade, thence up the Missouri river, with its meanders, to the place of beginning."

In the years 1818 and 1819 the territory now included in the counties of Ray and Clay — and much other territory besides — was surveyed and opened to entry, and thereupon settlers came in rather rapidly. In what is now Ray county, settlements were made on Crooked river as early as 1817 by the Vanderpools, Abraham Linville, John Proffitt, Isaac Martin, Isaac Wilson, John Turner, Lewis Richards, and one or two others, who were from Kentucky and Virginia.

THE FIRST AMERICAN SETTLERS IN CLAY.

No authentic information can be given of any permanent settlements made in what is now Clay county prior to the year 1819. In that year[1] there came John Owens, Samuel McGee, Benjamin Hensley, William Campbell, Thomas Campbell, John Wilson, Zachariah Averett and John Braley; and also, according to Smith's Atlas sketch, Charles McGee, George Taylor, Travis Finley, Cornelius Gilliam and Edward Pyburne. These located in the southern and southeastern portions of the county, some of them in the vicinity of where Liberty now stands.

In 1820 immigration began in earnest, and settlements were made on Fishing river, Big Shoal, along the Missouri, and throughout the southern portion of the county generally by Samuel Tilford, John Thornton, Andrew Robertson, Sr., Andrew Robertson, Jr., Col. Shuball Allen, Robert Murray, John Bartleson, Andrew Bartleson, John Dean, Henry Estes, Thomas Estes, Peter Estes, James Hyatt, Samuel Hyatt, Richard Hill, William Munkers, James

---

[1] According to Hon. D. C. Allen's sketch in Campbell's Gazetteer, 1875.

HISTORY OF CLAY COUNTY

Gilmore, Robert Gilmore, Ennis Vaughan, Andrew Russell, Eppa Tillery, Martin Palmer, Henry Mailes, Squire Hutchinson, Solomon Fry, Edmond Munday, William Lenhart, William L. Smith, Humphrey Best, David McElwee, Eldridge Patter, Thomas Hixon, Joseph Grooms, Hugh Brown, Joseph Brown, Thomas Officer, Robert Officer, Patrick Laney, and doubless others.

At this time the territory now embraced in Clay county formed a part of or at least was attached to Howard county. The county seat was at Old Franklin, where was also the United States Land Office at which the land was entered. November 16, 1820, Ray county was organized (named for Hon. John Ray, of Howard) and what is now Clay became a part thereof, being denominated at first Fishing River township. Afterward, in 1821, the western half was called Gallatin township.

The first county seat of Ray county was called Bluffton, which stood on the Missouri river, near where Camden now stands. It remained the seat of justice until 1827. The first county court was held in April, 1821, and of its members two of the justices, John Thornton and Elisha Cameron; the clerk, William L. Smith, and the sheriff, John Harris, were either then or soon afterward became citizens of Clay and held the same positions in our first county court.

AN INDIAN FIGHT.

Although there were numerous bands of Indians in close proximity to the settlements in Clay, and though many of these were semi-hostile, no outbreaks or collisions occurred between them and the pioneers until in the summer of 1821.

Up in what is now the northwestern part of the county lived the Vesser family, whose adult male members were not above suspicion in many regards. Especially were they accused of frequently acquiring property by questionable means. Their fondness for horses was a particular weakness. On one occasion, in the summer of 1821, they visited a camp of Iowa Indians up in the Platte country and carried away some horses belonging to the savages.

It was some time in the month of August, 1821, probably, when nine Iowa Indians came down into the Clay county settlements to take reprisal for the horses stolen from them by the Vessers. To the southeastern part of the county, three miles northeast of where Missouri City now stands (northwest quarter section 34, township 52, range 30), David McElwee had come from Tennessee the previous year, and built a house and opened a farm. At the time of the visit

HISTORY OF CLAY COUNTY

of the Indians, however, he was back in Tennessee on a visit, having taken with him his wife and daughter, the latter now Mrs. Margaret Howdeshell. He left behind to care for the house and farm his sons, James and William, and his daughter Sarah, all unmarried young people.

The nine Indians came to Mr. McElwee's one evening and took three horses belonging to the settler, from the stable, and seized another which they were prevented from carrying off only by the stubborn and plucky interposition of young James McElwee. The Indians seemed greatly elated at the ease with which they had "got even" with the whites in the matter of horse stealing, and at once sent off the three captured animals, in charge of two of their number, to the tribe. The other seven Indians went into camp for the night within fifty yards of Mr. McElwee's house.

The young McElwees were in great terror to be sure. But when their father left he had charged them that if they were ever in danger from the Indians they had only to let their nearest neighbor know it and they would soon be relieved. On this occasion they contrived to let Mr. Thomas Officer know of their situation and soon the entire settlement was informed that seven Indians had already taken three horses from the McElwee young folks and were threatening them by their presence with further damage and injury.

The next morning early came old Martin Parmer, and with him Patrick Laney, Thomas Officer, James Officer, David Liles, William Liles, James Woolard, Alex. Woolard and —— Brummett. With them were Mrs. Jane Laney, wife of Patrick Laney, and Miss Mary Crawford, who had come for companionship for Miss McElwee.

The Indians were a little startled by the appearance of the settlers but stoutly maintained that what they had done was justifiable and altogether proper. Old Martin Parmer was not in a mood to discuss the principles of the *lex talionis* and its applicability to this case. He never let an opportunity pass to have a fight with the Indians. Two years before, in a fight of his own bringing on, down on the Wakenda, in Carroll county, he and his party killed three Indians and wounded a number more. His voice was always for war — or, at least for a fight — when there was the smallest provocation.

The discussion in McElwee's door-yard grew warm, and at last Parmer said something to one of the Indians which so incensed him that he presented his gun at Parmer and cocked it, but before he could fire Parmer shot him dead.

A fierce and stubborn little fight then came off in the door-yard. Both

HISTORY OF CLAY COUNTY

whites and Indians ran to cover. Two of the Indians ran into the house where the ladies were, but seing them coming Miss McElwee ran out of doors and Mrs. Laney and Miss Crawford took refuge under a bed. The Indians outside were defeated and scattered, one of them being wounded. Those in the house closed the door tightly and bravely held the fort. But at last the whites climbed to the top of the house and began tearing away the roof, when the savages suddenly opened the door and sprang forth, hoping to escape by swift running. Some of the settlers were waiting for them and one was shot dead before he had gotten twenty feet from the door; the other escaped.

The fight was now over. Two Indians had been killed, and one at least was wounded. Three of the unharmed survivors made their way in safety back to the tribe, but the remaining one was never heard of. It was believed that he, too, was wounded, and crawled off into the woods and died. The one known to have been wounded made his way to Ft. Osage, where he was cared for until he recovered, and was then sent back to his tribe.

When the two Indians were running into the cabin Wm. McElwee and his sister Sarah both attempted to run out. Miss McElwee got safely away, but one of the Indians struck at William with a tomahawk. Young McElwee threw up his arm to protect his head from the blow, but the weapon descending cut off one of his fingers. This was all the injuries the whites received, though some of them heard bullets whiz uncomfortably close to their ears.

It is believed that this is the first time the details of this incident have been published, and that this account is the only correct one ever given to the public. It has been derived from the statements of Mrs. Margaret Howdeshell, a daughter of David McElwee, and a sister of Sarah, William and James McElwee. She is now living in Fishing River township, and through her son Samuel the facts above set forth have been learned.

Smith's sketch in the Clay County Atlas refers to this incident as having occurred in 1820, and calls it "a skirmish which occurred that year in the eastern part of the county, and in which *seven* [!] Indians were killed." Mr. D. C. Allen, author of the valuable and well written article on Clay county in Campbell's Gazetteer (1875), thus describes it: "In a skirmish in the southeastern part of the county, in 1820, seven Indians were killed; another about the same time had his hand cut off in attempting to burst open the door of David McElwee's house." The reader will see that both Mr. Smith and Mr.

97

HISTORY OF CLAY COUNTY

Allen were misinformed in regard to the facts in the case. Mr. Allen's informants caused him to believe that not only were " seven " Indians killed in the " skirmish," but that another row occurred in the same locality in which an *Indian* had his hand cut off, etc. The old settlers got the story mixed. It was William McElwee's finger which was cut off by an Indian, and this occurred in the only " skirmish " ever had with the savages in this county ; and moreover only two or possibly three Indians were slain, not " seven." There were only seven Indians in the party.[1]

ORGANIZATION OF CLAY.

During the year 1821 settlers had poured into the western part of Ray county in considerable numbers. The pioneers evinced a disposition to go out upon the frontiers to the " jumping off place," or to the extreme western boundary of the State, as far as they could go. So it was that Clay was well settled before Carroll, the eastern part of Ray, and a large portion of Chariton were.

Fishing River and Gallatin townships of Ray county were so well populated that it was determined to create out of them a new county to be called *Clay*, in honor of the then brilliant orator and coming statesman of Kentucky, Henry Clay. January 2, 1822, the Legislature passed the following act forming the new county : —

Be it enacted by the General Assembly of the State of Missouri, as follows:

1. A new county shall be established as follows : Beginning in the middle of the main channel of the Missouri river, south of the range line passing between range twenty-nine and thirty west of the fifth principal meridian, thence north and with said range line, pursuing the course thereof, when continued to the northern boundary line of this State ; thence west with the northern boundary line to the northwest range of this State ; thence south with said boundary line due south to the Missouri river, and to the middle of the main channel thereof ; thence down the middle of the main channel thereof to the place of beginning, which shall be called the county of Clay.

2. John Hutchins, Henry Estes, Enos Vaughn, Wyatt Atkins and John Poor, be, and are hereby appointed commissioners, with power to fix upon the most suitable place in said county whereon to erect a court-house and jail ; and the place whereon they, or a majority of them shall agree, shall be the permanent seat of justice for the said county of Clay.

---

[1] Since the above was written the statements are corroborated by one or two old settlers.

HISTORY OF CLAY COUNTY

3. The power and duties of the said commissioners within the county of Clay shall be the same as the powers and duties assigned by an act entitled " An act defining the limits of Howard county, and laying off new counties within the limits of said county as heretofore defined," to the commissioners appointed to point out and fix upon the most suitable place in the county of Ray whereon to erect a court-house and jail for the said county of Ray.

4. The said commissioners, or a majority of them, be and are hereby empowered to receive as a donation, or to purchase the land by them selected, and to lay off the same into lots or squares, and to expose them to public sale under the same restrictions as were imposed by the before recited act, on the commissioners of Ray county, and the powers and duties of the judge of the circuit court shall be the same in the said county of Clay, as in the said county of Ray.

5. The courts to be holden in the county of Clay, shall be holden at the house of John Owens, until said commissioners shall choose and fix on a temporary seat of justice for said county; and after the said commissioners have selected a temporary seat of justice in said county, the courts to be holden for said county shall be holden at the temporary seat of justice until a house for holding courts and a jail is provided at the permanent seat of justice for said county of Clay.

6. All executions to be issued after the taking effect of this act, from the circuit court of the county of Ray, shall be directed to the proper officers of the county of Clay, if the person against whom they may issue reside within the said county of Clay; and such executions shall be executed and returned by him in the same manner as if issued by the clerk of the county of Clay; and all accounts of executors, administrators and guardians now pending in the county of Ray, if such executors, administrators or guardians reside in the county of Clay, shall at the request of such executors, administrators or guardians, be certified by the clerk of the said county of Ray, with the proceedings had thereon, to the clerk's office in the county of Clay, and shall stand ready for trial or settlement as if they had commenced therein; and all justices of the peace. and constables now residing in the said limits of said county of Clay shall continue to execute all the duties of their offices, as justices and constables, in the county of Clay; and it shall be the duty of the county court for said county of Clay, at the first term of said court, to appoint a collector for said county, who shall immediately enter upon the duties of his office; and the taxes for the said county of Clay shall be collected and accounted for by the collector of said county in the same manner as is now required of the collector of Ray county.

This act shall take effect and be in force from and after the passage thereof.

Approved, January 2, 1822.

CHAPTER II.

HISTORY OF THE COUNTY FROM 1822 TO 1830.

General Historical Sketch from 1822 to 1830 — First County Courts — First Circuit Courts — Three Indian Horse Thieves — First Murder Case — Execution of the Murderess — The County in 1822 as Described by Dr. Beck — Martin Palmer, the "Ring-Tailed Painter" — Miscellaneous Items — Liberty Township — Roads and Ferries — Important County Court Proceedings in 1826 — Miscellaneous — Valuation of Property in 1829 — The Indian Alarm of 1828 — The Expedition into the Platte Country.

Upon the organization of Clay county, in January, 1822, the population was about 1,200. The area of the county at that time was very much larger than at present, but the population was almost entirely confined to the territory embraced within the present limits. The number of voters was 240.

Liberty was laid out and made the county seat in the summer of 1822, and the same year a dozen houses — nearly all log cabins — were built. Six small stores were in the county this year, two of which were Essex & Hough's and Robert Hood's. These were at Liberty. A few Indian traders were at the mouth of the Kansas and across the river at Fort Osage.

Other merchants in Clay county from 1822 to 1830 were William Samuels & Co., Ely & Curtis, Hickman & Lamme (afterward Hickman, Lamme & Ringo), Joshua Pallen, F. P. Chouteau, James Aull, James M. Hughes & Co., and Moore, Samuels & Croysdale. Some of the grocers[1] were James Aull, Hiram Rich, Gershom Compton and Laban Garrett. Noah Richards had a licensed dram-shop in 1828. All these were in Liberty.

Merchants' licenses were $15; grocers', $5 and $10.

From the records of the county court — indisputable evidence — it appears that among other industries Lewis Scott had a tanyard in 1825; Ely & Curtis operated a distillery in 1826; and John Baxter had a saddle and harness shop in Liberty in 1827.

Mills followed the first settlers. Smith's sketch in the Atlas says the first horse-mill was built near Liberty in 1821, by Samuel Tilford

---

[1] At that date a "grocer" sold more whisky than coffee and sugar, and a "grocery" was understood to be a place where ardent spirits were retailed.

HISTORY OF CLAY COUNTY

"and ground only corn." Probably there was nothing else to grind. The buhrstones of this mill were made of "lost rocks," as are sometimes called the granite boulders scattered over the county, relics of the glacial period. Four other mills were in existence certainly as early as 1826 — Manchester's mill, on Shoal creek.; William and Joel Estes' mill, on Fishing river; Smith's mill, on Smith's fork, and Hixon's mill.

David D. Moore had a mill on Big Shoal creek, in the southwestern part of the county, in 1830.

A serious obstacle to the settlement of Clay county was the difficulty of crossing the Missouri, then more so than now a turbid, troublesome stream, with its shifting currents and channels, its treacherous bars and shoals, and, when at a high stage, its almost irresistible tides. Trifles and insignificant circumstances often directed a settler's location, and many a man located on the south side of the Missouri because of the difficulty of crossing to the north side. The first ferries whose owners lived in this county were Joseph Boggs', established in 1825; Richard Linville's the same year; John Thornton's in 1826, and Frost's about the year 1828. Linville, in 1826, disposed of his ferry to an old Frenchman named Calisse Montargee, commonly called "Calisse" (pronounced *Caleece*). He ran it until in 1830, when he sold it to Benj. Hancock.

Old Calisse was an eccentric character. He was one of the first settlers in the county, coming here soon after the War of 1812, first as a trapper and *voyageur*. He had a landing on the river, known as Calisse's landing, on fractional section 18–50–32, or a mile south of the present site of Moscow. He ran his ferry from this landing.

Aaron Overton had a ferry over the Missouri, at the mouth of Rose's branch, in May, 1830. It and all the other ferries were propelled by oars, or sweeps, and it was a good half day's work to take the boat over to the south side and bring back an emigrant wagon.

Schools were established early. Smith's sketch states that a few steps south of the Baptist Church, in Liberty, was built a log schoolhouse as early as 1821, the first in the county, and that the first school was taught there by Judge Sibron G. Sneed. There may be and probably is a mistake in the statement that this house was built as early as 1821, but there was certainly a school-house in Liberty in 1823. In 1825 there was a good school-house near Benjamin Sampson's in the southwestern portion of the county (elections were held in it), but the name of the first teacher can not here and now be given.

101

There was also a church, or as the records call it "a meeting-house," near Mr. Sampson's, in 1825.

Upon the first settlement of the county Government land was $2 per acre, and the nearest land office was at Old Franklin, in Howard county. In about 1825 the price of land was reduced to $1.25 per acre, and the land office was removed not long afterward to Lexington.[1] A number of the farms in this county were taken as "New Madrid claims."

The term "New Madrid claim" may thus be explained to those who do not understand it: After the great earthquake at and in the vicinity of New Madrid, in December, 1811, Congress passed an act for the relief of the settlers who had been injured by that great convulsion of nature, giving each of them certain favors and privileges in regard to re-entering or locating land in other parts of the State. In some instances this relief amounted to an absolute grant of land. The act was passed February 17, 1815, and was entitled, "An act for the relief of the inhabitants of the late (?) county of New Madrid, in Missouri Territory, who suffered by earthquakes."

In 1827 a United States military post was established on the site of the present Fort Leavenworth, an incident of importance to this county, since it furnished a market for horses, mules and supplies, and also gave employment to a number of our citizens, contractors and others. In a letter to the compiler, Gen. R. C. Drum, Adjutant-General of the United States, says: "It appears from the records of this office that Cantonment Leavenworth, on the site of the present Fort Leavenworth, was first established by Cos. B, D, E and H, Third Infantry, under Col. Henry Leavenworth (who was its first commandant, and for whom it was named), about April 1, 1827."

In the summer of 1826 came the first "big rise" in the Missouri. The bottom lands were overflowed and the settlers thereon were forced to remove to higher ground. Though there was some inconvenience and even damage and distress at first, the flood proved a blessing in disguise to the county in general. Many of the pioneers were afraid of the highlands, and especially of the prairies, but now they preferred them to the bottoms, which, as they could see, were liable annually to be submerged by the mighty, tawny waters of the Missouri, bringing destruction and devastation and leaving malaria and pestilence. So now, the uplands of the county were tested and found to be good, and thus the whole county began to settle up.

---

[1] The Atlas sketch says this was in 1822, but there was no Lexington in 1822.

HISTORY OF CLAY COUNTY

Upon the first settlement of the country many of the pioneers shared the expressed opinion of Dr. Beck, given on another page, and held that the prairies were and always would be practically valueless; but there were others who knew good soil when they saw it, and did not hesitate to say that the Clay county prairies were fertile and would produce well. There was a serious obstacle in the way of their cultivation, however. At that day there were *no plows* strong enough to tear up the thick, tough sod. The plows then in vogue were light affairs, with small iron (chiefly cast-iron) points, and wooden moldboards. These were wholly insufficient for prairie breaking. After a time stronger plows were introduced, the prairie sod was trodden and became less substantial, and prairie farms became very popular.

FIRST SESSIONS OF THE COUNTY COURT.

February 11, 1822, the first county court of Clay county convened at the house of John Owens, which stood on what is now lot 186, on the northwest corner of Water and Mill streets, in the city of Liberty. There were present the county justices, John Thornton, Elisha Camron[1] and James Gilmor, who exhibited their commissions, signed by Gov. Alexander McNair, and took their seats. (Thornton and Camron had previously been justices of the county court of Ray county). William L. Smith was appointed county clerk, with Col. Shubael Allen and John Shields as secretaries. Smith had been clerk of Ray county.

The court first proceeded to the appointment of certain other officers of the county for the year 1822, viz.: William Hall, assessor; Jesse Gilliam, collector; Samuel Tilford, John Hutchings, Howard Averatt,[2] Richard Linville and Benjamin Sampson, commissioners "to preserve from waste the school lands lying in this county." All of these, except William Hall, were present in court and took the oath of office. John Harris was sheriff; he had been sheriff of Ray county.

It is said that the court room was Mr. Owens' sitting room, vacated by the family for the occasion. Old Zadock Martin was present, and seemed to hold the entire proceedings in contempt, and so the first order of the court was the imposition of a fine of $1 on Mr. Martin for his said contempt. Whereupon Zadock awoke to a realization of

---

[1] Judge Camron died in this county June 2, 1853, aged sixty-nine. As he wrote it himself his name was spelled as here printed, but latterly it is spelled with an *e*. The city of Cameron was named for him.

[2] Afterward and now spelled Everett.

103

the fact that this really was a court, with power to protect its dignity and punish affronts thereupon, and so he made apology, and the fine was subsequently remitted. Martin was afterward a county judge himself, and he it was who is said to have been the first American actual settler in Platte county, whither he removed in 1827, and established a ferry on Platte river, at the crossing of the military road from Liberty to Fort Leavenworth.

On the second day of the term the newly appointed assessor, Wm. Hall, appeared and took the oath of office. The court determined to establish a precedent for economy in the administration of the county government and made the following order: —

Ordered, That the sum of *one dollar* only per day be charged by the justices of this court for their services; and it is further ordered that the same economy be observed by all persons who shall have claims against the county.

Money was scarce that day, and the judges wisely determined that the county ought to live within its income. Mr. Owens was allowed $2 for the use of his house as a court room during the two days' session, and then the court adjourned.

The court made no order dividing the county into municipal townships — at least none is to be found. It seemed to accept the division which had previously been made by the Ray county court — of two townships, Fishing River and Gallatin. The line between these townships ran north and south, dividing the county nearly into halves.

A special session was held at Owens' March 9, 1822, at which Judges Thornton and Gilmor were present. Jesse Gilliam gave bond as collector, and Wm. Hall was appointed assessor in Gallatin township, and Pleasant Adams assessor of the State taxes for Fishing River.

At the regular May term, 1822, all the justices were present, and John Thornton was made presiding judge. George Halfacre and James Williams were nominated to the Governor as suitable persons to be commissioned as justices of the peace for Fishing River township. Preparations were made for holding the August election in the two townships, as follows: —

In Fishing river, the house of James Munker was designated as the voting place, and Thos. Officer, Howard Averatt and Bailey George were appointed judges of the election. In Gallatin township, the house of John Owens, in Liberty, was named as the voting place, and the judges of election were James McClelland, John Evans and John McKissick.

HISTORY OF CLAY COUNTY

The *first roads* established by the Clay county court were ordered surveyed or reviewed at this term. Those already in use had been make by the Ray court. The first road established by our court was one from Liberty to the intersection of a road leading to Bluffton, on the Missouri river, which was then the county seat of Ray county. This road was directed to be surveyed " from the county line, where the road leading from Bluffton strikes said line; from thence by Col. [Martin] Palmer's, taking the dividing ridge between Fishing river and the Missouri; thence with the said ridge to the line ranges 30 and 31, and from thence to the county seat by the nearest between and most practicable route." The commissioners were Joseph Hutchings, Jacob McKoy, Thos. Estes, Elisha Hall and Elijah Smith.

Other roads were established as follows: A road leading from the north end of Main street, in Liberty, " the nearest and best way to the prairie in the direction of Magill's." Commissioners, John Owens, Eppa Tillery, Ezekiel Huffman and John Hall. A road " leading from the court house [John Owens'] in Liberty, the nearest and best way to Andrew Russell's, from thence to the [State] boundary line." Commissioners, Mitchell Poage, South Malott, Aaron Roberts and Andrew Russell. The settlers had already begun to push out as far as possible, or was safe, and settlements were being made on the western frontiers, and roads were needed for communication with the outer world.

At this term David Manchester was appointed county surveyor, and Joshua Adams assessor for Fishing River township. Mr. Adams was selected to assist Mr. Hall, the county assessor, who, owing to the size of the county at that time, could attend to his duties in but one township, Gallatin, in time for the June levy.

Some idea of the character of the county at this time can be gained from the report of Jesse Gilliam, the county collector, who stated to the court that he had issued *six* retail licenses (at $5 each), thus showing that there were six retail stores in the county in the spring of 1822. These, of course, were not comparable with the establishments of to-day, but their stocks were limited to the necessaries of pioneer life at that day. Some of the merchants in the county this year were Essex & Hough and Robert Hood.

FIRST CIRCUIT COURT.

March 4, 1822, the first circuit court of Clay county was held at the house of John Owens — in Liberty — David Todd, judge; Wm. L.

Smith, clerk; Hamilton R. Gamble, circuit attorney,[1] and John Harris, sheriff. The court was in session two days, and had for grand jurors: Richard Linville, foreman; Zachariah McGree, Benj. Sampson, Robert Y. Fowler, Zachariah Averett, Howard Averett, John Ritchie, James Munker, John Evans, Thomas Estes, Andrew Robertson, Richard Hill, David Magill, Walker McClelland, Robert Poage, Samuel Tilford, David Gregg, Wm. Allen, Elisha Hall and James Williams. There was no trial jury until the July term, in the case of "The State vs. Jonathan Camron." Indictment for affray. The jurors were: Abijah Means, Richard Chaney, Abraham Creek, John Bartleson, James Gladdin, Francis T. Slaughter, Enos Vaughn, Andrew Copelin, John Carrell, Matthew Averett, Eppa Tillery and Samuel Magill. Verdict, "Not guilty." There was no fixed place for holding court, it being sometimes held under the arbor of a tree, until 1832, when the first court house was built.

The first attorney admitted to practice before our circuit court was Dabney Carr, at the first term.

Judge David Todd was born in Fayette county, Ky., in 1790. He came to Missouri at an early day and located at Old Franklin, Howard county. He was well known and long remembered as an able and upright judge and a pure man. Judge Todd died at Columbia, Boone county, in 1859. Hamilton R. Gamble was born in Winchester county, Va., November 29, 1798; came to St. Louis in 1818, and in 1819 to Old Franklin; was appointed prosecuting attorney in 1822; Secretary of State in 1824, and Supreme Court Judge in 1851. In 1861, when Claib. Jackson was deposed, he was made Provisional Governor. He died in 1864.

THREE INDIAN HORSE THIEVES.

In the month of May, 1823, a roving band of Iowa Indians passed through this county on their way down to the Grand river country. Three of these Indians stole three horses from Ezekiel Huffman and other citizens of this county, and carried them off to the encampment on Grand river, above where Brunswick now stands.

The chiefs of the tribe gave information to the authorities, and on an affidavit of John P. Gates, the Hon. David Todd, then judge of the first judicial circuit, issued a warrant directed to the sheriff of Chariton county, where the Indians then were, directing him to arrest the

---

[1] At this term Mr. Gamble was not present. Hon. Abiel Leonard, then deputy circuit attorney for the first circuit in the counties of Clay, Ray, Lillard, Saline and Cole attended.

three culprits, whose names were given as *Cha-pa-har-lar*, or Buffalo Nose; *Mon-to-kar*, or White Briar, and *Ton-tar-ru-rhue-che*, or Where he is Crossing. Subpœnas were also issued for *War-sen-nee*, or The End of Medicine; *War-hu-kea*, or Moccasin Awl; *Monk-she-kon-nah*, a Valiant Man, *Won-chee-mon-nee*, " chiefs of the said Ioway nation of Indians."

The Indians were duly arrested,[1] and brought before Judge Todd, at Fayette, on the 5th of July. Their preliminary examination resulted in their commitment to the Howard county jail. On the 7th they were again brought before Judge Todd by Sheriff Ben B. Ray, of Howard county. The judge ordered " the said Indians committed to the custody of the sheriff of Chariton county, to be forthwith remanded to the sheriff of Clay county, to await their further trial before the circuit court of Clay county on the first day of the next term, in default of giving bail in $200 each." [2]

But on the night of the 8th of July the prisoners contrived to escape from their guards, as witness the following return of the deputy sheriff of Chariton county, in whose custody they were: —

On the 7th of July the within named Indians were delivered into my custody. I summoned Thos. Smith, Joel King and Thos. Jack as a guard, who kept them under custody until the night of the 8th inst., when the said Indians made their escape and have not since been apprehended. ALEXANDER TRENT,

July 11, 1823. Deputy Sheriff Chariton County.

The Indians were never recaptured, but it is understood that the stolen horses were recovered by Huffman and his neighbors. This is the only instance now to be found where the Indians committed any serious offense against our people after the year 1822, or the organization of the county.

THE FIRST MURDER CASE — EXECUTION OF THE MURDERESS, A NEGRO WOMAN.

Some time in the summer of 1828 (probably in June), a slave woman named Annice murdered her children, and the crime having been discovered she was arrested and indicted. At the July term of the circuit court following she was arraigned and tried before a jury

---

[1] The arrest was effected by a posse composed of Maj. Daniel Ashby, John M. Bell, Peregrine Earickson and Christian Houser, who, the return says, were " on the search for three days."

[2] See the papers in this case, on file in the circuit clerk's office.

composed of Charles English, Benedict Weldon, Mayberry Mitchell, David Bevins, Abraham Creek, Josiah Thorp, John Hardwicke, Edmund Munday, David Hamilton, James Gray, Lewis Shelton and Nathan Chaney. Of these David Bevins and Josiah Thorp are yet living.

Annice belonged to a Mr. Prior, who lived near Greenville, in the northeastern part of the county. The family went away from home, and the negress decoyed her children to the woods and to a small stream, a branch of Fishing river. In a deep pool formed by a small water-fall she threw two (or three) of her youngest children and drowned them. She was chasing another, her oldest, when she was discovered.

The proof was positive as to the guilt of the accused, and Judge David Todd sentenced her to be hung on the 23d day of August following. There was no appeal of the case, no pardon, no commutation, no postponement of the execution, and the wretched creature was hung on the day appointed, by Col. Shubael Allen, the then sheriff. The execution came off in the northern part of Liberty.

DR. BECK DESCRIBES CLAY COUNTY IN 1822.

Beck's Gazetteer of Missouri, published in 1823, has the following concerning Clay county : —

Clay county was erected from Ray in 1822. It is bounded north and west by the boundary lines of the State, east by the county of Ray, and south by Lillard. Its form is that of a parallelogram, about 100 miles in length, and 21 in breadth; containing an area of about 2,000 square miles. The southern boundary is washed by the Missouri river; the interior is well washed by Fishing river, and several other small streams, running in a southerly and westerly direction. The lands are generally elevated, and in the northern part approaching to hilly. Of the fertility of this county and the inducements which it offers to emigrants, I need not adduce a more convincing proof than the fact that but two or three years since it was a complete wilderness without a single white inhabitant; while at present its population is not less than 1,000. The country north and west is owned and inhabited by hordes of Indians.

Clay county is attached to the first judicial circuit; sends one member to the House of Representatives, and with Ray, Lillard and Chariton, one to the Senate.

Speaking of the prairies in this quarter of the State, Dr. Beck says : —

The prairies, although generally fertile, are so very extensive, that they must for a great length of time, and perhaps forever, remain

HISTORY OF CLAY COUNTY

wild and uncultivated; yet such is the enterprise of the American citizens — such the immigration to the West, that it almost amounts to presumption to hazard an opinion on the subject. Perhaps before the expiration of ten years, instead of being bleak and desolate, they may have been converted into immense grazing fields, covered with herds of cattle. It is not possible, however, that the interior of the prairies can be inhabited; for, setting aside the difficulty of obtaining timber, it is on other accounts unpleasant and uncomfortable. In winter the northern and western blasts are excessively cold, and the snow is drifted like hills and mountains, so as to render it impossible to cross from one side to the other. In summer, on the contrary, the sun acting upon such an extensive surface, and the southerly winds, which uniformly prevail during this season, produce a degree of heat almost insupportable.

It should not, by any means, be understood these objections apply to all the prairies. The smaller ones are not subject to these inconveniences; on the contrary, they are by far the most desirable and pleasant situations for settlement.

There are those of this description in the county of which we are treating, surrounded by forests, and containing here and there groves of the finest timber, watered by beautiful running streams, presenting an elevated, rolling or undulating surface, and a soil rarely equaled in fertility.

"THE RING TAILED 'PAINTER.'"

In 1826 the first State Senator for the district composed of Ray and Clay was elected. Hitherto the district had been represented by Gen. Duff Green, of Howard. The successful candidate in 1826 was Martin Parmer (or Palmer), of Clay, who lived on Fishing river, in the southeastern part of the county. Parmer was a "statesman" somewhat of the David Crockett species, uneducated, illiterate and uncultivated, but possessing natural good sense, a considerable amount of shrewdness, and an acquaintanceship with the ways of the world. An incident that occurred during Palmer's career as State Senator is thus described in Wetmore's Gazetteer: —

When the time approached for the meeting of the Legislature, Palmer loaded a small keel with salt on the Missouri, above Hardeman's plantation, and having taken the helm himself, manned the vessel with his son and a negro. Uniting, as he did, business and politics, while afloat on the river he stood astride of the tiller, with a newspaper in hand (not more than six weeks old), out of which he was spelling, with all his might, some of the leading points of a political essay. At this critical period the assemblyman was reminded by his vigilant son in the bow of the break of a "sawyer head." "Wait a minnit," said he, "until I spell out this other crack-jaw; it's longer than the barrel of my rifle gun," but the current of the Missouri was no respecter of persons or words, the river " went ahead," and the boat ran foul of the nodding obstruction, and was thrown on her beam ends. The next whirlpool turned her keel uppermost. The cargo was discharged into the bowels of the deep; and there his " salt lost its savor." The negro, in a desperate struggle for life, swam for the shore, but the steersman, who, like a politician, determined to stick to the ship as he would to his party, as long as a timber or a fish floated, continued to keep uppermost.

Having divested themselves of their apparel, to be in readiness for swimming, the father and son continued astride the keel, until the wreck was landed at the town of Franklin. Here the old hunter, who was a lean citizen, was kindly supplied by a stout gentleman with a suit of his own clothes, which hung, like the morals of the politician, rather loosely about him. The sufferers by shipwreck were invited into the habitation of a gentleman who dwelt near the shore on which they had been cast.

While recounting their perils at the breakfast table, the lady, who was administering coffee, inquired of the politician if his little son had not been greatly alarmed. " No, madam," said he, " I am a real ring-tail painter, and I feed all my children on rattlesnakes' hearts, fried in painter's grease. There are a heap of people that I would not wear crape for if they was to die before their time; but your husband, *marm*, I allow, had a soul as big as a *court house*. When we war floating, bottom uppermost (a bad situation for the people's representative), past Hardeman's garden, we raised the yell, like a whole team of bar-dog on a wild cat's trail; and the black rascals on the shore, instead of coming to our assistance, only grinned up the nearest saplin, as if a buck possum had treed. Now, madam, I wish God Almighty's *yearthquakes* would sink Hardeman's d—ned plantation — begging your pardon for swearing madam, with my feet on your beautiful kiverlid here. May be you wouldent like me to spit on this kiverlid you have spread on the floor to keep it clean; I'll go to the door — we don't mind putting anything over our puncheon floors. " The river, marm," continued the guest, " I find is no respecter of persons, for I was cast away with as little ceremony, notwithstanding I am the people's representative, as a stray bar-dog would be turned out of a city church; and upon this principle of Democratic liberty and equality it was that I told McNair, when I collared him and backed him out of the gathering at a shooting match, where he was likely to spoil the prettiest kind of a fight. 'A Governor,' said I, ' is no more in a fight than any other man.' I slept with Mac. once, just to have it to say to my friends on Fishing river that I had slept with the Governor."

MISCELLANEOUS.

A special session of the county court in June, 1822, was devoted to arranging for the collection of taxes. A levy of 50 per cent of the amount of the State tax was made for county purposes, and it was ordered that "all taxes collected for county purposes be paid in gold or silver coin." In August following, however, this order was rescinded, the court saying that they "doubted the legality" of making nothing but gold and silver receivable for taxes. The collector was ordered to *pay back* what specie he had already received on the receipt of its equivalent in loan office or county certificates.

At the August term, 1822, the court made an order for the erection of the first public structure built by the county. This was a "stray pen" or pound for the restraining of animals running at large under certain circumstances. It was 60 feet square, built of posts and rails, by Jonathan Reed, and cost the county 29.87\frac{1}{2}$

Road commissioners, to lay off roads and allot hands to work the same, were appointed, viz.: For Fishing River township, John Hutchings and Thomas Officer; for Gallatin, John Thornton and James Gilmor. Chesley Woodward was appointed overseer of the road leading from Liberty to the prairie, "in the direction of Magill's."

In November, 1822, Jesse Gilliam, the county collector, made his first report. The total tax list of the county was 142.77\frac{1}{2}$, and of this he had collected 140.27\frac{1}{2}$, leaving a delinquent list of but $2.50. What the delinquent list would have been had the court insisted on the payment of gold and silver can only be conjectured, but doubtless it would have been much larger.

At this term the first guardians were appointed: Richard Linville and Thomas Frost were appointed guardians of Gilbert, Thomas, Josiah, Joshua, Benjamin, Polly, Ann and Hannah Frost, children under fourteen, of Elijah Frost, deceased.

The county court was in session nine days in the year 1822.

In November, 1824, the court appointed the first patrol, one company for the entire county, as follows: Captain, Leban Garrett; privates, Claiborne Rice and Charles Magee. There were only enough slaves in the county at the time to justify the appointment of but this one company.

The tax list in 1824 amounted to 225.52\frac{1}{4}$.

Merchants in 1824 were Wm. Samuels & Co., Ely & Curtis, Hickman & Lammes and Robert Hood.

In February, 1825, six saloons or dram-shops and one billiard table were licensed in the county. The latter was charged $50 for the privilege of running one year. Our first settlers were men like some of their descendants and loved their toddy. But while Clay county, in 1825, with a population of 4,000 had six saloons, in 1885, sixty years later, with a population of nearly 20,000, she has not one saloon, and has not had for many years.

In the fall of the previous year (1824) a road had been established through the county leading to " the Council Bluffs," and in the early spring of this year another was laid out from Liberty to the Missouri river, " at a certain blue bank."

Under an act of the Legislature, passed the previous session, the justices of the peace of the county constituted the county court, and at the March term, 1825, there assembled at Liberty George Burnett and Sebron G. Sneed, Esqs., of Gallatin township, and George Huffaker and Howard Averett, of Fishing River. They paid Benj. Simms " for repairing the court house and for furnishing benches " and also paid Nathaniel Patton, of Old Franklin, Howard county, for publishing in his paper, the *Boone's Lick Democrat*, the receipts and expenditures of the county for the year 1824. At that time the *Democrat* was the paper published nearest to this county.

Thornton Strother and Sebron G. Sneed were recommended to the Governor for commissions as justices of the peace of Gallatin township, at the August term, this year. At this time Sneed's house, in Liberty, was used to hold courts and elections in, and was called a court house. It is said that it was a vacant building owned by Judge' Sneed.

TOWNSHIP BOUNDARIES DEFINED — FORMATION OF LIBERTY TOWNSHIP.

At the March term, 1825, Liberty township was created by the following order of the county court : —

Ordered, That the following boundaries hereafter constitute the townships of this county : —
All that part of this county which lies between the line dividing Ray and Clay counties to the sectional line running north and south, dividing sections 9 and 10, in the tier of townships in range 31, be and constitute *Fishing River* township.

All that part of the county which lies between said sectional line dividing sections 9 and 10, in townships 50, 51, 52, 53, 54, 55, 56, and 57, in range 31, to the first sectional line running north and south in range 32, be and constitute a new township, to be called and known as *Liberty* township.

All of that part of the county which lies west of said sectional line dividing sections 1 and 2, in townships 50, 51, 52, 53, 54, 55, 56, and 57, in range 32, to the western boundary of the county constitute and hereafter be known and designated as *Gallatin* township.

In the following August these boundaries were changed. The

HISTORY OF CLAY COUNTY

western boundary of Fishing River was made the section line between sections 2 and 3, in range 31, which is now (1885) the eastern line of Liberty. The western boundary of Liberty was made the line between sections 2 and 3, in range 32, a mile west of the present boundary of the township. Gallatin township comprised the western portion of the county. All the townships extended northward from the Missouri river to the northern boundary of the State.

The previous year, at the August term, a petition was presented for the creation of Liberty township out of Gallatin, but the court refused to grant the prayer of the petitioners, saying: —

* * * Upon consideration, it appears to the court that the signers to said petition, or a large majority of them, reside in or near to the town of Liberty, the county seat, and therefore can not labor under much inconvenience in consequence of the size of the township; and it moreover appears that said petition, being presented so soon after the election, has been gotten up on improper grounds, and is, therefore, *rejected.*

ROADS AND FERRIES IN 1825.

In May a road was laid out from Liberty to Thornton's ferry, on the Missouri, "at or near the Blue bank." Another from Liberty to the Missouri river, "at the boat landing at the town of Gallatin." Another from Liberty "to the mouth of the Kansas river."

In September Joseph Boggs was licensed to keep a ferry across the Missouri river, "from the bank near where Wyatt Adkins lives." He was allowed to charge the following rates: "For a loaded wagon and team, $2; empty wagon and team, $1.50; loaded cart and team, $1; for a dearborn and horses, or gig and horses, $62\frac{1}{2}$ cents; man and horse, $37\frac{1}{2}$ cents; single person, $18\frac{3}{4}$ cents; horses, each, $18\frac{3}{4}$ cents; sheep, hogs, and cattle, 3 cents each." In November Richard Linville was licensed to keep a ferry on the Missouri, from a point in section 18, township 50, range 32, "where Louis Barthelette now lives," a mile south of the present site of Moscow. Judge Linville was allowed to charge the same rates as Boggs.

MISCELLANEOUS.

In the spring of 1825 Philip Logan and Wm. Murray engaged in an affray, or fisticuff, one day, in Liberty, and were arrested and convicted before Esq. Seron G. Sneed, who sentenced them to pay a fine and costs. Not having any money they were sent to Lillard county jail. When they had served "in gaol" a sufficient time to liquidate the fine they were released upon making oath that they were unable

HISTORY OF CLAY COUNTY

to pay the costs and the county court ordered their release. Thomas Young, another convicted and imprisoned fighter, asked for his release, but the court said he should remain in confinement "the time prescribed by the verdict of the jury." Logan and Murray were arrested the same summer charged with arson.

Elections in 1825 were held: In Gallatin township, at Benj. Sampson's; judges, Zadock Martin, Sr., Harmon Davis and Benj. Sampson. In Liberty, at the town; judges, John Evans, George Lincoln and John Bartleson. In Fishing River, at James Munker's; judges, Wm. Miller, Thos. Officer and Jeremiah Rose.

New merchants this year were Joshua Pallen and F. P. Chouteau, the latter a well known trader. This year, 1825, the county court records mention "a meeting house, near Benj. Sampson's," in the southwest part of the county.

COURT PROCEEDINGS IN 1826.

In February, township 51, range 31, including Liberty and the country east and south for five or six miles, was incorporated as the *first school township* in the county under the act of the Legislature of 1825.

At the same session the court provided for a seal of the following design: " *Device* — A plough and rake, with the sun immediately over the plough, the rays of which point in every direction." The words: "Seal of Clay county, Missouri," were to be " on the outer margin and circle."

In May the first steps were taken to build a court house; Wm. Averett was allowed $30 per year for the support of his insane son; and Abraham Lincoln (uncle of the " martyr President"), Reuben Tillery and Abraham Creek were appointed reviewers of a road from Liberty to Estes' mill, on Fishing river.

Elections were held this year in Gallatin township, "at the school house near Mr. Sampson's, in said township;" judges, Wm. Todd, Benj. Sampson and Hermon Davis. In Fishing River, at James Munker's; judges, Peter Writesman, William Miller and Travis Finley. In Liberty, at the court house; judges, James E. Hale, John Evans and Samuel Tilford.

This year Reuben Tillery, the county assessor, was twenty days in assessing the county.

MISCELLANEOUS.

Patrolers were appointed in 1827 as follows: In Fishing River township, Roland Starks, captain; Smith Story and Littleberry Sublette. In Gallatin, Hiram Fugate, captain; Robert Cain, John Gumm, Daniel Hughes, John S. Mallott. In Liberty, Thos. Estes, captain; David Lincoln, Lewis Scott, Robert Johnson. Their duties required them to patrol at last 24 hours in every month.

The Legislature of 1827 repealed the law providing that the justices of the peace should be *ex-officio* county judges, and in June, pursuant to this act, the county court of Clay assembled, being composed of Elisha Camron, Samuel Tillery and Joel Turnham, all of whom presented commissions signed by Gov. John Miller, appointing them county judges for a term of four years.

The *first deeds of emancipation* were issued in 1828. In February Henry Estes emancipated "Tom, a man of color," and John Evans set free "Sylvia, a woman of color." In May Joseph Collett, who was himself a "man of color," but free, purchased and emancipated "Hannah," a slave woman, and her two children, "America" and "Eliza." It is quite certain that the woman was or became Collet's wife. In 1836 Collet and his wife were granted license to remain in the State as long as they should be of good behavior. No other cases of emancipation are recorded until 1834, when John Robidoux, the founder of the city of St. Joseph, gave freedom to one Jeffrey Dorney.

The receipts of the county from all sources during the year 1829 were $1,231.39; the expenditures were $960.26.

Wm. L. Smith, county clerk, resigned in January, 1831, and Wm. T. Wood (afterwards the distinguished lawyer and jurist of Lexington) was appointed in his stead. David R. Atchison and Andrew S. Hughes were licensed to practice before the county court at this time.

VALUATION OF PROPERTY IN 1829.

Perhaps a definite idea of the value of personal property in Clay county in early days may be obtained from the appraisement of Archibald Holtzclaw's estate, in 1829, and the prices at which the property was sold. Mr. Holtzclaw's estate was very large and valuable, and his property was divided among his children at the following values : —

Jincy, a crippled slave girl, 30 years old	$100
Anthony, Jincy's child, 1 year old	100
Susan, a slave, 14 years old	300
Henry, a slave, 13 years old	336
Isaac, a slave, 25 years old	450
George, a slave, 13 years old	316

HISTORY OF CLAY COUNTY

Other personal property had the following sworn values: A horse and side-saddle, $40; cow and calf, $7.50; sow and five pigs, $1.50; sheep, each, $1; a flax wheel, $3; a cotton wheel, $3; flag-bottomed chairs, 50 cents each; Bible and hymn-book, $1.50; skillet, $1.25; a good horse, $25.

THE INDIAN ALARM OF 1828.

In the summer of 1828 there was another Indian alarm in this county. Some white men up in what is now Clinton county had sold some whisky to a band of Iowa Indians. The latter became uproariously drunk, and in the absence of a town, began to paint the prairies red. Of course, an alarm spread that the Indians were on the warpath, and were about to descend on the settlements in Clay.

Capt. Wm. Stephenson, of near Liberty, at the head of 63 armed and mounted men set out at once for the scene of the reported troubles, intending, if the Indians were really advancing, to meet them at least half way. The men furnished their own horses, rifles, provisions and equipments. Some of the members of this company were Anthony Harsell, Alex. B. Duncan, Thos. Vaughan, Wm. Campbell and "Pelig" Ellington.

The company was organized at Liberty, and rendezvoused the first night out at John Owens', three miles north of Smithville. From thence it went up on Big Platte — being accompanied by Gen. Andrew S. Hughes — then north of where Plattsburg now stands, and over on to Crooked river; from here it went as far back as the waters of Grand river, and then turned back and returned home, after an absence of 14 days. Not an Indian was seen. The men were afterwards declared to be entitled to 40 acres of land each for their services.

About the same time Capt. Leonard Searcy, the well known tavern-keeper of Liberty, took out a company for the protection of the cantonment and garrison at Fort Leavenworth. This company, like Stephenson's, accomplished nothing but the fatigue of its members and their loss of time. On its return it encountered a band of 15 peaceable, friendly Iowa Indians and brought them to Liberty, where they were released.

An incident that occurred during the stay of these Indians in Liberty is remembered by some of the old pioneers, as it was one instance wherein an Indian "played off" on a white man, Mr. Gill E. Martin, a young son of old Zadock Martin, being the victim. The Indians were excessively fond of sugar, and were known to consume inordinate quantities when they could get it.

Young Martin accosted a strapping "buck," and told him that if he would eat three pounds of sugar he would buy it for him. With extravagant demonstrations of joy and delight, the Indian accepted the proposition, and Martin bought the sugar. The savage set to work with great gusto and ate handful after handful. Martin and some companions stood watching him, eagerly awaiting the time when the limit of his appetite should be reached, and he should become first satiated and then sickened.

But when the Indian had eaten a pound or so, he coolly wrapped up the remainder and thrusting it under his blanket and prepared to take his leave. "Hold on!" exclaimed Martin, "you agreed to eat *all* of the sugar — stand to your bargain, sir!" With something of a shrewd look the "untutored savage" rejoined: "Ugh! All right — me eat him all — maybe some to-day — maybe some to-morrow — maybe some one odder day — Injun no lie — me eat him *all* — good-by!"

CHAPTER III.

HISTORY OF THE COUNTY FROM 1830 TO 1840.

General Sketch of the County from 1830 to 1840 — Early Days in Clay County — The Deep Snow of 1830 — Building the First Court House — The First Jail — During the Black Hawk War — Origin of the Platte Purchase — The "Hetherly War" — Clay County in 1836 — The Mormon War.

GENERAL SKETCH OF THE COUNTY FROM 1830 TO 1840.

In about 1830 steamboats began to make regular trips from St. Louis up the Missouri as high as Liberty Landing, and occasionally a boat laden with government freight ascended as high as Ft. Leavenworth, or even up to Council Bluffs. Landings were established at divers available points on the river in this county. Col. Shubael Allen established a landing on his plantation in about 1830. He had a licensed warehouse and near by Wm. Yates had a ferry in the spring of 1831. In the fall of 1831 Col. Allen obtained the ferry, and operated it from his warehouse. One informed on the subject thus writes of Allen's Landing in the Missouri volume of the U. S. Biographical Dictionary, p. 313 : —

From 1829 until Col. Allen's death (1841), Allen's Landing was the main point of exit and entrance of nearly all the business and travel of Northwest Missouri, in its communication with the outer world by the river, and hence there were visible at that point a degree of activity and a multitude of commercial transactions utterly unknown in these days of the degeneracy of the river traffic in Missouri. It was also for many years the starting point of a large number of the employ s of the American Fur Company in their expeditions to the plains and mountains of the great Northwest. The scene presented annually on the assemblage of these employes — embracing, as it did, swarthy French *voyageurs;* tall, half-breed Indians, straight as arrows, and dressed in wild garbs ; the display of arms of all kinds, the tents scattered over the lawn, the picketed animals, the many-colored garments — this scene was unique, semi-barbarous, but animated and highly picturesque.

Liberty Landing, in the boating season, was a point of some activity. Joel Turnham built a tobacco warehouse here in the winter of 1830–31, and had it licensed in February of the latter year ; James Roberts was inspector. A great deal of freight was shipped from St.

HISTORY OF CLAY COUNTY

Louis to this landing, and a great many passengers were landed here from the boats — emigrants and prospectors.

In November, 1831, Aaron Overton had a ferry at Overton's Crossing. Shrewsbury Williams operated one in 1832, and Samuel Gragg established one in the spring of 1833. Col. Allen's ferry was succeeded by Fielding McCoy's.

Some of the grocers in the city in 1834 were S. & A. S. Ringo, Shubael Allen, Charles Carthrae, Abraham Croysdale, George Wallis, J. & R. Aull, and Arthur, Turnham & Stephens.

The Big Shoal meeting-house was built in 1835, and is mentioned in the county records of 1836.

The first public bridge, that is, built by authority of the county, was erected across Fishing river, at the crossing of the State road, in the spring of 1836. Reuben Long, Solomon Fry and Littleberry Sublette were the commissioners. Soon after, another bridge was built by the county across a small branch near Uriel Cave's, on the Big Lick road; but as it cost but $37 it could not have been a very elaborate or important structure. To be sure, there were other bridges prior to these, but they were built by private subscriptions.

As the county was now pretty well settled, and roads were nearly as numerous as now, it became necessary to systematize the matter of establishing new roads and keeping them in repair. In February, 1836, the county court divided the county into 42 road districts, and appointed overseers.

The nearness of Fort Leavenworth to the county and the desire for military life, induced some of our young men to visit the barracks and enlist in the regular army. They imagined, from what they could see from the service, that the life of a soldier was one of smart uniforms, dress parades, and an easy time generally, with $8 a month and "board, clothes, and doctor's bills." Some of them who enlisted soon grew disgusted and desperate at the drudging, menial life they were compelled to lead, and deserted. Others sought to back gracefully out. In March, 1836, our *county court* took upon itself the responsibility of ordering one Charles D. Stout discharged forthwith from the U. S. service! Whether or not the military authorities obeyed the order can not here be stated.

Daniel Ferrill volunteered in Capt. Sconce's Ray county company, in 1837, and served in the Florida War. It is believed that two or three more Clay county men enlisted with Ferrill.

The population of the county in 1830 was 5,338; in 1836, it was 8,533.

119

The following were the post-offices and their respective postmasters in the county in 1836: Liberty, John Hendly; Barry, P. Flemming; Elm Grove, James Duncan; Platte, W. Turner.

The vote for President in this county in 1832 can not here be given, but in 1836 it stood: For Van Buren, Democrat, 347; for Harrison and Hugh M. White, Whigs, 282.

"An old resident" writing in the *Tribune*, in 1859, thus mentions the first Sunday-school in the county: —

In contrast with the present public opinion of the county, I will relate the history of the first Sunday-school established in Liberty. At the request of an aged minister of the gospel, I had purchased some Sunday-school books in Philadelphia, and when they arrived a school was opened in the court-house, and I consented to be one of the teachers. The news spread over the county that such an institution was established, and that I had taken part in it. Several of my friends advised me to quit — that it was calculated to "unite church and State," and that I would lose my custom if I persisted. I did quit, and the school soon broke up, the old minister not being able to procure help to carry it on.

Intercourse with Fort Leavenworth was frequent and quite intimate. Many parties, balls, and merry-makings in Liberty were participated in by Gen. Bennett Riley, Lieutenants Nate, Cady, Cooke, Walters, Wickliffe, and others. Liberty was noted for its dancing parties, which were frequently attended by excursionists from Lexington, Richmond, Independence and Leavenworth.

In 1834, Gen. A. S. Hughes brought to Liberty the old Indian chief, White Cloud, and his daughter, Sally. They attended a party at Leonard Searcy's tavern, and the next morning Miss Sally purchased a new leghorn bonnet, trimmed with flaming red ribbon. Her father bought for himself a fur hat, with the crown 15 inches high, but with a narrow brim. The father and his daughter paraded the streets in their new clothes, proud of their new acquisitions, and the observed of all observers.

EARLY DAYS IN CLAY COUNTY.

A writer in the Liberty *Tribune* of December 19, 1846, under the head of "Clay County 17 Years Ago," thus narrates certain incidents in the early history of this county. Who this writer was can not here be stated, as he signed himself "Old Settler," and his name can not now be identified: —

In the month of December, 1829, I saw for the first time the county of Clay and the town of Liberty. I remember it well. I entered the county by the way of Meek's (then Jack's) ferry, and I had not ridden more than a mile or two before I saw an opossum, and I got off my horse and killed it.

What changes have taken place since that day! The whole Platte country was then inhabited by the Iowa, Sac and Fox Indians; there were only one or two families in what are now Clinton, DeKalb, Gentry, Caldwell, Daviess and Harrison counties. Clay county was the *ultima thule* of Western emigration, and Liberty was regarded as the very paradise of Western towns. Compared to the neighboring towns it was so, for Richmond, Lexington and Independence scarcely deserved the name of towns, and Plattsburg was not then in existence.

In these days Liberty was a thriving town. It was the headquarters of the Upper Missouri, and Liberty Landing was the head of navigation, except that occasionally steamboats would go up to Fort Leavenworth. There was no warehouse then at our landing. The arrival of a boat was announced by the firing of a cannon four or five miles below, and by the time it reached Col. Allen's all the merchants would be there, as well as half the town and neighborhood. Freight was high but money was plenty, and everybody thought that there was no such a place as Clay county. The thought of ever being in want of a market for the surplus productions of the county never once entered into any of our minds.

The change is wonderful in this and the surrounding country since 1829. The Indians have left the Platte country, and now there are at least three counties in it that contain as heavy a population as Clay, viz.: Buchanan, Platte and Andrew.

In 1830 an election for Senator, Representative and sheriff took place. I attended a muster at Judge Elisha Cameron's and heard the candidates speak. Jacksonism at that time was in its zenith, and rode over everything else. A candidate had but little else to say besides declaring himself "a Jackson man." That was enough to defeat the best men who were opposed to Jackson. I recollect the speech of the famous "Neal" G—— [Cornelius Gilliam] at the muster above spoken of. He was a candidate for sheriff and of course was elected. He mounted a big elm log and said:—

"*Fellow-citizens*—I am a Jackson man up to the hub. I have killed more wolves and broke down more nettles than any man in Clay county. I am a candidate for sheriff, and I want your votes."

He then dismounted, and a "Hurrah for Neil" was given by the crowd. In 1832 the Jackson spell was somewhat broken, as the Clay men succeeded in electing the lamented Woodson J. Moss to the Legislature, along with Col. Thornton. The Whigs have been in the ascendancy ever since.

THE DEEP SNOW OF 1830–31.

October 29, 1830, the memorable "deep snow" commenced falling, covering the ground to a depth of 20 inches on the level, and drifting in many places twelve feet deep. A week or so afterwards another snow fell of about the same depth, and actually covering the ground, without drifting, to a depth of two feet in most places. January 3, 1831, another snow fell, which added to that already on the ground made a depth of nearly three feet. The situation may be imagined. Travel was almost impossible. The few roads were blocked, and no one pretended to go abroad except on horseback. In a short time there came a thaw, then a freeze, the latter forming a crust through which the deer would break, while wolves and dogs passed over in safety. Large numbers of deer and turkey perished, and could be caught with but little difficulty. The snow lasted till the first of March following, when it went off with a warm rain, and there were great floods resultant.

The season of 1831 was unfavorable for the settlers of this county. Corn was the chief staple then raised — the principal dependence of the people — and the corn crop of that year was a failure. Much of it was planted late, and the season turned out backward and cool and the summer was full of east winds. At last, in August there came a frost, " a killing frost," and nipped the corn so severely that it did not ripen. The grains were so imperfectly developed that but few of them would germinate and the next spring seed corn was very scare and very dear. Certain vegetables were also injured by the frost, and to many the situation was actually distressing.

BUILDING THE FIRST COURT-HOUSE.

Up to 1828 there was no attempt made to build a court-house for the county. There was no money in the treasury to build a suitable one, nor could a sufficient amount be raised by taxation, within a reasonable time, on the property then in the county. In May, 1826, Enos Vaughan was allowed $4.50 " as commissioner of the court-house and jail," but it does not appear what services he performed.

Temporary houses in which the courts were held were rented of John Owens and John Thornton up to 1828, and afterwards of Stephen A. St. Cyr, J. T. V. Thompson and others. In May, 1838, Wm. L. Smith, who as county commissioner had superseded Wm. Powe, Henry Estes and Wyatt Adkins, was authorized to contract for 100,000 bricks, and also for digging the foundation in the center of the public square, " 44 feet 4 inches square from out to out."

A large portion of the expense of building the house was borne by the citizens. In May, 1829, when Commissioner Wm. L. Smith resigned, he had expended $672.11, of which sum $415.11 had been

HISTORY OF CLAY COUNTY

subscribed by the people. Joel Turnham succeeded Smith, and let the contract for laying the brick and for the greater portion of the wood work. The architect of the building was Judge George Burnet.

The work dragged along until in May, 1831, when Richard C. Stephens was appointed commissioner, and it was under his supervision that the work was finally completed. Although some of the lower rooms were occupied in 1831, it was not until the spring of 1833 that the entire building, plastering, furnishing, etc., was finished. Joseph Bright did the carpenter work for $694.50; the lathing and plastering were done by John Dyke, Hezekiah Riley and Robert Burden. The tables were made by George C. Hall.

The court-house was of brick, two stories high. The first story was 14 feet and the second nine feet " in the clear." It was well lighted and had four doors or entrances on the ground floor, one at each cardinal compass point. As it was erected before the days of heating stoves the rooms were warmed by fire places, at least for many years. In 1836 lightning rods were placed upon it. This building was burned down in 1857, standing about 25 years, and was replaced by the present handsome, commodious and valuable structure.

In May, 1836, the public square was enclosed by post and square-rail fence, the rails being set in the posts " diamond position." There were four gates in the center of the four sides opposite each door of the court-house, and two stone steps led up to each gate.

THE FIRST JAIL.

For about ten years after its organization Clay county had no jail, or gaol, as it was commonly called. Prisoners were sent to the Lillard or Jackson county jail for safe keeping. In April, 1833,[1] our county court let a contract to Solomon Fry for the building of the substantial stone structure still standing in Liberty. Elisha Camron was commissioner. The building was completed and ordered paid for the following December, and it is said that it cost less than $600.

DURING THE BLACK HAWK WAR.

Details of the Black Hawk War, which broke out in Wisconsin in the spring of 1832, between the whites and the Sacs, Foxes and Winnebago Indians, belong to other histories. It is only with the part

---

[1] By a misprint the sketch in the County Atlas says 1828.

of that war with which Clay county was concerned that these pages have to deal.

The news that the war had broken out reached here in due season. Various circumstances contributed to form a belief on the part of many prominent men well versed in the characteristics of the savages that a general Indian uprising from the Lakes to Mexico was imminent. In this part of Missouri many of the people were acquainted with the Sacs and Foxes and knew that they were formidable enemies if they once went on the war path. Knowledge of the events taking place in Wisconsin and Illinois coming to the people of this county, there was considerable alarm and apprehension. Some of the more adventurous of the early settlers who had pushed out on the frontiers into where is now Clinton county, retired in good order to this county, fearing that the Indians would swoop down upon them from Iowa unawares and leave none to tell the tale.

Fearing for the northern frontier and the settlements in this and other portions of the State, Gov. John Miller early adopted precautionary measures. About the 10th of May, 1832, he ordered the generals commanding the Missouri militia to warn the members of their commands "to keep in readiness a horse, with the necessary equipments, a rifle in good order, with an ample supply of ammunition," etc. On the 25th of May, 1832, he ordered Maj.-Gen. Richard Gentry, of Columbia, to raise, without delay, one thousand volunteers for the defense of the frontiers of the State, to be in readiness to start at a moment's warning. Accordingly, on the 29th of May, 1832, orders were issued by Gen. Gentry to Brig.-Gens. Benjamin Means, commanding the seventh, Jonathan Riggs, eighth, and Jesse T. Wood, ninth brigade, third division, to raise the required quota, the first named 400, and each of the last 300 men.

Two companies of militia belonging to Gentry's division — a company from Pike county, commanded by Capt. Mudd, and a company from Ralls county, under Capt. Richard Matson, were sent to the northeastern border of the State about the 1st of July.

Accordingly, Capt. Matson's company set out for the northern part of the State, and after some days of scouting and marching reached a point eight miles from the Chariton river, in what is now Schuyler county, and began the erection of a fort, which, in honor of the captain of their company, the Ralls county men named Fort Matson. This fort commanded what was then known as the Chariton river trail, which led from Iowa down to the settlements near Kirksville. Three years before — that is to say, in 1829 — a party of Iowa Indians had

HISTORY OF CLAY COUNTY

made a raid on these settlements and killed a number of men and two women. It was believed that should the Indians come into the State one line of invasion would be over the Chariton trail, and in that event Fort Matson was designed as the first formidable obstacle they would encounter.

The Pike county company marched to the extreme northeastern part of the State, and built a fort ten miles from the mouth of the Des Moines river, within the present limits of Clark county; this fort, in honor of their county, Capt. Mudd's men called Fort Pike. The two companies were kept pretty busy for some weeks scouting, picketing and fort building, but not fighting, for they saw no hostile Indians.

These companies were afterward relieved by Capt. Jamison's and Hickman's companies of Callaway and Boone respectively, as narrated on page 53 of this volume, which see for a summary of the events that took place in the northeastern portion of the State.[1]

Coming now to the part taken in the Black Hawk War by Clay county, it may be stated that two companies, commanded by Capts. Geo. Wallis and Smith Crawford, took the field in August. Crawford's company was from the northern and northeastern portions of the county; Wallis' was from Liberty and the adjacent neighborhoods. Each company numbered about 60 men, who were all mounted, and every man furnished his own horse, arms, ammunition, and rations.

The battalion was under command of Col. Shubael Allen, who marched it northeast into the Grand river country, scouting that region thoroughly. From Grand river the battalion went westward to the boundary line, down which they marched to near Smithville, and came back by way of that village to Liberty, which they reached after an absence of 32 days. Not a hostile Indian, or, indeed, no Indians of any sort, were encountered on the entire march, which was void of interesting adventure or incident worth mention.

Mr. Anthony Harsell is now the only survivor of the Black Hawk War expedition from Clay county, known to the compiler, and from him much of the information contained in this article has been obtained.

ORIGIN OF THE PLATTE PURCHASE.

The accomplishment, in 1836, of what is known as the "Platte Purchase," deserves especial mention in a history of Clay county, because

---

[1] NOTE.—By an omission, too late to be corrected, no mention is made on pages 53-54 of the only real important services performed by Missouri militia during the Black Hawk War—those performed by Capts. Matson's and Mudd's companies—and so they are inserted in the history of Clay county.

HISTORY OF CLAY COUNTY

it was in this county that the idea of the acquisition of that purchase originated, and where the plans for the same were fully matured. Moreover it was Clay county men who carried out these plans.

As Col. Switzler, in his History of Missouri says, many intelligent citizens of Missouri have often propounded the inquiry, without having it answered, — When, where, and by whom was the suggestion first made that Missouri, a State already among the largest in territorial area in the Union, should extend her boundary so as to embrace what is now known as the " Platte Purchase?" The idea originated in the summer of 1835, at a regimental militia muster at Weekley Dale's farm, three miles north of the town of Liberty, in Clay county.

After the morning parade and during recess for dinner, the citizens present were organized into a mass meeting, which was addressed, among others, by Gen. Andrew S. Hughes, who came to Clay from Montgomery county, Kentucky, in 1828, and who soon afterwards was appointed Indian agent by President John Quincy Adams. Gen. Hughes was a lawyer by profession, a gentleman of acknowledged ability, and in wit and sarcasm almost the equal of John Randolph.[1] At this meeting, and in this public address, he proposed the acquisition of the Platte country; and the measure met with such emphatic approval that the meeting proceeded at once, by the appointment of a committee, to organize an effort to accomplish it. The committee was composed of the following distinguished citizens: William T. Wood, afterwards judge of the Lexington circuit; David R. Atchison, ex-United States Senator; A. W. Doniphan, too well known to be mentioned more fully; Peter H. Burnett, afterwards Governor, and one of the supreme judges of California, and Edward M. Samuel, afterwards president of the Commercial Bank in St. Louis, and who died there in September, 1869, — all of them, at the time of the appointment of this committee, residents of Clay county.

An able memorial to Congress was subsequently drafted by Judge Wood, embracing the facts and considerations in behalf of the measure, which all the committee signed, and it was forwarded to our Senators and Representatives at Washington.

Pursuant to the prayer of this memorial, in 1836, a bill was introduced into Congress by Senator Benton, and ardently supported by his colleague, Senator Linn, namely, an act to extend the then existing boundary of the State so as to include the triangle between the ex-

---

[1] General Andrew S. Hughes died while attending court at Plattsburg, Missouri, December 14, 1843, aged 54 years.

HISTORY OF CLAY COUNTY

isting line and the Missouri river, then a part of the Indian Territory, now comprising the counties of Atchison, Andrew, Buchanan, Holt, Nodaway and Platte, and known as the "Platte Purchase." The difficulties encountered were threefold: 1. To make still larger a State which was already one of the largest in the Union. 2. To make a treaty with the Sac and Fox tribes of Indians whereby they were to be removed from lands which had but recently been assigned to them in perpetuity. 3. To alter the Missouri Compromise line in relation to slave territory and thereby convert free into slave soil. Notwithstanding these difficulties, the two first mentioned serious, and the last formidable, the act was passed and the treaties negotiated, and in 1837, the Indians removed west of the Missouri river, thus adding to our State a large body of the richest land in the world.

THE "HETHERLY WAR."

In the summer of 1836 occurred in Northern Missouri certain incidents known in the aggregate as the "Hetherly War." With these incidents it is proper to deal in this volume, since two companies of volunteers from Clay county took part in the war, and at the time the entire population was greatly excited and at times apprehensive.

From the official records of Carroll county, from the statements of living witnesses, and from other sources of information, it is learned that in the spring of this year a band of desperadoes, robbers and thieves lived in that part of Carroll county known as the Upper Grand river country, and now included in Mercer and Grundy counties. This band had for its principal members a family named Hetherly, from Kentucky, composed of the following persons: Geo. Hetherly, Sr., the father; Jenny Hetherly, the mother; John Hetherly, Alfred Hetherly, George Hetherly, Jr., and James Hetherly, the sons, and Ann Hetherly, the daughter.

The Hetherlys lived far out on the frontier, and their cabin was a rendezvous for hard characters of all sorts. The antecedents of the family were bad. Old George Hetherly was regarded as a thief in Kentucky, and Mrs. Hetherly was a sister to the notorious Kentucky murderers and freebooters, Big and Little Harpe. The women of the family were prostitutes, and the men were believed to be villians of the hardest sort. One of Mrs. Hetherly's children was a mulatto, whose father was a coal black negro, that accompanied the family from Kentucky to Missouri. Bad as they were, however, the Hetherlys were perhaps not as black as they were painted, and many crimes were attributed to them of which, in all probability, they were innocent.

127

HISTORY OF CLAY COUNTY

Living with the Hetherlys as boarders, visitors or employes, were three or four young men whose reputations were none of the best, and who had doubtless drifted westward from the older States as they fled from the officers of the law from crimes committed.

Old Mrs. Hetherly is said to have been the leading spirit of the gang, prompting and planning many a dark deed, and often assisting in its execution. Tales were told of the sudden and utter disappearance of many a land hunter and explorer, who visited the Upper Grand river country and was last seen in the neighborhood of the Hetherly house. These stories may or may not have been true, but all the same they were told, and gradually gained credence.

Early in the month of June, 1836, a hunting party of the Iowa Indians from southern Iowa came down on the east fork of Grand river on a hunting expedition. As soon as the Hetherlys heard of the proximity of the Indians they resolved to visit their camp, steal what horses they could, and carry them down to the river counties and sell them. Taking with them James Dunbar, Alfred Hawkins, and a man named Taylor, the four Hetherlys visited the scene of the Iowas' hunting operations and began to steal the ponies and horses which had been turned out to graze. Fortune favored them and they managed to secure quite a lot of ponies, and escaped with them to the forks of Grand river. Here they were overtaken by a pursuing party of the Iowas, who demanded a return of their property. The demand not being either refused or instantly complied with, the Indians opened fire on the thieves. The first volley killed Thomas. Other shots being fired, the Hetherly gang retreated, leaving the ponies in the hands of their rightful owners.

Upon the defeat of their scheme the Hetherlys returned home, and began consulting among themselves as to the best course to pursue under the circumstances. Being much alarmed lest the Indians should give information of the affair to the whites and have the true story believed, it was resolved to anticipate a visit to the whites on the river, and go first themselves and tell a tale of their own. Dunbar had for some time shown symptoms of treachery to the party, or rather of a desire to break away from his evil associations. Soon after he was murdered and his body found.

In a day or two the Hetherlys made their appearance in the settlements raising an alarm that the Indians were in the country murdering and robbing, and claimed that they had killed Dunbar and other white men in the Upper Grand river country. The news was at first believed, and there was great excitement throughout the country. A

HISTORY OF CLAY COUNTY

part of the story — that the Indians were in the country — was known to be true, and the rest was readily believed. Carriers were sent to Ray, Clay and Clinton, and the people were thoroughly aroused.

Gen. B. M. Thompson, of Ray, commanding the militia forces in the district, ordered out several companies, and at the head of a regiment from Ray,[1] and Carroll moved rapidly to the scene of the reported troubles. The whole country north of Carroll county was thoroughly scoured. An advance scouting party penetrated the section of country where the Indians were, visited their camp and found them quiet and perfectly peaceable, and wondering at the cause of the visit of so many white men in arms.

Two companies from Clay were ordered out by Gen. Thompson. These were commanded by Capts. Wallis and Crawford, the same who had led the Clay militia in the Black Hawk War. Campbell's Gazetteer states that one of these companies was the " Liberty Blues," commanded by David R. Atchison, but W. A. Breckenridge, who belonged to Wallis' company, assures the writer that the " Blues " were not out.[2] The battalion, numbering about 150 men, was again commanded by Col. Shubael Allen. There accompanied the militia some volunteers, among whom were A. W. Doniphan and O. P. Moss.

Obedient to orders Col. Allen marched his battalion almost due north, nearly along the then western boundary of the State to a point in what is now DeKalb county, and then turned east to the reported scene of the troubles. This was done to discover whether or not there was a movement of the savages from that quarter or to flank the supposed hostile band reported to be advancing down Grand river.

The first night on the march after leaving the county, Col. Allen's battalion encamped at Joel Burnam's, in the southwest corner of Clinton county, near where Union Mills or Edgerton now stands. Here 30 or 40 Indians, Sacs and Iowas, were encountered on a hunting expedition, all friendly. Col. Allen held a council with them — it is not clear why. During the deliberations he stated to the savages that they would do well not to go on the war-path against the whites, whose soldiers, he assured them, " outnumbered the blades of grass on all these prairies ! "

Arriving at Grand river the battalion crossed and encamped one Sunday on its banks. No trouble of any sort was encountered.

---

[1] The two companies from Ray were commanded by Capts. Matthew P. Long and Wm. Pollard.

[2] Gen. Atchison himself, in a letter to the writer, corroborates this statement.

After thorough examination and investigation of the situation and the circumstances, Gen. Thompson became perfectly satisfied that the Indians were not and had not been hostile — were innocent of the offenses alleged against them, but, on the contrary, had been preyed upon by the Hetherly gang in the manner heretofore described. After consultation the officers returned the men to their homes and disbanded them, and the great scare was over. The Clay county men marched to Liberty, *via* where Haynesville and Kearney now are.

The depredations and crimes alleged against the Indians were now traced directly to the Hetherlys. A warrant for their arrest was issued, and July 17, Sheriff Lewis N. Rees, of Carroll county (yet living), with a strong posse, apprehended them, and their preliminary examination came off before 'Squire Jesse Newlin, who then lived at Knavetown, now Spring Hill, Livingston county. The examination attracted great attention and lasted several days. The result was that the accused were found to be the murderers, either as principals or accessories, of James Dunbar.

There was strong talk of lynching them, but on the 27th of July they were given into the custody of the sheriff of Ray county for safe keeping, until the October term of the circuit court. Old man Hetherly, his wife, and their daughter, Ann, were released on bail.

October 27, 1836, in obedience to a writ of *habeas corpus*, issued by Judge John F. Ryland, in vacation, the sheriff of Ray county brought into the circuit court, at Carrollton, the old man, George Hetherly, his wife, Jenny Hetherly, their sons, George, Jr., John, Alfred and James Hetherly, and Alfred Hawkins, all charged with the murder of James Dunbar. The accused were returned to the custody of the sheriff.

The grand jury found bills of indictment against the Hetherlys, and a separate indictment against Alfred Hawkins. Austin A. King took his seat on the bench, as judge of the circuit, in the room of Judge Ryland, at this term. Thos. C. Birch was circuit attorney, but having been of counsel for the accused in the preliminary examination, was discharged from the duties imposed upon him by the law in this case, and Amos Rees was appointed by the court special prosecutor.

On Tuesday, March 7, 1837, John Hetherly was acquitted. There being no sufficient jail in Carroll county, the Hetherlys were sent to the Lafayette county jail, and Hawkins to the jail of Chariton county, for safe keeping. Bills to the amount of $530 were allowed certain partiesfor guarding the prisoners.

HISTORY OF CLAY COUNTY

It being apparent to the prosecutor that no conviction could be had of the Hetherlys, nor of Hawkins, unless some of his fellow-criminals would testify against him, at the July term, 1837, before Judge King, a *nolle pros.* was entered against the Hetherlys, and they were discharged. Whereupon Hawkins was placed on trial, and the Hetherlys testified against him. He was ably and vigorously defended by his counsel, who induced some of the jury to believe that the Hetherlys themselves were the guilty parties, and the result was, that the jury disagreed, and were discharged.

At the November term 1837, Hawkins was again tried, at Carrollton, and this time convicted of murder in the first degree, and sentenced to death. The sentence was afterwards commuted to twenty years in the penitentiary, whither he was taken, but, after serving about two years of his time, he died, and thus terminated "the Hetherly War." What eventually became of the Hetherly family is not known.

CLAY COUNTY IN 1836.

The following description of Clay county in 1836 is from Wetmore's Gazetteer of Missouri, published in 1837 : —

This county, on the left bank of the Missouri river, is bounded on the south by it and west by the old State line, which is now changed by the addition of the territory recently acquired by Missouri. When the State was admitted into the Union, there was not a house in Clay county.[1] It is now one of the best settled tracts of country in Missouri or elsewhere. The high cultivation of the numerous and large farms, the substantial buildings, and the tasteful arrangements about the domiciles of the old settlers, would lead the visitor to suppose, if he were governed by appearance, that he was in the heart of the best settlements of one of the older States.

The pioneers who explored this region of country found the land so rich and the face of the country so attractive, that swarms of good citizens of Kentucky and elsewhere poured in, and the county was speedily settled and densely populated. Great wealth was carried to the country, and more has been acquired by the enterprise and industry of the inhabitants. They have not failed to avail themselves of the advantages presented in the frontier market, which they enjoy in common with their neighbors of Jackson county. This market the settlers of Clay at first enjoyed exclusively, having been cultivators before any settlements were made in Jackson.

The people of Clay have not complained of having too much prairie; and it is probable a larger proportion would have been ad-

---

[1] This is an error so palpable that it is a matter of wonderment how Wetmore made it. In 1821 there were a number of houses in this county. — *Compiler.*

vantageous. They have, however, the fashion of making prairie, where there is any deficiency, with the Knous[1] or Collins axes. The timber of Clay is good, and the county abundantly supplied with a variety of oak, black walnut and black ash. The bee hunters (a people rather less industrious than the insects which they destroy) have made sad havoc with the timber of Missouri. [?] They go ahead of the settler, and find honey in the tops of the tallest trees in the forests. These are necessarily felled to obtain the honey; and thus some of the best timber on the public lands is destroyed. Where the bee hunter is followed up by the tanner, much additional waste is committed on the public domain. But, after all these depredations, enough generally remains for all the purposes of the farmer; and heavy log-rollings are common occurrences. Fields of corn filled with bare and leafless trees are found in various parts of the county, and are among the surplus possessions of the farmers of Clay, as well as their countrymen of other counties.

The inhabitants of Clay are at present dependent upon the East fork of the Platte and Fishing river and some smaller mill-streams for their water power. But when the great mill sites on the main branch of Little Platte shall be improved, the western part of the county will be happily situated for milling facilities. These sites are in the territory recently acquired by the State. Limestone and sandstone abound in Clay, and the "lost stone" is used for milling purposes in ordinary or country work milling.

There are eleven grist mills that are run with water power in Clay, which are not sufficient for grinding bread stuffs for all the inhabitants of the county, and horse-mills are therefore still in use. There is likewise a steam mill a few miles from Liberty, on the Missouri river.

THE MORMON WAR.[2]

In 1832 the Mormons, under their Prophet, Joe Smith, came into Jackson, where the previous year large tracts of land had been entered and purchased for their benefit, and began to occupy and possess the land, with the intention, as they said, of remaining for "all time." But their years in that land were few and full of trouble. They were in constant collision with their Gentile neighbors, who frequently tied them up and whipped them with cowhides and hickory switches, derided their religion, boycotted them where they did not openly persecute them, and at last engaged in a deadly encounter with them, tarred and feathered their bishop, threw their printing press into the river, and finally drove them from their homes and out of the county.

---

[1] The Knous axes were made by Nathan Knous & Sons, of Fayette, Howard county.

[2] See pages 54–57.

Affrighted and terror-stricken, many of the Mormons took refuge in Clay. Every vacant cabin in the south half of the county was occupied by the fugitives. Many of them among the men obtained employment with the farmers; some of the women engaged as domestics, and others taught school. A few heads of families were able to and did purchase land and homes, but the majority rented. The Clay county citizens received them kindly, ministered to their wants and rendered them so many favors that to this day, away out in Salt Lake, the old Mormons hold in grateful remembrance the residents of the county of 1834–36.[1]

The Jackson county people were indignant at the reception given the Mormons by the citizens of Clay, and stigmatized some of our people as "Jack Mormons," a term yet used. On one occasion a delegation of eleven Jackson county citizens, led by Maj. Sam. Owens and James Campbell, came over to Liberty to hold a council with the Gentile citizens and Mormons of Clay in regard to the lands from which the Mormons had been driven. The title to these lands was in the hands of the Mormons, but the Gentiles wished to extinguish it by purchase, if it could be obtained at their — the Gentiles' — price. Accordingly they offered the Mormons an insignificant sum for their lands and farms, many of which were already in possession of certain citizens of Jackson, but this offer was refused. The Clay county people generally indorsed the refusal.

Returning home that night, in great ill humor with their neighbors on this side of the river, the delegation of Jackson met with a sad misfortune. As they were crossing the river at Ducker's ferry, when about the middle of the river the boat sank and five of them were

---

[1] An old citizen of Independence has recently published in the Kansas City *Journal* an interesting article on the Mormon troubles in Jackson county. One paragraph of this article is as follows: —

True history, however, must record the fact that the deluded followers of the so-called prophet, Joseph Smith, in their first effort to organize and establish a religious socialistic community in Jackson county, Mo., were unjustly and outrageously maltreated by the original settlers, that is seen in the tragic and pitiful scenes which occurred during the last part of their sojourn in this, their promised inheritance, their Zion, and New Jerusalem. With scarcely one exception, the settlers were aggressors so far as overt acts of hostility were concerned. During the last year of their stay the continued persecutions to which they were subjected excited the sympathy of many outside of the county, especially of the people of Clay county, who gave them an asylum and assistance for a year or two after their expulsion. Indeed, material aid and arms were furnished them by citizens of Clay before their expulsion; a wagon with a quantity of guns was stopped near the south part of Kansas City and seized by parties on the watch.

HISTORY OF CLAY COUNTY

drowned. Three of the unfortunate men were Ibe Job, James Campbell, and —— Everett. The casuality increased the indignation already felt against the people of Clay.

By the year 1838, all, or nearly all, of the Mormons had left Clay county and joined the Mormon settlement, at or near Far West or at other points in Caldwell and Daviess counties, and in October of that year the "Mormon War" broke out. Among the troops dispatched to Far West during that month were some companies of militia from Clay, belonging to Gen. Doniphan's brigade of Maj.-Gen. D. R. Atchison's division. Two of these companies were commanded by Capts. Prior and O. P. Moss.

Of Capt. Prior's company Peter Holtzclaw was first lieutenant. He, with 25 men from the northern part of the county, became separated from the main command and did not leave with it. The detachment marched across into Ray county and fell in with the Jackson county regiment which had refused to march through Clay, owing to the animosity existing, and had crossed the river at Lexington.

All the Clay county men were present in line confronting the breastworks when the Mormon camp at Far West was surrounded, and witnessed all the proceedings. They saw the white flag pass back and forth from the Mormons, and saw the robber, Capt. Bogard, of the Missourians, fire on it; saw the cannoneers stand with lighted matches beside their pieces, having sent word to Gen. Doniphan that they were ready to fire; saw suddenly a white flag go up; saw the Mormon battalion march out with "Gen." G. W. Hinkle, brave as a lion, at its head, and form a hollow square and ground arms, and then saw Hinkle ride up to Doniphan, unbuckle his sword and detach his pistols from their holsters and pass them over to his captor, who quietly remarked, "Give them to my adjutant." Then they saw Hinkle dash the tears from his face, and ride back to his soldiers.

The Mormons agreed fully to Doniphan's conditions — that they should deliver up their arms, surrender their prominent leaders for trial, and the remainder of them, with their families, leave the State. As hostages, Joe Smith, Sidney Rigdon, Lyman Wight, G. W. Hinkle, and other prominent Mormons, delivered themselves up to be held for the faithful performance of the hard conditions.[1]

---

[1] Col. Lewis Wood, of this county, who was present, states to the compiler that at a council of the leading militia officers held the night following the surrender, it was voted by nearly three to one to put these leaders to death, and their lives were only saved by the intervention of Gen. Doniphan, who not only urged his authority as brigadier, but declared he would defend the prisoners with his own life.

The Mormon leaders were taken before a court of inquiry at Richmond, Judge Austin A. King presiding. He remanded them to Daviess county, to await the action of the grand jury on a charge of treason against the State, and murder. The Daviess county jail being poor and insecure, the prisoners were brought to Liberty and confined in the old stone jail (still standing) for some time. Many citizens of the county remember to have seen Joe Smith when he was a prisoner in the old Liberty jail.

In due time indictments for various offenses, treason, murder, resisting legal process, etc., were found against Joe Smith and his brother, Hiram Smith, Sidney Rigdon, G. W. Hinkle, Caleb Baldwin, Parley P. Pratt, Luman Gibbs, Maurice Phelps, King Follett, Wm. Osburn, Arthur Morrison, Elias Higbee and others. Sidney Rigdon was released on a writ of *habeas corpus*. The others requested a change of venue, and Judge King sent their cases to Boone county for trial. On the way from Liberty to Columbia Joe Smith escaped; it is generally believed that the guard was bribed. Parley Pratt escaped from the Columbia jail. The others were either tried and acquitted, or the cases against them were dismissed. The entire proceedings in the cases were disgraceful in the extreme. There never was a handful of evidence that the accused were guilty of the crimes with which they were charged. Those that were tried were defended by Gen. Doniphan and James S. Rollins.

4

CHAPTER IV.

HISTORY OF THE COUNTY FROM 1840 TO 1850.

The Political Canvass of 1840 and 1844 — Elections of 1846 — The Great Flood of 1844 — Miscellaneous — Negro Killing — Tom Haggerty's Case — Clay County in the Mexican War — List of Capt. Moss's Company, and Sketch of its Services — The Political Canvass of 1848 — The Jackson Resolutions — Benton's Appeal — His Meeting at Liberty.

THE POLITICAL CANVASS OF 1840 AND 1844.

The Presidential campaign of 1840 was one of the most exciting in the history of the country. It marked the advent of the Whig party into power under Harrison and Tyler, and the Democrats, under Van Buren and Johnson, were overwhelmingly defeated. Even in Missouri, where the Whigs were in a minority, they were extremely active and held numerous monster meetings, at which their best speakers orated, and where they paraded log cabins, barrels of hard cider, live raccoons, and other emblems of their political heraldry. One meeting at Rocheport, Boone county, lasted three days. Gen. Doniphan was one of the speakers.

In Clay the Democrats were led by Gen. D. R. Atchison, Col. John Thornton and Capt. Geo. Wallis. The Whigs were marshalled by Gen. A. W. Doniphan, Maj. John Dougherty and William T. Wood. Notwithstanding that there is a recollection that in this canvass the Whigs carried the county, the records show they did not, the vote standing: Van Buren, 649; Harrison, 457; Democratic majority, 192.

But in 1844 the Whigs swept the polls by a good majority for Henry Clay and Frelinghuysen over Polk and Dallas by the following vote: Clay, 765; Polk, 552. The canvass had been full of interest, and the old Kentuckians rallied largely to the "favorite son" of their native State. The political hosts were under the same leadership as in 1840.

ELECTIONS OF 1846.

At the August election, 1846, Congressmen were first elected from Missouri by districts. Hitherto they had been chosen by a general ticket voted on by all the voters in the State. As now, Missouri was strongly Democratic, and the result had uniformly been the choosing

HISTORY OF CLAY COUNTY

of a "solid" Democratic delegation. The Whigs were growing in numbers, however, and as there was a tendency to bringing out Independent Democratic candidates, thus dividing the Democratic vote, the chances that Whigs might thereafter be chosen caused the majority in the Legislature to adopt the district plan, care being taken that each district be surely and safely Democratic.

The district in which Clay was situated (the Fourth) was composed of the counties of Adair, Linn, Grundy, Livingston, Carroll, Ray, Caldwell, Clay, Platte, Daviess, Clinton, Buchanan, Andrew, Holt, De Kalb, Harrison, Nodaway, Putnam, Gentry, Atchison, Mercer and Sullivan, all of Northwest and a portion of Northeast Missouri.

Hon. Willard P. Hall, then a private in Capt. Moss' Clay county company, of Doniphan's regiment, and in service, was the regular Democratic nominee (nominated at Gallatin), and opposed to him was Hon. James H. Birch, of Platte, who announced himself as an Independent Democratic candidate. The Whigs, largely in the minority, brought out no candidate, and a strong effort was made to practically unite them in the support of Birch. The latter stumped the district, denouncing his opponent as having enlisted not wholly out of patriotic impulses, but as a stroke of demagoguery, to excite sympathy and win admiration.

But Hall, who was already a noted lawyer and politician, marched along with his company toward Santa Fe, and wrote his reply to Birch and sent it back to his district, where it was printed and circulated and proved a most effective campaign document. When the election came off Hall was elected by nearly 3,000 majority.[1] Many Whigs voted for him. He and Birch had, however, in the early spring canvassed a portion of the district together, to secure the Democratic nomination.

The vote at the election in this county stood: —

Constitution of 1845 — For, 809; against, 211. Congress — Hall, regular Democrat, 564; Birch, Independent, 463. Legislature — Coleman Younger, Whig, 498; Henry Owens, Democrat, 575. Two members were chosen, and there was no opposition to Younger and Owens. Sheriff — Samuel Hadley, Democrat, 683; H. M. Riley, Whig, 468.

In the summer Hon. Sterling Price resigned his seat in Congress to become the colonel of a Missouri regiment in the Mexican War, and

---

[1] Though Hall was duly informed of his election he did not at once return home, bu with four others of the Clay company volunteered to accompany Gen. Kearney from Santa Fe to California, and was commissioned a lieutenant in Capt. Hudson's company.

HISTORY OF CLAY COUNTY

in November a special State election was held to fill the vacancy. The candidates were Hon. Wm. M. McDaniel, of Marion county ("Billy the Buster"), and Hon. Wm. M. Kincaid, of Platte county, the former a Democrat, the latter a Whig. Hon. J. T. V. Thompson, of Clay, was an Independent candidate, but was voted for in but a few counties. McDaniel was elected by about 500 over Kincaid, although the vote was small, and some 30 counties in the State did not hold an election. In this county the vote stood: Kincaid, 421; Thompson, 184; McDaniel, 30.

THE GREAT FLOOD OF 1844.

The extraordinary high water of 1844 will long be commemorated in the history of the Missouri valley. The river was higher in that year than in any other now known, exceeding the great overflow of 1826. The "June rise" of that year was extraordinary, and it was reinforced by the unprecedented flood in the Kansas river.

Judge Ransom, of Kansas City, an old settler, says that the rise in the Kansas was caused by heavy rains along the Republican and Smoky Hill forks, and other tributaries of the river in Kansas. The depth of fall of the Kansas at Kansas City, where it empties into the Missouri, is much greater than that of the Missouri at that point. Discharging great volumes of water day and night, the Kansas cut square across the Big Muddy and broke in huge breakers on the banks on the opposite side, and at last over into the Clay county bottoms, doing great damage. The weather was very peculiar; it rained a veritable "forty days and forty nights." Every evening, out of a clear sky, just as the sun went down, there arose a dark, ominous looking cloud in the northwest. Flashes of lightning and the heaviest thunder followed, and about ten o'clock the rain would begin to fall in torrents. The bridges were nearly all washed away. The next day the sun would rise clear and beautiful, and not a cloud would fleck the sky as a reminder of the disturbed elements of the night.

In Clay county the days on which the flood was the highest were June 14, 15 and 16. The river was over its banks everywhere, and all the low bottom lands were submerged everywhere.

The crops of that season were well advanced, and promised a glorious harvest; vast fields of wheat, oats, rye and corn were submerged, and the waters receded to leave them a desolate waste. Great suffering necessarily followed. The corn in the bottoms was especially luxuriant, and many persons were dependent upon the successful cultivation of that staple for a living. When it was destroyed their only resource for the necessities of life was the charity of the people.

138

MISCELLANEOUS.

In the summer of 1846 the prices of produce were as follows: Hemp, $2.50 per cwt.; wheat, 45 and 50 cents per bushel; flour, $2 and $2.50 per barrel; hams, 4 cents per pound; "hog round," $3\frac{1}{2}$ cents. Shipping rates to St. Louis from Liberty Landing were, for hemp, $6 and $7 per ton; wheat and corn, $16\frac{2}{3}$ cents per bushel; bacon, $2 per hhd.

About April 1 the steamer Wakendah struck a rock at the mouth of Fishing river and sank to the bottom. The boat and cargo were a total loss. A few days later the Tobacco Plant was snagged near Richfield and sank, but was soon after raised, brought down to Liberty Landing and repaired.

On May 6, 1846, a hurricane passed over the central part of the county, from southwest to northeast. Three miles south of Liberty it blew down a double log house belonging to a Mr. Simms and prostrated trees, fences, etc.

December 26, 1846, the first railroad meeting in aid of the Hannibal & St. Joseph railroad was held at Liberty. E. M. Samuel was chairman. A general meeting was called to meet at Fayette, March 8, 1847, "to consider the propriety of building a railroad from Hannibal to some point on the Missouri river," and the following named delegates were appointed from Clay county: Thomas W. DeCourcey, A. H. F. Payne, Walter S. Watkins, E. M. Samuel, Graham L. Hughes and Col. Henry L. Routt.

In the winter of 1847, when the old Masonic College was to be removed from Marion county, a strong effort was made to have it located at Liberty. The people worked hard for it. Even the ladies turned out, held meetings, made speeches themselves, and subscribed handsomely. The college was located at Lexington, however.

In the winter and early spring of 1848 a temperance wave struck Liberty and rolled from thence over the entire county, bearing along many, but unfortunately not washing away all the whisky. A lodge of the Sons of Temperance was organized at Liberty March 13, with Col. H. L. Routt as H. P.; Benj. Hayes, W. A.; H. M. Jones, R. S.; J. W. Ringo, F. S., and Isaac Palmer, treasurer. The lodge numbered 65 members, some of whom were among the most prominent citizens of Liberty. A large temperance celebration was held under the direction of the lodge in May.

HISTORY OF CLAY COUNTY

It was some time in the first few years of the decade beginning with 1840 that the murder of Chavez, a wealthy Spanish-Mexican, occurred. Chavez was a merchant and trader of Santa Fe, who had a branch house at Independence. At the time of his murder he was on his way from New Mexico to Missouri, and had several thousand dollars in his possession, chiefly in Spanish doubloons.

A party in Liberty was organized to go out on the Santa Fe trail, along which Chavez was known to be coming, and intercept him and his party and murder and rob them. This was done at a point near the crossing of the Arkansas river. Chavez was murdered and his money, or a large portion of it, was found secreted in one of the axles of a wagon.

Developments led to the arrest of several parties in Liberty and their trial in the United States court at St. Louis. John McDaniel, a young clerk of Liberty, was convicted and hung. Further particulars are not well enough remembered to be stated with exactness.

NEGRO KILLING.

In August, 1848, two negro slaves had an affray at Liberty Landing, which resulted in the death of one of them. The particulars are thus briefly given in the current number of the *Tribune:* —

On Saturday evening last a dispute arose between two negro men, at Liberty, the property of Robert Thompson and John D. Ewing, which resulted in the death of the negro belonging to Mr. T. On Monday morning the negro man of Mr. Ewing was tried before Justice Tillery and committed for further trial.

How the case was disposed of is thus stated in the same paper in October: —

The black man of Mr. J. D. Ewing, of this county, charged with murder of Mr. Robert Thompson's black man, had his trial on Monday last and was sentenced to receive 39 lashes and transported out of the State.

HAGGERTY'S CASE.

In the summer of 1848 one Thomas Haggerty was arrested and imprisoned in the Liberty jail on a charge of horse-stealing. He sent for Col. Alex. W. Doniphan to defend him. It is related that Col. Doniphan said to the prisoner: "It is very hard to clear a horse thief. It is far easier to acquit him of murder. There is more of bias and prejudice against men who steal horses than against men who take human life."

140

HISTORY OF CLAY COUNTY

Though this was not meant for a hint that he should commit murder, Haggerty acted upon it as such, and the same night fell upon another inmate of the jail, a negro, and wantonly murdered him, outright, in cold blood, and without any sort of provocation whatever. The negro was named "Tom" Lincoln, and was temporarily placed in the jail for safe keeping, preparatory to being sent South and sold to the cotton planters. Haggerty was indicted for murder, but in March, 1849, escaped from jail, went to California, and was never recaptured. He wrote one letter to Col. Doniphan, however, and detailed the manner of his escape.

CLAY COUNTY IN THE MEXICAN WAR.

The annexation of Texas was the alleged cause of the declaration of war by Mexico against the United States in April, 1846, but the more immediate cause was the occupation by the American army of the disputed territory lying between the rivers Nueces and Rio Grande. May 13, 1846, a counter-declaration by the American Congress was made, that "a state of war exist between the United States and Mexico."

President Polk called on Gov. Edwards of this State for a regiment of volunteers to join Gen. Kearney's "Army of the West." There was a hearty response from all quarters of Missouri, and, as in all other wars through which the country has passed, Clay county bore her full part.

May 30, 1846, a war meeting was held at Liberty. J. T. V. Thompson was chairman. Speeches were made, it was resolved to raise a company for the war, and a number of volunteers put down their names at once. As the company was to be mounted and a number of volunteers had no horses and were unable to buy them, a committee, composed of J. M. Hughes, M. M. Samuels, Alvin Lightburn and J. T. V. Thompson, were appointed to raise means to mount such volunteers as were unable to mount themselves.

As reported in the *Tribune* there was a generous and hearty subscription. James M. Hughes gave $100 in cash. A. Lightburn, W. H. Wymer, S. McGauhey, J. C. Christy, Garlichs & Hale each gave $20; Clark & Wilson, $25, and other parties smaller sums. Col. J. T. V. Thompson gave four horses, E. M. Samuel, two, and A. Lightburn, John R. Keller, Robt. Walker, Joseph Courtney, Garrard Long, Samuel Hadley, E. D. Murray, R. Neally and Robt. Atkins each subscribed one horse.

A company was soon raised. Volunteers poured in not only from

141

HISTORY OF CLAY COUNTY

all parts of this county, but from other counties. More men offered themselves than could be accepted. By the 6th of June the roll was full and the company left for Ft. Leavenworth, the place of rendezvous. They arrived the same evening, were mustered into service the next day, and immediately went into camp.

Upon the organization of the regiment, the following was the muster roll of the Clay county company, which became

COMPANY C, 1ST MISSOURI MOUNTED VOLUNTEERS.

O. P. Moss, Captain.
L. B. Sublette, First Lieutenant.
James H. Moss, Second Lieutenant.
Thomas Odgen, Third Lieutenant.
Thomas McCarty, First Sergeant.
James Long, Second Sergeant.

Wm. Wallis, Third Sergeant.
A. K. McClintock, Fourth Sergeant.
George H. Wallis, 1st Corporal.
Carroll Scaggs, Second Corporal.
John S. Groom, Third Corporal.
Martin Cloud, Fourth Corporal.

PRIVATES.

Abraham Estes, Bugler.
Henry B. Ammons.
John Brisco.
Wm. Beal.
Park Benthal.
Wash Bell.
James T. Barnes, Blks'ith.
James Burns.
Sherrod Burton.
James Cooper.
Smith Cumins.
Wash Crowley.
Ed. Crabster.
John G. Christy.
James Chorn.
Rufus Cox.
Allen Cox.
Wm. Campbell.
Hiram Chaney.
N. Paley Carpenter.
Hudson Clayton.
Wash W. Drew.
Harvey Darneal.
Matt. Duncan.
Wm. Duncan.
Theo. Duncan.
Riley Everett.
Henry Ellis.
Harvy W. English.
Spencer Faubion.
Matt. Franklin.
Riley Franklin.
John M. Findley.
Thos. Fielding.

Robert Fleming,
Geo. Fleming.
Wm. C. Gunter.
Hiram Green.
Carroll Hughes.
John T. Hughes.
Willard P. Hall.
Doc. Hall.
James Hall.
John D. Holt.
Chas. Human.
Bailor Jacobs.
Newton Jacobs.
And. Job.
John Leard.
Wm. T. Leard.
James Lamar.
Matt. Letchworth.
Richardson Long (Suthey).
Dick Long.
—— McNeice.
Wesley Martin.
Eli Murray.
Dewilton Mosby.
James McGee.
John J. Moore.
Abraham Miller.
Benj. W. Marsh.
Albert McQuidely.
Richard A. Neeley.
John Nash.
John Neal.
Edward Owens.
Jesse Price.

Wm. Pence.
Josiah Pence.
Peter C. Pixlee.
Ben. Pendleton.
—— Pendegrass.
Martin Ringo.
Alonzo Rudd.
Robt. Sherer.
John Shouse.
John Story.
James Sites.
Cunningham Scott.
James Saunders.
Thos. Stephenson.
Obadiad Sullivan.
Addison Smith.
Shelton Samuels.
Jos. Sanderson.
Wm. P. Snowden.
Riley Stoutt.
Joshua Tillery.
Henry Tillery.
—— Thompson.
And. Tracy.
Thos. Waller.
Wm. Wells.
James Wills.
Hardin Warren.
John Warren.
Gideon Wood.
James York.
John York.
Jack Laidlow. (Col'd.)
Capt. Serv't.

For some time it had been understood that one of Clay county's honored and most honorable citizens, Gen. Alex. W. Doniphan, would in all probability be the colonel of the regiment making up at Leavenworth. He was pushed forward for the position by the people of Clay of all parties and shades of opinion, and nothing was left undone by

HISTORY OF CLAY COUNTY

them to attain for him this distinction. The colonel of the regiment was to be designated by election, every member having a vote. All the electioneering therefore had to be among the volunteers. One specimen of how this was done may here be given.

Capt. John W. Reid's company, of Saline county, marched through to Leavenworth, via Liberty. When they reached Liberty the citizens received them and took excellent care of them. In a journal of M. B. Edwards, a member of the company, published a year or two since,[1] and detailing the experiences of his company, appears the following : —

Sunday, June 7, Liberty, Clay county, was reached. Here the company was well entertained, given suppers, beds, and breakfast at the hotels, excellent pasture and forage for the horses, and shown every attention. But although it may be wrong to impugn the good actions of the people of Liberty, I was rather disposed to attribute their conduct more to policy than to patriotism, for Hon. A. W. Doniphan, a prominent and popular citizen of the place, has declared himself a candidate for colonel of the regiment to which we are to be attached :

The election of field officers came off at Leavenworth, July 19 ; Gen. Doniphan was elected colonel, C. F. Ruff, lieutenant-colonel, and Wm. Gilpin, major. Doniphan and Ruff were both of Clay county ; Gilpin was from Jackson. Col. Ruff resigned September 17, following his election, and was appointed captain in the regular army. He was a rigid disciplinarian, too strict for the volunteers, and on that account very unpopular with them. Col. Congreve Jackson, of Howard county, succeeded Ruff as lieutenant-colonel.

At the time of his election as commander of the First Missouri Col. Doniphan was 38 years of age. He had, however, commanded a brigade of militia during the Mormon War, and unlike many another " colonel," had before " set a squadron in the field," and knew gunpowder from black sand. He, too, was a Whig, but his Democratic soldiers voted for him, and Gov. Edwards and President Polk gladly commissioned him. It was a singular fact, moreover, that while the Whigs, as a party, opposed the Mexican War, perhaps a majority of the Americans who fought in it were Whigs. It came to be called a Democratic war, and a Whig fight. Gens. Scott and Taylor were prominent Whigs, as were other general officers. Of the 114 men which at first composed the Clay county company, 90 were Whigs and only 24 were Democrats.

---

[1] History of Saline county, p. 240.

June 23, a delegation of citizens of the county, a large number of whom were ladies, went up from Liberty, on the steamer Missouri Mail, to Forth Leavenworth and presented the Clay county company with a beautiful flag. Mrs. Hannah O. Cunningham, wife of Prof. Oliver Cunningham, made the presentation address, and Capt. O. P. Moss responded. The flag was of silk, made by the ladies themselves, and bore the motto: *" The love of country is the love of God."* As the day was rainy and the ground where the company had assembled was unfavorable, the presentation was made on the hurricane deck of the boat.

The flag was carried safely through the war, brought home, and was unfortunately consumed in the fire which destroyed the court-house, in 1857. The flag had been deposited in the building for safe keeping.

The services rendered the country by Col. Doniphan and his regiment need not here be enumerated. Other volumes have been devoted to them, and they are read and known by every school boy who studies the history of his country, The remarkable expedition to Santa Fe and thence to Chihuahua won the plaudits of the American people, the commendations of military chieftains and the admiration of mankind.[1]

After a stay of 20 days Doniphan's regiment left Fort Leavenworth Friday, June 26, 1846, for Santa Fe, New Mexico, which place it reached August 18. *En route,* two Clay county men, James Chorn and Hon. Thos. McCarty, took prisoner a son of the Mexican General Salazar, a remarkable feat under the circumstances. At Santa Fe Willard P. Hall (then member of Congress elect) volunteered in Capt. Hudson's company, and accompanied Gen. Kearney to California.

The Clay company took part in the engagements at the Bracito, December 25, 1846, and at Sacramento, February 28, 1847, and then marched on into old Mexico.

Of the engagement at Sacramento, wherein, as is reported, and has been frequently published, only *two* Americans were killed (Maj. Samuel Owens, of Independence, who was not a soldier, and A. A. Kirkpatrick, of Capt. Walton's Lafayette company), while more than *three hundred* Mexicans were slain, — of this phenomenal battle, Gen. Taylor was pleased to say in orders : —

* * * The commanding general would at the same time announce another signal success won by the gallantry of our troops on

---

[1] For further mention of Doniphan's regiment, see p. 57

the 28th of February, near the city of Chihuahua. A column of Missouri volunteers, less than a thousand strong, with a light field battery, attacked a Mexican force, many times their superior in numbers, in an entrenched position, captured its artillery and baggage, and defeated it with great loss. * * * By command of

MAJOR GENERAL TAYLOR.

The vast superiority of the Anglo-Saxon race, though only one to four, carried all before them, and the battle was decided, though not finished, in an hour after it began. The battle of Sacramento was fought on the 28th of February, 1847. After the battle Doniphan took possession of the city of Chihuahua, and capital of the State, containing a population of 25,000 souls.

On the 24th of April, 1847, after remaining in Chihuahua two months, the regiment was ordered home, which news was received joyfully, and the men began their march for Missouri on the 26th of April, 1847, moving down into Mexico, to Gen. Wool's headquarters, where they were discharged, their year of service having expired. Upon being mustered out and receiving their pay, they marched to the seaboard.

On the 5th of June, 1847, Doniphan's regiment left Mexico for the United States, arriving at New Orleans on the 15th. Before it left Mexico it received the following very complimentary mention from Brig. Gen. Wool, commanding division : —

HEADQUARTERS AT BUENA VISTA, May 22, 1847.
Special Orders No. 273.
·I. The general commanding takes great pleasure in expressing the gratification he has received this afternoon in meeting the Missouri volunteers. They are about to close their present term of military service, after having rendered, in the course of the arduous duties they have been called upon to perform, a series of highly important services, crowned by decisive and glorious victories. No troops can point to a more brilliant career than those commanded by Col. Doniphan, and none will ever hear of the battles of Bracito and Sacramento without a feeling of admiration for the men who gained them. The State of Missouri has just cause to be proud of the achievements of the men who represented her in the army against Mexico, and she will, no doubt, receive them on their return with all the joy and satisfaction to which a due appreciation of their merits and services so justly entitles them. In bidding them adieu, the general wishes to Col. Doniphan, his officers and men, a happy return to their families and homes. By command of

IRVIN McDOWELL,[1] A. A. Gen. BRIG. GEN. JOHN E. WOOL.

---

[1] General in command of the Federal army at the first battle of Bull Run, Va., July 21, 1861.

HISTORY OF CLAY COUNTY

After an interesting experience of a homeward voyage, a grand reception at St. Louis, the survivors reached their Missouri homes. The Clay county company arrived at home about the 1st of July, and on the 15th were given a grand public reception and dinner in a grove, a little southeast of Liberty. There was a large procession in charge of Col. J. T. V. Thompson as marshal. Col. H. L. Routt delivered an address of welcome to the soldiers, and this address was responded to by Col. Doniphan. Other speakers were Gen. David R. Atchison and Hon. James H. Birch. The dinner was a magnificent affair. One cake was five feet in height, and the baker was Miss Mary Dale, now Mrs. John Morris. There were present thousands of people, one of the largest concourses that ever assembled in Liberty.

Not all of the volunteers returned. John M. Finley died at El Paso, of typhoid fever, aged 21. Wm. Duncan was another that died in New Mexico, at Bent's Fort. John D. Leard was shot by Ben. W. Marsh at the Valverde crossing of the Rio del Norte. Marsh was tried by court-martial but acquitted. James Wills died en route to Chihuahua, below El Paso. Gideon Wood was slightly wounded at the battle of Bracito.

THE POLITICAL CANVASS OF 1848.

This being the year of a Presidential election, politics engrossed a considerable portion of the attention of our people, and Whigs and "Locofocos," — as the Democrats were nicknamed — were vigilant and enthusiastic in the support of their parties.

The candidates for Governor were James S. Rollins, Whig, and Austin A. King, Democrat; for Congress, Edward M. Samuel, Whig, of Clay, and Willard P. Hall, Democrat, of Buchanan. The vote at the August election in this county was as follows: —

Governor — Rollins, 745; King, 531.
Congress — Samuel, 570; Hall, 578.
Legislature — Thos. F. Swetnam, Whig, 739; H. L. Routt, Democrat, 478.
Sheriff — O. P. Moss, Whig, 654; Samuel Hadley, Democrat, 645.

Hall was re-elected to Congress by a large majority, and in the State the vote for Governor was: King, 48,921; Rollins, 33,968.

Early in the year 1847 a movement was started in the country by the Whigs to make Gen. Zachary Taylor, then commanding the armies of the United States in Mexico, a candidate for President. The movement was popular, grew in public favor month by month, and at the Whig national convention in 1848 he was nominated without opposition. The Whigs were greatly delighted. Gen. Taylor was given the

146

sobriquet of "Rough and Ready," or "Old Zach," and a campaign of fuss and fustian was inaugurated, similar to that of 1840.

The fight on the part of the Whigs, or Taylor and Fillmore men, was spirited and vigorous. They were determined not to lose the battle this year through inaction on their part. A verse of one of their campaign songs ran : —

> Jimmy Polk we thought a joke in eighteen forty-four,
> When he was made the nominee 'way down at Baltimore.
> But we'll look out what we're about before it is too late,
> And we'll have no such cruel tricks played off in 'forty-eight.

In this district Col. Doniphan was at first elected by the Whigs as their candidate for election, but he declined, and William A. Witcher, also of Clay, was selected in his stead. Several meetings were held in the county this year, and at the November election, though there was a reduced vote, the Whigs easily carried the county, the following being the vote of the townships : —

Townships.	Taylor.	Cass.
Gallatin	46	43
Liberty	418	224
Fishing River	36	65
Washington	52	46
Platte	79	40
Total	626	418

At this election Mordecai Oliver, of Ray, was elected circuit attorney over Chas. J. Hughes, of Caldwell.

On the 9th of December the Whigs had a grand celebration at Liberty over the election of Gen. Taylor. A large meeting was presided over by Madison Miller, and Col. Doniphan, Mr. Witcher and Col. Pitt made speeches.

CENSUS OF 1848.

By the census of 1848 the county's population aggregated 9,426, as follows : —

Total white population	6,882
Total slave population	2,530
Total free negroes	14
Total	9,426

The population of Liberty was 728.

THE JACKSON RESOLUTIONS.

Early in the year 1849 there began a series of discussions in the Missouri Legislature concerning the slavery question, or, rather, the power of Congress over slavery in the Territories. On the 15th of January Hon. C. F. Jackson, Senator from Howard, afterward Governor of the State, introduced into the Legislature a series of resolutions, as follows : —

Resolved by the General Assembly of the State of Missouri: That the Federal constitution was the result of a compromise between the conflicting interests of the States which formed it, and in no part of that instrument is to be found any delegation of power to Congress to legislate on the subject of slavery, excepting some special provisions, having in view the prospective abolition of the African slave trade, made for securing the recovery of fugitive slaves ; any attempt therefore on the part of Congress to legislate on the subject, so as to affect the institution of slavery in the States, in the District of Columbia, or in the Territories, is, to say the least, a violation of the principles upon which that instrument was founded.

2. That the Territories, acquired by the blood and treasure of the whole nation, ought to be governed for the common benefit of the people of all the States, and any organization of the territorial governments excluding the citizens of any part of the Union from removing to such Territories with their property, would be an exercise of power by Congress inconsistent with the spirit upon which our Federal compact was based, insulting to the sovereignty and dignity of the States thus affected, calculated to alienate one portion of the Union from the other, and tending ultimately to disunion.

3. That this General Assembly regard the conduct of the Northern States on the subject of slavery as releasing the slave-holding States from all further adherence to the basis of compromise, fixed on by the act of Congress of March 6, 1820, even if such act ever did impose any obligation upon the slave-holding States, and authorizes them to insist upon their rights under the constitution ; but for the sake of harmony and for the preservation of our Federal Union, they will still sanction the application of the principles of the Missouri Compromise to the recent territorial acquisitions, if by such concession future aggressions upon the equal rights of the States may be arrested and the spirit of anti-slavery fanaticism be extinguished.

4. The right to prohibit slavery in any Territory belongs exclusively to the people thereof, and can only be exercised by them in forming their constitution for a State government, or in their sovereign capacity as an independent State.

5. That in the event of the passage of any act of Congress conflicting with the principles herein expressed, Missouri will be found in hearty co-operation with the slave-holding States, in such measures as

may be deemed necessary for our mutual protection against the encroachments of Northern fanaticism.

6. That our Senators in Congress be instructed and our Representatives be requested to act in conformity to these resolutions.

The foregoing resolutions were known as the "Jackson Resolutions," from the name of their mover, but their real author was Hon. W. B. Napton, of Saline county, latterly a Judge of the Supreme Court, who admitted the fact to the writer. Space is given to an account of the Jackson resolutions in this volume from the fact that at the time they engaged a large share of the attention of the leading politicians and prominent men of the county. The Representative of the county voted against them, and the sentiments of but few of his constituents were in their favor. There were many who thought their passage untimely, unwise, and that they foreboded eventually a dissolution of the Union. Many yet regard them as the beginning of the Civil War.

Col. Thomas H. Benton, Missouri's distinguished Senator, was especially opposed to the resolutions. He thought (and correctly, too,) that they were aimed at him, and designed to deprive him of his seat in the United States Senate, which he had held for nearly thirty consecutive years. The last section commanded him to act in accordance with the resolutions, the spirit of which he had often vigorously opposed.

In the House, Hon. Wm. T. Swetnam, the Representative from Clay, voted against every one of the resolutions, but they were adopted by a vote of 53 to 27 in the Lower House, and 24 to 6 in the Senate. Hon. Lewis Burns, of Platte, then the Senator from this district, voted for the resolutions.

Col. Benton appealed from the action of the Legislature to the people of Missouri,[1] and canvassed the State against the Jackson resolutions.

---

[1] SENATOR BENTON'S APPEAL.

To the People of Missouri: The General Assembly of our State at its last session adopted certain resolutions on the subject of slavery, and gave me instructions to obey them. From this command I appeal to the people of Missouri — the whole body of the people; and if they confirm the instructions I shall give them an opportunity to find a Senator to carry their will into effect, as I can not do anything to dissolve this Union, or to array one-half of it against the other.

I do not admit the dissolution of the Union to be a remedy, to be prescribed by statesmen, for diseases of the body politic, any more than I admit death and suicide to be a remedy, to be prescribed by physicians for the natural body. Cure, and not kill, is the only remedy which my mind can contemplate in either case.

In the prosecution of his appeal he visited Clay county, and on Monday, July 16, addressed a meeting in a grove half a mile from Liberty, having reached the town the previous Saturday. He intended speaking in the court-house, but the anti-Benton Democrats had gotten up a counter demonstration and procured the attendance of Col. James H. Birch, who was to reply to whatever Benton might say, and the latter declared he would not countenance "Jim Birch" in any manner whatever — would not speak in the same room where he had spoken, or was to speak. Col. J. T. V. Thompson, Howard Everett, F. Givinner, and other anti-Benton men got up a meeting in the forenoon, and so Benton spoke in the afternoon at 2 o'clock.

There were present to hear Benton's speech an audience of at least 1,000 persons, many of whom, however, were Whigs. Stimulated by the opposition he had met elsewhere, and goaded by the hostility of his enemies here, Col. Benton made a caustic but powerful effort. Rising by degrees to something of majestic denunciation he character-

---

I think it probable, from what I observe, that there are many citizens — good friends to the harmony and stability of this Union — who do not see the Missouri instructions and their prototype, the Calhoun address, in the same light in which I see it, and in the light which it is seen by others who best understand it. For the information of such citizens, and to let them see the next step in this movement, and where it is intended to end, I hereby subjoin a copy of the Accomac resolutions, lately adopted by a county in Virginia, and fully indorsed by the Richmond *Enquirer* as the voice of the South. I do not produce these resolutions for the purpose of arraigning them; on the contrary, I see something in them to admire, as being bold and open, and to the true interpretation and legitimate sequence of the Calhoun movement. I consider the Calhoun address and its offspring, the Missouri instructions, as fundamentally wrong; but to those who think them right, the Accomac resolutions are also right, and should be immediately imitated by similar resolutions in Missouri. I produce them to enable the people of Missouri to see what it is to which their Legislature would commit the State, and what it is they have instructed me to do.

I appeal from these instructions to the people of Missouri — the whole body of the people — and in due time will give my reasons for so doing. It is a question above party, and goes to the whole people. In that point of view the Accomac resolutions present it, and present it truly; and I shall do the same. I shall abide the decision of the people, and nothing else. Respectfully,

St. Louis, May 9, 1849. Thomas H. Benton.

Note. — The Accomac resolutions referred to by Col. Benton were a series of resolutions adopted at a public meeting at Accomac C. H., Virginia, March 26, 1849. Their author and mover was Henry A. Wise. The resolutions hinted strongly at secession or revolution in resistance to the "encroachment by the Federal government, and by the people of the North on the institution of slavery in the States, Territories and districts of the United States." Such expressions as "the time for action has arrived," "no time should be lost in preparing for the impending crisis," were common in these resolutions. — *Compiler*.

HISTORY OF CLAY COUNTY

ized the anti-Benton men as "nullifiers" and "incipient secessionists," [1] who would, if unsubdued, yet drag Missouri into civil war.

Adverting to the principal part of his speech he maintained that the spirit of nullification and treason lurked in the Jackson resolutions, especially in the fifth; that they were a mere copy of the Calhoun resolutions, offered in the United States Senate, February 19, 1847, and denounced by him (Benton) at the time as fire-brands, and intended for disunion and electioneering purposes. He said he could see no difference between them, except as to the time contemplated for dissolving the Union, as he claimed that Mr. Calhoun's tended directly, and the Jackson resolutions ultimately, to that point. Col. Benton further argued that the Jackson resolutions were in conflict with the Missouri Compromise of 1820, and with the resolutions passed by the Missouri Legislature, February 15, 1847, wherein it was declared that "the peace, permanency and welfare of our national union depended upon a strict adherence to the letter and spirit" of that compromise, and which instructed the Missouri Senators and Representatives to vote in accordance with its provisions. In conclusion, Col. Benton warned his hearers that the Jackson resolutions were intended to mislead them into aiding the scheme of ultimately disrupting the national union, and entreated them to remain aloof from them.

After the conclusion of Benton's speech in the grove, the anti-Benton men reassembled in the court-house and Col. Birch addressed them in reply to "Old Bullion." At the close of Birch's speech, resolutions condemning Col. Benton for his refusal to obey the instructions of the Legislature, and denunciatory of his course generally, were adopted. But Col. H. L. Routt, Dr. W. A. Morton, F. C. Hughes, Wm. D. Hubble, J. M. Litchworth, J. M. Keller, and other friends of the old Senator published a card in the *Tribune*, alleging that these resolutions were adopted by a "packed" audience, late in the evening, after nearly everybody had gone home.

A few days after the Benton meeting Gen. David R. Atchison, then Col. Benton's colleague in the Senate, spoke in Liberty in opposition to Benton and Bentonism, declaring that he (Atchison) was ready at all times to either obey the instructions of the Legislature of Missouri or resign and come home and allow some one else to be sent to the Senate who would obey.

---

[1] According to the *Tribune's* report.

CHAPTER V.

FROM 1850 TO THE TROUBLES IN KANSAS.

The California Gold Fever — The Political Canvass of 1850 — The Attempted Murder of Mrs. Dinah Allen — Lynching of Her Would-be Assassins — The Cholera — Elections of 1852, 1854, 1856 and 1858 — The Know Nothings — Tragedies — The Great Smithville Melee and Mob in 1854 — Murder of Wm. O. Russell, Esq., by "Pete" Lightburne — Lynching of "Pete."

THE CALIFORNIA GOLD FEVER.

The California gold fever, which broke out early in the year 1849, greatly excited the people of the West, and Clay county was one of the first communities to take the infection. In the early spring of this year many of our people prepared to set out for the new Eldorado, of whose abundant and easily acquired riches such marvelous tales were told — where, it was said, even the wave of the river and the spray of the fountain were bright with the glitter of drops of virgin gold.

On the 1st of May three wagons and eight men set out from Clay county, undeterred by the long distance to the Pactolian land, and not afraid of the terrible contagion, the cholera, which had broken out at different points in Missouri, and raged among the gold seekers from Independence to Fort Kearney, claiming each day its victims and dotting the route with their graves. These eight Clay county Argonauts were Maj. Lane, Jasper M. Hixson, Dr. Henry B. Hixson, J. H. Hixson, Daniel Mosley, Paley Carpenter, Thos. Conington and James York.

Among the other Clay county "'49ers," who went at different periods during the spring and summer, were W. W. Estes, "Big Tom" Estes, Albert Davis, Taylor Dougherty, John Minter, John W. Collins, Wm. Pixler, John Waller, Jas. Withers, Anderson Chanslor, Wm. Davenport, Perry Keith, Henry Ammons, Edward Crabster, and two or three of the Longs.

In 1850 there was a larger emigration. The stories of bad luck that came back were unheeded; the stories of fortunate finds and lucky strikes were greedily listened to, and the desire for sudden wealth tempted many to the perilous journeys and sore hardships undergone in that period by those who crossed the plains. Of those

HISTORY OF CLAY COUNTY

who set out in the spring of 1850 was a large party among whose members was Rev. Robert James, the father then of two little prattling boys, who afterwards became the noted bandits, Frank and Jesse. En route Mr. James wrote one letter to the Liberty *Tribune*, which is still preserved in the files of that paper. Not long after his arrival in California, Rev. James died.

Mr. Jasper Hixson was a regular correspondent of the *Tribune*, and, while the burden of his letters was the advice to friends and neighbors to let well enough alone and stay at home, yet the "one chance in a thousand" was quite sufficient to induce many to try their luck. Some of these made great sacrifices in order to obtain the necessary "outfit," and afterward had good cause to regret that they did so. Others fared much worse. For after divers hardships and privations, perils among Indians and false brethren, sufferings from hunger and thirst, and from heat and cold, the exhaustion of long and arduous travel, and the ravages of diseases, many of the Clay county gold seekers died in a strange land and never saw their homes again.[1] Only comparatively a few bettered their condition. Yet the emigration continued until about 1855.

THE POLITICAL CANVASS OF 1850.

Never since the admission of Missouri into the Union has there been a more exciting political canvass than that of 1850. It was an exciting period in the history of the United States that year. The question of the admission of California into the Union with a constitution prohibiting slavery; the compromise or "omnibus bill" under discussion in the U. S. Senate; the passage of a fugitive slave bill by Congress, and of "personal liberty" bills by certain Northern States, calculated to interfere with the operation of the fugitive slave

---

[1] The following are the names of those of the Clay county emigrants who died in California during the year 1850: —

Abel King, at Weber, in January; Randolph King, at Hangtown, in February; Daniel Moseby, at Sacramento, in June; Ben. Keyser, at Hangtown, in July; Benj. Clark, at Sacramento, in August; Rev. Robert James, Thos. Pence, ——— Albright, and ——— Maxwell, at Rough and Ready, in August; John Brock, killed at Hangtown, in August; ——— McCrory, at Weber, in November; Jas. A. Walker, at Weber, in October; Jas. Ellet, at Weber, in November; Benj. Carpenter, at Hangtown, in October; Wm. Morton, at Greenwood, in November; Geo. W. Wallis and Samuel M. Grant, at Nevada, in November; John H. Moseby, near Sacramento, of cholera; John McCrory, at Weber, in August; Henry Gill, at Johnston's Ranch, in September; Anderson Estes, at Nevada, in August; Geo. Estes, at Hangtown, in August; Wm. Homer, Samuel McKneiss, Sanford Bell, Geo. W. Huffaker, Washington Huffaker, two Ellises, and three Graggs, at various times and places.

law — these and other questions caused great agitation throughout the country.

In the early part of the year 1849, South Carolina — always a State "touchy" in the extreme, proposing nothing and never satisfied with anything — wanted to secede from the Union, and invited the other Southern States to go with her. A convention of the Southern States was called to meet at Nashville, Tenn., in June, 1850, to consider the situation and to take action " to preserve the rights and protect the interests of the South "— whatever that may have meant. The passage of the "Jackson resolutions" by the Missouri Legislature, in 1849, in some sense committed the State to sympathy and co-operation with the Nashville convention, but no delegates were authoritatively sent.

The Democratic party of the State was divided into two factions — the Benton Democrats, or the " hards," who indorsed Col. Benton's course and views, and favored his re-election to the U. S. Senate for the sixth term of six years, and the anti-Benton Democrats, or " softs," who opposed him, and were bent on defeating him in his contest for re-election. The Whigs —" the wily Whigs "— constituted the third party, and, taking advantage of the bitter and uncompromising warfare between the Democratic factions, made shrewd and careful preparations to capture the senatorial, certain legislative, and other prizes for themselves — and in the end they were successful.

It is a mistake to suppose that political canvasses were conducted thirty years ago with more of courtesy, more of gentleness, more of mild words, than they are to-day. The crimination and recrimination were as common with party papers as they have ever been or are likely to be. The Benton men charged the anti-Bentons with being " disunionists," " nullifiers," " aiders and abettors of treason and traitorous schemes," and bestowed upon them a choice lot of epithets calculated to bring them into the contempt of all classes of patriotic people. They extolled their leader, Mr. Benton, " to the skies," and denounced all his opposers, from his colleague in the Senate, David R. Atchison, to the humblest voter in the ranks.

The anti-Benton men were as severe on their opponents. They denounced Col. Benton as a " boss "— at least that would have been the term employed in these days — of whose imperious, domineering conduct and bullying spirit they had become thoroughly tired, and with whose record on the subject of slavery they had become thoroughly disgusted. The Benton men were called " lick-spittles,"

"Benton's slaves," "free-soilers," and even "abolitionists," and to call a man an abolitionist at that day in Missouri was to bestow upon him the sum of opprobious epithets. The Benton men, for the most part, denied that they were disunionists under all the existing circumstances, and professed unreserved loyalty to "the government established by Washington and Jefferson."

The Whigs kept aloof from the Democratic quarrel, occasionally patting each side on the back when they could do so without being observed by the other side, and all the time remaining in an attitude as if they stood with their arms folded and saying very meekly of their own party: "Behold how great an institution is Whiggery! See those unfortunate Democrats; how angry they are! We Whigs never quarrel, for Whigism means peace on earth and good will to men."

THE UNION MEETING OF 1850.

Early in the spring the following call for a public meeting was published in the Liberty *Tribune:*—

The friends of the Union of these States, without regard to party, will hold a public meeting on the first Monday in May, 1850, to congratulate Messrs. Clay, Webster, Cass, and other friends of the Union in Congress, for the noble stand they have taken against the spirit of secession and disunion. Let there be a full turn-out.

The meeting was quite numerously attended, and both Democrats and Whigs participated in the deliberations. Addresses were made by Col. Doniphan and others. A committee on resolutions was appointed, consisting of Col. J. T. V. Thompson, Howard Everett, Dr. W. A. Morton, Winfrey E. Price, Benj. Ricketts, Wm. Thomasson, Sr., Dr. F. Garlichs and E. M. Samuel. Whigs, Bentons and anti-Bentons were represented on this committee. However widely the members of the meeting may have differed at the time on minor political questions, they were each and all unconditionally for the Union — there was but one party on that issue. The Secessionists of South Carolina and other States had no sympathizers here then; neither had the fanatical abolitionists of the North.

The committee reported the following resolutions, which were unanimously adopted by the meeting: —

WHEREAS, A crisis has arrived in the history of these United States of North America, and clouds of fearful omen are rolling along the political skies, threatening not only the peace and harmony of the people, but even the destruction of the glorious Union under which we have so long been sheltered from the storms which have wrecked other Republics;

WHEREAS, We believe that this state of things has been chiefly produced by the ultraism of party spirit, and that want of charity amongst political parties which fails to regard men to be as honest in political as they are in social, moral, pecuniary and religious duties, we are further of opinion that this unhappy state of things has been greatly accelerated by the courting propensities of both the Whig and Democratic parties towards a dirty, wicked, unprincipled party called Abolitionists, who, instead of being courted by either party, should have been, from the first, denounced as dishonest by both.

We believe that, in this country, there never will be but two honest parties, and they are the Whig and Democratic; and we regard it as the solemn duty of both to treat all who leave their connection, (in order to the formation of new parties, whether called Abolitionists, Native Americans, Anti-Masons, Free Soilers, Secessionists, Disunionists, or what not) as too contemptible to woo or win. There is no other way to break up the new parties that we can conceive of, and we are decidedly of opinion that, in order to be courted, many of the factious parties with which our country has been afflicted have been organized.

We hope the day is at hand when the Whig and Democratic parties, each for itself, will repudiate all other aid except that of reason and honesty. We are rejoiced, however, to find that now, as heretofore in our history, when we have fallen upon times that "try men's souls," we have the men, in both the Whig and Democratic parties, who can be trusted.

We, therefore, the people of Clay county, in the State of Missouri, now assembled together, as Whigs and Democrats, do

Resolve, That our thanks are especially due, and are hereby tendered to Henry Clay, of Kentucky; Daniel Webster, of Massachusetts; Lewis Cass, of Michigan; Daniel S. Dickinson, of New York, and John Bell, of Tennessee, for the noble and patriotic stand they have taken in defense of the Union, and the noble spirit of compromise which they have evinced in the settlement of the agitating question of slavery.

Resolved, That we regard non-interference in reference to slavery in the Territories and elsewhere as the safe course for both North and South, believing as we do that an All-wise Controlling Providence can, and will, regulate the whole matter so as to promote His own glory and the best interests of both whites and blacks.

Resolved, That we are in favor of the Union *under any and all circumstances*, yet we regard the Wilmot proviso and all kindred measures with the most perfect abhorrence.

Resolved, That we are in favor of the early admission of California as a free and sovereign State of the Union.

Resolved, That we regard the calling of the Nashville convention as premature, believing that so long as Congress discharges its duty there is no danger to the Slave States. We will send no delegates to it.

Resolved, That the proceedings of this meeting be published in the Liberty *Tribune*, and that the papers in Washington City and St. Louis be requested to copy them, and that the secretary enclose copies to Mr. Clay, Mr. Webster, Mr. Cass, Mr. Dickinson, and Mr. Bell.

The result of the August election in this county in 1850 was as follows : —

Congress — Charles E. Bowman, Whig, 584; Willard P. Hall, anti-Benton Democrat, 445; J. B. Gardenhire, Benton Democrat, 54.

Legislature — Thos. T. Swetnam, Whig, 615; Ryland Shackelford, Whig, 639.

Sheriff — O. P. Moss, Whig, 438; Samuel Hadley, Democrat, 656.

There was no opposition to Messrs. Swetnam and Shackelford, both Whigs. The Democrats concentrated all their efforts on the election of Samuel Hadley as sheriff, and it was feared that should they nominate candidates for the Legislature, it would draw party lines, and as the county was strongly Whig, would endanger his chances. At that time Clay county was entitled to two representatives in the Legislature.

At the ensuing session of the Legislature (January, 1851,) there was intense interest over the election of the United States Senator. Col. Benton was, of course, a candidate for re-election, but as the Democrats were divided on the question of his indorsement, the Whigs held the balance of power and by the adroit management of their leaders succeeded at last, by the help of the anti-Benton Democrats, in choosing the Senator themselves — Hon. Henry S. Geyer, of St. Louis, who was chosen on the fortieth ballot, the vote standing, Geyer, 80; Benton, 55; B. F. Stringfellow, 18, and 4 scattering.

THE ATTEMPT TO MURDER MRS. DINAH ALLEN — LYNCHING OF THE ASSASSINS.

In the early morning of April 1, 1850, an attempt was made to murder Mrs. Dinah A. Allen, widow of Col. Shubael Allen, at her residence, in Liberty. The family had retired for the night, and the doors were all secured. About three o'clock in the morning Mrs. Allen was aroused from her sleep by a painful stinging sensation on the cheek, and rising from her bed stepped into the room of her sons and awakened them, telling them she was bleeding to death: She had been struck across the face with some sharp instrument, apparently

HISTORY OF CLAY COUNTY

either a knife or an axe, and the wound was at first believed to be mortal,[1] but did not prove so.

Mrs. Allen was a lady without a known enemy and was held in universal esteem. No conjecture could be ventured for the motive prompting the deed. The citizens generally made persistent efforts to discover the perpetrators, and at last they were found out.

A slave woman, named Anice, belonging to Mrs. Allen was suspicioned and thrown into jail. In a few days she confessed her guilt and implicated as her partner in the crime a white man, a citizen of Liberty, named McClintock. The confession reduced to writing and published in the *Tribune* of May 17, 1850, was as follows : —

Four days before the commission of the act McClintock told me that there was a good deal of money in the house of my mistress, and that I ought to kill her ; that he would assist me ; that we would get the money, and with that we would go to California, and that I would be his wife and be free. On Sunday night, the night of the commission of the crime, he came to the kitchen where I was sleeping, waked me up and we proceeded to the house. McClintock hoisted the window and got in the house, and pulled me through the window after him. He approached the bed, found my mistress asleep, and said to me, " She lays right." I took the ax, which belonged to McClintock, and made the lick. McClintock had the ax in his hand when I took hold. My mistress made a noise and we both ran out of the house ; he went to his own house, a few hundred yards off, and I went back to the kitchen and laid down on the bed.

Upon hearing this statement from Anice, the slave women, her partner, McClintock, was secured and placed in jail. There was intense excitement. A few weeks before, but subsequent to the attempt on Mrs. Allen's life, an attempt had been made by a negro servant woman to poison the family of Wade Moseby, of this county. Previous attacks had been made by slaves on their masters. An example was called for to remedy if possible this condition of affairs.

Thursday, May 9, a considerable number of the citizens of the county met at the court-house to take action in the premises. The meeting had among its members some of the best men of the county, and the proceedings (though of course wholly illegal) were quiet and orderly. That morning Anice had sent for the Rev. Moses E. Lard to come to the jail, and to him she repeated her confession. She was brought before the meeting, as was McClintock, and in the presence of the entire assemblage she reiterated what she had twice previously

---

[1] Liberty *Tribune.*

stated in reference to the crime, and told McClintock fairly to his face that he was the sole instigator and planner of the crime, and the cause of her participation therein. McClintock stoutly and indignantly denied any sort of participation or complicity in the outrage, and denounced the negress as a liar, unmitigated and shameless.

Under the law of Missouri at that time a slave was not allowed to testify in court against a white person, and as there was no other evidence of McClintock's guilt save what could be furnished by Anice, there was no prospect of his legal conviction and punishment. Even though his accomplice, the bondwoman, should offer to turn State's evidence, she would not be allowed to do so. The theory was that a slave was irresponsible, and could not be trusted to swear to the truth, where the life or liberty of a white person was involved.

But, curiously enough, while the *oath* of Anice would not have been received in court against McClintock, her unsworn statements were readily accepted, and there was but little expressed doubt of his guilt. The question as to what should be done in reference to Anice's case was argued by several able and respectable citizens. A motion was made that she should be hung, and this motion carried unanimously. There were persons in the house opposed to hanging her, but they did not vote. Then there were cries of " *Hang them both.*" " *Hang McClintock, too!* " It was agreed, therefore, to hang them both on the same tree, *nem. con.*

The meeting was composed of all classes of citizens, farmers, mechanics, merchants, lawyers, physicians and others. Its proceedings were generally indorsed by the best classes of citizens, though they were admitted to have been irregular and illegal, and no attempt was made to interfere with them.

The hanging came off half a mile north or northwest of the public square, on the then Plattsburg road. McClintock denied to the last that he was guilty, but the negro woman asserted that her confession was true.

THE CHOLERA.

The overflow of the Missouri river in the spring of 1851 did considerable damage to farms in the bottom lands, and the subsidence of the flood was followed by a few cases of cholera in the county. Anderson Edwards and another citizen and three slaves died in Liberty in July. The contagion was severe that year at Independence, Weston and elsewhere.

In the latter part of May and the first part of June, 1854, cholera broke out in Richfield, and seven persons died in one day. It was

HISTORY OF CLAY COUNTY

thought the disease was fostered by a rotting pile of potatoes near the village. At least eleven died during the period of the disease — Dent. Violett and his wife and two children, Wm. M. Barrett, Vincent S. Crawford, Mrs. Rogers, Mrs. Canach, Mrs. Brown, a daughter of Thos. C. Reed, and a daughter of James Reed.

ELECTIONS OF 1852.

Col. A. W. Doniphan, of Clay county, was nominated for Governor by the Whigs of Missouri in 1852, but declined owing to ill health, and James Winston, of Benton county (who had been nominated for Lieutenant-Governor), was selected in his stead, with Andrew King, of St. Charles, for second place. Sterling Price was the Democratic candidate. The vote in this county at the August election resulted : —

Governor — Winston, 732 ; Price, 491.

Congress — Mordecai Oliver, Whig, 840 ; Jas. H. Birch, Dem., 311 ; Austin A. King, Dem., 73.

Legislature — O. P. Moss and Nathaniel Vincent, both Whigs, elected without opposition.

Sheriff — Samuel Hadley, Democrat defeated J. D. Skaggs, by some 300 majority, but the latter contested, and the next fall Judge Dunn decided that Hadley had not received a constitutional majority.

As there were two Democratic candidates for Congress, Mordecai Oliver, the Whig, " running between " them, was elected, the vote in the district standing: Oliver, 7,598 ; Birch, 4,399 ; King, 4,107.

At the November election the Whig electoral ticket carried the county by a reduced majority. Gen. Winfield Scott and Wm. A. Graham were the Whig candidates for President and Vice-President, against Franklin Pierce and Wm. R. King, Democrats. The vote in Clay county stood: Scott and Graham, 626; Pierce and King, 406.

1854.

Mordecai Oliver was re-elected to Congress this year over Leonard, Lowe and John E. Pitt.

1856.

Governor — R. C. Ewing, Know Nothing, 775 ; Trusten Polk, Democrat, 831. Thos. H. Benton, Independent, none.

Congress — James H. Moss, K. N., 802 ; James Craig, D., 824 ; Joel Turnham, Dem., 808.

Representative — Robert G. Gilmer, K. N., 799.

Sheriff — Trigg T. Allen, K. N., 800 ; Samuel Hadley, Dem., 830.

James H. Moss, the Whig, or " American " candidate for Congress, was a resident of Liberty. He was defeated in the district by Gen. James Craig, of St. Joseph, by 2,500 votes.

HISTORY OF CLAY COUNTY

At the Presidential election the Know Nothings carried the county for Fillmore and Donelson, the vote standing, Fillmore, 756; Buchanan, 675.

1857.

January 12, 1857, Gov. Trusten Polk was elected U. S. Senator, to succeed Senator Geyer. A new Governor was to be chosen. The anti-Bentons, or regular Democrats, nominated Hon. Robert M. Stewart, of Buchanan county. The "Americans" brought out Hon. James S. Rollins, of Boone county, who was indorsed and supported by a majority of the Benton Democrats. Col. Benton had written a letter from Washington to his friends in Missouri, urging them to vote for Rollins. The vote in the county was: For Rollins, 643; Stewart, 585. In the State as canvassed, it stood: Stewart, 47,975; Rollins, 47,641; Stewart's majority, 334. The Rollins men declared that their candidate was fairly elected, but was cheated in the count by "doctoring" the returns from certain counties in the southwest part of the State, but the truth of this declaration was never fully established.

1858.

Congress —James H. Adams, Whig and American, 993; James Craig, Dem., 826.

State Senator —J. H. Layton, W. and A., 929; J. T. V. Thompson, Dem., 837.

Legislature —John Dougherty, W. and A., 877; B. L. Lampton, Dem., 895.

Sheriff — R. A. Neely, Whig, 939; Samuel Hadley, Dem., 882.

Craig was elected to Congress and Thompson to the State Senate.

THE KNOW NOTHINGS.

The Native American, or as it was called, the "Know Nothing" party deserves particular mention in these pages, as at one time it was a political organization very formidable in its character, and largely in the majority in this county. It was formed in the United States some time before the year 1840, but did not become strong or very prominent until the dissolution of the Whig party, in 1853.

The party was a strange one, as it was a secret political order, whose members were oath-bound, and which had its lodges or "councils," its signs, grips, and pass-words, and worked secretly to accomplish its openly professed objects. It was composed chiefly of old Whigs, although there were many ex-Democrats in its ranks. Its great basic principle was that "Americans must rule America;" in other words, that none but native-born citizens of the United States, and non-Catholics[1] ought to hold office. It also favored a radical change in the naturalization laws, insisting on a foreigner's twenty years' residence in this country as a prerequisite to citizenship.

The following resolutions constituted the first platform of the American party in Missouri: —

* * * * * * * * * * * *

2. A full recognition of the rights of the several States, as expressed and reserved in the Constitution, and a careful avoidance by the general government of all interference with their rights by legislative or executive action.

3. Obedience to the Constitution of these United States as the supreme law of the land, sacredly obligatory in all its parts and members — a strict construction thereof, and steadfast resistance to the spirit of innovation of its principles — avowing that in all doubtful or disputed points, it may only be legally ascertained and expounded by the judicial powers of the United States.

4. That no person should be selected for political station, whether native or foreign prince, potentate or power, or who refuses to recognize the Federal or State constitutions (each within its sphere) as paramount to all other laws or rules of political action.

5. Americans must rule America; and to this end native born citizens should be selected for all State and Federal offices in preference to naturalized citizens.

6. A change in the laws of naturalization, making a continual residence of twenty-one years an indispensable requisite for citizenship, and excluding all paupers and persons convicted of crime, from landing on our shores; but no interference with the vested rights of foreigners.

7. Persons that are born of American parents, residing temporarily abroad, are entitled to all the rights of native born citizens.

8. An enforcement of the principle that no State or Territory can admit others than native born citizens to the rights of suffrage, or of holding political office, unless such persons have been naturalized according to the laws of the United States.

9. That Congress possessed no power under the Constitution to legislate upon the subject of slavery in the States where it does or may exist, or to exclude any State from admission into the Union, because its constitution does or does not recognize the institution of slavery as a part of its social system and expressly pretermitting any expression of opinion upon the power of Congress to establish or prohibit slavery in any territory; it is the sense of this meeting that the territories of the United States and that any inflence by Congress with slavery as it exists in the District of Columbia, would be a viola-

---

[1] After a time the clause in the platform against Catholics was stricken out, except in regard to those who held to the supremacy of the Pope in temporal affairs.

HISTORY OF CLAY COUNTY

tion of the spirit and intention of the compact by which the State of Maryland ceded the District to the United States, and a breach of the national faith.

10. That we will abide by and maintain the existing laws on the subject of slavery as a final and conclusive settlement of the subject on spirit, and in substance, believing this course to be the best guarantee of future peace and fraternal amity.

The organization of the Know Nothing party was begun in Clay county in the fall of 1855. On the 1st of January, 1856, a meeting of the party was held at the court-house in Liberty. Hon. James H. Moss addressed a large audience in explanation of the principles of the new organization. Dr. W. A. Morton was chairman. A committee composed of Thos. McCarty, Simpson McGaugherty, T. R. Dale, Nathaniel Vincent and J. B. Talbott, reported a series of resolutions indorsing the National and State platforms,[1] and adding the following: —

That the Union of these States is the paramount object of patriotic desire. That we re-affirm and most cordially and unchangeably indorse the declaration of the lamented hero, sage, and statesman, Andrew Jackson, that, "*The Union must and shall be preserved.*" That, with equal ardor and affection, we re-affirm and indorse the answer of that great national statesman and patriot, Henry Clay, who, when asked when he would be ready for a dissolution of this Union, said, "*Never! never! never!*"

The lodges of the Know Nothings were called "councils." In this county, among others, there were councils at Liberty, Richfield, Smithville, Gilead, and in Washington township. In March, 1856, Liberty Council endorsed the nominations of Fillmore and Donelson, and the other councils subsequently took similar action.

It is said that one of the hailing signs of the Know Nothings was "Have you seen Sam?" meaning, it is presumed, "Uncle Sam," the mythical personage supposed to represent the Government of the United States. The American flag was always present in the council rooms, and the Federal constitution was a part of the constitution of the order.

For some years the native American party was a prominent and important factor in politics, but the influence and strength of the foreign and Catholic vote of the country were of course always against it; the Republican and Democratic platforms condemned its

---

[1] On the Kansas question the National platform declared that "none but those who have a *fixed* residence in the Territory," ought to vote.

HISTORY OF CLAY COUNTY

principles, and so it grew smaller by degrees until 1861. Then the Civil War came on and broke it up. And came near breaking up the country as well.

TRAGEDIES.

In an affray between two brothers-in-law named Farr and Woolbridge, at Barry, about the 1st of September, 1854, Farr killed Woolbridge, giving him five pistol shots and several knife wounds.

February 4, 1858, Solomon Binswanger was stabbed and killed in a drunken quarrel at Missouri City. Dr. Geo. C. Tuley, Geo. H. Wallis and Geo. W. Withers were arrested and indicted for murder in the second degree. The case against Withers was dismissed. In May, 1858, Tuley was tried at Liberty, convicted of manslaughter in the third degree, and sentenced to three months' imprisonment in the county jail and to pay a fine of $100. In April, 1859, Wallis was tried, but the jury disagreed, and he was allowed to plead guilty of manslaughter and received the same sentence as Dr. Tuley, but in October following he was pardoned by Gov. Stewart.

September 7, 1858, J. A. S. Major shot and killed Samuel R. Trabue, at Centerville. There was great excitement and indignation in the community over the tragedy. A public meeting condemned it, and extolled the character of Mr. Trabue as that of a " most worthy, temperate, mild, peaceful and order-loving citizen."

Richard Moore stabbed and killed Pat Cusick in a drinking house in Liberty, in June, 1859.

THE SMITHVILLE TRADEGY OF 1854.

Monday, August 7, 1854, a terrible melee occurred in Smithville, this county, which resulted in the death of two citizens of the place, John W. Douglass and S. J. Ross, and the lynching of three men accused of their murder, Samuel Shackelford, Wm. Shackelford and John W. Callaway. The following statement of the affair was furnished by the *surviving* (?) citizens of Smithville and published in the Liberty *Tribune:*—

There had been a gang of thieves and outlaws quartered in this vicinity, which fact had been established by a court of inquiry, according to the laws of the country. These thieves and incendiaries were notified to leave Clay and adjoining counties by more than 100 respectable citizens of this vicinity. Their answers were that they would not leave, and that 50 armed men could not make them leave. Thus the matter passed on until Monday, August 7, the day of the election, when they sent word that they intended to clean out the

HISTORY OF CLAY COUNTY

town, commencing on those who had used the most exertions in prosecuting them with the law, even telling their friends where they wished to be buried if they fell in the conflict.

They then armed themselves with two revolvers each and bowieknives and dirks. Thus equipped, they made their appearance in town. Their leader, Samuel Shackelford, commencing a conversation, in an insulting manner, with John W. Douglass, and alluded to Wm. Ross, both respectable citizens of this community. Mr. Ross replied in a calm manner, but was dared to the onset by Samuel Shackelford, and at that moment a person, a relation of Shackelford's, passed between them for a moment. Shackelford drew a revolver, the person passed on, and Shackelford shot Wm. Ross twice, wounding him severely, perhaps mortally. Shackelford then turned and shot Mr. Douglass twice, and then shot at M. Imhoff twice. Douglass then returned the fire on Shackelford twice, wounding him, and then Douglass drew a bowie-knife, he being the only citizen on the ground who was armed. Wm. Shackelford seized Douglass and got his knife and pistol, and then commenced the work of destruction on Douglass, inflicting several wounds, of which Douglass fell dead. He then shot twice or three times at M. Imhoff, but without effect.

Persons then interfered to stop the effusion of blood. Saml. Shackelford stabbed every person whom he suspected as his enemy, inflicting a mortal wound on S. J. Ross, and also cutting and stabbing Ira Witt, who was a stranger, and only engaged for peace, as also young Ross. John W. Callaway ran in and shot at M. Imhoff and missed him, as did Samuel Shackelford. Callaway then shot Wm. Slater, wounding him slightly in the leg.

By this time the fight became general. Stones and clubs were in order. The Shackelfords and Callaway retreated, and in doing so attempted to kill others whom they considered their enemies. Samuel Shackelford's pistol, which he drew with the intention of shooting Mr. Payne, missed fire, and he then threw the pistol at him. They then entered a drug store and locked themselves up for defense; but owing to Samuel Shackelford being wounded, and the people threatening to fire the house, they surrendered to the populace.

The people were frenzied. Ropes were called for, guns and pistols procured, and all hands calling for immediate vengeance on the murderers. Thus it passed on, until the people were alarmed in all directions, and notified of the circumstances. They came from Platte county. Ridgeley was a precinct, and it being a public day the people flocked in gangs to the place.

The cry was "Lynch them! hang the thieves and murderers!" Two or three hundred persons were present. Wm. Shackelford was then hung. John W. Callaway was next hung. He stated, before his death, that Samuel Shackelford was to blame for all the trouble; that Sam. Shackelford had induced him into stealing horses; that Sam. Shackelford stole the mule that he was arrested for, and he took it and sold it in St. Joseph; that they had concluded not to kill the people of Smithville and vicinity [and would not have made the at-

165

tempt] but for the over-persuasion of —— —— that he would stand up to them and see them through. The same was affirmed by Mrs. Shackelford, although they had agreed among themselves to go into the massacre before —— came. Sam. Shackelford was hung next, all to the same limb.

The peace officers made speeches against mob law, and used every exertion for the civil authority to have its proper course, but all to no effect. Order was confounded; confusion reigned. Men paraded the streets like dragoons in military service. The whole of this resulted from an effort on the part of the citizens to bring these thieves to justice according to law, for the commission of crime, their guilt of which they acknowledged. The people are satisfied with what they have done, so far as civil authority is concerned.

MANY CITIZENS.

P. S. — There had been an attempt made to assassinate Douglass at the dead hour of night, supposed to have been by these murderers, and he was threatened by them, which was the reason why he was armed.

Callaway, at the time of his lynching, was under $1,000 bond to answer a charge of stealing a mule from Calvin Smith, in the fall of 1852. The Shackelfords and Callaway were hung on a sugar tree, near the bridge across Smith's fork; the tree is still standing. The mother of the Shackelfords, and the wives of Callaway and one of the Shackelfords were present and witnessed the execution. They wailed, moaned, screamed, entreated, cursed and prayed by turns, striking the lynchers with their hands and with sticks, and striving frantically with all their might to rescue them. At the time he was hung, Sam. Shackelford's skull was crushed in, the wound having been inflicted some time previously, but he was "game" to the last.

MURDER OF WM. O. RUSSELL BY "PETE" LIGHTBURNE — LYNCHING OF "PETE."

On the night of February 12, 1855, Mr. Wm. O. Russell, a citizen of the county, living three miles southeast of Liberty, was mortally wounded by a negro slave named "Peter," the property of Maj. A. Lightburne. The circumstances, as best remembered, are that Mr. Russell owned Pete's wife, and for some offense she had given, had whipped her severely. This she told her husband and he vowed revenge. On the night and question "Pete" called at Mr. Russell's, after the latter had retired, and calling him up said he had been sent for a bill of lumber. Russell admitted the negro and asked him if he had brought a bill. The latter answered "yes." Mr. Russell stooped over to stir up his smoldering fire, when suddenly the negro drew a short but heavy corn-knife, which he had concealed in his bosom, and assaulted Mr. Russell so savagely and with such effect that he died two weeks later from his wounds.

"Pete" was arrested and imprisoned in jail. A mob of excited men gathered and were about to hang him, but his owner, Maj. Lightburne, spoke to them in such an earnest, remonstrating manner, that the design was abandoned at the time. March 5, the crowd reassembled, determined to lynch the criminal. Rev. Moses E. Lard and others addressed them, and urged them to allow the wretch to be punished according to law, but they dragged him from his cell and hung him to a tree in the court-house yard, before the sound of the speakers' voices had hardly died away.

CHAPTER VI.

DURING THE KANSAS TROUBLES UP TO 1861.

The Kansas Troubles—Clay County's Interest in Kansas Affairs—Sketch of the Situation in Kansas Territory Upon its Organization—The Election in 1854—Clay Furnishes Her Quota of Voters—The "Sons of the South"—Election in the Spring of 1855—The Parkville Mob Indorsed—The "Wakarusa War"—Seizure of the Liberty Arsenal by the Clay County Volunteers—Maj. Leonard's Report—The Arms Returned *Minus* What Were Retained—County Seat Fight in Kansas—Emigrants to Kansas Turned Back—End of the Fight—The Free Soilers Win—Explanation of the Course of Clay County. *Up to 1861*—Census—Miscellaneous—The Present Court-House—The Kansas City and Cameron Railroad—The Presidential and Gubernatorial Campaigns of 1860—After the Election—Trouble Brewing.

DURING THE TROUBLES IN KANSAS.

From the first to the last of the troubles in the Territory of Kansas, the result of an attempt at a decision of the question whether or not slavery should exist in the State upon its admission into the Union, the people of Clay county took a conspicuous part therein upon the pro-slavery side. The proximity of that Territory to this county, its likeness of soil and climate, made it a desirable objective point of emigration for people here when they should become tired of their homes, and those who had slaves wished of course to take them along. Then there was a strong desire to have Kansas made a slave State among slaveholders everywhere; and the politicians of the South had made this desire the measure of the devotion of Southern men to "Southern rights." Much was expected from Missouri generally, and a great deal from Clay and other border counties.

In the summer of 1853, when the Kansas-Nebraska bill was under discussion, the border counties of Missouri prepared for the conflict—for the conflict of ballots, and the conflict of bullets if necessary. A military company was organized in Liberty in July, with A. J. Calhoun as captain, John Dunn, N. S. Prentiss, Lewis Bennett, lieutenants, and R. Fisher, orderly sergeant. There was not much attempt at concealing the fact that the services of this company were to be called into requisition if necessary in the settlement of the political questions in Kansas.

By the provisions of the Kansas-Nebraska bill, which repealed the Missouri Compromise of 1820, slaveholders might or might not be per-

HISTORY OF CLAY COUNTY

mitted in Kansas, as the people thereof should decide. "The true intent and meaning of the act" was declared to be "not to legislate slavery into any State or Territory, or exclude it therefrom," but to leave the people thereof free to form and regulate their domestic institutions in their own way, subject only to the Constitution of the United States." Under this declaration the pro-slavery men claimed they had a right to settle in the Territory with their slaves; but this was denied by the anti-slavery men or Free Soilers, who claimed that "the normal condition of the public territories was freedom."

The full history of the Kansas troubles belongs to other volumes; but it will be necessary to refer to certain incidents in that history in order to understand clearly the part taken by Clay county. Under the first Territorial government an election for delegate to Congress was ordered to be held November 29, 1854. The candidates were: Whitfield, Pro-Slavery, and Flenniken, Free Soil. Andrew H. Reeder, of Pennsylvania, had been appointed Territorial Governor by President Pierce, and arrived in October. It was decided that all the voters on the border of Missouri who could possibly do so should go over to Kansas and vote! The law regarding the eligibility of voters was differently construed; the Free State men claimed that only *bona fide* settlers could vote, and the Pro-Slavery men that any man was entitled to vote if he had been in the Territory "an hour."

The people along the Missouri border from Andrew county to Jasper, and as far east in the State as Randolph, Callaway, and Cole, organized and prepared to set out for Kansas to cast their votes. Numerous meetings were held in this quarter. Senator David R. Atchison and others stumped the counties of Buchanan, Clay, Platte, and Jackson. A few days before the election Atchison spoke in Liberty. He had previously addressed the people of Platte county at Platte City, and said to them: "When you reside in one day's journey of the Territory you can, without exertion, send 500 of your young men who will vote in favor of your institutions." This he repeated to the people of Clay in his speech at Liberty.

There was the most intense excitement throughout the country, and it was thought that the interests of Missouri, and especially the interests of slavery, demanded the most radical efforts to prevent the Abolitionists from winning the first battle in the conflict over Kansas. Whatever the means employed, it was believed that the ends would justify them. Scores of citizens of this county, well armed and furnished with provisions and money by those who "could not go," went over into the Territory, voted "early and often," and returned home

169

within a few days! Hundreds of other Missourians did the same, and Whitfield was elected by a large majority!

All through the winter of 1854–55 nothing much was talked of in the county but the Kansas question. A regular organization of the Pro-Slavery men — a secret order called the "Blue Lodge," the "Social Band," the "Friends' Society," or the "Sons of the South," being known by different names — had been organized in Missouri and other Slave States, and "camps" were established in Clay county. The object was the preservation, perpetuation, and extension of the "peculiar institution," and the order had its hailing signs, grips, and passwords, and was near of kin and auxiliary to the "Knights of the Golden Circle." It took a leading part in the Kansas question.

March 30, 1855, an election was held in Kansas to choose members of the Territorial Legislature, or Council. Extraordinary efforts were made by both parties to carry this election. The Free Soilers had come in in considerable numbers the previous year, under the auspices of the "Emigrant Aid Societies" of the North, and fears were felt among the Pro-Slavery men that by some chance a majority of Free State men might be chosen to the Council, and a Constitution forbidding slavery chosen by that body. All Western Missouri was on the stir. The following notice was printed on handbills and circulated through this county, and published in the Liberty *Tribune*:—

Friends of the South! — The first election of members of the Territorial Legislature in Kansas comes off Friday next, the 30th inst. Friends of the South, the crisis has arrived, and now is the time for you to determine whether or not that rich and fertile Territory shall be governed by the miserable hirelings sent thither from the dens of Abolitionism in the East to rob you of your rights and your property. *We must act! We must act!* A meeting will be held at Liberty on Thursday, the 29th inst., to take such measures as may be considered proper under the circumstances. Let every friend of the South and her institutions attend.

A large and enthusiastic meeting was held at the court-house pursuant to the call, and numbers of our best citizens enrolled themselves into companies, and set out at once for Kansas. Those who could not go furnished arms, provisions, horses, and money to those who needed such assistance and were willing to go. All the men were armed.

At this election the men from Clay went into the Sixteenth district (immediately across the river, or in which Leavenworth was situated), or into the Third district — Tecumseh. Some were in other districts and at various polling places. A considerable company that went into the

HISTORY OF CLAY COUNTY

Sixteenth district did not arrive until late in the day of the election. At Stinson's, or Tecumseh, the Missourians were under the leadership chiefly of Hon. S. H. Woodson, of Independence. The pro-slavery men were armed and organized, but not uniformed; many wore badges of hemp or white tape tied in their button-holes to designate them from the Free State men. A great deal of promiscuous voting was done, and the Pro-Slavery candidates were declared elected by overwhelming majorities. On the face of the returns this was true.[1]

Upon the return of the Clay county "voters" their acts were universally approved and indorsed. It was determined to keep in readiness a strong force of "minute men" for future emergencies.

April 14, 1855, a large force of the citizens of Platte county assembled at Parkville, threw into the river the press and material of the *Industrial Luminary*, a newspaper owned and published by George S. Park and W. J. Patterson, and with decided Free Soil tendencies. Its first issue after the Kansas election had contained an article severely denunciatory of the proceedings of the Missourians in their interference with the election. Mr. Park was absent at the time, but Mr. Patterson was seized, and was about to be tarred and cottoned (or as some say lynched) when his wife threw her arms about him and could not be prevailed upon to leave him, and by a small majority it was voted to release him on condition that he leave the State and never return.

The citizens then held a meeting and passed a set of resolutions, declaring, among other sentiments, "That George S. Park and W. J. Patterson are traitors to the State and county in which they live, and should be dealt with as such; that we meet here again on this day three weeks, and if we find G. S. Park or W. J. Patterson in this town then, or at any subsequent time, we will throw them into the Missouri river; and if they go to Kansas to reside we pledge our honor as men to follow and hang them wherever we can take them." It was further declared that no Northern Methodist preachers should be allowed to preach in the county under penalty of " tar and feathers for the first offense and hemp rope for the second," and the meeting declared its intention to " attend to some other Free Soilers not far off."

On April 21 a large meeting of the citizens of Clay convened in Liberty, at the court-house, to consider the proceedings had and done

---

[1] At Leavenworth the vote was Pro-Slavery, 899; Free State, 60: at Tecumseh, Pro-Slavery, 366; Free State, 4. The total vote in the Territory was, Pro-Slavery, 5,427; Free State, 791.

HISTORY OF CLAY COUNTY

at Parkville. The following is the official report of the proceedings of this meeting, as published in the Liberty *Tribune*:—

KANSAS MEETING.

At a large and enthusiastic meeting of the citizens of Clay county, assembled at the court-house for the purpose of indorsing the action of the citizens of our neighboring county of Platte, in the destruction of the Parkville *Industrial Luminary*, Maj. John Dougherty was called to the chair, and Geo. W. Morris appointed secretary.

On motion, Henry L. Routt, Geo. W. Withers, Maj. Joel Turnham, Asa T. Foree, Wm. H. Kerr and Fountain Waller were appointed a committee to draft resolutions expressing the sense of the meeting. After a short absence the committee reported the following resolutions :—

WHEREAS, We have seen the proceedings of a meeting of the citizens of Platte county, held in Parkville on the 14th inst., and feel that the time has come when it becomes the duty of every man in our State that there may no longer be any misapprehension on the part of any of the citizens of our sister States ; therefore,

Resolved, 1. That the action of the non-slaveholding States in setting at defiance the laws for the protection of our property, in not only countenancing but justifying and abetting by their legislation, its systematic and public highway robbery of Southerners, by the insults and outrages heaped upon them whenever compelled to pass through or over to land upon the borders of the non-slaveholding States ; the declared purpose of those who perpetrate these outrages, not only to plant their hosts of felons upon our borders but to invade our State, strip us and drive us from our homes, demand the adoption of the most efficient means for our protection.

2. We will begin at home, and rid ourselves of the traitors harbored in our midst.

3. To speak or publish in a slaveholding community sentiments calculated to render slaves discontented, to irritate them to escape or rebel, is not an exercise of the " liberty of speech," but is an act of positive crime of the highest grade, and should receive summary and exemplary punishment.

4. Those who in our State would give aid and encouragement to the Abolitionists by inducing or assisting them to settle in Kansas, or throw obstacles in the way of our friends by false and slanderous misrepresentations of the acts of those who took part in and contributed to the gratifying results in the late election in that Territory, should be driven from among us as *traitors* to their country.

5. We fully approve the action of our friends in Platte in destroying the press of the *Industrial Luminary* and their resolutions to expel the traitors, Park and Patterson.

6. That we regard the efforts of the Northern division of the Methodist Episcopal Church to establish itself in our State, as a violation of its plighted faith — and pledged as must be its ministers to the anti-

HISTORY OF CLAY COUNTY

slavery principles of that church, we are forced to regard them as enemies to our institutions. We therefore fully concur with our friends in resolving to permit no person belonging to the Northern Methodist Church to preach in our county.

7. We urge the citizens of other counties, and pledge ourselves to act cordially and efficiently in executing the principles of the foregoing resolutions.

8. To show our full approval of the proceedings of our friends in Platte, we will attend at Parkville on the 5th day of May next, and in person indorse their action.

The resolutions were unanimously adopted.

The meeting was then addressed by Gen. B. F. Stringfellow, Maj. John Dougherty, W. E. Price, Judge Thompson, Geo. W. Withers, Henry L. Routt and Maj. James H. Adams.

On motion of Geo. W. Withers, 100 delegates from each township were appointed to meet our fellow-citizens of Platte in council in Parkville on the 5th day of May next.

On motion of J. H. Adams, a committee of five from each township were appointed by the chair to wait on all persons in the least suspected of Free Soilism or Abolitionism, and notify them to leave the county immediately.

The chairman appointed the following persons under the last motion: James T. V. Thompson, Joel Turnham, A. G. Reed, O. P. Moss, D. J. Adkins, J. H. Adams, G. H. Wallis, W. E. Price, S. Levi, Geo. W. Withers, David Morris, Thos. M. Gosney, L. J. Wood, Thos. J. Young, Edmund Tilman, A. T. Foree, Wm. Austin, A. C. Courtney, Ryland Shackelford, Henry Estes, Maj. John Dougherty, Wyatt Wills, Willis Winn, Fountain Waller, A. Murray.

On motion of H. L. Routt, all persons of this county who are subscribers for papers *in the least* tinctured with Free Soil or Abolitionism, are requested to discontinue them immediately.

On motion, the Liberty *Tribune*, Richfield *Enterprise* and St. Louis *Republican* were requested to publish the proceedings of this meeting.

On motion, the meeting adjourned.

JOHN DOUGHERTY, Chairman.

GEO. W. MORRIS, Secretary.

There was such intense and long continued excitement in the county over the Kansas question that our people became intolerant to a degree that they have since regretted. It was not safe to disapprove the measures adopted by the Pro-Slavery party to make Kansas a slave State. Even Editor Miller, of the *Tribune*, who mildly protested against the violent destruction of the *Luminary*, saying the better way to have suppressed it would have been " to let it die for want of patronage," had his orthodoxy on the slavery question openly doubted, and the Richfield *Monitor* assailed him savagely.

HISTORY OF CLAY COUNTY

Clay county was not alone in indorsing the proceedings at Parkville. Other counties, by resolutions adopted at large meetings, approved them. But in Johnson county, at an assemblage of the citizens at Warrensburg, in May, the people excepted to the proscription of the Northern Methodists, saying : —

The constitution and laws guaranteeing to us the right to worship God according to the dictates of conscience we regard as sacred, and the course pursued at meetings held in our own and sister counties in proscribing ministers of the Gospel of certain denominations, is tyrannical, arbitrary, illegal, and unjust, and unworthy the intelligence of an enlightened community.

Throughout the war in Kansas during the year 1855 this county furnished men and means to aid the Pro-Slavery cause whenever called upon. At the time of the " Wakarusa War," in December, Mayor Payne, of Kansas City, came over to Liberty and raised 200 men and $1,000 for the purpose of aiding Sheriff Jones and the other officers under Gov. Wilson Shannon, in capturing the Free State town of Lawrence, whose inhabitants were in rebellion against the acknowledged authorities of the Territory. Lawrence at that time was virtually in a state of siege, with men in arms and breastworks to resist a process in the hands of the sheriff.

The Clay county volunteers, to the number of 100 or more, under the leadership of Maj. Ebenezer Price, moved upon the Liberty Arsenal, then in charge of Maj. Luther Leonard, seized it, put Leonard and the employes under arrest, and took out three pieces of artillery, brass six-pounders, mounted ; 55 rifles, 67 cavalry sabers, 100 dragoon pistols, 20 Colt's revolvers, besides all the necessary equipments, accouterments, and a large amount of ammunition, including shot and shell for the cannon, thousands of cartridges for the small arms, etc., all of which belonged to the Government. The following report of this seizure was made by Maj. Leonard to the Department at Washington : —

REPORT OF CAPT. LUTHER LEONARD OF THE ROBBERY OF LIBERTY ARSENAL, DECEMBER 4, 1855.

MISSOURI DEPOT, LIBERTY, Dec. 4, 1855, (5 p. m.)
Col. H. C. Craig, Ordnance Department, Washington City:
SIR—I improve the first moments of liberty to report that to-day, about 3 o'clock p. m., this depot was surprised by about 100 armed men, who placed me under an armed guard, as also the operatives at the post, and proceeded to take possession of public property to a large

HISTORY OF CLAY COUNTY

amount, consisting in part of three six-pounder brass guns, mounted; artillery harness, artillery implements, rifles, pistols, Colt's revolvers, sabers, fixed ammunition, accouterments, etc., etc. The exact amount can not be ascertained until an inventory is taken of the property remaining. Resistance was useless, and I could only protest against this violent and unlawful seizure of the public property in my charge.

From the best information I can obtain, the parties to this robbery have taken the property to Kansas Territory, to engage in some disturbances said to exist among the inhabitants thereof. I have reported these facts to Col. E. V. Sumner, commanding Fort Leavenworth, asking his advice and assistance.

This unparalleled outrage leaves me in doubt how to proceed in the absence of special authority, and I shall, therefore, anxiously await your orders.

I am, sir, very respectfully, your obedient servant,

L. LEONARD,
Military Storekeeper.

Being well armed and well mounted the Clay county volunteers set out for the "seat of war." One party with five wagons and a cannon bore a large flag in the center of which was a large purple star. Upon their arrival at the Pro-Slavery camp on the Wakarusa they were received with hearty cheers, and their flag was hoisted on a tree in the center of the camp. The campaign was soon over and the men returned home.

Meantime, in May, the Free State men, claiming that the March election was a fraud, had held an election and chosen members of a Territorial convention, which met at Topeka in October and adopted a Free State constitution. The Pro-Slavery delegates chosen in March had assembled at first at Pawnee and then at the Shawnee mission, one mile from the Missouri line and four miles from Westport, where, sitting as a Territorial Legislature, a formidable Pro-Slavery code of laws, modeled upon, if not taken almost entirely from, the Missouri Statutes, was adopted. But these statutes were decided to be valid by two of the three judges of the Supreme Court of the Territory, S. D. Lecompt and Rush Elmore. The enactments were, however, uniformly disregarded and defied by the Free State men. It was to enforce these laws that the Clay county men marched to the Wakarusa.

On the 10th of December, Capt. Wm. N. R. Beall, of the First U. S. Cavalry, came over from Ft. Leavenworth with a company of cavalry to guard the arsenal from another threatened raid, and to try to recover the property that had been taken. The same day he reported that "the robbery was on a large scale," and that he had

175

HISTORY OF CLAY COUNTY

notified certain prominent citizens that the property must be returned. The next day he reported as follows: —

MISSOURI DEPOT, Dec. 11, 1855.

SIR — I have the honor to state that Judge Thompson, one of the leading men of Liberty, called on me to-day and informed me that the arms, stores, and ammunition taken from this place on the 4th inst. are in this vicinity, and that the parties who took them are anxious to return them. I informed him that if they were brought to the arsenal *gate*, I would *there* receive them. They are now being delivered, and I presume that within two days from this time I will have possession of all that they have to return. I have an accurate inventory taken of them as they arrive.

I am, sir, very respectfully, your obedient servant,

W. N. R. BEALL,
Captain First Cavalry Commanding.
Lieut. Adjt. R. RANSOM, First Regt. Cav., Ft. Leavenworth, K. T.

About $400 worth of arms and ammunition were never restored. Jefferson Davis was then Secretary of War, and no further efforts were made to obtain them, and no arrests were ever offered to be made of those who took them.

One rather humorous incident connected with this "free for all" balloting in Kansas occurred in October, 1855. An election was to be held October 8, in Leavenworth county, to select a county seat. Three towns were aspirants for the distinction — Leavenworth, Delaware and Kickapoo, all three on the Missouri. Leavenworth, in population and number of resident voters, outnumbered both Delaware and Kickapoo two to one, and it was of course believed by the people of the first named town that it was sure to win. But the people of Delaware and Kickapoo had learned how elections might be carried, from seeing the Leavenworth men manage territorial contests. So on election day the ferry-boat ran free between Weston and Kickapoo and hundreds of Missourians from Platte county crossed over and voted on the county seat question in favor of Kickapoo, and while Leavenworth cast 600 votes Kickapoo came smilingly to the fore with 800!

But Delaware was yet to hear from. Situated eight miles below Leavenworth, it was near to both Platte and Clay counties, in Missouri. A few days before the election notices of the election were posted in different parts of this county and published in the *Tribune*. These notices closed as follows: "Pro-Slavery men will find it to their interest to make Delaware the county seat. The ferry at Delaware will be *free* that day; there will also be a big barbecue there

176

HISTORY OF CLAY COUNTY

on that day, and a big ball at night." The Delawareans kept the polls open *three days*, until after they heard from both Kickapoo and Leavenworth, and then came up triumphantly bearing their poll-books which showed a vote of *more than nine hundred* for Delaware! At that time there were not more than 60 actual resident voters in the place. To say that Leavenworth was disgusted is to very imperfectly state the prevalent feeling. The first authority to which the case of the election was submitted decided in favor of Kickapoo, but the territorial court waived all "irregularities," and ruled on the side of Delaware.

In March, 1856, a large meeting was held at the court-house, and a considerable sum of money subscribed in aid of the cause. In June an organization, called the Pro-Slavery Aid Association, was formed, with Michael Arthur, president; David Roberts, secretary and treasurer, and T. C. Gordon, D. J. Adkins, J. T. V. Thompson, A. W. Doniphan, and others, as directors. This association sent men and means into Kansas during the year from time to time as they were needed, and performed important work for the Pro-Slavery cause.

Some of the Clay county men took part in various skirmishes with the Free State men in Kansas in 1856, and were at Ossawattomie, Turkey Creek and elsewhere. One man, R. M. G. Price, was killed by the accidental discharge of a gun of a comrade, J. M. Sullivan.

In the spring and summer of 1856 numerous bodies of emigrants bound for Kansas from the Northern States were stopped in Western Missouri, not allowed to enter the Territory, and many of them forced back to their old homes. At Weston and Leavenworth one or two boat loads of Eastern emigrants were stopped and turned back, and similar action was taken with others at Lexington, Wellington and elsewhere. In May eight families, with 12 teams from Illinois, traveling overland, were stopped in Platte county, and brought to Liberty by a guard of eight men headed by Robert Pate. Here they were turned over to the citizens, and Judge Thompson took charge of them. They were permitted to camp near town for two days, and then sent 10 miles east where they rented houses and lived until the troubles in Kansas were over. These Illinoisans were John Veteto, his two sons and their families, and Benj. Draper, John Wooster, James Hancock, R. Roberts and M. Dibble, and their families.

In June, 1856, an attempt was made in Liberty to mob Darius Sessions, who was a prominent member of the Know Nothing party, but accused of holding anti-slavery sentiments. Sessions was rescued with some difficulty, and a public meeting indorsed him as a true friend of Southern institutions, and condemned the assault upon him as unmerited and unwarranted. Hon. L. W. Burris was prominent in the rescue of Sessions, who was killed by the bushwhackers at Missouri City during the Civil War.

After a time, along in the latter part of the year 1856, although the Government authorities virtually took sides with the Pro-Slavery men, and dispersed the Free State Legislature at Topeka with Col. Sumner's dragoons, it became apparent that the Northerners would win, and that Kansas would never become a Slave State. A congressional committee, composed of John Sherman, of Ohio; Howard, of Michigan, Republicans, and Mordecai Oliver, the member of Congress from this district, a Pro-Slavery man — was sent out to investigate matters in Kansas, and the report of Sherman and Howard, one-sided though it was, stimulated the Northerners to renewed exertions, and they poured into the Territory in such numbers and made so many permanent settlements, that they soon controlled nearly everything.

A sort of treaty of peace was made between Senator Atchison and Gov. Charles Robinson, and though there were diver tragic episodes in 1857 and 1858, yet no serious difficulties occurred after the fall of 1856. The Free State men won as much by their generalship as by their numbers.

In explanation of the course taken by the Pro-Slavery people of this county during the troublous times of the settlement of Kansas it is, perhaps, but the simple truth to say that whatever was done generally in that period was deemed to be done in a spirit more of self-defense than in wantonness or recklessness. Situated as Clay county was, it was by no means desirable that Kansas should become a free State. Runaway slaves were common enough then when Iowa was the nearest goal of freedom to be reached. Let Kansas become free and filled with Northern and Eastern Abolitionists, who counted it God's service to encourage and assist runaway slaves, and there would be no security or safety for slave property in this county; the 3,500 slaves belonging to our citizens would be held only as long as it pleased them to remain in a state of slavery.

Eternal vigilance was the price of slavery. The very nature of the institution made this so. Very many of the slaves were constantly on the watch for a chance to escape, and improve every opportunity to run away. Their masters owned them and they were and had been recognized as property. They represented so much money, which the masters could illy afford to lose, in many instances, and it behooved them to guard well their own at all times. There was a constant state of apprehension and uneasiness among most slave owners — a fear not alone of an exodus, but of an insurrection on the part of the negroes. The horrible scenes of St. Domingo and Jamaica it was feared might be repeated here some time. The negro could not be always under lock and key or in chains, or under watch, and yet he could not be trusted to go about the most ordinary avocation unguarded. Hence there arose a proverb that a " white man is uncertain and a nigger *will* run away?"

The Abolitionists were continually meddling with the slaves and inciting them to mischief. They visited the Slave States in various guises and disguises. Sometimes as preachers, sometimes as peddlers, sometimes as travelers. A fair speaking, meek looking individual would visit a slave-holding community on a plausible errand, and a week after he left a dozen negroes would have absconded and struck out for the North Star! To imprison them did no good; to flog them did not discourage them; to hang one occasionally only multiplied them. There was law in plenty to protect slavery, but it seemed ineffective and was oftener inoperative and a dead letter.

Hence it was that our people were forced to adopt the most vigorous policy in dealing with Abolitionists, and to become distrustful, suspicious and afraid of all strangers, and Northerners especially. We grew even inhospitable toward those we did not know, for frequently when we received into our houses a man whom we thought a gentleman, it turned out that he was a " nigger thief," who had come among us to entice away what all the laws and courts in the land said was our *property*, and which we had acquired honestly, as we believed.

Of a truth eternal vigilance was the price of slavery. So long as slave labor was a recognized factor in our political and commercial economy, it had to be protected and watched over. This could have been done by our people quietly and without a resort to extraordinary measures, but for the exasperating conduct of the Abolitionists, who took delight in irritating the slave owners in every possible way. Not only did they steal or entice away the slaves, but after the fugitives were well on the road to Canada, the liberators would often send to the masters taunting and insulting letters, full of sarcasm, denunciation and contempt. Pamphlets and circulars were distributed liberally, denouncing slavery and slaveholders in the vilest terms. The former was described as " the sum of human villainies;" the latter were termed " traffickers in human flesh," " brutes who breed up their own children for the slave market, and sell their own daughters to become the concubines of other slave-breeders," etc., etc. It was but natural, therefore, that the slaveholding population of the South should have but small regard for Abolitionists, and should resort to severe means and methods in dealing with them. A few Abolitionists, zealous and earnest, were capable of an infinite deal of mischief. In the language of the Abolition song, old John Brown —

"Captured Harper's Ferry with but nineteen men so true,
    And frightened old Virginia till she trembled through and through."

And *one* fanatical, working "liberator" could set an entire county agog, and have whole neighborhoods up in arms; and so the greatest care and extremest vigilance were required and exercised to keep that one Abolitionist out of the country, or to make his reception such that he would not care to return after being expelled.

Then the legislation of many of the Northern States against the institution, especially in regard to the execution of the fugitive slave law, the speeches of Free Soil orators and the utterances of the Free Soil press, all excited and embittered the people, and led them to do certain things which it would have been better to have left undone.

In explanation of the severity with which Northern Methodists were dealt, it is to be said that upon the division of the Methodist Church, in 1844–45, an exciting controversy arose, and as the division resulted from a discussion of the slavery question, the Northern wing opposing the institution, animosities were engendered against that organization which required many years of time to extinguish. Abolitionists were not wanted in Missouri, and as every Northern Methodist was akin in sentiment to, if not altogether, an Abolitionist, his room here was preferable to his company.

As to the dubious and really reprehensible policy of exporting voters to Kansas who were not and so far as they really knew did not intend to become actual residents of the Territory, who went over one day and returned the next, it is only the truth to state that the Free Soilers were pursuing practically the same tactics. In New England and New York the Abolitionists and their sympathizers organized "emigrant aid societies," regularly incorporated associations, with thousands of dollars of capital, and these societies sent hundreds and thousands of men into Kansas to be and remain there, so far as the societies expected or cared, only until after the election. True, these importations of the aid societies remained longer in Kansas than our Missouri voters, but the principle that governed them in coming to the

HISTORY OF CLAY COUNTY

Territory was the same — they came "to help our side." The early elections in Kansas were nearly all farcical and fraudulent anyhow. Where the Pro-Slavery men had the upper hand they regulated matters their own way; where the Free State men were in the majority they did the same.

Coming to the circumstance of the raising of money and means to help along the slavery cause, to arm and equip men and sustain them in the field, did not even the Republicans the same? Collections were taken up throughout New England and in New York and Ohio, even in the churches, to buy arms for and generally assist the men who went to Kansas "to consecrate the soil to freedom." Powder and shot were bought with the receipts of mite societies to assist in this "consecration;" ministers of the gospel prayed God from their pulpits to assist the Free State army, and Henry Ward Beecher distributed among some of the "cohorts of freedom" Sharpe's rifles which had been purchased with the contents of the contribution boxes of Plymouth Church.

Jim Lane marched through Southern Iowa into Nebraska and then down into Kansas at the head of a small army of mounted men, having with them cannon and a goodly supply of shot and shell. Cannon were smuggled into the Territory and mounted at Lawrence and Topeka. To meet these, the Missourians carried over other pieces of artillery taking them wherever they could find them.

The whole matter of the Kansas question, when viewed fairly and impartially, and when the elements of fraud and violence are contemplated, resolves itself into the homely expressed case of "six of one and half a dozen of the other." Many things were done by each side which were very discreditable, but the faults were nearly, if not quite, equally divided, and the honors and dishonors were easy.

CENSUS OF 1850.

The total population of Clay county in 1850 was 10,332, as follows: Whites, 7,590; blacks, 2,732. The number of heads of families was 1,352; number of school children, 2,403; number of farms, 1,000; number of deaths during the year, 151; amount of hemp raised in the county during the year, 1,232 tons. The population of Liberty was 827.

CENSUS OF 1856.

White males, 4,856; females, 4,327; total whites, 9,183. Slaves, 3,353; free negroes, 45; total colored, 3,398. Total population,

HISTORY OF CLAY COUNTY

12,581. Number of whites able to read and write, 5,395. Number of horses, 4,410; cattle, 9,585; mules, 1,495. Valuation of slave property, $1,496,630; total valuation, $5,456,595. Amount of tax for the year, $11,543.17.

MISCELLANEOUS.

From 1850 to 1855, steamboating was very active on the Missouri. Frequently four or five fine boats passed up and down daily. Some of the steamers of 1853 making trips regularly between St. Louis and Weston, Leavenworth and St. Joseph were the Banner State, Isabel, F. X. Aubrey, Robert Campbell, Timour No. 2, Polar Star, Clara, Ben West and Sonora. In August, 1853, the Polar Star made one trip from St. Louis to Liberty Landing in 52 hours and 47 minutes, making all intervening landings and losing three and a half hours. This was regarded as exceptionally fast time.

Upon the death of Dr. Wm. Jewell, in Liberty, August 7, 1852, a large public meeting was held and eulogistic resolutions of the philanthropist's character adopted. A very large funeral procession paraded the streets.

In October, 1853, the Clay County Agricultural Society was formed. W. E. Price was the first president, and W. T. Withers, secretary. The first fair of the society was held on the grounds, near Liberty, October 12, 13, and 14, 1854. Exhibitors from all the adjoining counties competed.

A teacher's institute was formed at Liberty, June 10, 1854. Prof. James Love was the first president; R. W. Fleming, vice-president; N. R. Stone, recording secretary; O. H. O'Neal, corresponding secretary; B. F. Woods, treasurer; L. M. Lawson, librarian and A. W. Doniphan, R. C. Morton, David Brown, A. D. Brooks and B. F. Hawkins the board of managers. The organization existed some years and held numerous interesting meetings.

The drouth in the year 1854 was quite severe in this county, and the following October wheat was quoted at from $1.37 to $1.72 per bushel, and corn was worth 60 cents.

When the financial distress of 1857 came upon Clay county the people had their pockets filled with free bank paper, much of which proved worthless, and many men were pretty badly injured by the crash. However, there was plenty of good money in the country, and it was not long until the county had well recovered.

In January, 1859, there was $20,000 worth of slaves sold in Liberty in one day, the greater number belonging to the estates of John Capps

HISTORY OF CLAY COUNTY

and Joel Estes. Of the Capps negroes Sarah, aged 47, brought $447, Gincey, aged 28, and her children aged three years and fourteen months, $1,200; George, aged 22, $1,265; Howard, aged 19, $1,280. Of the Estes negroes, Margaret, aged 17, sold for $1,025; Mack, aged 9, $601; Carmy, 15 (unsound), $600.

Some time in June, 1859, a meeting was held in Liberty, in aid of a railroad " from Kansas City to the North Missouri, at some point in Randolph county." The road then contemplated was to pursue substantially the route over which now runs the Kansas City branch of the Wabash, St. Louis & Pacific, from Moberly, in Randolph county, to Kansas City. A large meeting in favor of a road on this line was held at Richmond in July.

Prof. Oliver H. Cunningham, the well known teacher, whose schools in Liberty from 1844 to about 1858 were attended by so many Clay county people, died in Richmond, in the spring of 1859.

BUILDING OF THE PRESENT COURT-HOUSE.

May 19, 1857, the county court decided to build the present courthouse, on the site of the old building, and appropriated $35,000 therefor. The plan was furnished by Peter McDuff, of Weston, who was appointed commissioner and paid $6 per day.

The contractors were Crump & Thompson, and the building was finally completed and accepted November 9, 1859, but it had been occupied by the courts and clerks for some time previously. The jail had also been used for the confinement of prisoners. The total cost of the building was about $41,000.

Aside from the holding of courts the first public use to which the circuit court room was put was when, in the spring of 1860, Prof. T. S. Rarey, the renowned horse-tamer, was allowed to use it for a series of lectures.

THE KANSAS CITY AND CAMERON RAILROAD.

Upon the completion of the Hannibal and St. Joseph railroad, in February, 1859 — and even before — a project had been on foot to build a branch of that road from Cameron to Kansas City *via* Liberty. The new town of Cameron had been laid out by E. M. Samuel and other Liberty men, who were interested in its prosperity almost to the extent that they were in their home town, and the enterprise was pushed vigorously.

In the early summer of 1860 the county was thoroughly canvassed on the question of the county court's making a subscription of $200,-

000 to the proposed branch road. The sense of the people was to be ascertained at a special election held June 11. The towns of Missouri City and Smithville opposed the subscription, but the vote was largely in its favor, as follows :—

Townships.								For.	Against.
Liberty	.	.	.	.	.	.	.	595	43
Gallatin	.	.	.	.	.	.	.	286	46
Fishing River	.	.	.	.	.	.		62	400
Washington	.	.	.	.	.	.	.	232	67
Platte	.	.	.	.	.	.	.	25	282
Total	.	.	.	.	.	.	.	1,200	832

The county court duly made the subscription, and a month or two later (in August) an additional appropriation of $25,000. Private subscriptions were also obtained to the amount of nearly $25,000 more.

In August the contract was let for the building of the road to J. A. Quealey, of Hannibal, for $300,000. This included the grading, bridging, tieing and laying down the iron. The leading officers of the Kansas City and Cameron road at this time were Dr. G. M. B. Maughas, president; S. W. Bouton, secretary, and E. M. Samuel, treasurer.

THE PRESIDENTIAL CAMPAIGN OF 1860.

In very many respects the Presidential campaign of 1860 was the most remarkable, not only in the history of Clay county, but of the United States. Its character was affected not only by preceding but succeeding events. Among the former were the excited and exciting debates in Congress over the repeal of the Missouri Compromise and the Kansas-Nebraska controversy; the passage by the Legislatures of various Northern States of the "personal liberty bills," which rendered inoperative in those States the fugitive slave law; the John Brown raid on Harper's Ferry, West Virginia, in the fall of 1859, and various inflammatory speeches of prominent leaders of the Republican and Democratic parties in the North and in the South.

There was the greatest excitement throughout the country, and when it was in full tide the Presidential canvass opened. The slavery question was the all-absorbing one among the people. The Republican party, while it had not received a single vote in Clay county, had carried a large majority of the Northern States in the canvass of 1856, and every year since had received large accessions to its ranks, and under the circumstances, there being great dissensions in the Democratic party, prognosticating a split, bade fair to elect its candidates. The Democratic Convention at Charleston, South Carolina, April 23, after a stormy and inharmonious session of some days, divided, and the result was the nomination of two sets of candidates — Stephen A. Douglas and Herschel V. Johnson for President and Vice-President, by the " regulars," and John C. Breckinridge and Joseph Lane by the Southern or States rights wing of the party.

The " Constitutional Union " party, made up of old Whigs, Know Nothings, and some conservative men of all parties, nominated John Bell, of Tennessee, and Edward Everett, of Massachusetts, on a platform composed of a single line — " The Union, the constitution and the enforcement of the laws."

The Republican party was the last to bring out its candidates. It presented Abraham Lincoln and Hannibal Hamlin, on a platform declaring, among other things, that each State had the absolute right to control and manage its own domestic institutions; denying that the constitution, of its own force, carried slavery into the territories whose normal condition was said to be that of freedom. Epitomized, the platform meant hostility toward the *extension* of slavery, non-interference where it really existed.

It was to be expected that Missouri, being the only border Slave State lying contiguous to the territories of Kansas and Nebraska, should be deeply concerned in the settlement of the slavery question. Her people or their ancestors were very largely from Kentucky, Tennessee, Virginia and other slaveholding States, and many of them owned slaves or were otherwise interested in the preservation of slavery, to which institution the success of the Republican party, it was believed, would be destructive. There were many of this class in Clay county. There was not only a selfish motive for the friendliness toward the " peculiar institution," but a sentimental one. It was thought that it would be unmanly to yield to Northern sentiment of a threatening shape or coercive character. If slavery was wrong (which was denied) it must not be assailed at the dictations of Northern Abolitionists.

The canvass in the State was very spirited. The division in the Democratic party extended into Missouri. The Democratic State convention nominated Claiborne F. Jackson, of Saline county, for Governor. The Bell and Everett party nominated at first Robert Wilson, of Andrew, and, on his withdrawal, Hon. Sample Orr, of

HISTORY OF CLAY COUNTY

Greene county. Judge Orr was selected in the room of Mr. Wilson by the central committee.

Very soon the politicians began a series of maneuvers designed to develop Jackson's views on the main question before the country, and especially as to which of the two Democratic presidential candidates he favored. For a long time the wily Saline county statesman succeeded in evading the question and defining his position; but at last the Missouri *Republican* and other Douglas organs "smoked him out." He announced in a well written communication that he was for Douglas, because he believed him to be the regular and fairly chosen nominee of the party; but at the same time he announced himself in favor of many of the principles of the Breckinridge party. He was called by some who disliked him "a Douglas man with Breckinridge tendencies," "a squatter sovereign on an anti-squatter sovereignty platform," etc.

When Jackson's letter appeared soon thereafter the Breckinridge men called a State convention and put in nomination Hancock Jackson, of Howard, for Governor, and Monroe M. Parsons, of Cole, for Lieutenant-Governor.

Being encouraged by the feuds in the Democratic party, the Bell and Everett men had high hopes of electing their gubernatorial candidate at the August election, and carrying the State for "Bell, of Tennessee," the ensuing November. To this end they did everything possible to foment additional discord and widen the breach between the two wings of their opponents; but they overdid the business. The Democrats saw through their tactics, and agreeing to disagree as to presidential candidates, practically united in the support of Jackson and Reynolds at the August election, and triumphantly elected them by a plurality of about 10,000. The vote stood: C. F. Jackson, Douglas Democrat, 74,446; Sample Orr, Bell and Everett, 64,583; Hancock Jackson, Breckinridge Democrat, 11,415; J. B. Gardenhire, Republican, 6,135.

In Clay county at the August election the vote was as follows: —

Governor — Sample Orr, 943; C. F. Jackson, 586; Hancock Jackson, 134.

Congress — John Scott, "Union," 977; E. H. Norton, Democrat, 710.

Legislature — L. W. Burris, "Union," 887; J. C. Garner, "Union," 29; A. Harsell, "Union," 199; J. S. Huston, Democrat, 540; G. W. Withers, Democrat, 88.

Sheriff — R. A. Neeley, "Union," 1,640; no opposition.

Norton was elected to Congress by a majority of 5,000.

186

PRESIDENTIAL ELECTION.

Nothing daunted by their defeat in August, the Bell and Everett men in Missouri kept up the fight for their Presidential candidates, and came within a few hundred votes of carrying the State for them in November, the vote standing : —

For the Douglas electors, 58,801 ; for the Bell electors, 58,372 ; for the Breckinridge electors, 31,317 ; for the Lincoln electors, 17,028. Douglas' majority over Bell 429, over Breckinridge, 27,484.

It is said that many Democrats voted for Bell because they thought he was the only candidate that could beat Lincoln. In the October elections the Republicans had carried Pennsylvania, Ohio and Indiana, and Lincoln's election was almost inevitable. Fusion tickets against the Republicans had been formed in New York, New Jersey, and other States, and many thought the Tennessee statesman might be elected after all.

Following was the vote in Clay at the Presidential election, 1860: Bell, 1,036 ; Douglas, 524 ; Breckinridge, 304 ; Lincoln, none. For circuit attorney D. C. Allen received 782 ; Samuel Hardwick, 662 ; John W. Otey, 212 ; A. C. Ellis, 20. Mr. Allen was elected.

During the campaign, October 22, there was a large meeting of all parties at Liberty. Gen. David R. Atchison, Senator James S. Green and Col. Samuel Churchill spoke for Breckinridge ; Messrs. Hovey and J. H. Moss for Bell, and Col. Jones for Douglas. A day or two later Hon. Henry Clay Dean, of Iowa, spoke for Douglas.

AFTER THE ELECTION OF LINCOLN.

The news of the election of Lincoln and Hamlin was received by the people of Clay county generally with considerable dissatisfaction ; but, aside from the utterances of some ultra pro-slavery men, there were general expressions of a willingness to accept and abide by the result — at least to watch and wait. A number of citizens avowed themselves unconditional union men from the first — as they had every year since 1850, when they met in convention from time to time, and these were men who voted for Bell, and men who had voted for Douglas, and even men who had voted for Breckinridge. Upon the secession of South Carolina and other Southern States, however, many changed their views. Indeed, there was nothing certain about the sentiments of men in those days, but one thing — they were liable to change ! Secessionists one week became Union men the next, and *vice versa.* There was withal a universal hope that civil war might be averted.

Already the best men of the country feared for the fate of the republic. Northern fanatics and Southern fire-eaters were striving to rend it asunder. The former did not want to live in a country (so they said) whereof one-half depended on the begetting and bringing up of children for the slave market, and so the constitution which permitted slavery was denominated an instrument of infamy, and the flag of the stars and stripes was denounced as a flaunting lie. The fire-eaters of the South were blustering and complaining that their "rights" had been or were about to be trampled on by the North, and therefore they were for seceding and breaking up a government which they could not absolutely control.

A majority of the people of the county, it is safe to say, believed that the interests of Missouri were identical with those of the other slave-holding States, but they were in favor of waiting for the development of the policy of the new administration before taking any steps leading to the withdrawal of the State from the Federal Union. "Let us wait and see what Lincoln will do," was the sentiment and expression of a large number. A respectable minority were in favor of immediate secession, and so declared publicly.

"Missouri is a peninsula of slavery running out into a sea of freedom," said Gov. Bob Stewart, in 1861. It was bounded on three sides by Free States, and " Black Republican " States at that — Kansas, Iowa and Illinois. Should she secede and become a part of a foreign nation her condition, as suffering from Northern Abolitionists and slave liberators, would be aggravated. When one negro ran away while the State remained a part of the Union, ten might be expected to "skedaddle" if she seceded. Thus argued many Pro-Slavery men at the time.

The Liberty *Tribune* said that Lincoln had been fairly elected President, and that there was no ground whatever for secession. "Lincoln is powerless to do harm if he would," argued the *Tribune*, "since both houses of Congress and the Supreme Court are against him, and he can have no legal power to interfere against the institutions of the South. Let the Union men stand firm."

Always attached to the Union, editor Miller was especially zealous in its defense at this critical juncture. The *Tribune* of December 7 contained reflections and aspersions against the motives that actuated the Secessionists of the Cotton States. A leading editorial charged that the Secessionists were taking steps to lead their States into secession : —

Not because they feel their rights to be endangered by the election

HISTORY OF CLAY COUNTY

and consequent inauguration of Lincoln, but because of deep-seated and long-cherished hostility to the Government in which we live. They have long desired a dismemberment of the Union; their desire to secede existed long before the establishment of the Black Republican party. Their actions are not based on the apprehension of danger from Lincoln, but they urge prompt action at this time because they believe other States, incensed at the result of the late presidential election, are now prepared to go with them. If they were satisfied that a justifiable cause for disunion would be furnished by any act of Lincoln's administration, they would wait for its occurrence, because they know that then there would be no division in the South.

A financial crash was imminent in this State and throughout the West, owing to the disturbed and menacing condition of affairs, and a public meeting at Liberty, November 28, declared in favor of a suspension of specie payments on the part of the banks, especially of the State bank and its branches at Lexington, Paris and Liberty.

As time passed, the spirit of alarm diffused itself more and more among the people. At a public meeting at Liberty, December 24, Col. H. L. Routt and Hon. J. T. V. Thompson were the speakers. They bade their hearers to prepare for action, for there was no prophesying then what they might be called upon to do. Thirty men enrolled themselves as "minute men," and elected H. L. Routt, captain; L. L. Talbott, John C. Dunn and G. W. Morris, lieutenants, and A. Gillespie, orderly sergeant. There was considerable comment on this action, many deeming it untimely; others unwise, but there were many who approved it.

The close of the year 1860 found the county in a highly prosperous condition. Crops had been fairly abundant, money was reasonably plenty, the country was finely improved and teemed with wealth, good schools and churches were plenty, enterprises were opening on every hand, a new railroad had been begun and was certain of completion, and altogether it would have seemed that the temporal future of our people was of the highest promise.

But a fell spirit of distrust and malevolence toward that vast section of our common country called the North had found lodgment in the minds of many. Prophecies of evil were continually shouted in the ears of the unwary. Memories of injuries suffered at the hands of the anti-slaveryites were revived, and every Northern gale and every Southern breeze fanned into flame the fires of sectional hate which had for a time been smoldering. The clear sky was overcast with clouds, and they were dark and lowering.

189

CHAPTER VII.

HISTORY OF THE COUNTY DURING 1861.

The Legislature of 1861 — Election of Delegates to the State Convention — The Work of the Convention — After Fort Sumpter — Capture of the Liberty Arsenal — Maj. Grant's Reports — After the Arsenal's Seizure — Preparing for War in Earnest — Organization of Military Companies — Gen. Doniphan Declines a Military Appointment — Departure of the Secession Companies for the War — The First Federal Troops — Events of the Summer and Early Fall of 1861 — Proclamation of Gen. Stein — Rallying to His Standard — The Battle of Blue Mills — The Killed and Wounded — Reports of the Leaders — Col. Saunders, Hon. D. R. Atchison, Col. Scott — List of Killed and Wounded in the Third Iowa — War Incidents of the Fall and Winter of 1861 — The Neosho Secession Ordinance.

THE LEGISLATURE OF 1861.

On the last day of December, 1861, the Twenty-first General Assembly met at Jefferson City. The retiring Governor, Robt. M. Stewart, delivered a very conservative message, taking the middle ground between secession and abolition, and pleading strenuously for peace and moderation. He declared, among other propositions, that the people of Missouri "ought not to be frightened from their propriety by the past unfriendly legislation of the North, or dragooned into secession by the restrictive legislation of the extreme South." He concluded with a thrilling appeal for the maintenance of the Union, depicting the inevitable result of secession, revolution and war. Many of Gov. Stewart's predictions were afterwards fulfilled with startling and fearful exactness.

The inaugural of the new Governor, Claiborne Fox Jackson, indorsed the doctrine enunciated in his famous resolutions of 1849 — that the interests and destiny of the slaveholding States were the same; that the State was in favor of remaining in the Union so long as there was any hope of maintaining the guarantees of the constitution, but that in the event of a failure to reconcile the differences which then threatened the disruption of the Union, it would be the duty of Missouri "to stand by the South;" and that he was opposed to the doctrine of coercion in any event. Gov. Jackson concluded by recommending the immediate call of a State convention, in order that "the will of the people may be ascertained and effectuated."

In accordance with the Governor's recommendation, the Legislature, on January 17, passed a bill calling a convention, to be composed of three times as many members as in the aggregate each senatorial district was entitled to State Senators—that is, three delegates from each senatorial district in the State—and appointing February 18 as the day on which they were to be elected, and February 28 the day on which the convention should assemble. Hon. J. T. V. Thompson and Hon. Luke W. Burris, respectively the State Senator from this district and Representative from this county, voted for the convention bill. The tenth section of this bill contained the following important provision:—

No act, ordinance or resolution of said convention shall be deemed to be valid to change or dissolve the political relations of this State to the government of the United States, or any other State, until a majority of the qualified voters of this State, voting upon the question, shall ratify the same.

Mr. Thompson voted especially for this section, which was introduced in the Senate by Hon. Charles H. Hardin, then the Senator from the Boone and Callaway district, and afterward Governor of Missouri in 1874–76. Thus the secession of the State was made an impossibility without the consent of a majority of the voters, although Hardin's amendment was adopted by the close vote of 17 to 15. After a much disturbed and very turbulent session the Legislature adjourned March 28.

ELECTION OF DELEGATES TO THE STATE CONVENTION.

The Thirteenth Senatorial District was composed of the counties of Clay and Platte. On the 28th of January the Unconditional Union men of Clay met in convention at Liberty. with Dr. W. A. Morton chairman. Resolutions favoring the Crittenden compromise and opposing coercion were unanimously adopted and Col. A. W. Doniphan and James H. Moss, of Clay, and Elijah H. Norton, of Platte, nominated for delegates to the State convention.

February 1 a "Southern Rights" meeting was held at Liberty. John R. Killer presided. Col. H. L. Routt spoke and was replied to by James H. Moss. Resolutions looking to secession in certain contingencies were introduced, and though the chairman declared them adopted, it was the general expression that they had been rejected by the meeting, a majority of whose members were Union men who, under the leadership of Mr. Moss, had come in and "captured" it.

Delegates from Clay and Platte met at Barry February 7, and regularly nominated, though not without dissent, Messrs. Doniphan, Moss and Norton. Certain "Southern Rights" candidates were announced independently.

On election day, February 18, there was much interest manifested in this county. At Missouri City even the ladies were interested. They assembled in a public meeting, indorsed the Crittenden compromise, declared for the Union and then, carrying the old flag, with 34 stars and 13 stripes, marched in procession to the polls and urged and entreated the voters to cast their ballots for the Union candidates, Doniphan, Moss and Norton, and assist in preventing civil war with all its enormities and horrors. Never before had the ladies of Clay county abandoned their domestic duties to engage even indirectly in politics, and their action on this occasion indicates what must have been the prevalent feeling among our people.

The election in this district resulted in an overwhelming majority for the Union candidates, as follows : —

Candidates.						Clay.	Platte.
A. W. Doniphan, Union	.	.	.	.	.	1,578	2,275
James H. Moss "	.	.	.	.	.	1,468	1,928
Elijah H. Norton "	.	.	.	.	.	1,480	1,891
J. F. Farbis, Secession	.	.	.	.	.	166	503
Kemp M. Woods "	.	.	.	.	.	66	134

The selection of Doniphan, Moss and Norton by a vote of nearly ten to one againt the Secession candidates, clearly and unmistakably shows that a large majority of the people of Clay and Platte were for the Union in the winter of 1861 — at least were opposed to secession at that time. But it is just as true, although not shown by official records, that they were strenuously opposed to coercion. There must be no war. It was folly and unwise for the Cotton States to secede, but there must be no attempt on the part of the General Government to bring them back into the Union by force of arms. In such an event, many openly declared, " we will stand by our Southern brethren."

THE WORK OF THE CONVENTION.

The convention assembled at Jefferson City, February 28, 1861. Sterling Price, of Chariton county, afterward the distinguished Confederate general, was chosen president. On the second day it adjourned to meet at St. Louis, where it re-convened March 4, continued in session until the 22d, when it adjourned to meet on the third Monday in December, subject, however, to a call of a majority of a committee of seven. Before adjourning, a series of resolutions was adopted, two of which were of superior importance, and here proper to be noted: 1. Containing the explicit declaration that there was no adequate cause to impel Missouri to dissolve her connection with the Federal union.   2. Taking unmistakable ground against the employment of military force by the Federal government to coerce the seceding States, or the employment of military force by the seceding States, to assail the government of the United States.

Mr. John F. Redd, of Marion, and Mr. Harrison Hough, of Mississippi, presented a minority report, declaring the Abolitionists of the North responsible for the then condition of affairs and favoring the holding of a convention by the non-seceding Slave States at Nashville, Tennessee, for the adoption of a plan of settlement of the existing difficulties on the basis of the Crittenden compromise.

The resolutions from the committee on Federal Relations being under consideration, Mr. Moss, of Clay, moved to amend the fifth of the majority (Gamble) series by adding the following: —

And further, Believing that the fate of Missouri depends upon a peaceable adjustment of our present difficulties, she will never countenance or aid a seceding State in making war on the General Government, nor will she furnish men or money for the purpose of aiding the General Government in any attempt to coerce a seceding State.

The Moss amendment was under discussion in the convention for several days, during which period several speeches were made upon it by the ablest and most prominent members.   Mr. Moss himself delivered an able argument in its favor, at the same time avowing himself an unconditional Union man, opposed to fanatical Abolitionists and coercionists alike; declaring that he verily believed a majority of the people of the seceded States were really Union men, but that a " reign of terror " existed among them, stifling their voices and awing them into submission.[1]   Following was the conclusion of his speech:—

In conclusion, I only desire to state that I hail from a county where Lincoln did not get a vote, and where the Secessionists got only less than two hundred.   My constituents are Union men, and they indorse my position, and they believe that all Missouri has is staked on the die — that she must have a peaceable settlement.   They do not want to go out of the Union, but they ask that their honor shall be safe in your hands.   We occupy the middle ground, and we can extend to both sections a friendly hand, and say we want peace, and our salvation depends upon it.

---

[1] See Journal of Proceedings of State Convention, first session, 1861, p. 75.   For the entire speech, p. 68 to 75.

HISTORY OF CLAY COUNTY

On the fourteenth day of the convention Mr. Moss' amendment was voted down by the following vote : —

Ayes — Eli E. Bass, of Boone ; Geo. Y. Bast, of Montgomery ; R. A. Brown, of Cass ; J. R. Chenault, of Jasper ; Samuel C. Collier, of Madison ; A. Comingo, of Jackson ; R. W. Crawford, of Lawrence ; R. W. Donnell, of Buchanan ; Geo. W. Dunn, of Ray ; R. B. Frayser, of St. Charles ; Joseph Flood, of Callaway ; N. F. Givens, of Clark ; H. M. Gorin, of Scotland ; A. S. Harbin, of Barry ; R. A. Hatcher, of New Madrid ; V. B. Hill, of Pulaski ; W. J. Howell, of Monroe ; Prince L. Hudgins, of Andrew ; J. Proctor Knott, of Cole ; J. T. Matson, of Ralls ; J. H. Moss, of Clay ; E. H. Norton, of Platte ; R. D. Ray, of Carroll ; J. T. Redd, of Marion ; S. L. Sawyer, of Lafayette ; E. K. Sayre, of Lewis ; J. K. Sheeley, of Jackson ; J. G. Waller, of Warren ; N. W. Watkins, Cape Girardeau ; Warren Woodson, of Boone — 30.

Noes — J. S. Allen, of Harrison ; Orson Bartlett, of Stoddard ; J. H. Birch, of Clinton ; Joseph Bogy, of St. Genevieve ; S. M. Breckinridge, of St. Louis ; J. O. Broadhead, of St. Louis ; H. E. Bridge, of St. Louis ; Isidor Bush, of St. Louis ; Robert Calhoun, of Callaway ; M. P. Cayce, of St. Francois : Wm. Douglass, of Cooper ; Charles Drake, of Moniteau ; John D. Foster, of Adair ; H. R. Gamble, of St. Louis ; T. T. Gantt, of St. Louis ; J. J. Gravelly, of Cedar ; Willard P. Hall, of Buchanan ; Wm. A. Hall, of Randolph ; John B. Henderson, of Pike ; Littleberry Hendrick, of Greene ; Henry Hitchcock, of St. Louis ; Robert Holmes, of St. Louis ; John Holt, of Dent ; Harrison Hough, of Mississippi ; John How, of St. Louis ; J. M. Irwin, of Shelby ; Z. Isbell, of Osage ; Wm. Jackson, of Putnam ; R. W. Jamison, of Webster ; J. W. Johnson, of Polk ; C. G. Kidd, of Henry ; W. T. Leeper, of Wayne ; M. L. L. Linton, of St. Louis ; John F. Long, of St. Louis ; Vincent Marmaduke, of Saline ; A. C. Marvin, of Henry ; J. W. McClurg, of Camden ; J. R. McCormack, of Perry ; Nelson McDowell, of Dade ; James McFerran, of Daviess ; Ferd. Myer, of St. Louis : W. L. Morrow, of Dallas ; J. C. Noell, of Bollinger ; Sample Orr, of Greene ; John F. Phillips, of Pettis ; Wm. G. Pomeroy, of Crawford ; C. G. Rankin, of Jefferson ; M. H. Ritchey, of Newton ; Fred. Rowland, of Macon ; Thos. Scott, of Miller ; Thos. Shackelford, of Howard ; J. H. Shackelford, of St. Louis ; Jacob Smith, of Linn ; Sol. Smith, of St. Louis ; J. T. Tindall, of Grundy ; W. W. Turner, of Laclede ; A. M. Woolfolk, of Livingston ; Uriel Wright, of St. Louis ; Ellzey Van Buskirk, of Holt ; G. W. Zimmerman, of Lincoln, and the President, Sterling Price, of Chariton — 61.

Absent — A. W. Doniphan, of Clay ; C. D. Eitzen, of Gasconade ; A. W. Maupin, of Franklin ; J. P. Ross, of Morgan ; Robt. M. Stewart, of Buchanan ; Aikman Welch, of Johnson ; Robt. Wilson, of Buchanan.

Sick — Philip Pipkin, of Iron.

HISTORY OF CLAY COUNTY

The convention adjourned March 22, to meet the third Monday in the following December, but was called together October 10, 1861. Messrs. Moss and Doniphan attended subsequent sessions, and voted with the other conservative members against the test oaths. Doniphan voted for the emancipation ordinance, adopted July 1, 1863, providing for the abolition of slavery in the State July 4, 1870. This ordinance was adopted by a vote of 51 to 30, but its provisions were rendered of no force by the adoption of the thirteenth amendment.

AFTER FORT SUMPTER.

The firing on Fort Sumpter by the Confederates, April 12, 1861; the proclamation of President Lincoln calling for 75,000 volunteers; Gov. Jackson's indignant refusal to respond to the requisition on Missouri; the excitement throughout the South; the uprising in the North, these are incidents in the history of the country, the particulars of which need not be set forth in these pages.

The reception of the news of the firing on Sumpter caused the most intense excitement in Clay county. Cheers for South Carolina and Gen. Beauregard rang out, and secession flags fluttered in the breezes at Liberty and Smithville. When Lincoln's proclamation was heard of, a great storm of indignation swept over the county, bearing down all but the staunchest Union men. Many who had opposed secession up till now, changed their views suddenly, denounced the administration, and avowed themselves " on the side of the South." The " submissionists," as the unconditional Union men were termed, were few and undemonstrative; the Secessionists were numerous and noisy.

CAPTURE OF THE LIBERTY ARSENAL.

The Missouri border was ablaze. In Clay county a long meditated act — an act forming an incident of a grand scheme — was accomplished, highly important in its results to the Secession cause. This was the capture of what was generally known as the Liberty arsenal, although it was really four miles from Liberty, and was called by the U. S. authorities the Missouri *Depot*. It is altogether probable — though the evidence can not be had, owing to the reluctance of certain parties to give it in such clear terms as is desirable — that a plan had been organized by leading Secessionists of the State, Gov. Jackson among the number, to seize not only Liberty arsenal, but the St. Louis arsenal, and even Ft. Leavenworth.

There is evidence, and the statement has been published, that while these captures or seizures were not to be made by the authority of

Gov. Jackson, yet they received his personal sanction and approval, and that of other prominent gentlemen of Secession proclivities in the State, as M. Jeff Thompson, John W. Reid, James S. Rains, S. H. Woodson and certain St. Louisans. Col. Peckham, of St. Louis, states that Col. Marmaduke (now Governor) was sent to Ft. Leavenworth and that the sum of $25,000, of which $5,000 was drawn from the bank at Arrow Rock, was placed at his disposal for the purpose of bribing Maj. Hagner, the officer in command, to surrender the post when called upon by an invading force from Missouri.[1] A letter written by the compiler of this volume to Gov. Marmaduke, and asking for an affirmation or denial of this statement of Peckham's, received no answer.

Saturday morning, April 20, as Maj. Nathaniel Grant, in charge of the arsenal, was at breakfast, a negro boy entered hastily and handed him a note. The note was not signed, but was written by a Union man, then living near the landing and read substantially as follows : —

A company of men from across the river camped in the bottom last night. I understand that another company is at or near Liberty, and that the destination of both is the arsenal. *Look out.* If you want to make a speech, get it ready.

A few minutes later about 200 armed and mounted Secessionists rode up to the arsenal gate, forced admission and demanded of Grant the surrender of the post and its contents. There was but little need of this demand, since the post was already in their possession. No thought of resistance was entertained at any time, for the force at the arsenal consisted of Maj. Grant and two employes, Armorer Giros and Wm. L. Madden. Had the note of warning come earlier it would have made no difference in this respect. Grant contented himself by protesting vigorously against the seizure, and this was allowed him with great good humor, and amid laughter and raillery,

The force that captured and seized the arsenal was about 200 Secessionists, composed of one company from Jackson county commanded by Capt. McMurray, of Independence, and a strong company from Liberty and Clay county under Col. Henry L. Routt, the whole under command of Col. Routt. The Jackson county company had crossed the river the previous evening. No authority was presented by Routt implicating Gov. Jackson or any other officials, but he significantly stated that he knew what he was about. Asked if he didn't fear that the Governor would order the arms returned, he replied, "*Never!*"

---

[1] Lyon and Missouri, p. 112.

The Secessionists held possession of the arsenal for a week, until all the stores and munitions had been removed. The Jackson county men took away some cannon, muskets, etc., with them and sent back for more. Lieut. J. W. Gillespie was guarding the stores that had not been removed and refused to give any portion of them up. Whereupon a fight over the spoils was imminent, and only prevented by a concession on the part of Lieut. Gillespie, who gave the delegation from Cracker's Neck half of what they demanded.

The property taken consisted of three six-pounder brass cannon, each weighing 882 pounds, mounted on field carriages; 12 six-pounder iron guns, unmounted; one three-pounder iron gun; five caissons, two battery wagons, two forges, besides all the ordinary artillery equipments and accompaniments, and several hundred rounds of artillery ammunition, chiefly solid shot and canister; 1,180 percussion muskets, complete; 243 percussion rifles, 121 rifle carbines, 923 percussion pistols, 419 cavalry sabers, 39 artillery swords, 20 cavalry and artillery musketoons, 1,000 pounds cannon powder, 9,900 pounds of musket powder, 1,800 of rifle powder, about 400,000 cartridges, besides accouterments and equipments for all small arms in great number, and in excess of the arms taken.

By far the greatest portion of the arms and munitions were taken possession of and hauled in wagons, provided for the purpose, to Liberty. Here they were distributed to the "minute men" of Clay and surrounding counties. Col. Routt's ice-house was converted into an armory, and here the military companies repaired from time to time and received their guns and other munitions of war, which in time did effective service against the Government to which they belonged. The powder in barrels amounted to thousands of pounds,[1] was hidden away in different portions of the country — in hay stacks, hollow logs, and elsewhere, and long after much of it gave its custodians no end of uneasiness, anxiety and trouble, for fear of its discovery by the Federal soldiery.

The day following Maj. Grant sent this report of the capture of the arsenal to the chief of ordnance at Washington:—

MISSOURI DEPOT, Sunday, April 21, 1861.

SIR — I embrace the first opportunity to inform you that the depot was taken yesterday, about 10 o'clock, by a body of armed men from this and the adjacent counties. While I am writing the depot yard

---

[1] In February, 1862, ten of these barrels were returned by D. S. Miller, who found them hidden in his straw stack.

and grounds are filled with men, who are rapidly moving the ordnance and ordnance stores from the post. Having no means of resistance, my protest against the forcible and unlawful seizure of the public property was of no avail, and I was informed that all the military stores would be taken. I send this to Saint Louis by boat to be mailed, and so soon as it can be done a detailed report of all the facts, so far as they can be ascertained, will be forwarded. Very respectfully, I am, sir, your obedient servant.

NATHANIEL GRANT,
In charge of Depot.

Col. H. K. Craig,
Chief of Ordnance, Washington City.

The following dispatch was sent from East St. Louis to the Secretary of War: —

East St. Louis, Ill., April 21, 1861.
Hon. Simon Cameron, Secretary of War:
Liberty Arsenal, in Missouri, was taken possession of by Secessionists yesterday, and 1,500 arms and a few cannons distributed to citizens of Clay county. The Missouri river is blockaded at Independence. All quiet here at present.

BENJAMIN FARRAR.

Two days later Maj. Grant made the following detailed report of the seizure: —

DETAILED REPORT OF MAJ. GRANT.

Missouri Depot, April 27th, 1861.
Col. H. K. Craig, Chief of Ordnance, Washington, D. C.:
Sir — On the 21st inst. I informed you — by letter sent to St. Louis by boat to be mailed — that this depot had been seized by armed men from this and adjoining counties, and that the arms, ammunition, etc., were being rapidly removed. The only reason assigned for this act was that the property was considered essential to the safety of the frontier; and they *assumed* that the State would eventually become responsible for it to the General Government, and they to the State. Having no force to repel them, nor to prevent the removal of the stores, I was compelled to submit.

The post was evacuated by the insurgents to-day, and during the period of their possession they removed all the cannon, gun carriages, caissons, battery wagons, forges, arms, accounterments, implements, ammunition and part of the tools, etc., from the depot. The post was occupied by a force varying from 100 to 200 men during the first three days, and was then left under a guard of about 20 men to remove the balance of the stores.

The Union feeling had been so strong in Missouri, and particularly in this county, that I had no apprehension that the post would be disturbed; but it appears that the late telegraphic dispatches from other States produced much excitement among the people, and meetings have been held and Secession flags raised in almost every town during the past week — this state of things being inaugurated by the seizure of the depot.

I understand, however, that this feeling is by no means universal, and that a majority of the citizens here disapprove the seizure of the public property; but this feeling of disapproval, being simply negative in its character, is powerless to prevent the violent measures advocated by those holding extreme political views, and the Conservatives, or Union men, who have done their utmost to preserve the peace and the Union, begin to despair, and are of the opinion that the State is fast drifting into the current of secession.

The exact condition of the property at the depot can not be accurately reported until I can make an inventory of the stores not taken, and this will be done with as little delay as possible. The forcible seizure of the public property in my charge leaves me at a loss how to proceed in the absence of special instructions.

I learn that the property has been distributed through several of the border counties.

I am, sir, very respectfully, your obt. servt.,

NATHL. GRANT,
In charge of Depot.

AFTER THE ARSENAL'S SEIZURE.

News of the capture of the arsenal was telegraphed to the outer world the same day, and created considerable sensation throughout the country, North, South, East, and West. It was *the first overt act of citizens of Missouri against the Federal government.* Lincoln heard of it and telegraphed to Leavenworth for an explanation. Harney heard of it at St. Louis and refused to believe it, but Lyon and Sweeney at the St. Louis Arsenal doubled their guards, planted two cannon at the gate, and sat up all night to watch the movements of a large crowd of Secessionists at the Berthold mansion, who were dispersed at a late hour by Mayor Daniel Taylor.

Among those who believed in secession the tidings were received with great joy and exultation. Clay county was cheered heartily; the act itself was applauded, and Routt and his men were the heroes of the hour. There can be no question that the capture or seizure was of inestimable advantage to the Secession cause, and so far was a success. In this county it decided, or helped to decide, the course of hundreds of men in twenty-four hours!

Monday following the seizure a large and enthusiastic Secession meeting was held at the court-house. Circuit court was in session, Judge Dunn on the bench. Eloquent and impassioned speeches were delivered by S. H. Woodson, Aaron H. Conrow, J. H. Adams, John T. Hughes, Dr. Maughas, G. S. Withers, J. C. C. Thornton, J. E. Pitt and J. W. Gillespie, of Clay, Jackson, Ray, Platte, and Buchanan counties. A fine Secession flag was raised amid the firing of the captured cannon and the cheers of the multitude, men and women.

Resolutions were adopted condemning President Lincoln for the call for troops, and indorsing Gov. Jackson for his "noble reply:" declaring that the State Convention did not represent the will of the people when it said that Missouri would remain in the Union, even if the Crittenden compromise was refused; favoring a new convention, and resolving —

That in the event there should be a new convention ordered, we pledge ourselves to support no man for delegate for said convention who will not aver himself a Southern Rights man, and that we will use all honorable means for the immediate secession of Missouri.

The stream of secession had swollen from insignificance to a mighty and almost resistless torrent, and was bearing down upon its current hundreds who had aforetime declared that, in the language of Henry Clay, the time could "*never, never,*" come for secession and disunion. Two months before the vote was ten to one against secession; now, if an expression could be had the vote would be largely in its favor. So much had old gray-haired Edmond Ruffin done for Clay county when he pulled the lanyard that sent the first shot against Sumpter.

But many of the conservative Union men were not demoralized or dismayed, by what had occurred elsewhere, and what had occurred in their midst. The next day after the Secession meeting they assembled at the court-house and held a meeting of their own. Dr. W. A. Morton was chairman. Col. Doniphan and James H. Moss addressed the audience in speeches full of fervor and feeling, pleading still for the Union, and crying peace, "when there was no peace." Doniphan said he could not take part in the war. He would not fight against the flag under which he fought and conquered in the war with Mexico, and he would not draw his sword against his neighbors, his kinsmen, and his friends in the South. The sentiment of the meeting was alike opposed to secession and coercion.

The proceedings of this meeting were marked with befitting gravity and deliberation. Resolutions were passed declaring that "secession is a remedy for no evil," approving Jackson's reply to Lincoln, and asserting that "the true policy of Missouri *at present* is to maintain an independent position within the Union, holding her soil and institutions against invasion or hostile interference from any quarter."

PREPARING FOR WAR IN EARNEST — ORGANIZATION OF MILITARY COMPANIES.

And now in the season of spring, when the winter was over and gone, and the time of the singing of birds and the blooming of flowers had come, there was the note of preparation for bloody and deadly conflict heard in our county of Clay, and the fancy of the young men did not turn to thoughts of love. There was mustering and there was forming and the setting of squadrons in the field. Military companies were organized everywhere throughout the county.

In Liberty the first company was organized. This, as distinctly announced, was for " home protection," and was called the " Liberty Home Guards." The members were to defend the town against everything hostile, but to assail nothing. It was composed largely of Union men. Capt. O. P. Moss, an unconditional Union man, and the veteran commander of the Clay county company in the Mexican War was elected captain; James H. Moss, Wm. G. Garth, and John Dunn, lieutenants, and Larkin Bradford, orderly sergeant. The Liberty Home Guards numbered 107 men, and the company was organized April 24.

But other companies were organized whose objects were not so pacific. A company at Liberty called the " Mounted Rangers," was formed contemporaneously with the Home Guards. Its members were " Southern Rights" men. H. L. Routt, like Moss, a Mexican War veteran, was captain, and L. S. Talbott, George W. Morris and J. W. Gillespie, the lieutenants. The men were well armed with the arsenal arms.

A cavalry company at Smithville was composed of 120 men, well mounted and armed. Theodore Duncan was captain, P. M. Savery, Wm. Davenport, J. E. Brooks, lieutenants, and J. W. Duncan, orderly sergeant.

In Gallatin township an infantry company of 80 men was officered by G. W. Crowley, captain, Amos Stout and R. H. Stout, lieutenants, and John Neal, orderly sergeant.

May 1, the " Washington Guards," 43 men, were organized at Greenville. L. M. Lewis, captain; G. W. Mothershead, M. D. Scruggs, Richard Laffoon, lieutenants; John A. Perry, orderly.

HISTORY OF CLAY COUNTY

At Gilead, on the 11th of May, a company for "home defense" was organized at a public meeting, of which Anthony Harsell was chairman. The officers were O. H. Harris, captain; W. W. Smith and Samuel Henderson, lieutenants, and Tapp Soper, orderly.

Some of these companies were afterwards broken up, and reorganized; others changed their officers, but nearly all of the members did more or less service for the Confederate cause, at one period or another, during the war.

About the 1st of May, Col. M. Jeff. Thompson, of St. Joseph, military inspector for this district under Gov. Jackson, came to Liberty, clad in full military uniform, with sword, sash, epaulets, etc., to look after the company organizations in this quarter. He made a speech at the court-house in which he said that in capturing the Liberty arsenal the Clay county men, though meaning well, had "acted the fool," as they had prevented the capture of the larger and more important arsenal at St. Louis! News of the seizure here, he said, had been telegraphed to St. Louis in time to put Gen. Lyon on his guard.

Upon the news of the capture of Camp Jackson the Missouri Legislature hastily passed the famous "military bill" and adjourned. Gov. Jackson ordered several companies of the Missouri State Guard to assemble at the capital for its defense, and on the 20th of May, Capt. Routt's company of "Mounted Rangers" and Capt. Theo. Duncan's Smithville cavalry company left the county, pursuant to orders, for Jefferson City. Before leaving Liberty, Capt. Routt's company was presented with a beautiful Missouri flag by a number of ladies, Miss Minnie Withers making the presentation.

Notwithstanding what had already occurred, and the fact that preparations for war were still making everywhere, many yet strove for peace. Numbers of citizens protested against the enrollment of companies openly and boldly, and Capt. O. P. Moss declared that Col. Routt had no more right to capture the Liberty arsenal, with its government arms and munitions, than John Brown had to seize the arsenal at Harper's Ferry. The *Tribune* still opposed secession and war, and denounced the "military bill" in unstinted terms.

GEN. DONIPHAN DECLINES A MILITARY APPOINTMENT.

Under the provisions of the "military bill" the State of Missouri was divided into military districts. Clay county was in the fifth district, composed of the counties of Atchison, Nodaway, Holt, Andrew, Buchanan, Platte and Clay. Gov. Jackson tendered the appointment

HISTORY OF CLAY COUNTY

of brigadier-general of this district to Col. A. W. Doniphan, of Clay, but he refused it, saying that he did not desire the honors of a brigadier at that time, as he had held that rank at the age of 29, and besides he had learned that Gens. Harney and Price had made a "treaty" by the terms of which peace was to be secured to the State anyhow.[1] Governor Jackson then appointed Gen. A. E. Stein, an ex-lieutenant of the regular army, to the command.

DEPARTURE OF THE SECESSION COMPANIES FOR THE WAR.

Pursuant to the Harney-Price agreement Gov. Jackson ordered the companies of the State Guards to return to their respective counties from Jefferson. But May 31st Gen. Nathaniel Lyon succeeded Gen. Harney in command of the U. S. forces at St. Louis, and on the 11th of June, in an interview with Gen. Price and Gov. Jackson, he kicked over the agreement, and gave the Governor and his general two hours to leave St. Louis. Jackson and Price left for Jefferson City on a special train, burned the Osage river bridge behind them and cut the telegraph wires, and the next day the Governor issued a proclamation calling into the field 50,000 State militia " for the purpose of repelling invasion and for the protection of the lives, liberty and property of the citizens of this State."

The Clay county companies had returned to their homes within a few days after their departure, but on the receipt of Jackson's re-call, Routt's, Duncan's and Mothershead's companies sprang into their saddles, and on the 13th departed for Independence, all well armed and well mounted, to assist the State Guards in driving out the Federal forces which had come to Kansas City under Capts. Sturgis and Prince. The same day occurred the skirmish at Rock Spring, in Jackson county, between the Missourians under Col. Halloway and the Federals under Lieut. D. S. Stanley, and in which Halloway was killed.

Sunday evening, June 16, while in camp on the Blue, Capt. Theo. Duncan was shot by a member of another Secession company, who some aver was a half-insane man. A few days later the Smithville company returned home, owing to the wounding of their captain, and to a misunderstanding and disagreement. Capt. Duncan died from his wound June 27, and was buried at Liberty, the first victim of the Civil War from Clay county. He had served in Moss' company in

---

[1] See " Proceedings of the Rebel Legislature," published by authority of the Twenty-Third General Assembly.

the Mexican War, and was not only a brave soldier, but a worthy citizen. The man who shot Duncan was killed the next day by some of the Clay county men.

A short time after the skirmish at Rock Spring the State Guards, Secession forces, were ordered to Lexington to perfect their organization. Lexington was in Gen. J. S. Rains' district, but hither many companies repaired from the north side of the river. In Clay Capt. Thos. McCarty organized a company of infantry, with A. J. Calhoun, J. C. Vertrees and R. P. Evans as lieutenants, and J. C. Dunn orderly. This company started for Lexington June 17, and on its arrival went into camp. In a few days four other Clay county companies were at Lexington — Capt. Talbott's, Capt. Holt's, Capt. Mothershead's and Capt. Crowley's. Capt. Talbott succeeded H. L. Routt to the command of the "Mounted Rangers," Routt having been promoted to the rank of lieutenant-colonel.

THE FIRST FEDERAL TROOPS.

On the morning of June 19th Clay county was first invaded by the Federal troops. A company of regulars, commanded by Capt. W. E. Prince, came over from Kansas City to Liberty, taking the people somewhat by surprise and creating no little consternation. About 20 of the State Guards were in town, mainly at the hotels, and were speedily made prisoners, and their arms and horses taken from them. They were released by taking an oath not to serve against the United States during the war, and mainly upon the solicitations of Capt. O. P. Moss, known to be a sound Union man, Capt. Prince gave them back their horses and private arms.

The Federals remained in town only a few hours. After cutting down the Secession flag which for some weeks had been floating undisturbed, cheering for the Union, and "chaffing" the Secession people, they returned unmolested to Kansas City. A day or two previously Capt. Prince had sent over a spy, who on his return had fully apprised him of the situation. Some of the Secessionists believed that certain Unionists had been in communication with the Federals, and were responsible for their visit, and serious threats were made against the supposed informers. The paroled prisoners paid no regard to their paroles, but taking the same arms and horses which had been restored to them entered the Southern army within a few days.

The next Federal soldiers that visited this quarter did not get off so easily and with equal success. Some time about the 12th of July Col. Stifel's regiment of St. Louis Germans (Fifth United States Reserve Corps), which had been at Lexington for some days, came up the Missouri on the steamer White Cloud to destroy the ferry-boats on the river and prevent the crossing of the State Guards from the north side to the south. At Blue Mills landing they were fired on from the Jackson county side by some State Guards in ambush, and had one man killed and twelve men wounded.[1] The ferry-boat was burned, as were a warehouse and store-room at the landing. At Missouri City the German Federals seized a number of fire-arms and carried them off.

A few days later the same force came up the river on the way to Leavenworth to procure a company for the reinforcement of the Federal garrison then being formed at Lexington. A number of young men of this county repaired to the bottom, and when the boat came up opened fire on it with their rifles and shot-guns. No serious damage was done, but the Federals returned the fire and the Secession boys ran away.

EVENTS OF THE SUMMER AND EARLY FALL OF 1861.

From the middle of July until the first part of September, 1861, the peace of the county was scarcely disturbed, save by the exciting news from Southwest Missouri, whither the State Guards had retreated after the fight at Boonville, and whither they had been followed by the Federal forces under Lyons and Sturgis.

July 5 Capt. McCarty's company took part in the battle of Carthage, and lost one man, Albert Withers, killed, and a number wounded. At Wilson's Creek, August 10, the following men from Clay county, under Gen. Price, were killed: Sergts. A. W. Marshall, John W. Woods and Amos Stout; Privates David Morris, John Grant and Richard Cates. The wounded were: Geo. Hollingsworth, mortally; Capt. Thos. McCarty, seriously, and Lieut. T. K. Gash, James Miller, J. B. Winn, C. S. Stark, Richard Talbott, Wm. Hymer and L. B. Thompson, more or less severely. The Clay county troops were attached to Col. C. C. Thornton's " extra battalion."

Some time after the battle of Wilson's Creek many of McCarthy's company returned home, and their stories of that desperate conflict were listened to with great eagerness and interest by their friends and neighbors. Recruiting for Price's army was greatly stimulated by the tidings of the Federal defeats at Carthage and Wilson's Creek, and many hastened to enlist before the war should be over! The Federals

---

[1] Adjutant-General's Report for 1865, p. 79.

at Kansas City and Leavenworth were quiet and kept well at home, and hundreds of men passed to and from Gen. Price with nothing to molest them or make them afraid.

About this time there was one Federal officer found who did not enforce the doctrine of the old maxim that in time of war the law is silent. In August it was learned that Henry Harrison, the absconding railroad contractor, was a soldier in the Federal army at Leavenworth. Harrison had escaped from the Liberty jail by knocking down his keeper and running away. Jailer Ford, himself a Secessionist, went to Ft. Leavenworth and demanded the fugitive, who thought, doubtless, that his enlistment would prevent his return to the well-known "rebel" county of Clay. But Capt. Prince, the commander of the post, gave him up without a word of objection or remonstrance, and even sent a strong guard with him to the river to prevent the possibility of his rescue or escape. The jailer reached Liberty with his prisoner in safety.

Near the 1st of September Col. Boaz Roberts and Majs. Thornton and Morris came up from Price's army, and brought word that the Southern troops needed clothing and other supplies. An open, public meeting was held at the court-house to take measures for their relief. The contributions were considerable. Committees were appointed for each township to secure additional aid, and especially to furnish cloth to the patriotic Southern ladies, who gladly agreed to make it up into clothing for "the boys" in the tented field.

In the latter part of August and during the first week in September several Union men either left the county through fear or were driven out by armed Secessionists. In Liberty Capt. O. P. Moss, James H. Moss, E. M. Samuel and Judge James Jones were forced to flee under the penalty of being "put out of the way," and they made their way up to the Union settlement of Mirabile, Caldwell county, where they were safe for a time. There must have been a serious state of affairs for the Union men, when men of such undoubted personal courage as the Mosses could be induced to leave by threats and hostile messages.

PROCLAMATION OF GEN. STEIN — RALLYING TO HIS STANDARD.

In the latter part of August Gen. Stein,[1] the commander under Gov. Jackson of this military district, issued a proclamation to the people in order to stimulate them to enlistment in the Southern ser-

---

[1] Gen. Stein was killed at the battle of Prairie Grove, Ark., December 6, 1862.

vice. Hitherto Gen. Stein's division had existed chiefly on paper. It contained but few men. The Clay county Secession troops were chiefly attached to Gen. Slack's division, and Stein was especially desirous of recruiting his command to something like respectable proportions. For some time it had been merely a laughing stock. Following is a copy of the proclamation referred to: —

To the People of the Fifth District.

I, as your Brigadier-General, call on you to arouse and come to the rescue of your State. Your State has been invaded by a Northern army, your rights have been trampled on, the privacy of your firesides have (*sic*) been disregarded. Will you tamely submit to the dictates of a tyrant? *No!* every man exclaims. Then come and meet the invader, transfer the war from your own homes, meet them in other parts of the State, and never stop until the last foe has "bit the dust," or been driven from your State.

Organize into companies of from 50 to 100. Come, and I will lead you to victory. Bring your shot-guns and rifles; they have been tried on the plains of Carthage and Springfield, and they did good work. Come, and do not wait for the army to get to your homes before you come out.   A. E. STEIN,

August 25, 1861.   Brigadier-General.

Stein's proclamation, albeit not seemingly a very spirited, thrilling or even well-worded document, was not altogether without effect. Soon after its appearance, or by the 10th of September, a considerable force of Secession troop rendezvoused at Lexington, under Col. H. L. Routt, of this county, encamping in the fair grounds in front of the Federals under Mulligan. In Clay L. B. Dougherty commanded a company, of which Lina Roberts, James A. Gillespie and L. A. Robertson were lieutenants. Two other companies raised in this county about the same time were Capt. John S. Groom's and Capt. P. C. Pixlee's. All three of these companies repaired to Lexington to await the coming of Gen. Price's army, then known to be on its way up from Springfield.

The following Clay county companies participated in the siege of Lexington and assisted in the capture of 2,800 Federals under Col. Mulligan, who surrendered September 20. Clay county men were present during the siege, which lasted eight days, and took a hand as members of other commands, but the regularly organized companies from this county were those of Capt. G. W. Mothershead, Gideon Thompson, L. B. Dougherty, John S. Groom and P. C. Pixlee. Out of perhaps 400 men engaged, Clay county had but two or three wounded at Lexington.

THE BATTLE OF BLUE MILLS.

Preliminary to an account of the battle of Blue Mills—if it be proper to call that insignificant collision of hostile forces, unimportant in character and indecisive in results, a *battle* — it is proper to detail the situation preceding and the circumstances which led to it.

When Gen. Price's army had reached the Osage river, on its way northward to Lexington, where the Federals were under Mulligan, the general dispatched swift messengers ahead with orders to the State Guards and other Secession forces in Northeast and Northwest Missouri to meet him at Lexington. Gen. Thomas A. Harris and Col. Martin E. Green responded with a force of 2,500 or 3,000, crossing the Missouri at Glasgow, after a brief but rather creditable campaign against the Federals under Pope and Hurlbut and the then Col. U. S. Grant.

In Northwest Missouri — in the counties of Gentry, Andrew, Nodaway, Holt, Buchanan and DeKalb — hundreds of men had organized for service in the Southern cause, but found it difficult and dangerous to get to the army of Gen. Price, where they must be in order to be effective ; for the Federals in this quarter, though not numerous, were vigilant and active and in addition to their being stationed in the principal towns they were keeping all the principal fords and crossings of the Missouri. But at last, about the 15th of September, these forces under their own leaders, having received the orders of Gen. Price, succeeded in uniting near St. Joseph, and set out at once for Lexington.

All told the Northwest Missourians numbered about 3,500 men, as follows : From the fifth military district (Gen. Stein's), there were five regiments of infantry, under Col. J. P. Saunders, and one regiment of cavalry, under Col. Wiltley ; from the fourth district (Gen. Slack's), there were five regiments of infantry, under Col. Jeff. Patton and one battalion of cavalry, under Col. Childs.[1] There was also Capt. E. V. Kelly's battery of three guns.

The total number is and was variously estimated. The Liberty *Tribune*, of September 20, 1861, said of the command : —

About 4,000 State troops passed through the city on Monday last, on their way to Lexington. Most of them were mounted and the baggage train numbered over sixty wagons. They had three cannon — two six-pounders and one nine-pounder.

---

[1] See D. R. Atchison's report.

Col. Saunders, in his report, mentions but 1,500, aside from Col. Boyd's and some other commands. From the best evidence now to be had it is quite probable that the number did not exceed 3,500.

On the evening of September 15th Gen. Price sent forward from Lexington Hon. D. R. Atchison, to hasten forward the recruits for whose arrival he was waiting to begin active operations against Mulligan and his cooped-up Federals. Atchison reached Liberty the next day, and met the troops and pushed them forward to Blue Mills Landing, where a considerable portion of them, including the artillery (Kelly's battery), crossed the same night. The remainder were waiting their turns.

At this time the Federals had forces at Cameron and at the Hannibal and St. Joe railroad bridge across Platte river. Those at Platte river were the Sixteenth Illinois infantry, Col. R. F. Smith, and some companies of the Thirty-ninth Ohio, Col. Groesbeck. At Cameron there were the Third Iowa infantry, Lieut. Col. John Scott, and four companies of Missouri Home Guards; of the latter, one company, 35 strong, was from Adair county, under command of Capt. Cupp; one — merely a squad — from Macon, under Capt. Winters; two from Caldwell county, one under Capt. E. D. Johnson and the other under Capt. M. L. James. All the troops at Cameron were infantry, except Capt. James' home guard company, which was mounted.

Learning of the movement of the Northwest Missourians towards Gen. Price's army, Gen. Pope, then in command of the Federal troops in North Missouri, determined to intercept them. Accordingly, pursuant to his orders, Col. Smith set out from Platte river bridge and Col. Scott from Cameron, with instructions to unite at Liberty the day before the Secession troops should reach that point.

Col. Scott moved more rapidly and more continuously than Col. Smith, and reached Liberty early on the morning of the 17th, "the day after the fair," as the Secessionists had passed through the day before, and half of them were already across the river and safely on the way to Gen. Price at Lexington.

Col. Scott was using the Caldwell county Home Guards, under command of Capt. Moses L. James, as an advance guard, they being mounted. At about 8 o'clock an encounter occurred between a detachment of this company, numbering 40 men, under the command of Lieut. James Call, of the Third Iowa, and the rear guard of the Secession forces, commanded by Col. Childs, and consisting of his battalion of cavalry, 300 men. This encounter took place about three miles south of Liberty, on the road to Blue Mills, or Owens' Landing, and resulted in the complete discomfiture of the Caldwell Home Guards, four of whom were killed outright and one wounded. The remainder retreated in some confusion, but all, or nearly all, ultimately joined Col. Scott at Liberty.

Scott was in something of a quandary. He feared to attack the Missourians (who, as everybody informed him, largely outnumbered his forces) unless Smith would join him, and Smith was " long, long on the way." The Iowan sent some of his mounted men out to meet Smith and hurry him forward. He also sent out other scouts to discover, if possible, the situation at the river. Some of these exchanged shots with the enemy, but could learn nothing except that they were crossing as rapidly as possible and seemed more eager to get to Gen. Price than to fight. Col. Scott thought if they were attacked they would stop to fight, and that he could hold them until Smith came up. Accordingly he concluded to attack them.

About 11 o'clock some of the fugitives from the skirmish with the Secession rear guard reached town and reported to Col. Scott, who now resolved to move his command down to the scene and if possible prevent the further crossing of the Missourians. He determined not to wait for Smith, but dispatched another messenger to him informing him of the situation.

Accordingly, with some 500 men of the Third Iowa, the Adair county Home Guards, the Caldwell county company, and 15 volunteer artillerists in charge of a six-pounder brass cannon — in all about 600 men — Col. Scott moved toward Blue Mills Landing. Reaching the pickets of the State Guards, the Federals were fired on and halted. The State Guards fell back, and after some little time spent in reconnoitering, Col. Scott concluded they had retreated, and again ordered the advance.

Col. Saunders, in command of the State Guards, had full knowledge of the movements of the Federals, and was well prepared to receive them. The ground was well calculated for an ambush, each side of the narrow road being thickly wooded and filled with vines and rank shrubbery, forming an almost impenetrable jungle, and well adapted for concealing a considerable armed force. Some years before a cyclone had uprooted a number of trees, which now formed admirable vantage points for the riflemen, and on the west side of the road ran a then dry slough with a considerable embankment, forming a good strong breastwork. Into this thicket Col. Jeff. Patton's regiment of Northwest Missourians was placed, on both sides of the road. Supporting them were other battalions and companies, and from the

HISTORY OF CLAY COUNTY

best information now to be obtained, the State Guards and the Federals were about equal in numbers — 600 on each side; the State Guards may have numbered 700.

As the Federals were marching gaily along, " eager for a fight," as they said, suddenly a galling fire was opened upon them from both sides of the road. A fierce little fight was begun and kept up for nearly an hour. But the advantage was with the Missourians from the start until the close, and the Federals were at last driven from the field, and retreated into Liberty in something like disorder and more of haste. Their artillery was of little service to them. The piece, as stated, was manned by German volunteers, under a sergeant, whose name is best remembered as Waldeschmidt, and the surprise was so perfect that only a few rounds could be fired,[1] and they were not effective. The alleged artillerists abandoned the gun, and it would have been captured had not a few plucky Iowans rallied to it and drawn it away.

The Federals returned the fire, but they declared they " saw nothing to shoot at," and so those of their shots which took effect were chance ones. Some of them were driven back into Mr. Beauchamp's wheat field, and here it is said they saw their enemies. A wagon improvised into a caisson and loaded with ammunition was left on the field.

The fight took place about four miles east of south of Liberty, or between the wooden bridge across the town branch, a little below the arsenal, and Mr. Beauchamp's, though extending a little beyond (n. e. $\frac{1}{4}$ sec. 33, tp. 51, range 31). The locality is a mile below where now (1885) the Wabash railroad crosses the county road to the ferry landing.

A few, and only a few, Clay county men took part in the Blue Mills fight, against the Federals, of course. These had joined Col. Saunders' forces as they passed through.

Returning to Liberty Col. Scott found that Col. Smith had come up with about 2,500 troops, and was in camp about the square in Col. Lightburne's orchard. Everything was now safe on the Federal side, and equally safe on the Secession side. Col. Saunders had not seen proper to follow up his victory, as it would seem he could have done — and if so should have done — and was content to get across the river without further molestation.

Col. Saunders says the piece was fired six times, but Col. Scott says it was discharged but twice.

HISTORY OF CLAY COUNTY

The Federals visited the field that night, and succeeded in removing nearly all of their wounded. The next day all were brought back and taken to the William Jewell College building, which was converted into a hospital. The Federal surgeons had their hands full for a day or two, and were assisted by Dr. W. A. Morton and perhaps another local surgeon.

The Federal dead were buried in the college grounds, a little north of the buildings, and there yet all or nearly all of them still lie,

"Under the sod and the dew, waiting the judgment day."

September 20 two companies of Home Guards from Kansas City, under Capts. Hyde and Thomas, came down to Liberty Landing on the steamer Majors, and marching thence to Liberty, removed all the wounded able to be transported to Kansas City, where they were cared for till they recovered. These companies also took away with them some blasting powder and a few tools that the Secessionists had left the previous April at the seizure. But there were no arms left for them to take.

THE KILLED AND WOUNDED.

According to the best information obtainable, discarding all wild and sensational reports made without grounds and never authenticated, the Federal loss in the Blue Mills fight amounted to 14 killed outright on the field — 7 in the Third Iowa, 1 of the German artillerists, and 4 of the Caldwell county Home Guards, and 2 of the Adair county Home Guards. In the Third Iowa there were mortally wounded: David H. Dill, Co. E, died September 28; Michael Wierna, Co. H, died November 19; Larian T. Washburn, Co. I, died next day, September 18. This information is obtained from official records, muster rolls, etc., yet on file in the offices of the adjutant-generals of Iowa and Missouri, and agrees with the memory of Dr. W. A. Morton, who was at the Federal hospital. The Federal wounded amounted to about to about 80 — 74 in the Third Iowa, 3 of the Caldwell Home Guards, and 3 or 4 of the German artillerists and Adair Home Guards.

The loss of the Missourians was 3 killed dead on the field — James W. Gillespie, of Patton's regiment; Dr. John Ross, of Wilfley's regiment; and William Pope, unattached — and it is believed that 2 more died of their wounds within a week. The wounded numbered 17 or 18.

Of course other publications, biased in favor of one side or the other, have placed the number of killed and wounded much larger. Immediately after the engagement each side grossly exaggerated the loss of the other — the wish fathering the thought in this particular — and each side, too, vastly over-estimated the forces of the other. The statements of the leading officers were seized upon by their respective partisans, and lost nothing in volume by their currency and circulation, until finally it came to be believed in certain quarters that 100 or more Federals were killed and three times as many wounded, and in certain other quarters that four score " rebels " had bitten the dust and a proportionate number wounded.

Happily official records, complete and perfectly authenticated, with no motive *now* for prevaricating or concealing the truth, do not leave anything to be *guessed*. In the light of these, and in the face of other testimony corroborative, and with no design of disparaging the veracity of either Col. Scott or Col. Saunders, it is but the plain, simple truth that when one said, " the loss of the enemy (the Missourians) * * * from accounts deemed reliable, is not less than 160," and " his total force about 4,400," and the other said, " the enemy (the Federals) admitted a loss of 150 to 200 killed, wounded and missing," and that " 42 were left dead on the field," — both were mistaken.

REPORTS OF THE LEADERS.

The official records of Col. Scott, commanding the Federals, Col. Saunders, commanding the Missouri State Guards, or Secession forces, and Gen. D. R. Atchison, a volunteer *pro tem.*, serving under the orders of Gen. Price, are herewith given as necessary portions of an account of the engagement at Blue Mills.

REPORT OF COL. SAUNDERS.

REGIMENTAL HEADQUARTERS,
LEXINGTON, September 21, 1861.

BRIG.-GEN. A. E. STEIN — I have the honor to submit to you the following report of an engagement on the 17th at Blue Mills ferry, between the State forces under my command, and a body of some 1,100 Federal troops. From the hour of leaving St. Joseph until I reached the river at Blue Mills, reports of the enemy hanging on our rear were hourly received. But upon the night of the 16th reliable information reached us of the enemy's presence in considerable force (estimated variously at from 1,500 to 3,000) upon the Centerville road, some 12 miles distant.

My command, consisting of my own regiment of infantry, embracing 11 companies, numbering about 400 men ; Col. Jeff. Patton's regiment of infantry of about the same number ; Lieut.-Col. Wilfley's

213

HISTORY OF CLAY COUNTY

regiment of cavalry of an equal number; Col. Child's battalion of some 300 men reached the Missouri river at about four o'clock on the 16th, but could not commence crossing until 2 o'clock a. m. on the 17th, the boats being occupied by Major Boyd's troops, who reached the ferry in advance of me. My orders being imperative to push on, I permitted no delay in crossing, with such facilities as were at my command. When about one-fourth of my train, consisting of about 100 wagons, were crossed about 8 o'clock a. m. my pickets were driven in. I had posted Col. Child's some four miles back upon the road with his battalion, and when his men were driven in, he took prompt steps to hold the enemy in check until I should be prepared to receive them.

The ready and judicious disposition of this officer in the morning, as well as his gallantry later in the day, deserves the highest commendation, and is especially brought to your attention.

After some sparring between pickets, Col. Childs succeeded in killing four and severely wounding one man, who was left upon the road and was afterwards given up to his friends.

After reconnoitering I concluded the enemy had retired and marched my men — who had been formed in order of battle — back to the river and proceeded with the work of crossing, when, at 3 o'clock, about one-half had crossed, reducing my effective force which could be rallied, to about 600, our pickets were again driven in.

I ordered Cols. Patton and Childs forward with such forces as could be hastily formed, and directed Lieut.-Col. Cundiff to go forward with the remainder of my regiment while I should rally and bring up all the available forces not yet over the river.

The enemy opened on us with grape from a brass six-pounder, which my men silenced at the sixth round, killing all their artillery men (except one, who was slightly wounded and taken prisoner) and their horses. The men from the rear now commenced reaching the scene of action, and adding their cheers to those in front, the enemy commenced flying, leaving their caisson on the ground containing 123 shell and a large lot of canister, grape and round shot. My men ran them some three miles, and only desisted when quite exhausted. The officers and men under my command behaved most gallantly, and deserve especial notice for their bravery and coolness during the action.

If I had had artillery, I doubt not I should have taken the piece opened upon us, with all the enemy's baggage.

My loss was 1 killed and 17 wounded, as follows: Of Capt. Fisher's company, W. P. McGee, dangerously wounded; P. Smith Roberts, slightly wounded.

Of Capt. Sullivan's company, J. B. Still, slightly wounded.

Of Capt. T. Owens' company, Wm. Willis, seriously wounded.

Of Capt. Edmonson's company, Wm. L. Carson, dangerously wounded; James White, slightly wounded.

Of Capt. Petram's company, Conrad Sharp, seriously wounded.

Of Capt. Finney's company, James York and Wheeler South, both slightly wounded.

HISTORY OF CLAY COUNTY

Of Col. Patton's regiment, James W. Gillespie, killed; Robert Austin, Geo. A. Bell, J. T. Thornton, slightly wounded.

Of Col. Wilfley's regiment, Dr. John Ross, killed; B. Allen, Chas. Thorp and Thos. Spencer, seriously wounded; James A. Burnham, slightly wounded.

The enemy admitted a loss of 150 to 200 killed, wounded and missing; 42 were left dead on the field. We got the prisoners, who are still in my hands. Several gentlemen not in any company or official capacity deserve especial mention for gallantry and activity; among those were G. W. Van Lear, of St. Joseph, and Wm. Pope, of Buchanan county; the latter fell mortally wounded in the very front of my advancing column.

Respectfully, etc.,

J. P. SAUNDERS,
Col. Missouri State Guards.

HON. D. R. ATCHISON'S REPORT.

LEXINGTON, Mo., September 21, 1867.

SIR — In pursuance of your orders I left this place on the evening of the 15th inst. and proceeded forthwith to Liberty, Clay county, Mo., where I met the State Guard on the march from the Northwest — five regiments of infantry, under the command of Col. Saunders, and one regiment of cavalry, under the command of Col. Wilfley, from the fifth district; five regiments of infantry, under command of Col. Jeff. Patton, and one battalion of cavalry, under Col. Childs, from the fourth district. I delivered your orders to the above commands to hasten to this point (Lexington) with as much dispatch as possible. They marched forthwith, and arrived at the Missouri river about four o'clock in the evening, when Col. Boyd's artillery and battalion and baggage were crossed over to the south, where the colonel took his position, Capt. Kelly planting his artillery so as to completely command the river. The crossing continued all night without interruption, every officer and man using his best exertions. We received news during the night that the enemy would be in the town of Liberty, about six miles distant from Blue Mills ferry, at an early hour the ensuing morning. We were crossing in three small flats, and much time was necessary to move the large train of some hundred wagons. Col. Childs with his command had taken post for the night about two miles from Liberty on the road to the ferry. Here he engaged the enemy's advance or pickets in the morning, killing four and wounding one, with no loss on our side. The enemy fled and we heard no more of them until 3 or 4 o'clock, when their approach was announced in large force, supposed to be about 900 men, with one piece of artilery (a 6-pounder). The men of our command immediately formed, Col. Jeff. Patton leading the advance, to meet the enemy. After proceeding about three miles from the river they met the advance guard of the enemy and the fight commenced. But the Federal troops almost immediately fled, our men pursuing rapidly, shooting them down until they annihilated the rear of their army, taking one caisson, killing about 60, and wounding it is said, about 70. The Federal troops attempted two or three times to make a stand, but ran after delivering one fire. Our men followed them like hounds on a wolf chase, strewing the road with the dead and wounded, until they were compelled to give over the chase from exhaustion, the evening being very warm. Col. Saunders, Col. Patton, Col. Childs, Col. Cundiff, Col. Wilfley, Maj. Gause, Adj. Shackelford, and all the other officers and men, as far as I know or could learn, behaved gallantly.

D. R. ATCHISON.

To GEN. PRICE.

COL. SCOTT'S REPORT.

HDQRS. THIRD REGIMENT IOWA VOLUNTEERS,
LIBERTY, September 18, 1861.

SIR :—In relation to an affair of yesterday which occurred near Blue Mills Landing, about five miles from this place, I have the honor to report :—

Agreeably to your orders, I left Cameron at 3 p. m. of the 15th inst., and through a heavy rain and bad roads made but 7 miles during the afternoon. By a very active march on the 16th I reached Centreville, 10 miles north of Liberty, by sunset, where the firing of cannon was distinctly heard in the direction of Platte City, which was surmised to be from Col. Smith's Sixteenth Illinois command. Had sent a messenger to Col. Smith from Haynesville, and sent another from Centreville, apprising him of my movements, but got no response. On the 17th, at 2 a. m., started from Centreville for Liberty, and at daylight the advanced guards fell in with the enemy's pickets, which they drove in and closely followed.

At 7 a. m. my command arrived at Liberty, and bivouacked on the hills north of and overlooking the town. I dispatched several scouts to examine the position of the enemy, but could gain no definite information. They had passed through Liberty during the afternoon of the 16th to the number of about 4,000, and taken the road to Blue Mills Landing, and were reported as having four pieces of artillery. At 11 o'clock a. m. heard firing in the direction of the landing, which was reported as a conflict between the rebels and for disputing their passage over the river.

At 12 m. moved the command, consisting of 500 of the Third Iowa, a squad of German artillerists and about 70 Home Guards, in the direction of Blue Mills Landing. On the route learned that a body of our scouts had fallen in with the enemy's pickets, and lost 2 killed and 1 wounded. Before starting dispatched courier to Col. Smith to hasten his command.

About two miles from Liberty the advance guard drove in the enemy's pickets. Skirmishers closely examined the dense growth through which our route lay, and at 3 p. m. discovered the enemy in force, concealed on both sides of the road, and occupying the dry bed of a slough, his left resting on the river and his right ex

HISTORY OF CLAY COUNTY

tending beyond our observation. He opened a heavy fire, which drove back our skirmishers, and made simultaneous attacks upon our front and right. These were well sustained, and he retired with loss to his position. In the attack on our front the artillery suffered so severely that the only piece, a brass 6-pounder, was left without sufficient force to man it, and I was only able to have it discharged twice during the action. Some of the gunners abandoned the piece, carrying off the matches and primers, and could not be rallied.

The enemy kept up a heavy fire from his position. Our artillery useless, and many of the officers and men already disabled, it was deemed advisable to fall back, which was done slowly, returning the enemy's fire, and completely checking pursuit. The 6-pounder was brought off by hand, through the gallantry of Capt. Trumbull, Lieuts. Crosley and Knight, and various officers and men of the Third Iowa, after it had been entirely abandoned by the artillerists. The ammunition wagon, becoming fastened between a tree and a log at the roadside in such a manner that it could not be released without serious loss, was abandoned.

The engagement lasted one hour and was sustained by my command with an intrepidity that merits my warmest approbation.

I have to regret the loss of a number of brave officers and men, who fell gallantly fighting at their posts. I refer to the enclosed list of killed and wounded as a part of this report.

The heaviest fire was sustained by Co. I, Third Iowa volunteers, which lost four killed and 20 wounded, being one-fourth of our total loss.

Maj. Stone, Capts. Warren, Willett and O'Neil were severely wounded, and also Lieuts. Hobbs, Anderson, Tullis and Knight. The latter refused to retire from the field after being three times wounded, and remained with his men till the close of the engagement.

Among the great number who deserve my thanks for their gallantry I might mention Sergt. James F. Lakin, of Co. F, Third Iowa, who bore the colors and carried them into the thickest of the fight with all the coolness of a veteran.

The loss of the enemy can not be certainly ascertained, but from accounts deemed reliable is not less than 160, many of whom were killed. His total force was about 4,400.

Your most obedient servant,

JOHN SCOTT,
Lieut.-Col. of the Third Iowa Volunteers.

S. D. Sturgis, Brig.-Gen. U. S. Army.

LIST OF KILLED AND WOUNDED IN THE THIRD IOWA.

[The following list of the killed and wounded of the Third Iowa Infantry, in the battle, has been kindly furnished for this history, properly certified, by Col. W. L. Alexander, Adjutant-General of

HISTORY OF CLAY COUNTY

Iowa. It is taken from muster rolls yet on file, and is compared and agrees with the Iowa Adjutant-General's report of 1863] : —

Maj. Wm. M. Stone, wounded in the head.

Company A — Wounded, First Lieut. D. J. O'Neil, in the arm; First Sergt. D. J. Duane, in the thigh; Corp. Wm. H. Munger, in the thigh; Privates, Elliott Critchfield, in the arm; James P. McCafferty, in thigh, John Schrage, in the leg.

Company B — Wounded, Second Lieut. Albert Hobbs, in shoulder; Sergt. John C. Woodruff, through left lung; Corp. W. F. Hart; Privates Benjamin Robins, in left arm, Josiah M. Woodruff, left thigh badly shattered.

Company C — Killed, Lester Squires. Wounded, Corp. Benjamin Hunting, in arm; Wagoner, Herman Drone, severely; Private, Wm. H. Phillips.

Company D — Killed, Wm. B. Miller. Wounded, Capt. George R. Willett, in knee; Second Lieut. Ole A. Anderson, in head; Private, Wm. B. Hickert, in knee.

Company E — David H. Dill, died September 28; Wounded, Sergt. Thos. Mulvana; Corps. Nathaniel Jennings and Wm. H. McCowin, in side; Privates, Geo. W. Groves, James F. Guthrie, Daniel Hill, Joseph H. Miller, Bartley N. Pardee, Wm. R. White and Wm. C. White.

Company F — Killed, Hasseltine D. Norton. Wounded, Second Lieut. Aaron Brown; Corp. L. B. Davis, severely; Privates, John W. Hawn, severely; David Ishman, severely; Joseph N. Johnson, Charles Lyon, Jacob Swank, Thos. Saunders, and Charles Winchell, severely.

Company G — Wounded, Corp. William Swan; Privates Francis M. Lotta, William Michael, John McCullough and John A. Rutter.

Company H — Wounded, Michael Wierna (died November 19), Capt. John H. Warren, in legs; First Lieut. James Tullis, in legs; Sergt. John McMannus, in arm; Privates Ed. A. Barbour, Isaac Gamble and Jesse McClure.

Company I — Killed, G. W. Bedell, Thos. M. Mix, Benj. F. Darland. Wounded, Lorain T. Washburn (died next day); First Lieut. John P. Knight, in arm, leg and chin; Sergts. David Forney and Isaac M. Henderson; Corp. William Burdick, in leg; Drummer Chas. E. Balcomb, in neck; Privates James Buel, in right leg; Leroy Carter, in leg; Peter S. Darland, severely; Richard C. Dolph, severely; Daniel W. Foot, Wolsey Hawks, Wm. H. Mirifield, in leg; Lewis D. Powers, in arm; Wm. L. Peppers, in leg and arm; A. S. Russell, severely in arm; Geo. W. Stocks, severely in head and arm; Geo. H. Smalley, in leg; Ferdinand Seick, Samuel Trowbridge, Joseph Wyborney, in left knee; Asa H. Warner, A. M. Wilcox, severely in leg; Thos. B. Walley and James E. White.

Company K — Killed, Private James H. Brownell.

The four men of the Caldwell county Home Guards that were killed

HISTORY OF CLAY COUNTY

were Linus Miller, Daniel Strope, John Smith and James Bogan. Three of Johnson's company were wounded — Capt. E. D. Johnson and privates Whitfield Early and Wm. O. Dodge.

Capt. Cupp, of the Adair county Home Guards, was killed in the action, as was a private of his company.

OTHER WAR INCIDENTS OF THE FALL AND WINTER OF 1861.

On Friday, September 20, a considerable Federal force under Gen. S. D. Sturgis came into Liberty from the north and east and united with the Third Iowa and Sixteenth Illinois. Sturgis' command consisted of the Twenty-seventh and Thirty-ninth Ohio regiments of infantry, and some Gentry county Home Guards. The next day, Sturgis at the head, the Ohio regiments departed for the west, going toward Fort Leavenworth. A day or two before their arrival at Liberty they had attempted to reinforce Mulligan at Lexington, but in the Missouri bottom, opposite and about four miles from Lexington (or near the present site of R. & L. Junction), they were diverted from their purpose by the presence of Gen. Rains' division of Missourians, sent across by Gen. Price to stop them, and they moved rapidly to the westward to get out of the way, burning some of their wagons.

Not long after September 21, the Third Iowa and Sixteenth Illinois, with the Missouri Home Guards, left, and in their case the citizens considered it a good riddance of a lot of bad rubbish. For with these commands, especially among the Home Guards, were a lot of rapacious and unscrupulous thieves and plunderers that out-jayhawked the Kansas jayhawkers. Hen roosts, pig pens, gardens, even kitchens and private houses were preyed upon and stripped by these scamps, and two stores in Liberty were completely "gutted." The Missouri Home Guards did the greater part of this pillaging; next to them were the Sixteenth Illinois men, and then came the Third Iowa, though it is said only comparatively a few of the latter regiment engaged in the plundering, but such as did were quite active.

Not so with the Ohio troops. These men were all gentlemen, and seemed to understand that the war was one between fellow-citizens of a common country. They came quietly into town, went into camp, and as quietly conducted themselves during their stay. They abused nobody, insulted no one, and there did not seem to be a thief among them. Even at this late day, these regiments, and especially the Thirty-ninth, and its old colonel, John Groesbeck, are pleasantly remembered. Brave men these were, and many a time afterward in the mighty battles in Tennessee, Mississippi and Georgia, did they accomplish great deeds of gallantry and moment, but not the least among their glories during their term of service were their acts of gentility, honor and chivalry toward the people of Missouri in the fall and winter of 1861. It is a pity that the same can not be said of all Federal regiments!

Upon the fall of Lexington there was great rejoicing among the Secessionists, and enlistments in the army of Gen. Price were further stimulated. About this time inflammatory appeals were made by certain leaders of the Secession forces to our people, asking for assistance in men and means, and denouncing Federals and Federal sympathizers in the severest terms. The following is an extract from a communication of Col. John T. Hughes, in the Liberty *Tribune*, of September 20 : —

* * * Were I Governor of this State I would notify Gov. Charles Robinson, of Kansas, that if he should again suffer his soldiers to cross into Missouri I would retaliate with a terrible vengeance. I would invade, occupy and hold, and desolate the entire State of Kansas with fire and sword, and sack and burn every town and city in the State. I would reduce it to its primeval solitudes.

* * * The exiled soldiers are returning, and this land will be drenched in blood, and widows and orphans be multiplied, and the wildest anarchy prevail, if there should be any attempt to support the Provisional Government of the traitor and usurper, Hamilton R. Gamble, by force of arms.

Col. Hughes appealed to the women to weave cloth and prepare clothing, and to the men to prepare leather and other supplies for the use of Price's army, and the appeal was not altogether unresponded to.

The bank at Liberty, which was a branch of the Farmers' Bank of Lexington, suspended specie payments in the summer, and early in the fall the coin was sent to St. Louis for safety.

Recruiting was kept up for the army of Gen. Price during the fall, and on December 1 there were at least five companies with "Old Pap" in his camps down in Southwestern Missouri: Capt. P. C. Pixlee's, L. B. Dougherty's, Gideon Thompson's, Robert Minter's and R. Scott's. Other men from Clay belonged to companies whose officers were from adjoining counties.

THE NEOSHO SECESSION ORDINANCE.

On October 26, "Claib Jackson's Legislature," as it was called, met in the Masonic Hall at Neosho, and on the 28th an ordinance of secession was passed by both houses. In the Senate the only vote against it was cast by Charles Hardin, then Senator from the Boone and Callaway district, and afterwards Governor of the State, and in the House the only member voting "no" was Mr. Shambaugh, of DeKalb. According to the records and to Mr. Shambaugh there were in the Jackson Legislature at the time but 39 members of the House and 10 members of the Senate, when by the constitution a quorum for the transaction of business was required to consist of 17 Senators and 67 Representatives. Be that as it may, the secession ordinance and the act of annexation to the Southern Confederacy were approved by the Confederate Congress at Richmond, recognized by that portion of the people of Missouri who were in favor "of cutting loose from the old Union," and Gen. Price fired a salute in honor thereof. And so those Missourians, then and afterwards in arms against the Federal flag, became entitled to the name of *Confederates*, and will so be denominated in future pages of this history, instead of being called "State Guards," "Secessionists," "Southern troops," etc., as they have hitherto been spoken of.

On Sunday, December 8, about 2,000 Federal troops, under command of Gen. Ben. M. Prentiss, appeared in Liberty and remained until the following Tuesday. During their stay quite a number of citizens of Confederate proclivities were arrested and forced to take an oath of loyalty to the Federal Government. Among these was Robert. H. Miller, editor of the *Tribune*, who was required to agree not to publish any more "secesh" articles in his paper. When he left Gen. Prentiss carried off with him Dr. Patton, Judge Vertrees, Deputy Sheriff J. J. Moore, Constable J. H. Ford, and 9 others.

CHAPTER VIII.

DURING THE YEAR 1862.

The "Gamble Oath" — It is Taken by a Majority of the County Officials — Miscellaneous — Parker's Raid on Liberty — The Reign of Penick — Organization of the Enrolled Militia — Miscellaneous Military Matters — November Election, 1862.

THE "GAMBLE OATH."

After the reorganization of the Missouri State Government by ordinance of the State Convention — with Hamilton R. Gamble as Provisional Governor, Willard P. Hall as Lieut.-Governor, Mordecai Oliver as Secretary of State, etc., — it was required that all county officers (and many others) should take an oath of allegiance, not only to the United States, but to the Provisional Government. In this county some of the officials refused to take this oath, but whether this refusal was upon the grounds that the Gamble government was illegal or that they considered Missouri, under the Neosho ordinance of Secession, one of the Confederate States, can not here be stated. For a time, owing to the disturbed condition of affairs incident to military occupation, public business was practically suspended.

But at last, after due deliberation, and upon a consideration of all the circumstances, it was concluded that it was best to accept the situation and to recognize the authority of the Federal and State Governments. Some of the officers took the oath willingly, others with a mental reservation. In January, 1862, the county court assembled at Liberty. All the officers had been reappointed, and had taken the Gamble oath. The justices were Thomas M. Chevis, Alvah Maret and Isaac Wood; clerk, Ephraim D. Murray. Public business was transacted as usual. In March the court assembled, and considering the cases of many of the justices of the peace of the county who had resigned rather than take the oath, reappointed nearly all of them, and the most of them afterward served.

In the circuit court Judge George W. Dunn had refused to take the oath, and ex-Governor Austin A. King was appointed in his stead. Circuit Attorney D. C. Allen would not take and subscribe to the oath, and D. P. Whitmer, of Ray, was commissioned. Circuit Clerk A. J. Calhoun accepted the situation.

HISTORY OF CLAY COUNTY

The following is a copy of the " Gamble oath : " —

I, —————————, do solemnly swear (or affirm, as the case may be) that I will support, protect and defend the Constitution of the United States, and the Constitution of the State of Missouri, against all enemies and opposers, whether domestic or foreign; that I will bear true faith, loyalty and allegiance to the United States, and will not, directly or indirectly, give aid and comfort or countenance to the enemies or oppressors thereof, or of the Provisional Government of the State of Missouri, any ordinance, law or resolution of any State Convention or Legislature, or any order or organization, secret or otherwise to the contrary notwithstanding; and that I do this with a full and honest determination, pledge and purpose, faithfully to keep and perform the same, without any mental reservation or evasion whatever. And I do further solemnly swear (or affirm) that I have not, since the 17th day of December, A. D. 1861, willfully taken up arms or levied war against the United States, or against the Provisional Government of the State of Missouri. So help me God.

After a time the " Gamble oath " was supplemented by one more binding, more exacting, harder to take, and still harder to observe. This was called the " ironclad oath."

MISCELLANEOUS.

In February a small Federal command under Lieut. Elias Lankford, then engaged in raising a company for service in the Sixth regiment, Missouri State Militia, Col. E. C. Catherwood's, came to Liberty as the advance of a force that was to occupy the county. Lieut. Lankford opened a recruiting office, but recruits came in very slowly. In all 32 men from this county joined Catherwood's regiment.

On the 10th of March Maj. A. Lightburne's extensive rope factory at Liberty was set on fire and burned to the ground, involving a loss of some thousands of dollars. The incendiary was a negro woman, the slave of L. N. Rees. She was arrested and confessed that she did the burning to be revenged on Maj. Lightburne, who some time previously had caused her to be whipped for stealing some clothing from him. The woman, with some other slaves, was sent off to another quarter of the State and sold. Somehow a report that the Federals at Liberty had burned the factory gained currency, but there was not the smallest particle of truth in it.

PARKER'S RAID ON LIBERTY.

On Friday, March 14, a band of mounted Confederate partisans, 40 in number, led by Col. B. F. Parker, of Jackson county, dashed into

223

HISTORY OF CLAY COUNTY

Liberty and held the place for a few hours. Soon after their entrance they called up to them a citizen named Owen Grimshaw, who had a short time previously enlisted in the Federal service, and after conversing with him for a moment, shot him in the shoulder, bringing him to the ground. The wound was a severe one, but did not prove mortal.

Capt. R. G. Hubbard, afterwards of Penick's regiment, had a recruiting office, with ten men. The Confederates attacked them and there was an irregular exchange of shots for nearly three hours, when Hubbard and his men surrendered to keep from being burnt out. After paroling the prisoners and tearing down the U. S. flag from the court-house, the raiders left as suddenly as they had entered, striking straight for their rendezvous in Jackson county, among the Sni Hills. Save Grimshaw nobody was hurt. Kit Childs was with Parker and acted as his lieutenant.

News of his raid was sent to Cameron, and Col. Catherwood, with four or five companies of militia and recruits, came galloping down to Liberty, making the march of 42 miles over heavy roads in 15 hours. After a little examination Catherwood realized that the raiders were out of all reach, and on Sunday, the 16th, he returned to Cameron, leaving at Liberty a company of his own regiment under Capt. E. D. Johnson, — Caldwell county men.

In a day or two came a reinforcement to Liberty from St. Joseph, under Col. T. T. Kimball, consisting of two companies of his six months' militia, commanded by Capts. Drumhiller and Phelps. These remained until about the 1st of April, when, their term of service having expired, they left for their homes, and then came Col. W. R. Penick, with his 500 men, and after that all Confederate raids on Liberty by small bands were prevented.

Col. Parker was subsequently killed, June 28, 1863, in a raid on Wellington, by a squad of McFerran's First M. S. M. On his person was found a commission as colonel of the " First Missouri Partisan Rangers," signed by J. S. Seddons, Confederate Secretary of War, and H. D. Walker, assistant adjutant-general of the Confederate army. Parker was the only Missourian that ever held a commission as a partisan ranger during the war. At least he was the only one *known* to hold such a commission. Quantrell, Todd, Anderson and others were never commissioned.

THE REIGN OF PENICK.

The Fifth regiment of cavalry, Missouri State militia, commonly known as " Penick's men " — or else as " Penick's thieves " — held

HISTORY OF CLAY COUNTY

possession of Clay and other counties in this part of the State for several months during the summer of 1862. Clay was known as a strong "rebel" county, and it must have been that the Federal commander of the district had an especial spite against our people when he sent down Penick's men to hold them in subjection. The regiment was recruited at St. Joseph and the men were all or nearly all from Northwest Missouri — some were from Kansas. Col. Penick himself was (and yet is) a citizen of St. Joseph; he was of Southern birth and rearing, a native of Boone county, Mo., and a slaveholder.

After not quite a year's service the regiment was broken up and dismissed from the Federal service, as the order said, " in view of the interests of the public service."

Upon Col. Penick's advent into Clay county the situation was fairly felicitous for a season of peace and quietude. The people were about ready to declare the war for the independence of the Confederacy a failure and to accept the situation generally.

On the 7th of April a Union meeting was held in Liberty to consider the condition of affairs, and men of both and all parties attended to counsel together for the public good. T. C. Gordon presided and Robt. H. Miller was the secretary, and published the proceedings approvingly in the *Tribune.*

A committee on resolutions composed of Hon. L. W. Burris, Geo. S. Story, A. M. Riley, Dr. W. A. Norton and Milliner Haynes reported a series of resolutions, declaring among other things that " any further efforts to separate Missouri from the Federal Union would be madness and folly," and requesting " our fellow-citizens to lay down their arms and return home." To all who were willing to heed the latter admonition Gen. Halleck was requested to " offer them the privileges on reasonable terms."

The resolutions were adopted without dissent. Col. Moss and Gen. Doniphan made speeches indorsing them, and going even further in demanding that hostilities against the Union should cease. These speeches were reported and Col. Moss' was republished in the St. Louis *Republican* and many other public journals.

About this time Hon. J. T. V. Thompson, a prominent Secessionist of this county from the start, a member of the " Claib. Jackson Legislature," who had followed Price's army into Arkansas and had been taken prisoner at the battle of Pea Ridge, was released after a brief term of imprisonment at St. Louis, upon taking the oath. A few days later he returned home and wrote the following open letter, which was published in the St. Louis *Republican*, as well as in the *Tribune* and other papers in this district: —

ST. LOUIS, April 2, 1862.

To E. M. Samuel, Esq.:

SIR — For more than thirty years we have stood in antagonistic political relations. In the present troubles we have seen and acted differently, but I hope, hereafter, will act together in bringing the State back to its allegiance to the United States Government of Missouri; in promoting peace and friendly feeling among our people and in the State generally. This I have a great desire to do, and will do when I return home. We have a common interest in putting down all bands of outlaws and guerrilla parties that now infest and may infest our State. I hope to be able, as I am willing, to act with all good men in bringing the State to its allegiance to the United States Government, and in sustaining the provisional government of Missouri.

That the course I took in the Legislature of Missouri since these troubles commenced (though dictated by honest motives at the time), was injurious to the State and to the Union, I freely admit, and I will hereafter, as a private citizen, do all I can to repair the injury and ruin resulting therefrom. I can, as you know, do much in my county and my old senatorial district, to restore peace, loyalty and good feeling among the people. I will use my influence to restore law and order, and will oppose, discountenance, and, if need be, assist in destroying all bands of men who aim to trample law and order under their feet. The State has already suffered enough, and I will, with you, and all other law-abiding men, urge the people to return to their allegiance to the United States Government, and to sustain our present Provisional Government, as the only means for peace and prosperity. I am fully convinced that this is the duty of all good men.

Respectfully,

J. T. V. THOMPSON.

Soon after his arrival at Liberty, Col. Penick began a system of general arrest and apprehension of those of our citizens who had identified themselves with the rebellion. These were for the most part taken at their homes and brought to Liberty, where the oath of loyalty was administered to them, and then upon giving an approved bond for the observance of their oath they were released and allowed to depart in peace, even if in mortification.

The first victims were B. W. Nowlin and S. D. Nowlin, who were released upon giving bonds of $5,000 each. Among those brought up in May was Franklin James, afterwards the notorious bandit, who took the oath and gave a $1,000 bond for the faithful observance of its terms.

Many citizens came forward voluntarily and took the oath, and in time so many had subscribed to the sworn and solemn pledges of faithful allegiance to the Federal government that it would seem Clay county was as loyal as any county in "bleeding Kansas." Our people had *sworn* to their loyalty, while the Kansans only protested theirs.

The oath required to be taken was printed on a blank duly filled out and signed by the party sworn, and was as follows : —

The undersigned solemnly swears that he will bear true faith and allegiance to the Government of the United States of America and support the Constitution thereof as the supreme law of the land ; that he will never take up arms against said Government, or those who may be acting under its authority ; that he will never, by word, act, or deed, knowingly give aid or comfort, or in any manner encourage armed opposition to the Government of the United States, but that, on the contrary, he will do all in his power as a citizen to prevent such opposition, and to discourage the same wherever it is being made. He makes this oath freely and voluntarily, with no mental reservations or restrictions whatever, honestly intending, at all times hereafter to keep the same, in spirit as well as in letter, and to conduct himself as a peaceable, law-abiding citizen of the United States. This I do solemnly swear, so help me God. (Signature.)

April 27, another large public meeting was held at Liberty ; many of Penick's men were present. Ex-Gov. King spoke and was followed by Col. Thompson, who graphically and humorously described his disastrous experience in following the fortunes of the Confederacy, and the result, and then seriously addressing his audience he declared that it was folly to think of contending longer against the mighty armies and vast resources of the Federal government : that the Confederate government would ultimately perish from the earth ; that there might be required three or four years more of war to demonstrate this, but the end would surely come, and the Confederacy fall, and if the war lasted two years more slavery would fall with it, while if the war ceased then ("now") slavery would be preserved. Col. Thompson declared himself emphatically for peace, and altogether opposed to bushwhacking, and finally said he would live honorably up to the terms of his release and to every syllable of the oath he had taken.

Some time in the latter part of the winter Col. H. M. Routt, who had returned from the Confederate army, tired of the war, was arrested at his home in Liberty and taken to St. Louis on a charge of treason, in leading the force that captured the Liberty arsenal. Expressing a willingness to take the oath of loyalty, and fully acknowledging the "error of his past ways," upon the influence of certain prominent Union men, he was granted a full and free pardon by President Lincoln, and soon returned home. He, too, like Col. Thompson, declared the war of secession had been and would continue to be a failure, and that its further continuance would be a gross wrong if not a crime.

Thus the two men who were the most prominent among the first Secessionists of Clay county, each a stalwart among the stalwarts, were the first to abandon the cause to its fate and to cry for peace. Col. Routt was the first prominent officer from the county to enter the Southern service, and was the first to leave it. Col. Thompson was among the first to proclaim the doctrine and policy of secession, and was the first to declaim against it. It is not untrue to say that they were consistent in both courses. Believing secession to be politic and right in April, 1861, it was proper they should advocate it and support it. Believing in April, 1862, that secession was wrong and impolitic, it was proper they should denounce it.

But Thompson and Routt made but few proselytes among the Clay county Confederates in arms. They not only refused to desert their new colors, but cursed them for " getting them into the scrape," and then getting out of the scrape themselves in the easiest but most discreditable way.

Now it is perhaps only the truth to say that it was Col. Penick's dictation and counsel — and it may have been his orders — that brought about these meetings and the speeches and acts of Thompson and Routt. He advised the people to a course of submission, and granted favors to those who obeyed him for a time. But after a brief season he lost nearly all of the advantages he had gained on account of the lawless conduct of his men. People learned to hate the Union cause because they somehow considered " Penick's thieves" its exponents.

ORGANIZATION OF THE ENROLLED MISSOURI MILITIA.

On the 22d of July, 1862, when Cols. Jo. Porter and J. A. Poindexter were leading large forces of newly recruited Confederates through North and Northeast Missouri, and Cols. John T. Hughes, John T. Coffee, Vard Cockerell, Joe Shelby and other Confederate officers were slashing about through Jackson, Johnson, Lafayette and Saline counties, and the Federal forces in the State seemed powerless to interfere with them — Gov. Gamble issued an order for the organization " of the entire militia of the State into companies, regi-

HISTORY OF CLAY COUNTY

ments and brigades," for the purpose of "putting down all such marauders, and defending the peaceable citizens of the State."

This order of Gov. Gamble's had a most wonderful effect in creating soldiers. It threw into partially active and irregular service on the Federal side many thousands of men, and it drove into the Confederate army nearly 10,000 other men who had from the first vowed that if they were *forced* to take up arms they would enlist under the banner of the stars and bars.

In Clay county the conservative Union men, chiefly under the leadership of Col. J. H. Moss, decided to obey the order at once, and organize the militia of this county under the auspices of the Conservative Union party, to protect the county against *all* "marauders," whether guerrillas and bushwhackers from Missouri or jayhawkers and red-legs from Kansas.

In the latter part of July three companies of enrolled militia were organized at Liberty. The first company had for officers, Anthony Harsell,[1] captain; T. N. O'Bryant and R. W. Flemming, lieutenants; second company, J. H. Moss, captain; Wm. A. McCarty, C. J. White, lieutenants; third company, W. G. Garth, captain; Arch. Lincoln, J. S. Thomason, lieutenants. A fourth company, organized for the defense of Liberty, and composed of "exempts," had O. P. Moss for captain, and A. J. Calhoun and Wm. T. Reynolds for lieutenants. The companies averaged 80 men each.

The companies of enrolled militia in Clay and Platte were organized in September into a regiment denominated the Forty-eighth Regiment of Enrolled Missouri Militia. Of the field officers of this regiment the following were from Clay county: James H. Moss, colonel; C. J. White, adjutant; W. T. Reynolds, quartermaster; W. A. Morton, surgeon. The following were the Clay county companies in the Forty-eighth.

Company D — Captain, Anthony Harsel; first lieutenant, T. N. O'Bryant, resigned January 8, 1863, succeeded by Benj. Jaggers, second lieutenant, R. W. Flemming.

Company E — Captains, J. H. Moss, promoted to colonel; Wm. A. McCarty, resigned February 11, 1863; A. W. Tracey. First lieutenants, W. A. McCarty, promoted to captain; W. S. Garvey, resigned December 7, 1862; A. W. Tracey, promoted to captain February 14, 1863; John W. Younger. Second lieutenants, C. J.

---

[1] The night after Capt. Harsell entered the service, the Confederates burned his house, with nearly all its contents.

229

HISTORY OF CLAY COUNTY

White, promoted to adjutant; James D. Baxter, resigned April 17, 1863; John Collier.

Company F—Captain, Wm. G. Garth. First lieutenants, Archibald Lincoln, resigned November 11, 1862; John S. Thomason. Second lieutenants, John S. Thomason, promoted to first lieutenant; Thomas J. Bowman.

Company H—Captains, John R. Green, promoted to major September 29, 1862; Solomon G. Bigelow. First lieutenants, Sol. G. Bigelow, promoted to captain; J. S. McCord. Second lieutenants, J. S. McCord, promoted to first lieutenant October 18, 1862; Taylor Hulin.

Company K—Captain, Darius Sessions, killed by the bushwhackers at Missouri City, May 19, 1863. First lieutenants, Ben. R. Everts, resigned January 2, 1863; Wm. T. Davis. Second lieutenant, De Wilton Mosely.

In consequence of the extraordinary reduction in numbers of this regiment by removals from the State, payment of commutation tax in lieu of military service, volunteering in the United States' service, etc., this regiment was disbanded November 1, 1863, and the commissions of officers, with the exception of Col. Moss, were revoked. Col. Moss was retained in commission, and instructed to reorganize the effective militia of Clay, Platte and Clinton counties. He was afterward made colonel of the Eighty-second Enrolled Missouri, one of the regiments of the "Paw-Paw" militia, fully mentioned elsewhere in this volume.

MISCELLANEOUS.

For a time Maj. M. L. James, of Catherwood's regiment, was in command at Liberty. He it was who had commanded the Caldwell county Home Guards in the Blue Mills fight. Drunkenness became so common among the soldiers, and was of such aggravated form that the major issued strict orders in May, that no more spirituous liquors were to be sold to his men, and the severest penalties were threatened against all offenders.

One incident regarding the estimation in which slavery was held in certain Federal sections ought to be mentioned, as a fact for one reason, as a curiosity for another. In the month of May, of this year 1862, four runaway Missouri slaves, the property of Mrs. Sarah Davis, were arrested near Topeka, Kan., and returned to their owner mainly by the assistance of the Federal military authorities. They were brought to Liberty and put in the county jail for safe keeping, taken in

HISTORY OF CLAY COUNTY

charge by the sheriff, and so on, all the same as before the war. But the rule was, even before as well as during the war, that when a slave escaped from Missouri to Kansas he was practically as free as if he had his deed of emancipation in his pocket.

During the first part of the month of August a number of stirring military incidents occurred in the adjoining counties. At Independence August 11, and at Lone Jack five days later, occurred two important and memorable conflicts between the Federals and Confederates, in both of which the Federals were defeated, though after stubborn fighting. For the numbers engaged the battle of Lone Jack was one of the hardest ever fought in Missouri, or perhaps anywhere, during the Civil War.

Perhaps 200 Clay county men took part in these engagements. Capt. Grooms, Col. Gideon Thompson and Col. Boaz Roberts were there at the head of considerable commands. At Independence Col. John T. Hughes, who had formerly been a prominent citizen of Clay, the author of "Doniphan's Expedition to Mexico," and who has been frequently referred to in preceding pages of this volume, was killed. Among the Confederate killed at Lone Jack was Wash Thompson. Other Clay men were killed and a number wounded.

At this time Confederate raiders were on both sides of the river. Down in Carroll county Maj. John L. Mirick had 500 men, too strong for a force of Penick's men under Maj. Biggers, sent against them, and the first week in August Penick himself went down with the remainder of his regiment, leaving Capt. Harsel with some newly enrolled militia in command. There was considerable uneasiness lest Liberty should be taken, but the strong Confederate bands in Jackson county could not cross the river, and the danger passed.

After the Lone Jack fight Lexington was seriously menaced by the Confederates. From Liberty Penick and his command and the enrolled militia companies under Capts. Moss, Harsell and Garth went down to reinforce the Federal garrison. Capt. O. P. Moss was the only officer in command at Liberty, or even in Clay county, for a few days. When Penick returned he remained but a day or two, and then, with his entire regiment, he left for Jackson county, leaving the enrolled militia to take care of Clay.

Thursday, August 14, Col. Penick, with 50 men, went from Liberty into Platte, to break up a band of alleged bushwhackers, though perhaps they were really Confederate recruits that had formed in the southeastern part of that county, three miles southwest of Barry. Nearing the camp Penick made inquiries concerning it of two citizens

231

HISTORY OF CLAY COUNTY

there living, but they declared that it was not within three miles. A few hundred yards further, the bushwhackers were encountered, in ambush, ready and waiting. At the first fire two Federals were killed outright, one mortally wounded and two others seriously hurt. The Federals were thrown into confusion, but rallied, and then both parties retreated. Penick took out the two citizens, who he claimed had betrayed him, shot them and burned the house and barn.

August 23, a band of Kansas jayhawkers and red-legs made a raid on the southwest portion of Clay. Word was brought to Liberty and Capt. H. B. Johnson, of Penick's regiment, in command, sent 30 enrolled militia, under Lieuts. Flemming and Thomason, after them. The raiders were found in the bottom between Liberty and Kansas City. The militia fired on them, attacking them as savagely as if they had been Confederate bushwhackers, wounded a number, took four prisoners and recovered 25 negroes and 30 horses, which the rascals had stolen from our citizens and were carrying off to Kansas. During the day a company of militia from Kansas City came over and co-operated with Flemming and Thomason in breaking up and driving out the marauders. It was now demonstrated that the enrolled militia of Clay, so long as commanded by Col. Moss and led by Lieuts. Thomason and Flemming, might be depended on to fight thieves and robbers, whether they were clad in Federal blue or wore " hodden gray " and butternut.

September 24 two Confederate officers, Col. Boaz Roberts and a partisan leader named Scott, while in Barry, captured Deputy Sheriff Wm. E. Rhea, who was out in the country collecting taxes. They took from him the tax-books, about 25 writs of execution, robbed him of his horse, pistol, $40 in money and then released him.

NOVEMBER ELECTION 1862.

Notwithstanding the presence of hundreds of soldiers in this county in the year 1862, and the thousand and one shocks to the law and order incident to " war's alarms," courts were held and other proceedings gone through with according to the forms of law, and the vote at the election of this year, while not very large and full, was fair and free, and the election itself was conducted without intimidation or any overawing on the part of the soldiery. So far as this county was concerned, the bayonet protected, and did not attempt to control the ballot box.

The only political issue involved was the question of emancipation, and there were few emancipationists in this county. No one could vote unless he had first taken the Gamble oath, and so all the voters were — or at least presumed to be — "loyal." The following was the vote in this county: —

Congress — J. H. Birch, 582; Austin A. King, 159; E. M. Samuel, 179. (Birch and King were anti-Emancipationists; Samuel was not committed.)

State Senator — John Doniphan, of Platte, 844; no opposition.
Representative — L. W. Burris, 828; no opposition.
Sheriff — Wm. W. Smith, 469; F. R. Long, 430.
Assessor — Greenup Byrd, Jr., 449; James Burns, 399.
County Judge — Alvah Maret; no opposition.
County Treasurer — B. F. Tillery; no opposition.

HISTORY OF CLAY COUNTY

CHAPTER IX.

DURING THE YEAR 1863.

Miscellaneous War Items of the Early Spring — The Raid on Missouri City and Killing of Capt. Sessions — Other War Incidents — After the Lawrence Raid — Threatened Invasion from Kansas Prevented — The "Paw Paw Militia," and Certain Military Incidents in This County During 1862 and 1863 — Interesting Testimony of Col. J. H. Moss — November Election — Sons of Malta — Military Murders.

Early in the spring of this year, before the leaves of the trees put out, or even the buds began to swell, the Confederate guerrilla bands in this part of Missouri were on the move. The first band in Clay county was led by Joe Hart, of Buchanan county, who had deserted the Confederate army to come back to Missouri and "bushwhack." About March 1, Capts. Garth and Tracy, of the enrolled militia, captured one of Hart's men and five jayhawkers near Missouri City. The bushwhacker was sent to St. Joe; the jayhawkers to Kansas City. Hart and half a dozen of his band ranged through the country in the neighborhood of Centerville (Kearney) claiming to be in search of a militiaman named Harris, whom they wanted to kill, but at the same time they were robbing citizens. From one man they took $60 in money and two horses; from everybody, arms.

April 29, Capt. Tracy and half a dozen militia were fired on, after dark, at a point 12 miles east of north of Liberty, by Hart's band. The bushwhackers retreated after the first fire, and Tracy captured two of their mules.

In adjoining counties, before spring had fairly arrived, the guerrillas and bushwhackers were at work. Coleman Younger, Dave Poole, Fernando Scott, and some others of Quantrell's band captured the steamer New Sam Gaty, at Sibley's landing, March 27, killing three of Penick's men after they had surrendered, robbing all the passengers, carrying off 20 negroes, and throwing into the river 100 sacks of flour and a dozen wagons.

THE RAID ON MISSOURI CITY.

On the 19th of May occurred a guerrilla raid on Missouri City made by a band of 12 guerrillas, led by Fernando Scott, who crossed the river at Sibley, and rendezvoused for the raid at the house of Moses

234

HISTORY OF CLAY COUNTY

McCoy, in Fishing River township. It is said that Frank James, Fletch. Taylor and Joe Hart were members of Scott's band. The following account of the raid was given in the current number of the Liberty *Tribune*, and is pronounced fairly accurate : —

One of the residents of Missouri City came in and reported either to Capt. Darius Sessions of the enrolled militia, or Lieut. Gravenstein, of the Twenty-fifty Missouri Volunteers, that he noticed two or three suspicious characters lurking about a short distance below that place. The captain and lieutenant with not more than three or four men — all we suppose they could muster at the time for duty — went out on a scout, and had not proceeded far before they were fired upon from the brush by a body of men at least three or four times their number. Finding their little force inadequate, they were compelled to beat a hasty retreat in a somewhat northerly direction. They were, however, hotly pursued by the bushwhackers. Capt. Sessions was shot dead, several bullets, it is said, entering his body. Lieut. Gravenstein, finding his pursuers fast gaining on him, and escape about hopeless, turned and offered to surrender but was killed on the spot without mercy. A private of the Twenty-fifth Missouri who was wounded in the arm, found by a citizen, and brought into Missouri City, was cruelly fired upon by several of these outlaws as they came rushing into town — neither his helpless condition nor the humane attentions of those around him dressing his wound, could save him. He was still alive when last heard from but his recovery is deemed hopeless. The ruffians broke into James Reed's store, forced open his safe, took therefrom some $170 or $180 in gold, destroyed all his valuable papers and other property. They also plundered and did considerable damage to Mr. B. W. Nowlin's store, and after charging about for some time in a threatening manner, departed to the woods below the city.

These men, those of them who came into the city, were under the leadership of Scott, a saddler who lived in Liberty some years ago, but for the past four or five years has resided in Jackson county. He is a native of Ohio. George Todd it is also said was at hand with another squad. Their pickets were seen early Wednesday morning on the bluff above the lower part of Missouri City. The number of guerrillas altogether was sixteen, although at first they were supposed to number a much larger force.

Capt. Garth, with what forces he could hastily gather up, immediately went in pursuit, but did not succeed in capturing any of them. In the absence of the militia the citizens of Liberty turned out *en masse* to defend the town, and it was done with a willingness and a "vim" that plainly indicated that the bushwhackers had but few if any sympathizers in Liberty.

The bushwhackers were all from Jackson and other counties but three — Vandivere, Easton and James — all of whom were of Clay. Vandivere boasted in the streets of Missouri City that he killed

Capt. Sessions because he reported on him and wouldn't let him stay at home. The rascals, when firing on the wounded man in town, declared that when any of their men were captured they were killed, and that they intended to do the same — that they neither asked nor gave quarter.

Mr. Benjamin Soper, residing some eight or ten miles north of Liberty, reported to headquarters on Thursday that fourteen of the above squad took possession of his farm, stationing out pickets, and notifying him and family that they were prisoners, and not to leave the place. That they remained all one day, and on leaving took one of his best horses, and warned him it would not be good for any of the family to be caught from home that night.

The body of Capt. Sessions was buried at Liberty with the honors of war. The remains of Lieut. Gravenstein were sent to his family at St. Joseph. This was the same Darius Sessions who, during the troubles in Kansas, was accused of Abolitionism, and came near being lynched in the streets of Liberty. He was saved by the intervention of prominent Pro-Slavery men, who vouched for his soundness, and a public meeting denounced the lawless proceedings against him. (See preceding pages of this volume.)

OTHER WAR INCIDENTS.

Along in the summer, after the raid on Missouri City — or Richfield, as that part of the town was then called — the county was badly infested with bushwhackers, who roamed about in every township, stealing, robbing, and sometimes murdering. Of an exploit of three of these partisans the *Tribune*, in August, contained the following : —

Three Southern Gentlemen in Search of Their " Rights." — On the morning of the 6th of August, Franklin James, with two others of the same stripe, stopped David Mitchell on his road to Lexington, about six miles west of Liberty, and took from him $1.25, his pocket knife, and a pass he had from the Provost Marshal to cross the plains. This was one of the " rights " these men are fighting for. James sent his compliments to Maj. Green, and said he would like to see him.

Owing to the disturbed condition of affairs it was impossible to collect the public revenue in the usual way, and in July the county court made the following order : —

CLAY COUNTY COURT, July 8, 1863.

WHEREAS, it is painfully apparent, and for many months past has existed in our county, which renders it unsafe and almost impossible for the collector and his deputies to collect in the usual manner and within the time prescribed by law, the State and county revenue, and the taxes assessed for military purposes, without calling on the militia to escort and protect them from the roving bands of thieves and marauders which infect our county; and that were said officers to essay, alone and unprotected, to visit tax-payers at their place of residence in the county, a standing temptation too powerful for these bad men to resist, would be given to waylay and rob said officers; and whereas, said collector is under heavy bonds to the State and county for the prompt collection and payment of said taxes — by far the greater part of which remains uncollected; and, whereas, the court desires to see the civil law and authority upheld and respected without the aid and assistance of the military forces in our midst, and to witness the speedy restoration of tranquility, good order, and all the safeguards of society: —

It is therefore ordered by the court that the tax-payers of Clay county who have not yet paid their taxes be notified and enjoined to repair as soon as practicable to the office of Col. F. R. Long, at the court-house, in the city of Liberty, and pay their taxes to said collector or his deputies; and, unless they promptly respond to this order, the court will be compelled, as an act of justice to the State, the county, the brave militia faithfully serving the cause of law and loyalty, and said collector, either to call into requisition the services of said militia to enable said officers to collect said taxes, or to order said defaulting tax-payers to be returned as delinquents.

And be it further ordered that this order be published in the Liberty *Tribune*, as many weeks as may be necessary to give full publicity thereto, and also by printed hand-bills posted in the most prominent places for observation in the county.

(A true copy. Attest).

EPHRAIM D. MURRAY, Clerk.
By THOMAS D. MURRAY, D. C.

On August 27, Capt. W. W. Garth, with a small squad of militia, came upon R. S. Osborn's bushwhackers near Chrisman's school-house and exchanged shots with them. The bushwhackers retreated without loss. A night or so afterward they robbed A. J. Calhoun of $30 in cash and a valuable horse, James Johnson of a horse, J. T. Field, J. Lewis, Richard Morton, Samuel Jones and others of horses, money, clothing, etc., and from Mrs. Richard Price they carried off an old negro man, whom they inhumanly murdered in a corn field near by.

Sunday night, September 6, Maj. John R. Green, of the provisional militia, in command at Liberty, sent a squad of men on a scout out on the Missouri City road. The militia hid themselves, and soon three bushwhackers came along the road and were themselves bush-whacked, the militia firing on them and killing one of their number,

Park Donovan. He had on his person several articles belonging to citizens of the county, among which was a powder flask he had taken from Elder R. C. Morton.

AFTER THE LAWRENCE RAID.

After the raid on Lawrence, Kas., by Quantrell's men, a large public meeting was held at Liberty, T. C. Gordon presiding, to take the sense of the meeting on the affair. Resolutions were passed condemning the raid as " infamous and cruel in the extreme, rivaling the bloodiest deeds of the red men of the forest or the carnivals of Oceanica," and expressing the hope that the " last fiend engaged in this heartrending outrage will be overtaken with swift destruction." The meeting was attended by all parties, including many ex-Confederates. When Ewing's " Order No. 11 " came out, requesting the citizens of Jackson and other counties to either repair to some designated military post or else leave their respective counties, Maj. Green, in command of Clay county, issued the following order:—

HEADQUARTERS, LIBERTY, MO., Sept. 9th, 1863.
Special Order.]
All persons who are leaving Gen. Ewing's district in compliance with his order (No. 11) are hereby prohibited from stopping in this county to reside. All those failing to comply with this order will be escorted beyond the lines of this county.

JOHN R. GREEN,
Major Commanding Post.
By ROBT. W. FLEMMING, Act. Post Adjt.

There was the greatest alarm and anxiety felt in this county and Platte for some time after the sacking of Lawrence. A number of Clay county men belonged to Quantrell's force, and the Kansas militia were threatening to invade Missouri and take dreadful retaliation for what the guerrillas had done. Gen. Thos. J. Ewing has declared that he issued " Order 11 " to prevent lawless bodies of Kansas troops from visiting the Missouri border and slaughtering indiscriminately the people and burning up the country, as they were threatening to do. However this may be, it is certain that Gen. Ewing notified Gen. Guitar, then in command of the district of Northwest Missouri, and also the Federal officers at Liberty to be on the lookout for Kansas raiders. August 27, he sent the following telegram to Gen. Guitar, who was then at Macon City:—

[By Telegraph from Kansas City.]
I am advised that an expedition is being fitted at Leavenworth

or a raid into Missouri; it is uncertain whether they intend to cross the river or attempt the lower border. I have notified commanding officers at Liberty, and directed my provost marshal at Leavenworth to keep the commanding officers at Weston advised. My troops at Fort Leavenworth can not be certainly relied on in the present state of feeling. I have doubts whether any expedition of consequence will really set out, as I have orders that it will be resisted; but you had as well be ready.

THOMAS J. EWING,
Brigadier-General.

Gen. Guitar returned the following answer: —

MACON, Mo., August 27, 1863.

To Brigadier-General Ewing, Kansas City, Mo. — I have this moment received your dispatch of this date, for which I am under obligations. I deeply sympathize with the unfortunate people of Lawrence, and with yourself, in the responsible and embarrassing position you occupy. By all means let speedy vengeance be visited upon the guilty; but, in the name of heaven and humanity, let us protect the innocent and inoffending. I need no assurance that it will be done as far as you are able. I shall be upon the alert, and I admonish the people of Kansas not to cross the Missouri river for the purpose of marauding and destruction; they will certainly be met if they do. I trust so dire a calamity will be averted. I am ready, if need be, to march every soldier in my command from North Missouri to the relief of Kansas, and to the Gulf if necessary. As I denounced and fought against the invasion of Kansas in 1856, as an outrage, so must I resist any invasion of Missouri for any illegal purposes. If they come to aid in maintaining the authority and laws of our glorious Government, I shall welcome them with fraternal hands.

O. GUITAR,
Brigadier-General Commanding.

The same day Guitar sent the following to Col. Williams at St. Joseph: —

MACON, August 27, 1863.

To Col. John F. Williams, St. Joseph, Mo. — I have this moment received a dispatch from Gen. Ewing, advising me he believed an expedition was being fitted out at Leavenworth, to make a raid across the river into Missouri — such a movement must be promptly met and resisted. You had better, perhaps, send Maj. Garth down opposite Leavenworth with "Co. B," to keep a watch upon their movements. You will notify Capt. Garth at Liberty, to move with his company to Wyandotte. You will also notify your troops above St. Joseph, near the river, to be on the alert, and take such steps as will checkmate any movement in that direction. If men cross into Missouri to repeat the outrages which Quantrell and his murderers have just consummated in Kansas, no matter under what pretext, I want them met with "bloody hands." Keep me promptly advised of every hostile indication or movement.

O. GUITAR,
Brigadier-General Commanding.

It was about this time that Gen. Guitar wrote his celebrated "hell-and-the-iron-works" letter to his brother-in-law, Maj. Reeves Leonard. This letter was dated at Macon, September 9, and was severe on the Abolition Federal officers, and declared that runaway negroes were not to be received in Federal camps. The letter closed with this paragraph:—

I write in haste, as I expect to go to St. Louis this evening to look after the Kansas invasion; so you see, I am placed between hell and the iron-works, but thank God I am a free man, amenable to no power save the laws of my country and my God, and under no constraint, except to do right as I see it. Keep the Rebs. and Rads. straight. If our Kansas friends come over I will endeavor to give them such a reception as becomes a brave and hospitable people.

THE " PAW-PAW " MILITIA AND CERTAIN MILITARY INCIDENTS IN 1862–63.

In the fall of 1863 Col. J. H. Moss received orders from Gen. Schofield, at St. Louis, to reorganize the militia of Clay and Platte counties. This he at once proceeded to do by organizing what came to be known as the Eighty-second Regiment of Enrolled Missouri Militia. This regiment and the Eighty-first, Col. John Scott, constituted what was derisively called the "Paw-Paw" militia brigade. Many members of the regiment had been in the rebel or Confederate service, and it was said that some of them had the previous summer laid out in the paw-paw thickets of the Missouri bottoms to keep out of the way of the Federals, and when frost came lived mainly on the paw-paws! From these alleged circumstances the two regiments were called "Paw-Paws" or the "Paw-Paw Militia."

The Radicals greatly disliked the Paw-Paws and wished to have them mustered out of service. The Legislature in January, 1864, appointed a committee to investigate them, and this committee summoned before it several prominent Union men of this county to testify as to the character of the militia and to the general condition of affairs in Clay then and previously. Extracts from the sworn testimony of some of these persons before the committee might be inserted here, but the testimony of Col. Jas. H. Moss, given below, contains the *main*

HISTORY OF CLAY COUNTY

facts in the testimony of all these men, so that is deemed unnecessary to enter into any repetition : —

TESTIMONY OF COL. JAS. H. MOSS.

Ques. by Mr. Davis. What was your reason for organizing the citizen militia, commonly styled the " Paw-paws? " Had you a commission for it? *Ans.* I had an order to that effect, being in command of a sub-district, as colonel of the Forty-eighth E. M. M.

Q. What was the situation of the country at that time? *A.* The border was overrun with outlaws of all sorts; bushwhackers, Southern recruiting officers, thieves and robbers, without any regard to politics. In addition to local troubles of that sort, great excitement prevailed in the State of Kansas on account of the raid on Lawrence, and an invasion of the State was threatened by Gen. Lane. Gen. Ewing had telegraphed to Gen. Guitar, commanding district of North Missouri, that armed organizations were formed in Kansas for the purpose of invading North Missouri, and expressed a doubt whether he would be able to control them, on account of the excitement prevailing in consequence of the Lawrence raid. I found the militia in service in a very demoralized and insubordinate condition. I found one portion of the county of Clay occupied by bushwhackers, Southern recruiting officers and robbers, and the other side by outlaws from the State of Kansas. I found, when I took command, that an order had been given by the district commander for one company to take position on the west side of the county, towards Kansas. The company which had been ordered to do this was in such a demoralized condition, that the officer in command gave it as his excuse for not complying with the order; the men had declared to unite with the outlaws of Kansas, in case of emergency. I found that the citizens, loyal and disloyal, were disarmed, and all the citizens were at the mercy of these outlaws, rebels as well as loyal men. I found it would be impossible to relieve the country from these troubles, without calling on all the citizens to participate in the work, and co-operate with the military. The companies of militia then on duty in the county, were, with the exception of one company, strangers to the people and to the localities, wholly inefficient so far as rebel bushwhackers and outlaws were concerned, and were unwilling to make warfare on robbers and outlaws from Kansas. For the purpose of defeating any attempted invasion from Kansas, such as was threatened by Gen. Lane and predicted by Gen. Ewing, and for the purpose of ridding the county of the bushwhackers, thieves and outlaws, I called together the entire male population of the county, and proposed to have companies organized in different parts of the county to hold themselves in readiness to answer any call for the defense of the county which I might make on them.

I then proceeded at once to re-organize the E. M. M. of the county; I organized two companies of the E. M. M. under the command of loyal officers, and armed them. I did not arm the companies of citizens, having had no occasion to call on them for repelling an invasion. In ten days from the time of the organization, there were no outlaws left in the county. We caught a good many and turned them over to the civil authorities. On several occasions I made details from the companies of citizens, and placed them under the command of my officers, of the regularly enrolled companies of the E. M. M.

Of these captured outlaws there are men claiming to belong to all political parties, but about four-fifths of them are Southern bushwhackers, thieves and outlaws. In addition to these captures, I have banished from the State a number of citizens that had connection with these outrages and outlaws.

A further reason for reorganizing these companies of enrolled militia, now called "Paw-paws," was, that my old regiment, the Forty-eighth, was virtually broken up; some of the companies reduced down to 25 or 30 men, and some without officers.

I enrolled three companies of E. M. M., and put two of them into service.

The citizens were not organized by me direct; they formed their organizations in the different neighborhoods by my direction, and under my authority, so as to be ready when I should have occasion to call on them. The whole object of calling on the citizens *en masse* was to prevent an armed invasion from Kansas, and co-operate with the companies in active service in ridding the county of rebel bushwhackers and outlaws. One of the most desperate outlaws in Missouri was caught by us and is now in jail.

Q. Did your men, the "Paw-paws," interfere with runaway slaves? *A.* Never. Orders were given to all the military in the State to have no connection with slaves, and this has been complied with.

Q. Has your force interfered with the enrollment of slaves? *A.* They have not; but, on the contrary, I recommended the enrolling officer, Lieut. Holmes, to Col. Broadhead, and have furnished him all the assistance in my power, in the way of protection and transportation, purchased supplies and furnished him money out of my own purse to aid in recruiting.

On one occasion there was a controversy between a recruited negro (belonging to a man by the name of Keller) and a citizen by the name of Cravens. Mr. C. owns a negro boy of about 14 years of age, who had been induced to go up to the recruiting office by the negro already recruited. Cravens meeting this recruiting negro in the street, asked him why he was attempting to get that boy of his to enlist. The negro replied and denied that he had made the attempt; Cravens replied: I saw you take him up into the recruiting office. The negro said: He (Cravens) was a liar. Cravens knocked him down; considerable excitement was occasioned, and the affair was immediately reported to my headquarters. I went down to the locality and ordered the recruited negroes to be taken to their quarters, and gave instructions that there should be no acts of violence committed upon the recruits, and any such cases should be reported to me immediately.

The recruiting officer (Holmes) became alarmed, and without applying to me, ordered some of my soldiers to guard his door. I understand the men refused; they were not subject to his orders, and had none from me. Some such language, it was reported, had been used by them. I saw the recruiting officer myself, and told him there should be no obstacles in his way; and there has been no difficulty since. I believe he recruited some fifty negroes in one day, and sent them to the railroad.

Q. What were the antecedents of Holmes? *A.* He was a Secessionist at the outset, said to have acted as Quartermaster to Thompson; but he has been an enthusiastic Union man for some years, and calls himself a Radical now.

Q. Do you know W. E. Rhea? *A.* I know him well.

Q. What were his antecedents? *A.* He is a Union man and has been for two years — and a Radical Union man now; there is no question as to his loyalty now; he started out on the wrong side, was in a rebel company just before Price's retreat from Lexington; we got him out of the company, and he has been an exemplary Union man ever since.

Q. Do you know Robert Fleming? *A.* Yes. He is a Union man, a Radical Union man, he calls himself. He has been a Union man for over two years. He was for a short time in a company of " State Guards," under Claib. F. Jackson.

Q. Do you know Capt. Garth? *A.* Yes. He started out a rebel, but is now a good Union man, and has performed his duties in the militia very efficiently.

Q. Who is Capt. Prixley? *A.* He was an officer in Price's army; I do not recollect when he came home. When I called on the citizens for assistance he offered his company of citizens to me, which I refused to accept, not wishing to have a man from Price's army commanding a company. The company has been disbanded and has never been in service.

Q. Has your force never interfered with runaway slaves? *A.* Two men from Jackson county had kidnaped a fugitive negro and brought him over to Clay county; one of my officers, Capt. Thomason, received a line from Gen. Ewing stating the facts, whereupon my men arrested the kidnapers and the negro, and returned them to Kansas City.

Q. What is the character of the men in the Paw-paw companies as to loyalty? *A.* I will state that they are now, and during the entire term of their service have been, loyal; some, in the early part of the rebellion, were disloyal, and connected themselves with the rebel service. The men all willingly and cheerfully took the oath of allegiance. I made them take an additional oath, to war upon Southern recruiting officers and bushwhackers; they took the oath cheerfully and have conducted themselves in a manner which satisfied me of their sincerity. They have not only hunted bushwhackers and Southern rebels who were in arms, but they have reported acts of disloyalty and disloyal language of citizens, who (the citizens) have been punished by me in consequence thereof. I refer to the men I have in service and belong to my regiment.

Q. What proportion of the men in the two companies of Clay county have been in the rebel service? *A.* Each company has 85 men; my impression is that from 15 to 20 in each company are of that class.

Q. Have any brigands or armed bands from Kansas invaded the Missouri border for plunder? *A.* Yes. There has been a system of plundering going on since the war commenced; outlaws from Kansas and Missouri have carried on a partnership work of plundering, murdering, arson, robbery, etc., which has ended in the desolation of the border counties, on the south side of the river, down to Arkansas, and the loss of life and property on the north side of the river. That system was in full operation when I took command in September last. The counties of Clay and Platte were being daily and nightly ravaged by armed men, white and black; some of them in the garb of Federal soldiers. On one occasion after I took command, a squad of my men caught some of Gen. Ewing's soldiers at night, committing depredations in my county, who were sent to the General's headquarters. Many other outrages and robberies were committed by soldiers; one of the most extensive was by men under Capt. Ryan, of the Fourth M. S. M., on their way from Buchanan county; they stole horses, money and jewelry, from men and women they met on the road.

Q. Have murders and robberies been committed by the enrolled militia previous to their disbanding? *A.* Not in my county; the companies I found in service in Platte and Clay, when I took command, were favoring the system of plundering practiced by the Kansas outlaws, and refused to fight them. They openly refused to fight these outlaws, who came with impunity into these counties, night and day.

NOVEMBER ELECTION 1863.

At the general election in Missouri in November, 1863, but two tickets were voted for, both "Union," of course. One ticket, headed by Barton Bates, W. V. N. Bay and John D. S. Dryden, for Judges of the Supreme Court, was called the Conservative ticket, and was voted for generally by the Democrats; the other, headed by H. H. A. Clover, Arnold Krekel and David Wagner, was denominated the Radical Republican or Charcoal ticket. This election is remarkable for being the first in Missouri at which, under a general law, the voting was by ballot and not *vive voce*.

The vote in Clay county was more than twelve to one in favor of the Conservative candidates, as follows: —

Conservatives — Bates, 1,328; Bay, 1,324; Dryden, 1,323.
Radicals — Clover, 92; Krekel, 92; Wagner, 87.

For circuit judge, Geo. W. Dunn, Conservative, received 1,220 votes, and D. P. Whitmer, Radical, 148.

"SONS OF MALTA."

In the fall of 1863 the extraordinary order of "Sons of Malta," or as it was here called, "Knights of Palermo," had an organization or "council" in Liberty, with many members. This alleged "order" was a most stupendous and at the same time a most ludicrous and laughable humbug. It pretended to have a ritual, signs, grips, etc., similar to Freemasonry, but really was no order at all. The initiation was all there was of it. The poor candidates, unsuspicious and confiding, were always blindfolded and tied and then put through a series of practical jokes — tossed in a blanket, deluged with dirty water, made to assume a variety of ridiculous postures, etc., and finally were fearfully and ponderously armored, panoplied and equipped, led in front of a mirror and the bandages on their eyes removed.

MURDERS COMMITTED.

Up to the 1st of January, 1864, there had been eighteen citizens of the county murdered by the military forces of both sides. Four Union men had been killed by the bushwhackers, and the Federals had killed fourteen men of Confederate proclivities. Of the latter Penick's men killed six, enrolled and provisional militia six, and the Twenty-fifth Missouri Infantry two.

CHAPTER X.

DURING THE YEAR 1864.

Jayhawker raid on Missouri City — The Federal Draft — Bushwhacker's Raid — Fletch Taylors' First Raid, and Murder of Bond and Daily — He Kills the Bigelows — His Letter to Capt. Garth — His Skirmish on Fishing River with Capt. Kemper — Miscellaneous War Items — Ford's and Jennison's Visit which They were not Invited to Repeat — Bill Anderson — Other War Incidents — Census — Presidential Election.

On the night of the 20th of January, 1864, a company of 40 thieves led by a man calling himself "Maj. Sanders," of Jennison's regiment of Kansas jayhawkers, crossed the river from Jackson county and captured Missouri City, then held by a small force of enrolled militia, under Capt. Geo. S. Story, of this county. Capt. Story was made prisoner and guarded, though in attempting an escape he was shot at. The robbers then plundered B. W. Nowlin's store of $2,000 worth of goods and fled.

In February the Federal draft caused no little disquietude in the county. Public meetings were held to encourage voluntary enlistments in the U. S. service, and the county court offered a bounty of $200 for each recruit so enlisting from this county. Under calls from the President previous to December 19, 1864, the full quota of men required from Clay had been 398, and the number furnished 407, making a surplus of 9. Under the call of December 19, 1864, the quota was fixed at 98, and 47 were furnished, leaving a deficiency of 51.

Up to February 20, 1865, the county had paid in bounties the sum of $9,000.

BUSHWHACKER RAIDS.

In the early summer of 1864 bands of bushwhackers and guerrillas invaded Clay county and began operations. Many Clay county men belonged to them, and they found numerous friends and sympathizers here who aided and abetted them when it was possible to do so with reasonable safety. The war had been in progress so long, and had been waged with such bitterness on the border of Missouri, that people had come to possess the most intense hatred and animosity on the subject. Many Confederate sympathizers favored anything that would

HISTORY OF CLAY COUNTY

injure the Federal cause, and as the bushwhackers claimed to be fighting that cause exclusively, and did really fight the military representatives occasionally, it was deemed proper to aid them by at least feeding them, sheltering them, giving them information, etc. On the other hand some of the Unionists deemed it possible and laudable to kill " rebels " at all times and under all circumstances, and aided all bodies of troops that were pro-United States and anti-Confederate.

About the 1st of June four bushwhackers — said to have been Chas. F. Taylor, Arch. Clements, Peyton Long and James Bissett — drew the first blood in Clay county. Long and Bissett had their homes here. Chas. F. Taylor (or " Fletch " Taylor, as he is commonly called) was from Independence, and Clements, the cruelest, most desperate guerrilla of the war, was from Johnson county. Fletch. Taylor was the leader. June 5 these four, all dressed in Federal uniform, came to the house of Bradley Y. Bond, a quiet, reputable citizen of this county, called him out and shot him. Mr. Bond had been in the Federal service in 1862, but was taken prisoner at Lone Jack, paroled, and had been at home subsequently.

The next day the same men, with one or two recruits, went to the house of Alvis Dailey, called him out of the field where he was at work, marched him before them, and as he was crossing a pair of bars shot him dead. Mr. Dailey was about 23 years of age, and had been a member of Capt. Garth's company of militia. The bushwhackers went to the house and said to the family that they had killed Dailey, and the one who claimed that he did the shooting said he had done it because Dailey belonged to the squad that killed Park Donovan, another bushwhacker, in the night fight the year before.

Now began that series of frightful scenes that occurred in Clay county in the summer and fall of 1864 when murders and killings were numerous, and robberies, plunderings and thefts were of such frequent occurrences as not to be mentioned, except as matters of course and of small consequence. Men were slain before the eyes of their wives and children, or else shot down without mercy by the roadside and their bodies left to fester and corrupt in the sun. Property was taken and destroyed on every hand, business of all kinds was prostrated, values were unsettled, everything was disturbed. Many people left the county, or had left, for the gold mines of Montana and Idaho ; others went to Iowa and Nebraska for safety, others fled they knew not whither.

Verily, those who had clamored so loudly for war in the beginning, and would be satisfied at naught else, should have listened to the in-

HISTORY OF CLAY COUNTY

junction of good old Chaucer who, 500 years before, had said of war (or " werre ") in his quaint old Saxon : —

Ther is ful many a man that crieth " werre! werre!" that wot ful litel what werre amounteth. Werre, at his beginning, hath so greet an entre and so large, that every wight may entre whan him liketh and lightly finde werre; but what ende schal falle thereof it is not lightly to know. For sothly whan that werre is oones bygonne, ther is ful many a child unbore of his mooder that schal sterve yong, bycause thilke werre, or elles live in sorwe and die in wrecchidnes; and therefore, er that eny werre be bygonne, men mosti have gret counseil and gret deliberacioun.

The bushwhackers swarmed through the county, crossing back and forth from Jackson when they pleased, and roaming where they listed. A negro, belonging to Abijah Withers, was shot by them in cold blood near Beauchamp's farm, south of Liberty. He was returning from town where he had sold a load of wood, and was shot, as alleged, " for fun."

Stables were robbed everywhere. In certain neighborhoods, the farmers slept in their barns and horse lots, thoroughly armed, and carefully guarding their horses. Money and other valuables were hidden away. Quite often the bushwhackers robbed Southern men as readily as " Feds.," one man's money being considered as good as another's.

June 15, George Shepherd and six other Jackson county bushwhackers rode into Missouri City, but did no damage. Other bands here were not harmless.

During the last week in June Fletch. Taylor's band, numbering now it is said 40 or 50 men, killed two men, Simeon G. Bigelow and John Bigelow, brothers and Union men, living in the northeastern part of the county. The Bigelows were Union men, and had come originally from one of the Northern States. Two years before they had belonged to Col. Moss' regiment of militia. The next day Bishop Bailey, another Union man, and a citizen of Smithville, was killed by Taylor's band, while on the road from Smithville to Liberty and four or five miles from home.

A day or two before the killing of these the Federals had killed a Mr. Smith, of Fishing River township, and left his body lying in the road, some miles north of Liberty. David Coffman, a bushwhacker, had been killed in the southern part of Clinton. He and a comrade named Davis came to Jeff. Pryor's and demanded horses and money. A few hours afterward he was overtaken in a lane near a Mr. Smith's,

248

on the road between Haynesville and Plattsburg, and killed by a squad led by a son of Mr. Pryor. Davis jumped his horse over a fence and escaped, but Coffman's horse, which belonged to Ambrose Stone, could not make the jump.

A short time after the killing of the brothers Bigelow and Bailey, Fletch. Taylor sent the following letter to Capt. Kemper, in Liberty : —

To Capt. Kemper, Commanding Post at Liberty:

SIR — In accordance with promises I made to Mr. Gosney, one of the peace committee, in relation to leaving Clay county, if the Radicals would also leave (which, I believe, was the understanding), I got my men together and proceeded toward Clinton county, and had got there when I heard about Coffman being killed. I immediately returned to avenge his death, and I did by killing the two Bigelows. I then started for Platte with some of my men, intending to stay out of these counties according to promises ; but hearing of one of my men being killed, I have come again to avenge his death — *and I will do it.* You now know why I returned, and I am going to stay here until the Radicals all leave this county ; and furthermore, I am going to fight all soldiers sent after me if they fall in my way. Sir, if you wish the peace of Clay county, you will use all your influence in keeping the Radicals out of here. And furthermore, I have found out that there has been citizens interrupted, imprisoned and driven from their homes, which is calculated to ruin this county more than any thing else ; for if the citizens are to be sufferers by you, I will make the Union party suffer as much, if not more — for by your interruption of them it recruits my company — whereas, if you and I would let them alone, we could fight one another, and we will be fighting men who have put themselves out for that purpose, and not fight the unsuspected citizen who is not in arms and deserving the fate which you wish to bring on him and his family.

Now, sir ; in conclusion, I will let you understand what I am going to do : I want peace, if it can be gained by honorable terms — and you can give it to the citizens or not. In the first place, if the Federals leave this county, I will leave also ; but if they stay, I will be about, and if you don't interrupt the citizens, I will be equally as kind. I will carry war on as you carry it on. You can't drive me out of this county. I will await your actions. You can make peace or war.— I will leave it to your choice. If I find that you are warring on the citizens, so be it ; *I will retaliate* — if you fight me alone, I will return the compliment. Your actions shall be my answer, or answer as you want.   I remain, sir, yours,

CHAS. F. TAYLOR,
Captain Commanding the Country.

To CAPT. KEMPER.
     Commanding the Town.

HISTORY OF CLAY COUNTY

The Bigelow brothers were killed only after a desperate resistance. Cornered in their house they refused to surrender and fought to the last as best they could. When their guns were empty they seized pieces of furniture and struck at their assailants until shot down. It is said that in this fight Jesse James, then a newly recruited member of Taylor's company, had his finger shot off.

SKIRMISH ON FISHING RIVER.

On Saturday, July 2, 1864, Capt. B. W. Kemper, of Co. C, Ninth M. S. M., who had been in command of the post at Liberty for some weeks, set out into the country after the bushwhackers. He struck straight for the Fishing river country, a locality rough, broken into hills, hollows and defiles by the river and its numerous little branches, and withal wooded and timbered — a favorite place for the " knights of the brush."

At first Kemper had a considerable detachment, but this he divided into three or four squads, the more effectually to scour the country. Sunday night a shower fell, and Monday morning a trail showing that a considerable number of bushwhackers had passed was struck by Kemper's party of about thirty men, and they followed it hard and fast.

A short distance below the ford over Fishing river, where the road leading from Liberty to the old Laidlaw farm crossed, a high, overhanging bank caused by a sharp curve in the stream overlooked and commanded the crossing. Upon and behind this bank about twenty-five guerrillas, under Fletch. Taylor, were in ambush awaiting their enemies. Unconscious of immediate danger the Federals rode into the ford and halted to allow the horses to drink. Immediately the bushwhackers from their place of concealment opened at almost point blank range a withering fire on the soldiers, who, surprised and terrorized no doubt, wheeled about in disorder and fled.

Two Federals were killed. Sergt. J. W. Kirby was killed instantly, and Private James Colston died in an hour. Capt. Kemper himself was severely wounded in the leg; Corporal John R. Ruberson was severely, and Private —— Colston slightly wounded. The bodies of the two killed were buried at Liberty the next day. The bushwhackers did not lose a man.

MISCELLANEOUS WAR ITEMS.

On the 28th of June Capt. John S. Thomason had reorganized his company of militia, which with Garth's and Younger's, and Capt.

Kemper's Ninth M. S. M., composed the only Federal troops in the county. Capt. Story's company had been disbanded in March. Gen. Roscrans issued order No. 107, allowing the people in districts where the bushwhackers were numerous to organize companies for protection and defense. A mass meeting was held at Liberty, July 11, and attended by all parties, for even many of Confederate proclivities were opposed to bushwhacking. It was determined to keep one or two companies of militia composed of citizens of the county constantly in service.

July 20, another very large mass meeting composed of 1,500 citizens from all parts of the county was held in Liberty, and the following resolution was one of many others adopted : —

Fourth. That guerrillas — whatever the name they assume — and bushwhackers are the ravenous monsters of society, and their speedy and utter extermination should be sought by all brave and honorable men — and that all who knowingly and willingly sympathize with, harbor, conceal, assist and feed them should be uniformly and rigidly held accountable and punished in accordance with the laws of war among civilized nations ; and we hereby distinctly, respectfully and emphatically protest against the action of the assistant provost marshals and others in authority in turning loose upon this and other communities men whose previous outrages and disloyal conduct called for a proper and salutary measure of punishment, many of whom have gone to the brush and are now fighting against the government and against their peaceable and loyal neighbors.

July 12, four or five of Catherwood's disbanded men, or men on furlough, had an encounter with about the same number of Capt. Thomason's company of militia in Centerville (now Kearney). Thomason's men were in a house when Catherwood's came up and fired on them. The Clay county men ran out and returned the fire, Catherwood's galloped off; Thomason's men followed them and killed one and wounded another.

Before Kemper's company left, Lieut. C. H. Gordon, its second lieutenant (now prosecuting attorney of Boone county), had a skirmish on Clear creek with two small companies of bushwhackers, Peyton Long's and Nin. Litton's. One of the latter's squad, James Justus, was killed.

July 15, 1864, Col. J. H. Ford, of the Second Colorado cavalry, was sent into this county at the head of a body of 300 Federal troops, consisting of detachments of the Second Colorado, Ninth Missouri State militia, and Jennison's Sixteenth Kansas. Ford marched straight for Liberty and encamped. His troops, or at least the Colorado men and the Kansas, turned themselves loose upon the citizens and committed the wildest excesses. The Kansas men were especially bad. They stole whatever they could, and openly plundered hencoops, pig-pens and smoke-houses, and abused the citizens with the foulest language. In Liberty many of them robbed the merchants of considerable amounts of goods. The next day Ford issued the following order in regard to all this robbing and stealing : —

HEADQUARTERS, FORD'S BRIGADE, LIBERTY, July 16, 1864.
GENERAL ORDERS.]
The colonel commanding desires to remind the officers and soldiers of his command that stealing, robbing and pillaging from the citizens of these counties must not be allowed. You are soldiers engaged in upholding the laws of your country, and protecting the lives and property of loyal citizens, and your conduct should be such as to inspire the belief that your object in visiting this country is not to destroy but to save. Battalion and company commanders will see that all such breaches of discipline are promptly and strictly punished. By order of   JAMES H. FORD,
    ROBERT S. ROE,   Colonel Commanding.
        Lieut. and A. A. A. G.

Fortunately the Coloradoans and Kansans did not remain long in the county. They left in three days, to everybody's joy. Between them and the bushwhackers it was six of one and half a dozen of the other.

On the 10th of August a Mr. Columbus Whitlock, who lived in the northern part of the county, and was considered a harmless, inoffensive Union man, was murdered by the bushwhackers. He was on his way to Smithville for a physician to attend his sick mother, when the bushwhackers caught him at Bill Hall's, took him with them to a point on Wilkinson's creek, within a mile of Smithville, and there shot him to death and stripped the body of a portion of the clothing. Three days before Mr. Whitlock had married a Miss Angeline Cox, of Platte county. He was buried at Mrs. Rollins'.

About the 10th of August the noted guerrilla Bill Anderson came into the county from a successful raid as far east as Shelbina, Shelby county. He had but a dozen men left, however, out of twenty-five, although not all had been killed. Instantly four or five little bushwhacking bands ran out of their coverts and joined the noted leader, who soon had a company of sixty-five men. At Mr. Creek's, in the eastern part of the county, a reorganization was effected, and Anderson given command.

About the 11th of August this company started eastward towards

HISTORY OF CLAY COUNTY

Ray and Carroll to form a junction with some Confederate recruits under Col. J. C. C. Thornton ("Coon" Thornton) and a force of bushwhackers under George Todd and John Thrail. The first day out a squad of militia from a company stationed at Fredericksburg, Ray county, was struck at Mr. Ford's, two miles east of Prathersville, and chased to their quarters.

Capt. Patton Colly, of Ray, who commanded the company of militia referred to (Co. E, Fifty-first E. M. M.), set out at once at the head of not more than thirty men. Anderson, after the first encounter, moved eastward until he struck the county line, when he moved down the road along the line a little over a mile on the farm of Mrs. Summers and went into ambush, leaving a rear guard behind to give him warning if the Federals should follow him, as he expected they would.

Within an hour or two Colly came up and at once proceeded to deliver battle. He attacked the rear guard and drove it, and Anderson then came forward and decided the fight very shortly. The Federals were routed and driven off in a hurry. Anderson himself killed Capt. Colly,[1] shooting him out of his saddle with a dragoon revolver. Two other members of Colly's company, named George Odell and Philip Sigel, were killed in the fight.

A short time before the fight came off Anderson's men had captured two members of Colly's company, Smith Hutchings and John Hutchings, who lived in the southeastern part of the county, and were returning to their company from a visit to their homes when captured. When the firing began Anderson killed these two at once, without mercy, and it is said that after the fight their bodies were mutilated.

In response to repeated calls for reinforcements, Gen. Fisk, in command of this district, sent Col. E. C. Catherwood with several companies of troops into this county. Catherwood's old regiment, the Sixth M. S. M., had been partly disbanded, and he had entered the U. S. service and was recruiting a regiment which was known as the Thirteenth Missouri Cavalry. Catherwood relieved Capt Kemper, who left the county with his company August 9, for Parkville. Catherwood arrived at Liberty August 3, and encamped in Steven's pasture.

Learning of the fight and death of Capt. Colly, Capt. Catherwood led a strong force after the guerrillas, too late to accomplish anything.

---

[1] According to the testimony of Ninian Letton, now City Marshal of Liberty, who was present as a member of Anderson's company, and says he saw the shot fired.

He followed into Ray county and turned back. Here the pursuit had been taken up by Capt. Clayton Tiffin with a company of militia, and he was joined by Capt. Calvert's company, and the two, on the 14th, fought a severe skirmish with Anderson on the Wakenda, in Carroll, losing ten men killed, while Anderson lost but one killed.

In the first week of September, and up to the 15th, a considerable force of guerrillas under Todd and Thrailkill operated in portions of Clay, Platte, Clinton, Caldwell and Ray counties, before starting for Boone and Howard. About the 15th they passed through the eastern portion of Clay, and Garth's and Younger's companies of home militia and some of Catherwood's men were sent after them.

After Bill Anderson was killed, October 27, 1864, many of his company deserted and some made their way into Clay, where forming into small squads, they continued to disturb the quiet of the country.

Sunday, November 13, a band of bushwhackers fired on some militia who were in the door-yard of Lieut. Smith, in the northern part of the county. Lieut. Smith and his little son were severely wounded. The militia returned the fire and the bushwhackers left. Eight days later — or, to be exact, on the night of the 21st — a band of them went to the arsenal, south of Liberty, and forced Maj. Grant to give them his uniform. The next morning, Lieut. Rhea, with a detachment of Catherwood's regiment, surprised five of the band in a house in the bottom, five miles below the arsenal. The bushwhackers retreated with one of their number wounded and leaving three saddles. One Federal was mortally wounded, dying the next day.

During the Price raid, in the latter part of October, and while the battles of Independence, Little Blue, and Westport were in progress, the excitement and alarm in this county were intense. Many of Confederate sympathies hoped that Gen. Price would defeat the Federals and cross the river and wrest the county from the Federals. The militia of the county were on the *qui vive* constantly, watching the fords or crossings, and guarding the towns. In Liberty the "curbstone brigade," an improvised company of militia, was called out on two occasions when the alarm was given that the raiders were coming.

But Gen. Price was, defeated at Westport and on the Little Blue and turned southward, and soon after his entire command was disastrously defeated, Gens. Marmaduke and Cabell and 1,500 men taken prisoners, and then his retreat became a straggling disordered rout into Texas, his train destroyed, his men starving, and his army saved from annihilation only by the hard fighting of Gen. Jo. Shelby's division at Newtonia. Then the hearts of our people of Confederate sympathies sank low and only the most sanguine among them had hopes of the triumph of their cause ever afterward.

CENSUS OF 1864.

A census taken in December, 1864, showed the total white population of the county to be 9,421, of which 4,671 were males and 4,740 females, showing a preponderance of females at that time owing to the absence of so many men in the war or in Montana and Idaho. The total number of slaves was 1,756, of whom 1,013 were females; free colored, 58. Total population, 11,235.

THE POLITICAL CANVASS OF 1864.

Amid all the turmoil of war, the political canvass of 1864 went on about as usual. Gen. George B. McClellan and Hon. George H. Pendleton were the national candidates of the Democratic party, and Abraham Lincoln and Andrew Johnson, the nominees of the Republicans. For Lieutenant-Governor on the Democrat ticket, with Gen. Thos. L. Price for Governor, was Hon. Luke W. Burris, of Clay. This fact gave the canvass something of interest to our people. Burris had been a Whig, but was now a cordial supporter of the Democrat party and policy, for Whigism was no more.

A short time before the election, during the Price invasion, when the Confederates had advanced as far as Lexington, Mr. Burris and Gen. Tom Price addressed a large audience composed very largely of soldiers and militia, whose presence and whose half-uttered threats to suppress the meeting did not prevent the speakers from uttering their sentiments — "Copperhead" sentiments although they were called.

The result in this county of the November election was as follows, the Democrats carrying the county by a large majority : —

President — McClellan, 777 ; Lincoln, 206.

Congress — E. H. Norton (Dem.), 635 ; R. T. Van Horn (Rep.), 157 ; Austin A. King (Dem.), 111.

Governor — Thomas L. Price, 786 ; Thos. C. Fletcher (Rep.), 195.

Convention — Against, 766 ; for 169.

Representative — Thomas C. Gordon (Dem.), 747 ; J. M. Jones (Rep.), 140.

Sheriff — F. R. Long, 232 ; Darius Gittings, 488 ; S. S. Clack, 134.

Assessor — T. R. Dale, no opposition.

CHAPTER XI.

SOME LEADING INCIDENTS FROM 1865 TO 1885.

Miscellaneous Military Incidents in 1865 — The Last of the Bushwhackers — Surrender of Oll. Shepherd's Band — The Drake Constitution — Robbing of the Clay County Savings Bank — Political Canvasses — The Railroads of Clay County — Hanging of Sam Walker — Census Statistics — The James Brothers.

In January, 1865, a band of bushwhackers from Jackson county kept the county in a constant state of disquietude by their predatory operations against the people. This band was led by "Wild Bill," a desperado who aped the character of Anderson in some respects and imitated the practices of Jennison in others.

About the 1st of January, "Bill" and his band robbed a Mr. Stone of what pleased them, shot at him and abused him and his wife, then went to A. Withers', in the bottom, and took a horse and some clothing. From here they visited other houses in the neighborhood robbing and plundering, finally retiring to their lair in the Sni hills over in Jackson. Three weeks afterwards they robbed the mail three miles below Richfield. A company of militia went out from Liberty after them, skirmished with them and drove them back into Jackson.

A battalion of the Third Missouri State Militia, under Maj. Angus Bartlett, was stationed in the county during the winter months. In April, under the militia law, a company of militia was organized in the county with John W. Younger as captain, and Ben. Cooper and David Smith as lieutenants.

In February, the following families in this county were served with notices of banishment from the county for "treason and notoriously disloyal practices," said the order; John Ecton's, Dr. Reuben Samuels', Mrs. J. H. Ford's, Wesley Martin's, Mrs. Rupe's and Kemp M. Wood's. The sentence of banishment against Mrs. Winfrey E. Price was revoked by Maj. Bartlett.

On the 29th of March, Wm. T. Reynolds, a prominent merchant of Liberty, and well known as a Union man, having served in the militia under Col. Moss, was shot in his store by a Federal soldier, and died from the wound April 20.

March 30 a skirmish occurred in the northern part of the county between Oll. Shepherd's band of a dozen bushwhackers and a company of citizens organized as militia. Shepherd's band was routed at the residence of Mrs. Fox and pursued some distance. Two of the bushwhackers were killed — Alexander Dever and his brother Arthur. The militia lost none. The Devers were both buried in one grave.

The news of the surrender of Gen. Lee and his army to Gen. Grant at Appomattox caused the hearts of the Southern sympathizers of this county to sink heavy within their bosoms. It was now evident that a bad investment had been make when stock was taken in the Confederacy, for it was clearly apparent that defeat, utter, complete and overwhelming, would soon overtake the cause of those who followed the stars and bars. The Confederate people of the county became resigned to the inevitable, and waited patiently for the end.

The news of the assassination of President Lincoln was received in Clay county with general regret. In Liberty the stores were closed, the town generally draped in mourning, and a large public meeting held to give expression to the prevailing sentiment of sorrow. A committee composed of A. J. Calhoun, F. Givinner, S. H. Hardwick and John Broadhurst reported a series of resolutions deploring the death of the President as a "great national calamity," condemning the act itself, and declaring that "under any circumstances we are devoted to the flag of our country."

THE LAST OF THE BUSHWHACKERS.

Sunday, May 28, the remnants of Oll. Shepherd's band of bushwhackers, which had been operating in various portions of the county for some time, came in and surrendered to Lieut. Benj. Cooper, of Capt. Younger's company of militia. The band numbered but five, as follows: Oll. Shepherd, captain; "Ling" Letton, James Corum, Alfred Corum and Milton Dryden. Previous to the surrender the following correspondence passed between Shepherd and the militia officers: —

MAY 25, 1865.

Capt. Younger, SIR: — I understand that peace is made. Myself and my little band, wishing to quit fighting and obey the laws of the country, I will send you these few lines to show you the terms that we are willing to surrender on: we must keep our side arms — for you know we have personal enemies that would kill us at the first opportunity. We have three revolvers that we captured from your men, which, if they belong to your company, we are willing to give up if you require it. I also have horses in my outfit that belongs to citizens of this county, that we are willing to return to their proper own-

HISTORY OF CLAY COUNTY

ers, for we did not take them for our profit — we took them to save our lives. I have a horse that I rode from Texas, that there is no use in a man talking about me giving up. When my men surrender, they expect to leave the State.

Now, Capt. Younger, these words I write in earnest ; there will be no use in talking about myself and band coming to Liberty if you don't allow us our side arms, and give us an honorable parole. We are willing to blot out the past and begin anew. If I come to Liberty, will let you know distinctly that I and my men intend to behave ourselves, and not throw out any insinuations nor insults to soldiers nor citizens, nor we don't intend to take any from them. Understand me, we blot all out and begin anew. Now, sir, Capt. Younger, if you wish peace and prosperity in this county, you will accept these propositions. Drop me a few lines in answer to this. Yours, respectfully,

OLIVER SHEPHERD, Captain.

To Capt. John Younger.

HEADQUARTERS, POST OF RICHFIELD,
RICHFIELD, MO., May 25, 1865.

Mr. Shepherd — SIR : I have just received a letter from you in which you state you are desirous of surrendering your forces. Sir, in reply to your proposition, I will say that the terms upon which you are willing to surrender *can not* be accepted by me. You wish to retain your arms — this you can not be permitted to do under any circumstances. If I accept your surrender it must be upon the same terms that others of your " profession " are being accepted ; upon which is a return of all arms and other property which may have been taken by you during your operations, and all arms which you may have had before, or which you may now have in your possession. With this, sir, I will close. Yours, etc.,

B. F. COOPER,

First-Lieutenant, Capt. Younger's Company, commanding Post.

LIBERTY, May 26, 1865.

Oliver Shepherd, James Corum, Alfred Corum, James Dever and others — Understanding from Tilman Bush that you have expressed a desire to surrender to the military authorities here, if such terms as you wish were granted you, I have but to say that your surrender must be unconditional. You will be required to give up your horses, arms and military equipment of every description, and upon doing so you will be guaranteed military protection, but you are not to suppose that you will be shielded from the civil law if it should be enforced against you for any offenses you have committed. I have no power nor disposition to assure you of such immunity, and it would manifestly be wrong to do so. DAVID SMITH,

Lieutenant Commanding.

The bushwhackers surrendered their horses and arms, notwithstanding Shepherd's assertion that there was " no use in talking " in

HISTORY OF CLAY COUNTY

regard to surrendering the latter. It is said, however, that some of the men hid two or more revolvers each before coming to town. Lieut. Cooper was faithful to his word, and protected his prisoners from some of the county militia who threatened to kill them. All of the bushwhackers left the county, for a time at least. Oll. Shepherd was killed by a vigilance committee in Jackson county, in 1868. " Ning " or " Ling " Letton is the present city marshal of Liberty, a reputable citizen, a worthy and faithful official, and since his surrender universally respected.

Under the " ousting ordinance " of the Drake constitution Gov. Fletcher, in May, removed the then county officers and appointed in their places James Love, circuit clerk, *vice* A. J. Calhoun, removed; county clerk, William Brining, *vice* E. D. Murray, removed; sheriff, James M. Jones, *vice* Darius Gittings, removed; county court justices, Joseph T. Field, John Chrisman, and Milliner Haynes, *vice* Alvah Maret, Isaac Wood and James M. Jones.

VOTE ON THE DRAKE CONSTITUTION, JUNE 6, 1865.

Townships.												*For.*	*Against.*
Liberty	.	.	.	.	.	.	.	.	.	.	.	31	528
Fishing River	.	.	.	.	.	.	.	.	.	.	.	25	102
Washington	.	.	.	.	.	.	.	.	.	.	.	1	121
Platte	.	.	.	.	.	.	.	.	.	.	.	38	26
Gallatin	.	.	.	.	.	.	.	.	.	.	.	..	113
Total												90	890

Majority against the constitution, 800.

ROBBERY OF THE CLAY COUNTY SAVINGS BANK.

On Tuesday, February 13, 1866, the bank of the Clay County Savings Association, at Liberty, was robbed of about $60,000 by a band of brigands, presumably from Jackson county, although it has since been ascertained that some of the members resided in Clay. At the same time, and incident to the robbery, a young man named George Wymore, a student on his way to a school, was without any sort of provocation whatever, inhumanly and mercilessly shot down by the robbers and instantly killed. The following account of the affair was given by the *Tribune* of February 16, 1866: —

Our usually quiet city was startled last Tuesday by one of the most cold-blooded murders and heavy robberies on record. It appears that in the afternoon some ten or twelve persons rode into town, and two of them went into the Clay County Savings Bank, and asked the clerk (Mr. Wm. Bird) to change a ten dollar bill, and as he started to do so, they drew their revolvers on him and his father, Mr. Greenup

Bird, the cashier, and made them stand quiet while they proceeded to rob the bank. After having obtained what they supposed was all, they put the clerk and cashier in the vault, and no doubt thought they had locked the door, and went out with their stolen treasure, mounted their horses and were joined by the balance of their gang and commenced shooting. Mr. S. H. Holmes had two shots fired at him, and young Geo. Wymore, aged about 19 years (son of Wm. H. Wymore), one of the most peaceable and promising young men in the county, was shot and killed while standing on the opposite side of the street at the corner of the old Green house. The killing was a deliberate murder without any provocation whatever, for neither young Mr. Wymore, nor any of the citizens of town, previous to the shooting, knew anything of what had taken place. Indeed, so quiet had the matter been managed, if the robbers had succeeded in locking the bank vault on the clerk and cashier, and had retired quietly, it would likely have been some time before the robbery would have been discovered.

The town was soon all excitement, and as many as could procure arms and horses went in pursuit, but up to this writing nothing is known of the result. Our citizens exhibited a commendable willingness to do all they could to assist in the capture of the robbers and their booty.

Thus has our city and people been grossly outraged by a band of thieves and murderers, and that, too, when the people thought they were in possession of permanent peace; and a worthy young man murdered, one of our most successful and ably managed monied institutions, and many private individuals, have been heavy losers. We hope to God, the villians may be overhauled, and brought to the end of a rope. Indeed, we can not believe they will escape.

The murderers and robbers are believed by many citizens, and the officers of the bank, to be a gang of old bushwhacking desperadoes who stay mostly in Jackson county. But it makes no difference who they are, or what they claim to be, they should be swung up in the most summary manner. Robbing and murdering must be stopped, and if it requires severe medicine to do it, so be it. Desperate cases require desperate remedies; and we believe our people are in a humor to make short work of such characters in the future. The people of Clay county want peace and safety and they are going to have it.

The robbers obtained about $60,000 in gold, currency and 7:30 U. S. bonds;—about $45,000 of the amount was in 7:30's.

The Clay County Savings Association issued hand-bills, which were sent throughout the county, and of which the following is a copy:—

$5,000 Reward.

The Clay County Savings Association, at Liberty, Mo., was robbed on the 13th inst., of SIXTY THOUSAND DOLLARS, by a band of bushwhackers, who reside chiefly in Clay county, and have their rendezvous on or near the Missouri river, above Sibley, in Jackson county.

The sum of FIVE THOUSAND DOLLARS will be paid by the Association for the recovery of the stolen money or in that porportion for the sum recovered. Every citizen, who values his life or property, will be expected to give his aid in capturing the thieves, as they are thoroughly organized and will no doubt continue to depredate on life and property, as they did here yesterday. Done by order of the Board of Directors.

JAMES LOVE, Pres't.

February 14, 1866.

A heavy snow fell within a few hours after the robbery, covering up the tracks of the robbers completely, and rendering it impossible to follow their trail far. It was learned positively, however, that they crossed the river into Jackson county and scattered themselves through the " Cracker's Neck " region and amid the almost impenetrable fastness of the Sni hills. It was almost wholly a matter of conjecture who they were; one man who met them declared he knew some of them, but afterward he refused to swear to his statement. This was in all probability really the heaviest bank robbing that occurred during the " reign of the robbers," in Missouri, Iowa and Kentucky, from 1866 to 1881. Despite assertions in sensational publications to the contrary, it is quite certain that no other bank was ever robbed by the Missouri bandits of so large a sum as even $50,000.

The robbery caused the temporary suspension of the savings bank, but the officers finally settled with their creditors by paying 60 cents on the dollar, a settlement that was satisfactory to all.

In August, 1866, one J. C. Couch, of Gentry county, was examined before a magistrate under a suspicion that he was one of the robbers, but he was discharged. A fellow named Joab Perry, who was lying in Independence jail on another charge, was taken out by the Clay county officials and brought across the river for examination, but escaped from custody and was never afterward arrested.

POLITICAL.

At the Presidential election, 1868, the vote in Clay county stood: Seymour, Democrat, 313; Grant, Republican, 291. For Governor — John S. Phelps, Democrat, 320; Joseph William McClurg, Republican, 284. For Congress — Gen. James H. Shields, Democrat, 319; R. T. Van Horn, Republican, 286.

In 1870, when the question of re-enfranchising the ex-Confederate sympathizers was before the people, and the candidates for Governor were B. Gratz Brown, Liberal Republican, T. W. McClurg, Radical Republican, the total number of registered voters in the county was 955.

The vote stood: Brown, 625; McClurg, 245. For the enfranchising amendments to the constitution, 838; against, 17.

In 1872 the vote was: For President — Greeley, Democratic and Liberal Republican candidate, 2,207; Grant, Republican, 528; Charles O'Conor, "straight" Democrat, 27. For Governor — Silas Woodson, Democrat, 2,472; John B. Henderson, Republican, 527. For Congress — A. S. Comings, Democrat, 2,477; D. S. Twitchell, Republican, 524.

In 1876 the vote for President was: For Tilden, Democrat, 2,848; Hayes, Republican, 509; Cooper, Greenback, 57.

In 1880 the vote was: For President — Hancock, Democrat, 2,969; Garfield, Republican, 589; Weaver, Greenbacker, 193. For Governor — Crittenden, Democrat, 2,979; D. P. Dyer, Republican, 586; Brown, Greenbacker, 196. For Congress — D. C. Allen, Democrat, 1,650; John T. Crisp, Democrat, 1,377; R. T. Van Horn, Republican, 547; Clark, Greenbacker, 179.

In 1884 the vote stood: For President — Cleveland, Democrat, 3,179; Blaine, Republican, and Butler, Greenbacker, fusion electors, 919; straight Blaine, 22; St. John, Prohibitionist, 58. For Governor — Marmaduke, Democrat, 3,093; Ford, Fusion, 903; Brooks, Prohibitionist, 136; Guitar, straight Republican, 9. For Congress — Dockery, Democrat, 3,217; Harwood, Republican, 803; Jourdan, Greenbacker 108.

RAILROADS.

The branch of the Hannibal and St. Joseph Railroad through this county was completed in the latter part of the fall of 1867 and first part of 1868. It was completed to Liberty about October 15, 1867. William J. Quealy, of Hannibal, was the chief contractor. This road was chartered before the war, and was originally called the Kansas City, Galveston and Lake Superior. Afterward the name was changed to the Kansas City and Cameron. It was merged into the Hannibal and St. Joseph February 14, 1870, and is still a part of the same. The first regular train over the bridge across the Missouri at Kansas City passed July 4, 1869. The "old reliable" Hannibal and St. Joe has been of incalculable value to Clay county. Besides giving our people an outlet to the markets of the world, at all times and seasons, it created in this county five new towns and villages, and caused the development of many tracts of unimproved land, and added largely to the value of much land already in cultivation.

The Wabash, St. Louis and Pacific — then called the St. Louis,

HISTORY OF CLAY COUNTY

Kansas City and Northern — was completed through the county in the fall of 1868.

The Chicago, Rock Island and Pacific began running its trains over the track of the Hannibal and St. Joseph, from Cameron to Kansas City, in the summer of 1871. It is not allowed to take on or discharge passengers or freight in this county, or even between Cameron and Kansas City.

THE GRASSHOPPER YEAR.

The year 1875 will long be remembered in Clay county as the "grasshopper year." In May vast swarms of grasshoppers, or Rocky Mountain locusts, made their appearance in this quarter of Missouri and devastated entire regions of country of vegetation, and of almost every green thing. In Clay they were, indeed, a burden. They made their appearance in such numbers that in many places the ground and entire surface of the earth was completely covered with them. Entire fields of wheat, and young corn, and meadows were devoured in a few hours. Gardens disappeared as though a fire had passed over them. Fortunately the pests departed from the county in a few weeks. Corn was replanted, and in the fall very good crops were raised.

HANGING OF SAM WALKER.

October 14, 1873, a negro named Samuel Walker shot and killed his wife, Katie, who at the time was employed as a domestic in a family at Liberty. Walker claimed that his wife was unfaithful to him. He came to Liberty from Platte county. One night he waylaid, shot and badly wounded a negro whom he suspected of visiting his wife, and a few nights thereafter shot the woman herself as she stepped out of doors for a bucket of water.

Walker was apprehended the same night in the chimney of a negro cabin down in the river bottom. He was indicted and arraigned in November following, and his trial continued to March, 1874, when he was tried and convicted, and sentenced to be hung May 15, two months later, a short shrift, certainly. On his trial he was defended by Col. Rucker. The evidence was conclusive against the prisoner, and he even confessed his guilt.

The execution came off at the appointed time, on what is called the show grounds, west of the railroad depot, in Liberty. A large crowd of both sexes, races, and all ages was present. The details occupied fully four hours. The condemned man had been visited the day before

263

by two Catholic Sisters of Charity, and then professed the Catholic religion, but on the scaffold he seemed to have gone back on Catholicism and to have become a good Protestant. He prayed, sung, exhorted, talked and bade farewell to all who would come up and shake hands with him, and the scene was by no means an attractive one. Sheriff Patton, the one-armed ex-Confederate soldier, had charge of the hanging.

THE FLOOD OF 1881.

In the spring of 1881 the Missouri river was higher than it had been since 1844. The bottoms were overflowed and much damage resulted. Harlem was all under water, and many buildings were destroyed. Some old settlers declared that the river was even higher in 1881 than it was in 1844. Certainly the damage was greater, for there was more to destroy. The ensuing season was drouthy, and crops were a partial failure. The next fall corn rose to $1 a bushel.

CENSUS AND OTHER STATISTICS OF 1880.

The total population of the county in 1880, according to the official census, was 15,572, of which 8,132 were males and 7,440 were females. The whites numbered 14,059; the colored people, 1,513. By townships the population was as follows: —

Townships.	Population.
Fishing River, including Missouri City	2,885
Gallatin	2,772
Kearney, including Holt and Kearney	2,667
Liberty, including Liberty Town	3,714
Platte, including Smithville	2,352
Washington	1,212
Total	15,572

The population of the incorporated towns and villages was as follows: —

Liberty, 1,476; Missouri City, 581; Kearney, 465; Smithville, 231; Holt, 162.

The native born population was 15,127, of which number of persons 10,586 were born in Clay county, 2,053 in Kentucky; 333 in Tennessee; 253 in Ohio; 244 in Indiana, 240 in Illinois, and the remainder in other States. The number of foreigners was 445, of whom there was born in Ireland, 166; in the German Empire, 117; in England and Wales, 53; British America, 35; Sweden and Norway, 16; Scotland, 14; France, 8.

HISTORY OF CLAY COUNTY

The number of voters in the county was 4,018.

The number of farms in 1880 was 2,015, and the number of acres of improved land, 184,455. The total value of the farms, including fences and buildings, was $4,860,571, the value of stock on the farms June 1st, was $1,250,961. The estimated value of farm products in 1879 was $879,411, consisting in part of 2,204,376 bushels of corn, 257,887 bushels of wheat, and 134,311 bushels of oats. The number of head of horses owned in the county in 1880 was 6,832; mules, 2,086; cattle, 19,743; sheep, 18,402; hogs, 53,516.

In manufactures the total value invested was $129,125; the value of products, $378,915. The number of operatives employed was 142 males and 11 females; amount of wages paid, $32,513.

RACE POPULATION IN 1860, 1870 AND 1880.

								1860	1870	1880
Whites	.	.	.	.	.	.	.	9,525	13,718	14,059
Colored	.	.	.	.	.	.	.	3,498	1,846	1,513
Totals	.	.	.	.	.			13,023	15,564	15,572

THE JAMES BROTHERS.

No attempt will be made in this history to give a detailed history of the noted bandit brothers known familiarly, not only throughout the United States, but in Europe, as the James' boys. It is only from the fact that they were natives of the county and for a time resided here that they are mentioned at all. Other publications profess to narrate their exploits and their career correctly, but whether they do so or not is no affair of the publisher hereof, and perhaps of but little consequence to any one. What is set down here may be relied on as accurate, however, and is given with the partial knowledge of its truth on the part of a large majority of the readers.

Alexander Franklin James was born in this county, January 10, 1843. Jesse Woodson James was born in the house where his mother now lives, in Kearney township, September 5, 1847.[1] Both boys were raised on their mother's farm, in this county, to their early manhood, except for a time during and immediately subsequent to the Civil War. What little education they possessed was obtained at the common county schools of their neighborhood. Neither of them ever attended any other sort of school.

In 1850 their father, Rev. Robert James, as mentioned elsewhere,

---

[1] Both dates are taken from the record in their mother's family Bible, and were set down by their father.

HISTORY OF CLAY COUNTY

went to California and there died soon after his arrival. He was a Baptist minister, a man of good education, and universally respected.

In 1851, the widow James — whose maiden name was Zerelda Cole — was again married to a Mr. Simms, also of this county, a widower, with children. At the time of her second marriage she was 26 years of age, and her husband was 52. The union proved unhappy, and in less than a year was terminated by a separation. The lady alleges that the chief trouble arose from the fact that her three little children, Frank, Jesse and Susie, whom she had always humored and indulged, gave their old step-father no end of annoyance. He insisted that she should send them away, and to this she once agreed, but her near relatives informed her that if she did so they would never more recognize her, and so she separated from Mr. Simms, who, she yet alleges, always treated her with kindness, and for whose memory she still has great respect. He died not long after the separation, and some time afterwards Mrs. Simms was married to Dr. Reuben Samuel, her present husband.

In the fall of 1861, when 18 years of age, Frank James volunteered in the Confederate service, becoming a member of Capt. Minter's company, Hughes' regiment, Stein's division. He was present at the capture of Lexington, and marched with Price's army into Southwest Missouri. At Springfield he was taken with measles, and on the retreat of Price's army before Gen. Curtis, in February, 1862, he was left behind in the hospital. The Federals, when they captured Springfield, took him prisoner, paroled him, and he returned home to his mother's farm in Kearney township. He was arrested by Col. Penick in the following early summer and released on a $2,000 bond. He returned to his home and went to work.

From time to time Frank James was accused of having aided and abetted the Confederate cause, in violation of his parole. The accusations may or may not be true, but in the early spring of 1863 he was again arrested, taken to Liberty and cast into jail. From here he contrived to make his escape, and soon afterwards, while a fugitive he determined " to go to the brush," as the phrase then was, and accordingly joined a small band of bushwhackers, under the leadership of Fernando Scott. This was in May, 1863, and a few days later he took part in the raid on Missouri City, when Capt. Sessions and Lieut. Grafenstein were killed. Thereafter he was a bushwhacker until the close of the War, winding up his career with Quantrell in Kentucky. During his career as a guerrilla Frank James participated in three or four skirmishes with the Federals in this county.

In May, 1863, soon after Frank James had gone to the brush, a detachment of Capt. J. W. Turney's company of Clinton county militia,[1] under Lieut. H. C. Culver, accompanied by Lieut. J. W. Younger, with a few Clay county militia, visited the Samuels homestead in search of James and his companions. Failing to find them, they sought by threats and violence to force the members of the family to give them certain information they desired. Dr. Samuel was taken out and hung by the neck until nearly exhausted, and the boy Jesse, then not quite 16 years old, who was plowing in the field, was whipped very severely.

A few weeks later, Dr. and Mrs. Samuel were arrested by the Federals and taken to St. Joseph, accused of "feeding and harboring bushwhackers." This was the charge preferred against Mrs. Samuel; but no charge whatever was ever filed against Dr. Samuel. Miss Susie James was not arrested. Mrs. Samuel had her two small children with her at the St. Joseph prison, and three months later another child was born. She was released by Col. Chester Harding after two weeks' imprisonment and sent home on taking the oath. Dr. Samuel was released about the same time. While Dr. and Mrs. Samuel was absent in St. Joe their household was in charge of Mrs. West, a sister of Mrs. Samuel.

Jesse James remained at home during the year 1863, and with the assistance of a negro man raised a considerable crop of tobacco. The next summer, in June, 1864, a year after he had been cruelly whipped by the militia, he too "went to the brush," joining Fletch. Taylor's band of bushwhackers, of which his brother Frank was a member. He was present when the Bigelow brothers were killed, and took part in the capture of Platte City, where he and other bushwhackers had their ambrotype pictures taken. The original picture of Jesse James is yet in possession of his family, but copies have recently been made and sold throughout the country. While with Bill Anderson's company on the way to Howard county, in August, 1864, Jesse was badly wounded by an old German Unionist named Heisinger, who lived in the southern part of Ray county, at Heisinger's Lake. Three or four bushwhackers went to Heisinger's, got something to eat and were looking about the premises when the old man fired upon them from a sorghum patch, put a bullet through Jesse James' right lung, and routed the party. This practically ended his career as a bushwhacker.

---

[1] Co. F, Fourth Provisional Regiment.

HISTORY OF CLAY COUNTY

His companions hid him away and one Nat. Tigue nursed him for a considerable time.[1]

It was a long time until Jesse was able to be in the saddle again. In February, 1865, in the rear of Lexington, when coming in with some others to surrender, he was fired on by a detachment of Federals belonging to the Second Wisconsin Cavalry, and again shot through the right lung. From this wound he did not recover for many months. He was nursed first by his comrades, then by his aunt, Mrs. West, in Kansas City, and at last taken by his sister, Miss Susie, to Rulo, Nebraska, where the Samuel family had been banished the previous summer by order of the Federal military commanders in this quarter. At Rulo, Dr. Samuel was making a precarious living in the practice of his profession — medicine — and here the young guerrilla lay until in August, 1865, when the family returned to their Clay county farm. Jesse united with the Baptist Church sometime in 1868.

When, as is alleged, the James brothers entered upon their life of brigandage and robbery, their associates were those of the old guerrilla days, and it is but true to say that this life succeeded to or was born of the old bushwhacking career. Not every old Confederate bushwhacker became a bandit, for many of the most desperate of Quantrell's, Todd's and Anderson's men became quiet, reputable citizens, but at the first every bandit in Western Missouri was an ex-guerrilla.

After the Gallatin bank robbery the civil authorities of this county began the chase after the now noted brothers and kept it up for years, or until Jesse was killed in April, 1882, and Frank surrendered. The pursuit was considered by each Clay county sheriff as a part of his regular duties and transmitted the same as the books and papers of his office to his successor.

Lack of space forbids an enumeration of the many adventures of the officers of this county in their efforts to capture the James boys and their partners. One fact must be borne in mind. Every sheriff worked faithfully and bravely to discharge his duties. The heroic and desperate fight near the Samuel residence[2] between the intrepid Capt. John S. Thomason and his brave young son, Oscar, and the

---

[1] While serving with the bushwhackers Frank was known as "Buck," and Jesse was called "Dingus" by their companions. While in a camp one day, shortly after he went out, Jesse was practicing with a revolver and accidentally shot off the end of one of his fingers. Shaking his wounded hand, and dancing about with the pain, he cried out, "O, ding it! ding it! How it hurts!"

[2] December 14, 1869.

HISTORY OF CLAY COUNTY

two brothers, when the Captain's horse was killed; the night fight made by Capt. John S. Grooms; the many expeditions by night and day, in season and out of season, by Thomason, Grooms, Patton and Timberlake, can not here be detailed, interesting as the incidents thereof may be.

Connected with the career of the bandit brothers, may be briefly mentioned the attempt of Pinkerton's detectives to effect their capture — an attempt blunderingly and brutally made and ignominiously ailing, resulting in the killing of little Archie Peyton Samuel,[1] the tearing off of Mrs. Samuel's right arm, the wounding of other members of the family, and the complete discomfiture of the attacking party of detectives. Whether or not, either or both of the James boys and another member of the band participated in this melee, and whether or not one of the detectives was killed, can not here be stated.

The murder of Daniel Askew, the nearest neighbor of Dr. Samuel, which occurred a few weeks after Pinkerton's raid, has always been attributed to one or both of the James brothers, though the charge is stoutly denied by their friends. Askew was called out one night and shot dead on his doorstep. A detective named J. W. Whicher, who, as he himself avowed, came to this county to plan in some way the capture of the brothers, was taken across the Missouri river into Jackson county and killed by *somebody*, in Jackson county, March 10, 1874.

That any considerable portion of the people of the county ever gave aid or comfort or countenance to the bandits who infested Missouri, whether the James boys, or who ever they were, is so preposterously untrue that there is no real necessity for its denial. Not one person in one hundred of the people of the county knew either of the James boys by sight, and but few more had *ever* seen them. After they entered upon their career of brigandage their visits to the county were so unfrequent and unseasonable and so brief that only the very fewest saw them, and it was not long ere those who once knew them intimately would not have known them had they met them face to face in open day; for from smooth-faced boys they were growing to bearded men, and no change is more complete than that from adolescence to manhood.

Moreover, it is most absurd, and most unjust, too, that any considerable number such as live in the county of Clay should be supposed to have any sympathy with villainy and villains of any sort. The

---

[1] Named by Jesse James for Archie Clements and Peyton Long, two desperate and notorious guerrillas during the war.

county is and has now been for years full of school-houses and churches and abounding with Christian men and women who fear God and keep His commandments, and keep themselves aloof from evil associations. Morality and love of the right are the rule among our people; immorality and viciousness the exception.

At any time within the past fifteen years five hundred men could have been raised in an hour to capture the James boys. Dozens of the best citizens of all classes have frequently volunteered to accompany the officers in their search for the bandits, and have lain night after night in the woods and watched roads and bridges, and done everything in their power to vindicate and uphold the law. Even when Jesse James was shot at St. Joseph a public meeting at Liberty applauded the fact and indorsed the manner of his taking off.

That the James boys had a few confederates in Clay county is barely possible. Who they were, however, can now never be known. It is probable that if they existed at all they were few in number, and their services and the character of their connection unimportant and unconspicuous.

CHAPTER XII.

MISCELLANEOUS.

Clay County Schools — County Teachers' Institute — William Jewell College, etc.

The first schools taught in the county were made up by subscription and taught during the summer or autumn. The school-houses were generally hastily improvised without much attention being paid to comfort or convenience. Sometimes a winter school was provided if a house could be found comfortable enough.

In township 52, range 30, — in the southeastern portion of the county — the people first thoroughly organized for school purposes. In February, 1836, the township was organized into two school districts, with Fishing river the dividing line between them. The southern district was called Franklin, and the trustees were James Dagley, George Withers and Sam Crowley. The northern district was called Jefferson; trustees, Winfrey E. Price, Michael Welton, Joel. P. Moore. In the spring Jefferson was divided into two districts, and the western or northwestern was called Clark, in honor of Jesse Clark.

In April, 1836, township 52, range 31, lying northeast of the town of Liberty, was divided into four school districts, Clay, Washington, White and Bell. Schools were established soon after in all these districts, and already there were good schools at Liberty. From the earliest period of its official existence Clay county has always taken a leading part in school matters among the best counties of the State.

The sixteenth sections in every congressional township in Missouri were from the first set aside for public school purposes, to be sold to the best advantage and the proceeds thereof properly applied, upon petition of two-thirds of the inhabitants of said congressional township. The Clay county court, in February, 1831, appointed Ware S. May to select the sixteenth sections in this county. Samuel Tillery was appointed commissioner, and he made sales from time to time up to the spring of 1834.

Under the act of February 9, 1839, public schools were instituted, and were aided from the interest of the township fund arising from the sales before mentioned. In 1842, the State began the distribution of a small fund. These schools were rather meager in their results until the act of February, 1853, set apart twenty-five per cent of the State revenue for the support of common schools. This act also created the office of county school commissioner, and Col. A. W. Doniphan was appointed to the office in November, 1853, which he filled until August 8, 1854, when he resigned, having been elected county representative. George Hughes was then appointed to fill the vacancy, and has held the office up to this writing (February, 1885,) with complete satisfaction to all.

The first annual report to the State Superintendent, by County Commissioner Hughes, was made November 4, 1854. The whole number of white children over 5 and under 20 years of age in the organized school township for that year was 2,426, and in the unorganized territory the children of school age were estimated to be about 500. The number of public schools was 32, and the number of teachers employed was 34. The average number of children attending public school was 1,264. The average salary paid teachers was $29 per month, and the length of school term was about five months and a fourth.

According to the report for 1884, the number of children in the county, between 6 and 20 years of age, was 4,708 whites and 420 colored. The total number attending public schools was 3,530 white children and 227 colored. The average number of days' attendance by each child was 80. The number of teachers employed during the year, 42 males and 53 females. The average monthly salary paid males was $47.82, and females $34.16. The whole number of white schools in operation during the year was 63, and for colored children there were eight. The total number of pupils that might be seated in the school rooms of the county was 4,125. The number of school houses was 61, of which 55 were frame, and six were brick. The total value of school property was $44,770.00. The average rate per $100 levied for school purposes was 49 cents. The whole amount received from public funds was $8,340.31, and the whole amount realized from taxation was $19,044.68. The amount paid teachers during the year was $20,445.45. The cost for tuition of each scholar was seven and a half cents. The average length of school term in each district was 124½ days.

County Teachers' Institute. — The County Teachers' Institute was first organized in 1854, and held its first annual session at Mt. Gilead Church, August 29, 1855 (James Love was president and L. R. Slone secretary). This is believed to be the first county teachers' institute ever held in the State. It continued to hold annual, and, sometimes semi-annual sessions, until the public schools were suspended, in 1861. When the public schools were again organized after the close of the Civil War, the county institute was also reorganized, and held annual sessions until monthly institutes and county normal institutes supplied its place in the educational work of the county.

WILLIAM JEWELL COLLEGE.[1]

The founding of this institution is the result of a necessity for higher education which was felt by the Baptists of Missouri at an early day in the history of the State. This feeling was manifested as far back as the year 1833. The Baptists in the State, even at that date, appreciated the supreme importance of establishing a college of the first order, wherein their youths, under denominational influences, might receive the benefits of education beyond an academic course.

Their General Association, on the 25th day of August, 1843, appointed Uriah Sebree, Wade M. Jackson, Roland Hughes, Fielding Wilhoite, David Perkins, Eli Bass, Jordan O'Brien, R. E. McDaniel, Wm. Carson, G. M. Bower, Jason Harrison, James W. Waddell and I. T. Hinton, trustees, to receive the offer of Dr. William Jewell of $10,000 toward the endowment of a college to be under the direction of the Baptist denomination, fix the same within 15 miles of the Missouri river, not east of Jefferson City, nor west of Glasgow, and "to do all other acts usual and necessary to organize and carry on a literary institution." On the 26th day of August, 1844, the General Association declined the offer of $10,000 made by Dr. Jewell, for the reason that in the opinion of that body it was not possible, under the circumstances of the Baptist denomination in Missouri at that time, to raise the sum required by him, as the condition of his donation; and so the persons named as trustees — in effect the committee on college organization — were discharged. The General Association met in August, 1847, at Walnut Grove, Boone county. The attendance of delegates was large and embraced quite a number of leading gentlemen of the Baptist denomination in the State. The movement in favor of the founding of a college was plainly taking a more definite shape and becoming more energetic. The General Association, with-

---

[1] Much of the information in this article has been derived from a sketch written by Hon. D. C. Allen and published in the History of the Baptists of Missouri. In many instances Mr. Allen's exact language is used.

HISTORY OF CLAY COUNTY

out dissent, as it appears, on the 26th day of August, 1847, adopted the following resolution, offered by Rev. S. W. Lynd, viz. : —

Resolved, That a committee of five persons be appointed as a provisional committee on education, whose duty it shall be to originate an institution of learning, for the Baptist denomination in this State, provided the same can be accomplished upon a plan by which its endowment and perpetuity may be secured.

Roland Hughes, William Carson, Wade M. Jackson, R. E. McDaniel and David Perkins were appointed the committee contemplated by the resolution.

The committee appointed in 1847 reported to the General Association on the 26th day of August, 1848. The report of the committee in substance was: That for the purpose of erecting and endowing a college in the State, they had secured subscriptions to the amount of $16,936 and that they believed, from the success which had attended their limited exertions, that a vigorous prosecution of the enterprise would finally end in success. On the recommendation of the committee the General Association passed the following resolution, viz. : —

Resolved, That so soon as the provisional committee may think it advisable to make a location, they be instructed to make such location according to the condition expressed in the subscription which the agents have been authorized to circulate.

At the same time the General Association appointed the gentlemen of the last preceding committee a committee also to make application to the General Assembly of the State for a charter for the college, and to appoint a board of trustees. Through the agency of this committee, the Fifteenth General Assembly of the State granted a charter for a college (which was approved by the Governor on the 27th day of February, 1849), in accordance with the wishes of the Baptists of Missouri. (Session Acts, 1849, page 232). The title of the act granting the charter is: "An act to charter a college in the State of Missouri." The preamble of the act begins as follows: —

"*Whereas*, The United Baptists in Missouri and their friends are desirous of endowing and building up a college in the State," etc.

The trustees named in the charter are as follows: Tyree C. Harris, Isaac Lionberger, Jordan O'Brien, W. C. Ligon, Robert S. Thomas, A. W. Doniphan, T. N. Thompson, W. D. Hubbell, Robert James,

HISTORY OF CLAY COUNTY

Samuel T. Glover, T. L. Anderson, R. F. Richmond, S. D. South, T. E. Hatcher, John Ellis, Wm. Carson, David Perkins, W. M. Jackson, Roland Hughes, William Jewell, W. M. McPherson, R. E. McDaniel, John Robinson, M. F. Price, E. M. Samuel and R. R. Craig.

It was about March 1, 1848, when the first definite and practical action was taken to secure the location of the college at Liberty. On that date a meeting was held at Liberty and committees were appointed for each township to solicit subscriptions to the endowment. J. T. V. Thompson, E. M. Samuel and Madison Miller were at the head of the movement. During the following summer the county was thoroughly canvassed and nothing left undone to secure for Clay county the location of the much desired institution. This work was continued for a year thereafter, or until the summer of 1849.

The provisional committee appointed by the Baptist General Association, August 26, 1848, called a meeting of the donors to the endowment, to be held at Boonville, August 21, 1849, for the purpose of determining the name of the college and fixing its location. The donors met pursuant to the call. The number of shares — each share being valued at $48 — represented was 883. The subscriptions, in addition, were $7,000 by the citizens of Clay county, for the erection of buildings only.

The Clay county donors were represented in the meeting by Col. A. W. Doniphan and Hon. J. T. V. Thompson, who, with E. M. Samuel, had been appointed at a meeting held in Liberty, August 3. Four towns in the State contested for the location — Liberty, Fulton, Palmyra and Boonville. Col. Doniphan presented the claims of Liberty. When it came to the vote on the location the contest was animated and eager. The subscription of Clay was larger than that of any other county, but did not constitute a majority of the votes, each share being entitled to a vote. Finally, the location at Liberty, Clay county, was made by the votes of Howard county being cast solidly for it. The final vote stood: For Liberty, 528; for Palmyra 194; for Boonville, 107; for Fulton, 44.

Immediately after the fixing of the location, Rev. Wm. C. Ligon moved that the college be named William Jewell College, in honor of Dr. Wm. Jewell, a prominent, well known and universally respected citizen of Boone county. Col. Doniphan seconded the motion, and it was adopted unanimously. Dr. Jewell was present in the meeting, and arose and returned his thanks for the honor. In conclusion he said he had long had his will written remembering this institution, and he now desired the secretary to write his obligation

275

HISTORY OF CLAY COUNTY

for $10,000 worth of land — 3,951 acres situated in Mercer, Grundy and Sullivan counties — which he desired to donate to the college. The conveyance was immediately completed. Subsequently, Dr. Jewell, in his will and by sums of money voluntarily expended out of his own pocket to contractors for the erection of the college edifice, gave the corporation not less than $6,000.[1]

The certificate of location and naming of the college was filed in the recorder's office of Clay County, August 25, 1849, and thereupon the name of the corporation became that which it still retains — "The Trustees of William Jewell College."

The site of the college was donated by Hon. J. T. V. Thompson, who, though not a church member, was all his life a friend and liberal patron of the institution. At first the corporation was liberal and almost non-sectarian in the organization of its faculty. From September, 1853, to June, 1861, one of the professors was uniformly a member of some other church denomination than the Baptist. This liberality was of decided advantage to the institution, in one respect at least.

The first meeting of the board of trustees was held November 12, 1849. The members at that time were Dr. Wm. Jewell, of Boone county; Roland Hughes, Wade M. Jackson, David Perkins, of Howard; M. R. Price, of Lafayette; W. C. Ligon, of Carroll; A. W. Doniphan, Edward M. Samuel, J. T. V. Thompson, R. R. Craig and Rev. Robt. James,[2] of Clay. Roland Hughes was elected first president of the board and Rev. Wm. C. Ligon, secretary. The board at this meeting decided to open a department of instruction — a preparatory school in the basement of the Baptist Church, in Liberty, the first session or term to begin January 1, 1850.

The school opened at the time specified, Rev. E. S. Dulin principal, with Rev. Thos. F. Lockett as assistant. The course of study

---

[1] Dr. William Jewell was born in Loudoun county, Va., January 1, 1789, and removed to Gallatin county, Ky., in 1800. He received a good education and took the degree of M. D., in Transylvania University. In 1820, he came to Missouri, and in 1822 located at Columbia. Accumulating something of a private fortune, he became a liberal patron of various laudable enterprises, and was well known as much for his general benevolence as for his public spirit. He gave $1,800 to secure the location of the State University at Columbia. He served two or three times in the Legislature as a representative from Boone county. In 1822, he united with the Baptist Church, and was a consistent member of that denomination until his death, which occurred at Liberty, August 7, 1852, of illness caused by over-exertion in a personal supervision of the work of erecting the building which bears his name. His noblest monument is William Jewell College.

[2] Father of the bandits, Frank and Jesse.

adopted was admirable and thorough. The faculty for the year 1850–51 consisted of Rev. E. S. Dulin, Rev. Thos. F. Lockett and Rev. Wm. M. Hunsaker, the latter being the principal of the preparatory department. Rev. E. S. Dulin, Rev. Terry Bradley, and James G. Smith constituted the faculty for the year 1851–52. Mr. Bradley was professor of mathematics and Mr. Smith principal of the preparatory department. Rev. Dulin terminated his connection with the college in June, 1852.

During the year 1852–53 the departments of instruction were simply under the patronage of the trustees, who permitted Rev. Terry Bradley and Geo. S. Withers to maintain a school in the rooms rented by the trustees, and take all the fees for tuition.

February 11, 1850, the trustees elected Dr. Jewell commissioner to superintend the erection of the college building. May 13 following, the board ordered contracts let for the erection, and work was begun on the foundations the ensuing fall. By August 7, 1852, the date of Dr. Jewell's death, the foundations were completed and the superstructure had been built to the height of twenty feet. Dr. Jewell supervised the work with the utmost vigilance and care. By the 1st of August, 1853, the building was complete except the flooring and plastering of the rooms of the south wing and what was then the lower chapel; these were completed about 1858. The building was occupied partially in the summer of 1853.

The architect of the college edifice was J. O. Sawyer, of Cincinnati, Ohio; the superintendent, B. McAlester, of Columbia; the brickmakers, Hunter & Alford, Lexington; the stonework was done by R. Ainsworth, of Jefferson City; the plastering by John Burbank, of Weston; the painting by A. H. Maxfield.

In the summer of 1853, the first faculty was elected with Rev. Robt. S. Thomas, of Columbia, as president; Terry Bradley, professor of Latin and Greek; James Love, professor of mathematics and natural sciences; Leonidas M. Lawson, tutor. The composition of the faculty for 1854–55 was the same as the previous year, with the addition of Wm. P. Lamb, who was principal of the preparatory department.

The first graduation in the college occurred on the third Friday in June, 1855. The graduating class consisted of five members.

From June, 1855, until September, 1857, instruction in all the departments was suspended for want of funds. By September, 1857, the financial condition of the institution had improved to an extent that warranted the reopening of the college, which was done. The faculty for the year 1857–58 was composed of Rev. William Thompson, LL. D., president, elected May, 19, 1857; M. W. Robinson, adjunct professor of ancient languages and literature; Jno. B. Bradley, professor of natural philosophy and astronomy; W. C. Garnett, principal of the academic department, and Grandison L. Black, assistant tutor.

August 12, 1861, the Civil War having broken out, and the country being in a highly disturbed condition, all departments of instruction were closed, and the college remained practically in a state of suspension for seven years, though irregular instruction was given at intervening periods during the war. After the battle of Blue Mills the college building was used for some days as a hospital for the reception and care of the Federal wounded. In August, 1862, the building and grounds were occupied by the Federal troops for some weeks, and some slight intrenchments constructed. No serious damage was done to the property by these occupations.

June 24, 1867, Rev. Thompson Rambaut, LL. D., was chosen to the presidency of the college, and for a year thereafter he and the trustees were engaged in reorganization, and September, 28, 1868, the college reopened with the following faculty: Rev. Thos. Rambaut, president; R. B. Semple, professor of Latin, French, and Italian; A. F. Fleet, professor of Greek and German; John F. Lanneau, professor of mathematics; James R. Eaton, professor of natural sciences and theology.

Dr. Rambaut resigned in January, 1874, since which time the duties of president have practically been performed by Rev. W. R. Rothwell, D. D., who came to the college in June, 1872, as professor of Biblical literature. The present faculty consists of Dr. W. R. Rothwell, professor of moral philosophy and theology; R. B. Semple, professor of Latin and German; James G. Clark, professor of mathematics and French; J. R. Eaton, professor of natural science; R. P. Ryder, principal of the preparatory department; A. J. Emerson, professor of English literature and history.

Ely Hall, named in honor of Lewis B. Ely, was built in 1880.

The total wealth of the college is about $150,000.

CHAPTER XIII.

LIBERTY TOWNSHIP.

Position and Description — Early Settlers — Liberty Landing — Country Churches — City of Liberty — First Incorporation — Liberty in 1846 — Churches of Liberty — Secret Societies — Biographical.

POSITION AND DESCRIPTION.

Liberty is the south-central municipal township of Clay county and its present boundaries are as follows: Beginning at the northeast corner, at the northeast corner of section 15, township 52, range 31; thence south to the Missouri river; thence up the river to the mouth of Big Shoal creek; thence up and along Big Shoal creek, on the eastern bank, to the southwest corner of section 22, township 51, range 32; thence due north to the northwest corner of section 3, township 52, range 31; thence east to the northeast corner of section 1, same township and range; thence south one mile to the southeast corner of said section 1; thence east one mile to the northeast corner of section 7–52–31; thence south one mile to the southeast corner of said section 7; thence east three miles to the beginning.

Although the country is naturally broken and hilly throughout the greater part of the township, some of the best farms in Missouri are here to be found. Without the least exaggeration some of the manor lands in Liberty are equal in point of development and improvement to many of the best estates in the famed blue grass region of Kentucky, or the much lauded farms of Central Ohio. To be sure many of the Liberty township farms have been cultivated for sixty years, but their possessors have not been slothful or unenterprising.

WATER SUPPLY.

The tributaries of Fishing river, Rush creek, Big Shoal and all of Little Shoal creek, furnish abundant water supply and adapt the township to stock raising, and this natural advantage is thoroughly well improved upon. The bottom lands along the Missouri are of course of the highest fertility, but difficult and hazardous of improvement, owing to the liability of overflow.

Among the many reputable farmers of this township may be mentioned J. W. Park, Esq., who resides near Liberty.

EARLY SETTLERS.

As to the first settlers in what is now Liberty township, it is probable that they were Richard Hill, Robert Gilmore, James Gilmore, Samuel Gilmore and Elijah Smith, who settled on Rush creek, in the southeastern part of the township, in 1820. The two first-named Gilmores, Hill and Smith came first in the spring and built cabins and put out small crops, leaving their families down in the Petite Osage bottom (commonly called Tete Saw) in Saline county. In the fall of the year they returned with their families.

Richard Hill settled on section 9, nearly two miles east of Liberty; the others were lower down the creek. All of these families were related. Samuel Gilmore was the father of Robert and James, and the father-in-law of Hill and Smith. Mrs. Mary Poteet, a widow lady, who was the sister of Elijah Smith, and the mother-in-law of James and Robert Gilmore, came with the party and made her home with her brother. She raised Mary Crawford, an orphan, who became the wife of Cornelius Gilliam, and was the first white woman married in Clay county. (See Fishing River township.)[1]

Other settlers came in quite numerously and located in the southern portion of the township in 1821, and in 1822, when the county was organized and Liberty laid out and made the county seat, there were still other additions made to the settlements in what is now the Liberty municipal township — then about equally divided between Gallatin and Fishing River, the two original townships of the county. Anthony Harsell says that in 1821 there was but one house north of Liberty — that of James Hiatt, who lived a little more than a mile from town, due north (section 31–52–31), now known as the Baker farm.

LIBERTY LANDING.

Liberty Landing, on the Missouri, three and a half miles south of the city of Liberty, was established many years ago. The site was for many years a place of importance. All merchandise for Liberty and other interior towns north was put off the steamboats here for many years. From 1858 to 1862 a large hemp factory, owned and operated by Arthur, Burris & Co., was conducted at this point. The

[1] Three weeks after the Gilmores came to their new homes permanently, David McElwee settled in Fishing River township, and from his daughter, Mrs. Margaret Howdeshell, the information concerning the early settlement of the township has been obtained.

machinery in this establishment cost about $30,000, and the firm handled thousands of tons of hemp. The business was broken up by the war and the machinery sold to McGrew Bros., of Lexington. At present there is a railroad station on the Wabash road at the Landing.

COUNTRY CHURCHES.

Little Shoal Creek, Old School Baptist. — This church has the distinction of being the first church organization in Clay county. It was constituted May 28, 1823, by the well known pioneer minister, Elder William Thorp. The constituent members were: William Monroe, A. Monroe, Enos Vaughn, Patsy Vaughn, A. Groom, Daniel Stout, Ailsey Hall, Patsey Stout, Elisha Hall, Elizabeth Monroe, Sally Stephens and Jane Groom. The first church building was a log house, erected in the year 1824. In 1881–82 the congregation built a good substantial brick house, costing about $2,300. The first pastor was Elder William Thorp, who served the church for 28 years. After him came Elder D. Bainbridge for six years; Elder Henry Hill, three years; Elder James Duval, 21 years; Elder Lucius Wright, two years. Elder James Bradley is the present pastor. Since the organization of the church it has received 317 members in all, but the most of them have backslid, leaving the membership of the church at the present time only 34.

Providence Missionary Baptist Church. — April 29, 1848, at the house of Peyton T. Townsend, this church was organized by Revs. Robert James and Franklin Graves, P. N. Edwards being the first clerk. The organization commenced with a membership of 44 persons, but has increased until at present writing there are 190. The first church building was erected in 1850, and was destroyed by fire in February, 1880, but was rebuilt the same year at a cost of $2,000. The pastors have been Revs. Robert James, John Major, I. T. Williams, A. N. Bird, W. A. Curd, G. L. Black and A. J. Emerson. The church is a brick building, and is situated in Liberty township, on the southeast quarter of section 15. The Sabbath-school has 25 scholars, the superintendent being J. P. Marr.

THE CITY OF LIBERTY.

Upon the organization of Clay county, in January, 1822, the land on which the city of Liberty now stands was owned by John Owens and Charles McGee. Owens had built a house on what is now the northwest corner of Water and Mill streets some time the previous year, and kept a sort of tavern, or house of entertainment. His house was

HISTORY OF CLAY COUNTY

a rather large and roomy affair, and, as elsewhere stated, was used to hold the first courts in, and for other public purposes. McGee and Owens donated 25 acres to the county for county-seat purposes, which donation was accepted, and soon after the town was laid out.

The legislative act creating the county appointed John Hutchins, Henry Estes, Enos Vaughan, Wyatt Adkins and John Poage commissioners to select a "permanent seat of government" for the county, and provided that, until such selection, courts should be held at the house of John Owens. William Powe was afterward appointed on the commission. In their report to the circuit court July 1, 1882, as a reason for their selection, the commissioners say: "That, in pursuance of the object of their appointment, they assembled together on the 20th of March last, to examine the different donations offered the county, and continued in session three days examining the sites for a town; that after mature deliberation and minute investigation the tract of land owned by John Owens and Charles McGee was thought best adapted for the object for which it was designed, as being more central for the population, surrounded with good and permanent springs, lying sufficiently elevated to drain off all superfluous waters, in a healthy and populous part of the county, and entirely beyond the influence of lakes, ponds, or stagnant waters of any kind; they, therefore, unanimously agreed to accept of the proposition of Mr. Owens and Mr. McGee of a donation of 25 acres each for the use of the county."

As soon as the town was laid out, which was in the early summer of 1822, improvements began to be made. The first sale of lots was on the 4th of July, and at that time nearly all of those fronting on the public square were disposed of. But up to about 1826 there were not more than a dozen houses in the place, and these, with perhaps one exception, were log cabins.

Early hotel-keepers were Leonard Searcy, who had a licensed tavern in the fall of 1826, and continued in the business for six or seven years; Laban Garrett, who opened a licensed tavern in December, 1827, and John Chauncey, who began in about 1832. These hotels, or "taverns," as they were universally called, were simple affairs, but were comfortable enough, furnished plenty of good, wholesome food, and were adequate to the demands of that day.

Probably the first store in Liberty was kept by Wm. L. Smith, the county clerk, who brought up a few goods with him from Bluffton in 1822, and sold them in his dwelling-house.

FIRST INCORPORATION.

Liberty was first incorporated as a town by the county court May 4, 1829, on the petition of " more than two-thirds of the citizens," under the name and style of "The Inhabitants of the Town of Liberty." The following were declared to be the metes and bounds : —

Beginning at the southeast corner of the northeast quarter of section 7, in the line of the New Madrid claim ; thence due west along said Madrid line to the southwest corner of said quarter section ; thence due north along the line of said quarter section to the northwest corner thereof; thence due east along said quarter section line to the northeast corner thereof; thence due north along the line dividing sections 7 and 8, to the beginning corner at the mouth of the lane between Andrew Hixon, Sr., and said town tract.

This incorporation really included 160 acres of land, being the northeast quarter of section 7, township 51, range 31. The first board of trustees was composed of Lewis Scott, John R. Peters, Eli Casey, Samuel Ringo and John Baxter.

Describing Liberty in 1829, the year of its first incorporation, a writer in the *Tribune* in 1846, says : —

The public square in Liberty then had two houses on the south side, one on the west,' two on the north, and two or three on the east. Hixon's, Wilson's, Bird's and Curtis' addition to the town were then in old Mr. Hixon's corn field. There was one tavern (the same now [1846] occupied by Judge Hendley) kept by Leonard Searcy. Parties and balls were frequent, and often times attended by ladies and gentlemen from Fort Leavenworth, Richmond, Lexington and Independence. Preaching was uncommon — at least I never heard much of it. There was no church in town, but I think the Baptists had two or three in the country ; perhaps at Big Shoal, Little Shoal and Rush Creek.

There was but little use for doctors at that time, as the chills and fever were unknown, except in the Missouri bottoms, where but few persons had then settled. I recollect that the first case of chills and fever that occurred in the uplands excited great alarm and astonishment. It occurred, I think, in Platte township. Liberty was always healthy. Not a death took place for several years after I came to it, except one or two persons who *came* to it laboring under consumption. Once a physician, Dr. Conway, was sent for to see a sick man at the Council Bluffs. It was regarded as a most hazardous undertaking, being in the winter season, and the doctor received a fee of about $250. There was no other physician nearer at that time ; now there are perhaps a hundred, and a trip to Council Bluffs is as little regarded as it formerly was to the falls of the Platte. These changes

HISTORY OF CLAY COUNTY

would surprise an individual who had gone to sleep for the period of 17 years, but in those who had witnessed them they excited but little.

The first settlers of Liberty were as clever, as sociable, and as good people as ever walked the earth. Many of them have gone to "that bourne from whence no traveler ever returns," and many of them are now still living. * * * There was a kind of brotherhood existing among the people of Liberty and Clay county when I first came among them; nothing like envy or jealously existed. They are perhaps more united yet than any other people in the State. This arose from the fact that the first settlers were almost entirely from Kentucky, and either knew each other, or else each other's friends before they came here.

Wetmore, in his Gazeteer of 1837, thus speaks of the place:—

Liberty, one of the well watered tracts of land with which Clay county abounds, was selected for the seat of justice, and is about four miles from the river. This location was made with a view to health, and the people are not disappointed. The springs at Liberty are a fair sample of the advantages enjoyed in this respect in various portions of the county, where the milk and butter part of good living are made perfect in well built spring-houses. There is but one objection that can be made to this town as a desirable place of abode, and that is contained in a single sentence once uttered by a matron who was emigrating thither — "It is so far off." But when emigrants shall begin to pass through Liberty, on their way to the Mandan villages, and to the forks of Missouri, that objection will vanish, and Liberty will be an interior, fashionable city, like that where the enthusiastic visions of a Kentuckian now rest — Lexington, the Athens of Kentucky.

There are 14 stores and groceries in Liberty. The court-house is a large, well finished brick building. The newspaper published at Liberty, with the very appropriate name of *Far West*, is a well conducted journal.

LIBERTY IN 1846.

A contribution to the *Tribune*, in December, 1846, in an article hitherto quoted from, describes Liberty as it was at that date:—

Liberty now contains 3 taverns, a printing office, 3 blacksmiths, 8 stores, 3 groceries, 2 drug stores, 1 hatter's shop, 1 tinner's shop, 4 tailors, 3 saddlers, 3 shoemakers, 1 carriagemaker, 2 wagonmakers, 1 tanyard, 1 bagging and rope factory, 5 physicians, 6 lawyers, 3 cabinetmakers, 2 milliners, 1 oil mill, 1 carding factory, a Methodist Church, a Reformer's Church, with neat brick buildings, and a Catholic Church under way; also a Baptist Church of stone; one school, kept by a Mr. Harrel, and a male and female school, under the superintendence of Mr. and Mrs. Cunningham. Our schools are equal to those of any town in the State in the ability of the teachers. Good houses to teach in are all that are lacking. The Missionary Baptists are making efforts to erect a church, and I doubt not will be successful. Efforts are also making to erect a large college, and judging from what has already been accomplished in the way of procuring subscriptions, it will go up on a scale commensurate with the wants of the surrounding country.

If there is a healthy spot in Missouri, it is in Liberty. It is finely watered, society is good, and in point of morals it is equal to any other place, and rapidly improving in that respect. There is stone enough in the streets to pave the whole town, and then enough left to macadamize the road to the Landing. These things will be done in due time. We have a " Union " Sunday-school, numbering 80 scholars, and quite a respectable library attached to it. The day will come, if good colleges are erected *speedily*, when Liberty will be to Western Missouri what Lexington is to Kentucky — the focus of intelligence and literature. When once improved as it should and will be, no place will be more handsome.

Two or three good coopers and a chair-maker would do well to settle in Liberty. The want of such mechanics is seriously felt by merchants' families and farmers.

March 28, 1861, the Legislature re-incorporated the town as " the City of Liberty," describing its site as " all that district of country contained within one mile square, of which the court-house in Clay county is the center, the sides of said square being respectively parallel to the corresponding sides of said court-house." The city is still governed under this charter and certain amendments.

At the outbreak of the Civil War, Liberty was a flourishing town, with numerous well filled stores, a good woolen mill, rope-walks, hemp factories, etc., and was well known throughout the country. Its schools gave it something of favorable notoriety, as well as its commercial advantages. A branch of the Farmers' Bank of Lexington had been located here.

The Liberty Insurance Company, with E. M. Samuel, Michael Arthur and Gen. Doniphan as its leading spirits, existed for some years after 1850.

The Civil War left the town much the worse for its experience, but during the four years of strife and demoralization business was kept up and the ordinary municipal affairs received proper attention. The building of the Hannibal and St. Joseph Railroad was an epoch of importance, giving an outlet by rail to the marts of the world and swift communication by mail and express with important commercial centers. Yet it is maintained by many that in another sense the building of

HISTORY OF CLAY COUNTY

the railroad injured Liberty more than it benefited it, as it gave facilities for going away from the town to trade, and caused sundry small towns to be built, thus diverting business away from the county seat, and affecting its material prosperity considerably.

CHURCHES.

Christian Church. — The origin of the Christian Church of Liberty was two small organizations formed in 1837. One of these organizations was called the " Church of God," and was composed of the following persons: Thos. T. Swetnam, Caroline Swetnam, Mason and Maria Summers, Howard, James, Anderson and Polly Everett, Johnny and Sally W. Reid, Martitia Young, James and Nancy Hedges, Walter Huffaker, Wm. F. Grisby, Thos. M. Chevis, Frank McCarty, John Thompson, Sally Thompson, A. H. F. and Mary Payne, Nancy Turner, and others, 35 in all. The first officers of this organization were chosen on December 24, 1837, and were as follows: Bishops, T. T. Swetnam and Mason Summers; Deacons, John Thompson, Thos. M. Chevis and James Hedges. The names of the members of the other organization have not been obtained. In May, 1839, these two organizations united and formed the Christian Church of Liberty. August 13, 1837, according to the minutes of the " Church of God," the " Church selected Liberty for the purpose of building a meeting-house, and chose the following persons to act as trustees: Thos. M. Chevis, Jonathan Reed, Joseph Reed and James Hedges." This building, the first church, is a brick and still stands at the foot of College hill, in the northeastern part of the town, having been remodeled, and used as a dwelling. It was completed about 1839. The present church building, also a fine brick, was completed in the fall of 1851, at a cost of about $4,000. In 1884 it was improved, the changes costing nearly $5,000, or more than the original cost. The pastors of this church have been Revs. A. H. F. Payne, who served from the organization up to 1850; Moses E. Lard, W. J. Pettigrew, A. B. Jones, Josiah Waller, R. C. Morton, Wm. H. Blanks, F. R. Palmer, A. B. Jones and J. A. Dearborn. Alexander Campbell visited the church at Liberty and preached in the years 1845, 1852 and 1859. The present membership is about 200.

Liberty M. E. Church South — Was organized about the year 1840. Some of the first members were P. B. Grant, J. B. Talbott, W. W. Dougherty and James Smithey. About 1842 a brick church building was erected, and in 1857 a frame building was constructed, cost about $1,800. It was dedicated in 1859 by Rev. R. A.

Young. Some of the pastors have been L. M. Lewis, Z. Roberts, W. G. Caples, W. A. Tarwater, H. G. McEwen, J. P. Nolan, G. W. Rich, Jno. Begole, E. M. Marvin, J. W. Johnsey, W. E. Dockery and J. S. Frazier. The present membership numbers about 50.

Second Baptist Church. — Nothing more has been learned of the history of this church than that it was organized by the eminent divine, Rev. A. P. Williams, D. D., May 19, 1843, with thirteen members, who had been dismissed from Rush Creek and Mt. Pleasant Churches — Old School — because of their views in regard to missions, etc. The Old School already had an organization at Liberty called the First Baptist Church of Liberty, and for this reason Rev. Williams called his church the *Second.* Elder Williams was first pastor, and in eight years increased the membership from 13 to 194. Eder B. G. Tutt, a most popular and efficient minister, is the present pastor. The church building, a fine structure, the best house of worship in the city, was completed in 1884.

St. James Roman Catholic Church. — In the year 1847 this church was organized, the following being some of the original members : G. L. Hughes, Cyrus Curtis, Philip Clark, Patrick Hughes, Maj. Leonard Mahoney, Thomas Morrison, Philip Fraher, James Fraher, Michael Fraher, Hugh McGowan, Owen Shearin, Patrick Barry, Joseph Morton and James Burns. The church building is a brick, and was erected in 1847 at a cost of $2,500. It was consecrated by Archbishop Kenrick, of St. Louis, in 1848. The pastors who had served this church have been Revs. Bernard Donnelly, P. A. Ward, Jas. Murphy, Matthew Dillon, John J. Caffrey, Daniel Healy, Dennis Kennedy, Z. Ledwith, W. Lambert, James Foley, Wm. F. Drohan, Fintan Mindwiller, Peter McMahan, Thomas Hanley, Michael Milay, Dennis J. Kiley, Joseph Beil and Peter J. Cullen, the present pastor. The present membership, including the small missions through the county, is about 214. Attached to the church are a pastoral residence and schoolhouse, both being two story brick buildings. The school building is at present rented to a company who use it for a non-denominational select school, known as Hawthorne Institute.

MASONIC.

Liberty Lodge, No. 31, A. F. & A. M. — At Liberty, has been in existence for 45 years. The dispensation was issued June 26, 1840, on petition of A. Lightburne, E. M. Spence, Josiah C. Parker, Lewis Scott, John M. McLain, Thos. M. Bacon, Henry Coleman and Henry C. Melone. The first master, under the dispensation, was Josiah C.

HISTORY OF CLAY COUNTY

Parker, who was installed July 18, 1840, by three past masters, Thos. C. Case, Henry C. Melone and E. M. Spence, and resigned August 29th following because of certain " unmasonic conduct." A. Lightburne was made senior warden August 15, 1840. The charter was not issued until October 9, 1840, the first principal officers being Josiah C. Parker, master, and A. Lightburne and H. C. Melone, wardens. The officers under the dispensation were Josiah C. Parker, master; A. Lightburne and H. C. Melone, wardens; Thos. M. Bacon, secretary; Henry Coleman, treasurer; Andrew McLain and Edward M. Spence, deacons; and John Gordon, tyler. The lodge meets in a hall built in 1875, at a cost of about $2,000. The present membership is 67.

Liberty Chapter, No. 3, R. A. M. — Was first organized under a dispensation, issued April 18, 1842; the charter was not issued until September 13, 1844. Some of the first members were: Alvin Lightburne, Frederick Gorlich and J. M. Hughes. The chapter meets in the Masonic Hall. There are at present 26 members.

Knights Templar. — Liberty Commandery, No. 6, K. T., was instituted by Geo. W. Belt, R. E. P. Gr. Com. of Mo., under a dispensation issued October 16, 1865, to Samuel Hardwicke, Rev. Ed. G. Owen, John S. Brasfield, Dan Carpenter, W. G. Noble, S. H. Masterson, L. W. Ringo, G. L. Moad and Thomas Beaumont. Of the first officers Samuel Hardwicke was commander, Ed. G. Owen, generalissimo, and John S. Brasfield, captain-general. (These were appointed by the State grand commander.) Under the charter, which bears date May 21, 1866, the first officers were: Samuel Hardwicke, commander; E. G. Owen, generalissimo; J. E. Brasfield, captain-general; A. Lightburne and W. W. Dougherty, wardens; Dan Carpenter, prelate; Peter B. Grant, recorder; W. A. Hall, standard bearer; D. C. Allen, sword bearer; W. W. Dougherty, warder. The present number of members is 15.

ODD FELLOWS.

The charter members of Liberty Lodge No. 49, I. O. O. F., were Madison Miller, who was also one of the first members of Baltimore Lodge, No. 1, the first lodge in the United States, Larkin Bradford, T. K. Bradley, Geo. W. Morris, T. Leonard, O. C. Stewart, Wm. Lamborn and J. W. Wetzel. The charter bears date March 5, 1851. The first officers were: Madison Miller, noble grand; Geo. W. Morris, vice-grand; T. K. Bradley, secretary; John Neal, permanent secretary; Larkin Bradford, treasurer. The present officers are L. W. Newman, noble grand; Canby Wilmot, vice-grand; Charles Patrick,

HISTORY OF CLAY COUNTY

secretary; W. H. Corbin, treasurer; B. B. Corbin, permanent secretary. L. W. Burris, of this lodge, is district deputy grand master. The membership is about 30. The lodge is in good financial condition, having some thousands of dollars loaned at interest. It is in the best condition, for the number of members, of any lodge in the State. The lodge hall is a brick, and was bought in 1878–79. Its furniture and all appointments are first class.

Clay Encampment, No. 12 — Was instituted in 1853, but is not now in working order.

BIOGRAPHICAL.

DARWIN J. ADKINS

(President of the Commercial Savings Bank, Liberty).

In any worthy history of Clay county the name that heads this sketch will always be given an enviable place among the leading citizens of the county and its self-made, wealthy business men. Mr. Adkins started out for himself when a youth only about 15 years of age and without a dollar, but before he had attained his majority he had succeeded in accumulating over $2,000 solely by his own work and good management. A history of his career in later years has been but a continuation of that of his youth and has been proportionally even more successful. He is now one of the two principal owners of the Commercial Savings Bank, one of the soundest and most reliable banking institutions in the western part of the State, and is also a large real estate owner and leading stock raiser of the county, owning a number of fine farms, from which he annually sells thousands of dollars' worth of stock. He also has a large amount of other valuable property and, in a word, is one of the prominent tax payers of the county. Such is the successful career of a man who cast himself out into the world on his own resources when but a mere boy and without a penny, a career that would reflect credit upon anyone man. Mr. Adkins was born in Scott county, Ky., October 9, 1821, and was a son of Judge Robert Adkins and wife, *nee* Miss Mary Snell, the Judge formerly of Virginia, but Mrs. Adkins a Kentuckian by nativity. The Judge's mother was a Miss Mille, and her parents were co-pioneers with Daniel Boone in Kentucky, having come out from Virginia in company with him on his first trip to the then wilds of the former State. In 1825, Judge Adkins came to Missouri with his family and located in Howard county, but returned to Kentucky soon afterwards. Ten years from their first trip, however, they came back to this State

HISTORY OF CLAY COUNTY

and settled in Clay county. Here the Judge bought several hundred acres of fine land, three miles north of Liberty, where he improved a large farm and lived until his death. He died of cholera in July, 1851. He became one of the well known and influential citizens of the county, and such was his high standing and popularity that although an uncompromising Democrat in a strong Whig county, as Clay county then was, he was repeatedly elected to the office of county judge, defeating each time the most popular Whig they could put up against him. He reared a large family of children, five sons and six daughters living to reach years of maturity and to become the heads of families themselves. Nine are still living, four brothers in Kansas City, three in this county and two sisters who are in Kansas City — Mrs. C. J. White and Mrs. Eliza Hall. Darwin J. Adkins was the eldest of the brothers and remained at home on the farm until he was 15 years of age, when, having secured something of an ordinary education, and having a taste for business life, he left the farm and came to Liberty, where he obtained a clerkship in a store. He clerked for about three years and not only obtained a good knowledge of the business, but also saved up a little means from his salary. He then went on a farm and also engaged in trading in stock. These interests he has ever since carried on. For some years he was engaged in the Southern trade in horses and mules, driving his stock to Shreveport, La., Alexandria, Miss., and other points. This was while he was yet quite a young man and he made some two or three thousand dollars before he was 21 years of age. In 1842, he was married to Miss Elizabeth Pence, a daughter of Edward A. Pence, formerly of Kentucky. He then gave up the Southern trade, and settled down on a farm, but continued in the local stock trading business. Later along he removed to Platte county, but after four years returned to this county, and bought the old Adkins family homestead, where he followed farming and handling stock until 1863. Subsequently he bought other places and resided at Liberty and on different farms until the time he settled permanently where he now resides. In 1856 he was largely instrumental in establishing the Farmers' Bank at Liberty, becoming one of its directors. This was finally succeeded by the Commercial Savings Bank in 1867. Since 1870 he has been president of this bank and he and Mr. Robertson own more than four-fifths of its capital stock. It has a stock of $50,000, all paid up, and the bank is in a most prosperous condition, paying annually a good dividend on the stock represented. Last year Mr. Adkins sold over $9,000 worth of stock off of his several farms. Mr. Adkins' first wife having died in April, 1852, he was married to Mrs. Mary A. Futsle, a daughter of Andrew Robertson, formerly of Tennessee. Her mother was a native of North Carolina. Mrs. Adkins' parents removed to Clay county way back in 1818, and she was born here in September, 1822. Mr. Adkins and his present wife have four children, namely: Magdaline, wife of Robert G. Robinson; Edward V., Robert I., and Emma, deceased wife of Michael A. Groom. By his former wife Mr. Adkins has two children: Ruth, wife of L. W. Pence, and Darwin J.

HISTORY OF CLAY COUNTY

N. Mrs. A. is a member of the M. E. Church South, and Mr. Adkins a prominent member of the Masonic Order.

LEONIDAS ADKINS

(Proprietor of the Liberty Livery, Feed and Sales Stables, Liberty).

Mr. Adkins is a representative of the old and respected family whose name he bears, mention of which has already been made in the sketch of his brother, D. J. Adkins, on a previous page. Leonidas Adkins was born on the old family homestead, near Liberty, April 6, 1838. He was reared on the farm and received a good practical education as he grew up, studying the higher branches at William Jewell College. Afterwards he engaged as a clerk at Liberty, and continued at that about five years. For the 24 years following, up to 1883, Mr. Adkins followed farming and stock raising in this county, and was satisfactorily successful. Early in 1884 he bought the stables and stock where he is now engaged in business. The building he has considerably enlarged, and has much improved the business, so that he now has one of the best establishments of the kind in the county. In 1858 Mr. Atkinson was married to Miss Martha J., a daughter of Hon. John R. Keller, of this county, whose sketch is elsewhere given. Mrs. A. is a graduate of the Liberty Female Seminary. They have five children: Robert, who is a partner with his father in business; Lila, James P., William, John C. and Churchill. Mrs. A. is a member of the Christian Church.

EDWARD V. (YCLEPT " CALHOUN ") ADKINS

(Farmer and Stock-raiser, Post-office, Liberty).

Mr. Adkins is well recognized as one of the neatest and most enterprising young farmers of the county. He is a man of thorough collegiate and university education, and is qualified for almost any business where intelligence, culture and energy are required, but has adopted farming and handling stock as his calling entirely from choice, preferring a free and open and independent life of a farmer to that of all others. In his farming operations he has brought his education and good taste to bear the same as he would have done in any other pursuit. He has a good place, large enough for his present purposes, and keeps it in the best of condition. His home and household and all its surroundings are in keeping with the general appearance of his farm, the credit for which is principally due to his refined and excellent wife, who is even more particular than her husband to have everything in presentable order. Mr. Adkins was born in this county May 19, 1845, and was a son of Downing O. Adkins, a well known and highly respected citizen of the county, who came here from Kentucky as early as 1832. Mr. Adkins, Jr., was reared on his father's farm (his father being a successful stock dealer as well as a prominent farmer), and given the best of educational advantages as he grew up. From the common schools he went to William Jewell College and then to Mount Gilead

HISTORY OF CLAY COUNTY

College, thence to Sidney College, Iowa, and from there to the State University of Missouri, where he completed his general education. Afterwards he took a commercial course at a business college in Lafayette, Ind., where he was honorably graduated. Returning from Indiana he at once engaged in farming in this county, which he has ever since followed. His farm contains 228 acres. November 8, 1882, he was married to Miss Susie H. Williams, a daughter of John Williams, of Shawnee Mission, Kas., but formerly from Marshall, Mich. She was an invalid at the time of her marriage, and survived her wedding day only a week more than a month. Her remains were buried in the cemetery near where Mr. Adkins now resides. She was a lady of singular sweetness and gentleness of disposition, and of a presence and bearing that won all hearts. But Death loves the shining mark, and in the morning of her life his cold and pulseless finger pointed her out for the grave — she was no more. While loved ones here have sustained a sad bereavement by her loss, heaven has been made brighter by her sweet, gentle spirit. Mr. Adkins was married to his present wife September 15, 1883. She was a Miss Emma E. Pence, a daughter of Capt. W. H. Pence, and a lady worthy in every way to occupy the place she does in the affection of her devoted husband. Mr. Adkins has not neglected the information to be had from travel, but has visited in different parts of the country no less than 17 States. After all the country he has seen he is satisfied there is no place like Clay county for a home. "There is no place like home."

HON. DeWITT C. ALLEN

(Liberty).

DeWitt C. Allen was born November 11, 1835, in Clay county, Missouri, and with the exception of a few brief intervals has passed his life in that county. His family is of English-Welsh extraction, and has been settled in America more than a century and a half, and his parents were persons of education and refinement. His father Col. Shubael Allen, was a native of Orange county, New York, whence he emigrated to Kentucky in 1816, and thence to Missouri in 1817, and finally settled in Clay county in 1820. His mother, Miss Dinah Ayres Trigg, was a daughter of Gen. Stephen Trigg, of Bedford county, Virginia, who emigrated to Kentucky near the close of the last century, and thence to Howard county, Missouri, in 1818. She was born in Estill county, Kentucky.

When Mr. Allen was five years old his father died, and he passed entirely under the influence and training of his mother — a woman of excellent judgment, fine literary taste, cheerful disposition, the most delicate sentiments of honor and integrity, and in every way fitted for the discharge of the duties devolved upon her. In temperament he is more like his father, but his character was molded by his mother. To her encouragement and advice he attributes mainly his achievements in life.

By mental constitution he was a student and lover of books, and

HISTORY OF CLAY COUNTY

his taste for study was strengthened by example. His historical and miscellaneous reading began at eleven years of age, and has been pursued with system and regularity. Before the completion of his thirteenth year, among other works, he had read all of Scott's novels.

In 1850, having previously received the benefit of excellent private schools, held, however, at irregular intervals, he entered William Jewell College, and was there graduated in 1855 with the first honors in the classics and *belles lettres*. His grade in mathematics was somewhat lower. His taste originally at college was for the mathematics, but as his acquaintance with the classics increased his fondness for mathematics became less strong. Having completed his collegiate course he accepted the position of principal of the preparatory department of the Masonic College at Lexington, Missouri, which he filled for a year to the entire satisfaction of the curators and patrons of that institution. He accounts the reminiscences of his stay at Lexington as among the most agreeable in his life. Society there was at the height of its brilliance and charm. The people, as ever, were hospitable and courteous, and he bears with him only memories of kindness and encouragement received from them. His previous life had been one of study and seclusion, and his experiences of society and the world were slight. Of the many persons there to whom he feels indebted for kind offices, he especially remembers his friends, Charles R. Morehead, Sr. (now deceased), and Mrs. William H. Russell. During the year succeeding his connection with the Masonic College he devoted himself to those historical and special studies (suggested to him by his friend, Col. Alexander W. Doniphan) which are considered by legal gentlemen as a proper introduction to the comprehensive study of the law, which he had chosen while at college as the profession of his life. From the summer of 1858 to May, 1860, he pursued his legal studies in the office of the late Richard R. Rees, Esq., in Leavenworth, Kansas. Occasionally during that period he assisted Mr. Rees in the trial of cases in order to acquire familiarity with the procedure in the courts. He recognizes his obligations to the advice and suggestions of Mr. Rees as being very great, particularly in the specialities of pleading, conveyancing and the drafting of orders, judgments and decrees. In May, 1860, he returned to his home in Liberty, Missouri, and began the practice of law. Since then he has devoted himself exclusively to the work of his profession. In November, 1860, he was elected circuit attorney of the Fifth Judicial Circuit of Missouri, composed of the counties of Clay, Clinton, Caldwell, Ray and Carroll. He discharged the duties of that office with fidelity and promptness until December 17, 1861, when, under the operation of an ordinance of the convention of that year, prescribing an oath testing the loyalty of officers, it became vacant in consequence of his refusal to take the oath. He was married May 18, 1864, to Miss Emily E. Settle, of Ray county, Missouri, daughter of Hiram P. Settle, Esq., of that county. She was born in Culpeper county, Virginia. They have three children.

During the years 1866–67 he was general attorney of the Kansas

293

HISTORY OF CLAY COUNTY

City and Cameron Railroad Company — now known as the Kansas City branch of the Hannibal and St. Joseph Railroad — and in that position labored assiduously with others to secure its early completion.

He was elected, without opposition, in January, 1875, to represent — in connection with Hon. E. H. Norton — the Third Senatorial District of Missouri, composed of the counties of Clay, Clinton and Platte, in the constitutional convention, called to meet May 5, 1875, and assisted in the framing of the present organic law of the State. In that body, composed of many of the ablest and most learned men in the State, he bore himself with ability and won the respect and confidence of its members. At its organization he was appointed a member of the committees on education and the legislative department, and was esteemed in them as an intelligent and indefatigable worker.

Mr. Allen has attained a high and honorable position at the bar. He deals with the law as a science, and sees the logical connection of its principles. He surveys the fields of legal lore with the clear, calm vision of a jurist. He is devoted to our system of jurisprudence because it contains the crystallized thoughts of the best minds of all ages and countries. He is noted for the power of his faculty for analysis, the quickness of his perception of the most remote analogies, the fineness and delicacy of his distinctions, and the rapidity of his detection of inconsistencies in argument. In forensic conflicts he brings into requisition the best materials of law and fact. His positions are always clear, logical and concise. His voice, though not strong, is distinct and penetrating, and his rhetoric faultless. When the occasion demands it, he ascends by easy gradations from the smooth, graceful and conversational style, suited to the courts, to a higher plane of oratory. His manner is earnest, and his ideas form in quick, unbroken succession. But his great power as a speaker is in the elevation of his sentiments, and his rich and sparkling thoughts. Ringing tones, electric fire and aptly chosen words merely form their drapery. He is a cultured, scholarly man. His style, both in speaking and writing, is peculiarly his own. He is an independent thinker and derives his information, when practicable, from original sources. He is systematic and exact in all things, and counts as worthless all knowledge that is not accurate. During the vacation of the courts he does not remain idle, but continues in his office engaged in work or investigation. He deals with his clients with the utmost candor. And one of his distinguishing characteristics is fidelity to his friends. He possesses a high sense of honor, and is bold and unyielding in defense of right.

Mr. Allen devotes his periods of leisure to literary reading — historical, philosophical, critical and poetical — but never allows it to infringe upon his professional study or work. He fully recognizes the truth so often urged by the sages of the law, that, of all men, the reading and thought of a lawyer should be the most extended. Systematic and careful study in the higher works of literature — historical, philosophical, critical and poetical — gives freshness, breadth and comprehensive grasp to the mind, variety and richness of thought, and a clearer perception of the motives of men and the principles of things, indeed of the very spirit of laws. Nature has given us both reason and fancy, and they were meant for use. Hence, he argues that the mind should both reason and bloom. Besides, a cultured fancy, guided by severe taste, is a source of invention in argument. He occasionally writes, but only as a matter of amusement or for the gratification of friends. His style of writing is clear, logical, chaste and impassioned. His thoughts are expressed with force and sententiousness. His fancy is delicate and subtle, and usually pervades his writings.

Mr. Allen is a charming conversationalist. His wide range of reading, habits of analysis and observation, intuitive knowledge of the motives of men and women, his fine fancy, rapid play of thought, and quick apprehension, combine with his genial good humor and innate charity to make him a brilliant and most agreeable member of society, and to render his triumphs in the *salon* equal to those at the bar. He is, as the result both of thought and observation, a staunch and enthusiastic friend of popular education, and is keenly alive to the advantages to be derived from an increase of facilities for university and scientific training for the young. During 10 years, or more, prior to the summer of 1881, he was one of the trustees of William Jewell College, and earnestly co-operated with his associates in the promotion of the interests of that institution. Probably to no one in the State is it more indebted for its present high state of efficiency.

Mr. Allen is not a member of any church, but he entertains a high respect for religion, and he conceives that reverence for it among the people is the life and soul of healthful, well ordered society. He is highly public spirited, and ready at all times to aid and encourage those movements which tend to increase the material happiness and promote the culture of his community. His highest conception of the due execution of a man's life work is the faithful performance of duty. In politics he is a firm, consistent Jeffersonian Democrat.

JOHN M. ALLEN, M. D.

(Physician and Surgeon, Liberty).

Dr. Allen was a son of the late Col. Shubael Allen, for many years a prominent and influential citizen of Clay county, but originally from Orange county, N. Y. Col. Allen is elsewhere referred to in this volume. Dr. Allen was born in Clay county, July 23, 1833. He was reared in this county, and educated at the common schools and in William Jewell College. At that institution he took a course of two years, immediately preceding 1852, and entered the college at its first opening, in January, 1850. His taste in study inclined to mathematics, and, after that, to history, natural philosophy and astronomy. Young Allen became a proficient mathematician, and he advanced in Latin as far as the Sophomore class. Early in 1852 he began the study of medicine under the tutorage of Dr. Joseph M. Wood, now of Kansas City, but then a resident physician of Liberty. In due time young Allen matriculated at the St. Louis Medical College, and he continued a student there until he was graduated with credit in the class of '54. He was a severe and unremitting student while at medical college, as he had previously been when taking his general college course; and the thoroughness he showed in his studies, and the progress made by him, attracted the favorable attention of his preceptors. Immediately after his graduation at St. Louis he was solicited by Dr. Pope, the dean of the St. Louis Medical College, to apply for the position of physician to the St. Louis City Hospital, an evidence of the high estimate Dr. Pope placed upon his attainments and ability as a physician. Dr. Allen, however, declined to make the application, preferring to enter at once upon the general practice of medicine. Returning home from St. Louis after his graduation, Dr. Allen located at Claysville, in the northeastern part of this county, and began the practice of his profession. When he arrived there he had but $6 in the world, and was $400 in debt. Stopping with Capt. William Cummons, a man whose largeness of heart was only equaled by his great purity of character and his almost religious veneration for North Carolina, his native State, young Dr. Allen frankly told him his financial condition, and that his assets consisted of a limited wardrobe, "Russell's Modern Europe," the Lord's Prayer and a small medical library. Capt. Cummons, who was evidently touched by reference to the Lord's Prayer, in the generosity of his great good nature, readily and graciously assured young Allen that he would gladly board him on trust, and would supply him with such reasonable sums of money as he might need. For this noble and generous act of kindness, and for the courtesy and consideration which was ever afterwards shown him in the family of Capt. Cummons as long as he remained with them, Dr. Allen cherishes a profound and lasting feeling of gratitude. The kindness of other friends, including that of those good men, Edward M. Samuel and Col. A. W. Doniphan, he holds in like remembrance. Declining, however, all loans, he remained at Claysville for about seven years, and built up an excellent practice, becoming one of the leading physicians of the northeastern part of the county.

When Mr. Lincoln fulminated his first proclamation against the South in 1861, Dr. Allen was temporarily absent from Claysville attending a post-graduate course of lectures at the St. Louis Medical College, in order to review his college course in medicine and surgery, and to acquaint himself with all the later and newer principles and theories of practice developed since his graduation in 1854. But believing that war was now imminent, and being determined to espouse the cause of the South, which he believed to be his duty as a loyal and patriotic citizen of Missouri, he at once returned home and proceeded to the enlistment of a company for the Southern service. On the organization of the company he was elected captain, and it became a part of Col. Benjamin A. Rives' regiment — who was killed at the head of his regiment in the battle of Elk Horn. But in May, 1861, Dr. Allen accepted the office of surgeon of Rives' regiment, which became a part of the Fourth Missouri division, State Guard. His term of service in the State Guard lasted for several months, after the expiration of which he and a number of other prominent gentleman in the Southern service from Missouri, organized the Third Missouri, of the First Brigade, in the regular Confederate service, he becoming regimental surgeon. He continued surgeon of that regiment until the fall of 1863, when, by order of Gen. Joseph E. Johnston, he was promoted to the office of chief surgeon of the district of Mississippi and East Louisiana, and attached to the staff of Gen. Wirt Adams, with whom he continued until the close of the war. Throughout the war Dr. Allen studiously avoided the exercise of his privilege as a surgeon of not participating in the various engagements in which his command took part, but invariably went to the front, when not occupied with his duties to the wounded. He took part in many of the great battles of the war, including, in Missouri, those of Carthage, Wilson's Creek, Dry Wood and the siege of Lexington; and beyond this State, those of Elk Horn, Corinth, Iuka, Grand Gulf, Fort Gibson and a number of engagements of less importance. After the war Dr. Allen returned home to Clay county, and located at Liberty, where he has ever since resided and been engaged in the active practice of his profession. He has been very successful as a physician and has taken a leading place among the prominent physicians of the State. He has always taken a pardonable pride in the good name and high character of the medical profession, and has diligently exerted himself on all proper occasions for its advancement. As early as 1856 he took an active part in the organization of the Clay County Medical Society, and from time to time after that was its president. In 1858 he became a member of the National Medical Association, and has ever since continued to be honorably identified with that organization. Later along he assisted to organize the Kansas City District Medical Society, and in recognition of his high standing in the profession and of the great value of his services in the organization of the society, he was made its first president. Dr. Allen, being a man of culture and decided literary tastes, takes a marked interest in the cause of education and literary matters. For many years he has been an active member of the Liberty Literary Club, a society of gentlemen at this place organized nearly 30 years ago, for the promotion of literature and social culture, and which contains among its members the professional men and *literati* of the place. He is also a strong advocate of temperance and has been connected with all the temperance movements in this county since 1848. Dr. Allen never signed a petition for a dram-shop license in his life, but by his individual efforts and numerous addresses and lectures has contributed in no small degree to the present advanced position of the people of Clay county on the temperance question. A man of good business habits and qualifications, he has been satisfactorily successful in accumulating the substantial evidences of material comfort and independence. At the beginning of his practice, over thirty years ago, he made it a rule to close up his books, either by cash settlements or requiring promissory notes, at the end of each year; and whilst he has earnestly avoided pressing the poor, he has been hardly less careful to make those pay who were able to, especially that class described in the couplet: —

"When the devil got sick, the devil a saint would be;
But when the devil got well, the devil a saint was he."

On the 15th of November, 1866, Dr. Allen was married to Miss Agnes McAlpine at Port Gibson, Miss. Mrs. Allen was a daughter of the late William R. McAlpine, Esq., of that place, and is a lady of marked culture and refinement.

As a citizen, Dr. Allen is public spirited, and readily appreciates those crises when the union of the intellect and energy of a community for action becomes necessary to secure results beneficial to all, and is at all times willing to bear his proportions of the burden of labor and expenditure needed to attain them.

GEORGE A. BALDWIN

(Superintendent of the Eleemosenary Farm, Post Office, Liberty).

Mr. Baldwin took charge of the county farm under contract of the county court in 1878, and has continued in charge of it ever since. The fact that he has been retained in this responsible position for so many years speaks well for his management of the place, his character in the service of the county, and the confidence in which he is held by the court and the people at large. There is an average of from ten to twelve poor persons on the farm all the time. In his treatment of them he is kind but firm, and so governs them that while they know they must respect and obey him, they nevertheless regard him with entire friendship, and show that they feel it a pleasure to have his good opinion. The county could probably not get a more suitable man for the position he holds than it now has. Mr. Baldwin is a native of Clay county, born in 1842. His father was Andrew B. Baldwin, distantly related to Maj. Roderick Baldwin, of the Warrensburg *Standard*, in this State. Mr. Baldwin's mother came of a good family. She was a Miss Harriet Moberly, a daughter of B. M. Moberly, formerly of Kentucky. They have four children: George T., Edna B., Ninety B. and Clyde A. One is deceased, Charles R. Mr. Baldwin and wife are members of the Christian Church, and he is a member of the I. O. O. F.

JOHN A. BEAUCHAMP

(Dealer in Groceries, Liberty).

Maj. Robbinson P. Beauchamp, the father of the subject of this sketch and a prominent lawyer in Western Missouri in an early day, came here from Southern Kentucky in 1825, and for a number of years resided at Liberty. He assisted to organize the first court ever held in Jackson county, and being a man of collegiate education, he understood surveying thoroughly and was induced to assist in 1825 in establishing the State boundary line of Western Missouri, from Iowa to Arkansas. Under John Quincy Adams' administration he was appointed Indian agent by President Adams, with headquarters at Ft. Leavenworth, in which position he continued until his death, in 1833. He died of cholera during the epidemic of that year, while on his way up the Missouri river on the boat Yellowstone, and was buried at Belleview, near Council Bluffs. He was married in Kentucky before coming to Missouri, his wife having been a Miss Dolly Winn, a daughter of Jesse Winn, Sr., of that State. She died at Paris, Tenn., in 1863. A family of five children were the fruits of their married life, including the subject of the present sketch.

John A. Beauchamp, who was the eldest son in their family of children, was born at Glasgow, in Barren county, Kentucky, December 19, 1817, and was still quite young when the family removed to Missouri. Partly reared at Liberty, at the age of thirteen he accompanied his parents to Ft. Leavenworth and remained there until 1832, after his father's death. His mother then went to Tennessee, but John A. obtained employment as salesman in a wholesale and retail house in St. Louis. He continued there for about five years and then returned to Liberty. But in 1838, in connection with a partner, he established a dry goods and grocery house at Richmond, in Ray county, and also a similar house at Camden, he, himself taking charge of the Camden store. He continued in that business for about nine years, at the expiration of which time he retired from merchandising and settled on a farm he owned just outside the suburbs of Liberty.

Mr. Beauchamp was actively engaged in farming on his place near Liberty for a period of over thirty years, or until 1880; and for nearly twenty years of that time he was extensively occupied in dealing in stock, trading, buying, selling, etc. However, for five years following 1865, he resided in town and carried on a clothing store, besides running his farm and stock-dealing. Three years ago he sold the farm and is still remaining in town, where he established a grocery store, which he has ever since been conducting. He has a full stock of groceries, provisions, queens' and glassware, etc., etc.

Mr. Beauchamp has been married twice. His first wife was a Miss Ann T. Lincoln, a daughter of George and Julia Ann (Gatewood) Lincoln, early settlers of this county from Kentucky. Her grandfather, Thomas Lincoln, originally of Rockingham county, Virginia, was a brother to Abraham Lincoln, the grandfather of President Lincoln.

Mr. Beauchamp's first wife died in 1853, leaving two sons, Robbinson P. and John S., both of whom are now themselves the heads of families and residents of Nebraska.

To his second wife Mr. Beauchamp was married in 1862. She was a Miss Sidney N. Owens, a daughter of Margaret M. and Samuel Owens, of Mason county, Kentucky. Five children are the fruits of this union: Lee, who clerks for his father in the store and is a graduate of the Liberty high school; Maggie, Marietta, Fanny and Nellie.

Mr. Beauchamp has held a number of local official positions and is

HISTORY OF CLAY COUNTY

a man as highly esteemed as any citizen of the county. He is a member of the Christian Church. His wife is a member of the Presbyterian Church.

WILLIAM E. BRASFIELD

(Farmer, Stock-raiser and Stock-dealer, Post-office, Liberty).

For many years Mr. Brasfield has devoted his time and attention principally to stock. He is one of those men of energy and natural business tact who generally succeed in whatever they engage. The qualities for successful business men are, to a large extent, natural, inherited, the result of a union, the conditions which tend to transmit to offsprings those characteristics and attributes in a large measure which afterwards go to make the successful man. It is said that the poet is born — not afterwards made by education. This is very largely true of many other spheres of activity, both mental and industrial. Unless one have the natural attributes for a particular calling, his career in that calling will always be an uphill struggle, and, at the best, only comparative success is possible. Mr. Brasfield came of a line of ancestors remarked for their energy and enterprise as business farmers; not only personally industrious themselves, but with a tact for making work around them move along, and for directing their affairs in a business-like way to the best advantage. Whatever they saw to be the most profitable as farmers they followed, whether at one time it was raising grain, at another fattening stock for the markets, or, again, breeding fine stock for the general trade. Being men of sterling intelligence and business acumen, they were generally able to perceive what branch of farm life was the most remunerative, and that they invariably pursued. So with Mr. Brasfield, the subject of this sketch. He has long seen that grain growing can not continue a profitable industry, and his sagacity in this respect has already been verified. Wheat in the Northwest is now being produced for a market that has reached as low a point as 35 cents per bushel, and the general average of prices will continue to go down. He, therefore, turned his attention to stock, and has profited by his good judgment. But ordinary, common stock is rapidly reaching the point where there is no profit for a Missouri farmer, on account of the cheap stock of Texas and the territories. Therefore, he is gradually converting his place into a fine stock farm. Mr. Brasfield has been very successful as a stock-raiser and dealer, and is one of the leading stockmen in the county. He has a fine stock farm of 434 acres, with 280 acres additional near by. His place is run nearly altogether in blue grass, reserving only enough for grain for stock feed in winter and for fattening purposes. He has an excellent grade of cattle on his place, and makes a business of raising and fattening beef cattle and hogs for the markets. He ships annually a large number of each. His specialty in the stock line, however, is breeding and raising fine saddle and harness stallions and fine jacks. For these purposes he has provided himself with some of the best stock in the country. He makes a special study of blooded horses and jacks, and selects his stock for breeding purposes from the classes, and, indeed, from the families of breeds which are recognized by common consent to be the best. Annually he sells a number of young stallions and jacks bred and raised on his place. He finds it but little more trouble and expense to raise a fine animal than it would to raise a scrub, whereas, with the first there is a large profit, and with the other little or no profit, if not a loss. Certainly he is correct in the idea that this is the only true and sensible theory of successful stock-raising. Mr. Brasfield was born in Chariton county, Mo., in December, 1827, but was reared in Clay county. His parents were Leonard and Lucretia Brasfield, who went from Virginia in an early day to Madison county, Ky. From there he came to Missouri in 1821, and located in Howard county. From there they shortly removed to Chariton county, and then settled permanently in Clay county in 1829. The father was a successful farmer of this county, and an enterprising stock-raiser. He died here in 1867; the mother died in 1871. William E., who was brought up to farming and stock-raising, went to California in 1849, and was absent two years, engaged in mining on Wood's creek with some success. Returning in 1851, he resumed farming, and raising and dealing in stock, and in 1854 took a drove of cattle across the plains to California, where he sold them to good advantage. He then came back, and ever since that time has confined himself to his farm and the stock business in this county. In 1855 he was married to Miss Sarah J. Estes, a daughter of William and Malinda Estes, the father a native of Virginia but her mother from Tennessee. They came to Missouri from Tennessee in 1817. They have four children: Amanda, the wife of John Dale; Annie B., the wife of William Davis; William L. and Hettie. Mr. Brasfield is a man who appreciates the importance of education, and gave his children the benefits of college instruction.

HON. LUKE W. BURRIS

(Clerk of the County Court, Clay county, Mo.).

The period of Mr. Burris' adult life up to the present time has been chiefly spent in two counties of this State, and from both he has been the recipient of enviable political honors. The county in which he was principally reared — Washington county — he represented with honor and ability in the State Legislature, after having held numerous other public trusts. Removing thence to this county after the close of his term as representative of Washington county, in 1853, he has been repeatedly honored here with the suffrages of the people in a manner not less creditable to him personally and as a trusted official than were the confidence and esteem in which he was held where he was reared. In 1864 he was the nominee of the Democratic party on the ticket with Hon. Thomas L. Price for Lieutenant-Governor, and if the people of Missouri could then have had, as they now have, "a free ballot and a fair count" he would undoubtedly have been elected.

HISTORY OF CLAY COUNTY

In the fall of 1870, after having twice represented Clay county in the Legislature, he was prevailed upon by his friends in this county to accept the office of county court clerk, to which he was elected by a highly flattering majority, and ever since that time he has been content to continue in that position, having been consecutively rechosen to the office by the people at each quadriennial election. At the close of his present term he will have served the people in this position for 16 years. Mr. Burris was a son of one of the pioneer settlers of Central Missouri. His father, David Burris, came to this State from Kentucky when a young man, away back in the early territorial days of the country. He first located in Howard county, and planted and raised a crop of corn the year when corn was first raised in that county, but soon afterwards made his home in Cooper county, near Boonville. He was an active participant in all the early Indian wars of the country, and was as brave an Indian fighter and deadly a shot with his trusted rifle as ever faced the foe of the forest or drew bead on a treacherous savage. Long after his death his widow drew a pension from the government on account of his services in protecting the homes of the early settlers of Missouri. He was married near Fayette in about 1812 to Miss Susan Monroe, a daughter of William Monroe, another brave-hearted pioneer settler from Kentucky. Their honeymoon and some years afterwards were spent principally in Cooper's Fort, for in those days no " pale-face " was safe where a red man's bullet could reach him from ambush. Luke W. Burris was born at Boonville August 2, 1817. In about 1830 the family removed to Texas, then a country even wilder and more weird than Missouri. But they returned in a short time to this State and settled in Washington county. In 1850 the father, though well advanced in years, still had the fire of the old pioneer in him, and felt equal to a journey across the plains to the Pactolian lands of the Pacific coast. He accordingly went to California and engaged in mining, but never lived to return. He died and was buried on the distant shore of the Pacific sea, where his remains still rest, wrapped in the sleep that shall be broken only by the final acclaim of immortal life. Mr. Burris was reared in Washington county, and as he grew up learned the lessons, by the experiences through which he passed, of industry, frugal habits and economy. These he has never forgotten. They have ever been characteristics of his subsequent life and conduct. Though brought up in a condition of society where the incentives for an education were by no means great, and where the opportunities for culture were even less, he had the intelligence and sagacity to see that learning, at least, a sufficient knowledge of books for all practical affairs of life, was of the first importance. Without the advantage of local schools, except for a period of about six months, he nevertheless applied himself to study. When 17 years of age, to use his own expression, he did not " know one figure from another ; " but by close attention to his books at home during what leisure he had from his daily employments, he succeeded in mastering the elements of an ordinary English education. He has always been remarked for his pleasant, affable manners, his kindly disposition and

HISTORY OF CLAY COUNTY

the frankness and generosity of his nature. He has, therefore, ever been a popular man among all who knew him wherever he resided. Well qualified by education and natural aptitude for the discharge of official duties, and a man of thorough integrity of character, it is therefore not surprising that most of his adult life has been spent in positions of public trust. When quite a young man he was elected constable of his township in Washington county, which he held with great satisfaction to the public and increasing popularity for several years. He was then elected county assessor, and at the close of his term, in 1844, in that office, was elected sheriff of the county. Following his first term as sheriff he was re-elected, and immediately after his second term, in 1850, he was elected a member of the Legislature, where he made an honorable and enviable record as a worthy and faithful representative. Mr. Burris came to Clay county in 1853, and for a number of years afterwards was actively engaged here in industrial pursuits. For five years he ran a saw and grist mill at Missouri City, and then was a member of the firm of Arthur, Burris & Co., of Liberty Landing, in a large hemp manufactory, up to the time of the war. In 1860 he was elected a member of the Legislature from this county as a Whig, and in 1862 was re-elected by the people generally without opposition. At the close of his second term in the Legislature from this county he became the Democratic nominee for Lieutenant-Governor, but, as stated elsewhere, he was defeated.

In the spring of 1865 he removed to St. Louis, and was engaged in the commission business for about four years, when he returned to Liberty. The year following his return he was elected county clerk, and, as stated above, he has continued to hold the office ever since that time. Though now past the age of 67 he is still active and efficient in the discharge of his official duties, giving his personal attention to his office. He is well known among the officials of the State as one of the best county clerks within its borders, and is not less popular in official circles where he is known than among the people of his own county. On the 12th of October, 1848, at Potosi, Washington county, he was married to Miss C. E. Mitchell, daughter of Thomas S. Mitchell, who died when she was quite young. She was a step-daughter of Dr. Henry Culver, and was born in Washington, D. C., but principally reared in Maryland. She was partly educated at St. Louis by the Mauro sisters. Mr. and Mrs. Burris reared but one child, a son, William M. Burris, now a prominent attorney of Kansas City. Mr. Burris and wife are members of the Episcopal Church, and he has been a member of the Odd Fellows' Order for over 40 years, holding all the positions in the different lodges with which he has been connected.

COL. ALEXANDER J. CALHOUN

(Retired Merchant, and Farmer and Fine Stock-raiser, Liberty).

There is probably not another family in the United States whose representatives have played a more important and honorable part in the history of the country than have those of the Calhoun family. With at least the name of one member of this distinguished family every civilized country has been made familiar, a name that stands second to none for ability and statesmanship, and patriotism and high personal honor in this or any other land. Whatever may now be the popular judgment upon the States Rights doctrines of John C. Calhoun, all admit that he was one of the greatest men, if not the greatest, and one of the most lofty and patriotic statesman this country ever produced. Others, perhaps, exceeded him in the gloss of eloquence, but as a logician, and for profound ability, he was without a superior. The Calhoun family have given other men of distinction to the country. In the annals of the National Legislature appear the names of no less than five distinguished representatives of this family, all either closely or distantly related. In the affairs of several States they have been prominent, also holding honorable positions of public trust, from the gubernatorial chair down, since early colonial times; and in the professions and in the various departments of science, in the industries and in business life, on the stage and in letters, representatives of the family have from time to time attained eminent distinction. Looking, therefore, at the history of this family as it is reflected in the history of the country, one may with all truth and propriety say that if Rome could ever boast her *gentes patriciæ*, the Calhoun family may with equal truth and propriety be called one of the patrician families of this country.

The American Calhouns descend from an ancient and honorable family of their name in Ireland. In the history of that country the name is frequently made mention of with credit and distinction. About the beginning of the second quarter of the last century three brothers of the name emigrated to America, all men of character and culture. Their first location in this country was in Pennsylvania. One of these brothers, Patrick Calhoun, became the father of Hon. John C. Calhoun; another (an older brother) became the father of Hon. John Ewing Calhoun, who preceded his cousin, Hon. John C., in the United States Senate from South Carolina; and from the third brother, descended the subject of the present sketch. Samuel Calhoun was the son of —— Calhoun, and from Samuel came Thomas Calhoun, the father of Col. Alexander J. Calhoun.

From Pennsylvania the three Calhoun brothers emigrated within some years of each other to South Carolina, Patrick Calhoun, however, stopping for a time in what is now West Virginia, where he intended to make his permanent home. But after Braddock's defeat the Indians became so emboldened that he was compelled to move on further South, and finally located permanently on the borders of the Cherokee territory in South Carolina, near where his brothers had previously settled. From South Carolina branches of the three families spread out into other States, including North Carolina, Virginia, Kentucky, Tennessee, Ohio, Indiana, Missouri and nearly all the Western and Southern States; and one branch settled in Massachusetts, of which Hon. William B. Calhoun, a distinguished member of

HISTORY OF CLAY COUNTY

Congress from the Springfield district, for about ten years prior to 1843, and afterwards an elector on the Clay and Frelinghuysen Presidendial ticket, was a representative of the branch of the family of which Col. Alexander Calhoun belongs. An interesting and well written account is given in a sketch of his life published in the United States Biographical Dictionary (Missouri Volume), in 1878, which we here reproduce, together with the body of the sketch : —

Alexander J. Calhoun was born in Wilson county, Tenn., November 10, 1814, and is a descendant of one of the old families of the Carolinas, and the son of a deeply revered and eminently pious gentleman. The first of the name emigrated from Ireland to America early in the history of the colonial settlement, and settled in South Carolina, where he reared a family. One of his sons, Samuel, was the grandfather of our subject. He was born in that State about 1740, in manhood was a soldier in the Revolution ; after the war he moved to North Carolina, thence to Tennessee in 1798, and settled in Wilson county, near the Big Springs, in 1801, where he died in 1833. His wife was Nancy Neely ; she was born in Pennsylvania in 1755, was of Scotch descent, and died in Tennessee in 1825. They had the following children: Hannah, married Hugh Roane ; John, Polly, married Flavel Garrison ; Thomas, Jane, married John Provine ; Nancy, married Montgomery McCorkle ; Samuel and James. Thomas Calhoun, the father of the subject of this sketch, was born in North Carolina, May 31, 1782. He was educated in that State, and moved with his parents to Wilson county, Tenn. He prepared himself for the ministry in the Cumberland Presbyterian Church, of which religious body he was one of the first members and was intimately connected with its founding and organization, in 1810, under Revs. Finis Ewing, Samuel King and Samuel McAdow. He was ordained and preached for that church full half a century. In 1808, he was married to Miss Mary Robertson Johnston, who was born in 1787, in North Carolina. Her father, Alexander Johnson, was born in the same State about 1760, was of Welsh descent, and died in 1800. Her mother, whose maiden name was Nellie Robertson, was born in Guilford county, N. C., about 1766, and died in 1839. The children of Alexander and Nellie Johnson were : John, Mary R., married Thomas Calhoun ; Robertson, William, Daniel, and Jane married Col. Gabriel Barton. There were born to Thomas Calhoun and his wife, Mary (Robertson) Calhoun, the following children: Ewing F., Nancy E., who married Blythe McMurray, and, after his death, John Foster, and died in Mississippi, in 1844 ; Alexander J., Persis B., Jane died in youth ; Thomas P., Samuel L. and Mary R. died in infancy. Alexander J. Calhoun, their second son, was raised and educated in his native county. In 1837 he moved to Columbus, Lowndes county, Miss., where he engaged in merchandising. In 1845 he moved to Clay county, Mo., where he farmed and taught school until 1853, when he was elected circuit clerk and held the position until 1865. He then returned to the farm and remained until 1874, when he was elected to

305

his former clerkship in Clay county, which position he now holds. Col. Calhoun received his title in 1840, by commission from the Governor of Mississippi as colonel of the State militia. He is a member of the Masonic fraternity, in which order he has been master, high priest and district deputy grand master. The Colonel is also a member of the Patrons of Husbandry and of the Good Templars. He is a member of the Cumberland Presbyterian Church. In politics he was a Henry Clay Whig, and since the death of that party has been acting with the Democracy. Col. Calhoun's first wife was a Miss Susan E. Huddleston, who was born in Washington, Ala., in 1819, and died in Clay county, Mo., in 1874. Her father, John Huddleston, was born in Georgia about 1793, of Scotch-Irish parents, and died at Pass Christian, Miss., in 1863. His second wife was Miss Bettie Alder, of Clay county, Mo , a native of Virginia, born in 1841. Her father, David P. Alder, was born in Virginia, September 11, 1803, but moved to Clay county, Mo., in 1850, and died there June 3, 1857. He had been county surveyor of Rockingham county, Va., and was deputy surveyor of Clay county after moving west. He was of English descent. He married Lydia A. Wall, of Kentucky, who was born in 1818, and died in Clay county in 1864. Their children were: Gardner, Bettie, married A. J. Calhoun; Maria, married James Grooms; Lurena, married Moses McCoy and after his death, W. P. Lucas; Madison, Lydia, married David Thorp; Worthington, now dead, and John died in 1874. Col. Calhoun had no children by his first wife. By his second wife he has one child, a son named Thomas Alexander, born May 4, 1876. His wife is a member of the Baptist Church.

JUDGE JOHN CHRISMAN

(Formerly of Liberty, now of Kansas City).

Judge Chrisman is a native of Kentucky, born in Fayette county, October 3, 1825. His parents were Joseph and Eleanor H. (Soper) Chrisman, his father originally of Virginia, but his mother a native of Kentucky. The Sopers were one of the pioneer families of Kentucky. They came there about the time, or soon after, the migration of Daniel Boone into the land of the Dark and Bloody Ground, and subsequently became quite prominent in the affairs of the State. Joseph Chrisman went out from Virginia to Kentucky when a young man, and was married to Miss Soper in Jessamine county. In 1851 he removed to Missouri with his family and located in Clay county, where he followed farming until his death, in 1875. He lived to the advanced age of 75 years. Mr. Chrisman, Sr., was quite successful as a farmer, and accumulated a comfortable property. Judge John Chrisman, the subject of this sketch, was reared in Fayette county, Kentucky, and his father being a man who appreciated mental culture, and being in good circumstances, gave him excellent educational advantages. After taking a course in the common and intermediate schools, he attended Transylvania University. Subsequently he taught school in Kentucky for a few years and then came to Missouri, accompanying his parents to this State in 1851. For some years after locating in Clay county he followed farming, but in 1864 removed to Liberty from his farm and began the study of law. In due time Judge Chrisman was admitted to the bar, and subsequently practiced his profession at Liberty for fifteen or twenty years. His business was mainly confined to office practice, and as a lawyer he was quite successful. Judge Chrisman made considerable money in his profession, and in 1884 removed to Kansas City in order to use his means to better advantage and to have a large and more lucrative field for the practice. In 1865 he was appointed a judge of the county court, and held the office one term. Subsequently he held other positions of public trust. In March, 1859, he was married to Miss Maria F. Petty, a daughter of William Petty, formerly of Virginia. She survived her marriage some sixteen years, dying July 15, 1875. Mrs. Chrisman left two children: William, now of Liberty, and Katie, who is just completing her education at Lexington, Missouri. Besides doing a general practice at Kansas City, Judge Chrisman is engaged in the real estate business. He is a man of good business qualifications and high standing. Being full of energy, he is rapidly establishing himself as one of the active, useful citizens of Kansas City.

JAMES G. CLARK, LL.D.

(Professor of Mathematics and French, William Jewell College, Liberty).

Dr. Clark is a native of Virginia. He was born at Millwood, in Clarke county, of that State, June 23, 1837. His father was James H. Clark. His mother's maiden name was Jane A. Gregory. She was originally from North Carolina. The father was a merchant by occupation, and a successful business man. However, he was broken up in fortune by the disasters incident to the Civil War. He died in Virginia in 1876. His wife, a lady of many estimable qualities of mind and heart, preceded him to the grave in 1859. Dr. Clark was reared in his native county, and spent his early youth principally at the schools of Millwood. At the age of 17 he matriculated at the State University of Virginia. Dr. Clark continued at the university until he had graduated in most of the departments of schools; thereupon he was elected assistant professor of mathematics in that institution, discharging the duties of the position with ability and satisfaction to all concerned for a period of one year preceding 1858. At the expiration of that term he was appointed instructor in the Alexandria Boarding School. Two years later he was elected to the chair of mathematics in Columbia College, Washington, D. C. Dr. Clark remained at the head of the mathematical department until the outbreak of the Civil War. He then resigned his position and enlisted in the Confederate army, becoming a member of the subsequently noted Rock Bridge Artillery, attached to Stonewall Jackson's brigade. During the winter of 1862–63 he was transferred to an engineer corps, but the following summer was made captain of artillery on ordnance duty in Cheatham's division of the Army of Tennessee. During the remainder of the war, or until the surrender of his command at Greensborough, N. C., in 1865, he continued in this service which began at the great battle of Lookout Mountain. After the war Dr. Clark was rechosen professor of mathematics at Columbia College. He subsequently continued to occupy that position for about six years, after which he again resigned, this time to engage in teaching a private school. On quitting Columbia College he taught at Washington City for a time and then at Richmond, Va. Early in 1873 he was elected professor of mathematics at William Jewell College, in Liberty, Mo., and, deciding to accept the position, he came at once to this place to assume the duties of the chair of mathematics to which he had been chosen. Ever since that time Dr. Clark has been identified with this institution, and throughout his entire connection with it he has been at the head of the mathematical department. In 1873 the duties of professor of the French language were also assigned to him, which he has ever since discharged. In view of what has already been said it is hardly necessary to remark that he is a scholar of superior and varied attainments. Having made teaching a profession, he has followed it with that industry and zeal which could hardly have resulted otherwise than they have in making him a teacher of ability, success and enviable standing. For many years he has made a special study of mathematics, and he has attained to a position of more than ordinary prominence among educators in that department of learning. Indeed, he has written a very able and valuable work on the "Infinitesimal Calculus." In 1880 Dr. Clark was honored with the degree of Doctor of Laws, by the Baylor University of Texas. In 1883, 10 years from the time he first became a member of the faculty of William Jewell College, he was elected chairman of the faculty, and now holds that position. Dr. Clark has long been a member of the Baptist Church, and has been a deacon in that denomination since 1875. In 1865 he was married to Miss Jennie Hume, a daughter of Rev. Thomas Hume, of Virginia. She survived her marriage, however, only a short time. To his present wife he was married June 30, 1868. She was Miss Kate M. Morfit, a daughter of Henry M. Morfit (deceased), late of Baltimore, Md. He was a leading attorney of that city, and a lawyer of wide and enviable reputation. Mrs. Clark was principally educated at Washington City. She is a lady of culture and refinement. Mrs. C. is a member of the Episcopal Church.

WILLIAM CLARK.

(Farmer and Stock Dealer, Post-office, Liberty).

Mr. Clark is a native of Kentucky, born in Nicholas county, July 11, 1847. His father was John L. Clark and his mother's maiden name, Mary Norton, both of that county. The family removed to Missouri in 1858, and located in Clay county, where the father bought a farm and engaged in farming, which he followed until his death, April 22, 1880. He possessed many sterling qualities. As a neighbor he was kind and considerate, and liberal and hospitable ; as a husband

and father he was affectionate and devoted; and as a citizen, he was just and honorable, and obedient to the laws. Few persons were so familiarly and favorably known as he. In personal bearing he was dignified, easy and affable; and in every sense he was a man whose presence will long be kindly remembered. He was a successful farmer and rarely failed in any of his business ventures. All who shared his intimacy could receive the benefit of his rare insight into the affairs of life. William Clark, the subject of this sketch, grew to manhood on the farm in this county, and afterwards continued farming, to which he had been brought up. October 8, 1868, he was married to Miss Mary Field, a daughter of Joseph T. Field, deceased. She was born and reared in this county, and educated at the Liberty Female College and the Kansas City High School. Mr. and Mrs. Clark have two children, Lutie and John F. Mr. C. has a good farm of 347 acres, which is well improved, and besides this there are 320 acres of fine Missouri river bottom land, partly improved. Mr. Clark is and has been for some years engaged in feeding and raising stock. He handles about 100 head of cattle annually. He has been quite successful as a stock man.

JUDSON COCKRELL

(Dealer in Groceries, Liberty).

John W. Cockrell, the father of the subject of this sketch and Hon. Francis M. Cockrell, United States Senator from Missouri, were the sons of the two brothers in the family of Cockrells of Virginia. Senator Cockrell's father, however, left the Old Dominion at an earlier day than that of the removal of John W. Cockrell's family to Missouri. John W. Cockrell was born in Virginia January 20, 1797, and was married there to Miss Elizabeth Mitchell, daughter of George G. Mitchell, who was born in Scotland. He received a classical education, lived and died in Staunton, Augusta county, Virginia, and was distinguished for scholarship, as hardly having his equal in education. Though dead he yet lives. They came to Clay county in 1846. He was a brickmaker, and built many of the first brick houses in this part of the country. He died here in about 1859. Judson Cockrell was in infancy when the family came to Missouri. He was born in Virginia, September 14, 1845. Reared in Clay county, he was educated at William Jewell College, and following the example of his father, he became a brick mason, and also learned brickmaking. He followed these continuously up to the time of engaging in the grocery business during the present year. He was fairly successful at his trades and accumulated some property. Mr. Cockrell has built a large number of houses at Liberty and in this vicinity, and is regarded as a thorough mechanic and upright, reliable builder. He engaged in his present business last spring, and is receiving a good trade, doing quite as well as he expected. He has a good stock of goods in the grocery line, and being an energetic, economical business man, he can hardly fail of success. In September, 1863, he was married to Miss Martha J.

HISTORY OF CLAY COUNTY

Mereness, a daughter of the late A. M. Mereness. Mr. and Mrs. C. had two children, John J., now a young man twenty years of age, and a clerk in his father's store in Liberty, Missouri; and one deceased. Mrs. Cockrell died in 1868, and Mr. C. has not since remarried. His mother keeps house for him, his father being also deceased, as stated above.

OVID H. CORBIN

(Of O. H. Corbin & Co., Owners and Proprietors of the Liberty Flouring and Woolen Mills).

Mr. Corbin is a native of Virginia, born in Stafford county, October 9, 1820. His father was Benjamin S. Corbin, and his mother's maiden name was Sarah Preston. The father was a carpenter by trade and followed that for a number of years. He then engaged in the milling business for some years before his retirement from active work. He was a soldier in the War of 1812. In 1849 he removed to Missouri with his family and located at Liberty, where he died in 1860. His wife died here in 1863. Ovid H., the subject of this sketch, was reared in Stafford county and came to this State in company with his parents in 1849. Under his father he learned the flouring mill business and also the millwright's trade. In fact, he was almost a natural mechanic. About the time he was of age he began working at the wagonmaker's trade, continuing that in connection with carpentering and millwrighting. In a few years, however, he turned his attention to farming, which he followed until he came to Missouri with his parents. Here he engaged in wagon and carriage making, and bought an established business in that line, which he continued until 1856, having in the meantime purchased the interest of his partner, with whom he had previously been in business. In 1856 he, with two others, bought the Liberty flouring mills, and four years later they added a plant of woolen machinery. Ever since that time they have been engaged in the manufacture of woolen goods and also running their flouring mill. They make all kinds of cashmeres, jeans, blankets, yarns, etc., etc. In their flouring mill they have three run of buhrs and are also prepared to grind corn, buckwheat, and other grains for breadstuffs. November 10, 1841, Mr. Corbin was married in Spottsylvania county, Virginia, where he had removed three years before, to Miss Sarah A., a daughter of Jesse Petty, of that county. Mr. and Mrs. Corbin have ten children, Mary F., William H., James M. (the two eldest sons being their father's partners in business), Beverly B., Benjamin F., George W. (he being the only one married), Laura E., Herbert T., Adelaide J. and Hattie B. The children have all received each a good education, either at William Jewell College or the Female Seminary. Mr. Corbin, now in his sixty-fifth year, has retired from active work at the mill and turned the management of it largely over to his sons, William H. and James M. He himself, however, is still quite active and well preserved. Whilst in appearance he is somewhat venerable looking, on account of his long, white

310

CAPT. ARCHIBALD C. COURTNEY

(Proprietor of the Arthur House, Liberty).

The Courtney family, so far as this country is concerned, was originally from Pennsylvania. Capt. Courtney's father, John Courtney, served in the American army during the Revolution. He was a farmer by occupation, and became a man of well-to-do circumstances. Mr. Courtney, the elder, was twice married, and after the death of his first wife was married to Miss Lucinda Martin; they were both of Pennsylvania, and each wife bore five children. Capt. Archibald C. Courtney was the third child by the last marriage, and was born in Garrard county, Kentucky, to which his father had previously removed, May 1, 1815. At the time of his father's death in 1830, he was about fifteen years of age, but he afterwards remained with the family until his marriage, working industriously, though at limited wages. Subsequently he engaged in stock trading and made several trips to Alabama and Georgia in that business, being quite successful. In 1840 Capt. Courtney came to Missouri on horseback and located on a farm of 200 acres near Kearney, where he subsequently followed farming for twenty years, and was very successful. He owned at one time about 600 acres of fine land. His reverses, however, commenced upon the outbreak of the war. Affairs were in an unsettled and dangerous condition but, despite his efforts, he was unable to retain a neutral position. Consequently, in 1863, as a matter of policy, he identified himself with the Home Guards, and became captain of a company, which duty he performed for a while. His company was never out of the county. As a matter of fact his company did much valuable service to the law-abiding classes of both sides by assisting to keep out those who were more bent on plunder and committing other depredations, than in serving the cause which they pretended to adhere to. During the war he removed his family to Liberty and all his movable property that had not been stolen, and with the horses he had left established a livery stable. His two sons having without his knowledge taken sides in the war, went as their sympathies directed, with the South, and made gallant soldiers under Price until the close of the struggle. Capt. Courtney continued in the livery business for a time after the war and then bought out a general store, which he carried on for about two years. This he also subsequently sold, but bought into another business house and ran that for a short time. He ran the Arthur House for about ten years and in 1879 rented it to another party. Since then he has lived in retirement, except for about a year, during which he was engaged in the hardware business. Capt. Courtney has served as justice of the peace and in some other local offices. His life up to the beginning of

HISTORY OF CLAY COUNTY

the war was very successful and he became comfortably situated, and he still has a modest competency, and can pass through the evening of life without the fear of destitution. Capt. Courtney is highly respected in this county and bears a name untarnished by a reproach. January 20, 1842, he was married to Miss Elizabeth A. Estes, a daughter of Henry Estes, one of the pioneer settlers of Missouri, referred to elsewhere in this work. Mrs. Courtney was born in Clay county, Missouri, and was only in her fifteenth year when she was married. She has been a most excellent helpmate to him and in the early days of his career herself helped in the laborious duties of farm life. Her energetic habits of that time have not left her in later years. Mr. and Mrs. Courtney have had twelve children, four dying when young. Those living are William J., an attorney at Kearney; Henry E., Jane, wife of John Merritt; Robert S., of Kansas City; Alexander M., a stock raiser of Colorado; Levinia, wife of Henry Smith, a member of the State Legislature, from Kansas City; James A. and Archibald C., Jr. Mr. and Mrs. C. are members of the Presbyterian Church, and Mr. C. has been a deacon in the church for half a century.

ELI R. CRAFTON

(Manufacturer of Spring Wagons, Carriages, etc., Liberty).

Mr. Crafton is a native of Illinois, born in Adams county, August 29, 1843. His father was John Crafton, from Kentucky, and his mother's maiden name Margaret Becket, who was born and reared in Indiana. They were married in the latter State and removed to Adams county, Illinois, about 1838. They resided there nearly thirty years and then settled in Linn county, Missouri. He was reared in Adams county, Illinois, and early in the second year of the rebellion enlisted in the One Hundred and Nineteenth Illinois Infantry, in which he served until the close of the war. He was in Banks' Red River Expedition under the command of A. J. Smith, and participated in the engagements at Alexandria, La., Sabine Cross Roads, Yellow Bayou, La., Tupelo and Nashville, Tenn., the siege and capture of Mobile and the fight at Montgomery, Ala., besides many others of less importance. He is naturally very proud of the services he rendered, and regards them as the greatest honor of his life. After the war Mr. Crafton returned to Adams county, Ill., and began an apprenticeship at the carriage and wagon-maker's trade. After completing that he continued to work at his trade, working later along at Quincy, Ill., St. Louis, Mo., St. Paul, Minn., and coming to Liberty in the summer of 1869. Here he continued at his trade as a journey workman until March, 1880, when he set up for himself, and has been in the carriage and spring wagon making business ever since. He has been satisfactorily successful and has established a good business, having employed now some four or five hands in his shop. August 3, 1870, he was married at Utica, Mo., to Miss Laura S. Sprinkle, a daughter of S. H. Sprinkle, formerly of Huntington, Ind.

HISTORY OF CLAY COUNTY

They have five children: Olive, Etta, Bessie, Ralph, and Lawrence. Both parents are members of the Episcopal Church.

GEORGE E. DAMON

(Manager of the National Flouring Mill, Liberty).

Mr. Damon is a native of Ohio, born in Lake county, August 2, 1847. His father was George Damon, a native of Massachusetts. His mother, whose maiden name was Mary Tyler, was a native of the same State. They were married in Massachusetts, and removed to Ohio in 1834, settling in Lake county, where they were of the pioneer settlers of the county. They resided in that county for nearly twenty years and then removed to Dane county, Wis. Before the removal of the family to Wisconsin the father was a wagon and carriage manufacturer. Afterwards he followed farming until his death, which occurred in April, 1861. George F. was born in Lake county, O., August 2, 1847. He completed his majority in Wisconsin, where he received a common-school education. At the age of twenty, however, he began learning the miller's trade, at which he worked in Wisconsin until the fall of 1867, when he came to Missouri. Here he first worked at Westport and then at Kansas City. In 1878, being a thorough pratical miller by this time, he bought an interest in the mill at Moscow and ran that mill for three years. Mr. Damon came to Liberty in 1881, where he bought an interest in the National Flouring Mill, which is owned by a joint stock company, known as the Clay County Milling Company, of which he is manager. These mills have the roller process of making flour and turn out as good flour as is to be seen in the country. They have a capacity of 100 barrels every twenty-four hours and do both a custom and merchant milling business. The building is a three story brick. September 3, 1873, Mr. Damon was married to Miss Lizzie E. Stanton, a daughter of Samuel Stanton, of Kansas City. They have two children, William E. and Edna.

WILLIAM H. H. DAVIS

(Retired Farmer and Stock-raiser, Post-office, Liberty).

Mr. Davis, an old and respected citizen of this county, was one of the early settlers of the county. He came to Clay county in 1836. Mr. Davis was directly from Saline county to this county, but was from Arkansas to Missouri. His parents, Samuel B. and Elizabeth Davis, went to Arkansas from Kentucky when he was in childhood, away back in 1821, and settled in Hempstead county. William H. H. Davis, who was born in Logan county, Kentucky, June 3, 1816, was reared in Arkansas, and came to Missouri when a young man. He became a farmer and stock-raiser in Clay county, and in the fall of 1839 was married to Miss America W. Estes, a sister to W. W. Estes. He afterwards continued farming and stock-raising and in 1850 went to California, but soon afterward returned. In 1859, however, he removed to Texas and made his home in that State until after the

313

HISTORY OF CLAY COUNTY

close of the Civil War, returning in June, 1866. After that time Mr. Davis was actively engaged with his farming and stock-raising interests until his retirement from active labor some years ago. His life as an agriculturist has been one of success. He accumulated an ample property for old age, and now has a fine stock farm of 600 acres, which is well stocked and well improved. Since his retirement, his son, William P., has had control of the farm, and is carrying it on with marked energy and success. In November, 1880, Mr. Davis had the misfortune to lose his good wife, the true and brave and generous-hearted, devoted woman who had been the partner of his joys and sorrows for over forty years, and with whose life his own being had become so thoroughly united that it seemed to him worse than death itself to lose her. But in that sad hour when the parting came there was one consolation, one hope that sustained him and made him brave to bear the heavy bereavement — the consolation and hope that the separation could not be long, and that in a few years their lives would again be united in a happier union, even, than they had known on this side the grave. Three children were the fruits of their long and happy married life: Thomas H., James J. (deceased), and William P. William P. Davis was born on the farm where he now resides, August 12, 1849, and learned the practical details of farming and stock raising as he grew up. In 1876 he was married to Miss Annie Brasfield, a daughter of William E. Brasfield, whose sketch precedes this. They have two children, J. W. Lesler and Nellie. Mr. Davis, Jr., like his father-in-law, Mr. Brasfield, makes a specialty of raising fine saddle and harness stallions and fine jacks. He has a representative of one of the best breeds of horses in this country. The stock originated in Virginia, and was named for a family in the Old Commonwealth, noted for their fine appearance, chivalric qualities, and all that sort of things, and the men for being remarkably "fast" — the Claibornes. They were one of the best families of Virginia, and knew that fact quite as well, if not better, than any one else. Mr. Davis' horse is named "Pat Claiborne," and any one can see at a glance that he is a regular, genuine, high-stepping, high-headed "pinked" Claiborne. He is one of the finest horses in the country, a horse of which his owner may well be proud. W. P. Davis makes a specialty of short-horn cattle, having his farm well stocked with some of the best blood, as well as good individuals. He has young stock for sale. The farm is situated three miles northeast of Liberty, on the Hannibal and St. Joe Railroad.

JOHN A. DENNY

(Retired Merchant, Liberty).

Mr. Denny, now retired from active business, is one of the oldest business men of Clay county, and one of its most highly respected citizens. He began merchandising at Liberty in 1852, having previously clerked at this place for several years, and continued in merchandising with little or no interruption until his retirement, one year

HISTORY OF CLAY COUNTY

ago. He was very successful in business, considering the population and wealth of the place and surrounding country, and accumulated a comfortable property. He is now, and for years past has been, a property holder of Liberty. Prior to the war he did a very large business for that time, carrying a stock of about $15,000. After the war his business was not so large as before, but was much safer, being done nearly altogether on a cash basis. Mr. Denny is still interested in farming, and has a handsome farm adjoining Liberty, on which he has resided for many years. Mr. Denny is a native of North Carolina, born in Guilford county September 12, 1814. His father was George Denny, who married January 14, 1808, Miss Jane Kenedy, both of early and well-to-do North Carolina families. They came to Missouri in 1835, and located on a farm in Clinton county, where they resided until their deaths. The father became a substantial farmer of that county, and remarkable for his longevity and the preservation of all his powers, physical and mental, until the very last. He left five sons and three daughters still living. He died in his ninety-sixth year, and only a few weeks before his death had been out hunting with a squirrel rifle, which he was able to shoot without the aid of glasses with wonderful accuracy. His death occurred March 24, 1879. His good wife preceded him to the grave some ten years. Mr. Denny, the subject of this sketch, was reared in North Carolina, where he received an advanced general English education, and also took courses of three years in Latin and Greek. He came to Missouri in 1836 and located in Clay county. Here he taught school for a few years, and then began as a merchant's clerk, as stated above. November 20, 1844, he was married to Miss Harriet A., a daughter of James Marsh, formerly of Kentucky, but an early settler in this county. Mr. and Mrs. Denny have four children living: Martha J., wife of H. F. Simrall, whose sketch is given elsewhere; Lunette, Ernest R., now merchandising in Liberty, and Minnie M., the latter now completing her course at Female College. One other is deceased, Portius E., who died at the age of 21, just before graduating at Westminster College. Mr. Denny and wife are members of the Presbyterian Church. He has taken a prominent part in temperance work, and thinks that the cause must advance until prohibition crowns the work. Mr. Denny has served as city treasurer, and in other local positions of public trust, but has never sought nor desired office.

WILLIAM W. DOUGHERTY, M. D.

(Physician and Surgeon, Liberty).

Among the prominent representative citizens of Clay county Dr. Dougherty occupies a well recognized and justly enviable position. He was a comparatively early settler here, and has been a witness to and active, useful participant in the progress the county has made from the condition of a sparsely populated frontier community to that of one of the leading counties in the State. His efforts have been united with those of the other old and useful citizens of the county in building up the county and making it what it is to-day. In view, therefore, of his long and prominent identification with Clay county, it would be an inexcusable omission not to present at least an outline of his life on these pages. Dr. Dougherty was born in Lawrence county, Ind., September 2, 1820, but he is a representative of an early and well known Kentucky family. The Doughertys settled in Kentucky from Virginia away back when the Blue Grass State was known as the "Dark and Bloody Ground," a name it received on account of the stubborn resistance the Indians made against the encroachments of the white settlers, and the many terrible massacres and house burnings that were visited upon the early white pioneers. Dr. Dougherty was a son of William and Ellen Dougherty, his parents being both originally of the same name, and cousins. The Doctor's mother died, however, when he was in infancy, and he was taken by his relations in Trimble county, that State, to rear. In 1831, when he was about 11 years of age, his relations, with whom he was living, removed to Missouri, bringing him with them and settled in Pike county. There he attended district and select schools for several years, and acquired the rudiments of a good, ordinary, practical education. But when about 16 years of age he accompanied his uncle, Maj. Dougherty, west to the mountains, his uncle being quite extensively engaged in the Indian trade. Young Dougherty spent four years among the Indians of the far, far West, at a time when white faces were hardly less rare there than the moccasined, painted savage is to-day in Missouri. Returning to Pike county in 1840, in 1844 he began to study medicine under Drs. Lane and Rodman, of Trimble county, Ky., going thence directly from Pike county. In due time young Dougherty entered the Medical Department of the University of Louisville, where he took a regular course and commenced the practice in the spring of 1845. After his first course he located at Madison, Ind., for the practice of his profession, but did not graduate for some years afterward, and was shortly married to Miss Hannah C. Dougherty, daughter of Col. Robert S. Dougherty, a second cousin to his father. Two years later Dr. Dougherty removed to Orange county, Ind., where he practiced for about three years. While there he lost his first wife and only child, and a short time before leaving Orange county he was married to Miss Mary A., a daughter of John Frazier, an eminent civil engineer of that day, and who surveyed the routes of most of the early Western railroads. In 1850 Dr. Dougherty removed to Missouri, and, after stopping a short time at St. Joseph, located at Liberty. Here he entered actively upon the practice of his profession, and soon built up a large practice. Dr. Dougherty has been a resident of this county ever since that time, for a period now of nearly 35 years, except for about two years which he spent in Platte county, preceding 1858. While in Platte county he was postmaster at Iatan, under the administration of James Buchanan, and also served as justice of the peace, besides attending to his general practice. Before going to Platte he had served as city councilman and mayor of Liberty, and afterwards he has served several times as city councilman. In 1868 he was nominated by the Democrats to fill a vacancy from this county in the Legislature, but on account of sickness was prevented from accepting the honor. In 1878, however, he was again nominated for the Legislature, and was elected by a large majority, defeating several of the most popular men of the county who were candidates. In the practical work of legislation he took an active and prominent part at Jefferson City. He introduced the bill to establish the State Board of Health, and also introduced and pushed forward to successful enactment the bill authorizing benevolent insurance companies in this State, principally in the interest of the Masonic order, of which he is a leading member. Dr. Dougherty was member of the committee on accounts in the House, and also of the committee on charities and benevolence, and on scientific and benevolent institutions. He made an enviable record in the Legislature, one that reflected credit on his high character and usefulness as a legislator. By his second wife Dr. D. has been blessed with a family of five children: Ella, the wife of John D. Share, of Wellington, Kas., a prominent dry goods merchant; Mattie, wife of William H. Martin, a successful lawyer of Bedford, Ind.; John, a partner with Mr. Share, at Wellington, Kas.; William W., Jr., in mercantile business at St. Louis; Charles L., who is now studying medicine under his father; and Minnie, who died in 1872, at the age of six years. The Doctor and wife are members of the M. E. Church South. Dr. Dougherty is a prominent member of the Kansas City District Medical Society, of which he was among the originators, and helped to organize, and afterwards was its president.

LEWIS B. DOUGHERTY

(Cashier of the Commercial Savings Bank, Liberty).

On the second expedition of Lewis and Clark to the Rocky Mountains in about 1799, Maj. John Dougherty, the father of the subject of this sketch, first came West from Kentucky. He was then only a youth some 17 years of age, but made one of the most resolute pioneers in the expedition. Traveling extensively over the West, he was finally located at Ft. Leavenworth, Kas., as Indian agent, where, having married in the meantime, at St. Louis, Mo., his son, Lewis B., was born December 7, 1828, and is believed to have been the first white child born in Kansas. In 1830 Maj. Dougherty removed to St. Louis, of which city Mrs. Dougherty was a native. Her maiden name was Mary Hertzog. Maj. Dougherty removed to Council Bluffs from St. Louis in about 1833, where he was stationed for some time as Indian agent. He was afterwards stationed at Ft. Leavenworth, and after some years resided again in St. Louis. Returning to Leavenworth later along he was there until 1837, in charge of the Indian agency. About this time he removed to Liberty and made his permanent home here. He became a leading and influential citizen of this county, and represented it in the Legislature, a colleague with Gen. Doniphan and William Wood. He opened a large farm, some six or seven miles from Liberty, on which he resided until his death. Maj. Dougherty died in January, 1761, well known throughout Clay county, and, indeed, over a large region of country surrounding he was as highly esteemed by all as he was well known. No man in the county stood higher in the opinions of the public and his neighbors. He was a man of high character, courage and generosity, and withal a man of great kindness of heart. Energetic, frugal in his manner of living, but never parsimonious, and a man of good business ability, he accumulated a comfortable property, which he left intact to his children at his death. Moreover, he had been generous in providing them with the best means for mental culture and otherwise fitting them for the activities of life within his power. A typical, good citizen, one whose industry and enterprise were not less valuable to the community than to himself and an exemplary man in his own family, his memory is revered by his children and all who knew him as that of one whose example is worthy of all imitation. Lewis B. Dougherty, the subject of this sketch, was reared on his father's farm near Liberty. He was educated at the State University in Columbia, from which he graduated in 1847. The same year of his graduation Mr. Dougherty went to Ft. Kearney, in Nebraska Territory, where he engaged in the suttling business, which he followed with success at that place four years. From there he went to Ft. Laramie, in Wyoming, about 1852, continuing in the same business at the latter place some four or five years. He was absent from Clay county in all about 10 years, and after his return in 1857 he settled on a farm, where he continued to reside, occupied principally with agricultural pursuits, some 12 or 15 years. When the Commercial Savings Bank of Liberty was organized, in he became a stockholder. About six years afterwards, in 1871, he was elected cashier of the bank, a position he has continued ever since to hold. The bank has a capital stock of $50,000. This is well known as one of the most substantial and reliable banks on the western border of the State, and for the enviable reputation it has made, a large share of credit is due to the good management of Mr. Dougherty. He is also still interested in farming, and has a valuable farm in the county, as well as a good farm in Vernon county, and one in Douglas county. In 1874 Mr. Dougherty was elected treasurer of the county and discharged the duties of that responsible office with efficiency and fidelity and to the general satisfaction of the public. December 7, 1858, he was married to Miss Anna Carey, a daughter of Daniel Carey, one of the pioneer settlers and substantial citizens of Platte county, but now deceased. Mrs. Dougherty was educated at Liberty and at the Camden Female College. Mr. and Mrs. D. have two children : Flora, now the wife of C. C. Courtney, of Kansas City, and John L. One besides is deceased, Mary, who died in 1880, at the age of eight years. Mr. and Mrs. D. are members of the Presbyterian Church, and Mr. Dougherty is a prominent member of the Masonic order, belonging to the Lodge, Chapter and Commandery. Mr. D. had two brothers and a sister who lived to reach mature years, but one of his brothers was killed at the battle of Franklin, Tenn., a member of the Third Missouri Confederate infantry, in the company of

HISTORY OF CLAY COUNTY

the subject of this sketch. His other brother, O'F. Dougherty, is a resident of this place, and his sister is the wife of Gen. C. F. Ruff, of Philadelphia.

O'FALLON DOUGHERTY

(Farmer, Stock-raiser and Stock-dealer, Liberty).

Mr. Dougherty was a son of Maj. John Dougherty and is a brother to L. B. Dougherty, whose sketch precedes this. In the former sketch an outline of the family history has been given. Mr. Dougherty was born in St. Louis June 5, 1832, but as the family subsequently removed to this county, he was principally reared here. His education was acquired at William Jewell College, where he took a thorough course of four years and subsequently graduated. After the close of his college course he returned to the farm and engaged in farming with his father with whom he continued until the latter's death. Mr. Dougherty inherited the old family homestead and stills owns it. He has a fine place of 1,162 acres, all improved except about 200 acres of timber. He has been extensively engaged in farming and raising stock for many years, to which his place is well adapted. His improvements on the farm are of an excellent class, a large comfortable, tastily built residence, good barns and other buildings, and good fences. November 30, 1865, Mr. Dougherty was married to Miss Sarah, a daughter of James and Eliza Nutter, early settlers of this county. Mrs. Dougherty was educated at the Liberty Female Seminary. They have two children : Katie and Mary Hertzog. In the spring of 1881 Mr. Dougherty removed to Liberty in order to educate his daughters. He is now just completing a handsome, spacious two-story brick residence in town, where he will make his permanent home. Mr. and Mrs. D. are members of the Baptist Church and he is a member of the Chapter and Commandery in the Masonic order. Mr. Dougherty's father, Maj. Dougherty, was at one time engaged in this county in the unusual pursuit of raising buffalo. He began with one cow and in a few years his stock of buffalo had increased until during one summer he had 23 head of calves. He was a great admirer of Henry Clay and sheared some wool from one of his best buffalo which his wife carded, spun and knit into a pair of mittens and a pair of socks. The Major sent them to the great Whig chief and statesman of that day, Henry Clay, from whom he received a most complimentary acknowledgment. After the death of Mr. Clay they were contributed by his heirs to the cabinet of *reliques* of public men at Washington, and they are now on exhibition in a glass case, with a card giving their history, in the Patent Office, in the Interior Department building.

JAMES R. EATON, A. B., A. M., Ph. D.

(Professor of Natural Sciences, William Jewell College, Liberty, Missouri).

Dr. Eaton is a native of New York He was born at Hamilton, Madison county, that State, December 11, 1834. He was a son of Rev.

Dr. George W. Eaton, one of the most accomplished scholars and eminent educators of New York. His whole life was devoted to the cause of education. The following concerning him and his services is reproduced from the report of the Commissioner of Education of the United States for the year 1872: —

Dr. James R. Eaton received his general education at the Madison University of New York. He graduated in 1856 and received the degree of Bachelor of Arts. Immediately following his graduation from the Madison University he entered the Hamilton Theological Seminary of the Baptist Church, in which he continued as a student for a period of two years, graduating in 1858 with the degree of Master of Arts.

Well recommended for ripe scholarship and for the natural characteristics necessary to a successful and useful career as an educator, Prof. Eaton, after his graduation at Madison, was tendered, in 1859, the chair of Adjunct-Professor of Mathematics and Natural Sciences in the Union University of Murfreesboro, Tenn., which he accepted. He filled that position and discharged the duties which it imposed with ability and eminent satisfaction to all concerned for two years. He was then offered and he accepted the professorship of Ancient Languages in Bethel College of Russellville, Ky. The events of the war, however, soon unsettled affairs in Kentucky so much that he resigned his position at Bethel College and left the State.

Prof. Eaton now went to New York, and soon afterwards received the appointment of superintendent of the advertising department and of the foreign mail delivery in the post-office of the city of New York. He continued at the head of that department in the New York city post-office until the close of the war. Prof. Eaton found official life in the civil service of the government by no means as congenial as the profession of teaching, and in 1866 he accepted the chair of Natural Sciences in the University of Louisville, Ky. He continued there for three years and until he came to Liberty, Mo., in 1869, to enter upon the duties of Professor of Natural Sciences and Natural Theology in William Jewell College, a position to which he had been called by the board of regents of this institution. He has occupied this position in William Jewell College from that time to the present, continuously, a period of 16 years. In the meantime, in 1876, his *Alma Mater*, Madison University of New York, honored him and herself by conferring upon him the degree of Doctor of Philosophy. The promise early given of a successful and useful career for Dr. Eaton as an educator has already been fulfilled to an eminent degree. With him teaching is a labor of love, the source of his greatest pleasure outside of his family and his church; and he has devoted his life, all his energies, to it with that zeal and disinterestedness, and that singleness of purpose — the mental and moral elevation and improvement of those committed to his charge — which stamp him a man of great nobility of character, and one fitted for the delicate and responsible duties of an educator, not less by the native qualities of his head and heart than by his superior attainments as a scholar. The Doctor is justly regarded as one of the leading educators of the State. For ten years

HISTORY OF CLAY COUNTY

he was president of the Education Board of William Jewell College, and until he resigned the position. His resignation was accepted with great reluctance.

Dr. Eaton is also active and prominent in the church and his services have been of great value to his denomination at Liberty and to the cause of religion. Though a scientist of profound learning and great ability and a devoted believer in the great principles established by scientific research, unlike many of greater pretentions but of unquestionably less depth of thought and thoroughness of investigation, he has never found anything to shake his faith in the Word of God, the doctrine of faith in Christ as contained in the Holy Scriptures. On the contrary, he has ever found science an unerring witness for religion, the faithful handmaid of religious truth.

Dr. Eaton devotes much of his leisure from his regular duties to general reading, and in the course of his studies of a general character he has collected an unusually large and valuable library, probably the best general library in this part of the State, outside of a large city. He has nearly twelve hundred volumes, all works of solid merit, and most of them standard authors on the subjects which they respectively treat.

On the 6th of June, 1872, Dr. Eaton was married at Liberty, Mo., to Miss Mattie E. Lewright. She is a lady of superior education and intelligence. She is a native of Missouri, born in Franklin county, and was educated by a private tutor, a gentleman who was a graduate of the ancient and famous University of Edinburgh, Scotland. She is a daughter of Wm. P. Lewright, formerly of Virginia.

The Doctor and Mrs. Eaton have one child living, Hubert L., a promising son aged about four years. Two others are deceased, both sons, Harold W. and Lewright B.

Dr. Eaton has an interesting and valuable collection of geological specimens, many of which he gathered himself in the West and elsewhere in the United States. He also has an interesting cabinet of *curios* of various kinds, collected from different parts of the world, and one of the finest collections of ancient and rare coins in the United States. His collection of coins, in fact, is said to be the best, though not the largest, one outside of Europe. It was exhibited at the Louisville Exposition in 1884 and one of the papers of that city made the following notice of it:—

"Among the new features at the Exposition will be the rare collection of coins belonging to Dr. J. R. Eaton, of William Jewell College. He has been 30 years making this collection, and it is probably the best and most complete one this side of the British Museum. All the coins mentioned in the Scriptures are here, from the gold *daric*, contributed to build Solomen's temple, to the *mite*, such as the poor widow cast into the treasury. Here also are the old Greek coins from the *didrachma* of Ægina, which must have been coined before the year 869 B. C., to the quarter *obolus*, the smallest coin ever circulated. The sacred *obolus* which was placed in the mouth of each corpse to pay the dead man's ferriage across the river Styx. The coins of Alexander the Great and his successors.

The collection embraces all the varieties of Roman coins. There is the original *As*. of bronze and weighing one pound, the largest coin in existence. It was recently exhumed at Naples and is a better specimen than the one in the British Museum. Besides these there are moderncoins of all nations now in use."

WILLIAM W. ESTES

(Farmer and Stock-raiser, Post-office, Liberty).

Whatever may be said of the productive quality of much of the farming land of Virginia, no one who knows anything about Virginians will question the fact that they know a good piece of land when they see it. In all the emigrations from different States to the West, Virginians have generally gotten the best of their fellow-emigrants from other States in the choice of good lands. Away back in the territorial days of Missouri, the more intelligent class of people in Virginia have made themselves familiar with the general character of the lands in this part of the country; especially well informed were those who expected to emigrate West. Among these was the father of the subject of the present sketch, together with a large number of other Virginians. Before coming to this State he had visited Kentucky when quite a young man, but returning to Virginia he was married and shortly afterwards, in company with quite a colony, came out to Missouri and settled in Saline county. That was as early as 1819. About two years afterwards he and a number of his fellow-emigrants came up the river, and crossing over, settled on the fertile lands of Clay county. This was one of the early settlements made in the county. Thomas Estes became a well-to-do farmer of this county and respected by all who knew him. He died here in 1854. His wife died in 1866. Their homestead was about a mile and a half northeast of Liberty. He left a large landed property at his death and a number of slaves. It should have been remarked before this, however, that after his first wife's death he was married again. By each wife he left a family of children. Of the first family only one is now living, and also one of the last marriage. William W. Estes was born in Saline county, March 7, 1821, but was reared on the family homestead in Clay county. In 1849 he, with a company composed of twelve young men of Clay county and twelve from Howard county, went to California overland, being about three months on the road. He spent two years in California engaged in mining. Returning in the fall of 1851, he came by way of Panama and New Orleans, and on reaching home settled down permanently to farming and stock-raising, which he has ever since followed. June 1, 1852, he was married to Miss Catherine Lincoln, a daughter of David Lincoln, one of the pioneer settlers of the county. She lived to brighten his home for nearly thirty years, but was at last taken away by death, September 25, 1881. She was a good and true and faithful wife and was esteemed by her neighbors and acquaintances only less than she was loved in her own family. But one child was reared to mature years. She is still living, Elizabeth D., the wife of James Bevins, who resides on the Estes' homestead and assists in the management of the farm. Mr. and Mrs. Bevins have two children, Katie C. and Plum, and have lost two, all of whom died in infancy. The farm contains 230 acres and is one of the choice farms of the

HISTORY OF CLAY COUNTY

vicinity. Messrs. Estes and Bevins are justly esteemed as among the best citizens of the community.

ROBERT C. EWING

(Farmer and Stock-raiser, Post-office, Liberty).

Mr. Ewing is a representative of a family, whose name he bears, that has given to several of the Western States, including Missouri, Ohio, Kentucky, Indiana and Illinois, some of their leading citizens. He was a son of J. B. Ewing, who came to this county from Kentucky in an early day, and who was a nephew of Rev. Finis Ewing, one of the noted preachers of his day, a man of finished education, fine presence, a magnificent orator and of profound piety. J. R. Ewing came to Clay county a young man in 1821. His parents had previously settled in Lafayette county, this State, at a very early day. He was married here to Miss Ruth Moore, a daughter of James Moore, formerly of North Carolina. After his marriage he settled on a farm adjoining the one where his son now resides. Robert C., the subject of this sketch, was born on that place, October 23, 1833. On the 5th of January, 1859, he was married to Miss Sarah Downing, a daughter of Charles Downing, formerly of Kentucky. After his marriage Mr. Ewing continued farming, which he had previously engaged in, for himself and by industry and good management he has become comfortably situated. Mr. and Mrs. Ewing have three children, Charles R., John D. and Robert C. One is deceased, Nettie. She died in the fall of 1881, being at the time the wife of Lilburn Arnold. Mrs. E. is a member of the Baptist Church.

JUDGE JOSEPH THORNBURG FIELD (DECEASED)

(Vicinity of Liberty).

He whose name heads this sketch was for many years, and until his death, regarded as one of the prominent representative citizens of Clay county. He was long a leading farmer and held many positions of public trust, as well as being prominently identified with business affairs and in every relation of life acquitted himself with great credit. He was born in Madison county, Va., December 10, 1798, and was the eldest of a family of nine children. In 1800 the family removed to Kentucky and settled in Bourbon county, where he grew to manhood, and resided until approaching middle age of life. In 1838 he went to Boone county, that State, where he made his home for several years and became a prominent citizen of that county. He was elected sheriff while there and discharged the duties of that office with marked efficiency and popularity. From Boone county, Ky., he emigrated to Missouri, and made a permanent settlement in Clay county. Here he was married in 1845 to Miss Mary A. Thompson, of Caldwell county, but formerly of Kentucky. She survived her marriage, however, only a short time, and left him one child, Sarah E., now the wife of John Chancellor. To his second wife Judge Field was mar-

323

ried in the spring of 1848. She was a Miss Margaret Wymore, daughter of Samuel Wymore, of this county, an early settler from Kentucky. Meantime he had bought land and improved a farm and by his industry and good management was steadily coming to the front as a prominent farmer and stock-raiser. Later along he was honored with different official positions in the county and among others was twice elected a member of the county court and served one term as county treasurer. As a county judge he is said to have been one of the most efficient ever honored with that position in Clay county, and in various other positions he held he acquitted himself with not less credit and popularity. He also became interested in banking and was director of the Liberty branch of the Farmers' Bank of Missouri. During the latter years of the career of the bank he served as its president, and under his management it obtained a wide and enviable reputation. By his economy and industry and admirable good judgment, he was enabled to acquire a comfortable fortune. He died at his homestead in this county March 19, 1881, at the ripe old age of 82. Judge Field was a valuable, good citizen, and as a friend, generous and faithful. As a husband and father, he was all that loved ones could have wished him to be, a good and true man in every relation of life and one whose memory is kindly cherished by those who knew him. In business affairs he was remarkably methodical and systematic and punctual and precise in all his transactions. His second wife died only a short time after her marriage, and he was subsequently married to Miss Amanda J., daughter of Leonard Brasfield, who came to this county from Kentucky in 1818. Four children were the fruits of his last marriage: Mary J., wife of William Clark; Ada, wife of Hon. James M. Bohart, of Clinton county; Joseph E. and Daniel B. The latter has charge of the old family homestead and is a young man of liberal education and of marked enterprise and personal worth.

JAMES D. FORD

(Mayor of Liberty and Deputy County Collector).

Prominent among the young men of Clay county who, by their own merits, are steadily and surely coming to the front in public and business affairs, is the subject of the present sketch. Mr. Ford, who is a young man of industry and sterling character, received more than an average general education at Liberty High School and at William Jewell College. Subsequently he followed farming for two years and then, in 1877, engaged in the grocery business at Liberty. Three years later he sold his interest in the grocery trade and became a clerk in the clothing house of J. J. Stogdale, one of the leading houses in that line in the county. Since Mr. Stogdale's election to the office of county collector, Mr. F. has had entire control of the store and also fills the office of deputy collector under Mr. Stogdale. In the spring of 1880 Mr. Ford was elected mayor of Liberty, and was the youngest mayor who ever occupied the office at this place.

HISTORY OF CLAY COUNTY

Although he has taken an active interest in politics for some years, and is regarded on all hands as one of the influential young men of the county, he has never himself been a candidate for office, except when he ran for mayor. March 13, 1884, he was married to Mrs. S. J. Haskill, a young widow lady, daughter of James H. Hubbard, of Plattsburg. Mrs. F. is a member of the Presbyterian Church. Mr. Ford was born at Liberty, March 13, 1856. His father is Capt. James H. Ford, a retired and highly respected citizen of this place. Capt. Ford was deputy sheriff when he entered the Southern army in 1862. Since the war he has held the offices of deputy sheriff and deputy collector. He came to this county from Kentucky in 1837, where he was afterwards married to Miss Mary Duncan, also formerly of Kentucky.

PHILIP FRAHER

(Of Fraher & Son, Manufacturers and Dealers in Boots and Shoes, Liberty).

Philip Fraher, the senior member of the above named firm, was born in Ballinamona, County Limerick, Ireland, April 2, 1822, and was the third son of Thomas Fraher and Johannah Herbert. He received a fair education, and learned the shoemaking trade. After completing his apprenticeship he carried on business on his own account for a few years, but, concluding to emigrate, came to the United States in May, 1846. After spending short periods in Massachusetts, Connecticut, Pennsylvania and New York City, he came West and located in Liberty, Mo., in March, 1851. He formed a business partnership with his brother, James, which was continued up to January 10, 1874, at which time the partnership between the brothers was dissolved, and the separate firms of Philip Fraher & Son and James Fraher & Sons were established. Previous to the late war the old firm of P. & J. Fraher did a large business in manufacturing boots and shoes to order, employing as many as thirteen hands during the busy season. Of late years the use of improved machinery by large manufacturers has so lessened the cost of production, and the products themselves have improved so much in style and quality, as to decrease the demand for the home-made article and increase the business in ready-made boots and shoes, in which the present firm of Philip Fraher & Son, in connection with their custom department, are extensive dealers, carrying the largest stock in the county and having built up a very satisfactory trade. Philip Fraher was married June 17, 1849, in St. Peter's Catholic Church, New York City, the Rev. Father Quinn officiating, to Miss Mary Anne Frazer, oldest daughter of Thomas Frazer and Elizabeth McLean, of Scrabby, County Cavan, Ireland. Miss Frazer was born May 15, 1828, and came to the United States also in 1846. After their marriage, she came West with her husband, locating, as above stated, in Liberty, Mo., where she died July 30, 1879, universally beloved and respected. Of this marriage there was born one son, Thomas J., who is a graduate of William Jewell College, and since attaining his majority has been associated with his father in business. He is a young man of good

325

THOMAS H. FRAME

(Editor and Proprietor of the Liberty *Advance*).

Mr. Frame was a son of Col. Thomas T. Frame, of Daviess county, this State, and was reared and educated in that county. He completed his education at the Gallatin High School, where he graduated in the spring of 1861. Following that, he began an apprenticeship at the printer's trade in the office of the *Sun*, at Gallatin, having decided to devote himself to the profession of journalism, and desiring to become familiar with the practical details of printing in order to make his success as a journalist the more assured. Mr. Frame worked at the case about three years and during that time also did considerable work as a writer for the paper in both its local and editorial departments. In 1865 he bought the *Torch-Light* newspaper, and afterwards was editor and proprietor of that paper for five years. While in charge of the *Torch-Light* he greatly improved it, both in mechanical make-up and influence, and its circulation and patronage steadily increased. Under his management the *Torch-Light* was brought to an enviable position among the country newspapers of the State. In 1870 Mr. Frame sold his newspaper office in order to accept a position at the head of the local department of the Kansas City *Times*, which had been tendered him. There, as in charge of the *Torch-Light*, his services were of much value to the paper. For five years he was connected with the *Times* as local editor, and it is well known to every one at all familiar with newspaper affairs in this State that while he was connected with the *Times* its local department was generally remarked for life, enterprise and ability. The *Times* became the popular local paper of Kansas City, and was looked upon as a model in this respect. But it is one thing to work on a salary, with little or no hope of accumulating means or establishing one's self in life, and another thing to have a business of one's own, the growth and increase in value of which is one's own profit. Mr. Frame preferred to return to country journalism, in the hope of securing a good paper and building it up. An opportunity of this kind was offered at Liberty. Accordingly, in 1875, he came to this place and took charge of the *Advance*, and two years later he purchased the office. His long experience in newspaper life enabled him to bring the *Advance*, by a few years of hard work and good management, to an enviable position of influence and prosperity. Its history for the last eight or nine years is one of gratifying progress in every feature that renders a newspaper valuable and influential. The circulation of the paper has largely increased. The office has been greatly improved by repeated purchases of new and additional material, and its advertising patronage is more than ordinarily large, considering the general business of Liberty and the county. The *Advance* is one of the leading Democratic country papers of the State, and Mr. Frame, himself, is

HISTORY OF CLAY COUNTY

recognized as a prominent and influential member of the Democratic party of Western Missouri. In 1884 he was delegate to the National Democratic Convention at Chicago. He is an earnest, consistent Democrat, but not an extremist, and as an editor he is a vigorous, pungent writer, one who gets his subject in hand before putting his views in print, and who expresses himself clearly, briefly and with more than ordinary pointedness and vigor. Mr. Frame is justly recognized as one of the representative, public-spirited citizens of Liberty. Twice he has been elected to the office of mayor, and in all matters of public advantage, either to Liberty or the county, he is ever ready to do his full share by contributing both his means, as far as he is able, and his time and personal exertions. February 4, 1871 Mr. Frame was married to Miss Rosa L. Riggins, a refined and accomplished daughter of B. L. Riggins, Esq., of Kansas City. They were married at Glasgow, Mo., where Mrs F. had been attending the Pritchett Institute for some time. Mr. and Mrs. F. have three children, Fredonia, Callie and Olin. He and wife are members of the M. E. Church. Mr.Frame's father, Col. Thomas T. Frame, was originally from Virginia. He was married in that State to Miss Myriam C. Catlett, and removed to Missouri with his family in 1830, locating in Daviess county. In a few years afterwards he was elected circuit and county clerk, and subsequently held one or both of these offices almost continuously for a period of nearly twenty years. In 1856 he was a candidate for State Treasurer, but was defeated by the Democratic nominee. He died at Jefferson City in 1861.

WILLIAM J. FRANCIS

(Farmer and Stock-raiser, Post-office, Liberty).

Mr. Francis came to this State when in childhood, away back in the "twenties." The family first settled in Gasconade county, where the father, Pearle Francis, died in 1850. The mother died in that county in 1863. William J. Francis was born in Lincoln county, Ky., in 1825. Principally reared in Gasconade county, Mo., he was married in 1852 to Miss Martha Waller, a daughter of Judge J. G. Waller, of Warren county, but originally of Henry county, Va. Meantime Mr. Francis had begun life for himself as a farmer, and was then engaged in that occupation. But during the Mexican War he had served a part of the time under Gen. Doniphan, but principally under Gen. Price, being nevertheless under Gen. Kearney also a short time. Mr. Francis removed to Clay county in 1866, and has been a resident of this county continuously ever since. His business has been that of farming and raising stock, and also dealing in stock. He has a good farm of 360 acres with more than average improvements. His farm is almost devoted exclusively to stock-raising, and is run in blue grass principally. In 1873 Mr. Francis had the misfortune to lose his first wife. She had long been a member of the Missionary Baptist Church, and was a true-hearted Christian lady and a devoted mother and wife.

She left six children: William W., Louisa B., wife of James Collier, of Fort Worth, Texas; Mary A., wife of French Boggess; Leoma A., Sarah E., wife of Gen. Price Boggess, and Emmet L. Mr. Francis' present wife was a Miss Abbie E. Ecton, a daughter of John Ecton, of Clay county. They have one child, Betsey Brooks. Mrs. Francis is an estimable lady, and she is a member of the Christian Church. Her husband belongs to the Missionary Baptist Church.

CAPT. WILLIAM G. GARTH

(Stock-dealer, Liberty).

The Garth family, or rather that branch of it to which our subject belongs, were early settlers in Central Missouri. His grandparents were from Virginia — the Russels on his mother's side, she being Miss Mary Ann Russel before her marriage to Jefferson Garth. Capt. Garth was born near Georgetown, Ky., November 19, 1832. His father moving to Missouri in his early childhood, he was reared on a farm overlooking the town of Columbia, where his father still lives, and even yet in his old age holds a prominent place in public enterprise. Capt. Garth's education was mostly received in the State University, to the location of which institution his father was a liberal contributor. In 1847 Capt. Garth enlisted in the U. S. army for five years or during the war, serving as a private under (now) Col. William H. Royal, of the U. S. army. The surrender of New Mexico returned him home at the end of the year, from which place the next year he started to California, making the overland journey of over 2,000 miles on the back of a mule. After a sojourn of two years in that then wild country he again turned his face homeward by way of Vera Cruz and the city of Old Mexico. The next three years he remained at his father's, farming and stock-raising, when, again leaving home, he located in Holt county, Mo., where he bought land and lived some two years. In the year of 1856 he was married to Miss Katharine Berry, daughter of John Berry, a prominent citizen of Liberty, Mo., to which place Capt. Garth removed and settled down to a useful, busy and active life, devoting himself to the handling of live stock. Successful in most his efforts, he is known in the various markets as a shipper whose judgment and ability can be relied upon. He owns three handsome farms; a substantial citizen of his county, his home for 24 years has been in the town of Liberty, identified with all its interests and enterprises. He served three years during the war as captain of a company of militia, which was organized and stationed in this county, and represented his county during one term of the Legislature. Capt. and Mrs. Garth have had two boys born to them, but reared but one (John B. Garth), who is now a young man, engaged in stock-raising in New Mexico. They are members of the Christian Church, and he is a member of the Blue Lodge of the A. F. and A. M.

CHRISTOPHER GEIB

(Dealer in and Manufacturer of Harness, Saddles, Etc., Liberty).

Mr. Geib commenced his trade as saddle and harnessmaker at the age of 15 in 1854 at Mineral Point, Wis., and has been at work at it as workman, foreman, or proprietor ever since. There is probably not a man in the State who understands the business better than he does. He served an apprenticeship of three years and a half at Mineral Point, Wis., and then worked in a large establishment at St. Louis until he entered the government service, May 5, 1860, and became foreman of the harness establishment at Fort Leavenworth Arsenal, and remained foreman 13 years. Since that time he has worked at different points, and once again for the government at Rock Island, Ill., being for a time at the head of a harness and saddle establishment for a company at Kansas City. During this time, until he located at Liberty in the spring of 1877, he has been at Wichita, Kas., Leavenworth, at different points in Iowa, at Rock Island and Kansas City. For a time he carried on business himself at Allerton, Iowa. When he began business at Liberty Mr. Geib had strong competition to meet, but being a fine workman, economical and an upright man, he soon gained the confidence of the people and overcame all opposition. He carries a good stock of saddles, harness and other goods in his line. Mr. Geib was married in 1862 to Miss Maria J. Johnson, daughter of Greenup Johnson, formerly of Kentucky. She was reared in Platte county. They have six children: Mary A., Annie, Emma, Christopher, Thomas and Allen. Mr. and Mrs. Geib are members of the Catholic Church. Mr. Geib was born in Luxemburg, Germany, September 13, 1839. His father was John Geib, and his mother's maiden name, Mary Rume. The family came to America in 1847 and settled at Mineral Point, Wis., where the father still resides. The mother died in 1877. Mr. Geib was educated at the common schools and a private academy.

MAJ. JAMES A. GILLESPIE

(County Collector, and late Proprietor of the Arthur House, Liberty).

When a lad about 11 years of age Maj. Gillespie was left an orphan by the death of his father. He was one of a large family of children. Some of the older children of the family had already grown to mature years, and one had married. In 1855, on the death of his mother, James A., with two others of the children, went to live with their married sister, Mrs. R. A. Stout, of Woodford county, Ky., where the family had long been settled. In 1856 Mr. Stout removed to Missouri and settled in Clay county, young James A., who was then in his nineteenth year, coming with him. Some years afterwards Mr. Stout returned to Kentucky, but young Gillespie remained in Clay county. In 1858 he obtained a clerkship in a general store at Liberty, and in 1860 engaged in business with Richard Evans, at Liberty (firm

HISTORY OF CLAY COUNTY

of Evans & Gillespie), until the breaking out of the war. He then enlisted in Thompson's regiment, of Stein's infantry brigade, under Gov. Jackson's call, and became second lieutenant of Capt. L. B. Dougherty's company. After about five months' service under Col. Thompson in the State Guard, he resigned and re-enlisted in the Southern service, becoming a volunteer in the regular Confederate army. At first he was a member of Col. John T. Hughes' battalion, but afterwards became a private in Co. B, Third Missouri infantry, but was shortly promoted to a first lieutenancy and ordered to report to the Twelfth battalion of Arkansas sharpshooters. He was with that battalion until the fall of Vicksburg, when he was directed to report at Washington, Ark., to reorganize his command, and was there given charge of a regiment with the rank of first lieutenant. At the battle of Saline river, though only holding a lieutenant's commission, he commanded a regiment, being made a brevet-major for the occasion. His brigade commander especially commended his gallantry and important services in this engagement. Subsequently he went to Northern Arkansas where he recruited a battalion for the Confederate service, and was elected its major. He served in that position until the close of the war, surrendering finally at Natchitoches, La. In the course of the war, among other engagements in which he participated were the battles of Lexington, Pea Ridge, Corinth, Iuka, Baker's Creek and Vicksburg. At Baker's Creek he received quite a severe flesh wound and was disabled for service for about a month. At the fall of Vicksburg he was, of course, captured, but was shortly paroled and exchanged, and, as stated above, was thereupon ordered to rejoin his command at Washington, Ark. After the war Maj. Gillespie returned to Liberty, and having lost all he had by the war, he shortly accepted a clerkship at Kansas City, where he was employed about six months. On the 2d of November, 1865, he was married to Mrs. Alice Breeden, daughter of Capt. John Sullenger, of Woodford county, Ky. In 1867 Maj. Gillespie engaged in the grocery business at Liberty for Mr. Dearing, which he continued for about six years. Returning to Kentucky in 1875, he made his home in Woodford and Scott counties until 1880, when he came back to Liberty and engaged in the hotel business. He had charge of the Arthur House for two years, and by his good management, hospitality and fair dealing as a landlord, placed the house in the front rank of popular hotels in this part of the State. Maj. Gillespie is an ardent Democrat, and takes an active and public-spirited interest in political matters. In 1884 he was a candidate at the general election for county collector, and was elected by a large majority. He is now (1885) serving the first year of his term in that office. He is a man of high standing, good business qualifications and justly popular wherever he is known. Maj. and Mrs. Gillespie have two sons: Elmer Lee and Willa Johnson. Maj. Gillespie was born in Woodford county, Ky., July 11, 1837. His parents were George E. and Louisa (Campbell) Gillespie, the father originally from Virginia, and the mother of a former Virginia family. James A. was the eighth in a family of 10 children,

330

HISTORY OF CLAY COUNTY

namely: Melvina, now Mrs. M. L. Wallace, of Hayes county, Texas; Fannie, the wife of R. H. Stout, present sheriff of Woodford county, Ky.; John W., present judge of the county court of that county; Charles, assistant in the Secretary of State's office at Jefferson City; the others now being deceased. The mother died in 1855.

JOSEPH C. GOODWIN

(Dealer in Furniture, Liberty).

Joseph Goodwin, the grandfather of the subject of this sketch, was a gallant soldier in the War of the Revolution, and commanded a company of brave Virginians in that long and terrible struggle for independence. He participated in a number of the leading battles of the war and assisted to win the final triumph of the Revolution at Yorktown. His son, Capt. William Goodwin, became the father of the subject of this sketch. Capt. William Goodwin was an officer in the militia organization of Virginia, holding the rank of captain. He married in that State Miss Mary Wells, and made Virginia his permanent home. Joseph C. Goodwin, the subject of this sketch, was born in Henrico county, near Richmond, March 27, 1824. Up to the age of sixteen his time was principally spent at school. He then began an apprenticeship of five years at the cabinetmaker's trade. Completing this, he subsequently worked at different places in Virginia, North Carolina, South Carolina, Georgia, Alabama and Tennessee. Later along he located at Bowling Green, Ky., and after awhile at Lexington, that State. There he was married July 15, 1853, to Mrs. Rosana, relict of John Young, and daughter of William Rickets. In 1853 Mr. Goodwin came to Missouri and located at Liberty. A year later, in 1856, he established a shop of his own which he carried on until the outbreak of the war, having a full stock of furniture. He also had a stock of dry goods and groceries. But during the war his business house was robbed. After that he removed to Lexington, Ky., and in 1864 to Illinois, engaging in merchandising at Zanesville. From there Mr. Goodwin removed to Augusta, Arkansas, and sold goods with a partner under the firm name of Goodwin & Bost, for about four years. But in 1869 he returned to Liberty and the following year resumed the furniture business and has been in business ever since. Mr. Goodwin is a substantial property holder at Liberty, owning a good business house and three residence houses. Recently he has been engaged in shipping apples, and this year shipped about 12,000 barrels. Mr. Goodwin's wife died in 1866. She left him one daughter, Rosana, who is the wife of Thomas Gasney.

JUDGE WILLIAM F. GORDON

(President of the Liberty Savings Ass'n, and Farmer and Fine Stock Raiser, Liberty).

The history of every community is made up, so far as its more interesting and important features are concerned, of the events and trans-

331

HISTORY OF CLAY COUNTY

actions of the lives of its prominent, representative citizens. No worthy representative history of Clay county would, therefore, be complete which failed to include at least an outline of the life of the subject of the present sketch, and something of the record of his family. Judge Gordon's parents came here among the early settlers of the county. His father, Hon. Thomas C. Gordon, was originally from Virginia, but was brought out at an early age to Kentucky by his parents, who settled in Clark county. Mr. Gordon, senior, grew to manhood in that county and in young manhood was married in Kentucky to Miss Charlotte Grigsby, of an early family in that State. They resided in Clark county for a time after their marriage and while there the subject of the present sketch was born June 24, 1831. The same year of his birth the family came to Missouri and settled eight miles northwest of Liberty, in Clay county. Here the father bought a large body of land and improved a farm. He owned a large number of slaves and engaged in farming quite extensively, which he followed with success. He also dealt in stock and all in all accumulated an ample property. Mr. Gordon, senior, represented Clay county for a number of terms in the Legislature and was a member of the House from this county at the time of his death, which occurred January 8, 1866. He was at the time at home from Jefferson City spending the holidays. For many years he had been a member of the Christian Church and was an earnest worker and liberal contributor in his church. Judge Gordon, the subject of this sketch, was the eldest in his father's family of eight children, four sons and as many daughters; all grew to mature years, and all, save one, lived to become the heads of families themselves. Two of the brothers and three of the sisters are still living. Judge Gordon was reared on his father's farm, eight miles northwest of this place, and spent his youth at farm work and in neighborhood schools until he was about 18 years of age. At this time the California gold excitement broke out and he was one of the first in the county to determine on crossing the plains and visit the land of stored wealth on the Pacific sea. He started across the Continent early in 1850, and took a drove of 150 head of cattle and a number of mules with him. He had a squad of fifteen men to accompany him as help and as guard against the Indians. They were on the way one hundred and ten days up to the day they for the first time grazed their cattle on the height overlooking the city of Sacramento. The Judge's impression of that scene as he describes it would make a subject worthy the pencil of a Diefenbach. There fed his cattle above the valley of the Sacramento, here and there in small groups, with a travel-stained and weary herder or cowboy near each group, either astride his trusted pony and with a long whip in one hand and his bridle rein in the other while the wide rim of his great sombrero quivered in the breeze; or, else, lying outstretched on the ground, refreshing himself with a peaceful slumber and naught above him but the clear blue sky, whilst his pony grazed around him all saddled and bridled for use at a moment's call and made secure by a long lariat staked to the ground. Below in the mist of the valley stood the

332

HISTORY OF CLAY COUNTY

quaint and wierd little city of Sacramento, with the steeple of its single cathedral piercing above into the clear light of the sky. The queerness of the dress of its few inhabitants and the promiscuity of their appearance and nationalities added an additional interest to the scene. Away off, thousands of miles from civilization, with the boundless, boundless sea on one hand and an almost impassable waste of country on the other, stopping there down the distant slope of the Cordilleras with no signs of civilized life near save the little semi-civilized city of Sacramento with its strange buildings, little, narrow, crooked streets and its admixture of people from every quarter of the globe, among the native Mexicans and Indians and half and quarter breeds, it was, indeed, a sight to be seen only in one generation in the history of a country. Judge Gordon remained in California, principally engaged in freighting and dealing in stock, for nearly two years, and then returned to his old home in Clay county, by way of Panama and New York. On his return home he visited Philadelphia, Pittsburg, Cincinnati and St. Louis, fully "doing" each city, as young men were then, as they now are, wont to "do" cities on their first visit. Coming on up home he settled down quietly and engaged in farming, having seen the world and interviewed the great "white elephant" to his entire satisfaction. Industry and close attention to his farming interests soon began to bear their usual fruits and in ample abundance. In a word, he shortly became one of the well established and prosperous farmers in the county. He also engaged in stock raising and in handling stock, after awhile turning his attention largely to fine short horn cattle. Judge Gordon finally bought and improved two other farms, the management of which he has been superintending for a number of years. Though engaging in the banking business as far back as 1865, he has nevertheless continued to carry on his farming and stock interests. Judge Gordon now has one of the best herds of short horn cattle in the county. He has been breeding and handling short horns for nearly twenty years, and was among the first farmers of the county to introduce them here. In 1865 he engaged in merchandising at Liberty as a member of the firm of Gordon, Reymon & Co., and continued in the business with success for about three years. He was one of the original organizers of the bank association of this place, which engaged in the banking business in 1865, and started at first on a capital of $1,000, but now has a capital of $36,000. His father was also one of the first stockholders of the association and was its first president. The Judge has been president of the bank since September, 1873. In 1878 he was elected presiding judge of the county court for a period of six years, but held it only two years on account of the change of law. On the 17th of October, 1853, he was married to Miss Rebecca Bland, a daughter of James Bland, formerly of Warren county. She was educated, however, at the Liberty Female College. On the 2d of April, 1872, she was taken from him by death, leaving eight children: Mary E., James B., Katie, wife of S. Burkhead; Frank Lee, Minnie, Carrie, William and Lena. On the 27th of January, 1875, Judge Gordon

HISTORY OF CLAY COUNTY

was married to Miss Louisa Oliver, a daughter of S. A. Oliver. His present wife was also educated at Liberty. They have one son, Oliver. The Judge and Mrs. Gordon are members of the Christian Church, and he is a member of the Blue Lodge, Chapter and Commandery, in the Masonic Order.

CAPT. JOHN S. GROOM

(Farmer and Stock-raiser, Post-office, Liberty).

The family name of the subject of the present sketch is one so long and worthily identified with Clay county, that no history of the county could fairly be considered complete which failed to make proper allusion to the Groom family. Capt. Groom's father, Joseph Groom, was a Virginian by nativity, but was reared in Kentucky. His father was a pioneer settler of Clark county, in that State, having removed there from Virginia during the latter part of the last century. Joseph Groom was reared in Clark county, and in early manhood was married to Miss Nancy Hudtison, a daughter of Col. Hudtison, another pioneer from Virginia and a brave old veteran of the Revolution. After their marriage Joseph Groom and wife removed to Missouri and settled in Clay county, back in 1824. The inhabitants of what is now Clay county could then have been numbered on one's fingers, so few and far between were the settlements in the county. He bought land and improved a farm and resides on the place he then improved to this day, now closely approaching a continuous residence on one farm of sixty years. His life, during the years of his activity, was one of industry and much usefulness, and from the beginning he has always preserved a character and good name that reflect only credit upon himself, his family and the community with which his life has been so long identified. Although now in his eighty-ninth year, he is still well preserved in mind and body, uncommonly so considering his advanced age. His good wife passed away some years ago, a motherly, noble-hearted old lady, loved and venerated by all who knew her. They reared a numerous family of children, all of whom are now worthy members of their respective communities. Capt. Groom, the subject of this sketch, was born about four years after his parents came to Clay county, November 28, 1828. He was reared in the county, and in youth attended the common schools of his neighborhood. On the outbreak of the Mexican war, early in 1846, he enlisted in the service under Col. A. W. Doniphan, becoming a member of Capt. O. P. Moss' company. With his command Capt. Groom took part in the expedition to Santa Fe, being finally ordered to New Orleans at the close of the war, by way of Matamoras, where he was honorably discharged. In common with his command he participated in the battles of Brazeta and Sacramento and in some lesser engagements. After his return from the Mexican War Capt. Groom engaged in farming, to which he had been brought up, and on the 24th of February, 1848, was married to Miss Catherine Hadley, a daughter of Samuel Hadley, deceased, an early settler of this county from Todd county, Ky. Capt. Groom continued farming after his marriage, and with good success. He bought a farm eight miles west of Liberty, where he resided some eight years, and in 1859 bought a place a mile from Liberty, west of town. The same year he was elected assessor of the county, and discharged the duties of that office something over a year, when the Civil War broke out. Like the great body of the property holders and the intelligence and character of the people of Clay county, he warmly espoused the cause of the South, and promptly enlisted in the Southern service. He organized Co. A, of Col. Thompson's regiment, being elected captain of the company, and soon, for the second time in his life, was taking part in the trials and dangers. and hardships of war. He was in the active service for nearly three years, and during that time participated in the battles of Lexington, Pea Ridge, Independence and Lone Jack. In the latter, one of the deadliest and most resolute engagements of the war, though not a great battle in point of numbers, he was shot through the shoulder and disabled for further service. The battle lasted for nearly eight hours, and every inch of ground was resolutely contested. Col. Vard. Cockrell commanded on the Southern side, and Maj. Emory S. Foster had command of the Federals. Both were Missourians, and had been reared neighbor boys together, and their men were all of neighboring counties. So, there, Greek met Greek, and it was a matter of personal pride in each side to win the battle. The Southerners, however, finally won the field. According to the numbers engaged, there were more men killed than in any other battle of the war. With the exception of two other fights, it is believed that this is true. After the battle Capt. Groom returned home for a short time and soon recovered, at least became strong enough, as he thought, to re-enter the service. He thereupon organized another company in Clay county, and at once started South with his men to rejoin the Southern army. But when about five miles from Liberty he was met by a body of Federals, and a fight ensued. During the fight Capt. Groom's horse was killed under him, and his men were routed and scattered, he himself barely escaping with his life; and for nine days afterward he was compelled to secrete himself in the brush, whilst the woods were literally "driven" for him, as hunters say when on a deer hunt. From Clay county he made his way to Denver, in Colorado, and remained there and in Nebraska until the close of the war, principally engaged in merchandising. After returning to Clay county he resumed farming again, but in 1866 established a store at Kearney, where he sold goods for about eight years. He was then, in 1874, elected sheriff, in which office he served for two terms. Immediately following that he was elected county collector, and served in that office for four years. He then bought the place where he now resides, in the vicinity of Liberty, a good farm of about 40 acres, where he is engaged in farming. He also has another farm of 320 acres, and other lands on the Missouri river. Capt. Groom is engaged in raising fine thoroughbred short horn cattle to some extent, and is having excellent success. On the 11th of August, 1864, he had the misfortune to lose his first wife. She left

HISTORY OF CLAY COUNTY

him four children : Fannie, wife of Richard Myall, of May's Lick, Ky.; Ruth, deceased, late wife of A. S. Brown; Jennie, wife of Charles Mosby, and Walter. To his present wife Capt. Groom was married in 1866. She was a sister to his first wife. There are no children by this union. Mrs. G. is a member of the Presbyterian Church, and her husband of the Christian.

MICHAEL A. GROOM
(Farmer and Stock-raiser, Post-office, Liberty).

Like a large majority of the people of Clay county, Mr. Groom is of Kentucky antecedents. His father, Joseph Groom, came to this county from the Blue Grass State in an early day, settling with his family about two miles west of Liberty. Mr. Groom, the subject of this sketch, was reared on his father's farm in this county, and in 1861, the beginning of the late Civil War, he entered the State Guard under Gen. Price and served in Col. Thompson's regiment, in Capt. Groom's company, until in 1862, when he entered the regular Confederate service, serving in the Trans-Mississippi department. During this time he took part in a number of leading battles and many lesser engagements and skirmishes until the surrender, after which he returned home, and resumed farming and also engaged in dealing in stock. He was married to Emma P., daughter of D. J. Adkins, in Clay county, November 5, 1867, and in 1882 he had the misfortune to lose his wife. She left him six children, namely : Elma, Ruth, Darwean, Artie E., Minnie G., and Lizzie E. Groom. Mr. Groom feeds cattle for the markets and is one of the energetic stockmen of the township. He has a good farm of about 500 acres, which is well improved, including a handsome brick residence and a new and commodious barn. His farm is principally run in blue grass for stock purposes. His present wife was a Mrs. Amelia Collins, widow of the late Jesse B. Collins, of this county, and a daughter of James M. Watkins. She has two children by her first husband, Jesse B. and Martha J. Collins. Mr. Groom is a man of warm domestic attachment and is greatly devoted to his family. With him there is in truth no place like home, and to both his own and his second wife's children he is all that a kind and affectionate father could well be. His first wife was an earnest and life-long member of the Christian Church and a devoted wife and mother. His present wife is a member of the Baptist Church and a worthy, excellent lady. Mr. Groom is a member of no secret order and often remarks that his own family is as pleasant and welcome a lodge as he cares to spend his leisure evenings in. Still, he is not insensible to the great good done by many of the secret orders and warmly approves the object for which they are instituted. He is a member of the Christian Church.

SAMUEL HARDWICKE
(Attorney at Law, Liberty).

For more than 25 years Mr. Hardwicke has been engaged in the active practice of his profession at Liberty and in the courts of this

State. A young man of a thorough classical education to begin with, a teacher of the classics in fact, and subsequently qualifying himself thoroughly for the bar by a regular and exhaustive course of study under Judge Norton, then one of the leading practicing lawyers of West Missouri and since 1876 a distinguished member of the Supreme Court, he entered upon his career. as an attorney at Liberty immediately following his admission in 1857, under auspices of a successful and honorable future in the legal profession. Nor has his record in the practice disappointed the just expectations that were formed of him at the beginning. For years he has held a prominent and honorable position among the leading lawyers of his judicial circuit, and he has long been recognized as one of the first lawyers in point of ability and success at the Liberty bar. Close habits of studiousness have always been one of his most marked characteristics, and while he is thoroughly wedded to his profession, a constant student of the science of law, by which he has become one of the best read lawyers in this part of the State, he has at the same time found leisure to gratify his taste for general literature and the classics. His knowledge of the law and his judgment upon legal questions command respectful consideration from the court and bar wherever his duties as a lawyer call him, whilst his culture, eloquence and ability as an advocate and his integrity, professionally and in private life, are recognized by all. Though an active, successful lawyer, Mr. Hardwicke is a man of unusually quiet manners, and of a retiring disposition, more given to the study of his books and to reflection than to the enjoyment of society or the pleasures of conversation. He has a fine law library, where most of his time is spent when not in the court-room or at home with his family. His library is by far the best in the county, and one of the best in the circuit. Samuel Hardwicke was born in Clay county, Mo., September 8, 1833. His father was Capt. Philip Allen Hardwicke, from Brooks county, Va., and his mother, Miss Margaret Gregg (then called "Peggy"), born in Tennessee, but reared in Howard county, Mo. She was the daughter of Hannon Gregg, whom Gen. A. W. Doniphan pronounced one of the strongest men in native intellect he ever met. Her brother, Josiah Gregg, was distinguished in science and as an author. Mrs. Hardwicke was brought out to this State by her parents when she was in childhood, and for a time they lived in Cooper's Fort for protection against the Indians. She was a witness to the death of Capt. Cooper, who was shot by the Indians in the fort. Mr. Hardwicke's grandfather was a gallant old Revolutionary soldier from Virginia, and received a grant of land from the State for his services in the struggle for independence. An incident in this connection is worth mentioning, as it gave rise to two ways of spelling the family name. In the instrument of grant, or patent, the name was spelled " Hardwick " instead of *Hardwicke*, the proper orthography. Since then some of his descendants have kept up the former way of spelling the name. In a very early day the grandfather, Hardwicke, died in Virginia. His son Philip was then a small boy. He was bound out to the cabinetmaker's trade. Before he was grown, however, he went to Logan county, Ky., where he helped to build the first house in Lebanon, a town in that county. About the time of attaining his majority Philip Hardwicke came to Missouri and located in Howard county. There he met and was married to Miss Margaret Gregg (then called " Peggy "), mentioned above. In the early Indian wars Capt. Hardwicke took an active and prominent part, and commanded a company of volunteers through several campaigns. In 1824 he removed to Clay county, having land about five miles north of Kansas City, where he improved a large and valuable farm and lived a useful and respected life until his death. He was a very successful farmer, and was a man of marked influence in the community. Often urged to stand as a candidate for official position he uniformly refused, being thoroughly averse to every idea and practice of the politician's life. He had no taste for the turmoil, confusion, slander, insincerity and double dealing incident to politics, and scrupulously avoided everything of the kind, though he believed earnestly in the *principles* of the old Whig party, and never failed to vote his honest convictions. In 1849 he joined the general movement of Argonauts to the Pacific coast, and died on his return the following year on the ocean, and was buried at Acapulco. Mr. Samuel Hardwicke was reared on his father's farm in this county, and received a general and classical education at the Sugar Tree Grove Academy, then an institution of more than local repute, which he attended for a period of three years. After this he was professor, in that institution, of Greek and Latin for a year, at the close of which he resigned his professorship to engage in the study of law. As stated above, he read law under Judge Morton at Platte City, and was admitted to the bar in the spring of 1857. He at once located at Liberty for the practice of his profession, and has been here continuously ever since, except during an absence of about eighteen months while at St. Paul, Minn. Mr. Hardwicke's professional career has already been spoken of. It is only necessary to add here that there has scarcely been a case of any importance in the county for years past with which he has not been identified as one of the counsel. Mr. Hardwicke has given little or no attention to politics, except to vote his honest convictions, and at times to help his friends. He has therefore neither held nor desired any strictly political position. When a young man he was city attorney of Liberty for a time, and in 1874 his name was canvassed by his friends for the Democratic nomination for circuit judge. His candidacy was very favorably received, and but for political trickery he would have been declared the regular nominee, for he fairly and honorably won the nomination. On the 27th of December, 1860, Mr. Hardwicke was married to Miss Ada Hall, a refined and accomplished daughter of the late John D. Hall, formerly a leading and wealthy citizen of this county. Mrs. Hardwicke was educated at Clay Seminary, where she graduated in the class of '59. Mr. and Mrs. Hardwicke have four children, namely: Miss Maude, a young lady of superior accomplishments, a graduate of the Baptist Female College of Lexington, where she won six medals for superiority in the

HISTORY OF CLAY COUNTY

many different departments of culture, and afterwards taught music in that institution; Claude, who was educated at William Jewell College, which he attended for six years — he is now conducting a cattle ranch in Arizona; Philip and Norton, both youths, still at home and attending school. Mr. H. is a member of the Cumberland Presbyterian Church, and his wife is a member of the Christian Church. Mr. H. is a prominent and active member of the Masonic Order, and founded the Commandery at this place. His mother is still living, at the advanced age of 81, remarkably well preserved in health and mental vigor.

PROF. GEORGE HUGHES

(County School Commissioner, Liberty).

Prof. Hughes is a native of this county, born in what is now Gallatin township, July 1, 1826. His father was Daniel Hughes, and his mother's maiden name Elizabeth Woods. Both were originally from Kentucky, his father from Bourbon county and his mother from Madison county. Mrs. Hughes was a daughter of Rev. Peter Woods, who early came to Missouri and was one of the pioneer Primitive Baptist preachers of the central part of the State. He settled in Cooper county. Mr. Hughes, Sr., came out to Missouri in 1824 and stopped for a time in Cooper county, where he met and was shortly married to Miss Woods. They then came to Clay county and located on land in Gallatin township, where he improved a farm, and where the son, the subject of this sketch, was born. Mr. Hughes, Sr., served as magistrate of the township for a number of years. He was also an earnest and useful member of the Primitive Baptist Church. Though not an extreme partisan he was an active and consistent member of the Whig party until its final defeat and disorganization in 1856. After that as against the Republicans he was a Democrat and voted the Democratic ticket. He died at his homestead in Gallatin township July 9, 1875, in the seventy-sixth year of his age. His wife, however, still survives in comparative good health, at the age of seventy-seven, and quite active considering her years. Prof. Hughes is the eldest of five children of the family living, three sons and two daughters. Four others lived to reach mature years, two brothers and two sisters. Prof. Hughes received his general elementary education in the public schools of the county, though afterwards he continued to study outside of the school-room and materially advanced himself in the higher branches. Indeed, he has been a constant student all his life, as well as a teacher most of the time for nearly forty years. In point of experience he is unquestionably the father of the teacher's profession in this county. In 1854 he succeeded Gen. Doniphan as school commissioner of the county, and has held the office ever since, a period of thirty years. For three years he was a teacher in William Jewell College immediately prior to its reorganization after the war. Subsequently he was three years principal of the Liberty High School for young ladies. Under his long administration in the office of school commissioner, the public schools of the county have made remarkable progress in

HISTORY OF CLAY COUNTY

numbers and efficiency. When he took charge of the office they were not considered the chief reliance of the youth of the county for an education. Now the public schools of Clay county are among the best and most successful to be found in any of the counties of the State, and are so constituted as to amply qualify those who attend them and complete the curriculum studies prescribed for all the ordinary business affairs of life. September 29, 1859, Prof. Hughes was married to Miss Margaret, a daughter of the late Andrew Russell, of this township, one of the early settlers of the county. They have two children, Frank and Ralph. The Professor and wife are members of the Christian Church. Prof. Hughes served three years as mayor of Liberty and was councilman for a number of terms. Prof. Hughes gives much of his leisure time to literary pursuits, being an active member of the principal literary societies of the community in which he lives.

DANIEL HUGHES

(Dealer in Drugs, Medicines, Paints, Oils, Etc., Liberty).

Mr. Hughes, who is a regular registered pharmacist and a druggist of experience and enviable reputation, began to learn the drug business nearly 20 years ago, when he was in his eighteenth year. He worked at it as a clerk for five years, and in 1870 formed a partnership with S. W. Warren, and began business on his own account at Liberty, buying out his former employer and succeeding him in business. Two years later he bought out his partner and became sole proprietor of the business, which he has ever since carried on alone, for a period now of over 14 years. He has been satisfactorily successful, and has one of the principal drug stores at Liberty. Mr. Hughes carries a large and well selected stock of goods in his line, and has a good trade. Personally, he is a man of pleasant, popular address, of an agreeable social disposition, and is much esteemed in the community. July 27, 1871, he was married to Miss Annie McCarty, a daughter of William A. McCarty, and niece of Capt. Thomas McCarty, deceased, former State Senator from this district. Mrs. Hughes was educated at Liberty, and is a graduate of the Female Seminary at this place. They have four children: Alla, George, Albert and Charles. Mr. and Mrs. H. are members of the Christian Church. Mr. H. is a member of the Masonic Order, including the Chapter, Commandery and Blue Lodge. Mr. Hughes was born in this county December 6, 1847, and was a son of Daniel Hughes, mentioned in the sketch of George Hughes, on a former page. Daniel Hughes, Jr., the subject of this sketch, was reared in this county and educated at the common and high schools and at William Jewell College.

GEORGE W. JONES

(Farmer and Stock Dealer, Post-office, Liberty).

Mr. Jones descends from an old Virginia family, one that has been settled in this county since the earliest days of that colony, as the large number of Jones in every quarter of the Union conclusively attest. He was born in Rappahannock county, Va., September 22, 1825, and was a son of William and Elizabeth E. (Easham) Jones, his father a veteran of the War of 1812, and a substantial planter of Virginia. George W. received an advanced education, attending New Baltimore Academy, under the tutorship of that distinguished educator Prof. Ogilvie. Afterwards he came West, locating at Buffalo, Mo., where or in the vicinity of which he taught school for seven years. Mr. Jones came to Clay county in 1847. Here he also followed teaching for some years. He had a number of negroes, but these he hired out to other parties for farm work, etc. He married Miss Elizabeth, a daughter of William Bywater, an early settler of Platte county, from Virginia. He then engaged in farming and raising stock in Platte county, and so continued up to 1862, when, on account of war troubles, he went to Virginia, which seemed a good deal like jumping out of the frying pan into the fire. Nevertheless, he obtained the favor of both sides in Virginia and was granted free passport through their lines to go and come as he pleased. There he did a thriving business in furnishing stock and supplies for the two armies. In the fall of 1863, however, he returned to Missouri, and located on a farm in Lafayette county. There he followed farming and also handling stock until the spring of 1881, when he came back to Clay county, and bought the place where he now resides. This is about two miles east of Liberty, and contains nearly a quarter of a section of land. Mr. Jones, besides farming in a general way and dealing in stock, makes a specialty of raising Poland-China hogs, of which he has some of the finest to seen in the country. Mr. Jones has been married three times. His first wife died a number of years before the Civil War. His second wife was a Miss M. A. Tillery, who only survived her marriage about two years. He was married to his third wife in the spring of 1863. She was a Miss Belle H. Hudson, a daughter of Capt. J. M. Hudson, of Saline county, this State. She is a member of the Christian Church, as he is, also, himself. By Mr. Jones' first marriage two children were reared: Alline E., the wife of James M. Elliott, of Cooper county, and William E., who was a graduate of the State University and of the Jefferson Medical College of Philadelphia, but died early in February, 1883, being at the time the leading physician of Jamestown, Missouri. Thomas L. Jones, the second son, was born of his father's second marriage. He is a substantial farmer in the vicinity of Liberty. By Mr. Jones' present wife there are four children: Mattie B., Jesse B., Unis B. and Dilburn D. He is a member of the Odd Fellow's Order.

JAMES M. KELLER

(Farmer and Short Horn Dealer and Breeder, Liberty).

Like most of the early settlers of Missouri, Mr. Keller is of Virginia descent. Both his grandfather, John Keller, and father, Jacob Keller, were natives of the Old Dominion. His grandfather served three years in the War of the Revolution and afterwards became one of the pioneer settlers of what became Jessamine county, Ky. There he served in several of the early Indian wars, as did also his son, Jacob Keller. Jacob Keller was married in Kentucky to Miss Mary M. Rice, formerly of Maryland, and became a large farmer and also extensively interested in distilling. He died in Jessamine county, at an advanced age, in 1824. James M., the subject of this sketch, was the third in the family of children. He was born in Jessamine county, Ky., October 13, 1809, and was reared in his native county, with farming experience and at work in the distillery. However, after his father's death he learned the gunsmith's and blacksmith's trades, continuing to work at that in Kentucky for about eight years. February 27, 1833, he was married to Miss Elizabeth Dillingham, a daughter of Henry H. Dillingham of Madison county, that State. Three years later Mr. Keller removed to Missouri, and opened a shop at Liberty, where he soon secured a large custom as a gunsmith and blacksmith. He continued at work in his shop until about 1857, when he bought land about three miles northeast of Liberty, to which he removed, engaging there in farming. Ever since that time he has been actively identified with farming and for many years past has been engaged in stock raising. Mr. Keller has a small herd of fine shorthorn cattle, which class of stock he is making a specialty of breeding and raising for the markets, and in which he has had good success. Mr. and Mrs. K. have three children, namely: Mary E., wife of James G. Adkinson of Kansas City; Pauline, a widow of Thomas J. Harper, deceased; Mrs. H. being now a resident of Liberty, and herself the mother of three children; and Amanda B., wife of D. K. Bogie, who resides on the Keller homestead, and is interested in the farming and stock business of the place. He is a native of Kentucky and a brother to Dr. Bogie, of Kansas City. He and wife have three children: Marcus, Keller and Mary H. Mr. Keller is a man who has led a life of industry and strict integrity and has brought to him and to the retirement of old age the esteem of all who know him.

HON. JOHN R. KELLER

(Farmer and Stock-raiser, Post-office, Liberty).

Among the old and prominent citizens of Clay county, the subject of the present sketch has long held a well recognized and enviable position. Mr. Keller is a son of Jacob Keller, reference to whom is made in the sketch of James M. Keller, elsewhere given. He was born in Jessamine county, Kentucky, December 18, 1812. Reared in that county, June 6, 1833, he was married to Miss Eliza J. Faulconer, daughter of Nelson Faulconer, of Fayette county, Ky. After his marriage he settled down in Fayette county, where Mr. Keller followed farming for about five years. But in 1837 he came on a prospecting trip to Missouri and traveled through several counties, particularly in the Platte Purchase. While on this trip he decided to make his home in Clay county, and, accordingly, dis-

HISTORY OF CLAY COUNTY

posing of his saddle horse, having come out from Kentucky horse-back, he went back by river, and at once went to work arranging his affairs for removal. In due time he returned to Missouri and bought a place of 320 acres, near to what is known to old settlers as Gladpen Springs, for which he paid about $17 an acre. Since then he has added to his landed estate until he now has about 700 acres, but still resides on the old homestead on which he settled when he first came to the county. Mr. Keller is very comfortably situated, has, in fact, one of the best homesteads in many respects in the county. He suffered considerable loss during the war, and was compelled to leave home for a time, but returned as soon as peace was restored and has ever since, as he had always been before, been regarded as one of the useful and prominent citizens of the county. In 1874 he was elected to the State Senate and served with marked ability in that body for two years. He also served on the State Board of Equalization and has filled other positions of trust, all with entire credit to himself and to the public service. Mr. and Mrs. Keller have a family of six children: Elizabeth, wife of M. B. Brooks; Sarah, wife of John D. Harper; George N., Thomas J., Martha J. and Joseph F. Mr. and Mrs. Keller are members of the Christian Church, and have been for 50 years. As the above facts show, Mr. Keller has been a resident or this county for nearly half a century. But he has not been a man to confine his full time and attention to the acquisition of means or property. He has been a man who has given much study to questions of public interest and has well informed himself upon the politics of the day and the political history of the country. He has also read a great deal in general literature, history and other branches, and is well informed. Nor has he neglected the information to be derived from travel, but has visited different parts of the country, and being always a close observer, he has profited much in this way. Mr. Keller is one of the intelligent, well informed representative citizens of the county.

MAJ. ALVAN LIGHTBURNE

(Retired Farmer and Business Man, Post-office, Liberty).

No name is justly entitled to a more enviable place in the history of Clay county than the one which heads this sketch. For nearly half a century Maj. Lightburne has been usefully and honorably identified with the growth and development of the county, with its advancement in every worthy particular. Abundantly successfully himself in the activities of life, his industry and business enterprise have been even of more value to the community where his fortunes were cast than to himself. Not only has he been useful in promoting the material interests of the county, but his public spirit and liberality have been worthily represented in every step taken for the higher social interests of the people — the establishment of advanced educational facilities, the encouragement of mental culture and moral improvements, and support of the churches, and the building up of a healthy, religious

HISTORY OF CLAY COUNTY

sentiment — the best safeguard of society. In a word, the influence of his life upon those around him has been only for good, and of marked force and value. The family originated in England, from whence some of his ancestors went to Ireland. Mr. Lightburne is a Kentuckian by nativity, born in Scott county, December 13, 1803. His father was Richard Lightburne, a son of Lieut. Richard Lightburne, of the Virginia State navy, who served in the American navy during the War of the Revolution. There were only two children, Staford and Deborah. The children of Richard Lightburne were all born and raised in Scott county, Ky.: Richard P., on the 23d of July, 1805, but died at Louisville, Ky., December 4, 1883; John S., born April 11, 1811, living in Clay county, Mo., and William L., born June 4, 1820, living at Stamping Ground, Scott county, Ky. Stafford Lightburne was the founder of the family in this country, whose immigration here was something of a romance. He was an Irish lad, about 16 years of age, in his native county, when he was " kidnaped " on a British vessel, which sailed for the New World. He was left on the cost of Virginia, and afterwards he found a home in a hospitable family in Caroline county, Va., where he remained until after he attained his majority. Stafford Lightburne was the father of Richard Lightburne, Jr., the father of the subject of this sketch. Richard Lightburne, Jr., came out from Kentucky when a young man, in about 1790. He was subsequently married in Scott county, that State, to Miss Temperance Sutton, formerly of Caroline county, Va. They made their permanent home in Kentucky after their marriage, and reared a family of children. Richard Lightburne, Jr., an energetic farmer by occupation, died in 1820. The mother survived until 1855. They had eight children, six sons and two daughters, and of their family of children, Alvan (Maj. Lightburne) was the eldest. Maj. Lightburne received a good common school education as he grew up, which was supplemented by instruction at private school and a course in a local seminary. Of a bright, quick, active mind and of studious habits, he soon became qualified for teaching, and for any ordinary business pursuits, so far as educational attainments were concerned. At the age of 17 he was appointed deputy circuit clerk, the duties of which position he discharged with efficiency and general satisfaction. Maj. Lightburne's father died the same year that the Major was appointed deputy circuit clerk, and from that time forward he had the care of his mother's family, with the responsibility and burdens his position as the eldest son imposed. The family was large, and had but little means to go upon, so that the chief dependency was upon him. But he proved himself worthy of his difficult position, and was at once a father to his younger brothers and sisters, a kind and affectionate son to his mother, and a competent, liberal provider for the family. He remained with them for some 14 years after his father's death, until most of the children had grown up and started out for themselves. After his close of service in the circuit clerk's office, his time was busily and profitably occupied with farming and teaching school, though principally the latter. He taught, however, for some 12 or

HISTORY OF CLAY COUNTY

14 years, during the usual school terms in his county. During the year 1831 he was a clerk on a steamboat, plying between Louisville and St. Louis. In 1832 he was elected constable of Scott county, the duties of which office were only second in importance to that of the sheriff, so that almost all his time was occupied. In 1834, having accumulated a little means, he went to Cynthiana, Ky., where he formed a partnership with Manlius V. Thompson, under the firm name of Lightburne & Thompson, for the manufacture of rope, twine and bagging, which they followed with success until they were burned out during the following year. His old partner, Manlius V. Thompson, was afterwards Lieutenant-Governor of Kentucky. From Cynthiana Maj. Lightburne returned to Scott county, where he established a rope factory. A year later he decided to cast his fortunes with those of the then new State beyond the Mississippi, Missouri; and he accordingly came out to this new country. This was in 1836. He came out on horseback and "prospected" all through the Missouri river counties of the State. Finally Maj. Lightburne located at Liberty, where he established a hemp factory, and a year later, in 1833, bought the farm adjoining town, where he now resides. The Major continued in the hemp industry for a period of 22 years, and was very successful. He retired from the business, however, in 1859, and after that devoted his whole time and attention to his farming interests. He became the owner of a number of valuable farms, and managed them with marked energy and enterprise. Though burned out twice while engaged in the manufacture of hemp, he never allowed himself to become discouraged, but went to work with redoubled energy to make up for losses, which he soon succeeded in doing. During the Mormon War he was a major of Missouri volunteers under Col. Doniphan, and was major of militia under the old militia laws of the State. He was mayor of Liberty, and from time to time has been prominently identified with enterprises for the improvement of the place and the advancement of the interests of the community. He was one of the leading spirits in securing the location of William Jewell College at this place and in founding that institution. As early as 1847 he went to work on the enterprise and spent the principal part of three years at work to secure the establishment of the institution and building it up, to the neglect of his own business. He made a thorough canvass of the people of the county for subscriptions, and by his and other citizens' efforts secured $24,767, which he turned over to the college committee. (About 1872 the subscription by town and county amounted to near $40,000). At the time of the committee for location, Hon. E. M. Samuel, Judge J. T. V. Thompson and Gen. A. W. Doniphan's departure from Liberty Landing, Maj. Lightburne arrived, handed subscription papers and said: "Gentlemen, you go to get the college; if the amount is not sufficient on your arrival at Boonville, add $3,000 or $5,000 more — secure the college." The proffered aid was not needed. For this noble institution, a credit to the State and an honor to the community in which it is located, people are under no greater obligations to any one than to Maj. Lightburne. His zeal and public spirit for

the college are entitled to additional credit from the fact that he was not interested in it so far as his own family are concerned, for he has never been blessed with children of his own. In numerous other enterprises looking to the educational, moral and social improvement of the community, as well as in those of a material character, he has been hardly less public-spirited and liberal of his time and means than in his efforts in behalf of the college. He has also been an active and prominent worker in the Masonic Order, and has held the offices of High Priest and Eminent Commander. He has also represented his lodge in the Grand Lodge and Grand Chapter. In whatever he has interested himself he has worked with zeal, energy and ability, and has made it a success. As early as 1837 he took an active part in founding the Female Seminary at this place, and putting it on a successful basis, contributing liberally to its fund. On the 3d of May, 1846, Maj. Lightburne was married to Miss Ellen J. Sutton, a daughter of Capt. William Sutton, of Scott county, Ky. She and Maj. Lightburne were children together, and were reared on adjoining farms. They played together in childhood, and in the morning of life formed that attachment for each other which has continued unbroken through the lapse of years, and has bound their lives together in a union which only death can sever. Their married life has been one of singular congeniality and happiness, and from the beginning each has seemed to study and labor to make the other happy. Mrs. Lightburne, though now advanced in years, is a lady of marked grace and dignity, and makes a most favorable impression upon all by her manifest superiority of intelligence, her amiability of disposition, and her gentle, motherly bearing. Maj. Lightburne is a man whose name stands a synonym for honorable and useful citizenship, and for purity and uprightness of character. For some years past he has been retired from business activities; and in the Indian summer of a well spent life is enjoying the comforts and pleasures which his industry has brought him and his good name and large circle of friends afford. He has a handsome residence property, a spacious and stately brick in the suburbs of town, provided with every comfort and convenience, where he is living in ease and retirement, esteemed and venerated for the nobility of his nature and the good that he has done. He and his good wife have reared several orphan children, for whom they have made ample provision, and by whom they are esteemed and loved as the best of parents. Certainly two lives, crowned as these have been and jewelled with so many noble deeds, are worthy to be commemorated in any just history of the county. Consistent members of the Christian Church for many years, and having lived lives in keeping with the teachings of the Father of all, they may now look back without regret, and forward to the final end with hope and joy.

JAMES T. MARSH, M. D.

(Physician and Surgeon, Liberty).

Dr. Marsh's father, James Marsh, came to Clay county with his family, from Kentucky, in 1827. Here he became a large landholder

HISTORY OF CLAY COUNTY

and leading farmer. He died here in 1840, leaving five children, four of whom are living, the Doctor, an older brother and two sisters. Dr. Marsh was born on the family homestead in this county February 18, 1833. In early youth he attended the common schools and afterwards took a course of two years at William Jewell College. He then entered Westminster College, in which he continued two years, graduating in 1857, with the degree of Bachelor of Arts. Immediately following his graduation he began the study of medicine. In due time young Marsh matriculated at the St. Louis Medical College, and subsequently took a course of two terms there, graduating in the class of '60. After his graduation Dr. Marsh located at Weston, in Platte county, but a year later removed to Clinton county, where he practiced until the spring of 1863. Dr. Marsh then came to Liberty, and has been in the active practice of his profession at this place ever since. Dr. Marsh is a member of the County District Medical Society and of the State and the National Medical Association. In the spring of 1860 Dr. Marsh was married to Miss Roxanna Brashear, a daughter of the late Cyrus Brashear, one of the pioneer settlers of Clay county. Dr. and Mrs. Marsh have four children, Carlton, Laura, Nellie and Morton. Mrs. Marsh is a lady of culture and refinement. She is a graduate of the Baptist Female College, at Liberty, and has long been a diligent and discriminating reader of the better class of literature. Dr. and Mrs. M. are members of the Presbyterian Church, and the Doctor is a member of the I. O. O. F.

JOSEPH F. MEFFERT, M. D.

(Physician and Surgeon, Liberty, Missouri).

It is no empty compliment, but the statement of a plain fact necessary to be written in any truthful biography of the subject of the present sketch, that Dr. Meffert, by his unusual energy, ability and ambition, has rapidly pushed himself forward in his profession, in point both of education and practice, until now, although a young man only little past the age of 27, he occupies an enviable position among the leading physicians of the State. Graduating with honor at William Jewell College in the class of 1878, he at once thereafter began the study of medicine under Dr. Records of this place, having a decided preference, and a more than ordinary aptitude, as the result is showing, for that profession. Making extraordinary rapid progress in his studies, he shortly matriculated in the Medical Department of the University of Louisville, Ky., and there by hard study he succeeded in graduating in June, 1879. Without stopping he entered the Kentucky School of Medicine where he graduated the following fall. From there he entered upon a course in the Hospital Department of Central University, of Kentucky, which he succeeded in completing the following spring. At that time the position of Hospital Surgeon and City Physician was vacant, which was to be filled by appointment, and the appointee to be selected by a competitive examination as to his qualifications and medical attainments. Dr.

HISTORY OF CLAY COUNTY

Meffert and a number of other physicians applied for the place, as it was quite a lucrative and prominent position in the profession. Upon competitive examination Dr. Meffert was selected as having shown the best qualifications among all those competing for the place. He desired the position not alone for its prominence in the profession and the salary, but also because the large and varied experience he would obtain there in a few years would be worth more to him than the practice of half a lifetime. He held the position for two years, until from overwork he was completely broken down and compelled to resign for rest and recuperation. However, he did not remain idle, but at once entered a medical institution at Buffalo, N. Y., where he spent several months, and afterwards occupied several months visiting the different hospitals of New York City and making a study of special cases. While there he received the appointment of physician to the State Lunatic Asylum of Arkansas, at Little Rock, which, however, he declined, for the reason among others that his presence was required at home, in Liberty, at that time to take charge of his father's business. On returning home at this place he shortly entered actively upon the practice of his profession and has continued in it ever since. He has a very large practice, having special cases, in fact, from other States, and, as has been said, occupies a position among the leading physicians of the State. He is administrator of his father's estate, and superintends the management of the property of the family. Dr. Meffert was a son of Frederick and Mary (Hubbach) Meffert, both formerly of Germany, but from Louisville, Ky., to Liberty. His father was largely engaged in the wholesale boot and shoe business in this State, first at Missouri City, Mo., then at Leavenworth, Kan., and finally he removed to Liberty in 1866, where he carried on a boot and shoe house for a number of years. He was a leading member of the Masonic Order and held a number of prominent positions in that order. During the last seven years of his life he was engaged in the drug business at Liberty. He died here August 20, 1884.

JOHN MESSICK

(Liberty, Missouri).

Considering that Mr. Messick is still comparatively a young man, and that he began for himself with little or no means to start on, his career has been a more than ordinarily successful one. At the age of 43, he is now one of the substantial property holders at Liberty. His means he has accumulated by successful business enterprise. He was born in Jessamine county, Ky., November 10, 1841. His father, John Messick, Sr., has resided in Indiana since 1861. Mr. Messick, Jr., received a good general education in the common schools and academy of Nicholasville, his native place, and at the age of 23 came out further West to Alton, Illinois, where he became clerk in a hardware store. After two years spent at Alton he had succeeded by economy in saving some money from his salary, and he returned to

Kentucky, where he was married, February 15, 1870, to Miss Margaret Sherley, a daughter of Elijah Sherley, of Jessamine county. Directly after his marriage Mr. Messick came to Missouri and located at Liberty, where he bought an interest in a hardware store already established. Five years later he bought the entire business and conducted it with unbroken and excellent success until February of last year, when he closed out to good advantage. He is now completing a large brick building in which to engage in the manufacture of carriages, and to carry on blacksmithing, repairing, etc. He also has a number of valuable properties at Liberty, and already is in comfortable circumstances. He is a man of thorough-going energy, a good business manager, and doubtless will continue his heretofore successful career. Mr. Messick has been married twice. His first wife died in February of the year following their marriage. In August, 1873, he returned to Kentucky and was married to Miss Nannie S. Speares, a daughter of Lee Speares, deceased, late of Fayette county, that State. By his last marriage there are four children: John, Jr., Charles, George and Miranda. Mr. Messick's mother was a Miss Jennie Hawkins, of Kentucky, but originally of Virginia. She died in 1848. His father is now married to his third wife and resides in Indiana.

THOMAS F. MESSICK

(Real Estate Dealer and Hardware Merchant, Liberty).

Mr. Messick has been a citizen of Clay county and resident of Liberty for only about ten years, but such has been his enterprise and success as a business man, that for some years he has held a worthy place among the leading and useful citizens of Liberty in business and general affairs. He began life for himself when a youth as clerk in a mercantile house, and afterwards continued in that employment for a period of about nine years, learning all the details of the business thoroughly. Not only that. But those habits of constant and close attention to business were formed and that knowledge of the fact was obtained that for one to succeed he must economize in every possible direction, which, together with good judgment, strict integrity and untiring industry, enabled him subsequently, when he came to engage in business on his own account, to make success an assured fact and to achieve it much sooner than would otherwise have been possible. Mr. Messick was partly reared in Indiana and came to Liberty in 1874. By this time, although he was a young man only about twenty-five years of age, he had succeeded in accumulating some means, which, on coming here, he invested in a hardware store. He, therefore, became a partner with his brother, John Messick, and the firm of Messick & Bro. continued successfully in the hardware business until last spring, when Thomas F., the subject of this sketch, sold his interest in the store. They carried a very full line of shelf and heavy hardware and also a large stock of farm machinery, wagons, etc., and did a good business. Aside from this, Mr. Messick was most of the time dealing in real estate, both town property and farms. At

Liberty, he built some seven or eight residence properties, several of them very handsome places, and four of them he still owns. His homestead property at this place is one of the neatest and handsomest at Liberty, a picture of good taste, convenience and comfort. He also owns two good farms in the vicinity. In handling real estate, exchanging, buying, selling, etc., he has had even better success than in merchandising. Mr. Messick is now giving his entire time and attention to real estate. December 22, 1870, he was married to Miss Lennie Harrison, a daughter of M. C. Harrison, deceased, of Montgomery county, Indiana. Mr. and Mrs. M. have four children, Harry, Emma, Mattie and Thomas. He and wife are members of the Christian Church, and Mr. M. is a prominent member of the Masonic order. He is also identified with the temperance cause and is an ardent believer in the doctrine of prohibition. He thinks that if it is right to sell whisky, sell it like hardware, dry goods, etc., are sold ; take away all restrictions. If *wrong, stop* it. Mr. Messick has been a member of the town council at Liberty. He was born in Jessamine county, Kentucky, September 22, 1849. His parents, John and Margaret Messick, removed to Indiana when he was about thirteen years of age, settling in Montgomery county, where he was reared. He was by his father's second marriage and was the only child of that union. After his mother's death his father was again married. By each of his father's first and last marriages there was a numerous family of children.

ROBERT HUGH MILLER

(Liberty).

Robert Hugh Miller was born in Richmond, Va., November 27, 1826. His parents were John E. and Mary A. (Rogers) Miller. His father's family was of Scotch extraction. About the year 1832, his parents immigrated to Barren county, Ky., and, after residing there nearly six years, removed to Missouri and settled in Monroe county. Soon after he was sent to Columbia, Mo., to learn the printing business, and there entered the office of the *Columbia Patriot*, published by F. A. Hamilton, W. T. B. Sanford, Thomas Miller and James S. Rollins, all of whom are now dead except the latter. Before the expiration of his apprenticeship, the *Patriot* ceased to exist, and entering the office of the *Missouri Statesman*, also published in Columbia, he remained there some months.

In April, 1846, in connection with the late John B. Williams, of the Fulton *Telegraph*, he established the Liberty *Tribune*, in Liberty, Clay county, Mo., whither he immediately removed and there he has ever since made his home. The connection between himself and Mr. Williams in the publication of the *Tribune* was terminated within a year after the first issue, and he became and has since remained the sole proprietor of that paper. The *Tribune*, in its history, has had no suspension, and but one failure of issue, which occurred in September, 1861.

HISTORY OF CLAY COUNTY

He was married June 28, 1848, to Miss Enna F. Peters, daughter of the late John R. Peters, of Clay county, Mo. She died December 3, 1867, leaving four children. May 3, 1871, Mr. Miller married Miss Lulu Wilson, daughter of the late Hon. John Wilson, of Platte county, Mo.

His educational advantages were such as could be obtained in his youth in the common schools of the country, and this he supplemented by research and observation. From his earliest acquaintance with politics to the dissolution of the Whig party, he was an enthusiastic member of it. Since then he has been a member of the Democratic party and earnestly co-operates in the advocacy of its principles. He was reared and educated under the influences of the Old School Presbyterian Church, and though not a communicant of any church, he retains a great respect and reverence for that grand and venerable body of Christians.

He has ever been an earnest advocate of all public enterprises inaugurated in Clay county — its railroads, schools, colleges, agricultural society, etc. — indeed, of all measures and conceptions whose purpose and tendency were to increase the wealth and social and moral well being of the people among whom he has so long lived.

Mr. Miller's characteristics are untiring industry, great tenacity of purpose, close adherence to approved forms, customs and usages, conscientious attachment to truth and right, and steady, unflinching devotion to friends.

JOHN J. MOORE

(Farmer and ex-County Collector, Post-office, Liberty).

Mr. Moore was born in Orange county, N. C., March 2, 1882. His father, Col. James Moore, was one of the prominent citizens of that county, and was colonel of militia and the founder of Mooresville, of which he was for many years postmaster. The mother, who was a Miss Margaret Robertson, was a lady of marked intelligence and of one of the best families in that part of the country. John J. Moore grew up in Orange county and remained at home until 1846, when he came to Missouri and made his home in Clay county. Here he shortly enlisted for the Mexican War under Col. Doniphan, and was out until the close of the war. He then returned to Clay county and followed farming for a few years, at the expiration of which time he engaged in the livery business at Liberty. For several years preceding 1861 he served as deputy sheriff of the county, and then enlisted in the Confederate service under Gen. Price. The first two years of the war he served east of the Mississippi, and the rest of the time in the Trans-Mississippi department. He was a member of the Forty-third Missouri infantry, and was with his regiment in all the engagements in which it took part. Returning after the war, he resumed the livery business and continued it with success up to 1872, when he was elected county collector. Two years later he was re-elected, and he was again re-elected in 1876, serving until March, 1879. Since the close of his last term Mr. Moore has been residing on the farm, which he owns,

351

HISTORY OF CLAY COUNTY

near Liberty, containing about 200 acres. In the summer of 1852 he was married to Miss Eliza, a daughter of John Lee, formerly of North Carolina. His wife was reared in the same neighborhood as himself, but just across the line in Caswell county. They have two children: William E., in the dry goods business at Liberty, and Ruth, the wife of John W. Norton, Esq., an attorney at Kansas City, a son of Judge Norton of the Supreme Court. Mrs. Moore is a member of the M. E. Church South, and Mr. Moore is a member of the I. O. O. F.

ELISHA A. MOORE

(Farmer and Stock-raiser, Post-office, Liberty).

During the war Mr. Moore was in the Union service, and did his full share of duty toward preserving the Union, which both Southerners and the loyal people of the North are now glad, or profess to be, is an established fact. He was born in Andrew county, Mo., April 8, 1845, but was partly reared in Clay county, this State, where his parents, William and Lucinda Moore, removed when Elisha A. was in infancy. His father was a native of South Carolina, and was a carpenter by trade. He came to Missouri when a young man. Mr. Moore's mother was a daughter of Judge Elisha Cameron, of Clay county. In 1850 the father, William Moore, went on a trip to California, and died there about a year afterwards. When Elisha A. was about eight years of age his mother came back to Clay county, and here he grew to manhood. In June, 1863, he enlisted in Co. B, Sixth Missouri cavalry, State militia, under Col. E. C. Catherwood. He served until the close of the war, and was honorably mustered out at St. Louis in 1865. He then came back to Clay county, but soon afterwards engaged in freighting across the plains, and followed that for several years, becoming wagon-master of a train. Returning in 1868, he now made Clay county his home for about a year. In June, 1869, he was married to Miss Mary C. Williams, of Jackson county, a daughter of Samuel S. Williams, formerly of Fleming county, Ky., but now deceased. After his marriage Mr. Moore followed farming in Jackson county for about six years, and bought a farm there. But selling out at the expiration of that time he came back to this county and settled on his present place, which he had previously bought. He has a good place of 135 acres, well improved, including a fine orchard of 300 bearing trees. Mr. Moore is president of the district school board, and has been a school director nearly ever since he came back to the county. Mrs. Moore is a member of the M. E. Church. They have four children: Mary Ellen, Arthur W., Walter H., and Charles C.

JAMES W. MOSBY

(Farmer and Stock-raiser, Post-office Liberty).

The Mosby family is originally of Virginia, and Gen. Mosby, of Confederate fame, is one of its prominent representatives. The sub-

HISTORY OF CLAY COUNTY

ject of the present sketch, however, comes of a Kentucky branch of the family. He was a son of Wade Mosby, a native of Woodford county, Kentucky. The father removed to Clay county, Missouri, as early as 1824. He was a farmer by occupation and died here in 1857. The mother, who was a Miss Rebecca Shouse before her marriage, died in 1865. James W. Mosby was born October 1, 1836, and was reared in this county. He was brought up a farmer, and in 1860 was married to Miss Sue Riley, a daughter of Alfred M. Riley, an early settler of Clay county. The result of this union has been one child, Charles, who is now a youth, twenty-four years of age. Mr. and Mrs. M. are members of the Christian Church. Mr. Mosby has a good farm of 320 acres, a half mile from Robinson's Station, on the H. & St. Jo. Railroad, and is comfortably situated. He breeds and deals in short horn cattle and feeds cattle and hogs for the wholesale market; in fact, he is quite a stock dealer, and is satisfactorily successful. He has always taken quite an interest in schools and does much to keep up a high standard of efficiency in the schools of his vicinity.

CHARLES MOSBY

(Farmer and Fine Stock-raiser, Post-office, Liberty).

Mr. Mosby is a son of James W. Mosby and was born on his father's homestead in this county in October, 1861. He was reared on a farm and in 1881, at the age of twenty, or, rather in his twenty-first year, he was married to Miss Jennie Grooms, a daughter of Capt. John S. Grooms, an old and prominent citizen of this county. Mr. and Mrs. M. have two children, James F. and John G. Mr. Mosby was reared a farmer and stock-raiser and has continued in the calling to which he was brought up. He has a handsome farm of 300 acres, situated two miles and a half north of Liberty, which is substantially and comfortably improved. He makes a specialty of raising fine Polland-Angus cattle and has a handsome herd of that breed of stock. On several of his stock he has been awarded premiums at different fairs. At the head of his herd he has a fine bull, Byron, imported from Scotland. Mr. Mosby also fattens a number of beef cattle and quite a number of hogs each winter for the wholesale markets. He is a farmer of enterprise and a man of good education. He was educated at William Jewell College, and afterwards took a course at Jacksonville Business College. Mr. M. is one of the prominent young farmers of the county. He has excellent young stock for sale at all times.

WILLIAM H. NEWLEE

(Dealer in Drugs, Medicines, Paints, Oils, Etc., Etc., Liberty).

Mr. Newlee was born in Claiborne county, Tenn., at Cumberland Gap, December 22, 1853. His father, C. A. Newlee, was from Virginia, and made his home in Tennessee when a young man. He was there married to Miss Mary C. Huff, and in 1857 they removed to Missouri and located at Liberty. He was a merchant tailor by

353

HISTORY OF CLAY COUNTY

trade and followed that here for a number of years. William H. was reared at Liberty and educated at William Jewell College. At the age of nineteen he commenced learning the drug business under Mr. Hughes at this place and continued under him for six years. In 1878 he became a member of the firm of Bradley & Newlee, dealers in drugs, and five years later he bought out Mr. Bradley and has ever since continued the business alone. He carries a complete stock of drugs, medicines and all other goods of kindred lines and his trade is steadily growing. March 16, 1880, Mr. Newlee was married to Miss Clara Miller, a daughter of David S. Miller, deceased, one of the early settlers of this county. Mrs. Newlee was educated at the Clay Seminary. They have two children : Arthur Martin, and Charles Embree. Mrs. Newlee is a member of the Presbyterian Church.

LANCE W. NEWMAN

(Attorney at Law and Prosecuting Attorney, Liberty).

Mr. Newman is a young lawyer who is steadily and surely making his way to the front in his profession, and as a prominent and useful citizen. A man of thorough collegiate education, a close student of and well versed in the law, he at the same time has, to a more than ordinary degree, the natural attributes essential to a successful career at the bar and in public life. Favored with a strong, vigorous constitution, full of life and spirit, he is also a man of studious habits, and closely and diligently applies himself to whatever he has in hand. Gifted with an active, well balanced mind, and of sober, mature judgment on all questions coming under his consideration, smooth and graceful in his address, a pleasing and forcible speaker, a man of a high sense of honor, unquestioned integrity and singular fairness and liberality, of a mind just and liberal, and generous of heart and character, he is very naturally highly esteemed by all who know him, and of much personal popularity. Mr. Newman, like the representatives of most of the early families in this section of the State, descends from old Virginia ancestry. His father, Peyton Newman, was a native of the Old Dominion, but was reared in Kentucky, whither his parents removed when he was a mere boy. He grew up in Boyd county, that State, but when a young man came to Missouri and located in Platte county, near the present town of Edgerton, where he bought land and improved a farm. That was as early as 1838, and he was one of the pioneer settlers of that county. There, a few years afterwards, he was married to Miss Susan, a daughter of Lance Woodward, an early settler of that county from Kentucky, but originally from Stafford county, Va. He (Mr. Woodward) is still living on his farm in Platte county, and is now in his eighty-ninth year. His daughter, Mrs. Newman, was principally reared in Madison county, Ky., where she resided before coming to Missouri. Mr. Newman, Sr., is a successful farmer and stock-raiser of Platte county. Lance W. Newman, the subject of this sketch, was reared on his father's farm in Platte county, and in early youth attended the common

HISTORY OF CLAY COUNTY

schools of the vicinity. Afterward he matriculated at William Jewell College, and continued a student here until he was honorably graduated in the class of 1880. After his graduation young Newman was appointed clerk of the probate court of Clay county, and while discharging the duties of that position he studied law under the tutorage of Maj. Samuel Hardwicke, whose sketch appears elsewhere. Two years later, after a thorough course of preparatory study, he was admitted to the bar, in 1882. About this time he was appointed justice of the peace, and he held this position until he resigned it to accept his present office, that of prosecuting attorney, to which he was elected in the fall of 1884. Meantime, in 1883, he had been elected city attorney of Liberty, and he discharged the duties of that office for one term. In the fall of 1884, as indicated above, he was a candidate for prosecuting attorney. He made the race in a free-for-all contest, and had two opponents, Messrs. James W. Fraher and James L. Sheetz, both highly popular and thoroughly capable young lawyers. The race was warmly but honorably and good-naturedly contested. Mr. Newman was successful by 103 plurality. Mr. N. entered upon his duties as prosecuting attorney in January, 1885. He will, unquestionably, make an able and successful, but, we believe, a just and not illiberal public prosecutor, one who will show good judgment and heart enough not to make his office an engine of inhumanity and injustice. Seeing to it that the laws are faithfully enforced, when their enforcement is necessary or can be made to accomplish any substantial good, he will doubtless, nevertheless, show mercy that is due and proper:

> " For earthly power doth show likest to God's,
> When mercy seasons justice."

Mr. Newman is not a married man; but if the whisperings of the wind can be relied upon, he is already suppliant at the feet of the fair mistress of the heart, for mercy unto himself; and doubtless he who can win the suffrages of his fellow-citizens can win the heart and hand of one more tender and sympathetic than even the most sensitive of the sterner sex.

DARWIN J. NUTTER

(Farmer and Stock-raiser, Liberty).

Mr. Nutter was reared in this county, and received a more than average general education as he grew up. He had the benefit of two years' course at the Georgetown College, of Kentucky. At the outbreak of the war, or rather in the fall of 1861, he enlisted in the Confederate service, under Gen. Stein, and was out about eight months. While encamped in Arkansas the malaria of its swamps fastened upon him and thoroughly shattered his health. On that account he received an honorable discharge Thence returning home, where he remained a short time, he went West to Colorado, both to eradicate the malaria from his system and to avoid the militia, who were as little to be endured as the malaria. Mr. Nutter was out there nearly four years engaged in the stock business, but returned in 1865, and resumed farming in this county, to which he had been brought up. He has followed that occupation ever since and has made it a satisfactory success. He has a good farm of nearly 400 acres, five miles west of Liberty, and has his place well improved and well stocked. He moved into town several years ago for the purpose of educating his children, but still carries on his farm himself. He is now town counselor and on every hand is accounted one of the worthy, substantial citizens of the place. September 19, 1873, he was married to Miss Lucy Corbin, a daughter of the late Dr. Corbin, of Nicholas county, Ky., who died there in 1853, just as he was preparing to remove to this State with his family. Mr. and Mrs. N. have four children: Theophilus, Warda, Gertie and Allie. Mr. Nutter, himself, was born in this county, November 5, 1841. He was a son of James and Elizabeth M. (Adkins) Nutter, both from Kentucky, his father from Scott county. They came here in about 1838, and the father, a successful farmer, died in 1846.

JAMES D. OLDHAM

(Retired Farmer, Post-Office, Liberty).

Mr. Oldham, now in his seventy-fourth year, has been a resident of Clay county for many years, and is well known as one of the worthy and respected citizens of the county. By a lifetime of honest industry he has situated himself comfortably in life and has ample provision for old age. He has a good farm of 200 acres well stocked and fairly improved and his home is provided with every necessary sober comfort to be desired. He was born in Shelby county, Ky., January 26, 1811, and was reared in his native county. His father, James T. Oldham, came from Virginia, when a youth, with his parents and grew up in Scott county. At about the age of twenty years, he located in Shelby county, where he was married to Miss Maggie R. Davis, in 1808. She was born and reared in Scott county, and her father's family was said to be the first family that settled in that county. Mr. Oldham, senior, died in 1824 in middle age. His wife survived until 1876. There were seven children in the family, all of whom lived to reach mature years. James D. Oldham, the subject of this sketch, after he grew up, was married in Scott county, Kentucky, November 14, 1836, to Miss Annie Neill, daughter of Rodman and Mary Noill. Thirteen years afterwards Mr. O. removed to Lawrence county, Indiana, with his family, where he resided for twenty years. He then came to Clay county, and has made his home here ever since. Farming and raising stock have been his regular pursuit, and in this he has been fairly successful. In 1877 Mr. Oldham had the misfortune to lose his good wife. She had borne him fifteen children, ten of whom are living: William, Baxter, John, Mary, August, Callie, Nevin, Nathaniel, Lee O. and Henry. James, Rodham, George, Nathan and Warren are deceased. Mrs. O. was

HISTORY OF CLAY COUNTY

an earnest member of the Presbyterian Church, and Mr. Oldham has himself long been a member of that denomination, and takes a commendable interest in the welfare of the church and the cause of religion.

CYRUS PARK

(Farmer and Stock-dealer, Post-office, Liberty).

Mr. Park was born in Madison county, Ky., September 7, 1838, and was reared in his native county. His education was completed at the high school, sustained by private subscription and located on his father's farm. Young Park took a thorough course in the English branches, mathematics, and also obtained a good knowledge of Latin. He remained on the family homestead with his father engaged in farming and handling stock for some eight or ten years after he reached his majority. But on January 2, 1868, he was married to Miss Mary E. Cobb, a daughter of Jesse Cobb, of Estill county, Ky., and the same year he removed to Missouri. Mrs. Park was born November 4, 1843, and was educated in Lincoln county, Ky., and at Madison Female Institute, Richmond, Ky. Mr. and Mrs. Park are both members of the Christian Church. On coming to Missouri, Mr. Park located in Clay county and followed farming, being also all the time engaged in trading in stock. He now owns a neat homestead just inside the town limits of Liberty, and near the college building. He bought this place in 1880, in order to be near the college, so as to educate his children. Mr. and Mrs. Park have had two children, Jessie E. and Marcus Taylor; the latter died January 11, 1884, in his fourteenth year. He was a singularly bright and promising boy and greatly loved by all who knew him. The following notice of his death is taken from the Liberty *Tribune.*

IN MEMORY OF MARCUS TAYLOR PARK,

Aged 13 years, 4 months and 15 days. Thus early in life has passed away one who bid fair to live out the allotted time of man. But alas! "the grim monster Death" claims as his victims the young and tender boy as well as the feeble old man. So on the morning of January 11th, 1884, while the stars were paling their beautiful light before the great king of day, Taylor's spirit tooks its flight to the golden shores that lie beyond the dark valley of death. His voice no more to be heard on earth, will join the heavenly choir to sing the chorus of the song so sweetly sung to his memory — "God's children gathering home."

But Oh! how hard it was to give him up. Although for twenty long and weary weeks he was the victim of disease and suffering, yet he never murmured or complained, always submissive to the wishes of fond and loving parents, who so faithfully and tenderly watched over him to the last.

During his sickness he would often say: "Pa I'm so anxious to get well. I want to live to be a good and useful man." And having known him from the day of his birth, I feel confident in saying that had his young life been spared, he would have been a noble Christian man — God's grandest work.

But such could not be; for while deeply enshrined in the hearts of parents, friends, teachers and schoolmates, God in his faultless wisdom thought best to take his pure spirit to a better world, while kind friends laid to rest his little body beneath the beautiful flowers that decorated his casket, there to wait till the resurrection morn, when Taylor, in a pure and spotless robe, will welcome his loved ones to the "Sweet by-and-by."

A FRIEND.

357

RICHARD L. RAYMOND

(Farmer and Fine Stock Raiser; Post-office, Liberty).

Mr. Raymond was about 14 years of age when his parents removed to this county from Nicholas county, Ky. His father, Hon. John M. Raymond, was a prominent citizen of that county, and had served in the Legislature of the State. Mr. R.'s mother was a Miss Sarah Griffith, from Harrison county, Ky. Her father had also served in the Legislature several terms, and was a member of the Senate when he died, and the family was one of the prominent influential families of the county. On coming to Clay county Mr. Raymond, Sr., settled about eight miles from Liberty, where he was successfully engaged in farming and stock raising until his death, which occurred in 1868. R. L. Raymond, the subject of this sketch, was born in Nicholas county, Ky., October 27, 1842. He was reared on a farm (after the age of 14) near Liberty, Mo. After arriving at his majority he followed clerking in a store for awhile and then formed a partnership with Judge Gordon and H. A. Bland, in connection with whom he sold goods for about five years. Subsequently he sold his interest in the mercantile business and resumed farming and raising stock, to which he had been brought up. For years Mr. Raymond has made a specialty of fine stock. His farm contains about 300 acres of choice land, and is well improved. The class of stock in which he is principally interested is fine short horn cattle, and he has a large herd of these, some 90, one of the largest and finest in the county. Besides, Mr. Raymond is interested with John Garth and James C. Leary in a ranch in New Mexico, where they own jointly about 1,000 head of cattle. Mr. R. is at present secretary of the Clay County Fine Stock Association. In 1881 he removed to Liberty, where he now resides. Mr. R. has a handsome residence property at this place, and is otherwise comfortably and pleasantly situated. December 1, 1868, he was married to Miss Mattie R. Wilson, a daughter of Thomas J. Wilson, deceased, late of Kansas City, but a native of Maryland, and one of the earliest settlers in Kansas City. Mr. and Mrs. Raymond have three children: Katie, Irene and Mattie R. He and wife are members of the Christian Church.

CAPT. ALLEN G. REED

(Farmer and Stock-raiser, Post-office, Liberty).

Capt. Reed, like perhaps a majority of the old residents of Clay county, is a Kentuckian by nativity. He was born May 26, 1812, in Clark county. Capt. Reed was a son of Capt. Joseph Reed, and a grandson of Samuel Reed, of South Carolina, who served under Washington throughout the War for Independence. Samuel Reed's wife was a sister of Col. Hampton, father of Gen. Wade Hampton, of colonial and revolutionary times, and who served with distinction in the War of 1812; he was for years a distinguished member of Congress,

HISTORY OF CLAY COUNTY

holding, also, other official positions of distinction, and being at one time the owner of over 3,000 slaves, besides being one of the largest plantation proprietors in the South. Gen. Wade Hampton, now of the United States Senate, and Capt. Reed are therefore second cousins, being the grandsons of brother and sister. Capt. Reed's father commanded a company in the War of 1812. His parents had emigrated to Kentucky in an early day from South Carolina. In 1810 Capt. Joseph Reed was married in Clark county, Ky., to Miss Catherine F. Griggsby. Over 20 years afterwards he removed with his family to Missouri, and settled in Clay county, buying land near Liberty, where he improved a farm and resided until his death. He died here in 1844. The mother died in 1850. Capt. Allen G. Reed, the subject of this sketch, was reared in Clark county, Ky., and at the age of 21, in 1833, preceded his father's family to Missouri. He came direct to Clay county, the family following during the next year. After farming for about a year in this county, he engaged as a clerk in a store at Liberty and two years later bought an interest in the store. In 1838 he bought a farm some six miles northwest of Liberty, retiring from the mercantile business, and followed farming for about eight years. He then engaged in partnership with Maj. John Dougherty, of Clay, in freighting west to Santa Fe and other points, and continued in the freighting business until 1846, becoming very successful and one of the largest freighters west. At one time he was running as many as 140 teams. Besides this he was engaged in merchandising during the last two years of his freighting experience. After quitting the West he bought out his partner's interest in the store at Liberty, and carried on the store at that place until 1858. Although actively engaged in merchandising at Liberty during this time, he had considerable outside business, and during a part of the time was again largely interested in freighting. In 1858 Capt. Reed failed in business, his liabilities being $10,000 and his assets $40,000. Thus he paid every dollar of indebtedness and subsequently went to Denver, Col., where he engaged in the stock business. He built the first brick house erected at Denver. While extensively engaged in the stock business, he was also largely engaged in railway contracting, furnishing ties to the Union Pacific Railroad, having his headquarters in that business at Laramie City, W. T. At one time he had as high as 400 men in his employ as railway contractor. But while his business was quite profitable, he was called upon to bear a misfortune which more than offset all the mere material success this life can afford. His eldest son Robert Reed was his paymaster, and after drawing the money at the express office at Laramie City to pay the hands with, he was murdered in cold blood in the streets of the place and in open daylight by several desperate characters for the purpose of robbery. It is a trite saying that one's misfortunes never come singly. So it proved with Capt. Reed. About the same time, having over 3,500 head of sheep in a mountain ravine, a sudden heavy rain came on, or water-spout broke above the head of the ravine, and the water was thus suddenly raised to the depth of from five to twelve feet, and his entire flock of sheep

359

were swept away and drowned. This took the last dollar he had but he was out of debt. Out there where sheep were rated at a high value at that time that reverse, of itself, was the loss of a respectable fortune. After this Capt. Reed returned home to Clay county and once more turned his attention to farming near Liberty on a handsome place of 250 acres. On the farm he has a valuable mineral spring, said by competent chemists to show as good medicinal qualities as the water of any springs in the State. It has not been developed and advertised, however, and is therefore not used as a resort, as doubtless it otherwise would be. Capt. Reed is a man of wonderful energy and fine business qualifications, one of that class of men whom even " bad luck " can't keep down. Mrs. Reed had some money left her from her father's estate, which her husband invested very wisely and to advantage in cattle. Upon their return from Colorado she was enabled to pay a second time for the farm here mentioned. Capt. Reed very modestly disclaims any credit arising from his supposed excellent financial condition, attributing it to his wife. Capt Reed has been married three times. His first wife, *nee* Miss Lucinda Adkins, was a sister to D. J. Adkins, whose sketch appears elsewhere. She left two children at her death: Irene, now the wife of A. T. Litchfield, and Robert who was murdered at Laramie City, W. T. In 1868 he was married to Miss Polly Neill, who survived her marriage only a few weeks. His present wife was a Miss Missouri A. A. Bivens, daughter of Tenman Bivens. They have three children: James F., sheriff of Clay county, whose sketch appears below; Katie, the wife of William H. Saeger, cashier of the Citizens' National Bank, at Kansas City, and Emma. Mrs. Reed and three daughters are members of the Presbyterian Church.

JAMES F. REED

(Sheriff of Clay county, Liberty).

Mr. Reed, the popular sheriff of this county, was born and reared here, and the confidence which the people have in him is therefore intelligently placed, for they have known him from boyhood and have had every opportunity to judge of his character and qualifications. It is easy enough for one of good address to go into a community of strangers and by proper effort to make a highly favorable impression, thus securing the esteem and confidence of those who know little about him. But it is not so with the one who has been born and reared in the community where he puts himself up for the suffrages of the people. If there is any kink in his character they know it and will repudiate him, for however big a rascal a voter may be himself he will turn up his nose and refuse to vote for a dishonest man with as much virtuous indignation as if he were the impersonation of purity and essence of all the excellencies of character. Mr. Reed was born at Liberty, April 11, 1852, and was a son of Allen G. and Missouri A. Reed, the father formerly of Kentucky, but the mother born and reared in this county. She was her husband's second wife, and is still

HISTORY OF CLAY COUNTY

living, a resident of this county. The father came here with his parents when a youth, and afterwards married and made this his home. His first wife died, and he was subsequently married to Miss Bivens. In 1859 he went to Pike's Peak, lived in Colorado ten years, and then returned to Liberty, Mo., where he still lives. James F. Reed grew up in this county, and has lived in this county all his life, except six years spent in Colorado and one year in Texas. When a young man he engaged in stock trading and farming. In 1878 he was appointed deputy sheriff under Mr. Timberlake, under whom he served for four years. In 1882 he was elected sheriff, and in 1884 was re-elected without opposition. While deputy sheriff he was city marshal for two years. March 20, 1883, he was married to Miss Fannie Wymore, a daughter of William H. Wymore, formerly of Kentucky. Mrs. Reed is a graduate of the Clay Seminary, and is a lady of refinement. She is a member of the Christian Church. Mr. Reed is a member of the Odd Fellows' Order.

CAPT. JAMES T. RILEY

(Dealer in Furniture, Undertaker's Goods and Carpets, Liberty).

Capt. Riley, who has had a very active career and one not without substantial success, was born and reared in this county, and at the age of seventeen began clerking in a country store near Mt. Gilead Church. After a year spent there he became clerk for Denny & Clark, of Liberty, and continued with them for four years. The next five years he clerked for Miller, McCarty & Co., at Liberty, the leading business house of the county. In 1860 he quit clerking to engage in the sheep trade, and bought a large drove of sheep, which he took to Texas for sale. After his return he resumed clerking and was engaged in that occupation when the war broke out. Early in 1861 he enlisted in the Southern service, becoming a member of Capt. McCarty's company under Col. John T. Hughes. Capt. Riley was in nearly all the engagements fought in this State in the early part of the war. At the battle of Carthage he received a flesh wound, which, however, was not serious. He was also slightly wounded at the battle of Oak Hill. After that engagement, early in 1862, being then in Texas, he became a member of Capt. J. W. Sedberrie's company, under Col. J. W. Sheight. This regiment was shortly ordered to Galveston and later along was consolidated with Col. Cook's regiment of heavy artillery, in which Capt. Riley served until the close of the war. For meritorious conduct and gallantry he arose from the ranks as a private to the commission of captain in command of Co. A. At the retaking of Galveston he was again wounded. At the close of the war he found himself without a dollar. However, he went to work in Texas and in a short time gathered up some little means with which he bought (partly on time) a drove of cattle at the low prices than prevailing. These he took to Memphis, Tenn., where he sold them, with a good profit left after the purchase money and all expenses were paid. After this Capt. Riley returned to Clay county, but went back to Texas

361

HISTORY OF CLAY COUNTY

in a short time, going, however, by way of St. Louis and New Orleans, and taking on his trip, in partnership with Maj. M. Dearing, a large quantity of supplies from St. Louis to the Crescent City, as a business enterprise. This also proved a profitable investment. In Texas, Riley and Dearing bought a drove of 400 head of cattle and brought them to Barton county, where they sold them at a good profit. Capt. Riley then returned to Liberty and became a partner in the firm of D. D. Miller & Co., in general merchandise. Five years later the firm became Stone & Riley. In 1878, Capt. Riley sold his interest in the above named firm and then engaged in the furniture business, which he has since continued. He has the leading furniture establishment of the county. In the spring of 1884 he established a branch furniture store at Kearney, which is doing a good business. December 1, 1869, Mr. Riley was married to Miss Mollie Stone, daughter of George Stone and sister of R. J. Stone, his former partner in business. Mrs. R. is a lady of education and culture, a graduate of Clay Seminary. The Captain and Mrs. R. have four children: Kate, Louise, Nannie and Mary Ross. Both parents are members of the Christian Church. He has served as city treasurer, and in 1880 was elected public administrator of Clay county, which office he filled for four years, and was re-elected in 1884. Capt. Riley was born in this county May 22, 1836, and was a son of H. M. and Caltha (Cotton) Riley, who came here from Fayette county, Ky., in 1727. They located near Gilead Church, where they resided a number of years and then removed to Liberty. The father died here in 1860.

JAMES S. ROBB

(Farmer and Fine Stock Raiser, Post-office, Liberty).

The family of which Mr. Robb is a representative settled in this country originally in Pennyslvania. Mr. R.'s grandfather, William Robb, who early removed to Kentucky, was a brother of Judge Robert Robb, who was adjutant-general in the War of 1812, and for many years district judge in Kentucky. Two other brothers, David and Joshua, located in Ohio. David made the race for Congress at a time when his district included nearly all of Eastern Ohio; he was defeated by his opponent by only four majority, after which Gen. Jackson, who was then President, appointed him Indian Agent. A son of Judge Robert Robb, Joseph Robb, held the office of judge and clerk of Lewis county, Ky., for 44 years. Mr. R.'s grandfather settled in Lewis county, Ky., and there William W. Robb, James S.'s father, was born and reared. He married a Miss Margaret M. Piper, and of this union James S. was born April 2, 1846, in Mason county, Ky., in which county his father settled. The father and mother are both living, and make their home with their children. There were two sons and a daughter in the family besides the subject of this sketch. The daughter is now the wife of Jasper Johnson, and resides in Illinois. James S. Robb was reared in Kentucky, and at the age of 18 began as a clerk and book-keeper in a wholesale store at Maysville.

HISTORY OF CLAY COUNTY

After about two years he engaged in farming and continued that until 1871, when he came to Pleasant Hill, Mo. He resided there for about two years, but was not in any active business on account of ill-health. In 1873 he removed to Greene county, Ill., and engaged in buying and shipping stock, which he followed for some five years with excellent success. August 29, 1879, he was married to Miss Annie B. Hodge, a daughter of Dr. John Hodge, deceased, late a prominent physician of Greene county, Ill. In 1879 Mr. Robb removed to Clay county, Mo., and three years ago bought the farm where he now resides. He has a good place of 280 acres, a mile south of Liberty, one of the choice farms of the county. He has a small herd, six head, of fine Jersey cattle, and a large flock of fine Cotswold sheep. Mr. and Mrs. R. have four children: Mary, Ella, Margie and Mabel. The Robb family was originally from Scotland, and have been Presbyterians from time immemorial.

WILLIAM R. ROTHWELL, D. D.

(Professor of Theology and Moral Philosophy in William Jewell College, Liberty, M o.)

Rev. Dr. Rothwell is a prominent representative of the old and respected family of Rothwells, of Callaway county, this State, but originally of Virginia. A somewhat extended notice of the Rothwell family is given in the History of Callaway County, recently published. It is also referred to in the histories of Randolph county, where Hon. Gideon F. Rothwell resides, and of Audrain county, of which Dr. Thomas P. Rothwell is a resident. From the United States Biographical Dictionary (Missouri volume), we reproduce the following sketch of Rev. Dr. Rothwell's life: —

William R. Rothwell was born in Garrard county, Ky., September 2, 1831. His parents, John Rothwell, M. D., and China Renfro, daughter of Dr. William Renfro, of Garrard county, Ky., were of Virginian birth and English descent. They had six children, three sons and three daughters.

In 1831, soon after the birth of the subject of this sketch, they emigrated to Callaway county, Missouri. William, from early childhood, was studious and gave great promise of becoming an eminent scholar. He attended the common schools in the county in which his father resided, and with the help of two short terms at academies, was prepared in 1851 to enter the Missouri University, from which he graduated with the degree of A. M., July 4, 1854, taking the first honor in a class of ten.

At the time of his graduation he had decided upon the medical profession, but his plans were changed by his being, in the same year, elected principal of Elm Ridge Academy, Howard county, Mo., where he received a very encouraging salary, and, being stimulated by success, he remained for two and one-half years, when he was elected the first president of the Baptist Female College, at Columbia, Mo., (now known as Stephens College). After one year of service there he was elected to succeed Rev. William Thompson, LL. D., as presi-

363

dent of Mt. Pleasant College, Huntsville, Mo., which position he held with great success for twelve years.

In 1860 he was ordained to the ministry, having been converted in 1853 under the preaching of Rev. Tyre C. Harris, Columbia, Mo., and was successively pastor of the Baptist churches at Huntsville and Keytesville, Mo.

During the years 1871–72 he was corresponding secretary of the Baptist General Association of Missouri, in which position he acquitted himself with marked ability. His letters and communications while corresponding secretary are noted as being among the most graceful and forcible that have emanated in the interest of that body.

In 1872 Mr. Rothwell was unanimously elected professor of theology and moral philosophy in William Jewell College, which position he still holds (1885). He was also the acting president of the college from 1873 to 1883.

In 1874 his *Alma Mater*, the University of Missouri, in honorable recognition of his distinction as a man of letters, conferred upon him the dignity of *Divinitatis Doctor*. Every moment of Dr. Rothwell's time since his graduation has been one of intellectual activity and usefulness.

In 1855 he married Louisa Hughes, daughter of Allen Hughes, of Howard county, Mo. In 1860 Mrs. Rothwell died, leaving one son, John Hughes Rothwell, now 26 years old, and a resident physician of Liberty, Mo., who gives rare promise of excellence in his profession, being a full graduate of William Jewell College and of Bellevue Hospital Medical College, New York.

In 1863 Dr. Rothwell married Miss Fannie A. Pitts, daughter of Rev. Y. R. Pitts, near Glasgow, Mo., and to them has been born a son, Younger Pitts Rothwell, now a member of the senior class in the college with which his father is connected.

Perhaps in few homes in the State could be found a more complete library than in Dr. Rothwell's. He has spared neither time nor expense in adding to it the standard works on theology and moral philosophy, besides valuable encyclopedias. His taste for literature and his desire for improvement has drawn about him friends of high social standing. He is in perfect sympathy with the Baptist workers throughout the State, and they enjoy the hospitalities of Dr. and Mrs. Rothwell's beautiful home.

Politically he is a Democrat, always voting, but not otherwise taking any great interest in politics.

Dr. Rothwell has a very commanding appearance, being six feet high and very erect. He is in the prime of life and mental vigor, is mild mannered, possesses easy dignity, and is very modest and unassuming. His sense of duty impels him to the front whenever principle or honor calls. He is a "ripe scholar," of elegant culture, and a man of liberal and expansive views. Perhaps no man in the State stands higher in the love and confidence of his denomination of Christians than he.

HORATIO F. SIMRALL
(Liberty).

The subject of this sketch was born in Shelby county, Ky., May 3, 1845. His parents were James Simrall and Cynthia Fritzlen Simrall, his father being of Virginia parentage and Scotch ancestry. Senator Simrall's mother, of German and Scotch ancestry, is yet living, a resident of Shelby county, Ky.; his father died in May, 1863. Mr. Simrall was educated at Shelby College, Ky., from which he graduated in the class of 1866, having taken the classical course. He was one of the teachers in that institution for the last ten months of his course. On leaving college he followed teaching and farming during the winter and summer respectively for about two years, at the same time devoting his leisure hours to the study of law. Following this he entered the Law Department of the University of Louisville, from which he graduated in 1868. One year after leaving the University he moved to Liberty, Clay county, Mo., and engaged in the practice of his profession, in partnership with Col. Henry L. Routt, which continued with mutual profit and satisfaction for about two years, when the firm dissolved. Mr. Simrall then entered into copartnership with James M. Sandusky, a young lawyer just admitted to the bar, which copartnership yet continues, and the firm enjoys a wide reputation and lucrative practice. Mr. Simrall brought to his profession a thoroughly trained mind; the habits of study, which characterized him at school and college, have never forsaken him. He is well versed in the legal profession and thoroughly familiar with all the leading decisions. Senator Simrall is a man of good *personnel*, generous in his impulses, liberal in his views, and courteous in manners. He is a fluent talker, and whether on the hustings or at the bar never speaks without striking at the heart of the subject. In politics he is a Democrat — thoroughly versed in the tenets of his party — and has several times held positions of public trust. He was prosecuting attorney of Clay county in the years 1875 and 1876 and 1883 and 1884. At the fall election in 1884 he was elected State Senator for the third district, composed of the counties of Clay, Platte and Clinton, having received the unanimous nomination of his party convention. In December, 1874, he was married to Miss Mattie J. Denny, a daughter of John A. Denny, Esq., one of the early settlers of Clay county. Mrs. Simrall is a graduate of Liberty Female Seminary. They have three children: Denny, Horatio F., and an infant son not yet named. Mr. and Mrs. Simrall are of the Presbyterian faith, and are both members of the local congregation at Liberty.

JOHN J. STOGDALE
(Clothier, Grain and Produce Dealer, and County Treasurer, Liberty).

Born near Moberly December 12, 1844, the subject of this sketch came of one of the early and respected families of Randolph county.

HISTORY OF CLAY COUNTY

In the pioneer days of that county his father, William Stogdale, located there from Virginia, being then a young man only about 18 years of age. He became an energetic farmer of that county, and was married to Miss Susan Gashwiler, a daughter of — Gashwiler, another early settler, and originally from Pennsylvania. She, however, was born while her parents were residents of Kentucky. In 1850 Mr. Stogdale, his brother-in-law, J. W. Gashwiler, afterwards Gen. Gashwiler, and a number of others, went to California. There Mr. Stogdale, Sr., died some eight months afterward, in the fall of 1850. Gen. Gashwiler remained permanently in California, and became one of the prominent and wealthy men of the State. He was very successful in mining, and became one of the millionaires of the Pacific coast. Indeed, it is a matter of record that a single check of his was honored for $1,000,000. John J. Stogdale, the subject of this sketch, was reared in Randolph county and given an advanced collegiate education. However, in 1862, at the age of 18, he went to St. Louis, where he was employed as salesman in the house of Collins & Son, in which position he continued for some two years. He then resigned his position and entered William Jewell College, following a course there of five years, at the end of which he graduated with marked distinction, being among the first in his class. At the annual meeting of the Alumni Association he delivered the address as one of the prominent post-graduates of the institution. After his graduation Mr. Stogdale engaged in the grocery business at Liberty, commencing in the first place on a small capital. This, however, was increased from time to time until 1872, when he sold out, having one of the leading grocery stores of the county. It was then that Mr. Stogdale established his clothing house, which he has ever since carried on with such marked success. He has an annual trade in the cloth line alone of over $40,000. He has also been in the produce trade for some time, especially the lines of apples and potatoes. In 1883 he shipped over 10,000 barrels of apples, and his shipments this year will exceed over 50 car loads. He has a large fruit evaporator for drying apples, at which he has employed about 20 hands. His present works require 120 bushels of apples to keep them running at full capacity. However, he is increasing the capacity of his works, and will shortly require 240 bushels daily. This is one of the successful industries of the place, and has been made such by his enterprise and business ability. Mr. Stogdale has always taken a marked interest in the cause of education, and has served in the office of school director for some three years, in order to assist in maintaining good schools at Liberty. In 1882 he was elected county treasurer, and such is his high standing and popularity that he received more votes in the county than were cast for both his competitors combined. In September, 1874, he was married to Miss Belle Miller, a daughter of R. H. Miller, editor of the Liberty *Tribune*. Mrs. S. was educated at the Liberty Female College. They have two children: Robert W. and Emma S. Mr. S. is a business man of energy and enterprise, and one of the representative citizens of the county. He is a man of pleasant, agreeable

HISTORY OF CLAY COUNTY

presence, and more than ordinarily popular manners, both personally and as a county official.

ROCKWELL J. STONE

(Dealer in General Merchandise, Liberty).

Mr. Stone began mercantile life as a clerk. He served two years in that capacity in the store of M. & D. D. Miller, at Liberty. Subsequently he went to Montana, but returned in the fall of 1866. The following spring Mr. Stone engaged in the dry goods business at this place, opening a stock in the building which he but recently moved out of, and where he sold goods for 14 years, continuously. Last fall he erected a business house on the south side of the square, which he moved into after its completion and now occupies. This is one of the neatest and best business rooms at Liberty, and is specially arranged for handling dry goods. Mr. Stone has built up a good business, and now has an annual trade of about $30,000. He also carries a line of boots and shoes and lines of other goods usually found in a dry goods store. February 3, 1874, Mr. Stone was married to Miss Julia L. Withers, daughter of Abijah Withers, one of the pioneers of this county. Mrs. Stone is a graduate of Hughes' Female Seminary. They have five children : George, Edwin, Miller, Lee, and an infant son, Dudley Steele Stone. Mrs. S. is a member of the Christian Church. Mr. Stone is one of the well respected and influential citizens of Liberty, and has served two terms as mayor.

CLINTON TILLERY

(Collector of Clay County, Liberty).

That success in life and advancement in public affairs are not limited to those whose early advantages have been the best and whose opportunities would therefore seem to be the most favorable, is daily illustrated by the lives of the men who have come to the front as representative citizens of their respective communities. Beyond all question personal worth is the controlling influence that shapes every man's future character, energy, ability and the qualities that win success in life. Unless one have these he may have had all the early advantages to be desired and in his career may be favored with abundant means and the help of influential friends, but still he can not compete with another who has the characteristics mentioned, however unfavorable the latter's early advantages may have been.

In presenting a sketch of the subject whose names stands at the head of the preceding paragraph, we have the example of a man who has risen to enviable prominence in the community where he was reared, almost solely by his own exertions and personal worth. He was born in Clinton county, June 19, 1849, and was left an orphan by the death of his father when quite young. His father, Joel D. Tillery, who came to this State from Kentucky when a young man, in 1842, was married to Miss Letitia Gilliam, formerly of Alexandria,

HISTORY OF CLAY COUNTY

Va. They made their home in Clinton county, this State, where they resided until early in 1851, when the father joined the general movement to California in quest of gold. He never lived to return, but died on the Pacific coast.

The mother, after her husband started to California, came to Liberty. Clinton was two years old when his father left for California. Reared in Liberty, his youth was spent at school and at work in a woolen factory, principally. By attending the common and high schools he succeeded in getting a good common English education, which was supplemented by instruction at William Jewell College for one term.

In 1867 he obtained a situation as clerk in a grocery store, and he continued clerking for about four years. During this time, by economy he was enabled to accumulate a nucleus of means with which to begin in business for himself, which he accordingly did, opening a grocery store at this place. He conducted his grocery business with success for about five years, when he sold out to advantage and assumed the duties of county treasurer, to which he was elected. Meanwhile, however, in 1874, he was elected mayor of Liberty, he being at the time only 25 years of age, and the youngest mayor who ever held the office. Elected treasurer in 1876, as stated above, he subsequently held the office for three terms, by consecutive re-elections, and was then elected county collector in 1882 and still holds that position.

Mr. Tillery has bought a handsome farm adjoining Liberty and is engaging quite extensively in breeding, raising and dealing in fine thoroughbred short horn cattle. It is his purpose to retire from his office at the close of his present term and devote his entire time and attention to his farming and stock interests. He is a man of energy and progressive ideas, and will doubtless soon take a prominent position among the leading agriculturists of the county.

October 9, 1874, Mr. Tillery was married to Miss Flora H., a daughter of Judge William H. Lane of this county. They have five children: Augustus, Trigg T., Jennie, Harry and Mary. He and wife are members of the Christian Church, and he is a prominent member of the I. O. O. F.

JAMES R. TIMBERLAKE,

(Stock-dealer, Ex-Sheriff of Clay county and Proprietor of Livery Stable, Residence, Liberty).

Mr. Timberlake, one of the most efficient sheriffs this county ever had and a man who has done much for the promotion of law and order in this community, and now serving as Deputy United States Marshall, is a native Missourian, born in Platte county, March 22, 1846. His father, John Timberlake, a Kentuckian by birth, born in 1809, was married in that State to Patsy Noland, some time after which, in 1830, he came to Missouri, locating in the Platte Purchase, in what is now Platte county, where he bought land and improved a

HISTORY OF CLAY COUNTY

farm. He remained here until 1864, when, owing to the unsettled condition of affairs here on account of war troubles, he went to Illinois for a short time. Returning soon after to Platte county, he made it his home until purchasing a place in Clay county, upon which he resided from 1866 to 1880. At that date he took up his location in Jackson county, near Independence, where he at present is situated. His first wife died in Platte county. The life of James R. has been a very active one. He remained at the home farm until 1864, and when his father went to Illinois the son entered the Confederate army in 1864, in Col. Slayback's cavalry regiment. He became second lieutenant of Co. B, Shelby's brigade, and as such participated in a number of engagements. After the close of the war he accompanied Shelby and Price to Mexico (leaving Texas in April, 1865), and continued in that country until December, 1865, traveling entirely through the heart of Old Mexico to California, which was reached the same month. He remained in that State until the following summer and then returned to his home in Missouri, though choosing his residence in Clay county. For two or three years after this he was peacefully occupied in the pursuits of farming and stock-raising. In the meantime, in 1872, he made a trip to Texas and brought back a herd of cattle which he disposed of to good advantage in Kansas. In 1876 Mr. Timberlake was appointed constable of Liberty township and served for two years, and so well were the duties of that position discharged that, in 1878, when it became necessary to select someone to fill the office of sheriff of the county, no more suitable man could have been chosen for that position. He was elected and at the expiration of his term of service was honored with a re-election. His services while discharging his official duties were marked with a fearlessness and conscientiousness which characterized him a typical sheriff, and in proforming his work he met with the hearty approbation of all officers of the court and the people generally. After his retirement from office, Mr. Timberlake went to New Mexico and in company with his brother bought two ranches, upon which they have since been actively and successfully engaged in the stock business. In 1883 he was appointed Deputy U. S. Marshal for the Western District of Missouri, a position which he still holds. He is now interested in a livery stable and has one of the largest establishments of this kind in Missouri — a stable which would be a credit to any city of larger size. November 25, 1874, Mr. T. was married at Liberty to Miss Katie, daughther of Grafton Thomason, deceased, one of the pioneers of Clay county. She was born at Liberty, but received her education in Platte. Mr. Timberlake is a member of Liberty Lodge No. 43, I. O. O. F. His wife is connected with the Christian Church.

JACOB A. TRUMBO

(Farmer, Post-office, Liberty).

Mr. Trumbo, if called upon, could doubtless furnish valuable information in regard to the facts of the controversy recently going in the papers as to the disposition made of the treasure of the Confederate Government after the evacuation of Richmond. He was one of Mr. Davis' guard. He was also for a time on the body-guard of Gen. Breckinridge. As a matter of fact he was one of the guard that secreted the gold of the treasury after the collapse of the Confederate Government, but never knew what became of this golden treasure. The notes from which this sketch is written barely refer to the facts here stated, so that no other particulars can be given. But he is most probably in possession of most valuable information in regard to this point on which historians widely differ. Mr. Trumbo, in the early part of his services in the Confederate army, was under Gen. John S. Williams, the veteran commander who fought with such distinction at Cerre Gordo, in the Mexican War, that he was ever afterwards called Cerre Gordo Williams, as Scipio was called Scipio Africanus, for his distinguished exploits in Africa during the Punic Wars. Mr. Trumbo came to Missouri in 1877, and has been a resident of this county ever since, engaged in farming. He has a good place of 250 acres in the vicinity of Liberty. His farm, unfortunately, was in the course taken by the memorable cyclone of the 13th of May, 1883. Although he and family escaped without the loss of life, or the killing of any stock, his buildings were literally scattered to the four winds of the earth. Fragments of his barns and other buildings were carried a mile or a mile and a half away. Since then he has rebuilt and repaired what could be repaired, and now has his farm in good condition again. He was born in Bath county, Ky., October 24, 1845, and was reared in that county. His parents were Adam A. and Hannah Trumbo, both of early and respected Kentucky families. Mr. Trumbo was married December 23d, 1869, in Bath county Ky., to Miss Mary E. Bradshaw. She survived until March 23, 1883, leaving him four children at her death: Adam A., Sallie A., James F. and Maggie L. To his present wife Mr. Trumbo was married August 11, 1884. She was a Miss Fannie Jacobs, a daughter of Henry Jacobs, of Franklin county, Ky. Mrs. Trumbo, his present wife, is a member of the Christian Church. His first wife was a member of the M. E. Church.

WILLIAM W. WILLMOTT

(Dealer in Lumber, Doors, Sash, Lime, Etc., Etc., Liberty).

The Willmott family is an old and prominent one, both in this country and in England. Representatives of different branches of the family have risen to positions of distinction in both countries. There are different orthographies of the name, according to whether the *l* and *t* or both are double or single in the spelling. John Eardley Wilmot was chief justice of the Court of Common Pleas of England during the first half of the present century; and his son of the same name attained to great eminence as a chancery lawyer. They were from Derby, England, where the original stock of the family was located. Judge David Wilmot, of Pennsylvania, a United States Senator from that State, was a distinguished representative of the family in this country. He was the author of the famous Wilmot "Proviso," that was an exciting subject of discussion throughout the whole country during the slavery agitation. Branches of the family in this country settled both in Pennsylvania and Virginia. Col. Robert Willmott, the grandfather of the subject of this sketch, was a gallant officer under Washington in the War for Independence. He subsequently removed to Kentucky and became a prominent citizen of that State. He was a leading member of the first constitutional convention of Kentucky, and served with marked ability for a number of years in the State Legislature. His son, John F. Willmott, the father of the subject of this sketch, became a wealthy planter of Bourbon county, Ky. He married a Miss Harriet Skillman, formerly of Virginia, and reared a large family of children. Among these William W., the subject of this sketch, was the third child, and was born October 14, 1829. He was reared on his father's farm in that county, and in young manhood, March 2, 1858, was married to Miss Mary J. Breckinridge, a daughter of Perry Breckinridge, who was a cousin to one of the most brilliant men this country ever produced, Hon. John C. Breckinridge. Mr. Willmott, the subject of this sketch, removed to Missouri in 1872 and engaged in the manufacturing business at St. Louis. Three years later he removed to Baton Rouge, La., where he engaged in cotton planting. After an experince there of four years he came to Plattsburg, Mo., in the winter of 1879, and the following spring located at Liberty, where he bought a lumber yard already established at this place, which, in partnership with his son, W. Canby Willmott, he has ever since conducted. They have a large stock of lumber and other building materials. and are doing an excellent business. Mr. Willmott and wife are members of the Christian Church, as is also their son, W. Canby, the only child they ever reared.

GEORGE W. WYMORE

(Farmer and Stock-dealer, Post-office, Liberty).

Mr. Wymore's parents, Samuel and Eliza (Downing) Wymore, came to Liberty from Fayette county, Ky., in 1843. George W. was then a lad about 14 years of age, having been born January 14, 1829. His father was for many years in the meat market business at Liberty, and dealing in cattle, hogs, etc., to some extent. George W. was brought up to this business, and became a thorough judge of stock. When he reached his majority he, too, engaged in the meat market business, which he followed for several years. He then established a livery stable, afterwards known as the Thompson House stables, which he built and stocked. He was in the livery business for about 20 years, and during all this time made a specialty in dealing in horses and mules, in which he had good success. Mr. Wymore is accounted one of the best judges of this class of stock in the county. He takes a special pride in handling horses and mules, and can get up a saddle or harness animal in better shape and in less time than perhaps any other man in the county. Mr. Wymore also has a neat farm two and

HISTORY OF CLAY COUNTY

a half miles south of Liberty, a place of over 200 acres. December 6, 1848, he was married to Miss Sarah Francis, a daughter of Walker J. Turner, formerly from Kentucky. They have 11 children: John H., Lila, wife of John Donaldson; Charles W., Andrew P., Mamie, wife of Adrean Arnold; Walter, now in New Mexico; Oscar, Bettie, Thomas McC., "Colonel Doniphan," and Mattie P. Mrs. Wymore is a member of the Christian Church.

JOHN H. WYMORE

(Ex-Town Councilman, and Proprietor of Wymore's Meat Market, Liberty).

Mr. Wymore is a son of George W. Wymore, whose sketch precedes this, and is engaged in the same business in which his father was engaged for a number of years, and that his grandfather began at Liberty over 40 years ago — the meat market business. Mr. Wymore, Jr., the subject of this sketch, is a very energetic young man, and understands his business thoroughly. He commenced for himself several years ago, and has been quite successful. Probably no young man in the county is a better judge of beef cattle and other fatted stock than he. He makes his own purchases and does his own butchering, or has it done under his immediate direction, so that he is not only enabled to carry on his business with a thorough understanding of its details, but to judge correctly of the character and quality of his meat sold at his market. Knowing that a good name in business is of more value than even capital itself, he is very careful to preserve the reputation of his market and suffers no meat to go out under a false recommendation. This is one of the main secrets of his success. November 13, 1851, he was born at Liberty. His education was received at the common schools, the Liberty High School and William Jewell College. October 10, 1876, he was married to Miss Ida M. Pratt, a daughter of M. E. Pratt, formerly of Kentucky. They have four children: George, Frank, Garthum and Mabel.

MARTIN WYMORE

(Dealer in Groceries, Queensware, Glassware, Etc., Liberty).

A historical outline has already been given elsewhere in this volume in a biographical sketch of one of the other representatives of this family. One of the pioneer families of Clay county, its members have always occupied an enviable position here among the respected and worthy citizens of the county. Nor is the subject of the present sketch an exception to this rule. A man of energy and unquestioned personal worth, he is esteemed by all as one of the representative business men of Liberty. Mr. Wymore is a son of Samuel S. Wymore already referred to. He was born at Lexington, in Fayette county, Ky., December 22, 1838. His father being engaged in pork packing and butchering, in connection with farming and stock raising, young Wymore was brought up to these occupations. In 1858 he engaged in the butcher business, and kept a meat market at Liberty on his own account, and afterwards continued the business for over 20 years. Mr. Wymore was quite successful and accumulated a substantial nucleus of means. In 1879 he retired from the meat market business and butchering and established a grocery store at Liberty. His success in this has also been satisfactory. He has one of the leading houses in this line in this county, and does an annual business of about $35,000. In the spring of 1860 he was married to Miss Isabella, daughter of James Bratton (deceased), late of this county. Mrs. Wymore was educated at the high school of Missouri City. They have 10 children, six of whom are living: Gertrude, Jennie, Maggie, Bennie, Ernest and Annie. Martin and James died in infancy; Lela and Mary both died the present year (1884), Lela in August and Mary in September, the former at the age of 18, and the younger at the age of 15. Mr. and Mrs. Wymore are members of the Christian Church.

PETER YOUNG

(Farmer and Stock-raiser, Post-office, Liberty).

Mr. Young is one of the substantial citizens in a property point of view as well as otherwise, of Clay county, and is unqualifiedly a self-made man. Every dollar he is worth he has made by his own hard work, frugality and good business sense. He was born in Belgium, though of French parentage, October 30, 1838. His father, John Young and mother, whose maiden name was Catharine Kolar, were both natives of the Gaulic Land of Vines, but went to Belgium early in life, where they were married. From the latter country they emigrated to the United States in 1849, and settled in Wisconsin, where they made their permanent home. The father died there (Ozouka county) in 1871. Peter grew up in that county and went thence to southwestern Illinois, opposite St. Louis, where he made his home for some 25 years. There he was largely engaged in vegetable farming and hauled thousands of loads of produce into the Mound City. Commencing for himself when a boy as a day laborer, he finally accumulated a comfortable property. In December, 1882, he removed to Clay county and bought the farm where he now resides, an excellent place of 200 acres, a mile and a half from Liberty. He also had 50 acres in another tract near by, and a farm in Jefferson county of 160 acres. January 27, 1866, he was married in Madison county, Ill., to Miss Annie, a daughter of Christian Smith, of Montgomery county, that State, but formerly of Darmstadt, Germany. They have eight children: Lizzie, John, Peter, Annie, Mar, Dora, William and Clara.

HISTORY OF CLAY COUNTY

CHAPTER XIV.

FISHING RIVER TOWNSHIP.

Position and Description — Early History, First Settlers, etc. — Voters at First Election in Township — Country Churches — Missouri City — Its Origin, Founder and Subsequent Career — Known formerly as Richfield — Murder of Wiley Herndon — Killing of two men named Titus by G. S. Elgin — Churches and Lodges in Missouri City — History of Excelsior Springs — When Surveyed and Started — Buildings Erected — Its Prosperity during 1881 — Incorporation — The Springs — The Medicinal and Healing Properties which They Possess — Churches at Excelsior Springs — G. A. R. Lodge — Prathersville — Location, etc. — Fishing River Baptist Church — Biographical.

POSITION AND DESCRIPTION.

Comprising the entire southeastern portion of Clay, Fishing River township is one of the most important municipal townships in the county. There are within its boundaries about 72 square miles, embracing one entire congressional township (52–30) and fractional parts of three others. Its legal boundary line begins on the county line between Ray and Clay, at the northest corner of section 1–52–30, and runs thence south to the Missouri river; thence up the river to the section line dividing sections 2 and 3, in township 50–31; thence due north to the northwest corner of section 14–52–31; thence east two miles, to the range line between ranges 30 and 31; thence north two miles to the township line between townships 52 and 53; thence east along the township line to the beginning.

The entire township, except the bottom lands, is rolling and broken. Along the Missouri river the alluvial lands comprise, in the extreme southeastern and southwestern parts of the township, a considerable extent of country. Near Missouri City the bluffs come up to the river and leave scant room between it and their base for the track of the Wabash Railroad. For miles up the river these bluffs, which are of the character known as mural, present their huge battlements against the encroachments of the river, protecting the country and presenting a picturesque and imposing appearance.

The nothern portion of the township is rolling and generally elevated. Many sections are rocky and the soil sterile and unimproved. Some of the bottom lands along Fishing river below Prathersville are as yet unreclaimed, being very low and even swampy. Doubtless the

374

HISTORY OF CLAY COUNTY

cutting away of the heavy timbers with which they are covered would do much towards their redemption. The western portion of the township contains some splendid farms in a most advanced state of improvement and cultivation.

Fishing river, from which the township takes its name, and its branches drain the northern portion of the township; Rush creek the southwestern, and Cooley's Lake, a nearly semi-circular body of water, nearly three miles in length, is in the southeastern. The latter is famous as a resort for hunters and fishers, and though abounding in fish at all seasons, and in all kinds of water-fowl in the spring and fall, there have been times within the memory of many when it went dry.

EARLY HISTORY.

Fishing River was one of the first permanently settled townships in Clay county. In the fall of 1820, David McElwee and his good wife, Mary, came with their family from Warren county, Tenn., to section 34–52–30, about a mile north of the head of Cooley's Lake. Patrick Laney, an Irishman by birth, but a Tennesseean by adoption, and his wife Jane, came with McElwee and settled half a mile northwest of the latter. Mrs. Margaret Howdeshell, a daughter of McElwee, who came with her father to Missouri, and yet lives, with a memory of early days unimpaired, states that when her father came to his settlement the nearest settlers to him were the Gilmores, Smith and Hill, on Rush creek, mentioned in the sketch of Liberty township.

In the winter of 1820–21, Thos. Officer settled one mile east of McElwee. Mr. Officer and James and Alexander Woolard located north of Fishing river, but in a year or two moved back to Kentucky. David and Wm. Lisles, brothers and unmarried, came with the Woolards, lived with them, and left the country with them. In the spring of 1821, Elisha and John Camron came to section 31–52–30, three miles north or northeast of where Missouri City now stands. John Camron was a widower, and his death, which occurred in the summer of 1821, is believed to have been the first that ever occurred in the county, of which an American settler was the subject. The body was buried on Judge Elisha Camron's farm.

Also, in the spring of 1821, two men named Spicer and Vickery settled on section 23–52–30, two miles or more southeast of Prathersville. Wm. and Thos. Slaughter settled in the forks of Fishing river nor far from Mt. Pleasant Church, in the spring of 1822. Ebenezer Price and Napoleon Price settled in the vicinity of Prathersville about the same time. Sam Oliver, who settled on section 26, was another early settler who came in 1821, but didn't like the country and returned to Kentucky in a year or two.

In the fall of 1821, after the fight with the Indians at David McElwee's, narrated elsewhere (see chapter I), the settlers in the country put up block houses into which they could retreat and "fort up," on the approach of danger. One of these "forts" or block houses stood on Elisha Camron's land; another was at the Gilmores', on Rush creek, near Liberty; and another was at old Martin Palmer's, on section 1–51–30, half a mile from Cooley's Lake, and just under the bluff, on the Camden road. Happily there was never any occasion for the use or occupation of these places of refuge.

The first wedding in Clay county occurred in the spring of 1821, under a sugar tree, a quarter of a mile east of Palmer's fort. The contracting parties were Cornelius Gilliam and Mary Crawford, and it is said that old Col. Martin Palmer, the "Ring-tailed Painter," performed the ceremony. Mary Crawford was an orphan, who was reared by Mrs. Mary Poteet, a sister of Elijah Smith, who lived on Rush creek. "Neil" Gilliam was afterwards sheriff of this county, State Senator, etc., and a gallant officer in the Florida War.

Rev. Finis Clark, a Baptist, was the first preacher in the country, and held the first services in the settlement along Rush creek, at private houses. Drs. Conley and May, of Liberty, were the first physicians who practiced in the township. There was considerable sickness in the county in 1820–21–22, and many of the pioneers became disgusted and disheartened, and soon returned to their former homes.

There was an abundance of game in the country in early days. Many of the hunters along Fishing river frequently went on excursions to the prairies, up in what is now Clinton county, to kill elk, which were numerous and easily caught when chased into the timber. The formidable antlers of the bucks hindered their progress through the brush, and it was not difficult to come up with them. Deer were plenty, and at first the principal article of flesh food was venison.

Bears were rather scarce. The hunters soon drove them out. One night "Neil" Gilliam, who then lived south of Liberty, heard a bear among his hogs. Running hastily out, barefoot and in his home-spun underwear, he caught up an ax and assaulted the beast, expecting to either kill it or drive it away. The bear ran and "Neil" ran after it. It was cold weather, but in his excitement Gilliam followed it, so the old settlers say, *eight miles*, or to Cooley's Lake, where he over-

HISTORY OF CLAY COUNTY

took it and killed it. Mr. Thomas Pevely supplied Gillam with clothing, a pair of shoes, trousers and a coat to return home.

At the first election held in Clay county, in August, 1822, the following were the voters in Fishing River township, which at that time, however, comprised the entire eastern half of the county, although a majority of the voters lived in what is now Fishing River: —

Pleasant Adams,
Joshua Adams,
Howard Averett,
William Averett,
Zach Averett,
Matthew Averett,
James Allen,
Shubael Allen,
John Bartleson,
John Boyles,
James Buckraye,
James Collins,
William Collins,
James Carroll,
John Carroll,
John Collier,
Jonathan Camron,
Elisha Camron,
Abram Cotts,
Absalom Cornelius,
John Cornelius,
Benjamin Cornelius,
Joseph Crockett,
David Crockett,
John Chapman,
Jonathan Denton,
William Davis, Sr.,
William Davis,
James Dagley,
Jeffrey Fletcher,
Berryman Gwinn,
Isham Grooms,
Robert Gillam,
Henry Greene,

Lewis Greene,
Bailey O. George,
John Hardwicke,
Alex. Hardwicke,
Lewis Hardwicke,
James E. Hall,
Edward V. Hall,
Samuel Hyatt,
Robert Hutchins,
Smith Hutchins,
William Hutchins,
Moses Hutchins,
Joseph Hutchins,
Samuel Hensley,
David Holmes,
George Huffaker,
James James,
John Livingston,
William Livingston,
John Linville,
Patrick Laney,
John Lincoln,
William Lenhart,
John Ledgwood,
William Martin,
Andrew Means,
Berryman Munkers,
William Munkers,
Richard Munkers,
James Munkers,
Isaac McCroskey,
Robert McCoy,
Jacob McCoy,

Alex Newman,
James Officer,
Thomas Officer,
Nehemiah Odle,
James Page,
Robert Page,
Thomas Peebley,
Nathaniel Powell,
Martin Palmer,
Humphrey Pritt,
Edward Pyburne,
Jonathan Roberts,
Jonas Roberts,
Nicholas Roberts,
Edward Roberts,
John Roberts,
Jere Rose,
Jonathan Reed,
Page Stanley,
Terah Smith,
A. Smith,
William Shelton,
Wilson Spencer,
John Thompson,
John Toplenure,
John Trotter,
John Vesser,
Samuel Vesser,
James Williams,
William D. Williams,
John Wilson,
Peter Writesman,
Benedict Welden.

The judges of this election were Elisha Camron, James Munkers and John Hutchins. The clerks were George Huffaker and James Officer. The votes of William Erastus and James Henry were rejected.

CHURCHES.

Erin Church — In the southeast corner of the southwest quarter of

377

HISTORY OF CLAY COUNTY

section 24, in Fishing River township, was organized October 16, 1877, with Joseph Turner, James M. Hill, Simon Hutchings, Marion Harris, Nancy Hutchings, Sarah Thurney, Susan M. Harris, Nancy Lewis, Mary E. Wyatt and Sarah E. Summers as its original members. The present membership is about 42. The names of the ministers who have served this church as pastors are Revs. Joseph Prather and Lafayette Munkers. The present frame church was erected in 1878 at a cost of $1,000. A grave-yard is connected with this property, in which 250 interments have been made.

Pleasant Hill Baptist Church. — In 1857 T. N. O'Bryan with four members, Jefferson Turner and wife, Elizabeth Free and Jane Quick, organized the above named church. At first meetings were held in school-house No. 1, and, in fact, until 1883, when a church building was erected in section 23, four and a half miles southeast of Liberty, the cost of which was about $600. Rev. Watson is now pastor of the membership, which numbers about 25.

German M. E. Church, — Located on section 14, four miles southeast of Liberty, was constituted an organization in 1847, by Rev. Henry Hogrefe, with the following original members: William Unger and wife, George Elliott and wife, Peter Elliott, Jacob Weber and wife, Henry Free and wife, Rudolph Irminger and wife, Samuel Weber and wife. In 1870 a church house, 22x32, was erected at an expenditure of $900. After Mr. Hogrefe, who was the first pastor, came the Revs. Elders Neidermeier, Rouse, William Shreck, Holzbeierlein, Muehlenbrock, William Maye, Prege, Brunly, Brinkmeier, Steinmeier, Bower, Menger, Eichenberger, Korphage, Buchholz, Koenig, and Rev. Kaltenbach, the present incumbent. The present membership of the church is 32. Mr. John Weber is superintendent of the Sabbath school of 20 scholars.

Mount Zion Baptist Church — Was organized in April, 1853, its constituent members being John G. Price, William B. Hoges, James T. Withers, William H. Price, James Munkers, Thomas Holdes, Daniel H. Sans, Thomas Y. Gill, George H. McNealy, Elizabeth L. McNealy, Louisana Hogen, Sarah E. Withers, Amanda Mosby, Agnes Munkers, Susan G. Withers, Margaret S. Gaur, America Price, Julia Gill and Martha Withers. The present membership is 29. Those who have served as pastors are Elders William H. Price, Henry Hill, William T. Brown and James Duvall. The present brick church building was erected in 1853, at a cost of about $1,500. This was the first brick church built in the county outside of Liberty. It is located on the northeast corner of the southeast quarter of section 30, township 52, range 30. James P. Withers and William Price are the only male members living that were members at the constitution, and Amanda Mosby and Mrs. T. P. Withers were the only female members.

Mount Pleasant Church — Was organized September 18, 1830. The original members were Joseph P. Moore, William B. Slaughter, Andrew B. Baldwin, Abram (a servant of J. P. Moore), Jonah Moore, Elizabeth Slaughter, Jane Welton, Mary Storz, Jane Posey, Mary Baldwin, Lucy (a servant of James P. Moore), and Catherine (a servant of William B. Slaughter). The present membership is about 25. Elder Newton is the present pastor. The present frame church was built in 1879, its cost being about $1,500. It is located on the southeast corner of the northwest quarter of section 15.

Woodland Christian Church — Was organized in about 1870 or 1872. Some of the first members were James M. Bohart, Richard P. Funk, Solomon Welton, J. W. Bradley and A. J. Roberts. The present membership is about 100. The names of the ministers who have served this church are Elders Josiah Waller, Baird Waller, Wm. Stephens, John Perkins, J. Trader, and Revs. Williamson and Akers. The church building is a frame, and was erected in 1872, its cost being about $2,000. It is located on the east half of the northwest quarter of section 29, in township 52, range 30. Near this church is a cemetery.

Zoar German M. E. Church. — This church was organized in 1845 by Rev. Heinrich Nuelsen. The original members were Rudolph Irminger, Susanna Irminger, John Irminger, Heinrich Irminger, Elizabeth Irminger, Anna Irminger, Samuel Weber, Henry Weber, Jacob Weber, Maria Weber and Margaret Frey. The pastors that have served this church have been the same as those of Bethel German M. E. Church, both churches being under the same charge. The church building is a frame, and was erected in 1873 at a cost of $700. The present membership is 33. The Sabbath-school superintendent is John Weber.

MISSOURI CITY.

The origin of the town of Missouri City was the establishment, at the mouth of Rose's branch, about 1834, of what was called Williams' Landing. The founder, Shrewsbury Williams, built a large house in which he lived, kept tavern and sold a few goods for some years. He also owned and operated a ferry across the Missouri. When travelers got off the steamboats at his landing Mr. Williams en-

HISTORY OF CLAY COUNTY

tertained them, and though his house was not regularly equipped as a hotel, it was considered and termed a " tavern."

In the year 1840 Eli Casey brought a stock of goods to Williams' Landing and opened a small store, with Linneus B. Sublette, now of Missouri City, and Dr. Frank Cooley as his clerks. Old Wiley Herndon came about the same time and kept a small store. In 1846 there were about a dozen houses at the mouth of the branch, including James Riggs' hotel, and the place was called Richfield. Some time afterwards Bell, of Brunswick, put up a large tobacco factory and warehouse at Richfield, placing them in charge of L. B. Sublette and Scales as his clerks. Hundreds of tons of tobacco were purchased and shipped from this point.

In about 1844 the shipping current of the Missouri began the formation of a bar in front of old Richfield, interfering and preventing the landing of steamboats, and a joint stock company, composed of Graham L. Hughes, John Shouse, John Keller and others laid out a town just below, but mainly on the top of the high bluff overlooking the Missouri, which they called St. Bernard, probably after the famous Alpine mountain, which they fancied it resembled. The company erected a large two-story hotel on the top of the bluff, which may have been likened to St. Bernard's famous Hospice, only there were no dogs to hunt for travelers, and no hooded monks to care for them. Afterwards John S. Houston sold goods in this house, and was the first postmaster. The post-office was called St. Bernard.

Just below and adjoining St. Bernard was a tract of land which had been entered in the name of Abram Fry, who sold it to Stothard, who sold it to Wm. L. Smith, who sold it to John G. Price and G. W. Withers, who laid out another town, which they called Richfield.[1] Then Thos. Williams, a son of Shrewsbury Williams, bought a tract of land of his father just east of Richfield, and laid out a village which he called Atchison, in honor of Hon. D. R. Atchison. Thos. Williams sold a portion of his land to R. G. Gilmer, who laid out Gilmer's addition.

Mr. Gilmer established the first store east of the hill. Pres. N. Edwards, B. W. Nowlin and — Lomax were other early merchants in Richfield. Thos. Y. Gill built the first hotel, which was afterwards kept by Mrs. Elizabeth Hardwicke. March 14, 1859, the three towns of St. Bernard, Richfield and Atchison were incorporated by the Legislature as one and called Missouri City.

Richfield had been incorporated by the county court November 5,

---

[1] This may be considered *New* Richfield, as the hamlet which stood at the mouth of Rose's branch is remembered as *Old* Richfield.

380

1855, the first board of trustees being composed of Wm. Owens, L. W. Burris, R. G. Gilmer, J. S. Story and Daniel Gano.

From 1850 to 1861 Richfield was probably the largest hemp market above Lexington. Withal it was an important shipping point, and annually thousands of tons of freight, produce and merchandise were taken on and discharged by the steamboats, one or more of which, during the boating season, daily landed at the wharf. Sometimes produce came from as far north as the Iowa line, and goods were landed here for merchants doing business in Gentry, DeKalb and Andrew counties. Robert G. Gilmer and John D. Holt were in partnership in the business of general merchandising, and their transactions amounted to many tens of thousands of dollars annually. There were two mammoth warehouses for the reception of hemp, tobacco and other produce and the storage of freight, which were generally well filled.

The Civil War prostrated Missouri City, closed many of its stores, shut up its warehouses, carried off many of its citizens, and at times it was at the mercy of predatory bushwhackers and jayhawkers, who did not hesitate to take advantage of its defenseless condition and " raid " it.

When Fernando Scott's bushwhackers (among whom was Frank James) killed Capt. Sessions and Lieut. Grafenstein, in May, 1863 (See Chapter IX.), they charged into town. Coming upon the wounded Federal of the Twenty-fifth Missouri who had been taken into Mrs. Hardwick's hotel, they fired at him as he lay upon a lounge, and put several revolver balls into his body. Mrs. Hardwick interposed her own person between the wounded soldier and his would-be murderers, and strove hard to save him, but the bushwhackers thrust her aside and kept up their brutal work until they believed they had " finished " their victim, who feigned death, and though riddled with bullets, eventually recovered. Some time afterward this soldier accompanied his command on an expedition up the Missouri, the troops being conveyed on a steamboat. When the boat reached Missouri City it landed, and numbers of the soldiers ran ashore to " clean out the town " as they declared. The soldier was one of the first to jump ashore, and running to Mrs. Hardwick's hotel he asserted that not a thing about the premises should be molested. "These people were kind to me once," he said, " and I remember them." His efforts in behalf of the benefactress were of avail; she was not disturbed, and the soldier was instrumental in repressing the general disorderly conduct of his comrades.

HISTORY OF CLAY COUNTY

In the fall of 1854, at the time of the Price raid, a Confederate soldier, named Stallings, who had come up from Arkansas with the invading army, made his way to his home in this county in the bottoms, below Missouri City, on a brief furlough. While at home he was made a prisoner by a scouting party of Clinton county militia, under Capt. McMichael. He was guarded in Missouri City that night, and the next morning the militia started with him for Liberty, but a little west of Missouri City he was taken off a short distance from the road and shot. It is said that the shooting was done either by Capt. McMichael himself, or in his presence and by his express orders. Stallings was not a bushwhacker but a regular Confederate soldier, and his murder was certainly inexcusable.

Since the war, and especially since the building of the Wabash Railroad, in 1868, Missouri City has improved in extent at least. Two or three additions have been laid out and partly occupied. Lying under a high steep bluff, on a narrow bottom, continually becoming narrower by the encroachments of the river, the situation of the town is not favorable. The one long street passing through on which nearly all the business houses are situated presents a busy aspect at times, however.

Upon the the first establishment of Richfield a Union church was built, in which all denominations had the privilege of worshiping. This was torn down. The M. E. Church South and Christian Churches were built before the war. During the war the Federal troups stationed here were quartered in the Christian Church.

Old Wiley Herndon, mentioned as one of the first storekeepers in Richfield, was murdered some time before the war, and it is believed that his body was robbed of a considerable sum of money. The body was found tied and gagged, and the fatal wound had been delivered in the temple with some sharp instrument. Herndon was an old bachelor, and lived alone in his grocery. A young man named Book, an engineer in John G. Price's rope factory, who slept in his engine room, was arrested on a charge of the murder, but acquitted on preliminary examination.

Another tragedy that occurred in Missouri City was the killing, in November, 1866, of two men named Titus, by one G. S. Elgin. After the killing Elgin fled to the residence of his father-in-law, near Weston. Here he was overtaken by John C. Titus, Noah Titus and John Bivens, relatives of the men he had killed at Missouri City, taken out and murdered. All the parties to the latter killing were indicted in Platte county, and for safe-keeping were placed in the Liberty

382

HISTORY OF CLAY COUNTY

jail, from which they escaped in the spring of 1867, by blowing open the jail door.

CHURCHES.

Missouri City M. E. Church South — Was organized in 1854 with the following as original members: O. P. Gash and wife; Joseph A. Huffaker, wife and one sister; Mr. and Mrs. Crasford, and Mr. Bratten and wife, and some five or six others whose names can not now be recalled. Rev. M. R. Jones, who organized this church, was the first preacher in charge. Next came Rev. Rich, followed successively by Revs. L. M. Lewis, Mayhew, McEwing, W. A. Tarwater, Samuel Huffaker, Wilson, Wilburn Rush, Joseph Devlin, E. F. Bone, Babcock, W. C. Campbell, F. Shores, L. F. Linn, W. B. Johnson, W. E. Dockery and last J. F. Frazer. The number of the present membership is about 80. The frame church building in which services are held, was constructed at a cost of about $2,000, in the summer of 1857. In 1882–83 it was remodeled at an additional expense of about $1,500. The Sabbath-school has been flourishing since 1867, at which time Joseph A. Huffaker was superintendent. E. P. Donovan now holds that position. The average attendance is about 60.

Missouri City Christian Church. — This church, as its name indicates, is located at Missouri City, where on Main street there was built in about 1859, at an expense of some $2,500, a good brick edifice, in which the present membership of about 150 persons worship. As organized in about the year 1856, the members were E. D. Bell and wife, T. C. Reed and wife, Nancy Reed and two daughters, Richard Funk and wife, B. F. Melon and wife, George W. Bell and wife, Merritt Fisher and wife and Milton Hull. Rev. Richard Morton, who was prominent in this formation, was the first pastor, and he was succeeded by Revs. F. R. Palmer, J. W. Waller, Preston Akers, Bayard Waller, Henry Davis, Jacob Hugley, Revs. Perkins and Carter, the present pastor in charge. E. M. Grubbs is superintendent of the Sunday-school, which has an average attendance of about 70.

ANGRONA LODGE NO. 193, A. F. & A. M.

The dispensation of this lodge was issued in March, 1858, under which it worked until May 28, 1859, when a charter was issued. The first members and officers were A. L. Chapman, master; Jno. W. Collins, senior warden; Newton Fields, junior warden; T. Everett, secretary; S. Elgin, treasurer; R. H. Moore, senior deacon; Wm. Adams, junior deacon; T. Y. Gill, stewart and tyler; J. M. Allcorn, John A. Prather, Joshua Vaughn, S. Charlston, J. Johnson, John Linn, J. M. Donovan, Victor W. Tooley, D. E. Yarbrough.

EXCELSIOR SPRINGS.

The site of Excelsior Springs was first improved and redeemed from its primeval condition by an old Mormon immigrant some 40 years ago. In time the little narrow valley along the east fork of Fishing river, on which the town stands, became a wheat field. For many years the people of the vicinity had known that a mineral spring ran out from the north bank of the creek, but they had never believed that it possessed remarkable curative powers. They called the water "copperas water." This spring is the one now called Excelsior Spring.

According to an historical and descriptive pamphlet issued by the town company in 1882, Excelsior Spring was discovered in June, 1880, and found by the merest accident to possess medicinal properties. Harvesters engaged in cutting wheat where the town now stands found a stream of clear cold water issuing from the bank of Fishing river, and remarked that there was a mineral taste to it. A negro standing by, who was badly afflicted with scrofula, heard the ensuing discussion on the healing qualities of mineral springs, and resolved to try the water of this one on himself.

A few weeks' use of the water effected a complete cure, to the great astonishment of all who knew the circumstances of his case.

Other persons in the neighborhood, afflicted with various ailments, were also induced by a vague hope to try the water, and it was found to be equally efficacious in rheumatism, liver complaints, diseases of the kidneys and bladder, dyspepsia and piles.

The fame of the spring was noised abroad, until the attention of J. V. B. Flack, D. D., a prominent minister of Missouri City, was called to the matter. He listened to the various statements of cures effected, examined the spring, and became sufficiently interested to have an analysis of the water made by Wright & Merrill, of St. Louis.

Chemistry showed that the mineral properties of the water were those to which science has always attributed the greatest curative power. The evidence was strong enough to convince the most skeptical. In the meantime the tidings had spread from farm to village, and from village to city, until, before the close of the season, hundreds of invalids were encamped among the neighboring groves and quartered with the hospitable farmers

Dr. Flack advised the owner of the land, Mr. A. W. Wyman, to lay out a town and sell such of his property as would be needed for the accommodation of health seekers; and finally, becoming part proprietor, he undertook the management of the new enterprise.

HISTORY OF CLAY COUNTY

The town was surveyed about September 1, 1880, by County Surveyor Thomas B. Rogers.

The first building of any kind in the place was a small confectionery, a "peanut stand," conducted by James Pierson. The second building was Flynn's grocery store. The first general store building was put up by Dr. Flack in the winter of 1880 and 1881, and the store was opened in February of the latter year with a $2,000 stock. The building is still standing, on the northwest corner of Broadway and Main street. The second store was M. G. Froman's, on the west side of Main street. The first hardware store was owned by Stapp & Snapp, and conducted by the junior partner, J. W. Snapp.

The first hotel was the "Cottage Home," built by Mr. Riggs, on the west side of Broadway and Main, in the fall of 1880. The "Excelsior House" was completed in the spring of 1881 by Joe Wert and A. W. Wyman. Mr. Wert was the first landlord.

The first school was taught in the spring of 1881 by Mrs. Robert Caldwell and Miss Susie Hyatt in a shed-room owned by Mr. Prather. Some time in the fall of 1880 Dr. Flack preached the first sermon and conducted the first religious services in a grove near town. Near the same time (fall of 1880) there was a large political meeting in the grove, in the creek bottom, which was conducted under the auspices of the Democrats. It was during the famous Allen-Crisp contest, and Col. Crisp, Judge Dunn and Dr. Flack were among the speakers. The post-office was established in March, 1881, and was at first and for about two years thereafter called Viginti, instead of Excelsior Springs. The first postmaster was J. B. Holton; the second, D. O. McCray.

In the spring of 1881 a boom was begun in Excelsior Springs, and kept up during the summer. Indeed, the town was built nearly to its present proportions within a year after it started. In the spring of 1882 a Union Church was built, the first in the place. Here all denominations united in religious services under the Christian Union organization, with Rev. J. V. B. Flack, D. D., as pastor. The organization now has a membership of 180. A Sabbath-school in connection — Dr. G. W. Fraker superintendent — has about 100 scholars. The Baptist church was partially built in the fall of 1884. It is not yet entirely completed. The opera-house was built in the spring of 1882.

The first child born in Excelsior Springs was Rolla Holt, a son of Mr. and Mrs. P. G. Holt. The first death was that of a traveling man in the spring of 1881. He was an invalid, and came to the

HISTORY OF CLAY COUNTY

springs for temporary relief, — and obtained relief from all earthly ills. The first physician was Dr. S. T. Bassett, of Richmond, formerly of St. Louis, and who now resides in Richmond.

In the spring of 1881 the hack running between Vibbard, on the Wabash Railroad, and Excelsior Springs was robbed three miles east of Excelsior by a band of brigands, suppose to be connected with the James boys' gang. Less than $50 in money and a few watches, etc., were taken from the few passengers. The incident was widely reported in the public press and served to advertise the springs, and so in the end was of more advantage to the town than detriment.

February 7, 1881, Excelsior Springs was incorporated by the county court as a village, the site comprising all of the northeast quarter of the southwest quarter of section 1, township 52, range 30 — 40 acres in all. The first trustees were William Riggs, J. D. Graham, W. C. Corum, L. P. Garrett and W. B. Smith. Kugler's addition comprises the northwest quarter of the southeast quarter, and Farris, Dunn & Isley's part of the southeast quarter of the southwest quarter of the same section.

July 12, 1881, the town was incorporated under the law as a city of the fourth class. The first officers were: Mayor, E. Smith; clerk, J. C. Dickey; aldermen from the First ward, N. L. Rice and J. C. Dickey; aldermen from the Second ward, Phil. G. Holt and L. W. Garrett; marshal, J. D. Halferty; attorney, John H. Dunn. These officers, with the exception of the attorney, served through 1882. J. L. Sheets was attorney in 1882.

In 1883 the officers were: Mayor, John H. Dunn; clerk, J. L. Sheets; aldermen, first ward, J. W. Snapp and J. V. B. Flack; aldermen, second ward, R. B. Clevenger and Thomas L. Hope; marshal, Aaron Roberts; attorney, E. Smith.

In 1884 the officers chosen were: Mayor, C. L. Cravens; clerk and attorney, E. A. Benson; aldermen, First ward, P. G. Holt and J. W. Snapp; aldermen, Second ward, H. C. Fish and D. O. McCray; marshal, J. M. Odell; treasurer, J. S. Prather.

The city has an indebtedness of $1,600 all funded. Its population in 1883 was given as 1,375, and is now *estimated* at 1,500. The school district contains 258 scholars. The school is at present taught in the Baptist Church; two teachers are employed. The district expects to build a new school-house the present season, costing $5,000. The town expects confidently to, within a year or a little more, become a point on the St. Joseph and Southeastern Railroad (narrow gauge), and has hopes of becoming a station on some other railway coming from the East and connecting with the Hannibal and St. Joseph.

The springs are four in number — the Excelsior, the Saratoga, the Relief, and the Empire — and are situated in the three angles of the little valley forming the site of the town. The Excelsior is a clear, cold stream of water, strongly impregnated with gas, and issues with considerable power and volume from the rocks. The temperature of the water is about 52°, at all seasons, and the flow is computed at the rate of 100 barrels a day. Relief spring is strongly magnetic, so that a blade of steel immersed in it for some minutes becomes sufficiently charged to attract a needle. The Empire and Saratoga are similar to the others.

Chemical analysis has shown that these waters are strongly charged with iron, alumina, soluble silica, chlorides and carbonates of magnesia, lime and sodium, altogether about 25 grains to the gallon; besides this there is a large volume of gas which has not yet been measured. The subtle laws of chemistry are, however, unable to explain the origin of the medical virtues, or unfold the secret of this wonder-working agent, which has restored to perfect health many sufferers who had been pronounced by the medical profession to be beyond all hope of recovery.

Experience has proven by hundreds of actual tests that, while the water is not a panacea for all the ills that flesh is heir to, it will benefit and cure many diseases that are both obstinate and prevalent. Rheumatism, scrofula, ulcers, gout, neuralgia, dyspepsia, liver complaints, kidney and bladder diseases, are acted upon by these waters as by magic, and often entirely cured in the short space of two or three weeks. Sore eyes, various diseases of the skin, piles, many forms of female diseases, chronic malaria, chronic diarrhœa, general debility and nervous prostration, have all been treated with marvelous results. The leading qualities of the water are alterative, tonic, highly soothing, and anti-irritant. In cases of deranged liver its alterative properties are very marked, and in that form of dyspepsia attended with restless, sleepless nights, its soothing effects are simply marvelous. In cases of irritated membranes, whether of bowels or lungs, its anti-irritant action is also eminently conspicuous. The large proportion of iron in the water renders it especially useful as a tonic, all cases of great debility and prostration of the system, from whatever cause, being speedily benefited by these waters, which are so refreshing and restorative that a good appetite is proverbially one of the first acquisitions of the many who visit the springs.

HISTORY OF CLAY COUNTY

CHURCHES.

Christian Union Church — Located at Excelsior Springs, was organized February 8, 1881. The names of a few of its original members were as follows: J. V. B. Flack, D. D., M. S. Flack, Rev. L. H. Worthington, Mary Worthington, Sampson Glasscock, L. Worthington, I. N. Williams, P. G. Holt, L. P. Garrett, Dr. S. T. Bassett, Laura Williams, Gideon Stein, O. Harris, P. Hedges, Lide Crowley, Bettie Shackelford and Annie Barger. One hundred and sixty communicants compose the present membership. Rev. J. V. B. Flack is its pastor. The present frame church was built in 1881 at a cost of about $2,000. There are 100 scholars in the Sabbath-school, its superintendent being Sampson Glasscock.

This is an unsectarian church adhering to the fundamental and essential truths of the Bible as their basis of operation. Any and every Christian can harmoniously co-operate with this church.

Excelsior Springs Baptist Church (Fishing River township) — Was organized in February, 1884, at the Opera House, its original members being Hiram Mathews and wife, Berryman Garrett, Mrs. Holt, William Dillon and wife, Robert Minter, Albert Campbell and wife, Austin Boone, L. Shipp and James Huey and wife. The present membership numbers about 60. This church was organized by Revs. W. A. Croach and S. J. Norton. Its present pastor is Rev. M. P. Hunt. This congregration is having a frame church building erected, which will soon be completed, its cost being about $11,000. There are 80 scholars in the Sabbath-school, its superintendent being E. Messick.

Grand Army of the Republic — Post 211, Department of Missouri, G. A. R., was organized by C. N. Burnham, of Cameron, October 2, 1884. W. E. Benson, post commander; C. N. Perkins, senior vice-commander; —— Clevinger, junior vice-commander; —— Killgrove, chaplain; Austin Boone, quartermaster; C. Overman, officer of the guard; —— Odell, officer of the day; J. Combs, adjutant. The opera hall of Excelsior Springs is the place of meeting of this post.

PRATHERSVILLE.

The little hamlet of Prathersville was established about the year 1870. Rev. J. A. Prather, a Presbyterian minister, built a steam mill on Williams' branch, near where it empties into Fishing river, and soon after some stores and shops were put up. A church was built by the Presbyterians and Baptists, and in time the village came to have twenty or more houses. Its nick-name, " Shoo Fly," was given it in derision of its small size and general insignificance, but the

388

locality is a pleasant one, the country surrounding first-class, and it is not impossible that some day the village will be of considerable importance.

Fishing River Baptist Church — Situated at Prathersville, was organized in about 1868. Its constituent members were L. T. Pettz, P. G. Smith, N. H. King, Richard King, Thomas W. Wilson, Nancy Wilson, John McCracken and Martin Price. The present membership is about 85. The ministers who have served as pastors to this church are Revs. John Harmon, William Ferguson, S. H. Carter, T. H. Graves, Dr. Rothwell, Asa N. Bird and S. J. Norton. The present frame structure was erected in 1874, at a cost of $700. The number of scholars in the Sabbath-school is 60, H. H. Ring being the superintendent.

BIOGRAPHICAL.

ANDREW R. ALLCORN

(Dealer in Drugs, Books, Stationery, Etc., Missouri City).

Mr. Allcorn is a son of James M. Allcorn, well known to all, and was born in this county, August 1, 1850. He was principally reared at Missouri City, and received a good common school education. In youth he learned the carpenter's trade under his father, and afterwards followed it for about eight years. While engaged in that he worked for a time in the southern part of this State. Returning to Missouri City in the summer of 1870, he remained during the fall and then went to Colorado, spending about two years and a half after that in that Territory and in Arizona and Wyoming. In 1873 he came back to Missouri City and has been a resident of this city ever since, except during two years spent in business at Lawson, in Ray county. In December, 1878, he engaged in the drug business at Missouri City on his own account, having previously had nearly five years' experience as clerk or proprietor in this line of business. His experience as a druggist has been one of substantial success, and he has one of the prominent drug stores of the southern part of the county. During the last six or seven years, being a man of enterprise and always disposed to turn an honest dollar by trade, he has made several changes in stores, stock, etc., but has continued in the business all the time. He has also handled some real estate and dealt in live stock, in both of which he has had good success. March 16, 1880, Mr. Allcorn was married to Miss Fannie E. Mitchell, daughter of W. B. Mitchell, of this county. They have one child, Nellie.

HISTORY OF CLAY COUNTY

Mrs. A. is a member of the M. E. Church. He is a member of the Masonic Order.

THOMAS R. BALLARD

(Dealer in Groceries, Missouri City).

Dr. J. B. Ballard, the father of Thomas R., removed to Missouri with his family from Albemarle county, Va., and settled in Carroll county, where he followed the practice of his profession for a number of years. In 1869 he removed to Clay county, and was engaged in the practice at Missouri City until 1878, when he located at Marshall, in Saline county. He died there in the fall of 1884. He was a very capable and skillful physician, and had a good practice at Missouri City, as he always had wherever he resided. During the war, on account of the war troubles, he went to Nebraska with his family, in 1864, but returned to Carroll county five years afterwards and removed thence to Missouri City, as stated above. His wife's maiden name was Annie M. Johnson. She died in 1872. The subject of this sketch was the third child in the family. He was born in Carroll county, December 17, 1847, and was principally reared there, being educated in the common schools. He accompanied his parents to Nebraska and afterwards to Missouri City. He began as a clerk in a store at the age of 20, under N. C. Maupin. In 1871 he engaged in the dry goods business with Mr. Maupin, which they continued together at Missouri City for about three years. Mr. B. then sold out and went West, to the mountains, returning, however, late in the fall of 1874. He then engaged in the grocery business at this place, and has continued in that line of business ever since. He commenced with a small capital, but now does a business of about $12,000 a year. He carries a full line of groceries, provisions, glassware, queensware, etc. April 29, 1875, he was married to Miss Alwilda George, daughter of the late William M. George, of this county. She was born in 1855. They have one child, Mattie Augusta Ballard, born in 1879.

WILLIAM BUXTON

(Farmer, Post-office, Missouri City).

Mr. Buxton was a young man in his twenty-seventh year when he came to Clay county with his parents in 1837. That was the time when the Mormon troubles were at their height, and he became a member of the militia for the expulsion of the polygamists from the State. He also engaged in farming about the same time, and in a short time in raising stock. He has ever since followed farming and stock-raising without material interruption. He has a good stock farm, and feeds annually about 50 head of cattle for the markets. Mr. Buxton was a son of William Buxton, Sr., and wife, nee Rachael Trail, both of Kentucky, and he was born there in Mason county, May 1, 1810. In 1836 the family removed to Missouri, and stopped the succeeding year at Lexington. The next spring they came up into Clay county. The father subsequently died here, but the mother survived until 1881. She

HISTORY OF CLAY COUNTY

was a woman greatly beloved in her own family and by all who knew her. As a mother she was one of the most devoted of women. Such were her motherly affection and solicitude that her children thought and felt that there was no one else on earth so good and kind as she. Especially was this so with the subject of the present sketch. He thought and still thinks that there never was another woman equal in all the better qualities of the heart to her, and such was his affection for her that even when he was a youth he made a vow that he would never marry as long as she was spared to make home bright and happy. He kept his vow, and as his good mother survived until only a few years ago he has never married. Hence he has remained a bachelor until now, far unto the evening of life. On his farm Mr. Buxton has a quiet, tastily kept family burying ground, where sleep under the shadows of the tomb the remains of his sainted mother and venerated father. Handsome marble slabs mark the last resting place of each, and also of others of the family. Mr. Buxton has wisely anticipated his own final dissolution and has made proper provision for his interment in the family burying ground among those of his loved ones who have gone before. Where he is to be buried he has had a handsome marble monument erected to mark the place where his remains shall slumber until the radiant dawn of the resurrection morn.

Dr. RICHARD CARTER

(Physician, Missouri City).

Dr. Carter, who is now in his seventy-sixth year, has been engaged in the active practice of medicine for more than half a century. In the treatment of cases he has been remarkably successful, and in the accumulation of a comfortable property he has been fairly so, though he has never been considered, or desired to be, a money making man. His whole life rather has been centered in his profession — it has been the object of all his thoughts and labors. Dr. Carter came to Clay county in 1832, and since that time has passed through three epidemics of cholera, in all three of which his success was little less than astonishing. In but one case of this kind among all that he was called on to attend did the patient die, and in that instance she was in a dying condition when he reach her bedside. His specialty from the first has been that of chronic diseases. These he treats largely with non-mineral remedies, though he does not hesitate to resort to minerals when they will best answer the purpose. For a generation his reputation has been recognized far and wide in this part of the State as a specialist in chronic diseases. In the general practice also he has long held a place among the leading physicians of the county. Dr. Carter comes of a long line of physicians, both in this country and in England. His ancestors, as far back as he can trace them on his father's side, have been men of reputation in the medical profession. His grandfather, Dr. Richard Carter, was a graduate of the British Academy of Medicine and Surgery in England, and came to this country prior to the Revolutionary War, settling in Virginia.

391

He became a leading physician in Central Virginia and quite wealthy. His university knowledge of medicine he united with a vast fund of knowledge obtained by a special study of Indian medicines in Virginia, and of the botany and geology of this country. Indeed, he became one of the most reputable physicians in the State. His son, Richard Carter, the father of the subject of this sketch, followed his father's example and studied medicine. He, too, made a specialty of Indian remedies, and visited among them for months at a time, practicing with Indian doctors in order to obtain a thorough knowledge of their practice. The science of medicine and surgery he studied under his father. In an early day Dr. Richard Carter (the second) removed to Kentucky, in about 1810, and settled in what afterwards became Shelby county. He practiced medicine there for a number of years, and had an immense practice. For the treatment of chronic diseases he was often called a distance of 50 and 100 miles. Hundreds and hundreds of people lived to testify to his remarkable skill and ability as a physician. He died in Shelby county, Ky., in 1825. His wife was a Miss Catherine Bell before her marriage, originally from Virginia. Dr. Richard Carter (the third), the subject of this sketch, was born on the south branch of the Potomac river July 4, 1809, the day that James Madison was the first time inaugurated President of the United States. He was reared, however, in Kentucky, and educated at Georgetown College. Even when a youth he began the study of medicine under his father. He continued to study under his father for about five years, when he and a brother went to Southern Kentucky, and began to practice as partners. They practiced there together until 1829, when Dr. Richard Carter, the subject of this sketch, came to Missouri. He settled in Clay county, near Missouri City, where he practiced medicine until 1832, when he located at Liberty. There he practiced for a number of years and then removed to the vicinity of Missouri City, where he has ever since continued to practice. Dr. Carter is still quite active, considering his age, and his powers as a physician and man of thought are unimpaired. In a property point of view, as otherwise, he is comfortably situated. February 18, 1830, he was married to Miss Dorotha A. Norvell, a daughter of Robert Norvell, formerly of Sumner county, Tenn. Mrs. Carter died in 1882. She had borne him three children, all of whom grew to mature years: George, now deceased; Christopher C., of Missouri City, and Sarah J., widow of James Henshaw. Dr. Carter's grandmother, in the agnate line, or the wife of the original Dr. Carter of Virginia, was partly of Indian descent, being in fact one-fourth Indian. This fact entitles the doctor and his descendants to as much land in the Indian Territory as they choose to fence in, and then all the land around the fence for half a mile away.

ELZA P. DONOVAN

(Dealer in Lumber, and other Building Materials, Missouri City).

Mr. Donovan is a native of Kentucky, born in Mason county, January 30, 1836. His father was James Donovan, and his mother's maiden name, Mary West. They were from Virginia. In 1855 they removed to Missouri and settled in Clay county. Elza P. was then in his tweny-first year and had been reared on a farm, although he had also learned the carpenter's trade. After coming to this county he followed his trade exclusively and became a prominent contractor and builder, his business extending across into Ray and Jackson counties. Mr. Donovan continued in that line of business for over 20 years, or until 1876, when he bought the lumber yard and stock of which he is now proprietor. He has ever since done a good business, though not a large one, but his customers are generally substantial, reliable men and he has few losses to bear for that reason. His business amounts to about $10,000 a year. October 15, 1857, he was married to Miss Saran E. Allcorn, a daughter of James M. Allcorn, an early settler of this county, originally from North Carolina. Mr. and Mrs. Donovan have seven children: Minnie, now teaching in the public schools of Missouri City; Lena, a young lady just completing her education; James, Charles, Edwin, Fannie and Edna. Mr. and Mrs. D. and their two daughters are members of the M. E. Church South. Mr. D. is a member of the I. O. O. F.

JOSEPH E. FIELD

(Farmer, Post-office, Liberty).

Joseph E. is a nephew to Thomas Field, whose sketch appears in this volume and a son of Joseph T. Field, who came to this county from Virginia in 1838. Joseph Field, Sr., became a prominent farmer of the county and served two terms as a judge of the county court. He was also quite successful in stock-raising. Judge Field's wife was a Miss Amanda Brasfield before her marriage. Her parents were natives of Virginia. Judge Field died here in 1881. His wife, Joseph E.'s mother, is still living. Joseph E., the fourth of their family of five children, was born in this county May, 6, 1855. His education when he was a youth was concluded at William Jewell College. Having been reared on a farm he very naturally chose an agricultural life as his favorite and permanent calling. Mr. Field has continued at the occupation of farming and also been engaged in raising and dealing in stock for some years. Although still quite a young man, he is rapidly coming to the front as one of the successful farmers of Fishing River township. He has a handsome farm, more than ordinarily well improved. His residence alone was erected at a cost of $6,000. His other improvements correspond with his dwelling. June 30, 1881, he was married to Miss Annie M. Griffith, a daughter of James A. and Mary Griffith. Mrs. F. is a member of the Presbyterian Church. Mr. and Mrs. F. have two children, May L. and Amanda J.

H. C. FISH

(General Manager of the Relief Springs and Land Company, and of the firm of Fish & Henry, Owners and Proprietors of the Excelsior House, Excelsior Springs).

Mr. Fish, one of the prominent and leading citizens of Excelsior Springs, is a representative of the old and well known Fish family of

New York, of which Hon. Hamilton Fish is a distinguished member. The Fish family came originally from Kent, England, and one of its early and prominent representatives there was Simon Fish, Esq., a distinguished lawyer, who died in about 1531. He is remembered in history not only as a great lawyer, but for having written a satirical play on Cardinal Wolsey, on account of which he was banished from the country for a time. While absent he wrote another satirical work known as the Supplication of the Beggars on the Catholic clergy. Mr. Fish, the subject of this sketch, was a son of Capt. Samuel C. Fish, of New York, a somewhat noted sea captain in his day, and who died in 1840, then only at the middle age of life. Capt. Fish was married at Baltimore to Miss Mary A. Williams, who survived him nearly 40 years. She died in Ohio at the age of 75, in 1882. H. C. Fish, the subject of this sketch, was born in Beverly, Ohio, and was the youngest of eight children in the family, four of whom are living. He was reared at Beverly and educated at the college in that place. At the age of 20 he began to learn the plasterer's trade which he acquired and followed for four years. The next four years he was in the milling business, in connection with steamboating, which latter he followed altogether for a period of about seven years. In 1868 Mr. Fish came to Kansas City and was appointed to the position of general western freight agent for the North Missouri Railroad. In 1872 he engaged in the omnibus transfer business at Kansas City, carrying on that business in connection with the Coates' House, of which he was proprietor for some two years. At about the expiration of this time Mr. Fish was appointed general eastern traveling freight agent for the Atchison, Topeka and Santa Fe Railroad, and went East in the discharge of the duties of that position. Finally, he became largely interested at Excelsior Springs, buying, in connection with others, the Springs and large amounts of contiguous lands. Thereupon the Relief Springs and Land Company was organized, of which he became the general manager. He and Mr. John W. Henry, formerly of Cincinnati, Ohio, took charge of the Excelsior House, which they have ever since been conducting. Mr. Fish has very naturally taken an active and public-spirited interest in the growth and prosperity of the Springs, and has been a very useful and liberal-minded citizen in promoting all movements beneficial to the place. The Relief Springs and Land Company own about 600 acres of fine land contiguous to the Springs and have made an addition to the place of 250 handsome lots, properly intersected with streets, alleys, etc. In 1856 Mr. Fish was married to Miss Annie E. Sales, a daughter of Joel Sales, formerly of Rhode Island. Mr. and Mrs. Fish have two children, Frank C. and Charles W. Frank is a cashier in the office of a large cattle commission house at Kansas City, and Charles W. is assistant ticket agent there at the Union depot. An only daughter, Cora Etta, is deceased. She died at the age of 16. She was a gentle and queenly-hearted girl, a favorite among all her associates, and hardly less than idolized in her own family. Life to her seemed fraught with a future of much happiness, for her disposition was one to make kind and true friends wherever she went, and her presence was always a pleasure to those around her. Though still quite young, she was possessed of rare graces of form and features, and, above all, was favored with a bright and cheerful mind, one in which the light of cheerfulness seemed never to fade. A dutiful daughter, devotedly attached to her parents and brothers, she was at the same time a pleasant and true friend as a playmate, and as a student at school was ever faithful in her studies, bright and quick to learn and obedient to her teachers. Cora Fish is remembered by all who knew her as a rare good girl, one who seemed too dear to her acquaintances to lose. Her death has left a void in the hearts of her loved ones that can never be filled on this side the grave.

REV. J. V. B. FLACK, D. D.

(Excelsior Springs).

Rev. Dr. Flack was born and reared in the State of Ohio. His father's name was John V. Flack, and lived to a ripe old age. His mother's maiden name was Mary Maddox, and died in early life, leaving the son to be cared for by an uncle and aunt. J. V. B. Flack was educated at Holmes University, and at the age of 21 began his life-work — that of preaching the Gospel. He was very successful and soon took front rank as a pulpit orator and a revivalist. He traveled and labored extensively, and over 8,000 persons were converted under his ministrations in 1884. He was made a Doctor of Divinity by Rutherford College, of North Carolina, one of the best colleges in the South. He has been the editor of a religious paper for many years, being elected by his church people at General Conference. He was for eight years the presiding officer of the General Conference. He also edits an independent paper called *The Sentinel of Truth*, at Excelsior Springs, Mo. Dr. Flack married at 26 years of age, on the 28th of July, 1867, Miss Marrieta Smith, the daughter of Judge Samuel Smith, of Illinois, then becoming his wife. As the fruits of their marriage seven children, five boys and two girls, have been born to them, five of whom are living. Dr. F. is the original founder of Excelsior Springs, and brought that very popular watering place and health resort before the public until now it is a young and growing city of the fourth class. Through his efforts the Christian Union Chapel was built at Excelsior Springs, and a free pulpit provided for all Christians. He has been a very active and energetic business man for many years, and a pronounced advocate of the temperance work in the different States. He is in continual demand as a preacher and lecturer. He has dedicated 23 church houses and united some 200 in matrimony. Has preached 300 burials. He is the author of several works on the Unity of the Church, and a compiler of a Union Hymn Book. Politically, he has always been a Democrat. He is known largely throughout the States, and evangelizes throughout several States from year to year. In short, Dr. Flack has been one of the most active men of his times, and is now, at the age of forty-five, in the prime of his life and usefulness.

HENRY C. FOLEY

(Farmer, Post-office, Liberty).

Elijah Foley, the grandfather of Henry C., was an early settler of Kentucky from Virginia, and Richard Foley, Henry C.'s father, and the son of Elijah Foley, was born in the Blue Grass State, and reared there. When in young manhood he was married to Miss Mary Funk, formerly of Maryland, and afterwards continued to reside in Kentucky until 1852. While a resident of Fayette county, that State, Henry C. Foley, the subject of this sketch, was born October 25, 1833. When he was about 19 years of age the family removed to Missouri, and he accompanied them. They settled on a farm in Clay county, where the father died in 1856. The same year of his father's death, Henry C. returned to Kentucky, and in a few years was married there, in 1859, to Miss Rebecca Brock, a daughter of Winfield Brock, deceased. After his marriage he resided in that county until 1865, and then returned to Missouri, and bought a farm three miles north of Liberty, where he has ever since made his home. February 22, 1878, he had the misfortune to lose his wife. She left him six children at her death : Foster R., Florence, Mary, Dandy J., Keller and Eliza. Mr. F. is a member of the Christian Church. His farm contains 286 acres, and he has other valuable land in the county. His place is well improved.

WILLIAM E. FOWLER

(Attorney at Law, and of Fowler & Thomson, Land, Loan, Pension, Patent, Fire and Life Insurance Agents, Excelsior Springs).

Mr. Fowler, a young man now in his twenty-fourth year, located at Excelsior Springs, from Ohio, in the spring of 1883. Like many of the better citizens of this place, he was drawn here by the reputation of the waters of the Springs. For some years previous to coming to Excelsior Springs he had been hard at work in the acquisition of his general and professional education. Ambitious to fit himself thoroughly for an active and useful life and to begin his career at the earliest day possible, he had unquestionably overworked himself and drawn too heavily on his physical strength and energies. The result was that although he succeeded in preparing himself for his profession at an earlier age than is common with young attorneys, at the very time he expected and wished to begin active work at the bar he found himself physically exhausted and his health shattered. This illustrates one of the most striking differences between the systems and policies of European and American institutions of learning. In Europe physical health and development are as studiously considered and provided for as the culture of the mind. But in this country, particularly in the West, such is the hurry and push of life and the anxiety of students to get into affairs, that little or no attention is paid to the physical man, and his general health is sacrificed to the exigencies of rapid advancement through his college course. Mr. Fowler went to

HISTORY OF CLAY COUNTY

school at Beverly, Ohio, the place of his nativity, and then from school he entered a law school at Baltimore, Md., one of the best institutions of the kind in the country, reading law in the office of Hon. F. P. Stevens, a well known Baltimore attorney. He graduated at Baltimore in the year 1882. From there he at once returned to Ohio and entered upon the practice of his profession at Beverly. But soon finding that his physical energies were exhausted, he was compelled to make a change of residence for his health. Excelsior Springs was highly recommended to him and he accordingly came to this place. Here he received marked benefit from the use of the waters of the Springs and by auxiliary treatment, and soon decided to make this place his permanent home. He therefore entered upon the practice of his profession here, and thus far he has been greatly encouraged by the favor with which he has been received, both personally and as an attorney. In the agency business he and Mr. Thomson are doing well, and have reason to be greatly pleased with their success. Mr. Fowler was born at Beverly, Washington county, Ohio, May 19, 1861, and was the firth of seven children of Joseph and Mary Fowler, his father, a grandson of Capt. John Fowler, of Revolutionary fame. Capt. Fowler participated in the battle of Lexington, where he was severely wounded, and was with Washington on that eventful night when the American army crossed the Delaware. Mr. Fowler's father, Joseph Fowler, referred to above, is one of the old and highly respected citizens of Washington county, a merchant of long experience, and he is one of the best insurance agents in the Eastern States.

CHARLES FUNK

(Farmer and Stock-raiser, Post-office, Liberty).

Mr. Funk was born in Clay county, July 14, 1854. His father was Richard Funk, now deceased, formerly of Jessamine county, Ky., and his mother was a Miss Sarah J. Bell before her marriage, a daughter of Fielding Bell, from Mason county, Ky., who came to this county in 1836. Charles Funk grew up on his father's farm in this county, and received a common school education. January 13, 1876, he was married to Miss Mary Richardson, a daughter of Samuel H. Richardson, deceased, formerly of Madison county, Ky. Mr. and Mrs. Funk have three children: Pattie, Richard H. and Charles Ralph. Mr. Funk has a good farm and is comfortably situated. Neither he nor his father ever held an official position, nor sought or desired one. Both are domestic home men, industrious, energetic farmers, and well respected citizens, or rather the father was in his lifetime, and Mr. Funk, Jr., still is.

GEORGE WASHINGTON GEORGE

(Farmer, Post-office, Missouri City).

"Grandfather" Joseph Groom, of the vicinity of Liberty, is said to be the oldest living resident of the county, being now well advanced

HISTORY OF CLAY COUNTY

in his eighty-ninth year. But Mr. George, the subject of this sketch, though many years "Grandfather" Groom's junior, has been a resident of the county longer than Mr. Groom. "Grandfather" Groom came here in 1824, then a young man 28 years of age. Mr. George was brought here by his parents when he was in childhood, in 1819. He has, therefore, been a resident of the county for 66 years. When Mr. G.'s parents settled in this county there were not half a dozen white families in the present limits of the county, and not as many in all the territory west of the Chariton, on this side of the Missouri, as now reside in Liberty township. His parents, Baley O. and Jemima (Withers) George, came from Kentucky, though his father was originally from Virginia. On settling in this county they located about six miles east of the present site of Liberty, where the father entered land and improved a farm. He became a prominent man of the county, and served in different positions of public trust. He was a judge of the first election ever held in the county. At the age of 70 years he died here, in 1865. His wife died in 1863. Eight sons and five daughters of their family were reared to years of maturity, and four of them, including two of the daughters, are still living. George W. was the second of their children, and was born in Madison county, Ky., April 15, 1815. He was principally reared, however, in Clay county, this State, and his educational advantages were limited to those of the schools of that period. As is well known, there are different periods of advancement in the progress of civilization. In this Western country the first was the period of the hunters and fur traders; then came the pioneer settlers with their families, known as the log-cabin, stock-chimney period; after that was the period of the hewed log-house and stone chimney, with now and then a plank floor, instead of broad-ax dressed puncheons; later along sawmills and brickyards were established, and neat frame and comfortable brick residences were built; and then came railroads, agricultural machinery, handsome architecture and all the comforts and graces of advanced social, business and industrial life. So, in the matter of education, different epochs are as distinctly marked: First, was the round log school-room without a floor, with a fireplace occupying one entire end of the building, and with no light except such as came through the unclosed entrance of a wooden-hinged, clapboard door. Those were the days of goose-quill pens, the "Testament" and the "Life of Marion" for readers, and teachers who invariably pronounced fatigue "fatigew," and bigamy "bigmary;" afterward came puncheon floors, a log sawed out of one end of the building to admit light, a long sycamore plank to write on, teachers who taught that the world was not flat, and other comforts and conveniences of a rather advanced civilization. But finally came frame and brick school-houses, and at last patent cast-mounted seats and desks, and the inevitable, ubiquitous and thoroughly intolerable, spectacled, gingery, effervescing "professor." Alas! the infliction he puts upon the public more than offsets all the benefits of modern educational facilities. Mr. George was reared and educated before the era of puncheon floor school-houses; but, nevertheless, by close application and a good deal of study at home he succeeded in obtaining a sufficient knowledge of books for all practical purposes in that early day. After he grew up he was married in this county to Miss Elizabeth F. Neeley, a sister to Richard A. and William L. Neeley, whose sketches appear in this volume. Mr. George continued farming after his marriage, to which he had been brought up, and in 1847 settled on the place where he now resides. For three years before he resided in Buchanan county. Returning then to Clay, this has ever since been his permanent home. He has been fairly successful and is comfortably situated. He owns about 350 acres of land, and his farm is well improved. He and his good wife reared five children: William (now of Rich Hill), Fannie, Richard W., Thomas N. and Clement B. One, Susan, died in early maidenhood.

JUDSON M. GRUBBS

(Of J. M. Grubbs & Co., Dealers in Groceries, Queensware, Glassware, etc., Missouri City).

Mr. Grubbs was about ten years of age when his parents, Hardin and Elizabeth (Lively) Grubbs, removed from Spottsylvania county, Va., to Clay county, Mo., in 1856. The father was a mechanic by trade and worked at carpentering, cabinetmaking and wagonmaking as occasion rendered most available or profitable. He died here August 5, 1865. He was twice married and it should have been remarked that his second wife, the mother of the subject of this sketch, died before the family left Virginia. The father was also a farmer by occupation and had a comfortable homestead in Virginia. Judson M., born in Spottsylvania county, Va., January 1, 1846, was principally reared, however, in Clay county, Mo. Brought up on the farm, he remained at home until he was 20 years of age and then engaged as clerk in a general store, which he followed for some eight years. After this he began the grocery business on his own account at Norborne, in Carroll county. He sold goods there for about two years and then returned to Missouri City, whereupon he and his brother, E. M. Grubbs, formed their present partnership, and engaged in the grocery business at this place. Their experience here has been satisfactory and they have built up a large trade and established one of the leading grocery houses of the southern part of the county. They have an annual business of about $20,000. November 9, 1876, Mr. Grubbs was married to Miss Bettie L. Aker, daughter of Preston Aker, of Ray county. They have three children: Roy E., Ralph H. and Ethel M. Mr. and Mrs. G. are members of the Christian Church, and Mr. G. holds the office of deacon.

MOSES C. HUTCHINGS

(Farmer, Post-office, Missouri City).

Mr. Hutchings, although comparatively a young man, has nevertheless, by his energy and industry, established for himself the name of

HISTORY OF CLAY COUNTY

being one of the thoroughgoing farmers of Fishing River township. He is a worthy son of the county by nativity, born on his father's homestead in Fishing River township December 17, 1841. His father being a farmer by occupation, Moses was brought up to that calling, and during the war he served faithfully in the Home Guards under Capt. D. P. Whitmer for a term of nine months. He then enlisted in the State militia and served under Capt. Colley six months. Through the remainder of the war he served under Capt. M. T. Real. On the 22d of October, 1874, Mr. Hutchings was married to Miss Maggie A. Koehler. Four children are the fruits of their happy married life: Mary J., Elijah, Benjamin and Ange E. Mr. Hutchings has a good farm of 78½ acres. His parents were Moses and Matilda Hutchings, his father a native of Tennessee, but his mother originally of Indiana. They came to this county in an early day.

CHARLES W. JACOBS, M. D.

(Physician and Surgeon, Excelsior Springs).

Dr. Jacobs, who is the city physican of Excelsior Springs and the regular attending physician to the Excelsior Bath House and at the two leading hotels at the place, is a physician of thorough training and superior attainments. After a thorough course of general reading he took a course of four terms at the Eclectic Medical College of Cincinnati and graduated with high honor in the class of 1880. He then located at Richmond, in Ray county, where he was born and reared, for the general practice of medicine in connection with his brother. Dr. Jacobs (Charles W.) was having a more than ordinarily successful experience at Richmond when his health failed, the following year after he located there, caused primarily by hard study while preparing for his profession and directly by severe cold contracted from the exposures of an active country practice. His lungs became critically affected, and in the hope of receiving benefit from travel and the purity of mountain air he went to Colorado. Dr. Jacobs received marked benefit by his visit to Colorado and returned much improved. Resuming his practice at Richmond, the hard work and exposures incident to a large practice soon brought back his lung trouble, and he was compelled to quit the regular country practice again. He then came to Excelsior Springs, and has obtained much good from the use of the water and baths at this place in connection with his own treatment. He has become thoroughly convinced from his own experience that many who believe themselves to be seriously if not hopelessly afflicted with lung trouble could be materially benefitted, if not entirely cured, by the use of the waters of Excelsior Springs, under proper medical directions and treatment. Having made a special study of the medicinal properties of the water here and of the classes of affections it is best adapted to remedy, he is peculiarly well qualified for the responsible position he holds, that of consulting physician for the Springs. His success here in the treatment of lung diseases and other afflictions of a persistent, difficult character has in many cases been remarkable. A number of cures have been effected which were hardly even hoped for by the patients themselves, so long had they hoped against hope without a ray of realization. Dr. Jacobs is a man of culture and a gentleman of dignified, refined manners. A man of fine feeling and of the warmest sympathy for the suffering, he brings to bear in his practice not only professional skill and ability, but, what is often more valuable, that manifest solicitude or welfare of his patients, which is always a balm to the sick. He is justly very popular as a physician and citizen. Dr. Jacobs is a worthy representative of one of the old and highly respected families of Clay county. His father, Maj. Clayton Jacobs, was for years one of the leading merchants of Richmond, and was abundantly successful. He is now retired on an ample competence. Maj. Jacobs held various official positions in Clay county, including those of collector of the revenue, sheriff, assessor, etc. He was from Lincoln county, Ky., and served in the Mormon War in this State, assisting to drive the polygamists out of the country. For 20 years he has been an elder in the Christian Church, and is a church member of half a century's standing. His good wife, a motherly and noble-hearted old lady, is still spared to make the evening of his life as happy as their earlier years have been. Dr. Jacobs was born at Richmond, and was given good advantages and received an excellent general education. Of his parents' family of children all have become useful and prominent members of society.

JAMES L. JENNETT

(With Dykes, Chrisman & Co., Dealers in General Merchandise, Prathersville).

Capt. Jennett is a native of Virginia, born in Halifax county, on the 5th day of September, 1838. He was a son of James H. and Susan T. Jennett, and was brought to Missouri at the age of seven years by his parents, who settled in Franklin county, this State, in 1845. Capt. Jennett was partly reared in Franklin county and received a common school education. During the war he served in the Southern army, Fifty-ninth Virginia Regiment, under Gen. Wise, of Virginia, and participated in the battles of Cheat Mountain, Seven Pines, Malvern Hill, in the sieges of Charleston, S C., and Petersburg, Va., and numerous other engagements. He was publicly complimented by his general for gallantry and bravery while in South Carolina. Early in 1865 he was captured at Burkville, Va., and was a prisoner at Washington when President Lincoln was assassinated. He was then transferred to Johnson's Island, where he was held a prisoner until after the close of the war. On being released at the close of the war he returned home to Franklin county. Capt. Jennett came to Clay county in 1869, where he has ever since resided. He has held several local offices in this county and served as special deputy sheriff and city marshal of Kearney for several years. The Captain is a member of the mercantile firm of Dykes, Chrisman & Co. They are engaged in gen-

HISTORY OF CLAY COUNTY

eral merchandising, both at Prathersville and Kearney, and are doing a good business at each place. In 1866 Capt. Jennett was married to Miss Hattie Patton, of Franklin county, Mo. They have four children: Nellie, Edna, Harry and Lula. A son, James F., died in infancy. Mrs. Jennett is a member of the Baptist Church at Kearney. The Captain is a member of the A. F. and A. M.

TILFORD JENKINS

(Farmer, Post-office, Missouri City).

Mr. Jenkins has a farm of 80 acres in Fishing River township, and was born in Fayette county, Ky., in 1827. He was a son of Willis Jenkins, and has his place fairly improved. His father was originally from Virginia, and Mr. Jenkins, himself, is an energetic farmer and also carried on a blacksmith shop on his farm. In 1858 Mr. Jenkins, the subject of this sketch, was married to Miss Elizabeth Weaver, which happy union has resulted in nine children, namely: Mary A., Willis, Catherine, Edward L., Laura, Leona , Louisa and William S. The other one died in infancy. Mrs. Jenkins is a member of the Christian Church. Mr. Jenkins was educated in the common schools. He went for some time to Capt. Lawrence Dailey, who was a gallant old soldier boy in the War of 1812.

MELVIN McKEE

(Farmer and Fine Stock Raiser, Post-office, Prathersville).

David and Elizabeth McKee, the parents of the subject of the present sketch, came to Missouri in 1833 and settled in Platte county, where they made their permanent home, and reared a family of children. The father was a farmer by occupation and young Melvin was reared to that calling in this county. In 1857 he was married to Miss Pheoba A. Gromes, a union that has proved one of singular contentment and happiness and has been blessed with eight children: Charles, William, Samuel, Julia, Bettie, Ella, Mattie, Curtis, the last, being deceased. Mrs. McKee is a worthy and exemplary member of the Christian Church. Mr. McKee has always made farming and, in late years, raising fine stock, his regular pursuit. He has a good farm of 200 acres, well improved. His residence building was erected at a cost of $2,500, and his barn was put up at a cost of $1,000. Mr. McKee is a director of the school district and has been for a number of years. He has a good herd of thoroughbred, short horn and high grade cattle, some of which are as handsome animals as are to be seen in the county.

DAVID O. McCRAY

(Postmaster, Excelsior Springs).

Mr. McCray is a native Missourian, born in Caldwell county, March 10, 1855. He was the eighth in a family of 11 children, seven

402

HISTORY OF CLAY COUNTY

of whom are now living, of William and Nancy (Carroll) McCray, who came to Missouri at an early day, and settled in Caldwell county. William McCray became a large farmer and stock-raiser of that county and still resides there, having an extensive stock farm of 1,100 acres. When he first removed to Caldwell county the nearest government land office was at Plattsburg and he went to that place on foot and entered 500 acres of land at the then price of 12 1-2 cents an acre. During the war he was a strong Union man and two of his sons were in the Union army, the eldest, Frank, losing a leg at Lone Jack. David O. was reared on the farm in Caldwell county, and received a high school education. He then began an apprenticeship at the printer's trade, which he acquired, and afterwards he became the editor of the Lucas county *Republican*, at Chariton, Iowa. Since then he has had editorial charge of eight papers at different points in Kansas, Iowa and Missouri, the last one being the *Herald* at this place. In January, 1883, he was appointed postmaster at Excelsior Springs and still holds the office. He also has a news stand in connection with the post-office and a circulating library. Mr. McCray was married to Miss Carrie Stevens, a daughter of Dr. E. W. Stevens, a prominent citizen of Cameron, Mo., May 1, 1878. Mr. and Mrs. McC. have one child, Lena M.

FOSTER MEANS

(Farmer and Stock-raiser, Post-office, Missouri City).

'Squire Means is now in his sixty-second year, and until two years ago was never sick an hour in his life; even then he was only indisposed for a few days. The fact that he has always lived an active, temperate life, directed from the beginning by good judgment, is mainly the reason that he has been so fortunate in the matter of good health. He has always avoided going to extremes in everything or unnecessarily exposing himself, although he never stood back when anything proper was to be done, whatever the risk or hardship might be. He has been, and is yet, an active, energetic workingman, and although now closely approaching old age he bears his years so well that one would be far from taking him to be as old a man as he really is. 'Squire Means was born in this county in 1823. From infancy he has lived on a farm, and, since he became old enough to do for himself, has been a farmer on his own account. He has been fairly successful, and has a good homestead. Like most of the farmers of this vicinity, he raises some stock, and is interested in short horn cattle. In 1844 he was married to Miss Jemima Munkers, of one of the early families of Clay county. The 'Squire and wife have reared but one son, Albert E., who is still on the farm with his parents. In 1858 'Squire M. was elected a justice of the peace of Fishing River township and continued to hold that office until toward the latter part of the war, when he was ousted by the superlatively loyal faction of thrifty patriots of that day, because he was adjudged not to be as loyal as he might be. Since 1862 he has taken a prominent part in

HISTORY OF CLAY COUNTY

politics, having been a member of the Democratic Central Committee, etc. The 'Squire was a son of Andrew and Sarah W. Means, who came to Missouri in 1817, first locating in Howard county. Five years afterwards they settled in Clay, where they lived until their deaths. The father was from North Carolina, originally, but the mother was a native of Virginia.

MABRY MITCHELL

(Dealer in General Merchandise, Prathersville).

Mr. Mitchell has been engaged in business at Prathersville for about four years. Previous to that he was engaged in the produce trade at Denver, Col., for some time, or rather in shipping produce from this part of the country to that market. He is a native of Clay county and has spent most of his life within its borders. He was born in Liberty, November 18, 1826, and was a son of Mabry and Martha A. Mitchell, pioneer settlers of the county. His father was a native of South Carolina, and came West in 1819. Reared in the county, for a number of years young Mitchell was engaged in farming and raising stock and to some extent in dealing in stock. In 1845, April 15, he was married to Miss Evaline Leakey. She died September 10, 1875. Mr. Mitchell was married to his present wife November 15, 1877. She was a Mrs. Martha E. Davidson, daughter of Jonathan Atkins, a pioneer. By his first wife he has three children: Mary E., now Hiatt; Sarah F. (now Brown), and Samuel H. Mrs. Mitchell is a member of the Primitive Baptist Church, and Mr. Mitchell is a member of the Missionary Baptists. He is also a member of the A. F. and A. M., and forever a supporter of the temperance cause.

ROBERT H. MOORE (DECEASED)

(Vicinity of Prathersville).

Mr. Moore died at his homestead in this county in July, 1882. He had been a resident of this county for nearly 30 years and was one of its well respected citizens, and industrious, energetic farmers. He was a worthy member of the Masonic Order and his loss was greatly deplored by the fellow-members of his lodge and all who knew him. During the late war he was a gallant soldier in the Union army under Gen. Leslie Combs. He came of a family that had previously proved its devotion to the cause of liberty and free government, in the War for Independence. His father, Peter Moore, served in the army of the Revolution and participated in the battle of Brandywine, where he was severely wounded. He subsequently died of his wound. Mr. Moore, deceased, the subject of this sketch, came to Clay county in 1853 and resided here until his death. His widow still resides on the homestead in this county. She was a Miss Amelia R. Nichols before her marriage. They were married in 1853 in Kentucky. Three children are living of their family: Margaret, Flora and George T. George T. superintends affairs and carries on the farm. He is now

HISTORY OF CLAY COUNTY

absent in Kentucky, looking after property in which he is interested.

JOHN H. MOSBY

(Farmer, Stock-raiser and Stock-dealer, Post-office, Liberty).

Mr. Mosby parents, Wade and Rebecca Mosby, came to Clay county from Kentucky in 1822. They made this their permanent home, the father being a farmer by occupation. John H. was born after the family settled here, in 1824. Reared in this county, he was married in 1855 to Miss Sarah Hall. Meanwhile he had been to California and returned. He went overland to the Pacific coast in 1850, and was absent about two years. While there he was principally engaged in mining. Most of the time he was on the Yuba, in the vicinity of Nevada City, but for a time was on the Poor Man's creek, which was then thought to be of little or no value as a mining district, but which afterwards was found to have some of the richest deposits in the country, and became a wealthy mining region. Returning in 1852, Mr. Mosby engaged in farming and stock-raising in this county. His whole time, for the past 30 years, has been busily occupied with his farming and stock interests. He has a large farm of 600 acres, one of the best farms in Fishing River township, and he is extensively engaged in raising and dealing in stock. He has a handsome herd of short horn cattle, and feeds annually about 100 head of beef cattle, besides a large number of marketable hogs. Mr. Mosby is one of the leading farmers and stock-raisers of this part of the county, and is in comfortable circumstances. His place is well improved, including a handsome residence, erected in 1871, at a cost of $5,000. He also has large and comfortable barns and other outbuildings, and his lands are mainly devoted to blue grass for stock pasturage, but enough is reserved for grain for the ordinary purposes of stock raising. Mr. and Mrs. Mosby have a family of five children: Addie, the wife of Charles Dye; Ettie, Ida, Gertie and William. They have lost three: Edgar, Mamie and Ernest. Mr. and Mrs. M. are members of the Christian Church.

DEWILTON MOSBY

(Farmer and Stock-raiser, Post-office, Liberty).

Mr. Mosby's farm contains 560 acres, and, like his cousin John H., he makes a specialty of the stock business. He fattens for the markets annually from 50 to 75 head of cattle and a large number of hogs. August 23, 1873, he was married to Miss Martha M. Archer, of this county. They have five children: Jesse D., Rosa L., Emmet A., Nicholas and Bonnie M. Nicholas was named for his grandfather, Nicholas Mosby, who came to this county from Kentucky in 1837. Nicholas Mosby, the elder, was born in Woodford county, that State, and was reared in Kentucky, where he married Miss Mary Shouse. Some years afterwards he came to Missouri and settled in Clay county. He was an energetic farmer, and soon became comfortably situated.

His son, Dewilton Mosby, the subject of this sketch, was born in Kentucky, April 23, 1825, and was about 12 years of age when the family came to Clay county. He was reared on a farm, and in 1846 enlisted for the Mexican War. He served under Col. Doniphan and was honorably discharged at New Orleans after the final defeat of the Mexicans. He then came home and resumed farming. In 1850 he went to California, driving an ox team across the plains, and five months were occupied with the trip. After his return again he went to farming, and has followed it ever since.

ALBERT G. MOSBY

(Farmer and Stock-raiser, Post-office, Prathersville).

The subject of this sketch is a brother to Dewilton Mosby, already mentioned, and was born in Woodford county, Ky., in 1829. He was therefore in childhood when his parents came to Missouri, in 1833, and settled in Clay county. Brought up in that county in that early day, he, of course, had to experience hard work incident to Western farm life — improving land, and farming before the era of farm machinery, and when everything done had to be done by hard work. While this was pretty severe on some who had no taste for straight-forward manual labor, to the subject of this sketch it was not as disagreeable as might be expected. He was early trained that the most honest way to make a living was by honest industry, and that if he hoped to succeed in life, without reproach, the surest and safest course was to rely upon honest labor. Accordingly, he came up a hard-working, upright man, which he has ever since continued to be. He has relied on his own exertions alone for success, and has not been disappointed. Now, and for years past, he has been comfortably situated on a good farm, where he has every necessary convenience to make life a satisfaction and pleasure. His place contains about 640 acres, and besides raising large quantities of grain and other products, he feeds annually for the wholesale markets about 150 head of beef cattle, and nearly an equal number of hogs. His farm is mainly run in blue grass for stock purposes. In 1850 Mr. Mosby was married to Miss Mary A. Hodges, daughter of Judge W. V. Hodges, of this county, but formerly of Kentucky. Mr. and Mrs. Mosby have six children: Eva M., now the wife of William T. Pixley; Lunette, now the wife of Dr. C. B. Hardin; George A., Lee J., John H. and James D. Mr. and Mrs. M. are members of the Primitive Baptist Church. Mr. Mosby also has a large grain farm in the Missouri river bottoms in this county.

HENRY F. MUDD

(Farmer, Post-office, Missouri City).

Mr. Mudd is a representative of the well known Mudd family in this State and Kentucky, but originally from Maryland. Dr. Mudd, an eminent physician of St. Louis, is a representative of the same family. Members of the family are also prominent in Lincoln county and in other counties of this State, as well as in Kentucky. There is a tradition in the Mudd family, which seems authentic, that the entire stock of that name in the United States descended from two brothers who formed a part of Lord Baltimore's Maryland colony. Mr. Mudd himself was a school teacher for many years, but has long been retired on a farm near where he is engaged in the peaceful pursuit of agriculture. He was a son of William and Eliza Mudd, formerly of Kentucky, and was born in Ralls county, Mo., in 1830. In 1858 he was married to Miss Lydia C. Nichols. They have four children: James R., William T., Sarah E. and Henry F. Mrs. M. died in 1881. She was of Baptist parentage and embraced the Catholic faith only a short time previous to her last illness. Mr. Mudd is also a member of that church. He has a good farm of 100 acres, where he resides with his children.

RICHARD N. NEELEY

(Farmer, Post-office, Liberty).

This old and respected citizen of the county was born in Bedford county, Tenn., April 6, 1815. His father, Clement Neeley, was from Fairfield district, S. C., and went to Tennessee when a young man. His mother, *nee* Susan Harrington, was from North Carolina, but partly reared in Kentucky. They removed to Missouri in 1816, and located in Howard county. Six years later they came to Clay county, and the following spring settled on the place where Mr. N., the subject of this sketch, now resides. Consequently he has been living on this same place for a period of nearly 62 years. The father died here December 8, 1865. A family of three brothers and two sisters were left. The eldest brother died of cholera in 1833. A sketch of the younger of the two brothers left appears elsewhere. Mr. Neeley was reared on the farm where he now lives, and when he was about 17 years of age he and his eldest brother went to Gallatin, where they established a stock ranch. He clerked there at the first Presidential election, held after Daviess county was organized. Three years later he returned to Clay county and resumed farming, to which he had been brought up. In 1846 he enlisted under Col. Doniphan for the Mexican War, and followed the standard of the doughty old Mexican veteran until the flag of the Union waved in triumph above the marble halls of the Montezumas. After the war he returned home, and, January 14, 1850, was married to Miss Mary A., a daughter of Thomas Harrington, an early settler from Tennessee. Ever since then he has been settled on the old homestead, and also engaged in farming and stock-raising. For a number of years, however, he sold goods on the road in this State, a business that is now called drumming, the only difference between this and that being that now they travel on the railroad instead of a dirt road, as then, and sell by sample, instead of directly to the customer. Then the old-fashioned, common-sense name was peddling. Another difference is that the

HISTORY OF CLAY COUNTY

men who sold the goods then generally owned them, but now the seller is usually traveling clerk, but gives himself the altitudinous title of "commercial traveler." Mr. Neeley's line of goods consisted of clocks, and he had a number of young men on the road under him. He also did an extensive collecting business for wholesale merchants as he passed through the country. Mr. and Mrs. Neeley have reared two children, Clement and Maggie E. Mrs. N. is a member of the Christian Church, and he is a prominent member of the Odd Fellows' Order. Before the war Mr. Neeley was elected sheriff of Clay county, and was afterwards re-elected, serving until hostilities began. One other fact remains to be mentioned. In 1853 he engaged in the livery business at Liberty, and continued in the business about four years, in partnership with Judge A. Moore, whose sketch appears in this work. Mr. Neeley is now unfortunately afflicted with paralysis, but retains much of his mental vigor, and physically is still able to get about his own house. His life has been one of uprightness and integrity, and he has the good wishes of all who know him.

CAPT. SAMUEL D. NOWLIN

(Of Simmons & Newlin, Dealers in Dry Goods, Clothing, Hats and Caps, Boots and Shoes, Etc., Missouri City).

For many years Capt. Nowlin's father, Bryan W. Nowlin, was an enterprising merchant in this section of Missouri, in Clay and Ray counties. He was from Kentucky and came here when a young man. He first followed teaching school and taught in Cooper and Saline counties. Then turning his attention to merchandising, he followed that business for a time at Liberty and afterwards at Fredericksburg, in Ray county. Returning to Clay county in about 1852, he established a store at Missouri City, which he carried on until 1865, but was nearly broken up by the war, having lost a great deal by depredators from both sides. Mr. Nowlin, Sr., now resides at Prathersville. He was twice married. His first wife, who became the mother of the subject of this sketch, was a Miss Lucy N. Davis, a sister of W. H. H. and Albert G. Davis of this county. She died August 9, 1869. His second wife was a Mrs. Bowls, widow of the late S. D. Bowls. Capt. Nowlin was born in Ray county, August 18, 1838. He was principally reared in that county. Under his father his opportunities for learning the mercantile business were good and he learned all the practical details of running a country store. June 30, 1861, he was married to Miss Sarah M. Peery, daughter of Thomas Peery, of Howard county. The following September, Capt. Nowlin enlisted in the State Guard, Southern service, under Col. Thompson, and served for about seven months. He was elected first lieutenant of Co. C, and took part in the battles of Lexington, Pea Ridge and Springfield. At Springfield he was promoted to the position of adjutant of Thompson's regiment, with the rank of captain, and served in that position until the close of his term of service. At Van Buren, in Arkansas, March 16, 1862, he was honorably discharged. After that

408

HISTORY OF CLAY COUNTY

he was at home during the remainder of the war. For two years after the war he was engaged in the grocery business at Missouri City, and then turned his attention to farming, which he followed with success in the county until February, 1883, when he became a member of the present firm. Capt. Nowlin's first wife died December 27, 1864. She left two children, Thomas B., now a clerk in a dry goods house at Kansas City, and Sarah M., a young lady at home. April 28, 1868, Capt. Nowlin was married to Miss Martha C. Skinner, a daughter of Robert J. Skinner, of Montgomery county. Her father was an attorney and died at St. Joe while attending court there. By his last marriage Capt. Nowlin has five children: Zadie W., Cleon L., Tracy C., William N. and Harrison D. Mrs. Nowlin is a member of the Christian Church.

JOHN H. PIBURN

(Farmer and Stock-raiser, Post-office, Missouri City).

Among the energetic agriculturists and thorough-going men of Fishing River township, the subject of the present sketch is justly accorded an enviable position. By his own work, enterprise and business qualities he has accumulated a comfortable start in life and is already one of the substantial farmers of the township. He was born in Clay county, October 10, 1841, and was a son of David Piburn, a native of Tennessee. Edward Piburn, the grandfather of John H., was one of the pioneers of Missouri. He came here with his family in 1818 and settled in Howard county. From that county he removed to Clay county in 1820 and here made his permanent home. David Piburn was in infancy when the family came to this county. He grew up on the farm and subsequently married Miss Matilda Shouse, a daughter of John Shouse, who settled here from Kentucky in 1824. Mr. Piburn (David, the father of John) still resides in this county. He served in the Mormon War and helped to drive the followers of Joe Smith out of the State. John H. Piburn was brought up to the life of a farmer and was still at home when the war broke out in 1861. He then enlisted in Col. Thompson's cavalry regiment for the Southern service and served out the full time of his enlistment. During that time he took part in the fights at Rock Creek, Pea Ridge and a number of skirmishes. In the spring of 1862 he went west to Denver to void the war troubles, and afterwards followed freighting across the plains for a time. Finally, however, he located at Nebraska City, where he remained until after the restoration of peace. In the spring of 1866 he returned home and resumed farming to which he had been brought up. He also engaged in trading in stock, which he continued to 1873. February 18, of that year, he was married to Miss Cordies Rice, a daughter of William and Laura (Brasfield) Rice, early settlers in this county. After his marriage Mr. Piburn located the following year on the farm where he has ever since resided. He first bought a tract of 60 acres, but to that he has since added from time to time until he now has about 300 acres. For some years past he

HISTORY OF CLAY COUNTY

has also been engaged in the threshing machine business, and for the last two years has run a steam thresher. His cash receipts from threshing has been about $20,000. During the winter of 1884–85 he bought and established a new steam saw mill, which is located near Missouri City and is doing a good business. In 1880 and 1882, Mr. Piburn made two trips to Arkansas and the Indian Territory to buy stock, and was satisfactorily successful in the sale of the stock bought. Mr. and Mrs. Piburn have three children: Charles Ross, Gertie May and James Lester.

JOHN A. POSEY, M. D.
(Physician and Surgeon, Missouri City).

Among the physicians and with the public generally, Dr. Posey is recognized as one of the leading members of his profession in Middle-Western Missouri. He took a thorough course at the St. Louis Medical College, and afterwards had the benefit of a year's practice as assistant physician to the St. Louis City Hospital. Since then he has been in the active general practice for about 16 years, and has had a large and varied practice. He is a prominent member of the State and District Medical Societies, and has been president of the latter, which meets quarterly at Kansas City. He has also for many years been an active member of the Clay County Medical Society. Dr. Posey was born on his father's farm, in Fishing River township, this county, December 19, 1838. His father was James F. Posey and his mother's maiden name was Julia A. Singleton. Both were from Kentucky, and his grandfather Posey was one of the old pioneers of that State from Virginia. Dr. Posey was reared in this county and concluded his general educational course with two years at William Jewell College. In 1863 he began the study of medicine under Dr. B. M. Beckham of Clayvillage, in Shelby county, a leading physician of that county, and the following fall entered the St. Louis Medical College. He continued through two terms at the latter institution and graduated with honor in the class of '67. In the meantime, however, between his first and second terms, he was engaged in the practice of medicine at Barnsville, in Clinton county. After graduating he was elected assistant physician of the St. Louis City Hospital, and after serving in that position a year he located at Missouri City, where he has ever since been engaged in the general practice. Dr. Posey is a man who keeps fully abreast of the times in his profession, and is a liberal subscriber for different medical journals, periodicals, etc., and for the latest and best works on medical and surgical subjects with which he occupies his leisure time in order to give his patients the benefit of the most thorough information attainable and all the new and improved remedies. November 16, 1870, he was married to Miss Amanda Wysong, daughter of L. B. Wysong, of Prathersville. Mrs. Posey's family was originally from Virginia, but she was born and educated in Ohio. The Doctor and wife have three children: Mary E., Harvey B. and John Lester. Mrs. P. is a member of the M. E.

HISTORY OF CLAY COUNTY

Church, and the doctor is a member of the Christian Church, and the A. F. and A. M.

JOHN S. PRATHER,

(Of Prather & Crockett, Dealers in Dry Goods, Notion, Hats and Caps, Boots and Shoes, Groceries and Provisions, Excelsior Springs).

For some years prior to engaging in business, Mr. Prather was farming in this county. He came here from Kentucky, where he was born and reared. The county of his nativity was Fayette, and the time of his birth in 1848. His father, John M. Prather, was sheriff of Estill county for some years and a prominent citizen of that county. He died there in 1862. He had also been a farmer for many years and was quite successful in his chosen occupation. Mr. Prather, Jr., was reared in Estill county, and in 1872 was married to Miss Louella Roberts, a daughter of Dennis Roberts, a farmer of Clay county, Mo. In the meantime, however, Mr. Prather had come to this State and located in Clay county. He came here in about 1868, and followed school teaching for a number of years, and then turned his attention to farming. In 1879 he began merchandising at Moscow, and two years later came to Excelsior. Prather & Crockett carry a large stock of goods in their line and are doing an excellent business. Both are business men of good qualifications and thorough reliability, and are justly popular in the community not only as merchants, but as citizens in all the walks of private life. Mr. and Mrs. Prather are members of the Christian Church. They have six children: Clay, Reba, Benjamin, Thomas, John and Roy.

WILLIAM R. PRICE

(Farmer and Stock-raiser, Post-office, Missouri City).

Maj. W. E. Price, the father of the subject of this sketch, came to Missouri from Jessamine county, Ky., in 1824, and entered land in Fishing River township, in Clay county, where he improved a farm and resided until his death. He was a major of a regiment during the Mormon war, and afterwards served as sheriff of the county. He died here January 4, 1880, at the age of 84. His wife is still living, now in her eighty-seventh year. She is remarkably bright and active, considering her advanced years, and is seemingly in as good health and spirits as she was in the morning of life. William R. Price was born on his father's farm in this county October 4, 1829, and remained at home until he was 19 years of age. He then, in 1850, went overland to California, and was absent in the West, barring several visits home, until 1865. He was principally in California, but parts of the time was also in Nevada and New Mexico. His regular occupation out there was handling stock and ranching, in which he had good success. Being at home about the time that the war broke out he enlisted in the Southern service under Col. Thompson, and was out about a year. During that time he took part in the fights at Lexington, Independence, Pea Ridge, and several

411

others. Returning home in the spring of 1862, the next year he went back to California. In 1865 he made another visit home, and on his return trip to the West was robbed by a band of predatory Indians, resulting in a loss to him of about $6,000. This almost completely broke him up, and on that account he returned to Clay county and rented a farm, going to work again with resolution to get another start. He has been in this county ever since, and now owns the farm which he rented to begin with. He first bought a part of the place in 1867, and has subsequently made two other purchases, by which he has become owner of all of it, a fine farm of 300 acres, and one of the best places in the county. February 24, 1881, Mr. Price was married to Miss Katie W. Dudley, a daughter of Elder James W. Dudley, of Audrain county. Mr. and Mrs. Price have two children: Virginia Russell and James Dudley. Mr. and Mrs. Price are members of the Old School Baptist Church.

WALTER C. PRICE

(Farmer and Stock-raiser, Post-office, Missouri City).

During the war Mr. Price served about seven months in the Southern army under Gen. Sterling Price. While in the army he took part in the battle of Pea Ridge, and one or two engagements of less importance. W. C. Price was reared in this county, and has long been accounted one of the substantial farmers and respected citizens of the county. His father was early chosen justice of the peace of Fishing River township, and afterwards he held that office for a number of years. Besides farming, being a man of energy and enterprise, he was from time to time identified with other interests, among others that of bridge building, and he built a number of bridges in the county. In agricultural affairs he always showed marked public spirit. He was largely instrumental in organizing the first agricultural society ever formed in this county, and in recognition of his prominence and services in the matter he was elected the first president of the society. Walter C. Price was born in this county in 1832, and was a son of Ebenezer and Sarah Price, who came here from Kentucky in 1826. His father, as has been said, was a farmer by occupation, and Walter was brought up to farming and handling stock. In 1860 he was married to Miss Mattie Young, of this county. They have five children: William Y., Winfrey E., Sallie E., Mary and Kittie. Mrs. Price is a member of the Baptist Church, and the 'Squire is a worthy member of the Masonic Order.

ALBERT B. REED

(Farmer, Post-office, Kearney, Clay county, Mo.).

Mr. Reed is superintendent and has control of what is known as the H. D. Brown farm, owned by Samuel Archer, and which contains nearly 500 acres. There is a good orchard on the place, numbering about 600 trees. Mr. R. is an experienced and practical farmer and makes a good farm manager and during the war he was in the State militia for a time under Capt. John Younger. He was a son of James and Emerine Reed, of Shelby county, Ky., who settled in Indiana in 1838, and after living with his parents there, Albert accompanied them to Monroe county, Mo., in 1858, and remained with them for one year when, in 1860, he commenced working for John Vaughn. In 1861 he became overseer or took charge of the farm of Mrs. Jane Kipper, four miles north of Paris, Monroe county, where he remained and had full control until December, 1864, then coming to Clay county. His parents had removed here in 1862. Since 1878, Mr. Reed has been located on his present farm. He was born in Shelby county, Ky., on the 13th of January, 1834, and came to Clay county in 1864. He was married here in January, 1867, to Miss Ellen Dagley. The have three children: James W., Joseph A. and Marshall A. Mr. R. and wife are members of the Christian Church.

HUGH J. ROBERTSON

(Cashier of the Savings Bank, Missouri City).

The above named banking institution was founded shortly after the war with R. J. Golmer, president, and H. J. Robertson, cashier Its capital was $50,000. Through all the years that have intervened since that time the bank has maintained a high reputation for solidity, business integrity and accommodating, obliging management. It is one of the most popular institutions of the kind, as it is one of the oldest, in the county. Much of the credit for its good management and popularity is due to the efficiency with which the subject of the present sketch has discharged his duties as cashier and to the high personal esteem in which he is held. Mr. Robertson is a native of this county, a son of Hon. Andrew Robertson, deceased, and was born on his father's homestead in the vicinity of Missouri City, November 16, 1830. His father came here in a very early day, in 1820, and represented the county in the Legislature during the years 1831 and 1832. He was from Tennessee to this State. His wife was a Miss Ruth Robertson, a cousin of his. He died on his homestead in this county, at a ripe old age, in 1870. In their family were three sons and four daughters, only three of whom are living. Hugh J. Robertson was reared on the farm and educated at Chapel Hill College. September 3, 1850, he was married to Miss Elizabeth Chancellor, a daughter of James Chancellor, of this county After his marriage Mr. Robertson engaged in the mercantile business at Missouri City, which he followed until after the outbreak of the war. On account of the unsettled condition of affairs during the war he suspended business, and after the restoration of peace engaged in his present banking business. Mr. and Mrs. Robertson have eight children: Andrew, now of New Mexico; Oscar, assistant cashier of the bank; Mary R., Elizabeth, Rebecca, Dixy, Caroline and Hugh J., Jr. Mr. Robertson is one of the highly respected and popular citizens of Missouri City. He served two terms as mayor of the place and in other local positions of public trust. Under President Johnson's administration he was postmaster at this place.

A. W. ROBERTSON, M. D.

(Physician and Surgeon, Prathersville).

Dr. Robertson's family, or rather his father's family, came to this State from Kentucky, and located in Platte county in 1847, where they still reside. The Doctor was born there on the 9th of May, 1847. Reared in that county, he had good school advantages in youth and acquired a good general English education. In 1867 he began the study of medicine under Drs. Wilson & Bonifant, at Weston, and in the fall of the next year matriculated at the St. Louis Medical College, where he took a full course of two terms, graduating with credit in 1871. Dr. Robertson located at Prathersville immediately after his graduation, in 1871. He has been actively engaged in the practice of his profession at this place ever since that time. He has had excellent success as a physician in the treatment of cases and has not failed to reap some of the substantial rewards of a large practice. However, he is by no means an avaricious man and studies far more the science of his profession than the means of accumulating property. He is a thoroughly capable and skillful physician, and is so regarded by all that know him who are qualified to judge of his professional attainments. February 3, 1873, he was married to Miss Lillian Pixley, of this county. They have three children: Fred, Edna and Curtis. The Doctor and wife are members of the Baptist Church.

WILLIS M. SIMMONS

(Of Simmons & Nowlin, Dealers in Dry Goods, Clothing, Hats, Caps, Boots and Shoes, Etc., Missouri City).

Mr. Simmons has occupied his time since he began to do for himself with two occupations, principally, namely, milling and merchandising. He was born in Madison county, Ky., September 18, 1835, and was reared in his native county. In 1857 he came to Clay county, Mo., and went to work in a mill. Three years later he bought an interest in the Claybrook flouring mills, and was engaged in running that for about five years. He then came to Missouri City and ran the mills at this place for the proprietors for some five years. In 1870 he quit the milling business and became a member of the firm of Long & Simmons, general merchants, at Missouri City. He has been engaged in merchandising ever since. During this time he has had several partners at different times, and the present partnership of Simmons & Nowlin was formed in 1882. They carry a large stock in the lines mentioned above and have an excellent trade. On the 22d of March, 1860, Mr. Simmons was married to Miss Eliza Brasfield, a daughter of Leonard Brasfield, who came to this State from Virginia by way of Kentucky. Mr. and Mrs. Simmons have four children: George, express agent at Missouri City; William L., clerk in the store of Simmons & Nowlin; Stonewall Jackson and Robert E. Lee. Mr. and Mrs. S. are members of the M. E. Church South. He is a member of the Masonic Order. For four years following 1870 he was justice of

HISTORY OF CLAY COUNTY

the peace for Missouri City township. Mr. Simmons' parents were William H. and Mourning (Walden) Simmons, the father of an old Maryland family, but the mother of a Virginia family. They came to Clay county and settled in Washington township in 1858. The father, a farmer by occupation, died here in 1867. The mother died here also.

WILLIAM B. SMITH

(Proprietor of the Missouri City Livery, Feed and Sales Stables, and Missouri City and Excelsior Springs Stage Line).

Mr. Smith is now in the third year of his experience here in his present line of business, and has thoroughly established his business on a firm footing. He has a good establishment in this line, an excellent building for the purpose, which is well stocked with riding and driving horses and with carriages, buggies, etc. By close attention to business and fair dealing he has won the good opinions of the community and the traveling public as a liveryman, and receives a liberal share of their patronage. Mr. Smith came to Missouri from Illinois in 1878. He at once located at Missouri City, and has been a resident of this place ever since, except for one year, which he spent at Excelsior Springs. Prior to engaging in the livery business he clerked in a dry goods store for about three years, but at Excelsior Springs he was engaged in the drug and grocery business on his own account. He was born in Menard county, Ill., November 4, 1844. His father, Judge Samuel Smith, was originally from Dutchess county, N. Y., and in his younger days was a school teacher by profession. In 1836 he came West and located in Cass county, Ill. Subsequently he lived in Menard county for a while, but returned to Cass and made that his permanent home. He was judge of the Cass county court for a number of years. William B. was reared in Cass county and remained there until he came to Missouri in 1878. He has been married twice. His first wife was a Miss Mary A. Whitsell, daughter of Hiram Whitsell, of Clinton county, Mo. She survived her marriage but five years, dying in 1879 and leaving one child, Artelia M. His second wife was a Miss Roberta A. Winfrey, daughter of W. H. Winfrey, deceased, formerly of Carroll county, Mo. Mr. Smith and his present wife have no children. She is a member of the Christian Church.

HON. CHARLES M. SWETNAM

(Farmer and Stock-raiser, Post-office, Liberty).

In 1882 Mr. Swetnam was nominated by the Democrats of this county at a primary election to represent the county in the State Legislature, and was elected by a very large majority. At the primary election he received more votes than the total number cast for both of the other two candidates. He made a useful representative in the Legislature, and his record was warmly approved by the people of the county. Mr. Swetnam is a man of large popularity, and very justly so, for the reason that he possesses to a marked degree many of the

415

HISTORY OF CLAY COUNTY

qualities which command the respect and appreciation of the public. A man of thoroughly upright character, superior general intelligence and agreeable manners, he wins the good opinion of all with whom he comes in contact. Mr. Swetnam's father, Hon. Thomas T. Swetnam, was also a representative from Clay county in the Legislature. He was elected for two terms, at the election of 1848 and the one of 1850. Previously he had served eight years as assessor of the county. He was a substantial farmer and stock-raiser, and highly respected by the people of the county. He was from Kentucky to this county in 1835, and died in 1859. His wife, who was a Miss Caroline Young before her marriage, also of Kentucky, survived until 1878. Hon. Charles M. Swetnam was born on his father's homestead in this county July 1, 1848. He was reared on the farm, and as he grew up acquired a good education in the public and high schools of the county. After attaining his majority he and an older brother, Thomas B., engaged as farmers, partners, in farming on the old family homestead, which they have ever since continued. They have a good farm and are quite successful. They also raise considerable stock, which they find a profitable branch of industry. Mr. Swetnam is a member of the Masonic Order.

JOHN H. TRIMBLE.

(Dealer in Dry Goods, Clothing, Notions, Hats, Caps, Boots, Shoes, Etc., Missouri City).

Mr. Trimble, a prominent merchant of the southern part of the county, is a native of Kentucky, born in Clark county, May 1, 1829. He is one in a family of children of William and Margaret (Fry) Trimble, both of early Kentucky families. The parents removed to Missouri in 1865, and located at Plattsburg, where the father died in 1872. John H. was reared in Clark county, Ky., and received a good common school education. February 4, 1850, he was married to Miss Margaret Raney, a daughter of William Raney, of Harrison county, Ky. Six years later Mr. Trimble removed to Missouri, and settled on a farm six miles north of Missouri City. He farmed there, and he also engaged in stock raising, including fine short horn cattle, and dealing in stock, until the spring of 1883, when he bought and established a store at Missouri City, and moved to this place. He carries a large stock of goods in his line, is a careful, judicious buyer, a good business man and accommodating to his customers, and has, therefore, had a successful career as a merchant. He has an excellent trade and is doing a good business. Mr. Trimble is prominently identified with the Democratic party in this county and takes an active interest in political matters, though he has never been himself an aspirant for office. Mr. and Mrs. Trimble have eight children: John T., now in Colorado; James L. and Benjamin F., both also in Colorado; Annie L., wife of Jasper Clevinger, of Ray county; Sarah C., Dora E., and Maggie. Mrs. T. is a member of the Baptist Church, as is also Mr. Trimble. He is furthermore a member of the

HISTORY OF CLAY COUNTY

A. F. and A. M., including the Blue Lodge, Chapter and Commandery in each of which he has held prominent positions.

JOSIAH J. VAUGHN (DECEASED)

(Vicinity of Blue Eagle).

Mr. Vaughn lost his life in the Southern army in 1862. He was an orderly sergeant in Reeves' regiment, and was severely wounded at the battle of Pea Ridge, and died of his wound at a hospital in Arkansas. Mr. Vaughn had been a resident of Clay county for some 10 years prior to the war. He came to this county from Kentucky with his family and engaged in farming. He was a man of marked intelligence, good general education, and a thoroughly energetic farmer. He made many friends here, and was highly esteemed by all who knew him. Mr. Vaughn was a prominent member of the Masonic Order, and took an active interest in the welfare of the Order. He assisted to organize several lodges in this vicinity of country. His widow is still living, and resides on the homestead with her two unmarried children. She was a Miss Mary T. Stewart, from Kentucky. They had five children: Francis J., Peterson S., Nancy E., Justin E. and Mary E. Mr. Vaughn and his wife were both born in Kentucky. Francis J., their eldest son, at whose instance this sketch is inserted, was born in the native county of his parents in Kentucky, and accompanied them to this State, and in 1861 joined the Southern army, but shortly afterward he was taken prisoner and confined at St. Louis for a time. He was then exchanged, and re-entered the Southern service. After the war he returned home and engaged in farming. He has a neat farm of 80 acres, and is comfortably situated.

GEORGE H. WALLIS

(Farmer and Stock-raiser, Post-office, Liberty).

When the Mexican War broke out, Mr. Wallis was a young man about 19 years of age, and had been reared in Clay county. Animated by the ardor of youth and the patriotic impulses which are inherent in every true son of Missouri, he promptly and gallantly offered himself as a volunteer to assist at the risk of his life in carrying the flag of his country down in triumph to the capital of the Montezumas. He became a member of Capt. Moss' company, under Col. Doniphan, and accompanied the old Missouri hero, Doniphan, throughout all his campaigns in New Mexico and beyond the Rio Grande in the land of the Cactus Republic. Mr. Wallis received an honorable discharge with the balance of his company after the war, at New Orleans, and came thence to his home in Henry county. From the hardships and dangers of military life he now took upon himself the labors and responsibilities of farm life. He at once went to work with energy and resolution, and soon had the satisfaction of seeing the substantial evidences of prosperous industry accumulate around him. In a word,

Mr. Wallis made gratifying progress in the direction of becoming a well-to-do and prominent farmer and stock-raiser. In August, 1848, he was married to Miss Mary H. Mosby, a daughter of Wade and Rebecca Mosby, referred to in the sketch of their son, John H. Mosby. Seven children have blessed the married life of Mr. and Mrs. Wallis, but two of these, alas, have been taken away by the merciless hand of death. The children living are Mary H., Sarah M., Margaret J., Artimesia, John H., William D. and Robert H. The two deceased are George N. and Katie. Mrs. W. is a member of the Christian Church. Mr. W.'s farm contains 240 acres, which is well improved. His residence was erected at a cost of $5,000, and he also has comfortable and commodious outbuildings. Mr. Wallis makes a specialty of raising and feeding hogs for the market, and is quite successful. In 1854 he was elected justice of the peace of Fishing River township, and he served in that office for four years.

JEREMIAH WHITE,

(Farmer, Post-office, Missouri City).

The well known Baptist minister, Henry Hill, was the clergyman who officiated at the marriage of Mr. White, the subject of the present sketch, to Miss Elizabeth McQuiddy, in 1836. The ceremony took place in Clay county, Mo., in which Mr. White had located, direct from Kentucky, some two years before. He had been baptized by "Raccoon" John Smith. Since the time of first locating here he has been a continuous resident of the county (except while temporarily absent in California) for a period of half a century. In personal appearance Mr. White is a man of medium build. Indeed he can not be said to be more than an ordinarily fleshy man, weighing in the vicinity (something past the mark) of 160 pounds; and although now well advanced in years, like most men in good health, he is quite good humored, and jocularly remarks that he has managed to pick up only five, pounds in Clay county in 50 years. In 1850 he went to California seeking his fortune in the Pactolian sands of the Pacific Coast. Locating at Sonoma, he was there employed as chain carrier under the afterwards famous Mr. Peabody, then an humble surveyor in the land beyond the Cordilleras kissed by the last rays of the setting sun. He received $5 a day under Mr. Peabody and afterwards ran a livery stable for Spriggs & Cooper at Sonoma. Subsequently, he set sail on the billowy waters of the Pacific, bound for his home in the heart of the Continent, by way of the Palm-leaf Isthmus of Panama and the Crescent City of New Orleans. Finally reaching home, he resumed farming and stock-raising, which he has continued ever since. He and his good wife have been blessed with nine children, namely: Benjamin, Martha, Mary N., Harriet S., John, Daniel T., Franklin, Jeremiah and Emma. Sarah M., the eldest, died at the age of nine years. Mr. White was born in Fayette county, Ky., September 15, 1812. He came to Clay county, Mo., in 1834.

THOMAS M. WILSON

(Farmer, Post-office, Prathersville).

Thirty years ago Mr. Wilson came to this county from Kentucky. He was a son of William Wilson, who settled in Kentucky from Virginia in an early day. Thomas Wilson was reared in the Blue Grass State, and was there married to Miss Martha Faucett. On coming to Missouri they settled in Clay county, where they made their permanent home. Mrs. Wilson died here in February, 1882. Mr. Wilson has a good farm which is fairly improved and is a comfortable homestead. His wife left him one child, Mary, who is now married. During the late war Mr. Wilson served in the State militia for a short time under Capt. William Garth.

CHAPTER XV.

PLATTE TOWNSHIP.

Position and Description — Early Settlements — Organization — First Justices — First Post-office — Tragedies of the Civil War — Churches in the County — Town of Smithville — "Yankee" Smith and his Eccentric Characteristics — His Death and the Epitaph on his Tombstone — Incorporation — Churches at Smithville — Odd Fellows' Lodge — Gosneyville — Churches — Biographical.

POSITION AND DESCRIPTION.

Platte township comprises the northwestern portion of Clay, its present boundaries being as follows: Beginning at the northwestern corner of the county; thence south along the county line between Clay and Platte to the southwest corner of section 22, in township 52, range 33, thence due east to the southeast corner of section 21, township 52, range 32; thence north to the southeast corner of section 33, township 53, range 32; thence east to the half section line north and south through section 35, township 53, range 32; thence due north to the county line between Clay and Clinton; thence west along the county line to the initial point.

The greater portion of the township is well timbered and watered, and the principal farms have been hewed and dug out of the timber. Generally the face of the country is broken, and the land rolling and elevated. The numerous branches of the Platte — Smith's fork, Camp branch, Owen's branch, Second creek, Wilkinson's creek— afford plenty of water and render the country hilly in their vicinity. The eastern part of the northern portion of the country was originally — at least many sections — prairie.

Some of the best farms in the county are in Platte township. Considerable labor was expended in making them, and those who performed this labor in most instances did not live to enjoy the full fruits thereof. It has been left for their successors to realize the good fortune. Many large farms and wealthy farmers—albeit the latter are plain and simple in their lives — are to be found in Platte township.

EARLY SETTLEMENT.

Among the first *bona fide* settlers in Platte township was Humphrey Smith, the old "Yankee," mentioned elsewhere. His mill, at what afterwards became Smithville, was the nucleus or head of subsequent settlements. Smith came in the summer of 1822. His son, Calvin, says his nearest neighbors were eight miles off, and were Ezekiel Huffman, Tarlton Whitlock, David Magill, Abraham Creek and James Wills.

Prior to 1824 there were in what is now Platte township Rice B. Davenport, five miles east of Smithville; Capt. James Duncan, at Elm Grove, one mile south of Davenport; Capt. Wm. Duncan, three miles south of Smithville, and in the fall of 1824 came Eleven Thatcher, to his claim, two miles south, or about one mile north of Duncan. One account given fixes the date of the settlements of the Duncans as in the spring of 1824. In the eastern part of the township (west half of section 14—53—32) a squatter named Castle White lived in 1826. The dates and locations of other settlers in the township, prior to the creation of the township, in 1827, can not now be obtained, but it is known that there were at least thirty families in what is now the township before 1828.

ORGANIZATION.

Upon the organization of the county what is now Platte township was included in Gallatin. But in time it became necessary to have a third township, this portion being then thickly settled, and needing separate organization. Accordingly at the special term of the county court, in June, 1827, Platte township was created, with the following boundaries : —

Beginning on the boundary line of the State where the sectional line dividing sections 22 and 27 strikes said boundary line, in range 33, from thence due east along said sectional line dividing 22 and 27, to the sectional line dividing sections 21 and 22, in range 32, and from thence due north along said sectional line between 21 and 22 in range 32, to the township line dividing 52 and 53, and from thence due east to the western boundary line of Fishing River township, in section 36, township 53, and from thence due north to the northern boundary line of the county.

The first justices of the peace of the township were Wm. Duncan and James Duncan. The first constable was Jesse Yocum. Elections were held at James Duncan's, and the judges were James Winn, Wm. Yocum and John Loyd.

The first post-office in the township was at Elm Grove, the residence of Capt. James Duncan, six miles southeast of Smithville. It was established some time prior to 1835. This was the first post-

HISTORY OF CLAY COUNTY

office in this region of country, and was resorted to for years by the settlers in the Platte Purchase, and by many others.

TRAGEDIES OF THE CIVIL WAR.

During the Civil War a number of the citizens of Platte township were killed at or near their homes. The bushwhackers killed Bishop Bailey and Columbus Whitlock, and the Clay county militia killed Thos. D. Ashurst while on the way with him to Liberty, as narrated elsewhere.

John Ecton, Jr., had been in the Southern army, but had returned and was living quietly at home. A Federal detachment took him from his work of breaking hemp, carried him away and killed him.

In the first week of June, 1863, a squad of Federal State militia took prisoner Rev. A. H. F. Payne, a prominent member of the Christian Church, residing in the southern part of Clinton county, but well known and universally respected in Clay. They carried the prisoner with them on a raid through this township and halted one night at Smithville, where Mr. Payne passed his last night on earth at the residence of Col. Lewis Wood. The next day he was taken out, near his residence, and shot to death.

Near the time when Rev. Payne was killed Capt. John Reid was shot by a detachment of Federals at a point about three miles northeast of Smithville. Capt. Reid was a prisoner and was mounted on a fine swift horse. He sought to escape by the superior speed of his horse, and dashed away, but the Federal bullets were swifter than the horse, and he was shot out of his saddle. Many a prisoner was shot during the war in an *alleged* attempt to escape, but it is said by good Southern friends of the Captain, that he really was attempting to obtain his freedom when he was killed.

COUNTRY CHURCHES.

First Baptist Church of Platte. — This is probably the oldest church located in the limits of Clay county, and certainly the first one of Platte township, having been organized at Duncan's school-house, on Saturday, June 23, 1827. It is located on the northeast quarter of section 36, in township 53 north, range 38 west. Here the church building, originally constructed of logs, stood, but in 1876 a frame building was erected, costing $1,000. The first members were William Vance, Barbara Vance, Richard Jesse, Frances Jesse, Juliet„C. Jesse, John Thatcher, Woodford F. Jesse, William Corum, Bersheba

HISTORY OF CLAY COUNTY

Corum, Abijah Brooks, John Lloyd, Nancy Lloyd, Eleanor Corum and Polly Nance. Abijah Brooks was the first church clerk, being succeeded by Woodford Jesse. The church now has 15 members, and its clerk is Edward P. Moore. Revs. D. W. Riley, William Thorp, Eppa Tillery, Thomas Turner, Darius Bainbridge, William Warren, T. W. Todd and John E. Goodson have been the pastors in charge.

Mount Olive Christian Church. — This church is located on the northwest quarter and southwest quarter of section 8, township 52, range 32, where stands an excellent frame building, erected in 1875, and costing about $2,000. In connection with it is a handsomely laid out cemetery. Twenty-six persons comprised the original membership, as follows: Louis Grimes and Jacob R. Wilson, who were made elders; Samuel Hunt, William Christa, B. T. Gordon, G. C. Clardy, chosen as deacons; Bennett Smith, who was made clerk; Ellen Christa, Ruth Grimes, Mattie Wilson, Isaac P. Wilson, Isabella Wilson, Joel E. Grimes, Sallie Grimes, Sallie Hunt, Ellen Hunt, Nancy E. Smith, Sarah M. Crow, Mattie H. Crow, Lavena Blackstone, Elizabeth Dickerson, Giles C. Clark, Mattie Adams, Jeff T. Thompson, Lizzie Grimes, Ruth B. Grimes. The pastors who have filled the pulpit here are W. C. Rogers, Bayard Waller, A. B. Jones, H. B. Clay, S. R. Hand and Rev. Mr. Watson. The present membership is about 100. There are 25 scholars in the Sabbath-school, the superintendent being Mr. Gusten.

SMITHVILLE.

The town of Smithville stands on section 23, township 53, range 33, or one mile from the Platte county line and about five miles from Clinton county. It is a small village, but a trading point of already great advantage to the people of the surrounding country, and it promises now, with a railroad in quite reasonable prospect, to become at no very distant date a town of no small importance and consequence.

The first settler on the present site of Smithville was Humphrey Smith, who came in the spring of 1822, and two years later, or in 1824, built a mill on the fork of Platte river, which still bears his name. He was born in New Jersey in 1774, lived in Pennsylvania from 1784 to 1800, in Erie county, N. Y., from 1800 to 1816, and then removed to Howard county, Mo., where he resided three years and a half; then he removed to what is now Carroll county — then Chariton —

HISTORY OF CLAY COUNTY

where he remained until 1822, when he came to Clay. He was universally known as "Yankee" Smith.

With something of Yankee enterprise and shrewdness Smith located where he did and built his mill in order to catch the patronage of the government Indian agencies in the Platte country, and also the custom of the settlers who, he rightly conjectured, would push out in considerable numbers to the extreme frontier. The mill at first was but a "corn-cracker," but in a few years, when wheat was first raised in the country, Smith added a bolting apparatus, and it is said that this was the first flouring mill in Clay county. It stood near the site of the present mill, and Smith's dwelling-house, a log cabin, was built on the south side of Main street where the Liberty road turns south, and east of the road. The mill was operated by Smith and his sons for thirty consecutive years, and then purchased by Col. Lewis Wood. It was washed away by a flood in 1853.[1]

"Yankee" Smith was all his life an avowed Abolitionist. He declaimed against what he considered the *sin* of human slavery at all times and under all circumstances. For his principles he was mobbed in Howard county and driven away. His family fled to what is now Carroll, and he joined them as soon as it was safe to do so. But no sort of persecution, blows, mobbings, threats, denunciation, or raillery moved him or deterred him from speaking his mind. Frequently some bully would approach him and call out: "Smith, are you an Abolitionist?" "I am," was always the reply. The next instant he would be knocked down; but he would rise and calmly say: "O, *that's* no argument. You are stronger than I, but that don't prove you are right." Finally his soft answers turned away the wrath of those opposed to him, and he was allowed to hold and express his opinions in peace.

Smith always declared that slavery would be abolished in the United States, but he did not live until his eyes had seen "the glory." In June, 1857, he died of small-pox. It has always been supposed that he caught the disease from an infected Abolition paper, called the *Herald of Freedom*, published at Lawrence, Kas., and to which his son, Calvin, was a subscriber. The postmaster, James Brasfield, who handed Smith the paper, took varioloid, and Smith himself had small-pox in a violent and fatal form. At first his disease was not known,

---

[1] The first mention of Smith's mill in the county records appears in the proceedings of the county court in the summer of 1826, in connection with the reviewing of a road from Liberty thereto.

and persons who called to see him were infected, and spread the contagion through the neighborhood. Many died therefrom, and the incident was one long and sadly remembered.[1]

Humphrey Smith had a store at his mill before 1828, and soon after a little village sprang up. Calvin Smith, a son of Humphrey, managed the store at first. Next to him were Henry Owens and John Lerty, both of whom were small merchants here before 1840. James Walker was another early merchant. Dr. Alex. M. Robinson, afterward a prominent Democratic politician of Platte, Dr. J. B. Snaile and Dr. S. S. Ligon were the first physicians in the community.

Old settlers assert that as early as 1845 Smithville was a place of as much importance as at present, with nearly the same number of houses, and a great deal more whisky! The failure of the Parkville Railroad prevented the full development of the place, and entailed considerable loss on many of the citizens who were subscribers to the stock. Although always without railroad facilities the town has ever had a good trade. At present — April, 1885 — there is good prospect for securing to the town the St. Joseph and Southeastern Railroad within a year.

Smithville has been several times incorporated. The first incorporation was by the county court, August 7, 1867; this was amended April 8, 1868, but the trustees appointed never qualified, and July 6,

---

[1] As stated, Humphrey Smith died in June, 1857. He was buried in a small graveyard in Platte county, four miles northwest of Smithville. The following inscription appears upon his tombstone: —

"IN MEMORY OF HUMPHREY SMITH, BORN IN 1774, DIED JUNE, 1857.

" Like leaves on trees the race of man is found,
Now green in youth, now withering on the ground;
So generations in their course decay,
So perish these when those have passed away.

"This patriot came to Missouri in 1816, from the State of New York; labored to make the territory into a Free State, for which he was mobbed by armed slaveholders, scourged, bruised and dragged at midnight from his house. His ever faithful wife, coming to his assistance, received injuries at the hands of the mob which caused her years of affliction. He was compelled to leave the State. His wife and family fled from Howard county to Carroll county; there joining his family, he moved to Clay county, where for many years he kept up the struggle against the 'negro thieves or man stealers.' They denounced him as an Abolitionist, because he was in favor of human liberty for all men. His request was, 'Never let the men stealers know where I am buried until my State is free, then write my epitaph.'

" Here lies Humphrey Smith, who was in favor of human rights, universal liberty, equal and exact justice, no union with slaveholders, free States, free people, union of States and one and universal republic."

following, the county court appointed Erastus Smith, Jacob Kraus, Otis Guernsey, Theodoric Fitzgerald and Matthew McGregory in their stead. February 4, 1878, there was another incorporation, the territory incorporated being described as "all that portion of the southwest quarter of section 23, township 53, range 33, lying south of Smith's fork of Platte river." October 8, following, there was a reincorporation as "a town," with J. D. DeBerry, J. C. Brasfield, William Clardy, W. H. Rhoads and John Swartz as trustees. The town is now running under this incorporation. The population of Smithville is at present about 250.

CHURCHES.

Church of Christ at Smithville. — There are but few facts mentioned in connection with the histroy of this church which have been preserved, and some of the most important items of interest can not now be given. The organization of the church was effected October 13, 1843, and though the present membership comprises 151 communicants, the membership in that early day was composed only of Alexander B. Duncan, Preston Akers, Henry Owens, L. J. Wood, Christopher C. Baily, James G. Williams, Sr., Jonathan Owens, James H. Thorp, John Grimes, James Krauss, Margaret Krauss, Helen M. Duncan, Rachel C. Buchanan, Lucinda G. Grimes, Eleanor Breckinridge, Elizabeth Ecton, Juda Strode, Missouri A. Owens and Joseph Shafer. Some of the pastors have been Moses E. Lard, Preston Aker, A. H. F. Payne, William H. Robison, G. B. Waller and John W. Tate, the present pastor. In 1848, at a cost of $1,000, a plain, unostentatious brick church edifice was built. In 1883 a new building was erected at an expenditure of $4,500. This is one of the handsomest brick churches in the county. G. W. Clardy superintends the Sabbath-school, which numbers 80 pupils. Mr. J. F. Justus is church clerk.

Smithville Baptist Church. — J. D. DeBerry and wife, Mary A. DeBerry, J. B. Colley and wife, S. P. Herndon, Eliza and Emeline Herndon, Mary J. Parker and Clarissa H. Basley were the constituent members of this church, which was organized in the spring of 1873, and which now includes in its membership 108 persons. Rev. Mr. Livingston was instrumental in its formation. The first pastor was L. D. Lampkin, and he was succeeded by R. H. Jones, W. W. Wilkerson and A. Barton, after whom again came Mr. Jones. In 1882 the frame church building in which they now worship was constructed at a cost of about $1,700.

ODD FELLOWS LODGE.

Vigilant Lodge No. 289, I. O. O. F., at Smithville, was organized November 28, 1872. The original members were John H. Marr, S. S. Johnson, F. O. Estes, G. H. Hays and John Swartz. A. B. Crawford, L. J. Wood, Erastus Smith and Samuel Venrick were initiated the first night. The present officers of the lodge are R. P. Wood, noble grand; L. P. Moore, vice grand; J. R. Shafer, secretary; John Swartz, treasurer; A. K. Elliott, chaplain; John R. Swartz, conductor. The present membership is 27. John Swartz, who was the first treasurer, is the only one of the charter members now remaining.

GOSNEYVILLE.

Gosneyville, a small hamlet in the northern part of Platte township (on the southeast quarter of section 5, township 53, range 32), has half a dozen houses, two churches, stores, etc. It was never regularly laid out, and has no official history. Many years ago John Gosney established a blacksmith shop here, and for him the village was named. The post-office is called Paradise.

CHURCHES.

Gosneyville M. E. Church South. — This church was organized at the old Corum school-house, near Smithville, in 1843, by Rev. E. M. Marvin and Rev. Amos Tutt, and was the first M. E. Church organized in Platte township. The original members were: Geo. W. Douglas, Jane Douglas, Mahala McGee, James O. McGee, Julia McGee, Thomas McGee, Samuel J. McGee, Jane McGee, Polly Hulse, Mary Hulse, Moses McCall, Abner Loyd, William Slayton and John K. Rollins. The first pastor was Rev. Amos Tutt. The church is a frame building, and was built in 1868. The present membership is 127. Rev. Winston is the present pastor of the church. Connected with the church is a Sunday-school, with B. F. Rollins as superintendent.

Gosneyville Christian Church — This church was instituted July 18, 1868, by Rev. Preston Aker and Josiah Waller. The constituent members were John Gosney, Thomas D. Sparks, F. M. Graham, A. J. Lawrence, Samuel Moore, N. W. Litton, Bird Benton, Wm. H. Shannon, Rufus Patcher, Peter L. Holtzclaw, Henry Anderson, W. M. Endicott, Archibald Holtzclaw, Franklin Holtzclaw, Amos Anderson, James L. Vaughn, John Anderson, Francis McCracken, John W. Youtsey, Peter Youtsey, James C. Youtsey, David Summers, A.

HISTORY OF CLAY COUNTY

E. Mackabell, Geo. E. T. Parker, Alex. C. Scott, Jasper Perrin, John Bernard, Robert A. Hamilton, Peter C. Callaway, Henry Snow, T. K. Ross, Saml. Fleming and William Grooms. The church now has about 65 members. In 1870 a plain frame edifice was built, costing $1,500. Revs. Thos. Williamson, Bayard Waller, A. J. Pickrell, Benj. Hyder, — Blake and R. C. Watson have all ministered to this church as pastors.

BIOGRAPHICAL.

JAMES F. ADAMS

(Manufacturer of and Dealer in Saddles, Harness, Etc., Etc., Smithville).

Near the historic hermitage of Gen. Jackson, in Wilson county, Tenn., Mr. Adams was born on the 19th of August, 1819. His parents were James and Sarah (Bernard) Adams, and were originally from Virginia. They had removed, however, from that State to Kentucky and thence to Tennessee. In 1842 they came to Missouri and settled near Ridgeley, in Platte county, where the father followed farming and stock-raising. He died in 1866 at St. Joe, while on a trip to that place. The mother had preceded him in 1852. They had a family of nine children, six of whom are living. James F. Adams, the subject of this sketch, was reared in Tennessee and came out to Platte county the year previous to the removal of his father's family to the county. In Tennessee he had learned and worked at the saddle and harnessmaker's trade and this he resumed at Ridgeley, in Platte county. In 1857, however, having previously bought a farm, he engaged in farming and continued that for nearly 20 years, or until 1876 when he came to Smithville and once more went to work at his trade. Mr. Adams was married in 1843 to Miss Mary Owen, a daughter of Nicholas Owen, an early settler of Clay county from Kentucky. Mr. and Mrs. Adams have six children: Mary E., who has the misfortune to have been blind from infancy, resulting from a fever; Sarah M., wife of Robert Reed, of St. Joe; Lou M., wife of W. L. DeBerry; Maggie, wife of Dr. J. L. Mezner; Julia M., wife of Ernest Nelkerson, and James E. During President Polk's administration Mr. Adams was postmaster at Ridgeley.

GIDEON C. BLACKWOOD

(Owner and Proprietor of Oak Grove Stock Farm, Post-office, Liberty).

Oak Grove stock farm is situated six miles northwest from Liberty on the road leading from that place to Smithville. It contains 400 acres and is handsomely improved. The buildings, including the residence, barns and outhouses, are of a superior class, and the place is not only well fenced, but divided up into convenient fields, pastures, meadows, etc., for farming and stock purposes. The land is principally run in blue grass, though enough is cultivated to produce a sufficiency of grain and other products for home use. It is also well watered, and in every sense is one of the choice stock farms of the county. The land is very fertile, and has never been impoverished by misuse either from over tillage or injudicious pasturing. Mr. Blackwood keeps his place in excellent condition and order, and takes hardly less pride in the appearance of the farm than in its utility. He makes a specialty of breeding and raising fine stock. It has been a rule of his for years always to breed the best stock to be had in the country, and never suffer a scrub of any sort to come on the place. He has a handsome herd of fine short horns, from which he annually sells a number of young bulls and heifers. His short horns are all of registered breeds, and are either registered themselves in the American Short Horn Herd Book, or are entitled to register upon proper application. He also has fine breeds of horses, hogs, sheep and other stock. Besides his fine stock interests, he makes a business of dealing in stock generally. Mr. Blackwood is a native Missourian, born in-Clay county, April 7, 1858. His father was William Blackwood, originally from Gaston county, N. C., and late a substantial farmer of this county, but who died April 14, 1878. Mr. B.'s mother, who is still living, was a Miss Mary J. Stapp before her marriage, a daughter of Abijah Stapp, of Howard county. Gideon C. Blackwood is a young man unmarried.

JAMES W. BOGGESS

(Farmer, Post-office, Smithville).

Among the prominent farmers of Platte township is the subject of the present sketch. Mr. Boggess' father, Dennis H. Boggess, was an early settler here from Kentucky. He was married in this county to Miss Nancy Corum, also originally from Kentucky. She died in 1863, leaving four children, four of whom are living. The father was an enterprising farmer of the county and a man well thought of by all who knew him. James W., the subject of this sketch, was born in this county, July 3, 1844. He attended the common schools in his youth and learned the occupation of farming as he grew up, together with raising and handling stock. He thus acquired a decided taste for the calling of farmer and stock-raiser and adopted it as his permanent pursuit. He has been quite successful and is one of the substantial agriculturalists of the township. He was married in Platte county, Mo., February 18, 1869, to Miss Elizabeth Srite, a daughter of John and America Srite, formerly of Kentucky. Mr. and Mrs. B. have had seven children, four of whom are living: William A., Carrie, Emma and Owen. Mr. and Mrs. B. are members of the Christian Church.

CAPT. ALPHEUS BOREGARD

(Post-office, Paradise).

From his father, John Boregard, the subject of this sketch inherited that patriotic love of country and desire for military activities which prompted him, when the call for troops was made to defend the Stars and Stripes, to enlist as a plighted soldier for the Union. At the breaking out of the war he entered the Third regiment, West Virginia calvary, U. S. A., and served until the close of the war. We can not take the space to follow him through his four years of campaigning in the various parts of the country or to give any idea of the dangers and hardships through which he passed. Suffice it to say, that as a soldier he was distinguished for bravery among as brave a body of men as ever kept step to martial music, or faced death without fear on the field of battle. He participated in all the campaigns and battles in which his command took part and was ever found in the front rank fearlessly and relentlessly fighting. For service in the battle of Five Forks he was made captain of a company, an honor conferred upon him for his courage and intrepidity. Capt. Boregard was born in Jackson county, Va., now West Virginia, September 10, 1834, and was a son of John and Sarah J. (Postlethwaite) Boregard, both Virginians by birth. The former was born October 12, 1789, and the latter in February, 1787. After their marriage in Virginia, they went to Meigs county, O., in 1842, where they both died, the father, January 15, 1863, and the mother May 15, 1872. The father was a potter by trade, and also followed farming. Mrs. B. was a member of the Baptist Church. Alpheus was reared in Meigs county, and was educated in the district schools of the neighborhood. He first learned the trade of ship building and afterwards that of carpenter and joiner, at which he worked until the outbreak of the war. After his return from that conflict he returned to Ohio, where he was engaged in the grocery business at Pomeroy. In May, 1868, he removed to Kansas City, Mo., following carpentering and building that year and in the fall removed to Clay county, where he is now occupied in tilling the soil and working in the occupation of a farmer. His landed estate embraces 120 acres in cultivation, upon which is a neat residence. In February, 1865, Capt. Boregard was married in Ohio to Miss Eliza Hall, who died in 1860, leaving three children : Alice, John A. and Maxie Belle. His second wife was Mrs. Melissa Boone, to whom he was married in Spencer county, Va., February 12, 1863. She was the widow of Dr. D. G. Boone, who was killed at Spencer Court House, August 6, 1861, by Confederate troops. Nine children have been born to them : William H. C., Otto D., Ferdinand DeSoto, Ada G. and Maud are living, and four are deceased. Capt. B. is connected with the I. O. O. F.

JOHN C. BRASFIELD

(Of Brasfield, Spratt & Thatcher, Dealers in General Merchandise, Post-office, Smithville).

Mr. Brasfield began mercantile life at the age of 18 as clerk, in 1859, in a general store at Smithville. There he continued as such until the breaking out of the late Civil War. Going to Pike's Peak in the spring of 1861, he remained there a short time and then returned the same year and entered the Confederate army, under Maj. Savory, in Price's army, serving about one year. During that time he was corporal of a company. He returned home in the spring of '63, and in the fall of that year went to Leavenworth, Kas., where he resumed the occupation of clerking in a wholesale dry goods establishment. Upon coming back to Missouri, in 1864, he embarked in business for himself, buying a small general stock of goods at Smithville, where he continued up to the spring of '66. He now disposed of his store at this place and removed to Platte county, locating at Linkville, where, for about 18 months, he conducted a store, or until was he burned out. Retracing his steps then to Smithville, in partnership with his father and father-in-law, he bought and fed 140 head of cattle, but in 1869 again went to Platte county, where he was occupied in farming until the year 1871. He now established himself once more in the mercantile business at Smithville, and, with one exception, has remained here since in his present calling. The firm of Brasfield, Spratt & Thatcher is one of the oldest established business houses in the county, and one of the best known and most reliable. Mr. Brasfield is himself also interested in real estate and has laid off an addition to the town of Smithville, known as Brasfield's Addition, which contains about 15 good dwellings and in the neighborhood of 40 excellent lots. Mr. Brasfield was born in Platte county, Mo., in 1841. His parents, Thomas W. R. and Elizabeth Brasfield, came to this State from Clay county, Ky., in 1832 or 1833. The parents of the former settled in Clinton county, while his mother's parents (Lynn and Eleanor Breckenridge) located in Clay county. After the marriage of Mr. B.'s parents they removed to what is known as the Platte Purchase, where they were among the earliest settlers. The father was a merchant by occupation, and was fairly successful in business. He died in Platte county in 1874, his widow departing this life at Smithville in 1882. Mr. Brasfield was married in December, 1864, to Miss Minerva, a daughter of Daniel and Sarah Thatcher, of Platte county. They have four children: James W., Eleanor, John S. and Morton. Three are deceased, all dying in childhood. Mr. and Mrs. B. are members of the Christian Church. Mr. B. is connected with the A. F. and A. M., is a Chapter member, and also a Knight Templar. He also belongs to the I. O. O. F.

WILEY R. BRASFIELD

(Dealer in Drugs, Medicines, Etc., Smithville).

Mr. Brasfield is a younger brother to John C. Brasfield, whose sketch precedes this, and was born in Liberty township, this county, in 1848. As he grew up he had the advantage of a course in the Kansas City High School in addition to the usual course in the common schools. After concluding his high school course, in 1869, he engaged in farming in Platte county, the occupation to which he had been brought up, and he continued farming in that county with success for about ten years. In 1879, however, he came to Smithville and engaged in the drug business, which he has followed ever since. His store, now in the sixth year of its career, has long since passed the doubtful or experimental period of its career and has become established as one of the solid and fixed business houses of the place. He has a trade that he can always safely rely upon, it matters not what other houses come and go, a trade that is almost as secure for an income of a certain sum per annum as a Government pension. Besides this he has new customers coming to him all the time, so that his trade has a steady and substantial growth and increase. He understands his business thoroughly, treats everybody fairly and sells at reasonable prices. Hence it is nonsense to suspect that he is not bound to succeed. In 1872 he was married to Miss Alwilda, a daughter of John L. DeBerry, of Platte county. However, Mr. Brasfield's first wife died about four years ago, leaving him two children: James E. and Lula K., besides losing two in infancy. The mother was an earnest member of the Baptist Church. To his present wife Mr. Brasfield was married in 1882. She was a Miss Florence Hord, a daughter of Elias Hord, a farmer and stock-raiser of this county. She is a member of the Christian Church, as is also Mr. Brasfield. He is furthermore a member of the A. F. and A. M.

M. BYRD

(Of Byrd & Co., Dealers in General Merchandise, Smithville).

Mr. Byrd was born in the valley of the Shenandoah, in Shenandoah county, Va., in 1828, and was the second child in a family of nine children of William and Mary S. (Shafer) Byrd, both of old Virginia families. The father was a millwright by trade, and removed to Missouri with his family in 1832. He first located in Clay county, but six years afterwards settled in Platte county, where he followed farming in connection with his trade for many years. He finally gave his entire attention to farming. He was also justice of the peace for a number of years. Mr. Byrd, senior, survived to the advanced age of 89, dying in 1882. His wife lived to be 76 years of age, preceding him to the grave by one year. He left a good farm in Platte county, which has fallen to his children. Young Bird, the subject of this sketch, was reared in that county, and at the age of 17 went to work

HISTORY OF CLAY COUNTY

at the carpenter's trade, which he followed for over ten years, in connection, however, most of the time, with farming. In 1856 he engaged in the drug business at Smithville, and about three years later in the dry goods and grocery line. In 1862 he quit merchandising and bought a mill, which he ran for about three years, and then went to Idaho. Returning from the West in 1879, where he had been engaged in raising stock and carpentering to some extent, as well as in hotel keeping at Boyce City, he shortly afterwards resumed merchandising at Smithville in a general store line, which he has ever since followed. In 1852 he was married to Miss Phœbe Silvey, a daughter of James H. and Lucy Silvey, formerly of Kentucky. Mr. and Mrs B. have reared but one child, a son, Alfred O., who is his father's partner in business. He was married in 1882 to Miss Alma, a daughter of Dr. J. L. Hezner, of Smithville. They have a little daughter, Sallie G.

GILES C. CLARDY

(Of Clardy, Owen & Co., Dealers in Hardware, Agricultural Implements, Etc., Smithville).

Mr. Clardy is an uncle to Hon. Martin Linn Clardy, member of Congress from the Farmington district, in this State, and was born at Bowling Green, in Warren county, Ky., June 10, 1813. The family was originally from Virginia, and his father, Norman S. Clardy, came from that State to Kentucky in about 1800. Mr. C.'s mother was also from Virginia, a Miss Rachel Johnson before her marriage. They came to Missouri in about 1836, and, after a short residence in Carroll county, settled in Platte county, where they made their permanent home. The father lived to reach the age of nearly 100 years, having been born in 1778 and dying in 1876. The mother lived to be 85 years of age. Both died in Ste. Genevieve county, where the father's brother, J. B. Clardy, the father of Hon. M. L. Clardy, settled in a very early day. Giles C. Clardy, the subject of this sketch, was reared in Kentucky, and became a successful and popular school teacher. He came to Missouri in 1837, and afterwards taught some years in Clinton and Platte counties. In 1840, however, he engaged in farming in Platte county and followed it for nearly 30 years. But selling out in that county in 1868, he subsequently resided for awhile in Clay and then Bates counties, and in 1874 came back to Clay county and engaged in his present line of business at Smithville. His son, Giles W. Clardy, is one of his partners in business. Mr. Clardy, the subject of this sketch, was married in 1835 to Miss Araminta Adams, a daughter of James and Sarah A. (Bernard) Adams, formerly of Tennessee. Mr. and Mrs. Clardy have three living children: Garland C., Martha A., wife of E. B. Thatcher, and Giles W. Four others are deceased, two in infancy and two in later years. Mr. C. is a member of the Primitive Baptist Church, and also of the A. F. and A. M. His father, referred to above, Norman S. Clardy, was, in his day, one of the leading farmers and slaveholders of Platte county. In his lifetime he amassed a comfortable fortune.

433

ALEXANDER B. CRAWFORD

(Farmer and Stock-raiser, Post-office, Smithville).

Mr. Crawford, like many of the staunch citizens of Clay county is a native of Kentucky, having been born in March, 1824, in Nicholas county. He was reared on a farm there, receiving instruction in the common schools, being trained also in that school of hardships and adventures which gave its pupils great strength of character and greater fortitude, and made them more courageous and better fitted for the hard struggles of life than does the atmosphere in our college walls. His parents, Alexander B. and Charlotte (Riggs) Crawford, were originally from Maryland, but were reared and married in Kentucky, which continued to be their home until their death. The father, a brave and patriotic citizen of that State (then territory), upon the call for volunteers to defend the young colonies in their efforts for independence, bravely enlisted as a soldier and served during the War of 1812. The sterling characteristics which prompted him to enlist in that struggle remained with him during life, and ever afterwards characterized his years of labor. He died in April, 1876, his wife having preceded him in September, 1866. They had both been members of the M. E. Church. Alexander B. Crawford, the subject of this sketch, adhered to the calling which he had followed in early life, and for a time was also occupied in driving stock, continuing it until he came to Clay county, Mo., in 1859. Having a desire to enter into mercantile life, he embarked in the drug business in Smithville in 1861, following it for three years. In 1864 he took up his location at Bainbridge, Clinton county, and for two years operated quite successfully a saw and grist mill at that place. On April 1, 1867, returning to Smithville, he opened a store of general merchandise. This he carried on until 1870. At that time his desire to re-engage in farming caused him to dispose of his mercantile interests, and he has since been occupied with agricultural pursuits. He has a large farm, embracing nearly 400 acres of improved and cultivated land, admirably adapted for farming purposes. Mr. Crawford was married on April 4, 1871, to Miss Mary E. Barnard, in Clay county. She was a daughter of Landa Barnard, of this county, but died in 1872. She was a member of the M. E. Church South. Mr. Crawford is a member of the I. O. O. F. He takes a deep interest in all questions of public welfare and advancement, whether local, State or National.

STEPHEN C. DUNCAN

(Farmer and Breeder and Shipper of Thoroughbred Short Horn Cattle, Post-office, Smithville).

Mr. Duncan has a large stock farm of 1,263 acres, nearly all in blue grass, and one of the finest stock farms in Platte township. He makes a specialty of raising and handling thoroughbred short horn cattle, producing no grain whatever except for feeding purposes on the farm.

HISTORY OF CLAY COUNTY

A clear-headed, practical business man, he does everything of a pecuniary nature from a common sense, business point, believing that it pays best to feed what grain and grass he may raise to stock, putting them on the market in the shape of cattle, hogs, sheep and other farm animals. Mr. Duncan has led a very active life, and one not devoid of substantial results. He was seven years of age when his parents came to this county in 1840, having been born in Henry county, Ky., December 15, 1833. He was the son of Stephen and Lucy (Browning) Duncan, both natives of Bourbon county, Ky., the former of whom was born October 17, 1797. After their marriage, in the county of their birth, they removed to Saline county, Mo., in 1838, and to Clay county in 1840, thence settling in Clinton county, Mo. There the father died April 6, 1877, but his wife had departed this life in Saline county in 1838. He was a farmer by occupation, and he belonged to the A. F. and A. M. Both were members of the Christian Church. Stephen C. Duncan, the sixth of seven children, was reared in this county, and here received an ordinary common-school education. He accompanied his father on his various moves above mentioned, and in April, 1855, in partnership with him, engaged in the purchase of short horn cattle in Clinton county, being one of the pioneers in that branch of industry. He continued to be thus occupied with his father until 1863, and has followed it alone since that time, buying, feeding and shipping cattle during that perio . After leaving Clinton county he returned to this county, locating on the farm which he now occupies, mentioned above. His herd of short horns number 170 head — as fine animals as are to be found within the limits of this or any other county. These facts show that Mr. Duncan has been quite successful as a farmer and stock-raiser. He has been twice married. March 5, 1863, Miss Mary E. Davenport became his wife. She died September 10. 1869, having been a member of the Christian Church. He was married a second time November 10, 1870, in Clinton county, Mo., to Miss Maria Winn, a daughter of James and Malinda Winn, *nee* Hutsell, originally of Bourbon county, Ky., who came to Clay county in 1825. Mrs. Duncan was born and reared in Clinton county, and was educated at Camden Point High School in Platte county. They have three children : Lucy, the eldest, a most attractive young lady just blooming into young womanhood ; Mattie and Mabel. Mr. Duncan has been a member of the Christian Church since 1854, and is one of its present elders. His wife is connected with the same church, and he is a member in high standing of the A. F. and A. M. Politically he is a Democrat. He is popularly known, but none the less respected, as " Duff " Duncan.

JONATHAN A. FUNK

(Farmer and Stock-raiser, Post-office, Barry).

Mr. Funk is well known as one of the prominent farmers of Platte township. His farm contains 690 acres and it is largely devoted to stock-raising, being well improved for that purpose. Much of it is devoted to pasturage, though enough is reserved for grain for all necessary purposes. Mr. Funk came to Clay county in 1857 from Cass county, this State, but was originally from Kentucky. He was born in Jessamine county, Ky., February 12, 1830, and was a son of John and Nancy (Rice) Funk, his father originally from Maryland, but his mother born and reared in Jessamine county, Ky. The father died in that county March 3, 1861, at the age of 65. She died in 1866 at the age of 66. They had a family of nine children, six of whom are living. Jonathan A. Funk was reared in Jessamine county, Ky., and early learned the carpenter's trade, which he followed there for about six years. He then turned his attention to farming and stock-raising, and in 1852 came to Missouri, locating in Howard county. Three years later he removed to Cass county, and finally to this county in 1858. August 31, 1858, he was married to Miss Sallie Jartin, a daughter of Andrew and Jane Jartin, formerly of Kentucky. Mr. and Mrs. Funk have had seven children, five of them now living: Mattie M., Harry C., Pinkie R., Lutie M. and John A. Two are deceased, Arthur and an infant. Mr. and Mrs. Funk are members of the Presbyterian Church.

SAMUEL G. T. GREENFIELD

(Farmer, Post-office, Smithville).

Mr. Greenfield has a comfortable homestead near Smithville, and is one of the energetic farmers of Platte township. He was born in Todd county, Ky., October 4, 1822, and came to Clay county, Mo., at the age of 20, in 1842. He was married the first time to Miss Mary Brooks, daughter of Abijah and Harriet Brooks, of Clay county, Mo., on the 5th day of April, 1845. Subsequently he married here February 15, 1851, Miss Nancy Motherhead, a daughter of Nathaniel and Lucinda Motherhead, formerly of Kentucky. Mr. Greenfield has followed farming as his permanent calling, and is a thorough, practical farmer. He was a son of Samuel and Mary (Thompson) Greenfield, his father a native of Kentucky, but his mother originally from North Carolina. His father, a blacksmith by trade, died in Kentucky, October 4, 1823. He had served in the War of 1812. The mother survived until 1867, and was a life long member of the Methodist Church. There were five children in the family, three of whom are living.

MOSES KING

(Farmer and Stock-raiser, Post-office, Liberty).

When the war broke out in 1861 Mr. King was a youth in his eighteenth year. He was reared in this State and came of Southern parentage. Very naturally, therefore, in the enthusiasm of youth, he entered the Southern army. For three years he served in the ranks with unfaltering courage and fidelity. A part of the time he was under Gen. Marmaduke, and was under the command of the present Governor of the State at the battle of Helena, Ark., in 1863. The

HISTORY OF CLAY COUNTY

rest of the time he was under Gen. Joe Shelby, the irrepressible cavalry leader of Missouri, the gallant cavalier of the war, who made it a rule to ride rough shod over everything in his front with his command, infantry, artillery, or what not. After the war Mr. King came home and engaged in farming. He has a good place of about 140 (rented) acres, eight miles northwest of Liberty, and is also engaged in raising and trading in stock. In 1873 he was married to Miss E. A. Divine, a daughter of Matthew Divine, originally of Ireland. She, however, was born in New York, where her parents resided a number of years. Mr. and Mrs. King have two children: Edna M. and Edward L. Mrs. King is a member of the Catholic Church. He was born in Chariton county, Mo., October 20, 1843, and was a son of Morgan King, of Missouri.

ALWORTHY F. LEACH

(Farmer, Stock-raiser and Breeder of Clydesdale Horses, Post-office, Kearney).

Among the most prominent men in Platte township, one of its worthy, well informed and highly respected citizens and a man well and favorably known, is Mr. A. F. Leach, the subject of this sketch. On his parental side he is of Irish descent, his father, Cotton M. Leach, having been born in New Hampshire September 14, 1780, of Irish parentage. He married Miss Fannie Hayes, a native of Concord, Mass., who was born October 27, 1785. She was related to Cotton Mather, the renowned American metaphysician, and was a niece of Judge Joseph Story, a justly celebrated writer on the United States Constitution; her ancestors came over in the Mayflower and she was related distantly to Hon. Wilbur F. Story, late editor of the Chicago *Times*. Cotton M. Leach having grown up in New Hampshire, received an academic education there; his wife was reared in New York where she had the benefit of a college course. After their marriage in New York they removed to Ohio and settled in Twinsburg, in Portage county, in 1817, from which place they removed to Ft. Madison, Ia., where the mother died October 9, 1846. The father, who was a trader and speculator in lands, stock, etc., then went to Illinois to live with his son, the subject of this sketch. He died there (in Adams county) January 15, 1852. Until his removal to Iowa he had been a member of the M. E. Church, but there being no organization of that denonination there he became a Congregationalist, as his wife had also been. He was also a member of the A. F. and A. M. Alworthy F. Leach, the sixth in the family of nine children, six sons and three daughters, was born in Twinsburg, Portage county, O., June 23, 1818. He was reared there, the limited education which he received at the common schools being supplemented by instruction from his mother. At the age of 15 years he commenced to learn the carpenter's and joiner's trade, which he followed until his marriage. After that event he took up the study of medicine in Adams county, Ill., but never engaged in the practice. He also studied law, and in 1850 was admitted to the Quincy bar, several years

HISTORY OF CLAY COUNTY

thereafter being passed in the practice of his profession. On the 13th of July, 1840, Mr. Leach was married in Adams county, Ill., whither he had removed in 1838, to Miss Rebecca Enlow, a daughter of Thomas and Sarah (McCrorey) Enlow, originally from Pennsylvania, but of Irish ancestry. Mrs. Leach was born, brought up and received her education in Washington county, Pa. They have five children: Frances has been twice married, first to Joel James, who died, and then to James Brooks, a farmer in Pike county; Albert married Miss Belle McAtee, and is a prominent agriculturist in Adams county, Ill.; Walter married Miss Alice Hamlin; Byron married Miss Lina Fields, and both he and his brother Walter are occupied in farming in this county; Almira is the wife of Dr. William H. Leach of Knappy City, Cal. He is a prominent physician there and is a graduate of both the Cincinnati and Philadelphia Medical Schools. In 1874, Mr. Leach became a citizen of Clay county, Mo. He and sons now have a farm here of 450 acres, all under fence and in a high state of cultivation, upon which he is engaged in the stock business quite extensively, principally in the raising and breeding of Clydesdale horses. His farm is one of the finest for stock purposes in this township and he is one of the most progressive farmers in the vicinity.

J. A. MITCHELL

(Dealer in Furniture, Undertaker's Goods, Hardware, Etc., Smithville).

Mr. Mitchell was a youth of about 16 years of age when his parents came to this county and settled on a farm, which his father bought near Smithville. He remained on the farm with them until he was about 24 years old, when, in 1879, he came to town and opened a restuarant and also ran a butcher shop. In addition to these he, in a short time, carried on teaming between Smithville and Kansas City. Disposing of his other interests, in 1881 he bought a furniture and undertaker's establishment at Smithville, and has been conducting these lines of business ever since. In the spring of 1884 he added a stock of shelf and heavy hardware, and altogether is doing a good business. In 1878 he was married to Miss Annie, a daughter of Stephen and Amelia Duncan, of Clay county. They have one child, Edmond, and have lost one, who died in infancy. Mr. Mitchell's parents are Merrimon B. and Annie M. Mitchell, from Woodford county, Ky. His father has a good farm of 250 acres near Smithville.

WM. H. PATTERSON

(Proprietor of the Eagle Flouring, Grist and Saw Mills, Smithville, Mo.).

Mr. Patterson is not only a thorough miller, but one of the best millwrights in the western part of the State, if experience and employment in construction of first-class mills counts for anything. The ground and mill site upon which the Eagle mills now stand, he bought from Capt. Kemp M. Woods, in 1867, going in debt for the same. Building the mills soon afterwards, he took special pains to use

HISTORY OF CLAY COUNTY

nothing but the very best of material and leaving no part of his work half finished. Mr. Patterson has recently added to his mills all the latest and most improved machinery, including every modern improvement — recommended by the milling fraternity. The result is that his mills are unsurpassed either in Clay or Platte county. They have a capacity of 60 bbls. of flour and 10,000 feet lumber per diem. His flour Royal Eagle and Silver Drop has an enviable reputation, and is generally preferred to all other brands wherever introduced. It may not be generally known, but it is a fact nevertheless, that there is a vast difference in the quality of sawing done by different mills, even among those where the saw runs true, making lumber of accurate angles, dimensions and surfaces. Lumber from the same class of timber, or from same stock for that matter, sawed at different mills differs widely in market value. From one the surface may be rough, so that it costs twice as much to have it planned as it would the same class of lumber with a smoother surface from another saw. All good saw-mill men understand this, and those who take a pride in their business or care for their reputation see to it that this saw is kept perfectly sharp and in good order, and that it runs at the proper speed — and is regularly fed by the stock carriage so that a smooth surface is left on the board. Mr. Patterson takes a special pride in this feature of the lumber produced at his mills, and hence among lumbermen and carpenters it has obtained a wide and enviable reputation. Mr. Patterson was born on Barnhart's Island, St. Lawrence county, New York, in 1838, and was the second of six children of W. H. and Minerva Patterson (*née* Barnhart) who were both born and reared in the State of New York. W. H. Patterson, Sr., who was of French descent, moved to Canada, and was an extensive grain and lumber dealer there at the time of his death. At the age of 18 years the subject of the present sketch came West to grow up with the country, first stopping at Chicago and working there for a little over one year, and then coming on to Western Missouri to the home of his uncle, Robert Barnhart, then a merchant of Weston, Platte county, Mo. Afterwards he procured employment with Wilson & Estes, engine builders, at Leavenworth City, now known as the Great Western Manufacturing Company, and remained in their employ some three or four years, learning the millwright trade. In 1862 he went to St. Louis, Mo., and worked at his trade building mills and putting up machinery in the employ of A. K. Halteman & Co. About two years after he returned to his former home in Platte county, Mo., and in 1864 at Weston, Mo., he enlisted in Capt. Wash Wood's Company, Eighty-seventh regiment M. S. M., and served until about the close of the war, receiving an honorable discharge. He then took up his occupation of millwrighting, following the same until 1867, when he came to Smithville, Mo., and has ever since, for the last eighteen years, been engaged in the milling business. Mr. Patterson was married in 1872 to Johana Martin, a daughter of Wesley Martin, an ex-soldier of the Mexican War and a resident of this county, now deceased. Mr. and Mrs. Patterson have two children, Robert Lee and

HISTORY OF CLAY COUNTY

Minerva. Two are deceased, Charlie and Mattie. He and wife are both members of the Christian Church. Mr. Pat erson is indeed one of the reliable and substantial men of the county. He is highly respected among his numerous friends, and we may safely say hasn't a known enemy.

S. A. RILEY, M. D.

(Physician and Surgeon, and of Gentry & Riley, Druggists, Smithville).

Dr. Riley has been a resident of Smithville less than a year, but being a young physician of thorough education and a gentleman of good address and irreproachable character, he has made a very favorable impression on the community, and has every prospect of a successful and highly creditable career here both in his profession and as a citizen in business and private life. He is a native Missourian, born in DeKalb county, May 2, 1860. When he was a lad, about four years of age, his parents removed to Jackson county, where young Riley was reared on his father's farm near Independence. After taking a course in the primary and preparatory schools he entered Woodland College at Independence, and from there, in due time, matriculated at the State University. After concluding his university course he began the study of medicine under Dr. J. C. Rodgers, of Kansas City, and in the fall of 1880 entered the St. Louis Medical College. Dr. Riley took a regular course of two terms at St. Louis, and graduated in medicine with marked credit in the class of '83. He then at once located in Cass county and engaged in the practice of his profession, but not liking the location and having friends at Smithville, he was induced to remove to this place. Already he is receiving much encouragement in his practice, not only by the number, but particularly by the class of patrons who call upon him for medical attention. It is believed that he will shortly be in possession of a very satisfactory and increasing practice. He is also a partner with Mr. Gentry in the drug business. Mr. Gentry is a young man of good business qualifications, full of energy and thoroughly reliable, and has every requisite for a popular and successful druggist. These young gentlemen are both full of life and vim, and have started out in the world to accomplish something worthy of themselves as citizens of intelligence and character. Their drug house commands a good custom, and has already been placed upon a profitable footing. They keep good and pure drugs which they dispense at reasonable and fair prices, so that they could hardly fail of being a popular house in the drug line. Dr. Riley's father, J. G. Riley, is one of the substantial citizens of Jackson county. He also has a stock ranch in Colorado, and is a man of high standing and much business enterprise. The Doctor's mother, who was a Miss Elizabeth Buckingham, died September 14, 1884.

JOHN J. RICE, M. D.

(Physician and Surgeon, Gosneyville, Mo.).

In the medical profession in this county are to be found a number of physicians — men who have risen to success and local prominence

HISTORY OF CLAY COUNTY

in their profession, and solely by their own industry and perseverance as students and practitioners; and taking the secret of their success as a criterion by which to judge the future of the younger members of the profession, it is not difficult to point out those who are to occupy the places of these old and prominent physicians when they have passed off the stage of action. Prominent among this class of young men in Clay county is, without question, the subject of the present sketch. Dr. John J. Rice is a son of Richard C. Rice, a native of Woodford county, Ky., and now a leading agriculturist and stock man, residing in Liberty. His mother was formerly Lucinda Ferguson, of Marion county, Ky., where they were married. John J. Rice was the second of eight children, and passed his early life in attending to farm duties. His educational opportunities were above the average, he having received a classical course at Harmonia College, Perryville, Ky. After leaving this institution he engaged in the occupation of school teaching, which he continued for two years at Sorghotown, Daviess county, Ky. Having decided to make the practice of medicine his calling for life, he pursued a regular preparatory course of study for that purpose, under Dr. T. E. Lamping, of Owenboro, Ky. He took several courses of lectures in the Cincinnati College of Medicine and Surgery, and graduated from that institution on the 4th of March, 1881. The same year he came to Gosneyville, Clay county, Mo., and began the practice of his chosen calling at this place, where he has made gratifying progress in his profession as a practitioner. Studious and progressive in his ideas, and faithful and attentive to his practice, he is rapidly winning the confidence of the community in his skill and ability as a physician. He is a member of the Clay County Medical Society, also of the County Board of Health. On the 24th of May, 1882, Dr. Rice was married to Miss Emma Rollins, a daughter of John K. and Ella Rollins, of this county. She was born and reared here, her education being received at the Stewartsville Female Seminary, Stewartsville, Mo. They have one child, DeWitt T., born February 4, 1884. Dr. Rice's church preference is the Missionary Baptist. He is a member of the A. F. and A. M. His wife belongs to the M. E. Church South. His father, as should have been mentioned before, was a soldier in the Mexican War. He came to Clay county in 1872. He and his wife are now members of the Missionary Baptist Church, and Mr. Rice is also connected with the A. F. and A. M.

ANDREW B. ROSS

(Farmer and Proprietor of Ross' Mill, Post-office, Paradise).

Every old citizen in this section of the county very well remembers Mr. Ross' father, William Ross, for he lived in the county for nearly 35 years, and was one of its worthy, good citizens. His wife, Nancy Ross, was a Miss Hawkins before her marriage, and a native of Tennessee. They came to Clay county, Mo., in 1841. William Ross for a time was a substantial farmer, but in about two years after his

HISTORY OF CLAY COUNTY

settlement here built a water-mill on the site of the present structure which was subsequently burned. In 1856 he built a saw and grist mill, which he continued to operate until his death, October 22, 1875. This mill is the one now conducted by his son, the subject of this sketch. It is a two-story building, fitted with two runs of buhrs, and has a capacity of 15 barrels of flour per day, sawing also 3,000 feet of lumber. Andrew B. Ross, like many of the better citizens of this county, is a Kentuckian by birth, having been born in Madison county, April 28, 1839, being the fourth in a family of nine children. He accompanied his parents to Clay county, Mo., while in infancy, and has here continued to make his home. While growing up he very naturally followed his father's example and early became interested in the milling business, devoting much time to that occupation. He has always followed it, and having had such excellent opportunities to learn the trade in Missouri, in subsequent years he has risen to considerable prominence in the milling circles, where he is esteemed not less as a business man than as a private citizen. During the war Mr. Ross served in the army of the Potomac for four years, enlisting first under Gen. Bee, who was killed at the battle of Bull Run, and afterward under Gens. Whiting and Archer, respectively. About two years after the close of the war, on August 11, 1867, he was united in marriage with Miss Martha A. Gentry, a daughter of David and Louisa Gentry. She was born, reared and educated in this county, but died March 24, 1883, leaving five children: Nannie L., Mary E., John W., Andrew B., and Laura B., the second daughter, who died November 14, 1873. Mrs. Ross was a member of the M. E. Church South, as her husband now is. He is also connected with the I. O. O. F. Mr. Ross, in connection with his milling interest, carries on farming to some extent, having 40 acres of land under fence and in cultivation. His mother died here November 29, 1871.

WILLIAM H. SHANNON

(Farmer and Stock-raiser, Post-office, Smithville).

The father of Lewis S. Shannon, who was also the grandfather of the subject of the present sketch, was one of the pioneer settlers in the State of Kentucky, having lived there in a period when settlers were very few, the country being populated mainly by the original and perhaps rightful owners of the then wilderness — the aborigines. Game was plenty, and, in fact, the early days in that country were only examples of the pioneer days in this vicinity in subsequent years. Lewis S. Shannon was a native of Woodford county, Ky., and married Elizabeth Ellison, of Henderson county, this State. To them were born ten children, the eldest of whom was William H. Shannon, who was born in Frankfort, Ky., July 28, 1821. After the marriage of his parents, they came to Missouri in 1857, locating in Clinton county, where they lived until their death, the father having been occupied with agricultural pursuits. He died in 1859 and his wife in 1866. Both were consistent and prominent members of the Mission-

HISTORY OF CLAY COUNTY

ary Baptist Church. William H. was reared in the State of his birth, but his educational opportunities were necessarily limited, the primitive schools being much inferior to those of the present day. However, by self-application, he secured a sufficient knowledge of business for the ordinary affairs of life, and also learned the carpenter's trade. In 1840 he took up his residence at Richmond, in Ray county. Two years afterwards, October 11, 1842, he was married, Miss Amanda White becoming his wife. One child was born to them, which died in infancy. Mrs. Shannon also died in September, 1847. She had been a member of the Christian Church. After this Mr. S. returned to Kentucky, where he remained 10 years, and while there he was justice of the peace in his township. He was also married, January 22, 1852, in Anderson county, to Miss Mary C. Thompson, a daughter of Anthony Thompson, of Woodford county, Ky. Her birthplace was in Ohio county, Ky., but she was reared and educated in Franklin county, Ky. They have had five children: Thompson J. married Miss Bettie Willis, and is a carpenter in Smithville, Mo.; William E. married Miss Mary J. Youtsey, and is engaged in farming in this county; Laura May and Oliver E. are still at home. James H. died at the age of eight years. In 1857 Mr. Shannon returned to Missouri and settled in Clay county on the farm where he is now living. This embraces 110 acres either in cultivation or blue grass pasture. He and his wife are members of the Christian Church, in which he has been an elder for 20 years. He is also connected with the A. F. and A. M. They are among the most highly esteemed residents of the township.

JOHN SWARTZ

(Dealer in and Manufacturer of Boots, Shoes, Etc., and *Lehrer der Deutschen Schule*, Smithville).

Mr. Swartz is a Teuto-Frenchman by descent and nativity and was born in Abberbach, France, January 9, 1838. His father was Casper Swartz, also a native of France and mayor of Abberbach, in the parish of Seltz. The mother was a Miss Mary Mustar of Alsace. In their family were ten children, seven of whom are living. John Swartz, the subject of this sketch, was the second in their family and was reared at Abberbach up to the age of 18 years, when he came to America, landing at New Orleans. He had previously served two years of an apprenticeship at the blacksmith's trade. In the summer of 1855 he went to Keokuk, Iowa, and began at the shoe maker's trade. Thence he went to Hannibal, and later along to Palmyra, where he worked a time, then at Macon City, then Glasgow, then Kansas City and finally to Clay county, stopping a while at Barry, and locating permanently at Smithville in 1859. Early in the war he enlisted in the State Guard under Gov. Jackson's first call and was out about six months. At the fight of Lexington the captain of his company was killed and after that the men were scattered, some entering other companies and others returning home. After Mr. Swartz's return he remained at Smithville for a short time and then went to Leavenworth where he

443

resumed his occupation. In about three weeks, however, he returned home again and was shortly taken prisoner. After this he enlisted in the regular United States service, becoming a member of the Ohio infantry, in which he served until the close of the war. After the war he came back to Smithville and resumed his trade, that of making boots and shoes, and also soon brought on a stock of goods in that line. He has been in the business at this place ever since. He has an excellent reputation as a workman and commands a liberal patronage. He also has a good trade for his business as a boot and shoe dealer. In 1861 Mr. Swartz was married to Miss Susan Reeves, formerly of Kentucky. They have one child, John R. During the war, on account of some differences which it is not necessary to discuss here, a separation took place between Mr. Swartz and his first wife and a divorce was the result. Each have remarried, Mr. Swartz's present wife having been a Miss Mary Johnson, with whom his married life has been one of great satisfaction and pleasure. She was a daughter of William Johnson, from Tennessee to this county, in about 1857. There are three children by this union: Lewis, Pauline and French. John R., his eldest son by his first wife, is now engaged in the grocery and confectionery business at Smithville. He is also an Odd Fellow and conductor of his lodge. His mother is now the wife of A. D. Simpson, of Buchanan county. Mr. Swartz and his present wife are members of the Christian Church. Mr. Swartz is also treasurer of the Odd Fellows Order at this place. Mr. Swartz has a good German education. and in 1884 established a German school at this place which he still carries on. His school has proved a success and is liberally patronized by the people of the community, particularly by those of German nativity or descent.

ELEVEN L. THATCHER

(Farmer and Stock-raiser, Post-office, Smithville).

Eleven Thatcher, Sr., was one of the early settlers of Clay county. He came here from Kentucky and became a well-to-do farmer and highly respected citizen. His death occurred some 10 or 12 years ago. By all old residents of the county he is well remembered as a man of large heart, strong intelligence, courage and industry, and as one of the best of neighbors and friends. His good wife preceded him to the grave some five or six years. She was a Miss Sabina Hornback, of Kentucky, before her marriage. They reared a family of five children, most of whom are living, and are among the better class of citizens of their respective communities. Eleven L. Thatcher, their fifth son, was born on the family homestead in this county, November 24, 1840. He was reared to the occupation of farming and stock-raising, and acquired a good common school education as he grew up. At the age of 27, on the 16th of December, 1867, he was married to Miss Rosa D. Wood, a daughter of Col. Lewis J. Wood, formerly of Kentucky. Already Mr. Thatcher, Jr., had engaged in farming on his own account, and in this he afterwards con-

HISTORY OF CLAY COUNTY

tinued. He is now comfortably situated. His farm contains 480 acres, and he is quite extensively engaged in dealing in stock. He is also largely interested in breeding and raising fine stock. His thoroughbred short horns are all of registered stock, and he also has a herd of high grade cattle. His hogs are of fine breeds, and the Clydesdale horses are his favorite stock in the equine line. He has several representatives of the pure Clydesdale breed. Mr. Thatcher is one of the most enterprising and progressive farmers and stock-raisers of the county. Mr. and Mrs. Thatcher have two children: Lewis J. and James W. He and wife are members of the Christian Church, and he is a member of the A. F. and A. M.

WILLIAM P. THATCHER

(Farmer and Stock-raiser, Post-office, Smithville).

Mr. Thatcher is a worthy representative of that old and highly respected family of Clay county whose name he bears. Reference to his father has already been made in the sketch of E. L. Thatcher. William P. was born in this county in 1834. On reaching young manhood he started out for himself with little or nothing to begin on. But he had been reared to hard work and to regular, economical habits, and being a young man of good intelligence, fair common-school education, and with an honest purpose to rise in the world only by industry, he went to work without hesitation or discouragement, and in a short time had the satisfaction of seeing the legitimate fruits of honest toil accumulating around him. But in a few years the war came on. That was a great backset to him, as it was to most honest men in this part of the country. He went into the Southern army and took part in numerous engagements, including those at Lexington, Pea Ridge and Blue Ridge. At the latter fight he was fired on by a whole platoon of Federal soldiers, but either he was protected by the shield of the Lord, or the soldiers did bad shooting; anyhow, he came out unharmed. Resuming farming, he did the best he could under the circumstances, and after affairs became settled went at it again in dead earnest. Since then he has had a very successful experience. He now owns a fine farm of 440 acres, well improved, including an excellent class of buildings, and he is quite largely engaged in breeding and raising fine stock, and in fattening and dealing in marketable stock. His short horns are thoroughbreds and of registered stock, and he is breeding and raising fine calves for sale. In 1857 he was married to Miss Louisa Lampton. They have two children: William B. and Addie L. Mrs. Thatcher is a member of the Christian Church, and he is a member of the A. F. and A. M. and the Smithville Temperance Lodge No. 423,964.

EDWARD C. TILLMAN

(Farmer, Post-office, Smithville).

Mr. Tillman is a native of North Carolina, born in Chatham county, July 18, 1807. His father was John Tillman, also of that State, and

445

his mother's maiden name, Susan Fields. The .Tillman family has been quite prominent in politics in North Carolina and Tennessee for generations. Mr. Tillman was reared in Chatham county, and was one of a family of 12 children, eleven of whom lived to reach mature years. They and their descendants are now distributed in several States. After growing up Mr. T. traveled quite extensively for about ten years and then located in 1833 in Todd county, Ky., He came to Clay county in 1842, and entered the land on which he now resides. He has ever since been engaged in farming. He was married in Todd county, Ky., December 6, 1838, to Miss Keziah Thompson. They have three children living: Susan, the wife of M. H. Masterson, of this county; Mary A., the wife of Henry Humes, a stock trader of the county, and John W., who married Margaret Wilkerson and is farming on the home place. His wife died August 9, 1874.

JAMES WILLIAMS

(Farmer and Stock-dealer, Post-office, Smithville).

Bourbon county, Ky., and the 3d of March, 1826, were the place and date of Mr. Williams' birth, and his parents were James and Elizabeth (Wright) Williams, both of old and respected Kentucky families. Mr. W.'s father, a house carpenter by trade and who had served with credit in the War of 1812, died in 1863. The mother is still living, at the age of 86, having been born in 1798. There were eight children in the family, all yet living. James, the subject of this sketch, was reared to the occupation of farming and house carpentering and came to Missouri in 1851, settling in Clay county after a residence of two years in Platte county. He has resided in this county ever since, and for many years followed his trade, during the latter part of his life in connection with farming. In 1851 he was married in Montgomery county, Ky., to Miss Docia C. Judson, who survived her marriage 12 years, leaving five children living of the six born to them, namely: John T., of Oregon; Daniel, of this county; Susan E., wife of Perry Bazoo, of this county; Mary, wife of Samuel J. Bradley, of Clay county; James N. and Julia, deceased. Mrs. W. was a member of the church. Mr. Williams has a comfortable homestead near Smithville.

KEMP M. WOODS, JR.

(Real Estate Agent, Notary Public, Railway Director, President of the Town Board, and also Member of the School Board, Smithville).

Mr. Woods, though still this side of the fourth decade of life, has already had an active business career, and one that has placed him in a position of some prominence in affairs. He was born and reared in Clay county, and received an advanced general and classical education as he grew up, completing a regular collegiate course. From his grandfather, Phineas Skinner, he inherited a large landed estate, some 900 acres, located in different counties, but principally in Jackson, Mercer and Grundy counties. Since then he has dealt to a considerable extent in real estate, buying, selling, exchanging, etc., and has also had much to do with lands as agent for other parties. He now owns in his own right about 1,000 acres, which, however, includes little or none of the original tracts received by inheritance. His interests, besides real estate, have been identified with farming mainly, and railway contracting. He has also been somewhat interested in the State business, and still is to some extent. Like most young men of life and energy, he has not neglected to avail himself of the information which only traveling affords, but has taken the time and means to see something of the world, particularly the Western part of the country. Mr. Woods was one of the organizers of the St. Joseph and Southeastern Railway Company and one of its charter members, being now also a member of the board of directors of the company. This company contemplate building a line of railway from St. Joseph in a southeastern direction through Buchanan, Platte, and into Clay county to Smithville. The road, as has been intimated, is already chartered, and work has been commenced. In 1876 Mr. Woods was married to Miss Lillie M. Wiglesworth, a daughter of Wm. T. and Mary F. Wiglesworth, of Woodford county, Ky. Mr. Woods has been located at Smithville since the fall of 1881, and is now president of the town board at Smithville, and also a member of the school board. He is doing an excellent real estate business, and is one of the leading, progressive citizens of the place. He was born in this county in 1847, and is the youngest of the family of Kemp M., Sr., and Sarah (Skinner) Woods, early settlers here from Kentucky. His father, Kemp M. Woods, Sr., has given to his four sons, including Kemp M., Jr., 400 acres of land each, located in Platte and Clay counties.

CHAPTER XVI.

KEARNEY TOWNSHIP.

Boundaries, General Surface, etc. — Early Settlements — Tragedies of the Civil War — County Churches — Town of Kearney — Centreville — Location of Kearney and for Whom Named — Incorporation — Kearney's Churches — Holt — Location of this Village — Church and Lodge Records — Biographical.

BOUNDARIES, GENERAL SURFACE, ETC.

Kearney township was organized June 4, 1872, with the following boundaries: Beginning on the line between Clinton and Clay counties, at the northeast corner of section 36, township 54, range 31, thence along the county line to the half section line running north and south through section 35, township 54, range 32; thence due south to the township line dividing townships 52 and 53; thence east one mile and a half to the southeast corner of section 36, township 53, range 32; thence south one mile, thence east one mile, thence south one mile, thence east to the range line between ranges 30 and 31; thence north along the range line to the beginning.

Anthony Harsell was appointed by the county court the first justice of the peace *pro tem.* The township was named for the town of Kearney.

The general surface of the township partakes of the character of that of the county, and is rolling and broken, but some of the most valuable farms of the county are situated herein. The northern portion of the township — at least the northeastern — is heavily timbered, and much of it is unimproved. This is true of much of the eastern portion, along Clear creek, and new farms are being opened, clearings made, and land reclaimed from the wilderness in pretty much the same fashion as 50 years ago.

Settlements were made in this township at a very early day. In the northwestern part of the township, two miles south of Camp branch (east half section 23, township 53, range 32), Anthony Harsell settled in the fall of 1827, and here he is yet living. A mile and a half northeast of Harsell, William Livingston had come in 1825; James McCown settled one mile north of Harsell in 1826; Hezekiah Riley and James Marsh settled east of Harsell in 1827, the latter in the spring and the

HISTORY OF CLAY COUNTY

former in the fall. In the spring of the same year Edward Clark located one mile south.

For some years after the township was first settled bears and panthers were unpleasantly numerous. As late as the winter of 1836 a large bear was killed on Camp branch, two miles north of Harsell's spring.

Over on Camp creek, on one occasion, John McCown, Jr., killed a large panther which his dog had attacked and was being worsted in the encounter.

Among the tragedies of the Civil War, not especially mentioned elsewhere, may be mentioned the murder of two citizens of this township, Esq. David L. Ferrill and Dr. John Norris. They were Confederate sympathizers, and their murder was accomplished by some of Col. Catherwood's regiment, the Sixth Missouri State militia. Esq. Ferrill was an old and well respected citizen of the township. His sons were in the Confederate army, and his grandson, Red. Munkers, was a bushwhacker, but Esq. Ferrill himself was an old man about 70 years of age, and had never been guilty of overt acts against the Federal authority. One day in September, 1864, a squad of militia, led by Lieut. James N. Stoffel, of Co. A, Catherwood's regiment, took out the old man and hung him to a tree near his residence.

John Norris had served six months under Price, but for some time he had been living peaceably at home. One night, a short time after Esq. Ferrill was hung, a squad of Catherwood's men took him from his home and shot him.

Richard Sloan was a member of the party that hung Ferrill. He was a citizen of this township, and in September, 1866, he was waylaid and shot and his body left lying in the road.

CHURCHES.

Mount Gilead Christian Church. — This church is an outgrowth of what was originally a Calvinistic Baptist Church, as it was first organized. In March, 1844, there was a division in the congregation, some of the members still adhering to the Baptist denomination, while others, among whom were some of the old and most prominent Baptists, constituted themselves into a body of Christians. The church building first put up was erected in 1844, but becoming defective and unsafe from the ravages of time, it was torn down and in its place a handsome brick edifice was built in 1873, costing $2,569.95. It stands on section 29, northwest quarter, township 53, range 31. The first members were Elders Mason Summers, Timothy R. Dale and wife, Alfred M. Riley and wife, Hezekiah Riley, Robert Officer and wife, Weekly Dale and wife, James Riley and wife, George Dallis,

449

HISTORY OF CLAY COUNTY

Alexander Mooney and wife, A. H. F. Payne and wife, and John Dykes and wife. The deacons were Hezekiah Riley, Robert Officer and Weekly Dale. Following Augustus H. F. Payne, who was the organizer, the pastors have been Revs. Williamson, A. B. Jones, J. T. Tate, J. W. Perkins, and the present pastor, J. W. Trader, who has in his membership 130 persons. As now constituted, the elders of the church are A. J. Porter, P. T. Soper and George Smith; the deacons, T. M. Gosney, Albert Lincoln, Benjamin Soper, A. J. Phelps and Samuel Smith; clerk, Locke Riley. The first Sunday-school connected with this church was organized on the last Lord's day of May, 1868. The superintendent was O. G. Harris, assisted by E. G. Gill; the secretary was P. T. Soper. The school now has an attendance of 70 scholars. The superintendent is Abner Porter.

Clear Creek Old School Baptist Church — Located in section 14, Kearney township, was organized August 6, 1840. Its original members were Benjamin and Nancy Soper, Joel and Rachel Estes, Annie Palmer, Charles Waller, Margaret Waller, Henry and Lucinda Estes, Robert and Sarah Thompson, Alvira Arnold, Arabella Arnold, Harriet Arnold, William and Nancy Yates, and Elizabeth Groomer. The present membership is about 31. The names of the pastors who have served this church are Revs. John Edwards and Wolverton Warren, who has been the pastor for about 20 years. The present frame church building was built in 1853 at a cost of about $1,000. The constitution was formed by the following body, of whom John Edwards was moderator: William Clark, Henry Hill, John Atkins and E. Fillery, none of whom survive.

Bethel German M. E. Church — In this township, now includes in its membership 47 persons. As originally constituted, in 1845, by the efforts of Heinrich Nuelson, the constituent members were Fred Hartel, Peter Hartel, John Suter, Conrad Hessel, Jacob Hessel, Louis Feigat, Charles Fowler, Nicholas Frick, and perhaps others. After Heinrich Neulson, the first pastor, the pulpit was filled by Heinrich Hogrefe, Rev. Neidermeier, John Raus, Joseph Zimmerman, William Shreck, Andreas Holz Beierlein, Henry Muehlenbrock, H. Dryer, Peter Hehner, Carl Steinmeier, P. Mayer, Rev. Priegal, Henry Bruene, H. Brinkmeier, J. J. Jung, H. Deiner, C. Bauer, H. M. Menger, H. Eorphage, J. J. Eichenberger, J. W. Buchholtz, George Koenig, F. Kaltenbach. Until the building of the present frame church in 1875 (costing $1,000), services were held at private houses. It is now in good condition both spiritually and financially, and is having steady growth. An important adjunct to the church is the

450

HISTORY OF CLAY COUNTY

Sunday-school of 40 pupils, the superintendent of which is Conrad Hessel.

THE TOWN OF KEARNEY.

What is now the southeastern portion of the town of Kearney was originally called Centerville, and was laid out by David T. Duncan and W. R. Cave in the spring of 1856. Duncan lived on and owned the north half of the site of Centerville. Cave purchased the south half from his father, Uriel Cave, the original owner. The first houses were built by Adam Pence and W. R. Cave, and theirs were the first families in the village.

Barney Spencer, a Kentuckian, owned the first store in Centerville, which was conducted for some time in the beginning by his brother-in-law, Sam Trabue. The second store was owned and run by John Wade, of Ohio. These stores were established in the spring of 1857. John Gilboe had the third store. A school-house was built in about 1858 by W. R. Cave.

Upon the outbreak of the Civil War Centerville contained about 20 families, but when it closed there were only two or three. During the war only two houses were destroyed, however, and these were burned by the Federals — Ford's and Jennison's men. They were owned by John Corum and John Gilboe, but at the time they were burned Dr. Cravens lived in Corum's house, and W. R. Cave had a small grocery in Gilboe's building. The Federals claim that they did the burning in retalliation for the killing of Mr. Bond by the bush-whackers.

The murder of John Julius, an old man and a reputable citizen, by Lysander Talbott, shortly after the war, was the only tragedy of note that ever occurred in Centerville. The killing was wholly unprovoked. Talbott was on the "war path" and "wanted to kill somebody." He was arrested, indicted, took a change of venue to Clinton county, escaped from jail, went to Texas, and was himself killed in a row.

April 12, 1869, Alfred Pyle shot and killed Charles Smith, in a difficulty in Kearney, but Esquire Corbin acquitted Pyle on the ground that he had acted in self-defense, and he was never afterwards indicted.

The town of Kearney was laid out upon the building of the Hannibal and St. Joe Railroad in the spring of 1867, by John Lawrence. The first house was built by George H. Plitt, and is still standing on the southwest corner of Washington Avenue and Railroad street, fronting the depot on the east. It is now used as a hotel — the Oklahoma House. Plitt occupied it as a store room, but afterwards

451

HISTORY OF CLAY COUNTY

conducted a hotel. The building was erected before the railroad depot. Plitt was proprietor of a lumber yard, and the leading spirit of the place for some time. Perhaps James Hightower had the second store.

The town was named by John Lawrence for Fort Kearney, Neb., and not for a certain worthy citizen of the community. It is understood that Lawrence was at one time a resident of Fort Kearney before he came to Clay county. Soon after its establishment the village began to be peopled very rapidly. Stores and shops of all kinds were built, and in a little time Kearney and Centerville were practically united.

Kearney was incorporated "as a town or village" by the county court, April 5, 1869. The first board of trustees was composed of George H. Plitt, Peter Rhinehart, R. B. Elliott, D. T. Dunkin and George Harris. As the location of the town is very attractive, and as the buildings are all comparatively new, the town itself presents a handsome appearance. Washington avenue, the principal street, is well lined with stores and shops, and the business done is considerable.

The present school-house was built a dozen years ago, and the *Clipper* newspaper, a five-column sheet, was established by Thos. H. Frame, in July, 1883. The first church was the Missionary Baptist, which was at first called Mount Olive. It is worthy of note that John S. Majors, Esq., took an active and prominent part in the building of this church, contributing to it from first to last $1,000. It is a fine brick structure and still standing.

CHURCHES AT KEARNEY.

Kearney Christian Church. — On the 25th of August, 1868, Lucy E. Coryell, Elizabeth Petterfield, Eliza Netherton, Hannah Pollock, Abraham Netherton, Shelton Brown and wife, William H. Hawkins, D. T. Duncan, John S. Groom, James Reed and wife, Alfred Arnold and wife, George S. Harris, William Hall, G. D. Hall, Mrs. A. Rodgers, R. H. Burden and wife, Emily Craven, Nancy E. Pile, J. S. Sirpan, Elizabeth Rodgers, Alida Harris and Robert Morris formed themselves into an organization now known as the above church. This original membership has been added to from time to time until it now numbers 100. Among those who have filled the pulpit here are Preston Akers, J. D. Wilmot, Joseph Davis, T. J. Williamson, Rev. Martz, Preston Akers a second time, James W. Waller, J. W. Perkins, B. C. Stephens and William S. Trader. The church building, which they occupy is a frame structure, built for about $2,000, in 1869. M. W. Sullivan is superintendent of the Sabbath-school of 40 pupils.

452

HISTORY OF CLAY COUNTY

Baptist Church. — No report has been received, though promised, from this organization, originally called Mt. Olive, and briefly mentioned elsewhere.

THE TOWN OF HOLT.

The village of Holt, situated on the Clinton county line, on the northeastern half of section 35, township 54, range 31, has been in existence only since the completion of the Cameron branch of the H. and St. Joe Railroad. It was formerly the site of a heavy body of timber in a little bottom on a branch of Clear creek. The land was owned by Jerry A. Holt, an old North Carolinian, whose residence is just across in Clinton county, and who came to Missouri in about 1835. There are many other families of North Carolinians in this region.

Holt was laid out in the fall of 1867, and named for Uncle Jerry Holt, the owner of the land. Timothy R. Dale was the surveyor. The first house was built on lot 5, in East Holt, by J. C. Dever, and the building was occupied by Mr. Dever first as a store. It was burned down in 1873. Soon after Mr. Dever built a hotel called the Dever House which still stands on lot 10 in West Holt. The second store was built by Samuel Garrison on lot 11 in East Holt. In the spring of 1869 Capt. Joab Lamb built the third store on lot 8 in Holt East. The second house in Holt West was built by Richard Fitzgerald, in the spring of 1869.

The railroad depot was built in the spring of 1868; but previous to its construction the section house was used as a freight depot. The first station agent was Hiram Towne, and his brother, D. W. C. Towne, succeeded him. The public school building was erected in the summer of 1873. The mill was completed in the spring of 1883, by A. P. Cutler, S. L. Cutler, J. K. Morgan and J. F. Lampson, who composed the firm of Cutler, Morgan & Co. The first church, the M. E. South, was completed in the spring of 1883.

In 1868 the post-office was established. Capt. Joab Lamb secured the office, and was the first postmaster, but in a short time he was superseded by D. W. C. Towne. Prior to its establishment Haynesville, Clinton county, was the nearest post-office. The first practicing physician in the place was Dr. J. M. Brown, of whose abilities many of the old citizens speak disparagingly, but yet it is admitted that he had fair success.

Holt was incorporated February 4, 1878. The first board of trustees was composed of Boston L. McGee, A. P. Cutler, Adam Eby, J. C. Dever, Wm. H. McIntyre. Upon the organization of the board A.

453

HISTORY OF CLAY COUNTY

P. Cutler was made chairman; Boston L. McGee, clerk; D. W. C. Towne, treasurer, and Wm. M. Troxler, collector and marshal.

The Baptist Church was completed in February, 1885, and is an imposing, capacious structure, neatly furnished and equipped. The present population of the village is about 250. In 1880 it was 162. The average attendance at the public school is 54.

CHURCHES AT HOLT.

M. E. Church South — Located at Holt, in Kearney township, was organized in 1837 at Pleasant Grove, but was afterwards moved to Haynesville, and from there to the present place. The membership now is about 91. The pastors who have served this church are Revs. B. C. Owens, T. H. Swearingen and J. T. Winstead. This is a frame church and was built in 1883 at a cost of about $1,650. There are 50 scholars in the Sabbath-school and its superintendent is Wm. Laken.

Christian Union Church — Located at Holt, in Kearney township, was organized in November, 1879. Its constituent members were B. L. McGee, Adam-Ebly and wife, W. O. Greason, Jerry Holt and wife, G. M. Isley and wife, William Holt and wife, William Albright and wife, M. M. Albright and wife, and many others. The present membership numbers about 85. G. W. Mitchell is the present pastor and he was the organizer of the church. There are 50 scholars in the Sunday-school, which is superintended by B. L. McGee.

Holt Baptist Church. — Among the more recent acquisitions to the ecclesiastical element of Clay county is the Baptist Church at Holt, which was organized in 1884. The same year a frame house of worship was erected which cost $1,700. Among the first members were W. P. Garrett and daughter Bettie, John L. Clark and wife, Byron Allnut, L. P. Garrett, Joseph Downing, Mrs. Emsley Whitsell, A. S. Garrett and wife. The membership now numbers 60 persons. Prof. A. J. Emerson organized the church and Rev. M. P. Hunt is the present pastor.

HOLT LODGE NO. 49, A. F. & A. M.

Was first organized at Haynesville, May 19, 1854, but was removed to Holt in 1877, where it still is. Some of the first officers were Henry B. Hamilton, worshipful master; John R. Ling, senior warden, David W. Reynolds, junior warden. David L. Willhoit is the present worshipful master. The hall was erected the same year of the removal of the lodge to Holt, and cost about $600. The number of membership is 52. The lodge is without incumbrance, has money at interest and is in a flourishing condition generally.

454

BIOGRAPHICAL.

PRESLEY D. ANDERSON
(Of Anderson & Bros., Dealers in Groceries, Etc., Kearney).

Mr. Anderson is a native of Kentucky, born in Woodford county, April 14, 1835. His father was Spencer Anderson, and his mother's maiden name, Catherine Hicks. Both were of early Kentucky families. Mrs. Anderson inherited her father's homestead in Kentucky, where she made her home after marriage, and where all her children were born. But in 1852 they came to Missouri and located in Clay county, purchasing a farm near Kearney the following year. They resided there until the breaking out of the war, and the father became a prosperous farmer. He was also a contractor and builder, and a very capable carpenter by trade. He completed William Jewell College, which had previously been put under contract, but had not been completed. Before coming to this State he had erected a large number of important buildings, public and otherwise. He died in this county January 8, 1881. His wife preceded him to the grave in 1872. Of their family of children only five are now living, namely: Mary E., wife of Thomas M. Gasney, president of the Kearney bank; Dr. Joseph Anderson, of Colorado; Rachel A., wife of William D. Wright, of Denver, Colorado; R. S. Anderson and the subject of this sketch, partners in business. Presley D. Anderson was reared on the farm near Kearney and educated principally at select schools in Kentucky and Missouri. He also attended William Jewell College, at Liberty. In 1861 Mr. Anderson was married to Miss Helen M. Almy, a daughter of Hiram and Rebecca Almy, formerly of New York, but who came to St. Louis in an early day and to Liberty in 1852. In 1860 Mr. Almy removed to Saline county and engaged in farming and in trading in stock. He died at Palmyra in 1865. His wife is still living and making her home with the subject of this sketch. In the first of the war Mr. Anderson served a short time in the Southern army, but was compelled to retire from the army on account of ill health. In 1862 he went to Kentucky, but returned to Clay county in 1864. He was in the battle at Lexington. After the war he engaged in farming and stock raising, but in 1872 came to Kearney and for two years kept a hotel. He then followed bridge building, and in 1883 engaged in his present business at Kearney. Mr. and Mrs. A. have had seven children: Fannie, wife of Samuel A. Pence; Katie, Allie, David, Ella Eva, Willie and Ida. The last two died in childhood. Mr. Anderson is a prominent member of the Masonic Order, and he and wife are members of the Baptist Church.

HISTORY OF CLAY COUNTY

ROBERT S. ANDERSON

(Of Anderson Bros., Dealers in Groceries, Etc., Kearney).

Mr Anderson is a brother to Presley D. Anderson, whose sketch precedes this, in which something of a history of the family has been given. Robert S. was born in Woodford county, Ky., April 25, 1842, and was the second in the family of children. He was reared on the farm and educated principally at private schools and at William Jewell College. In 1868, having come to Missouri with the family when a mere boy, as stated in his brother's sketch, he engaged in the saw mill business, which he followed for eight years. He then became clerk in a general store and continued clerking until 1882, when he purchased a stock of goods at Holt, in Clay county, and began merchandising on his own account. Mr. Anderson continued at Holt until the spring of 1883, when he sold out on account of the ill health of his family at that place. He then went to Colorado for their health and remained until the winter of 1883–84, when he became a partner with his brother in his present business. In 1880 he was married to Miss Emma J. Clause, daughter of George and Elizabeth Clause, of this county; but formerly of Mason county, Ky. They came to Missouri in about 1864 and settled in Platte county, but afterwards came to Clay county in about 1858. Mr. Clause died here in 1868. He left his widow with seven children, two of whom have since died. Mrs. Anderson died October 1, 1883. She was an earnest and consistent member of the Baptist Church. Mr. A. also lost a child, who died in infancy. Mr. Anderson is a member of the Baptist Church. He has a good farm of about 100 acres near Kearney. He is a member of Kearney Lodge No. 311, A. F. and A. M., at Kearney.

HENRY D. ANDERSON

(Farmer and Fine Stock Raiser, Post-office, Kearney).

Mr. Anderson was born in Clay county in 1847, and was the second of six children, five of whom are now living, of Joseph D. and Mary (Young) Anderson, both parents natives of Kentucky. The Andersons, however, were originally from New Jersey and the Youngs from Virginia. Mr. and Mrs. Anderson's parents on either side have long been deceased. Mrs. Anderson's parents died over 30 years ago, but since their decease there has not been a death in the family, and there are now living nine children and 42 grandchildren. On the 10th of June, 1884, a family reunion was held, at which all the children were present, together with sons-in-law and daughters-in-law, and it was a most enjoyable affair. To the outsiders present it was quite an interesting sight, somewhat different from the illustration of the Logan family presented in *Puck* a few months ago, but even more pleasant to look upon. Henry D. Anderson was reared on his father's farm in this county, the family having settled here in 1834. Mr. Anderson, Sr., died in 1858, and the mother now makes her home with

456

HISTORY OF CLAY COUNTY

her children and rents the old family homestead. Henry D. in young manhood attended the commercial school of Buffalo, N. Y., and also the Toronto (Canada) Business College. In 1874, having returned to Clay county, he was married to Miss Bettie Gosney, a daughter to Thomas M. and Susan Gosney, of this county, from Kentucky. In the meantime Mr. Anderson had engaged in farming and stock raising, which he has ever since followed. He makes a specialty of stock, and has on hand a handsome herd of fine, thoroughbred short horn cattle; his farm is set in blue grass, and is one of the choice stock farms of the vicinity and contains 212 acres, and is well improved. Mr. and Mrs. Anderson are members of the Christian Church. They have one child, Thomas J., but three others have died in infancy.

W. H. ARNOLD

(Owner and Proprietor of the Kearney Elevator).

Mr. Arnold's father, Fauntleroy Arnold, was one of the first settlers of what is now Kearney township, in Clay county. He was from Kentucky, born in Woodford county, in 1807, and came here when he was in his twenty-first year, in 1828. His father, Lewis Arnold, was a native of Virginia, but early settled in Kentucky, and served from that State in the Northwestern campaign under Gen. Harrison. Fauntleroy Arnold served in the Mormon War under Capt. Shackleford. Shortly after coming out to Clay county he entered and pre-empted 280 acres of land, all of which but forty acres are still in possession of the family. He died here in 1857, after being an invalid for some years, resulting from exposures undergone while in, and going to and coming from, California during the gold excitement. He was a member of the Primitive Baptist Church. His widow is still living. She was a daughter of Mr. Carter, of Lexington, Ky., and was born in 1812. She resides on the family homestead near Kearney with two of her children. She is also a member of the Primitive Baptist Church, and has been for many years. W. H. Arnold was born near Kearney on the 25th of July, 1832, and was reared on a farm. At the age of 22, in 1854, he went to Leavenworth, Kan., and thence to Harrison county, Mo., two years later. In 1871 he returned to Clay county and followed farming here, where he has a good farm of 160 acres, for eight years. In 1879 he removed from his farm to Liberty, for the purpose of educating his children. After sending them to school there for two years he returned to the farm and in 1883 came to Kearney and built the elevator, which he now owns and conducts. His elevator has a capacity of 10,000 bushels and the past year he handled 35,000 bushels of grain. It is the only elevator at Kearney and has proved an entirely successful enterprise. Mr. Arnold has served as deputy assessor of the county and in other positions of public trust. In 1856 he was married to Miss Mary Jane Brawner, daughter of David O. and Sarah (Uttinger) Brawner, who came from Jessamine county, Ky., in 1835. Mr. and Mrs. Arnold have five children: Charles F. D., a graduate of William Jewell College, now

HISTORY OF CLAY COUNTY

a Baptist minister; F. G., a hardware merchant at Holt; John T., a farmer by occupation; Willie J., wife of S. B. Wilhoit, and James M., a graduate of the St. Joe Commercial College, and now clerk and book-keeper for the elevator.

WILLIAM B. ARNOLD

(Farmer, Post-office, Kearney).

In about 1825 Mr. Arnold's parents, Lewis and Arabella Arnold, came to Missouri from Garrard county, Ky., and made their home in the then wilderness of Clay county. Here the father improved a farm. At an early date he went to the Rocky mountains for his health and died while absent. He left five children, four of whom are now living: John, William, Henry, and Lucy, the wife of William Grooms. Mary F., the wife of Henry Shaver, died some years ago. The mother subsequently married Rev. William Warren, formerly of Kentucky, and of the Primitive Baptist Church. Five children are the fruits of her last union, all living except the youngest. William B. Arnold, the subject of this sketch, was born in this county in April, 1833, and was reared with farming experience. In 1856 he was married to Elizabeth Collins, and then located on a farm as a householder in the township of Kearney. He has ever since been engaged in farming and also handles some stock. His farm is mainly a grass and stock farm. Mrs. Arnold was a daughter of S. N. and Jane (Tilford) Collins, originally of Virginia, but came to this county by way of Kentucky. Her (Mrs. Collins') father was a pioneer of this county, and made the first clearing on the site of the present town of Liberty, away back when the Indians circulated the superstitious and ridiculous story that the Missouri river rose out of the earth in the distant West, where the sun sinks to rest behind the shadows of the mountains. Mr. and Mrs. Arnold had five children, two of whom are living: Alice, wife of Herman Davis, and Claude. Three are deceased, having closed their infant eyes in the sleep of death before looking on to understand the wrong and sin of the world. In 1872 Mr. Arnold was married to Miss Cleopatra Ann Hurt, daughter of Joel and Sallie Hurt, formerly of Virginia. Her father is now deceased. By the last union there have been two children, both of whom are deceased. Mr. and Mrs. Arnold are members of the Missionary Baptist Church.

FRANKLIN G. ARNOLD

(Post-office, Holt).

Franklin Grimes Arnold was born in Harrison county, Mo., on the 24th of February, 1859. His father, W. H. Arnold, was the son of Fauntleroy Arnold, originally from Kentucky, but who came to this State and here made his permanent home. W. H. Arnold, who was a native of Missouri, was married in Clay county to Mary Jane Browner, a Kentuckian by birth, though she had been reared in this State. Her parents were Mr. and Mrs. David O. Browner. The

458

parents of the subject of this sketch were denied the benefits of even a common school education such as could now be obtained. The father, a farmer by occupation, was very successful as such, industrious, energetic and possessed of good characteristics. He is still living (as is also his worthy wife) and takes a deep interest in the current affairs of the day. Politically he is a Democrat, and has a high regard for religion. He has been active in the Grange movement, and has also served as justice of the peace. After having lived in Clay county for 13 years he made his home in Harrison county some ten years, then returning to Clay county in March, 1872. To them were born five children: C. L. F. Arnold, Franklin J., J. T., W. J. and J. M., all of whom have reached mature years and three of whom are married. Two are in the mercantile business, one is a farmer, one a minister and one daughter is the wife of S. B. Wilhoit, a farmer. Franklin J. was brought up in the county of his birth to the life of a farmer, not being very well favored with educational advantages. For three years he has been occupied in the hardware business, but has recently disposed of his interests in this branch of business, desiring to resume agricultural pursuits in the coming spring. The present position in pecuniary affairs to which he has achieved, has. been acquired only through his own efforts, as no assistance was given him with which to start in life. Like his parents, he has divided his life between Harrison and Clay counties — 13 years in the former and 15 in the latter. He is now connected with the Masonic fraternity. November 14, 1883, Mr. Arnold was married at Holt to Miss Mary Jane Holt, a most estimable lady. She was born in Clinton county, Mo. Mr. A. is one of the highly esteemed residents of this community.

BENJAMIN A. ATCHISON

(Farmer and Fine Stock Raiser, Post-office, Kearney).

Mr. Atchison is engaged in the same pursuit which his father, William Atchison, made a life occupation. His father was a very successful farmer, and was one of the first men of Clay county who introduced the breeding and raising of fine stock. He became a large landholder, and at one time owned over 1,500 acres of choice lands in the county. Mr. Atchison, Sr., was twice married. His first wife was a Miss Catherine Baker. She left him six children at her death: David R., James B., William, Lewis C., Catherine and Mary. His second wife, who is still living, and the mother of the subject of this sketch, with whom she makes her home, was a Miss Sarah Robertson. There were two children by this marriage: James F., the other one besides Benjamin A., died in March, 1882. The father died in 1871. He was a brother of Hon. David R. Atchison, ex-United States Senator from this State, and for whom Atchison county, Mo., was named. In July, 1881, Benjamin A. Atchison was married to Miss Ella Lee Trumbo, a daughter of John A. and Ora Trumbo, formerly of Woodford county, Ky. Mr. and Mrs. A. have two children: James F. and Ora Lee. Mr. Atchison's farm contains 260 acres.

DAVID M. BEVINS

(Retired Farmer, Stock-raiser and Mechanic, Post-office, Kearney).

Mr. Bevins, now (February, 1885,) just past the age of 80 years, has been a resident of Clay county for nearly 60 years, and has been closely and usefully identified with the history of the county throughout all this time. He was born in Madison county, Ky., January 17, 1805, and was the eldest in his parents' family of 12 children. They were pioneer settlers of that county. When in his seventeenth year his father sent him to Missouri to enter land for the family, and begin the improvements of a farm. He came here horseback in 1821, and after leaving the settlements in the eastern part of this State he found the country so sparsely populated that several days he rode from dawn until nightfall on the main route of travel without passing even a solitary house. Mr. Bevins came to what is now Gallatin township, in Clay county, and entered a tract of 160 acres in the timber. That winter he cleared eight acres, and the following spring put in a small crop, building, in the meantime, a comfortable log cabin. He also entered an additional 160 acres, and in the summer of 1822 his parents, Truman and Annie Bevins, with their family of children, came out from Kentucky. He continued with the family two years longer, and then went out for himself to work with a whip saw, the day of circular saws not yet having dawned in this part of the country. He sawed lumber for several years, and furnished the lumber for the first business house ever erected at Liberty. In a short time he also took up the carpenter trade, and followed contracting and building for several years. He built the old arsenal building at Liberty away back in 182–. In 1830 Mr. Bevins was married to Miss Hulda C., a daughter of James Riley, who came out from Fayette county, Ky., in 1828. In the meantime he had entered and bought considerable land, and soon turned his attention to farming and stock-raising, at which he was very successful. He raised and handled all kinds of farm stock — horses, mules, cattle, hogs, sheep, etc., — and is still interested in farming and stock-raising. From time to time Mr. Bevins continued to add to his landed estate, until it aggregated over 5,000 acres, all choice land, specially selected by him. He and his good wife, however, have reared a large family of children, and in providing for them they have been very liberal. Mr. Bevins has divided his lands among his children until he now has only about 1,000 acres left. Of these 807 acres are in the family homestead. As these facts show Mr. Bevins has been abundantly successful in the affairs of life, and has an ample competency. Although now past 80 years of age, one would hardly take him to be more than 65, and he still takes an active interest in the conduct of his farm. He is making a specialty of sheep, and has a fine stock of 300 head. Mr. and Mrs. Bevins have reared a family of nine children, namely: Harriet, the wife of John S. Martin, deceased; Mary A., the wife of Hon. E. C. Cook, ex-representative of Clinton county; Oliver P.,

HISTORY OF CLAY COUNTY

David R., who was killed in the Southern army, at the battle of Franklin, Tenn.; Thomas T., of Clinton county; James, Alice, wife of Cass Atchison, nephew of Gen. Atchison, and Riley E. Three others died in infancy. Mr. and Mrs. B. are members of the Christian Church. The family of Mr. B.'s parents were David M., Walker W., Tyra T., Malinda, Minerva, Mary Ann, Martha, Margaret and America. Malinda married a Mr. Hudson; Minerva married a Mr. Merryman; Mary Ann married a Mr. Karey; Martha married a Mr. Cain; America married a Mr. Reed, and Margaret married a Mr. Adkins. All except Tyra are living.

GEORGE E. BISHOP

(Butcher and Dealer in Country Produce, Kearney).

Mr. Bishop is a native of England, born in Kent county March 24, 1838. He was the eldest in a family of ten children of Edward and Eliza (Ditton) Bishop, both of old English families. His father died there in 1871 in his sixty-first year, but his mother is still living, a resident of England. Nine of their family of children are also still living. Mr. Bishop, the subject of this sketch, is the only one in this country. He was reared in Kent county and brought up to the occupation of raising sheep, which his father followed. He received an ordinary school education, and at the age of 27 years began keeping a public inn, or tavern as we use to call them in this country, now denominated hotel, as it sounds more fastidious and Frenchy. He followed that business for five years, or until he came to the United States in 1871. In this country he at once located at Kearney, and for a time was engaged as a laborer, doing also, however, something in the line of trading in stock. In 1878 he opened a butcher shop, which he has since carried on with success. For some years he has furthermore been engaged in handling country produce, buying all kinds of farm products commonly classed as produce, including butter and eggs, hides, etc., and shipping them to the wholesale markets. In 1869 Mr. Bishop was married to Miss Martha A. Frampton, a daughter of James and Elizabeth Frampton, of England. Mr. and Mrs. Bishop have five children: Ellen M., Bertha E., Fredie F., Edmond and Albert J. They have lost two, Katie, aged six years and ten months, and Emma, ten months old. Mr. and Mrs. Bishop are members of the Episcopalian Church. Mr. Bishop has a fine city residence; also a small place of 30 acres, and makes a specialty of raising fine hogs and brown Leghorn chickens. His purpose is to give his entire attention to Durock Jersey-red hogs and brown Leghorn chickens.

CHARLTON B. BURGESS

(Farmer and Breeder of Short Horn Cattle, Post-office, Kearney).

Among the younger agriculturists of the county who have become prominent in their calling, through their own efforts, is C. B. Burgess, comparatively a young man, now but thirty-six years of age.

461

HISTORY OF CLAY COUNTY

He was brought to Clay County, Mo., by his parents, while still in infancy, and grew up in this vicinity, attending, in common with sons of other farmers (for his father was a farmer) the common schools. He was favored, however, with more of an education than could there be obtained, attending for some time the Mount Gilead High School, where he received an excellent course of instruction. He had been born in Mason county, Ky., March 8, 1849. His father, Joseph V. Burgess, and his mother, Charity (Morris) Burgess, were Kentuckians by birth, and were reared and married in that State. They came to Clay county in 1850, and before the father died, November 24, 1858. The mother is yet living. They were both members of the Christian Church, as the mother still is. Charlton was the youngest of the three children in the family. On the 10th of November, 1874, Miss Margaret Anderson, daughter of Joseph D. and Mary Anderson (whose maiden name was Young), of Clay county, became his wife. She was also a native of this county, and was educated at Mount Gilead High School. They have two children, Nora and Mary A. Mr. Burgess owns a farm of 210 acres, well improved, and in a good state of cultivation. He makes a specialty of the stock business, and particularly of short horns, and at this time has upon his place about 50 head of thorough bred short horn cattle. His wife is a member of the Christian Church.

JAMES COSTELLO

(Of Burnes & Costello, Dealers in Lumber, Etc., Kearney).

Nearly 35 years ago Michael Costello came to Missouri from Ireland, settling at Liberty, in Clay county, where he married Catharine Keatley. They made that place their permanent home, and the father, after a residence there of nearly 30 years, which was well occupied with useful industry, died December 15, 1868. He waas life-long member of the Catholic Church. The mother is still living, a resident of Liberty. Five of their children are living, namely: Mary, Katie, Annie, Nellie, and the subject of this sketch. Two others died in early years. James Costello was born at Liberty, February 3, 1856. His parents not being people of means, his educational advantages were quite limited. At the age of 12 he left school and was employed in different kinds of work for some time. In 1880 he was employed in the lumber business in Liberty, which he followed until early in 1883, when he formed a partnership with P. B. Burnes, under the name of Burnes & Costello, and engaged in the lumber business on their own account at Kearney. They carry a full line of lumber and all kinds of building material, and also lime, hair, doors, sash, blinds, mouldings, etc. Their experience has been quite successful in the lumber business and their trade, already a good one, is steadily increasing. Mr. Costello, who is of Irish ancestry, is a young man entitled to much credit for the energy and success with which he is making his way up in life. The qualities that have brought him to his present position in business, and as a respected,

HISTORY OF CLAY COUNTY

useful citizen, at his present early age, will doubtless carry him forward through the long years before him to a much more advanced station in life.

JOSEPHUS COURTNEY

(Farmer, Post-office, Kearney).

The subject of this sketch was the youngest of the family of children referred to in the sketch of his brother, which is given elsewhere, where something of an outline of the history of the family has been given. Josephus Courtney was born in Clay county in 1844, and like his brother was brought up to a farm life. In 1868 he was married to Miss Nettie Arnold, daughter of J. B. Arnold, who came to this State from Kentucky in 1851, and after a residence of 10 years in Franklin county, removed to Clay county, where he now resides. Mrs. C.'s mother died here in 1863. Her father is still living, now a retired farmer, and formerly, for about nine years, justice of the peace. After his marriage Mr. Courtney continued in the occupation of farming and also engaged in raising stock, in which he has ever since been interested. He has a good farm of 267 acres, principally a stock and grass farm. Mr. and Mrs. Courtney have six children: Ebba, Maggie N., Willie R., Rosa J., Robert B. and Melissa E. They have lost one, an infant. Mr. Courtney's farm is well improved, including a handsome two-story brick residence.

NATHAN E. CRAWFORD

(Farmer and Stock-raiser, Post-office, Holt).

The second in a family of 12 children, of Maj. Smith Crawford and wife, née Jane Reed, Nathan E. was born in this county on the 10th of September, 1830. His father, Major Crawford, was well known in an early day in this county. He came from Alabama here, but was a native of Tennessee. After coming to Missouri, he served with distinction in the Black Hawk War, and was major of a regiment of Missouri volunteers. He was also quite active and prominent in public affairs, and was suddenly taken off by death while on a campaigning tour. His death occurred before he could reach home, and his remains were interred at the cemetery, near his old homestead. His wife, to whom he was married in Alabama, survived him several years. Only four of their family of children are now living. Nathan E. was reared on the farm in this county, and in young manhood learned the carpenter's trade. He followed his trade for some years, but subsequently located on a farm, and finally turned his entire attention to farming. In 1881, however, he removed to Holt and engaged in merchandising, but two years later sold out and returned to his farm. Mr. and Mrs. Crawford have five children: Smith, Hattie, wife of Robert Shackleford; Andrew J., Lydia and Willis. They have lost three, Lutie and Mollie, at tender ages, and Mamie, at the age of 13 years. Mr. and Mrs. Crawford are members of the Baptist Church.

463

HISTORY OF CLAY COUNTY

JOSEPH P. DITTO

(Farmer and Stock-raiser, Post-office, Holt).

On his father's side Mr. Ditto is a representative of a family that has been long settled in this country and has rendered valuable service in time of war as well as being worthily identified with affairs in times of peace. The family settled originally in Maryland and from that then colony William Ditto, the grandfather of the subject of this sketch, enlisted under Washington in the War for Independence. He was engaged in that memorable struggle from the beginning until its close, for seven long years. His son, Abraham Ditto, the father of Joseph P., who early went to Kentucky, served in the War of 1812 from that State. His wife was a Miss Martha Foree, and both he and wife were natives of Baltimore. In the War of 1812 he held the rank of a commissioned officer and did valuable service for his country. The Ditto family is of Scotch descent, and came over to this country prior to the Revolution. Mr. Ditto's mother was a daughter of Joseph Foree, originally of Fairfax county, Virginia, and who also served in the War for Independence. The Forees are of French descent. Joseph Ditto was born in Shelby county, Kentucky, July 12, 1824. He was the fifth of twelve children, only three of whom are living. Reared on the farm in Kentucky, he remainded there until 1858, and then came to Missouri and located near Plattsburg, in Clinton county. The following year he was married to Miss Eliza A. Albright, a daughter of Daniel Albright, and in 1866 Mr. Ditto came to Clay county, buying a farm near Kearney, where he settled. He has ever since been engaged in farming and most of the time in trading in stock. He has a good farm of 100 acres. Mr. and Mrs. Ditto's family consists of Bettie, wife of J. N. Hunter; Prior D., Florence, Erasmus, Lego, Corda, Prentice and Daniel. Three are deceased, two in childhood, and William L., a young man grown, in the spring of 1884. Mr. Ditto is a member of the M. E. Church South. Mrs. D. is a member of the Christian Union.

JAMES W. EASTIN

(Farmer and Fine Stock Raiser, Kearney).

In the matter of fine horses, at least for saddle and driving purposes, Kentucky has the reputation for pre-eminence, not only in this country but in Europe. There the breeding and training of fine riding and driving stock was early made a favorite pursuit with farmers and others, which they have ever since followed. Thus they not only succeeded in developing the finest horses in their line to be found in any country, but built up a school of fine-stock men who are not surpassed in skill and judgment in any country. Take a fine-horse Kentuckian anywhere and he stands in the front rank of professional fine-horse men.

Missouri has also attained some reputation as a producer of fine

HISTORY OF CLAY COUNTY

saddle and driving horses as well as other fine stock. But whatever name she has made for herself in this direction is very largely due to former Kentuckians, who, on coming and settling here, brought their taste for, and skill in, raising and training fine horses and other stock with them. This State has every advantage for the purpose, equal if not superior to the advantages of Kentucky; and if our farmers would more generally turn their attention to this branch of industry, they would doubtless soon make the State a rival of the Blue Grass Commonwealth, a consummation devoutly to be wished by every Missourian who feels any pride in the fame of his State. Seeing, however, that our people do not take the interest in this pursuit they should, we ought to feel only the more grateful to the few among us who do, the worthy, true sons of Kentucky, who, having made homes in this State, are ambitious to make her fame equal to that of their mother commonwealth.

Prominent among Missourians from Kentucky who have virtually devoted their whole lives to the fine-stock interests of this State, particularly to breeding and training fine horses, is the subject of the present sketch, a fine horse raiser, who has done his full share toward placing Missouri in the front rank of fine-stock States. Nor has anyone, even in Kentucky, more reason to feel proud of the record he has made in his branch of industry than Mr. Eastin. He has produced stock whose fame has circled the earth. One of his horses, the celebrated "White Stocking" breed, raised and trained by him in this county, he sold to Dr. Wallace, of New York City, for $10,000 in spot cash. Other horses which have attained a wide reputation have been bred and brought up by him; among fine-horse men in this State he stands second to none, either in point of success, good judgment in passing upon the qualities of a horse or skill in training him. Mr. Eastin has a fine-stock farm of 400 acres near Kearney, one of the finest places in the county, devoted exclusively to this purpose. His place is run almost entirely in blue grass, divided up into convenient pastures and arranged with rare good judgment for handling stock. Its barns and other outbuildings are of a superior class, and in addition he has a handsome, tastily built and imposing two-story brick dwelling, containing ten rooms, a very picture of a home for a successful farmer and stock-raiser. However, he owns good property in Kearney, including his residence, as well as other dwellings, business houses, etc., and makes his home here as a matter of convenience in posting himself daily in regard to the markets and in communication with stock men at other points by mail and telegraph. He rides out to his fine-stock farm nearly every day to see his stock and attend to the place.

As has been said, Mr. Eastin is a Kentuckian by nativity, born in Madison county, November 22, 1820. Reared in Kentucky, he was married in that State in 1846 to Miss Kezia Bishop, a daughter of John Bishop, a fine stock raiser of Madison county. Afterwards, in 1851, Mr. Eastin came to Missouri and located for a short time in Platte county, where he engaged in farming. But in 1851 he came

HISTORY OF CLAY COUNTY

to Kearney, then known as Centreville, where he carried on the business of handling fine horses and dealing in stock generally, in connection with a livery stable. He also owned and conducted a general store at this place. Handling fast horses, however, he made a specialty, and his livery stable was run more as being advantageous to his stock business than with any other object in view. He also carried on a stock farm in connection with his stock business. Mr. Eastin bought his present large stock farm near Kearney in 1876.

Considering that he is advancing well along in years, he is a man of wonderful energy and activity, and seems to be as warm and enthusiastic in the stock business as would ordinarily be expected of a man in the meridian of life. Nevertheless, he is aware that in the usual course of nature he must in a few years more retire from active life, and he is wisely shaping his affairs with that object in view. But he has the satisfaction of knowing that he has an ample competence for old age and has made a name as a fine stock raiser which he can contemplate in retirement without regret, to say the least.

In 1877 Mr. Eastin had the misfortune to lose his devoted and good wife by death. She had been a member of the Christian Church for many years. Two sons of their family of children are living, Frank W. and William H.

Subsequently Mr. Eastin was married to Miss Anna D. Burgess, of Clinton county, a daughter of O. B. Burgess, formerly of Mason county, Ky. By his present wife Mr. Eastin has two children, John R. and Walden J.

Mr. Eastin is a worthy member of the Masonic Order. His parents were Reuben J. and Nancy Eastin, who settled permanently in Clay county, of this State, from Kentucky, in 1851. Both are deceased. Six of their children are living.

J. C. ENGLAND

(Grocer and Member of the Town Council, Kearney).

Mr. England was one in a family of twelve children of Capt. James and Nancy (Campbell) England, of Garrard county, Ky. The father, however, was originally from Virginia. He was a carpenter and farmer by occupation, and died in 1856 at the age of 74. The mother survived up to January, 1884, until her ninety-second year. She had been a member of the M. E. Church for over 60 years. Eight of their family of children are living. John C. England was born in Garrard county, Ky., March 24, 1825, and was reared in Kentucky. At the age of 17 he began to learn the blacksmith's trade, which he followed for a period of twenty years. In 1855 Mr. England came to Grundy county, Mo., but not liking the country he returned to Kentucky. He followed blacksmithing up to 1862, when he began merchandising in the grocery line in Garrard county. In this he continued for twenty years, and then came to Kearney, Mo., and established his present business here. He keeps an excellent stock of goods, and has a good trade. In 1884 he was elected a member of the

466

HISTORY OF CLAY COUNTY

town council, and is now serving out his term as a member of the council. In 1849 Mr. England was married to Miss Amanda Smith, a daughter of Jacob Smith, a merchant of Mercer county, Ky. They have five children: Thompson A., wife of Mundy Curd, a farmer of Kentucky; James W., Alice S., Warren H., in Chicago, and John C., a clerk in a store at Chillicothe. They have lost two children in childhood.

AMBROSE S. GARRETT

(Of Wilhoit, Garrett & Co., Dealers in General Merchandise, Holt).

Mr. Garrett was partly educated at William Jewell College, where he took a course of several terms after quitting the common schools. Havingbeen reared to farm life he continued at that after leaving college until the spring of 1884, when he came to Holt, and became a member of the present firm. He is well respected as a business man and otherwise at Holt, and has a favorable outlook for a successful business experience. His father resides on a farm near this place, and Mr. Holt, Jr., is still interested in farming with his father, and also to some extent in raising stock. Mr. Garrett was reared in Clay county, though born in Kentucky, March 12, 1848, in Shelby county, that State. His parents, William P. and Angeline (Stone) Garrett, removed to Missouri with their family in 1853, locating where the father now resides, near Holt. The mother died in 1877. A short time before his mother's death Mr. Garrett, Jr., was married in this county to Miss Ella Wilhoit, a daughter of Thomas Wilhoit, a substantial farmer and stock-raiser of Clay county. Mr. and Mrs. G. have three children: William G., Pearle H. and Agie. The parents are members of the Missionary Baptist Church.

THOMAS M. GOSNEY

(President of the Kearney Bank, Kearney, Mo.).

Thomas M. Gosney was born in Clark county, Ky., January 13, 1815, his father, Richard Gosney, being of German descent and his mother, Jane, *née* Lackey, of Irish ancestry, though both were Virginians by birth. They were reared, educated and married in Clark county, Ky., and removed to Clay county, Mo., in 1845, where the mother died August 27, 1846. The senior Gosney then made his home with the subject of this sketch for seven years, after which he removed to Monroe county, Mo., where he was married a second time. He departed this life on the 16th of June, 1856. In early life he was a hatter by occupation, but during later years was engaged in farming. He was a member of the Old School Baptist Church, his wife having been connected with the Christian denomination. They were the parents of 15 children, six sons and nine daughters, 13 of whom lived to be grown; eleven were married, but only four are now living. Thomas M. Gosney was the seventh child in his father's family and, like his brothers, grew up upon the farm in his native county, receiving only such education as could be received in the primitive common schools of the day. Having accompanied his parents to this county in 1845, he has made it his home ever since and has risen by his own aid in life from a small, obscure and almost unknown tiller of the soil, to one of the most prominent, influential and highly successful men of the county. His first start to obtain a competence was in working as a farm hand and driving stock to the South, having for 14 years, while still in Kentucky, gone to South Carolina and Georgia with stock. With the exception of 40 acres of timber, he now owns 500 acres, all under fence, upon which is a good residence and also excellent outbuildings. This is admirably adapted for stock purposes. He has turned his attention for the last 20 years principally to stock-raising and feeding beef cattle; he has had ready for market nearly every year from two to four car loads of beef cattle besides quite a number of fat hogs. He has not bought over 100 barrels of corn in 20 years. As has been estimated, he is recognized as a man of excellent financial ability, in recognition of which he was elected president of the Kearney Bank and in which he is one of the prominent stockholders. A man of high, social and moral standing in his community, he is recognized everywhere for his true, sterling worth and inestimable value to the county in which he has chosen to make his home. A warm friend and supporter of education, he has proven his appreciation of the school system of this county by having without compensation furnished a number of persons with the means necessary to obtain good school facilities. During the existence of that party, he was a Whig in politics and since that time has been an ardent Democrat. In March, 1847, Mr. Gosney was married to Miss Susan E. Gosney, a daughter of Rev. Fielding Gosney, of Monroe county, Mo. She died November 10, 1854, leaving one child, Susan E., wife of Henry Anderson, a prominent farmer of Clay county. Mrs. G. was a member of the Christian Church. For his second wife Mr. Gosney married Miss Mary E. Anderson, June 1, 1859. She was born, reared and educated in Woodford county, Ky., and is a lady of many estimable qualities. Her parents were Capt. Spencer and Catherine (Hicks) Anderson, of this county. Mrs. G. is a member of Kearney Missionary Baptist Church, while her husband is connected with Mount Gilead Christian Church, in which ne is now and has been a deacon for a number of years. He became a member of the Christian Church in Kentucky in 1838, uniting with Mt. Gilead in 1845. He has since had his membership there.

WILLIAM O. GREASON

(Dealer in General Merchandise, and Justice of the Peace, Holt).

Mr. Greason has been at Holt for over ten years, having come here from North Carolina in 1873. However, one year prior to that he had spent in Clinton county, of this State. He has been engaged in general merchandising at Holt ever since coming to the county. Mr. Greason is a man of excellent education, good business qualifications, and is justly popular both as a merchant and a citizen in and around

HISTORY OF CLAY COUNTY

Holt. He was born in Guilford county, North Carolina, in 1851, and when he was a youth lost his father, who died in the Confederate service at Charlotte, N. C., February 15, 1865. Mr. Greason, Sr., was one of the substantial and highly respected citizens of Guilford county, in his native State. William O. was reared in that county and educated at Yadkin College, where he took a course extending through a period of about six years. He was then appointed deputy sheriff of Guilford county, although he was only 19 years of age. Mr. Greason continued in the office of deputy sheriff until he came to Missouri, in 1872. In 1881 he was married to Miss Maggie A. Fitch, a daughter of John F. and Sarah J. (Dicky) Fitch, formerly of Kentucky. Mr. and Mrs. Greason have no children, having lost their only child, a little son, in infancy. Mr. G. is a member of the C. U. Church, and Mrs. G is a member of the M. E. Church South. Mr. Greason's mother, whose maiden name was Elizabeth J. Rankin, is still living, a resident of North Carolina, on the old family homestead. His father's Christian name was Gideon. In 1882 Mr. Greason was elected a justice of the peace, and has continued to serve in that capacity ever since he qualified for the office after his election. He has made an efficient and capable magistrate, one in whose integrity and good judgment the community have implicit confidence.

JOHN T. HARMON

(Farmer and Stock-raiser, Post-office, Kearney).

Mr. Harmon was next to the eldest in the family of children of Jacob I. Harmon, additional reference to whom is made further along, and was born in Garrard county, Kentucky, December 15, 1843. He was a lad six years of age when his parents removed to Clay county, Mo., where they made their permanent home, and young Harmon was accordingly reared here. His school advantages were quite limited, and his father not being a man of large means, he was compelled to start out in the world for himself without a dollar. When the war broke out in 1861 he was a youth about eighteen years of age, and at once enlisted in Co. D, Fourth Iowa infantry, under Capt. Burton, of Col. Dodges' regiment, and was afterwards out in the active service for nearly two years. In 1863, however, he was honorably discharged on account of physical disability. He then went West, across the plains, principally for the benefit of his health, and returned in 1864. The following year Mr. Harmon was married to Miss Sarah, a daughter of George and Louisa (Brooks) Oder. At the time of his marriage, Mr. H. had a good team and three mule colts, which was all the stock he possessed. Nevertheless, he went resolutely to work, and made a good crop the first year. He was soon able to buy the necessary farm stock to carry on farming; though he owned but 65 acres of land when he married. From that beginning he has steadily prospered, and is now one of the substantial citizens of the county. He owns over 500 acres of fine land in different tracts, and in his home place, which is well improved, has 347 acres.

469

HISTORY OF CLAY COUNTY

This was the T. T. Bevins farm which he bought in 1881. He is a remarkably hard working man, and possesses unconquerable energy. What he has now he has made by his own hard labor, economy and good management. Although he has been successful by honest daily industry, it still looks a little hard that some who never did a hard day's work in their lives should be able by a simple dicker or trick or twist in the grain market to make five times as much, and five times five, as Mr. H. has succeeded in gathering together by a lifetime of labor and self-denial; in other words, the farmer works in the rain and burning sunshine, and in all the changes of weather to raise a bushel of wheat, while the grain speculator makes as much as the price of thousands of bushels in two minutes, and without even ungloving his delicate, tender hands, — a condition of affairs which renders such an anomaly and wrong as that not only possible, but the regular rule must necessarily be radically wrong; and some day the people will become educated up to the point of seeing it and remedying it. Mr. and Mrs. Harmon have six children: James H., Mary F., wife of Adam Foreighner, Lizzie B., Sarah T., Walter D. and Louisa. Three others they lost in infancy. Mrs. H. is a member of the Christian Church. The Harmon family is of German descent. Mr. H.'s great grandfather, Jacob Harmon, was reared in this country and served in the War for Independence. Jacob J. Harmon, the father of John T., was a son of Reese and Nancy (Nelson) Harmon, originally of Pennsylvania. Her father, Wm. Nelson, also served in the American army during the Revolution. He was of Irish descent. Jacob I. Harmon was born in Garrard county, Ky., December 13, 1819, and in 1838 was married to Miss Mary Conn, daughter of Rev. John and Elizabeth Conn, of Kentucky. In 1849 Mr. H. came to Missouri, and settled in Clay county. Two years later he went on the plains, and afterwards, for about seven years, followed teaming in the far West, either on his own account, for private parties, or for the Government, generally coming home, however, to raise a crop during each cropping season. Ever since that he has followed farming exclusively, in this county. During the war he was in the militia for a short time; and in 1865 he was absent from the county some months on account of the unsettled condition of affairs. Since then he has been engaged in farming, and has served as deputy sheriff of the county and as constable of the township. He and wife are members of the Presbyterian Church, and he is a member of the Blue Lodge and the Royal Arch Chapter, A. F. and A. M. He has a good farm comfortably improved and is pleasantly situated in life.

FREDERICK HARTEL

(Farmer and Stock-raiser, Post-office, Kearney).

After an active and useful career of more than a generation, not without reward in the substantial evidences of success, as well as otherwise, Mr. Hartel has now comparatively retired from the regular duties of business and industrial affairs, and is spending the evening of life

HISTORY OF CLAY COUNTY

in comparative ease and contentment. He commenced for himself at an early age, and from that time until the present his career has been one of unceasing industry and activity. Like many of our better foreign born citizens he is a native of Hesse-Darmstadt, Germany, where he was born November 15, 1808. He was the fourth of six children of Abraham and Anna Marie Hartel, and after being reared and educated at his native place accompanied his parents to the United States. Subsequently they located in Missouri, taking up their home in Clay county in 1842, where they afterwards died. The subject of this sketch, Frederick Hartel, has continued to live here since that time, a period now of over forty years. Though not numbered among the wealthiest men in the county he is, as before mentioned, in comfortable circumstances, having a farm of 100 acres under fence and in cultivation. His family is one of which any husband and father might well be proud. In October, 1845, Miss Barbara Hoff became his wife, and to them have been born six children: Louis, Jacob (deceased), Frederick, Kate, Conrad and William. Louis married Miss Agnes Sell, and is a farmer in Clinton county, Mo.; Kate is the wife of Prof. John H. Frick, professor of mathematics and natural sciences in Central Wesleyan College at Warrenton, Mo. A sketch of his life and mention of the college with which he is connected are given in the History of St. Charles, Montgomery and Warren Counties, recently published by the authors of the present volume. Frederick is engaged in raising and shipping stock. Conrad married Miss Lizzie Irmiger, and is living on the farm with his parents. He is an industrious young man, and is more than ordinarily successful in the management of the homestead. William is a student in the Theological Department of Boston University in Boston, Mass., and is a graduate of Central Wesleyan College. Jacob married Miss Susan Frick. He and wife are now both deceased. Mr. and Mrs. Frederick Hartel and all of their children are members of the German M. E. Church.

WILLIAM H. HAWKINS

(Proprietor of Hawkins' Boot and Shoe Shop, Kearney).

Mr. Hawkins has long been engaged in the occupation which he now follows. His father, Capt. John C. Hawkins, was in the same business before him. However, in later years his father was also a farmer, and William H. was partly reared on a farm. He received a common school education. Having gone to Texas, in the meantime, in 1862, he entered the Confederate army, becoming a member of Co. F, Eighth Texas regiment, under Col. Overton. He did not serve, however, throughout the war, but after being in Col. Overton's regiment, returned to Milan county, Texas, where he had previously resided. In 1866 Mr. Hawkins came back to Clay county, Mo., and resumed shoemaking, which he had previously followed in Texas. He has followed shoemaking also continuously ever since. However, in 1866, he made another trip to Texas and was absent about a year engaged in farming. Mr. Hawkins has a good run of custom at

HISTORY OF CLAY COUNTY

Kearney, and is doing as well as could be expected in a place the size of this. In 1868 he was married to Miss Mary J. Groom, a daughter of Amos and Sallie (Chaney) Groom, early settlers from Kentucky. Mr. and Mrs. H. have one child: Mary M.; they have had the misfortune to lose six in childhood. He and wife are members of the Christian Church. Mr. H. is a strict temperance man. His father, Capt. Hawkins, came from Woodford county, Ky., and located at Liberty in about 1829. Subsequently he engaged in farming in Clay county. He was in the Mormon War, and helped to drive the disciples of polygamy out of the States. There was where he received his title of captain. He died in 1868, in the sixty-fifth year of his age. His wife, whose maiden name was Mary E. Turnum, died in 1857. They had 12 children, 11 of whom are living. William H., the seventh in their family of children, was born June 14, 1840.

GEORGE S. HENDERSON

(Dealer in Hardware, Farm Implements, Etc., Kearney).

Mr. Henderson was a youth seventeen years of age when his parents came to Missouri in 1853, and had received an elementary knowledge of books in the log school-houses of the period. But here he went to work at hard labor on the farm and was beginning to get something of a start when the war broke out in 1861. He then enlisted in Capt. Tom McCarty's company for the Southern service, and served until 1863, when he was taken sick and compelled to return home. In 1865 he went to St. Louis county, where the family had removed in the meantime, and remained there until 1866 engaged in farming. At that time he was employed by Messrs. E. M. Samuel & Sons, commission merchants, to travel for their house, which he followed for a year. After his employment with Messrs. Samuel & Sons, Mr. H. went to Holt county and engaged in the saw milling business. Two years later he bought a saw mill at Rulo, Neb., but in 1874 came back to Clay county, where he was interested in a farm and engaged in farming. In 1876 Mr. Henderson was married to Miss Nannie B. Leach, a daughter of Daniel and Elizabeth Leach, formerly of Scott county, Ky., but afterwards of Platte county, and later still of this (Clay) county. Mr. Henderson bought his present stock of goods in February, 1884, and has been engaged in business ever since. He and wife have two children: Daniel H. and G. DeMatt. Mrs. H. is a member of the Christian Church. Mr. Henderson was formerly interested in short horn cattle. He is a man of energy and enterprise and will doubtless prove one of the successful men of the county. Mr. Henderson's father was James Henderson, originally of Mason county, Ky., but whose parents came from Virginia. He was a large trader from Kentucky with the South before the railroads, and made as many as 13 trips from New Orleans to Kentucky on horseback. He dealt largely in mules and also in bacon, and transported his bacon either by wagons or by flatboats to the South. He was a man of great energy and thorough reliability. He came to Missouri with his family

HISTORY OF CLAY COUNTY

in 1853, locating first in Lafayette county, but settled in Clay county the following year. He died here in 1877 in the seventy-second year of his age. His wife, who was a Miss Brittyann Howe before her marriage, lived to reach the age of 66, dying in 1870. They were both members of the Old School Presbyterian Church, and are buried at Mount Gilead, Clay county, Mo. They had a family of five children, four sons and one daughter; the daughter is dead.

JACOB HESSEL (DECEASED)

(Late of Kearney Township).

On the 13th of August, 1881, died at his homestead in this county, Jacob Hessel, where for over 25 years he was known as one of the highly respected and influential citizens of Kearney township. He was a man who achieved success in life solely by his own exertions and personal worth, and his intelligent appreciation of the conditions and opportunities of life around him. From early circumstances but little or no better than the average of those of the youths among whom he was reared, he rose to a creditable degree of success in life, both in standing and influence. He came of a well respected German family, and was the youngest of five children, born February 14, 1824, in Germany. In 1845 he left the country of his nativity and came to America, locating in Clay county, Mo., in 1846. He was a farmer by occupation, but when the news of the discovery of gold in California reached the citizens of this county, he was drawn into the tide of Western emigrants, and went to the golden coast of that far-off Eldorado, remaining for three years. However, he then returned to Clay county, and here made his home until his death. Successful in the material affairs of life, he had accumulated 216 acres of land, all of which is now under fence, and 160 acres are in cultivation and blue grass pasture. On October 16, 1855, he had been married to one of the fairest daughters of the old Fatherland, Mrs. Malia Bauman, whose maiden name was Moeller. Their family consisted of seven children: William is now in Denver, Col.; Louis is a student at Central Wesleyan College, at Warrenton; Carrie is attending the same school; Mary is living with her mother; Jacob died September 15, 1883; Edward and Henry live on the old homestead and carry on the farming and stock-raising operations. They are enterprising and progressive young agriculturists, and have achieved quite a reputation in the stock business, having sold during the past year two car loads of cattle and one of hogs. Mr. Hessel was a member of the Bethel German M. E. Church. His wife and her children are connected with the same denomination.

CONRAD HESSEL

(Farmer, Post-office, Kearney).

Mr. Hessel is another example of what energy, industry and perseverance, when intelligently applied, have accomplished for those of foreign birth who have seen fit to locate within the boundaries of this country. Like many of the oldest residents of this county who have become possessed of means and gained a competence sufficient to enable them to pass their later years in ease and retirement, is a native of Germany, having been born there February 8, 1821. Other members of this family have also settled in Clay county from Germany, mention of whom is made elsewhere. The youth of Conrad was passed as those of other youths of the country, and when 22 years of age he left the place of his birth and emigrated to the United States, locating first in Ohio, in 1843, and then in 1847 in Clay county, which has continued to be his home for a period of about 40 years. His beginning in this county was indeed an humble one. Poor in purse, and by no means thoroughly conversant with the customs of this country, he commenced at once with characteristic thrift and industry to situate himself comfortably in life, which he has done, though at a cost of many years of hard toil and labor. The fruit of his success is now seen in the handsome homestead which he owns, a beautifully cultivated farm of 525 acres. In 1855 he was married to Miss Christina Heinz, and to them were born seven children: Fred, Kathrina, Elizabeth, Conrad, Louis, Barbara and Christina. Three of these are married, viz.: Frederick married Miss Katie Weber, and is now engaged in farming in this county; Elizabeth, wife of O. H. Weber, also a farmer, and Kathrina, now Mrs. William H. Stein, whose husband is pastor of the German Methodist Church at Hays City, Kas. Conrad is superintendent of the Sabbath-school connected with the Bethel M. E. Church, of which Mr. and Mrs. Hessel and their children are members. His domestic life has been one of great contentment and happiness, and he has reared a worthy family of children. A progressive farmer and an intelligent citizen, he is held in high respect by all who know him.

JOHN L. HODGES

(Stock Trader, Post Office, Kearney).

It was as early as 1826 that the family of which Mr. Hodges was a member settled in Clay county. His parents were among the pioneer settlers of the county, and became well-to-do and highly respected residents of Fishing River township. His father, Judge Hodges, served as an officer in the Black Hawk War, and was afterward elected a judge of the county court for a number of terms. He was one of the most popular men in the county, and was elected by an almost unanimous vote of the people. He died here in January, 1873. His wife, whose maiden name was Louisana Lingfelter, of German descent, died in April, 1881, in her seventy-seventh year. Judge Hodges had a fine farm of some 400 acres, most of which is still in possession of the family. He was a slaveholder before the war and a man of strong Southern feeling, though he took no active part, on account of his advanced years. Still, he enlisted in the State Guard, for home protection. He was an earnest and consistent member of the Old School Baptist Church, as was also his wife. He was quite zealous for the church, and a liberal supporter of both it and the cause of good schools. Of their family of eleven children seven are living, all sons except one, Amanda, the wife of A. G. Mosby, and all residents of Clay county, except Albert, who went to Oregon in 1850. John L. Hodges was born in this county March 11, 1851, and at the age of 20 enlisted in Co. F, under Capt. Pixley, of the Missouri State Guard, of which company he was orderly sergeant. He was in the battles of Lexington and Pea Ridge. But on account of inflammatory rheumatism, brought on by the exposures of camp-life, he was compelled to return home. In 1865 he was married to Miss Sarah E. Riley, a daughter of William P. Riley of this county. Mr. Hodges has been engaged in farming and stock-raising and also dealing in stock up to four years ago. He had a good farm, but sold his place in 1880 and removed to Kearney, where he is engaged exclusively in dealing in and shipping stock. He is considered one of the best judges of stock in this part of the county, and has had a successful experience as a stock dealer. Mr. and Mrs. Hodges have three children: John L., Jr., Anna M. and Allen O. They have lost one, William H., at an early age. Mr. H. and wife are members of the Christian Church.

JOHN T. HUFFAKER

(Of Mitchell & Huffaker, Dealers in General Merchandise, Holt).

As is well known Clay county received its largest early immigration during the "Thirties," at which time there was almost a flood tide of pioneer settlers, principally from Kentucky. Among the hundreds of other families who came during the first years of the "Thirties," was that of the father of Mr. Huffaker, Washington Huffaker. He settled in this county in 1831, and was the first sheriff of the county after its organization. He was subsequently a county judge for a number of years, and held other official positions. Judge Huffaker was one of the prominent and highly respected citizens of the county. He was a successful farmer and died here in 1863. His wife, who was a Miss Sarah Shackleford before her marriage, died in 1864. They reared a family of seven children, all of whom are living and are themselves the heads of families. John T. was born on the farm in this county in 1850. On growing up he became a farmer and followed farming and stock-raising until 1879, when he engaged in business at Holt with the Rev. Mr. Mitchell. Mr. Huffaker has served as mayor of Holt and in the town council. In 1880 he was married to Miss Laura Holt, a daughter of Col. John B. Holt, the founder of the town of Holt, and one of the leading wealthy citizens of the county. He was a gallant soldier in the Mexican War, and served in the Confederate army through the Civil War, rising by his ability and intrepidity as an officer to the command of a company which became noted for its valor on many a hard fought field. He is now living a quiet, retired life at Holt, in the possession of a competence, but best of all of an honored name and clear conscience. Mr. Huffaker, the subject of this sketch, is a leading and prominent Mason, and a worthy and exemplary member of the Christian Church.

HISTORY OF CLAY COUNTY

JOHN N. HUNTER

(Postmaster, Holt).

Mr. Hunter is a native of Nebraska, a fact which can perhaps be truthfully asserted of no other citizen of Missouri, at least of none not younger than he and probably a few others in the whole country, Nebraska included. His father, R. M. Hunter, was one of the pioneers of Nebraska, going there away back in the " Fifties," before the scream of the locomotive was heard on the plains, or the buffalo and Indian had been pushed on against the apron of the Cordilleras. He was born in Nemaha county, Neb., in 1859. His mother's maiden name was Miss Hollenbeck, a native of Illinois. His father was originally from Ohio, and was a saddle and harnessmaker, a trade that was very profitable in Nebraska in an early day, when one could exchange a good saddle for nearly enough buffalo robes to wall in and cover an ordinary sized house. There was also a good demand for saddles and harness among the white pioneers and emigrants bound for the golden shore, washed by the Pacific sea. However, on account of the severity of the climate in that early day when all the country was open and the biting frost came flying across the country with the speed of the wind, apparently guided only by the portentous sun dogs that seemed to absorb the warmth from the cheerless star of day, the family left Nebraska and came further south, to Missouri, where the elements and animal life were not so much at war with each other as they are in the young State of the plains. After residing in Atchison county for awhile, they settled in Clay county, near Holt. In 1879 they removed to Kansas, where they now reside. Mr. Hunter, Jr., was partly reared in the vicinity of Holt, and has made this his home continuously from the time the family first came here. In 1883 he was appointed deputy postmaster of Holt, and a short time afterwards was himself made postmaster. He has held the office ever since. He also carries a stock of books and stationery in connection with his duties as postmaster. In 1876 Mr. Hunter was married to Miss Elizabeth Ditto, a daughter of J. P. Ditto, of Clay county. Mr. and Mrs. H. have two children, John J. and Leonard W. They have lost one in infancy, Ida May. Mr. and Mr. H. are members of the Christian Union Church. Mr. Hunter's father also followed farming and handling stock, in which he is still engaged to some extent.

GEORGE M. ISLEY

(Of Morgan & Isley, Millers, Holt).

Mr. Isley has been in active business life for over thirty years, and is a man, who by experience, energy and business qualifications, is justly entitled to be classed among the better class of business men of the county. He is a North Carolinian by nativity, born in Alamance county, June 27, 1832. He was the eldest in a family of children of Austin and Polly Isley, both of early North Carolina families. On his father's side the family is of German descent, but has been settled in this country for generations. The father is still living and is a retired stock-raiser, having been quite successful in life. The mother died only about four years ago. Mr. Isley, Jr., or the subject of this sketch, was reared in his native county, and at the age of 21 engaged in merchandising at Gibsonville, that county. He continued in business as a merchant for about five years, at the expiration of which he was appointed postmaster at Gibsonville and also station agent on the railroad. Mr. Isley had charge of these offices for some seventeen years. He then removed to Raleigh, where he bought and took charge of a large distillery. Two years later, however, he sold out at Raleigh and removed to Missouri, locating in the vicinity of Holt. Here he also established a distillery and carried on a farm, which he purchased on coming to this county. He still owns the farm, and is engaged in farming, in addition to his milling business. He bought a half interest in the flouring and grist mill at this place, becoming a member of the firm of Morgan & Isley in 1875. He has ever since been engaged in milling. In 1855 Mr. Isley was married to a Miss Shoffner, a daughter of Daniel and Barbara Shoffner, of Alamance county, N. C. Her parents are both now deceased. Mr. and Mrs. Isley have had seven children, all living and residents of Holt. Thomas and Augustus are engaged in the livery business at this place and are young men of energy and enterprise. Mr. and Mrs. Isley are members of the Christian Union Church. Mr. I. is a member of the Masonic order and is one of the Democrats who has been voting the straight ticket (except while North Carolina was out of the Union) ever since 1856, without seeing a Democratic President inaugurated. That interesting event he was fortunate enough to enjoy on the 4th of March last.

WILLIAM H. LaRUE,

(Of Stowers & LaRue, Druggists, Holt).

Mr. LaRue was a teacher by profession, having come from Indiana to this State, and after coming here taught some three years in Clay county before engaging in the drug business. However, he had had experience in handling drugs and in pharmacy and had a good knowledge of the business before he became a member of the firm with which he is now connected. The firm of Stowers & LaRue have a neat drug store, keeping constantly in stock a full assortment of fresh and pure drugs. They also carry other lines of goods usually found in a first-class drug store. Being both good business men and upright and obliging in their dealings, they have of course succeeded in attracting a good trade. Mr. LaRue was born in Greene county, Ind., April 18, 1860. His parents were Jesse and Nancy (Dugger) LaRue, his father being a carpenter and contractor by occupation. The family on either side was from Tennessee and Virginia, respectively. The mother died in 1883, but the father is still living. William H.

was reared in Indiana and educated at the common and Normal Schools and the State University. Prior to entering the Normal School, however (at which he graduated), he had taught school and after concluding his educational course he resumed teaching, coming West to Missouri for that purpose. He came to Holt, Clay county, Mo., in March, 1881. The following year after coming to Missouri Mr. LaRue was married to Miss Lura L. Harris, a daughter of William Harris, of Clay county. They have one child, a daughter, Jessie, Mr. and Mrs. L. are members of the M. E. Church South. He is a member of the Masonic fraternity.

WILLIAM B. LEACH

(Dealer in Hardware, Tinware, Cutlery, Farm Implements, Wagons, Buggies, Etc. Kearney).

Mr. Leach engaged in his present business in 1880, as a successor in the business to George Spears. Mr. Spears had previously carried it on for some years, but in the spring of 1880 committed suicide in his store by shooting himself. Mr. Leach afterwards bought the stock and continued the business. He has materially enlarged and improved the stock of goods and added much to the patronage of the house. It is now one of the leading houses of this class in the northeastern part of the county. Mr. Leach was born in Scott county, Ky., July 23, 1840. When he was a lad about seven years of age his parents removed to Missouri and settled in Platte county, where young Leach grew to manhood. In 1867 the family removed to Clay county, where they still reside. In the meantime William B. had grown up and gone out into the world for himself. In 1861 he enlisted in the army, but after a term of service of less than a year, returned to Platte county, and the same year went to New Mexico. He came back, however, in 1862, but in June of that year went to Montana Territory, and was engaged in trading in stock for the following six or seven years. He was also in Utah, Idaho and British America. He went to the noted Kootney mines on a prospecting tour. In 1869 he returned to Missouri, and as his father's family had removed to Clay county, he stopped at Kearney. Here he engaged in farming and handling stock to some extent, which he continued until 1880, when he bought out the Spears stock of goods as stated above. While handling stock in the West Mr. Leach was also engaged in farming. In 1876 he was married to Miss Cassie McGinnis, daughter of James McGinnis, of Kearney, but formerly of Kentucky. They have one child, a little son. Mrs. L. is a member of the Christian Church and he is a member of Lodge No. 311, A. F. and A. M., at Kearney.

L. W. LEAVELL

(Farmer, Fine Stock Raiser and Stock-dealer, Post-office, Kearney, Mo.).

Clay county has long had the reputation of being one of the best stock-raising counties in the State. Not only do the farmers here

HISTORY OF CLAY COUNTY

give their principal attention to stock-raising, for which the county is remarkably well adapted, but they are generally a class of men of enterprise and information, who take pride in securing the best stock for breeding purposes to be had. This practice has had a beneficial result in two ways: it has not only been profitable to the farmers themselves, but has given the county an enviable name as a fine stock county. Prominent among the farmers who have done their full share toward advancing the stock interests of Clay county is the subject of the present sketch, Mr. Leavell, who came here in 1854. He was a well-to-do fine stock raiser of Kentucky, and after coming here bought about 1,700 acres of fine land. Having some forty odd or fifty negroes, he improved a large farm, and engaged in farming and stock-raising quite extensively. His negro property was soon afterwards taken from him by operation of the war, but he has, nevertheless, had a prosperous career in other respects. For years he has been recognized as one of the leading farmers and stock-raisers of the county. He is a man of high character and superior intelligence and information, and occupies a prominent position in the community. He was born in Todd county, Ky., December 12, 1821, and was reared to a farm life, receiving a common-school education as he grew up. In 1838 he was married to Miss Harriet D. Winn, a daughter of George Winn, of Christian county, Ky., a prominent and wealthy citizen of that county. Eight children have been the fruits of their union, namely, Frances, now the wife of Rev. G. W. Rogers, of Dallas, Texas; Sarah, the wife of Samuel C. Greenfield, of this county; Georgia A., the wife of Dr. Silas Denham, of Clay county, Mo.; Daniel W., now a resident of Kansas; Eugenia S., wife of William Rust, also a resident of Kansas; Leonidas, W. Llewellyn, Lane and Robert Ernest Lee. Three others are deceased, who, however, lived to mature years. Lycurgus L., their eldest son, who died in California; Harriet L., who died whilst the wife of John J. Eastin, and Montgomery D. Mr. and Mrs. Leavell are members of the Baptist Church, and Mr. L. is a Royal Arch Mason. Mr. Leavell's farm contains 860 acres. The balance of his land is divided up among his children. He has a handsome homestead, including a commodious and tastily built residence, and substantial, neat appearing barns and other outbuildings, He is very comfortably situated in life.

ALBERT LINCOLN

(Retired Farmer, Post-office, Kearney).

Only the few who have given the subject any thought and investigation have any idea of the important part Virginia has taken in the history of the country, and of the vast influence she still exerts, perhaps now not so much directly as indirectly. Leaving out of the account what she has done directly and is still doing, her indirect influence in affairs is not even approached in importance by that of any other Commonwealth in the Union. She not only gave to the country its great Northwest Territory, out of which have been formed some of the most populous, prosperous and progressive States of the Union, but largely gave the sturdy pioneers and brave settlers who founded these States and made them what they are. Besides this she peopled Kentucky, presenting the territory and the population of the Blue Grass State to the Union as a proud and free and generous gift. All Southern Ohio was mainly settled by her sons, or the sons of her eldest and fairest daughter, Kentucky, as were also most of Indiana and Illinois, and a large percentage of the other Northern States, and of the Pactolian Commonwealth of the Pacific coast, California. So, the younger States of the South were largely peopled from the Old Dominion, including Missouri and Arkansas. Likewise there is Texas, settled almost exclusively by Virginians, Kentuckians, Missourians and West Tennesseeans, settlers who sprang originally, almost without an exception, from Virginia families. Any comprehensive genesis of the population of the West and Southwest would show that more then 75 per cent of the people are of Virginia descent. But it is not in this respect alone that the Old Dominion holds a distinguished and pre-eminent position in the history of the country. Take the names of the great men that shed the brightest lustre on our career as a nation, and they are in a large majority of cases the names of Virginians, either by nativity or descent. Hardly less is this true of the present, than of the past. At the beginning, the "Father of our Country" was a son of the Old Mother Commonwealth. So, also, with most of the other early characters of prominence and distinction. Nor has there been an important epoch in the history of the country since that time in which the name of a Virginian has not stood out above and brighter than all others. In the great crisis of the Civil War the brightest names that illuminated that dark period were either of or from the Old Dominion. This was true on both sides. To the North and the Nation, Virginia gave Abraham Lincoln, a man who, on the Union side, was nearer than all others after the pattern of Washington, a brave, pure, true, great man On the side of the South we had Lee and Stonewall Jackson, names that any country might well be proud to boast. Now and at all times Virginians have occupied the first places in the history and in the hearts of their countrymen. Jackson, the "Iron President," Harrison, the "Hero of Tippecanoe," of Indiana, the great Clay, and hundreds of others traced their lineage back to Virginia. And it is a remarkable circumstance that the Washingtons, Lincolns and Lees were all orginally settled in Northern Virginia. From there branches of these families spread out into other parts of the State and into other States. But in the present sketch we have only to do with the Lincoln family — Albert Lincoln, whose biography is here given, being one of the descendants of that family. The Lincolns came to this country from England in early colonial times and settled, in the first place, in Northeastern Virginia. — Lincoln, ot that section of the Old Dominion, was the great-grandfather of President Lincoln and the grandfather of Abraham Lincoln (the father of the subject of this sketch), who became one of the pioneer settlers of Western-Central

HISTORY OF CLAY COUNTY

Missouri. Judge James E. Lincoln, of Liberty, is also a descendant of the same family. His father, George Lincoln, was a son of Thos. Lincoln, of Fayette county, Ky., but originally from Rockingham county, Va. Thomas Lincoln was a brother of Abraham Lincoln, the grandfather of President Lincoln. Judge Lincoln's father and Albert Lincoln's father were brothers. George Lincoln was one of the pioneer settlers of Clay county. He and Albert Lincoln's father, Abraham Lincoln, who were brothers, were both blacksmiths by trade, and both from Kentucky to this State. Abraham Lincoln, however, came to Missouri at an earlier day than the removal of George Lincoln. He, the former, settled in Saline county, or what is now Saline, before the county was formed, and in early territorial times. Subsequently he removed to Clay county, in about 1823; and later still (but yet at an early day), he settled on the Platte Purchase, where he located a claim; but while temporarily absent his place on the Platte Purchase was taken possession of or "jumped," as they termed it then, by another party, who hadn't even a color of right to it. Still, Mr. Lincoln being a quiet, upright man, preferred to lose his claim rather than engage in a lawsuit, or have any personal trouble with the claimant. He therefore decided to make his permanent home in Clay county, and afterwards resided here for many years, until his death, engaged at his trade and in farming. He was a man of sterling worth, strict integrity and strong, natural good sense — characteristics everywhere of the Lincoln family. His wife came of an old and respected family of Kentucky, but originally of Virginia. Her Christain name was Agnes Feming. They had a family of five children, all of whom lived to reach mature years and to become the heads of families themselves. Only three are now living. Albert Lincoln, whose name stands at the head of this sketch, was born in Saline county, April 18, 1819, but as his parents subsequently removed to Clay county, he was partly reared in this county. He learned the blacksmith's trade under his father, as he grew up, and afterwards followed it for some years. In 1844 Mr. Lincoln was married to Miss Armilda Soper, a daughter of Benjamin Soper, formerly of Kentucky. In about 1850 Mr. L. engaged in farming, and soon afterwards quit blacksmithing altogether and turned his entire attention to farming and stock-raising. Ever since that time he has made agricultural life his sole pursuit. A man of industry and good intelligence, he has always lived comfortably and has never been embarrassed by the reverses that often overtake men of more venturesome disposition. His greatest desire has been not to accumulate large means, but to live an upright, quiet, unobtrusive and respectable life, and to rear his family of children in comfort and creditably; but above all to rear them with the ideas of personal honesty thoroughly instilled into their minds, and with the conviction that only by honest industry should success be sought or hoped for. In all this he may be truthfully said to have been successful to the utmost of his desires. No man has traveled down the pathway of life to the shades of old age with a name more spotless than his. Albert Lincoln stands as high in the

481

HISTORY OF CLAY COUNTY

esteem of all who know him for integrity and personal worth as any man whose citizenship ever did honor to the country. Mr. Lincoln has a comfortable farm of 160 acres, and is now living in retirement from the severe activities of life. Nevertheless, he is a man of industry and perseverance and still assists, when necessary, at farm work. Though closely approaching the allotted age of three-score and ten, he is well preserved and is unusually active, considering his years. He and his good wife have reared a family of four children, one of whom is now deceased. The living are: John W., Newton H. and Benjamin F. Archibald died in young manhood in 1860. Mr. and Mrs. L. are members of the Christian Church.

LARZ A. LOGAN

(Farmer and Stock-raiser and County Assessor, Post-office, Kearney).

Among the officials of Clay county L. A. Logan, the subject of the present sketch, is deserving of more than a passing notice. Though only having been elected to his present office in 1882, sufficient time has elapsed to judge of his ability for the position to which he was chosen, and doubtless the people of this county will show their appreciation of his services by electing him to discharge the duties of this office for another term when it becomes necessary to do so. He is a Kentuckian by birth, having been born June 17, 1832, in Shelby county. After leaving there in 1857, he came to Missouri, but subsequently went to Colorado and Montana where he remainded until 1866, then returning to Platte county, Mo. In 1872 he took up his home in Clay county and here, on the 18th of January, of that year, he was married to a daughter of one of the old pioneers of Clay county, Miss Jennie E. Duncan, whose father was Alexander Duncan. They have been blessed with four children, one of whom, however, is deceased, Mary Ann. Those living are Gwathmey P., Matt. D. and Aytchmonde. When Mr. Logan came to this county he settled on 80 acres of land, but in 1879 moved to the place on which he now lives. Here, in addition to his agricultural pursuits, he is occupied to some extent in the stock business, more especially in the breeding of short horn cattle. His landed estate embraces some 300 acres. He and his wife are members of the Mount Gilead Christian Church.

JOHN S. MAJOR

(Farmer, Fine Stock-Raiser and Cashier of the Kearney Bank, Kearney).

Mr. Major, in addition to his duties as cashier of the Savings Bank, is interested on his farm near this place in breeding and raising fine stock of different kinds. His interest in stock includes horses, cattle and hogs, and he deals to a considerable extent in all of these. He makes a specialty of Pure Bates and Bates Topped short horns cattle, of which he has some unusually fine representatives. His other stock also are generally of superior grades and his experience with fine stock

HISTORY OF CLAY COUNTY

and in the stock business, generally, has been one of success and entire satisfaction. Mr. Major became identified with the Kearney Bank on its first organization. Indeed, he was one of its original stockholders and was instrumental in organizing the bank. It was organized in 1882, with a paid-up stock of $10,000, and has since had an entirely prosperous career. It has ever since paid an annual dividend of 25 per cent. It is one of the well-conducted, substantial banking institutions of the county, and is the only bank at this place. Mr. Major is a native of Clay county, born in this township February 22, 1852. His father was Dr. Herman S. Major, a leading and successful physician of this part of the county, originally from Kentucky, but now deceased. Dr. Major was also extensively engaged in farming and stock-raising and was prosperous. He graduated at the Louisville Medical College in 1850, and came to this county the following year. The same year of his graduation he was married to Miss Mary L. Swearingen, of an old and highly respected Kentucky family. The Doctor died here in 1869. His widow, Mrs. Major, is still living and residing on the old family homestead near Kearney. They had a family of nine children: Charles S., a farmer of Clinton county; William W., now in the bank at Kearney; Mary R., a twin sister to William W., and the wife of R. E. Bevins; Slaughter G., a farmer of this county, with whom his mother resides on the old homestead; Susan Y., a twin sister to Slaughter G.; Sallie B., Reuben H., Hermonetta, now deceased, and John S. John S. was reared in this county and educated at Kentucky Military Institute, near Frankfort, Ky., and at William Jewell College, of Liberty. In 1876 he was married to Miss Jennie Anderson, a daughter of Joseph and Mary Anderson, who came to this county from Clark county, Ky., in 1843. The father died here in 1859. Mr. and Mrs. Major have one child and have lost one.

SLAUGHTER G. MAJOR

(Farmer and Stock-raiser, Post-office, Kearney).

Mr. Major was born in this county in July, 1860, and was the fifth in the family of children of Herman and Mary Major, reference to whom is made in the sketch of John S. Major, another son of theirs, which precedes this. Slaughter G. was reared on the farm and received his primary education in the common schools. In 1878, at the age of 18, he entered William Jewell College, in which he took a course of three years, graduating in the class of '81. Besides taking a general English and classical course, he graduated in German and French. After his graduation he returned to the farm where he was reared, and resumed farming and stock-raising, to which he was brought up. He has continued occupied with these industries ever since that time. He and his brother, Reuben, and their sister, Sarah B., remain at home with their mother, their father having previously died. Mr. Major is at the head of the affairs of the farm and is showing marked good judgment and enterprise in its management. The place contains 240 acres and is well improved. He has about

483

HISTORY OF CLAY COUNTY

75 head of good cattle on the place aside from a small herd of short horns and other stock, and he feeds annually for the markets about 40 head of beef cattle and a larger number of hogs. The younger brother, Reuben, is now completing his course at college.

ZENAS F. MILBOURN

(Proprietor of the Kearney Livery, Feed and Sales Stables, Kearney).

Mr. Milbourn has a first-class establishment in the livery line, including a capacious and neatly built stable and a full stock of riding and driving horses and buggies, carriages, drummers' wagons, etc. He has been in this line of business some years and has had a successful experience as a liveryman. His stables have an established reputation and a patronage which is steadily increasing in extent and profit. Mr. Milbourn is a native of Maryland, born July 4, 1848. His father was Zenas F. Milbourn, Sr., formerly of Virginia, and his mother's maiden name was Adeline C. Marcellus. She was born and reared in Maryland. Mr. Milbourn Sr., went from Loudoun county, Va., to Maryland, where he was married, in Baltimore, to Miss Marcellus, a young lady of French descent. After some years' residence in Maryland he returned to Virginia. During the war he served in Co. A, Eighth Virginia regiment, and was wounded at Ball's Bluff, October 21, 1861, by which he was disabled for the service, and thereafter returned home. He is still living in Virginia but his wife died in 1856. Of their family of children three are living. Zenas F. Milbourn was reared in Virginia and in 1861 entered the Southern army. He was a member of Mosby's command and was out until the close of the war. Just before the breaking out of the war he had begun to learn the shoemaker's trade, and after the war he finished his apprenticeship at Baltimore. In 1868 Mr. Milbourn, Jr., removed to Ohio, where he followed his trade a year and then came to Missouri, working at different points until 1870, when he came to Clay county. Here he worked at his trade until 1878, and then engaged in the livery business at Kearney in partnership with Z. M. Tapp. Five years later he sold his interest in the stable and built the one he now occupies, where he has ever since been engaged in the business. June 23, 1871, he was married to Miss Mary L. Peper, a daughter of William Peper, of Mason county, Ky. Mr. and Mrs. Milbourn have one child, Zenas F., Jr. They lost one child in infancy. Mr. Milbourn has a good farm of 180 acres, where he is engaged in raising fine short horn cattle. Mr. and Mrs. M. are members of the Christian Church.

REV. GEORGE W. MITCHELL

(Christian Union Minister, Holt).

Rev. Mr. Mitchell's father's family was one of the early families to settle at Independence, in Jackson county. They remained there, however, only a short time, removing thence to Lafayette county, where they resided for a period of about 25 years. The father,

484

HISTORY OF CLAY COUNTY

Benjamin F. Mitchell, was a farmer and carpenter, and removed from Kentucky to this State. After farming some years in Lafayette county, he made his residence at Lexington. But in 1866 he removed to Haynesville, in Clinton county, where he resided until his death, which occurred at the age of 70, in 1877. The mother, the wife of Mr. Mitchell, Sr., preceded her husband to the grave in 1860. She was a Miss Margaret Franklin before her marriage. At her death there were five children, including the subject of this sketch, who was about 17 years of age. He was born in Lafayette county in 1842. As his parents shortly removed to Lexington, he had the advantages afforded by the schools of that place, and received a good general English education. However, at the age of 18 he went to work at the blacksmith's trade, which he afterwards followed for some six or seven years. In 1866 he engaged in general merchandising at Haynesville, remaining in business there for about 13 years. Mr. Mitchell then removed to Holt, and became a member of the firm of Mitchell & Huffaker, general merchants, with which he has ever since been connected. He has long been a member of the Christian Union Church, and in 1875 he felt that it was his duty to prepare himself for the ministry and exert whatever power and influence in the pulpit he might have for the highest and best interest of humanity, the salvation of souls. He accordingly studied the Scriptures thoroughly, and informed himself in general theology, particularly the theology and polity of his own church, and in 1876 he was licensed to preach. Two years later, Mr. Mitchell was regularly ordained a preacher of the Gospel. Ever since becoming a licentiate of the church he has been an active preacher, and has done much good for the cause of religion and of the church. In 1864, Mr. Mitchell was married to Miss Josephine Harris, a daughter of Solomon Harris, a farmer of the vicinity of Excelsior Springs. Mr. M. and his good wife are blessed with a family of ten children. Mr. Mitchell has a good farm of 120 acres on the Clay and Clinton county line. He is a member of the A. F. and A. M., including the Royal Arch Chapter, and is a member of the school board at Holt. At a series of revival meetings, held by Mr. Mitchell in 1883, and extending over a period of 47 days, 35 at Haynesville, and 12 at Holt, no less than 160 converts were made.

A. NETHERTON

(Manufacturer of and Dealer in Saddles, Harness, Etc., Kearney).

Mr. Netherton was born in Jefferson county, Ky., October 18, 1830, and was the youngest in a family of five children of John and Betsey (Wells) Netherton, both of Maryland. They came to Kentucky in an early day, and the father is still a resident of that State, in Bullitt county. The mother died in 1884. Mr. Netherton's grandfather was a physician by profession and served in the War of 1812. They reared a family of five children: Eliza, wife of William Hall, now deceased, his widow being a resident of Louisville, Ky.; William, a farmer of Kentucky; Richard, a farmer of Callaway county, Mo.;

HISTORY OF CLAY COUNTY

James, a farmer of Kentucky, and the subject of this sketch. Mr. Netherton attended the common schools until he was about 16 years of age and then began to learn the saddle and harness-maker's trade. In 1856 he came to Missouri and first located at Parkville, then in Platte City, and in 1858 at Plattsburg. He remainded at the latter place until 1861, when he went into the Confederate Army under Col. John T. Hughes, becoming a member of Co. K, Hughes' regiment and Gen. Platte's division. He was in the engagements at Carthage, Wilson's Creek, Dry Wood and Lexington, and in the early part of 1862 went to Clinton, where he engaged in farming near that place, but times became so critical there that he came to Haynesville, in Clinton county, where he worked at his trade until 1864. He then went to Indiana, and was married there in March, 1865, to Miss Eliza Hollingsworth, a daughter of Elias Hollingsworth, a farmer of Marion county, Ind. In 1867 Mr. Netherton removed to Centreville, Mo., now Kearney, and has made this his home ever since. He has a good trade in the saddle and harness business, and keeps an excellent assortment of goods on hand. Mrs. Netherton is a lady of great energy and excellent business qualifications, but no less refined, and of agreeable, winning manners. While her husband attends to his saddle and harnessmaking business she, with commendable industry, keeps a neat hotel at Kearney, which has a good patronage and is doing well. It is the only hotel in the place. But although without competition she keeps it with as much determination to excel as if there were any number of competing houses in the place.

A. L. NORFLEET, M. D.

(Physician and Surgeon, Kearney).

Dr. Norfleet is a young physician who has been to more than ordinary labor and expense in the acquisition of his professional education, having started out with the determination to qualify himself thoroughly for his calling. He was principally reared in Lafayette county, this State, and at the age of 20 began the study of medicine under Dr. J. B. Wood, of Waverly. Subsequently he took regular courses at the St. Louis Medical College, and graduated with marked credit in the class of '81. He afterwards practiced medicine in Lafayette county until early in 1882, when he located at Kearney. Here he has ever since resided and practiced his profession, except most of the year 1883, when absent attending medical lectures, either at New York or Philadelphia. He attended medical college at both of those cities for the purpose, as stated above, of acquainting himself with the most advanced learning in his profession in the Eastern States. Returning thence to Kearney, he resumed his practice here, and has already succeeded in taking a leading position among the most prominent physicians of the county. He is highly esteemed at Kearney, personally as well as professionally. On the 18th of January, 1858, Dr. Norfleet was born in Miller county, Mo. He was the eighth in a family of ten children of Larkin and Frances (Gaw) Norfleet, who came to

HISTORY OF CLAY COUNTY

Missouri from Kentucky in about 1854, and located in Miller county. In 1865 they removed to Johnson county, and four years later to Lafayette county, where they now reside. Dr. Norfleet is a well known and much esteemed minister of the M. E. Church South.

CAPT. WILLIAM H. PENCE

(Farmer and Stock-raiser, Post-office, Kearney).

Among the old and highly respected citizens of Clay county whose lives form the woof and warp of the history of the county, is the subject of the present sketch. Capt. Pence, now a man in his sixtieth year, has been a resident of the county almost continuously from childhood. His parents, Adam and Annie (Suell) Pence, came to this county from Kentucky as early as 1825. They located three miles west of Liberty, where the father entered land and improved a farm. He subsequently returned to Kentucky with his family and remained a short time, after which he bought land near Kearney and settled here permanently. He became a successful farmer and a large land-owner, and is still living at the advanced age of 81. His good wife, 80 years of age, is also living. Seven of their family of eleven children are now themselves the heads of families, and all but two, Josiah and Doniphan, residents of this State. The latter reside in Kentucky, and Doniphan has been sheriff of Nelson county for about seven years. In an early day, the father followed the distilling business for some years, but farming was his permanent occupation. Capt. Pence was born in Scott county, Ky., in 1825. Reared, however, in Clay county, Mo., he entered the army, under Doniphan, for the Mexican War, and participated in the expedition to Santa Fe, El Paso, Chihuahua, and on down to Monterey, where a junction was formed with Gens. Taylor and Wood. After the war, Capt. Pence came home by New Orleans with the other Missouri volunteers. In 1849 he went to California, and was successfully engaged in trading for several years, but met with a reverse that more than offset all the profits of the business. He was a regular trader, engaged principally in supplying different mining districts with goods from Sacramento or San Francisco by pack-mule transportation, something after the fashion of the merchants in the Land of the Pyramids, only they use camels to transport their goods, and call their trains " caravans." On one of these expeditions to a mining district in the northern part of California, Capt. Pence had a train of about 26 pack mules, loaded with goods, and when away up in the mountains a heavy snow storm came on, the snow finally becoming so deep that travel was impossible. Being thus snow-bound, the snow continued to fall until it became about fifteen feet deep. There was no hope of it passing off before starvation would overtake the train. Still Capt. P. and his assistants resolutely fought against fate until their packmules were all either starved or frozen to death. Seeing a like fate staring them in the face, themselves, they improvised each a set of snow shoes, and, abandoning everything, made their way on foot to the nearest settle-

HISTORY OF CLAY COUNTY

ment, after indescribable suffering from cold and hunger. Capt. Pence's loss was about $7,000. After that he was, of course, compelled to quit the business as a trader, but still having a little means left he engaged in a small way in stock trading in the Sacramento Valley, where he owned a ranch and some stock. But in 1852 he sold out in California and returned to Clay county. Here, the following year, he was married to Miss Dinitia Estes, a daughter of Henry and Lucinda (Cronin) Estes, who came here from Virginia in about 1820. Mr. Estes was one of the party who laid off the town of Liberty. Capt. Pence, after his marriage, resided on a farm in Platte county that he owned for about a year, and then returned to Clay county, where he has ever since made his home. He has a good farm of 300 acres, all well improved, and raises considerable stock, including some thoroughbred short horn cattle. He also deals in stock to some extent. In 1861 Capt. Pence entered the Southern army under Gen. Price, becoming captain of Co. C, of Col. Thompson's regiment, where he served a term of about six months. Subsequently he returned home, and for a time was a member of a company of paw-paw militia, organized in the county, to prevent the Kansas jayhawkers from robbing and plundering the people. In 1871 Capt. Pence had the misfortune to lose his first wife. To his present wife he was married in 1880. She was a Miss America Smith, a daughter of Hon. J. M. Smith, an attorney of Buchanan county, but who was murdered by the Home Guard on his return home from St. Joseph in 1864. Capt. Pence has held the office of road overseer for the past 29 years, and is a Mason of long and honorable standing. He has been treasurer of the lodge at Kearney for the past eight years. Eight of his family of children are living, and one deceased, the latter having been Lucinda, the wife of Edward Miller. The Captain and wife are members of the Christian Church.

A. W. PIPES

(Farmer and Stock-raiser, Post-office, Kearney).

The fifth in a family of ten children, Mr. Pipes was born in Mercer county, Kentucky, February 19, 1828. His father was Nathaniel Pipes, and his mother's maiden name, Margaret Harmon. Both his grandfathers, John Pipes and John Harmon, were soldiers in the Revolutionary War under Washington. The Pipes were of English descent and settled in North Carolina. The Harmons were of German extraction and settled in Pennsylvania. Mr. Pipes was reared in Mercer county, Kentucky, and continued to reside there after he grew up until 1855, when he came to Missouri to locate a land claim. In the meantime he had taught school in Kentucky for several years, and afterwards also followed merchandising at Mitchellsburg, being also postmaster at that place. After locating and securing some valuable lands in Missouri and Kansas, he returned to Kentucky and engaged in dealing in hogs and corn quite extensively, in which he had good success. In 1856 he was married to Miss Rachel Brand, a daughter of James A. and Catherine (Blink) Brand, formerly of Maryland. On both sides his wife was probably of German descent. After his marriage Mr. Pipes removed to Marion county, Kentucky, where he bought a farm, which he conducted with success, and also carried on the stock business, dealing principally in cattle, hogs and mules. He remained there until 1882, and then sold out and went to Texas, locating in Denton county. But not being satisfied with the country, he soon afterwards returned to Missouri and bought the farm where he now resides, in Clay county. He has a good farm and deals in cattle and hogs, and mules and horses. Mr. and Mrs. Pipes have seven children : Alonzo L., Laura K., wife of James W. England, James N. (Nat), Obie S., Mary L., Lizzie M. and Imogene. Two others died in infancy. Both parents are members of the Christian Church, and Mr. P. is a member of the A. F. and A. M.

ABNER J. PORTER

(Farmer, Post-office, Kearney).

Mr. Porter commenced life for himself as a brick-mason while yet a youth, and after learning that trade worked at it a number of years. Finally, however, after the Civil War he turned his attention to farming and has been principally engaged in farming and stock-raising ever since. He is a native of Virginia, born in Orange county in 1827. He was the second in a family of ten children of Samuel S. and Mary A. (Becker) Porter, both of old Virginia families. They came to Missouri in 1843 when Abner J. was about sixteen years of age. They settled in Clay county, and here the father became a prosperous farmer. He owned at one time about 600 acres of land. Mr. Porter, Sr., died in 1875, at the age of 80 years. His wife died in 1864, at the age of 61. Both were members of the Baptist Church. Seven of their family of children are still living. Abner J. Porter began learning the brick trade in 1848, and worked at it until he enlisted in the State Guard in 1861. In the meantime, in 1849, he was married to Miss Susan Dykes, a daughter of John and Susan Dykes, formerly of Kentucky, and who came to Clay county in 1827. Of this union were born nine children : George, John W., Benjamin D., Abner J., Emerson, Shearly S., Mary S., wife of L. B. Keas, and Alice and Nettie, the last two deceased. The mother of these died in 1873. She was a member of the Christian Church. To his present wife Mr. Porter was married in 1880. She was a Miss Sarah J. Lafore, daughter of William Lafore. She is also a member of the Christian Church, as is likewise Mr. Porter himself. Mr. Porter owns about 550 acres of land in two places. His home place contains 395 acres and is well improved. Mr. Porter is a prominent farmer and stock-raiser, and is one of the highly respected citizens of the northern part of the county.

LEWIS O. RILEY

(Farmer and Fine Stock Raiser, Post-office, Kearney).

Mr. Riley's father, Alfred M. Riley, who died in this county about three years ago, was one of the old and well respected citizens of the county. He came here from Kentucky in 1830, and was a farmer by occupation. He also taught school for many years, and took a warm interest in the cause of education and in church matters. He was an elder in the Mt. Gilead Church for about 40 years. Elder Riley was twice married. His first wife, who was a Miss Lucy J. Tapp (the mother of the subject of this sketch), died in 1849, leaving eight children, five of whom are living. His second wife was a Miss Ann Morris. Of this union four children of the six are living. Lewis O. Riley, the subject of the present sketch, was born on the farm near Kearney in 1839. In 1861 he entered the Southern army under Gen. Price, and was in the infantry service for about six months. About this time he was married to Miss Isabelle Smith, a daughter of George and Mary (Harris) Smith, of Clay county. After his marriage Mr. Riley settled down to farming on a tract of 200 acres of land given him by his father. He has ever since been actively engaged in the duties connected with his farm. For a number of years he has made something of a specialty of stock, particularly fine short horn cattle, of which he has a handsome herd. Mr. R.'s farm now contains 326 acres, and is one of the most comfortable homesteads to be found in this part of the country. Mr. Riley is a member of the Clay County Short Horn Association, and is in every sense an enterprising, go-ahead agriculturist. Mr. and Mrs. Riley have seven children: Mary, Annie, Gertrude, Arthur, George A., William S. and Charles A. They have lost four, including Horace, who died, at the age of twenty years, last spring. The others, Lucy, Lizzie and Lewis, died in childhood.

J. D. SAUNDERS

(Dealer in Furniture and Undertaker's Goods, Kearney).

Mr. Saunders came out to Missouri in 1882 from Virginia, where he had been engaged in the furniture and undertaking business, and settled in Kearney. A young man of limited education but of business qualifications, he was employed by Mr. James T. Riley, of Liberty, this county, to manage and carry on his branch store in that line in the town of Kearney. He carries a full line of furniture and all kinds of undertaker's goods required at this market. Mr. Saunders has a good run of custom, especially in the furniture line. In the undertaker's line his trade is all that could be expected, considering the health and longevity of the people in and around Kearney. He was born in Franklin county, Va., April 19, 1852, and was the eldest of nine children of John Q. and Nancy S. (Webster) Saunders, his father of an old Virginia family but his mother of Pennsylvania descent. The family came to Missouri in 1880 and settled in Callaway county, near Mexico, where they now reside. The father entered the Southern army in 1862 and served throughout the war without receiving a wound, notwithstanding he participated in the battles of Gettysburg, Vicksburg, Seven Pines, Petersburg and others. Mr. Saunders, the subject of this sketch, was educated in the common schools, and at

HISTORY OF CLAY COUNTY

Greenville and Tusculum College, East Tennessee, in the latter of which he spent two years. He commenced life for himself at the carpenter's trade, which he followed until 1867, or for a period of about ten years. He then engaged in the furniture and undertaking business, which he followed until 1882 at Rocky Mount, Va. Thence he came to Missouri, as stated above. In 1878 Mr. Saunders, Jr., was married to Miss Ellen Hurt, a daughter of Joel L. and Sallie Hurt, of Bedford county, Va. Mrs. Saunders' father died in 1878. Her mother is still living, a resident of that county. Mr. and Mrs. Saunders have two children, William D. and Lawrence Cleveland. Mrs. S. is a member of the M. E. Church.

WILLIAM SEYMOUR

(With Bradley & Co., Dealers in Hardware, Agricultural Implements, Etc., Kearney).

Mr. Seymour is of English-Scotch parentage, and was born in Jefferson county, N. Y., July 8, 1842. His father, Calvin Seymour, a native of England, was a wealthy farmer and prominent citizen of Jefferson county. The mother was a Miss Almyra McKnight before her marriage, originally from Scotland. Each came to the United States at an early age, and after they grew up were married in New York. The father died in 1859, at the age of 70 years; the mother in 1860, at the age of 60 years. Both were members of the Presbyterian Church. The father was also a prominent officer in the Masonic Order. He was a member of the Old Line Whig party, and a great admirer of that prince of statesmen, "Harry of the West." William Seymour was reared in Jefferson county and concluded his education at Watertown Academy, where he spent four years, graduating in the class of '59. He then commenced an apprenticeship at the tinner's trade, in which he continued until the war broke out. Early in 1861 he enlisted in Co. A, Ninety-fourth New York infantry, and was at once ordered South. He served throughout the war. He took part in the first battle of Bull Run, where he was wounded. In 1863 he was transferred to the Twentieth New York cavalry, and at the close of the war was orderly sergeant of his company. Mr. Seymour took part in a number of the principal battles of the war, including the second battle at Manassas, the battle at Cedar Creek, and the one at Alda. He was also present at the surrender of Lee at Appomattox. After the close of the war he returned to New York, and in 1873 came West as far as Frankfort, Ky., where he worked at his trade. Afterwards he went to Dayton, Ohio, where he had charge of a tinware and stove house, and in 1877 he went to Ft. Smith, Ark., where he was also engaged in the tinware and stove business. Three years afterwards he came to Missouri, locating at Smithville, and in 1884 he came to Kearney, where he engaged in his present business with Mr. Bradley. Their business has already been described in Mr. Bradley's sketch, which appears on a preceding page. In 1873 Mr. Seymour was married to Miss Fannie Partridge, a daughter of Charles Partridge, formerly of England. Mr. and Mrs. S. have five children:

HISTORY OF CLAY COUNTY

Reuben, Peal, Fannie, Charles and Mary. Mrs. S. is a member of the Episcopal Church.

P. TAPP SOPER
(Farmer, Post-office, Kearney).

Mr. Soper was the eighth in a family of thirteen children of Benjamin and Nancy (Tapp) Soper, the father a native of Maryland, but the mother born and reared in Kentucky. They were married in Kentucky and came to Missouri in 1830, settling in Clay county, where the father followed farming and carpentering, having been brought up to the first occupation and being a natural mechanic. He lived a worthy and respected life in this county and died in 1877, at the age of 81. He had served as justice of the peace for about twenty-five years and had always taken a warm interest in public schools, being for many years an active and useful member of the district school board. 'Squire Soper was of German descent, though the family had long been settled in this country. His wife died in 1879, at the age of 78. Both were members of the Primitive Baptist Church. Their children were Almedia, Louisiana, Martha E., Ann M., Almilda, John L., Fannie E., James W., P. Tapp, Emeline, Nannie N., Benjamin F. and Alfred B. Five of the above are deceased, Almedia, Ann M., John L., James W. and Nannie N. John L. was murdered by an assassin from ambush at the age of 50 years. He was out in his barnyard feeding stock at nightfall and was shot down in cold blood. The mystery of his murder was never unraveled, although the greatest efforts were made to ferret out the crime, both by the unfortunate man's relatives and the public authorities. This, at least, has proved one exception to the often-quoted couplet of Dryden : —

> " Murder may pass unpunished for a time,
> But tardy justice will o'ertake the crime."

The difficulty that rendered investigation little less than hopeless was that Mr. Soper was not known to have a personal enemy. Some years before he had been quite dissipated, but had fully reformed and long prior to the time of his death had worthily established the reputation of being one of the most steady, quiet and exemplary citizens of the community. He was a man of marked intelligence and great energy and was rapidly coming to the front as one of the representative men of the county. The mystery of his murder will probably never be made clear to those who knew him in life, and to whom his sad and untimely taking-off was a great bereavement, until the light of the Judgment Day, which is to reveal all things, shall come ; then the fate of the murderer will be sadder and far more pitiable in proportion, as the tortures of the lost exceed the ills of this life, than that which overtook Mr. Soper on the fatal night of his death. P. Tapp Soper, the subject of this sketch, was born in this county, July 11, 1835. He was reared on his father's farm, and afterwards continued farming as his regular occupation, engaging also in raising and handling stock.

HISTORY OF CLAY COUNTY

Mr. Soper is now comfortably situated on a good farm of over 100 acres. In December, 1861, he enlisted in the Southern service at Lexington, Mo., becoming a member of an infantry regiment in the Missouri State Guard. Six months later, after the expiration of his term of State Guard service, he enlisted in the regular Confederate army and continued in the army until the close of the war, being paroled at Shreveport, La., June 16, 1865. After his first six months' term he was under Gen. Shelby, and during his entire service participated in no less than forty-two engagements, and had two horses killed under him, but never himself received a wound. In how many instances, alas! was the reverse of his experience true. How often it was the case that one horse bore different riders, even on one field of battle, where the brave reinsmen, one after another, fell, whilst the gallant war-horse which bore them passed through the battle unharmed! After the war Mr. Soper returned home and resumed farming. In 1866 he was married to Miss Georgie Cook, a daughter of James and Lucy Cook, formerly of Kentucky. Her father died in 1841, and her mother afterwards became the wife of Col. Moses Hubbard, who also is now deceased. The mother made her home with Mrs. Soper until her death, which occurred in 1878. Mr. and Mrs. S. have seven children, James M., Mary L., Nannie S., Fannie M., Alexander C., Dollie and Lida M. They have lost four in infancy. Both parents are members of the Christian Church.

JOHN V. STROETER

(Farmer and Stock-raiser, Post-office, Kearney).

Mr. Stroeter is one of those thrifty, intelligent German-American citizens, almost invariably law-abiding and useful to the community where they live, who came over to this country when young men, without means and for the purpose of establishing themselves comfortably in life by honest industry and attending strictly to their own business. This is his record here exactly. He was born in Prussia in 1835, and was one of a large family of children. After receiving a partial education in his native country, he came to the United States in his seventeenth year and made his home in Wisconsin. There, for several years, he worked on a farm during the cropping seasons as a laborer at six dollars a month, with board, washing and mending included, and during the winters he worked for his board, nights and mornings and of Saturdays, and attended school during the balance of each week. His parents, Emanuel and Maria (Kæstner) Stroeter, came over in 1854 with their family, and soon afterwards he went to live with them. But in 1860 he started out for himself as a farmer, and five years later he removed to Madison county, Ill. Meantime, in 1860, he was married to Miss Elizabeth Mueller, a daughter of Conrad and Anna Mueller from Hesse-Darmstadt. Mr. Stroeter continued to reside in Illinois until 1882, when he came to Clay county and bought the farm where he now resides, one of the handsomest farms in this part of the county. It contains 214 acres and

HISTORY OF CLAY COUNTY

is well improved, including a fine brick residence, one of the best barns in the county and other betterments to correspond. Mr. and Mrs. Stroeter have seven children: Edward, Amelie (wife of George Mueller), Ida, Henry, George, Emma and William. Mr. and Mrs. S. are members of the Evangelical Church.

T. G. TEANEY

(Farmer, Post-office, Kearney).

October 1, 1825, was the date of Mr. Teaney's advent into this life, and the place of his birth was in Montgomery county, Va. His parents were Samuel Teaney and Johannah (Dobbins) Teaney, who were both born and reared in the Old Dominion, and were married there in 1821. The father was a wagon maker by trade, and by descent of German stock. In 1837 they started to Missouri, but stopped two years on the way in Tennessee and six years in Kentucky, finally locating in Henry county, this State, in 1843. There the father died the following September, and the mother in the fall of the next year. The father had been a soldier in the Mexican war. They left a family of eight children, six of whom are living. T. G. Teaney started out for himself before reaching his majority and came to Platte county, where he worked as a farm hand for about two years. He was then married in 1847 to Miss Nancy, a daughter of Samuel and Phœbe Ann Wiley, formerly of Madison county, Kentucky. After his marriage Mr. Teaney located on a farm in Buchanan county, where he continued six years. He then removed to the vicinity of Weston, in Platte county. For fourteen years Mr. Teaney resided near Weston. From there he came to Clay county in 1867. Mr. Teaney has a good farm in this county of 130 acres. His first wife died here in 1873. She had borne him ten children, all of whom are living, namely: Samuel T., Jason O., Phœbe A., wife of Abraham Shaver; Annette, wife of Marshall Baker, John A., Margaret, James M., Mary F., Charles D. and William H. In 1879 Mr. Teaney was married to his present wife, whose maiden name was Elizabeth Cave, a daughter of Urial and Susan Cave. She had been married to D. T. Duncan, who died in 1873. Both her parents are also deceased. She had five children by her first marriage: Lizzie, wife of Dr. W. L. Porterfield; Sarah, wife of Charles Middaugh; Rose, wife of Madison Eaton, Susie and Urial, the latter of whom died three years ago, in his twenty-seventh year. Mr. and Mrs. Teaney are members of the Baptist Church. Mr. T. served in the Mexican War.

THOMAS WAGY

(Farmer, Stock-raiser and Feeder, Post-office, Kearney).

Mr. Wagy became a citizen of Clay county, Mo., in 1869, when he removed here from Adams county, Ill., which had been his home for many years. He has since lived in this county and has become thoroughly identified with its interests, ever lending his aid and influence

HISTORY OF CLAY COUNTY

in promoting its prosperity and advancement. A warm friend of the public school system, he has ably and staunchly advocated and supported such measures as would tend to the betterment and promulgation of school facilities in this State, and especially in the community in which he lives. His parents were Henry W. Wagy, a farmer by occupation and Virginian by birth, and Eleanor (Stone) Wagy, originally of Ohio. They were married in the latter State, and in 1830, leaving there, settled in Adams county, Ill., which continued to be their home during life. The father died June 4, 1879, and his widow January 13, 1881. There were eight children in the parental family, of whom Thomas was the third. He was born in Licking county, Ohio, February 22, 1830, and was very young when taken to Adams county, Ill., where he spent his youth and early manhood, receiving such education as could be obtained from the limited common schools. Farming occupied his time and attention (and in which he was very successful) until his marriage October 24, 1850, in Pike county, Ill., when Miss Martha Decker became his wife. She was a daughter of Moses and Malinda Decker, *née* Boren, of Pike county, where she herself was born, reared and educated. The fruits of this union were six children: Jasper, Ellen, wife of John G. Hassel, a farmer in this county; Mary, wife of E. J. Shouldis; Park, married Miss Minnie Robinson and is proprietor of a livery and feed stable at Lawson, Ray county, Mo.; Nevada and Albert Jasper, those unmarried being still at home with their parents. His present homestead contains 200 acres of improved land, upon which is a neat residence, besides other substantial buildings, and here he is actively engaged in agricultural pursuits. He is a member of the A. F. and A. M. Mrs. Wagy is a member of the M. E. Church.

PLEASANT WILHOIT

(Of Wilhoit Bros. & Garrett, Dealers in General Merchandise, Kearney).

Mr. Wilhoit began merchandising in April, 1882, at Holt, and has continued in that line of business ever since. The present firm have been quite successful at merchandising, considering the time in which they have been engaged in it, and their house now takes rank among the leading establishments in their line at Kearney. Their customers include many of the best and most substantial citizens of the vicinity, and their trade is almost altogether for cash. They have quite a large custom, and are doing an excellent business. All the members of the firm are gentlemen of recognized standing for business integrity and enterprise, and they have the entire confidence of the public. Prior to engaging in merchandising Mr. Wilhoit taught school for a number of years and then followed farming. He was educated at Plattsburg and in Greenville, at which places, together, he attended school after taking the usual common-school course, for about three years. He followed teaching continuously for about eight years, except for one year, during which he was in the Southern army. In 1864 he was under Capt. Cundiff, of Shanks' brigade, and served until the close of

HISTORY OF CLAY COUNTY

the war. In 1869 Mr. Wilhoit located on a farm in Clay county, which he owned, and was afterwards engaged in farming for about thirteen years, or until he began merchandising. Mr. Wilhoit was born in this county, November 6, 1835, and was a son of Andrew Wilhoit, referred to in a sketch of David Wilhoit, which follows this. Pleasant Wilhoit was reared on the farm and was brought up to active industry in farm-work, learning fully all the details of agricultural life. He attended the neighborhood schools, and at the age of 20 began his high school course. In 1873 he was married to Miss M. E. Snody, an adopted daughter of Uncle Dick Clark, her father having died when she was infancy. "Uncle" Dick Clark was an uncle of her mother's. Mr. and Mrs. Wilhoit have three children: Luther Elmer, Walton Hugh and Minnie Emma. Two are deceased: Lella and Maude S. Both parents are members of the M. E. Church, Mr. W. having been a member ever since he was 16 years of age; he now holds the office of deacon in the church. He is also a member of the Masonic Order.

DAVID L. WILHOIT

(Of Wilhoit & Bro., General Merchants, Holt).

Back during the latter part of the last century, three brothers by the name of Wilhoit came to this country from Germany and settled in North Carolina. From those, it is believed, all in this country of that name have sprung. Mr. Wilhoit's grandfather, James Wilhoit, married and removed to Tennessee, where he reared a large family of children. Of his children, Andrew Wilhoit, the father of Mr. W., was born in the latter State in 1812. He grew up and removed to Missouri, where he met and was married to Miss Jane Gentry. They settled in Clay county, and here the father, a farmer by occupation, died in about 1859. Mrs. Wilhoit survived until 1877. Both were members of the M. E. Church, and the father was a class leader and deacon in the church. They had a family of 13 children, including the subject of the present sketch. David L. Wilhoit was born in Clay county in 1841, and was reared to a farm life. In early manhood he engaged in farming for himself, and in a few years in raising stock. Mr. Wilhoit continued on the farm until 1883, when he and his brother, Preston, formed a partnership, and established a general store at Holt. Their venture proved a success, and they are doing a good business. Mr. W. still owns his farm, which he has rented out. In 1864 he was married to Miss Eliza Yates, daughter of William Yates, of Clay county. They have two children, Cordelia B. and Ocie.

WILLIAM WRIGHT

(Farmer and Fine Stock Raiser, Post-office, Kearney).

Mr. Wright is a native of Ireland, and came to this country when a young man about 19 years of age, in 1863. He was born in the county Antrim, in May, 1844, and was an only child of William and Elizabeth (Hill) Wright. The father is still living, and a resident of

HISTORY OF CLAY COUNTY

that county. Young Wright's youth, up to the age of 14, was principally spent at school. He was then employed to attend fine stock, and as a gardener in his native county, being soon afterwards made foreman on the place. Working in these employments for some five years, he learned them thoroughly, and became a skillful and well qualified handler of fine stock, becoming also an excellent judge of stock. After coming to the United States he continued work as a fine stock man, obtaining employment in New Jersey. Five years later he came as far West as Kentucky, where he worked at the same business, and in 1883 he removed to Missouri, and bought the Emerson Green place, in Clay county, a fine farm of 200 acres. Here he is engaged in general farming and in raising and handling stock. In 1869 Mr. Wright was married to Miss Jane Gilberth, daughter of Joseph and Mary Gilberth, who came from Ireland in 1869. Mrs. Wright was born in the county Derry, Ireland, in March, 1846. Mr. and Mrs. Wright have six children: Mary E., William H., Joseph, John, Henry and Edward. He and wife are members of the Presbyterian Church.

ARTHUR YATES

(Farmer and Stock-dealer, Post-office, Holt).

Mr Yates, although hardly yet more than entered upon the middle of life, has already established himself as one of the leading agriculturists and stock men of the northern part of the county. His farm contains 180 acres, which is well improved and well stocked, and besides this he has four other farms, altogether aggregating over 860 acres. His farms are all well fenced and otherwise substantially improved, and are run principally in grass for stock purposes, although he also raises enough grain and other produce for general farm uses. Now, only in his forty-third year, he started out for himself when a young man without any means, and has accumulated all he possesses by his own industry, energy and good management. Mr. Yates is also an extensive dealer in stock and buys and ships to the wholesale markets on a large scale. In this he has been very successful, and is reputed one of the best stock men in his part of the county. Mr. Yates was born on his father's farm in Kearney township, April 16, 1842, and was the sixth in a family of eight children of William L. and Elizabeth (Gow) Yates, from Mason county, Ky. They came here in 1831, and the father died September 24, 1869, at the age of sixty-six years. Mrs. Yates died in 1844. Both were members of the Baptist Church. Mr. Yates, Sr., was subsequently married twice, his second wife surviving her marriage only a short time, and leaving one daughter, Nannie. His third wife is still living. She was a Miss Rebecca Watkins. Mr. Yates, Jr., the subject of this sketch, was reared on the farm and on the 27th of November, 1862, was married to Miss Agnes Shackelford, daughter of James and Mary Schackelford, formerly of Kentucky. Her father is deceased, but her mother is still living. Mr. Yates and wife have six children: Shelby, William, Arthur, Roy, Mabel and Jesse. Two others are deceased: Archie and Ruby. Mr. and Mrs. Y. are members of the Christian Church.

CHAPTER XVII.

WASHINGTON TOWNSHIP.

Location and Physical Features — Hamlets of Greenville and Claysville — Early History — Organization — Mount Vernon Missionary Baptist Church — Biographical.

LOCATION AND PHYSCAL FEATURES.

Washington township forms the northeastern portion of Clay county, and is composed of all of congressional township 53 and the lower tier of sections of township 54, in range 30. Much of the territory is very broken, rough, and rocky and worthless for agricultural purposes. Many small streams, all of which ultimately run into Fishing river and its forks, head in the township. In many places picturesque bluffs are found along these streams, and the scenery is beautiful to look upon, but hardly appreciated by those owning the land.

The township contains but two small hamlets, Greenville and Claysville. The St. Joe branch of the Wabash Railroad runs through the northeastern corner of the township, a distance of about two miles, and Lawson, in Ray county, is the nearest station and general shipping point. Kearney and Holt, on the Hannibal road, give the people something of competition in the matter of railroad facilities.

Greenville (Claytonville P. O.) is located in the southern part of the township, on Williams creek, 16 miles northeast of Liberty and about six east of Kearney. It contains a school-house, two churches (Methodist and Christian), and about 75 inhabitants. It is one of the oldest villages in the county.

Claysville (Prospect Hill P. O.) is about two miles northeast of Greenville, within half a mile of the Ray county line, and four miles south of Lawson, the nearest railroad station. It contains perhaps 50 inhabitants, or less.

EARLY HISTORY.

As early as 1824 Travis Finley settled on section 26 in this township, two miles southeast of Greenville. Archibald McIlvaine, Stephen Baxter and others were also early settlers. Ryland Shackelford located northwest of Greenville soon after Finley came, and Mr. Shackelford often declared that when he made his location, and for a year afterwards, there was not a white settler between him and the North Pole.

At the May term of the county court, 1830, Washington was created as a municipal township out of Platte and Fishing river. The boundaries were originally the same, practically, as at present, the two western tiers of sections being taken off in 1872 when Kearney was formed. The boundaries as ordered by the county court when the township was organized were as follows: —

Beginning at the point on the county line between Ray and Clay counties where the line between townships 52 and 53 strikes the same, thence due west along said township line for eight miles to the section corner on said township line between sections 34 and 35, in range 31; thence due north along said section line between sections 34 and 35, in range 31, to the northern boundary line of the county.

Singularly enough the court omitted to describe the northern and eastern boundaries of this township. They will be understood, however, to have been the northern boundary of the State, and the line between Ray and Clay extended to that boundary.

It was certified to the Secretary of State that there were at least 95 taxable inhabitants in the township upon its creation. John P. Smith and Harlow Hinkston were the first justices of the peace, John Wright the first constable, and Stephen Baxter, Archibald McIlvain, and Richard Clark the first election judges. The first election was held at the house of Stephen Baxter.

MOUNT VERNON MISSIONARY BAPTIST CHURCH,

located on section 15, township 53, range 30, was organized in 1857 by Rev. William Barrett. The names of the original members were Waltus L. Watkins, Mary N. Watkins, Kate Watkins, Spencer Anderson, Kitty Anderson, Mary Anderson, Rev. William C. Barrett, Jackson Garrett, L. B. Garrett, Samuel Hollingsworth, T. W. Barrett, Louisa Barrett, Olivia Barrett and Nancy K. Barrett. The present membership is 64. The names of those who have served as pastors are Revs. William Barrett, who filled the pulpit for three years, Thomas Montgomery, Asa N. Bird, J. W. Luke, G. L. Black and J. J. Fetts, who is the present pastor. This brick edifice was erected in 1871 at a cost of $5,000, more than one-half of which was contributed by Waltus L. Watkins.

BIOGRAPHICAL.

CHESTER BETHEL

(Farmer and Stock-raiser, Post-office, Lawson).

Notwithstanding the great hurrah and hubbub raised in this State over the James boys and Clay county as an awful robber-infested region by a few unscrupulous journals for political effect, and more interested in partisan success and capturing the offices than in the welfare and good name of the State, intelligent Northern men, both Republicans and Democrats, are constantly pouring into Missouri and making their homes upon its rich and favored lands. Clay county is no exception in this respect to the other counties of the State. Large numbers of Northern men have settled in this county since the war, and within the last four, six and twelve years. Among the many others that might be referred to is the subject of the present sketch. Mr. Bethel came to this county in the winter of 1871–72, and is one of the substantial farmers of the county. He has a finely improved place situated near Lawson. Besides farming in a general way, he is also engaged in raising stock. He was born in Jersey county, Ill., June 17, 1847, and was a son of Bluford Bethel and wife, *née* Nancy Seymour, the father originally from Tennessee, but reared in Illinois, and the mother born and reared in that State. His father was a substantial farmer of Macoupin county, and died there in August, 1875. His mother died July 28, 1858. She was a member of the Missionary Baptist Church. The father was a member of the A. F. and A. M. Mr. Bethel was reared in Jersey county, and was the fourth in his parents' family of eight children, five of whom are living. He was educated in Macoupin county, and after coming to Missouri in 1871, was married to Miss Emma Witt, December 4, 1874, a daughter of Pryor and Eliza J. (Tunnel) Witt, of Greene county, Ill. Mr. and Mrs. Bethel have two children: Nancy Alice and Mary Effie. Mr. B. belongs to the Order of the A. F. and A. M.

ROBERT A. FORD

(Farmer and Fine Stock Raiser, Post-office, Lawson).

Mr. Ford is one of the self-made men of Clay county. When he was in infancy, his father died, leaving his mother with a large family of children, and no means to speak of to go upon. The children, after they had struggled along through their earlier years, and come up old enough to work, had not only to look out for themselves, but to assist toward providing for the family. But the mother was a true and noble woman, and kept her family together during her lifetime. She died in 1857, when the subject of this sketch was about

HISTORY OF CLAY COUNTY

17 years of age. There were nine other children, and nine of the ten are still living. When the family came to Clay county, in 1851, Mr. F. was a lad about eleven years of age. He was here in 1861, when the war broke out, and entered the Confederate army or State Guard, under Gen. Price. After serving out his term of enlistment for six months, he returned to the county, and in 1863 went to Colorado. Three years later he came back, and has been a resident of the county ever since. He learned the occupation of farming as he grew up, and handling stock, and has made these his permanent pursuits. Starting out without anything but his industry, energy and intelligence, he has, nevertheless, become one of the substantial farmers and successful fine stock raisers of the county. He has a herd of 60 head of high grade cattle, and nine head of regular registered short horns. His farm is nearly all in blue grass, and is finely improved, his handsome brick residence alone costing $17,000. His place contains 220 acres of as fine land as there is in the county. Mr. Ford was born in Fauquier county, Virginia, March 13, 1840. His parents, Austin and Jane (Allison) Ford, were both born and reared in that county, and after their marriage came to Missouri, in 1840, locating in Clark county, where the father died the following year. He had been a soldier in the War of 1812, and was a farmer by occupation. The mother, with her family of children, removed to Clay county in 1851, where she died in 1857, as stated above. October 6, 1867, Mr. Ford, the subject of this sketch, was married to Miss Mary E. Story, a daughter of Thomas and Lucy A. (Baldwin) Story, of this county. Mr. and Mrs. F. have seven children living, Oscar N., John T., Jesse J., Ella T., Walter N., Maggie L. and Robert A. Three others, Flora Belle, James T. and Arthur F., died at tender ages. The oldest, Oscar N., an exceptionally bright youth, 14 years of age, is already an unusually accomplished penman. His work in general penmanship, card writing, etc., equals that of many professional penmen.

RUFUS M. MAJORS

(Farmer and Stock-raiser, Post-office, Lawson).

Rufus M. Majors was born in Clay county, September 7, 1841. His father was Elisha Majors, formerly of Burke county, North Carolina, and his mother's maiden name Catherine Huffaker, of Wayne county, Ky. Mr. Majors' grandfather, John Majors, a native of Maryland, was a soldier in the Revolutionary War. Mr. Majors' parents were married in Wayne county, Ky., and remained there until 1837, when he removed with his family to Clay county, Mo. He made his home in this county until his death, which occurred October 24, 1878. He was a successful farmer and worthy citizen of the county. His wife died here April 27, 1876. But three of their family of eight children are living, Michael, a farmer of Vernon county, and Elizabeth, the wife of B F. Elston, a farmer of Clinton county, being the other two, besides the subject of this sketch. Rufus Marion Majors was the seventh in the family of children, and was reared on the farm

HISTORY OF CLAY COUNTY

in this county. He received a district school education, and on the 22d of August, 1880, was married to Miss Sarah M. Wilhoit, a daughter of Thomas and Mourning (Benton) Wilhoit, of this county. Mr. and Mrs. Majors are members of the Missionary Baptist Church. Mr. M. has a good farm of 270 acres, all under fence and in an excellent state of improvement.

JUDGE ROBERT W. MIMMS

(Farmer, Post-office, Holt).

The Mimms family is one of pioneer ancestry in the history of the country, and one not altogether without note. One of the representatives of the family render distinguished services in the Revolution in the South Atlantic States, and a remembrancer of his career stands to this day in the shape of the ruins of Old Ft. Mimms in Georgia. Another member of the family was a gallant officer in the Northwestern campaign under Gen. Harrison, and Ft. Mimms, in Michigan, was named in honor of his services. The family is believed to have come to this country at about the time of the first settlement of Jamestown or with some of the colonial immigrants to Virginia soon afterwards. From Virginia branches of the family dispersed themselves throughout most of the Southern and Western States. Judge Mimms comes of the Kentucky branch of the family. He was born in Logan county, Ky., March 20, 1830, and was a son of John W. Mimms, whose father was one of the pioneer settlers of that State. The Judge's mother was a Miss Mary James before her marriage, originally of Goochland county, Va. The Judge's parents continued to reside in Kentucky until 1856, when they came to Missouri and his father established Mimms' Hotel, at Kansas City, well known in the days of the border troubles as the stopping place of thousands who passed that way going to or coming from "Bleeding Kansas." Mimms' hotel building, if it could talk, would be able to tell many a stirring and thrilling incident of those trying and terrible times. There, under the same roof, the Red-leg and the Border-ruffian, the Jawhawker and the Slave-driver, the emigrant sent out by the New England Aid Society, with nothing but his black carpet-sack, his Bible and his rifle, to colonize Kansas, and the adventurous, restless, fearless Down-Souther, with his long hair, piercing eyes, navy revolvers and double-barrel shotgun, who came out to see that Kansas was not permitted to fall into the hands of "the sniveling, negro-loving Yankee," as he always termed his New England brother, met and refreshed themselves at the same board. Not unfrequently hot words of scorn and hatred were hissed at each other across the table, but Mr. Mimms was a man of peace and without fear, and under his roof the hospitality of his house was made the protection of every guest, from wheresoever he came, North, South, East or West. The truth of history, however, compels the statement that many insulting words quietly spoken between partisans of the opposing factions who stopped at Mimms' Hotel were afterwards avenged by the rifle or

HISTORY OF CLAY COUNTY

shotgun, or the pistol or dirk, on the stakeless and lonely prairies of Kansas. Such were the unhappy times of that unhappy day. But through it all "Uncle John Mimms," as he was known far and wide, though a Southern man and a brave and fearless one, maintained an attitude as landlord of strict impartiality, and won the respect and affection of all who ever pulled his welcome latch-string. He was an ordained minister of the Missionary Baptist Church, and died at his home, in April, 1869, profoundly mourned by a wide circle of friends and acquaintances. His wife died eight years afterwards. Judge Mimms, who was the eldest in a family of twelve children, was reared in Kentucky, and came to Missouri in 1847. He first resided in Cass county, but came to Clay county the following year. In 1850 he went to California and spent eight years in that State, mining, etc., with varying success. Returning home in 1858, he subsequently went to Colorado, in 1861, and was elected treasurer and collector in Park county in 1862. In 1863 he went to Montana, locating at Helena. He represented Helena in the Territorial Legislature two terms, and was the author of the Sunday and High License laws of the Territory. He was soon elected judge of the police court of that city, a position he held for two years. In that day at Helena, not only a good knowledge of the law was required of a criminal judge, but a full measure of personal courage. A judge who was suspected of having anything like fear about him would have been made the laughing stock of the place and every mining camp in the vicinity, and his court would have fallen into the most helpless and puerile contempt. His weapon of defense was the weapon of moral suasion and good will toward all men. Consequently, he kept the peace and administered justice with even scales and without fear. As a judge and as a citizen he became one of the most widely known and popular men in the Territory. But in 1868 Judge Mimms, in whose heart some of the softer sentiments had begun to steal like the rays of the morning sun at early dawn, returned to Clay county, and in a little while afterwards was made the happy husband of one whom to him was fairer than the evening air clad in the beauty of a thousand stars, and much dearer than all the rest of the constellations, with the sun, moon and Mother Terra thrown in. The Judge's wife was a Miss Martha A. Thomason, to whom he was married September 8, 1870, a daughter of Robert and Sarah (Lindsey) Thomason. Her father was a soldier in the War of 1812, under Col. R. N. Johnson, of Kentucky. The Judge and Mrs. Mimms have three children: John R. L:, Mary Lizzie and Lucy Ethel. Ruth died at a tender age. The Judge and wife are members of the Missionary Baptist Church. The Judge is an energetic farmer of Washington township, and owns a neat and comfortable homestead.

JOHN W. SHOUSE

(Farmer and Stock-raiser, Section 29, Post-office, Kearney).

Mr. Shouse has had an extensive military career, in that he not only served gallantly for three years as a Confederate soldier in the War of

HISTORY OF CLAY COUNTY

1861 under Gen. Price, but also for a time was under Gen. A. W. Doniphan in the war with Mexico. He came ordinarily from Kentucky, his parents, John and Sarah (Slaughter) Shouse, having also been born in that State, where they were subsequently married. In 1827, leaving the State of their birth, they came to Missouri and located in Clay county, where they made their home until their death; the father died in August, 1863, and the mother in 1875. John W. Shouse, the fourth in a family of six children, was born in Franklin county, Ky., April 12, 1825, and was in infancy when his parents removed to Clay county. He was reared here to agricultural pursuits and received such educational advantages as the school opportunities of that early day afforded. One of the earliest settlers in the county, he has remained here ever since and his career as a tiller of the soil and private citizen has been not less creditable than his career as a soldier. His farm of 160 acres is one of the neatest places in Washington township, is all under fence and has upon it good improvements. When the Civil War broke out Mr. S., imbued with patriotic enthusiasm, organized a company for the Confederate army, of which he was made captain, which position he held until his health failing he was compelled to resign, and soon thereafter returned home. On the 1st of June, 1848, Capt. Shouse was married in Clay county to Miss Elizabeth Writsman, a daughter of Peter and Polly Writsman, *née* Officer. Mrs. S. was born, reared and educated in this county. To them have been born ten children, as follows: Thomas R., a farmer of this county, who married Miss Flora Lynn; James O., who married the first time Miss Bettie Dagley; she died October 27, 1879, and he then married Martha Whorton; he is also engaged in farming; Florence R., wife of William I. Price; Lola A., now Mrs. James Moberly of Clinton county, Mo.; Mary C., wife of William M. Riley; and John N., Frances M., Sarah E., Richard and Edna, who are still at home with their parents.

WALTUS L. WATKINS (DECEASED)

(Lawson Vicinity).

On the 24th of January, 1884, died at his residence, in this county, near Lawson, Waltus Locket Watkins, the subject of the present sketch. The life of Mr. Watkins, as is well known to every one acquainted with the affairs of Clay county, was long and prominently identified with the best interests of the county. The record of his career presents his life pre-eminently in two aspects, — one as an active and useful citizen in the business and industrial affairs of the county, and the other as a man of the most generous and philanthropic impulses, laboring at all times, when an opportunity was presented, for the spiritual, moral and educational good of the community of which he was a member. Nor were his services unimportant in either respect. As a citizen of enterprise, he stood among the first in the county; and in works for the social welfare of the community, he was second to none in private life. Mr. Watkins descended from a sterl-

HISTORY OF CLAY COUNTY

ing race of men, with whom matters of principle were supreme to everything else; who would stand by what they believed to be right though the world were against them and fidelity brought them ruin — the brave-hearted, honest, faithful Protestants of Catholic France, the French Huguenots. His first ancestor in this country, on his mother's side, Gen. Bartholomew Dupuy, was a distinguished representative of that fearless and true sect of Frenchmen. He had been a gallant officer in the French army, but on account of his Protestant faith and his refusal to forswear it, he was driven from the army and from France. Coming thence to this country in about 1700, he located in Virginia, where he became a prominent citizen and successful man of affairs, leaving at his death, a large family of children. To one of Gen. Dupuy's descendants, Miss Jane Minter, Mr. Watkins' father, Benjamin Watkins, was married, in Virginia. Of this union came the subject of the present sketch, and twelve other children. After their marriage they removed to Kentucky and settled in Woodford county, where Waltus L. Watkins was born on the 80th of October, 1806. Reared in Kentucky, he remained there until he was about 25 years of age and then came to Missouri, in 1831, and settled in Liberty, Clay county. In the meantime he had learned the machinist's trade in the East, and had also worked in cotton and woolen industries. It is a fact worthy of note, in passing, that he worked on the first railway locomotive ever built in the United States. After coming to Clay county he built the first cotton and woolen mill ever established in the county, and also introduced the first circular saw ever brought to the county. These were in connection with a grist mill, and his was one of the pioneer grist mills of this part of the country. It was patronized by people from a distance of seventy-five miles. In 1839 he moved to the land on which the family now reside, on which he improved a fine farm, erecting a handsome brick dwelling and making all of his other improvements of a superior class. He added to his lands from time to time by additional purchases and entry till they aggregated 5,000 acres, from which he sold several fine farms. On retiring from business he sold to his successors, John Watkins & Bros., 3,600 acres of fine lands, his milling property and live stock. The woolen, flouring and grist mills, now conducted by his sons, John Watkins & Bros., consisting of John H., A. Judson and Joe B. Watkins, he erected in 1860, at a cost of $30,000, the largest establishment of the kind in the State, outside of the large cities. The mills have a capacity of three sets of cards, 1,080 spindles, 25 looms and two sets of buhrs. He was also an extensive farmer and stock-raiser, and dealt largely in stock. All these various lines of business his sons keep up. The "Watkins Mills" manufacture on an extensive scale cassimeres, flannels, jeans, blankets, yarns, etc. John Watkins & Bros. also have a fine herd of 500 head of thoroughbred and high grade short horn cattle, from which they annually sell some of the best representatives of that breed to be met with in the country. Mr. Watkins, their father, was for many years an earnest member of the Mt. Vernon Missionary Baptist Church, and one of its most liberal supporters as well as a generous contributor to other churches, and the cause of education. Toward the erection of his own church building he contributed $1,200 in cash and spent the majority of two years working for the building and the completion of the church. He also built a comfortable and commodious brick school house near his farm, which was long used as a public school building. For the erection of other school houses and churches he contributed, from time to time, thousands of dollars. For a long time he was one of the trustees of William Jewell College, and contributed largely to that institution. Mr. Watkins was for many years an earnest advocate of temperance, and even in the time of the Washington Temperance Society, when home-made whisky was more common than wild honey, he was a member of that society, and ever after held his pledge of temperance sacred and inviolate. He had a high sense of honor. His duties to society, morality, religion and his financial obligations were his supreme law. On the 4th of March, 1834, Mr. Watkins was married to Miss Mary Ann Holloway, of Jessamine county, Ky., a daughter of Spencer and Catherine (Reed) Holloway. Mrs. Watkins is still living, residing on the old family homestead with her children. Eight of her family of eleven children are living, namely: George S., John H., Martha A., Mary E., Waltus J., Jr., Caroline E., A. Judson and Joe Barry. John H., Alfred and Catherine J. are deceased, the first being the eldest of the family, and for him his brother John H., living, was named. Mrs. Watkins and several of her family are members of the Missionary Baptist Church.

CHAPTER XVIII.

GALLATIN TOWNSHIP.

Boundary and Physical Features—Villages in this Township—Barry—Harlem—Moscow—Arnold's Station—Minaville—Churches—Biographical.

BOUNDARY AND PHYSICAL FEATURES.

Gallatin township comprises the southwestern portion of Clay county, and is bounded on the east by Liberty township and the Missouri river, on the south by the river, on the west by Platte county, and on the north by Platte township. It contains some excellent lands and fine farms, but there is also a great deal of rough and unproductive tracts in the township. Big Shoal creek and its branches drain the greater portion of the township.

Gallatin was one of the original townships of Clay county, comprising in 1822 the western half of the county. Settlements were made along Big Shoal in 1822. David Manchester's mill was a noted point in 1825. It is alleged that a few French families lived on Randolph] Bluffs in 1800.[1] In the neighborhood of Barry settlements were made about 1830, and there was a post-office at Barry in 1836, with P. Flemming as postmaster.

Gallatin township boasts of the enterprising and public spirit of its citizens, and is noted for its fine horses, cattle and live stock generally. The horse shows at Barry in their season are occasions of note and are attended by farmers from all parts of the country.

The villages of Gallatin township are five in number, viz: Barry, Harlem, Moscow, Arnold (or Blue Eagle), and Minaville, or North Missouri Junction.

Barry was established first as an Indian trading post about the year 1830, before the Platte Purchase, when what is now Platte county belonged to the red men. Its location immediately on the boundary line (west half of center section 10 and east half of center of section 11, township 51, range 33) puts half the town in Clay and half in Platte. It has a population of about 200, contains two churches, Cumberland Presbyterian and Christian, a good school, stores, shops, etc. It is 10 miles west of Liberty, and about the same distance

---

[1] *Vide* Campbell's Gazetteer.

HISTORY OF CLAY COUNTY

north of Kansas City. Some of the citizens are now moving to connect the village with Kansas City by a macadamized road.

Harlem lies in the extreme southwestern part of the township, on the north bank of the Missouri, immediately across the river from Kansas City. It dates its origin from the completion of the railroad through it to Kansas City. Prior to 1880 the location was subject to complete overflow by every "June rise" in the Missouri, but in that year the United States Government built a strong levee to the northwest, and large additional appropriations have since been made from time to time to strengthen this work so as to prevent future serious overflow. The great flood of 1881, however, nearly drowned out the village. The following lines of railroad pass through Harlem: The Hannibal and St. Joseph, the Wabash, St. Louis and Pacific, the Kansas City, St. Joseph and Council Bluffs, and the Chicago, Rock Island and Pacific — the latter running over the track of the H. & St. Jo. At present the population of Harlem is about 200.

Moscow is located on the northeast quarter of section 7, township 50, range 32, eleven miles southwest of Liberty and five and one-half miles from Kansas City. The nearest station is Arnold's, two and a half miles away. It contains two churches, Baptist and Christian, a good mill, general stores, shops, etc., and has a population of about 150.

Arnold's Station, on the Hannibal and St. Joseph (sect. 1/4 of 9–50–32), seven miles northeast of Kansas City, was founded upon the completion of the railroad by M. S. Arnold, Esq., for whom the place was named. From its earliest history it has been quite a shipping point. It is reported that the average shipments of hogs, cattle, wood, ties, grain, etc., per month is about 25 cars. March 4, 1880, the western portion of the town was destroyed by fire, involving a loss of $2,800. The buildings destroyed were soon replaced by better structures, costing in the aggregate over $5,000. It is claimed that the present population of Arnold's Station is 200. The post-office is called Blue Eagle.

Minaville, or North Missouri Junction, is located on the northeast quarter of section 11, township 50, range 32, eight miles from Kansas City and six miles from Liberty. It is the point where the Hannibal and St. Joseph and the Wabash Railroad tracks formerly connected, and dates its existence from about 1868. It contains perhaps 125 inhabitants.

CHURCHES.

Barry Cumberland Presbyterian Church — At Barry, on the county line, between Clay and Platte counties, was organized June 3, 1826, by R. D. Morrow, with 27 members, among whom were Henry J. Weeden, Jonathan English, Jeremiah Burns, Benjamin Craig, Herman Davis, Easter (or Esther) Davis, John English, Jane Burns, Polly English, David P. Gill, William Hulott, Thomas Adams, Matilda Simrall and Hugh Brown. The present membership numbers about 102. Some of the pastors who have served this church are Revs. Robert D. Morrow, O. D. Allen, A. D. Miller, W. Schenk, W. O. H. Perry, and J. H. Norman. The present frame church was built in 1859, costing about $2,000. The Sunday school has about 45 scholars, its superintendent being Dan Carpenter.

Barry Christian Church. — In the winter of 1840 a frame house of worship was built at Barry for a congregation which had been formed as a church organization on the 26th of April of that year. Among the original members were Thomas Chisis, Annie Chisis, William Beal, John Callerman, Bass Callerman, Archibald Woods, Jane Woods, Adam Woods, Mary Woods, James and Catherine Cerry, Ann Ham, and Catherine Endicott. Some of those who have filled the pulpit of the church are John Callerman, Bayard Waller, Josiah Waller, G. R. Hand, Preston Aker, A. E. Higgason, J. A. Lord, S. G. Clay, W. S. Ramey, William C. Rodgers, and others whose names are not now recalled. In 1859 a second church edifice was erected; it is also a frame one. The present membership is 120. The Sabbath school of 81 members is superintended by Samuel Dooley.

Ebenezer Christian Church at Minaville — Was organized in 1865, with John Foster, Thomas and Betsy Stevens, John Tipton, Lucinda Tipton, John J. and Mary Brost, Elizabeth Lindenman, Thomas and Dinah Gibbons, John F. and Susan Foster, Eleanor Foster, and James and Lucinda Stevens as constituent members. This membership has been increased until it now numbers 40. The pastors in charge have been Richard Morton, Bro. Pickerall, Joseph Wollery and Bayard Waller. They occupy a frame house of worship, built at a cost of $1,500 in the same year of the organization.

Big Shoal O. S. Baptist Church — Located eight miles southwest from Liberty, was organized May 21, 1823, by Rev. William Thorp. The number of the present membership is 46. This church building is of brick, erected in 1854 at a cost of $2,200.

Bethel Baptist Church — Located on the Barry road, five miles west of Liberty, was organized in Pleasant Valley school-house, in 1872, by Elder James Rouse. Their present house of worship, a frame building, was erected in 1883, at a cost of $1,500. The present membership is 26.

HISTORY OF CLAY COUNTY

Antioch Christian Church — Located five miles northeast of Kansas City, was organized in 1854. The number of the present membership is 75. This church building is frame, erected in 1858 at a cost of $1,800.

Faurbion Chapel M. E. Church South — Located eight miles southwest of Liberty, was organized in 1837. The number of the present membership is 60. Their present house of worship, a frame structure, was erected in 1870, at a cost of $2,150.

MASONIC.

Rising Sun Lodge No. 13, A. F. & A. M. — May 6, 1852, this lodge was organized. Of the first officers and members there were but two names furnished, Wm. Conway, master and James W. Smith, senior warden. The membership now numbers 51. The present officers are C. M. Crouse, master; E. F. Knighton, senior warden; J. R. Funk, junior warden; G. W. Thompson, treasurer; Wm. Samuel, secretary; Lon Darby, senior warden; J. C. Woods, junior warden; G. W. Elzea, tyler.

BIOGRAPHICAL.

JOEN ALLEN

(Farmer, Post-office, Harlem).

Mr. Allen, besides being an energetic farmer, takes a warm interest in the cause of temperance, which he believes to be a movement fraught with more good to humanity than any great reformatory measure that has challenged the consideration of men for centuries. He is thoroughly persuaded that intemperance has been the cause of more crime and sorrow, more sadness and affliction in the world than all other causes combined. Thus believing, it is but natural that being a man of large sympathies and warm philanthropic impulses, he should actively interest himself in the temperance movement. He is a prominent member of the Christian Temperance Union at St. Joseph, and contributes much in the way of counsel, work and actual means when necessary for the good of the cause. Mr. Allen is also a magistrate and administers justice for his neighbors and all in his township. During the war he served with credit in the enrolled militia for a period of about twelve months. He is a Kentuckian and came to Missouri some years ago, settling in Clay county. He was married in Casey

HISTORY OF CLAY COUNTY

county, Ky., to Miss Mahala P. Mills in 1854, but she died in 1856. She left him three children, two of whom are living: Nimrod D. and Mary E. Susan is deceased. Mr. Allen's second wife was a Miss Mary D. Bradhurt, daughter of Jacob and Sallie Bradhurt of this county. His marriage to her occurred January 14, 1869. Four of their five children are living: James O., John E., George and Sarah E. Mr. Allen has a farm of 121 acres, which is well improved. He was born in Casey county, Ky., February 11, 1834. He was one in a family of thirteen children of James and Samuel (Bromson) Allen. Six of the children are living and both the parents, the latter still residents of Casey county, Ky.

WILLIAM M. BELLEW

(Farmer, Post-office, Acme Springs).

Mr. Bellew was a son of John Bellew, who went originally from Alabama to Kentucky, then coming to Missouri. The father first settled in Mercer county away back in 1837. He was married there in 1840 to Miss Cincinnati Dunkerson, formerly of Kentucky. He was a farmer and stock-raiser by occupation, and made his home in Mercer county for nearly thirty years. But in 1864 he removed to Pottawatomie county, and four years afterwards to Cass county. Later along he removed to Bates county, and thence to Clay county in 1872. He died here in the spring of 1882. He was an energetic and respected farmer, and a worthy member of the A. F. and A. M. The mother is still living. They were blessed with a family of fourteen children, six of whom are living. Both parents were members of the Missionary Baptist Church. William M. Bellew was born in Mercer county March 3, 1842, and was reared in that county. In 1862 he enlisted in the Union service, Co. F, Twenty-seventh Missouri infantry, under Col. Thomas Kerley, of St. Louis, and Capt. Clark. Mr. Bellew served for about 14 months, and during that time participated in the siege of Vicksburg and a number of engagements. Meantime, on the 26th of June, 1860, he was married to Miss Mary F. Smith, a daughter of Albert and Hester Smith, formerly of Kentucky. Mr. Bellew's first wife died in 1864, leaving two children, John and Charles. His present wife was previously a Miss Mary Allen, a daughter of William J. and Patsey Munson. By his present wife there are three children: William T., Minnie M. and Fannie H. Mrs. Bellew is a member of the Baptist Church. Mr. Bellew is engaged in farming, and came to Clay county in 1885. He is an industrious, energetic man, and is well respected by his friends.

JOHN T. BARBOUR

(Farmer, Post-office, Barry).

Robert Barbour, the father of the subject of this sketch, came from England in 1836, and settled in Clay county the following year. He was a farmer by occupation and resided in the county for many years,

HISTORY OF CLAY COUNTY

but was accidently killed at Leavenworth, Kan., in 1862, by a runaway team. He had been married in the county in 1842, when Miss Isabella McGuire became his wife. She was from Ireland. Eight of their family of children are living, as is also the mother. She is a member of the Missionary Baptist Church. The father was an Episcopalian. John T. Barbour, the subject of this sketch, was born July 27, 1844, and was reared in the county to a farm life. He traveled considerably in the Western States and Territories and in 1861 enlisted under Col. Thompson in the Confederate army, where he served a term of six months, taking part during that time in the battle of Lexington. He was married in Clinton county to Miss Mollie E., a daughter of Thomas and Eliza Arnold, formerly of Kentucky, in December, 1882. Since then he has been engaged in farming in the county. He and wife are members of the Christian Church.

William H. Barbour, brother to John T., was born July 2, 1848, and was married in Cass county, December 9, 1877. His wife was a Miss Mary Cooper, a daughter of Benjamin and Mary Cooper, of that county. William H. and John T. are engaged in stock feeding and dealing in stock. They are good stock-men, understand their business thoroughly and are full of energy and enterprise.

RICHARD S. BARNES

(Farmer, Post-office, Blue Eagle).

Richard Barnes, Sr., the father of the subject of this sketch, was a lieutenant under Col. Johnson in the War of 1812 and afterwards drew a pension from the Government in recognition of his services. He was a Virginian by nativity and a mechanic by trade, but afterwards devoted his time and attention largely to farming. In an early day he removed to Kentucky and then, in 1823, to Boone county, Mo. Two years later he came to Clay county, where he made his permanent home. He died here in 1861, at an advanced age. His wife, who was previously a Miss Elizabeth Adkins, of Woodford county, Ky., died in this county, November 23, 1876. Both were members of the Baptist Church, and took a prominent part in religious matters. They had a family of eight children, six of whom are living. Richard S. Barnes, the subject of this sketch, was born in this county December 27, 1826. Reared here, in 1853 he went to Oregon and a year later dropped down into California, where he was engaged in mining, ship building, etc., for about two years. Returning thence to Missouri, the following year he went back to California, and was in that State and Nevada until 1865. Previous to going West he had enlisted for service in the Mexican War, but his company was never ordered out. Mr. Barnes was married in this county, February 6, 1868, to Miss Fannie, a daughter of Henry and Sarah Nall. Mr. and Mrs. B. have five children: Lewis H., Edward T., Charles G., Earl N. and Willie E. Mr. Barnes has been one of the active and energetic farmers of Clay county ever since the war, and has had good success. He owns an excellent farm of 370 acres, all choice land and well im-

HISTORY OF CLAY COUNTY

proved. In the matter of religious conviction Mr. Barnes is a disciple of Nature, believing that the only true idea of God is to be formed from the visible manifestation of His works, in the beauty and harmony and order of Nature. He is entirely content to let sectarians differ and contend over written creeds, whilst he looks up and does reverence and honor to the majestic God of the Universe, regardless of bibles, korans and all the other books that have been prepared in the distant past for the guidance of the highest and best interests of humanity.

JUDGE JOHN BROADHURST

(Farmer and Stock-raiser, and Judge of the County Court, Post-office, Acme).

The Broadhurst family were early settlers in Western Missouri. The Judge's parents, John Broadhurst, Sr., and wife, whose maiden name was Mary Teemer, came to this State away back in 1816. They were from North Carolina, and on coming here first located in Howard county. The father was a blacksmith by trade, and he followed his trade at Old Franklin for about eight years. But in 1824 he pushed on up the river with his family, and made his permanent home in Clay county. Here he followed blacksmithing for some years, but finally turned his attention to farming. He became a substantial farmer and stock-raiser of the county. He had served under Gen. Jackson in the War of 1812, and in his old age drew a pension on account of his services. He died on his homestead in this county in 1876, at an advanced age. His wife preceded him to the grave in 1875. At the time of her death they had been married 65 years, having been married in Buncombe county, N. C., in 1810. Six children were the fruits of their married life, all of whom lived to be grown, and two of whom are still living. Judge Broadhurst was born in this county, October 24, 1826. He was reared to the occupation of farming and stock-raising. This he adopted as his permanent calling after he grew up, and has been fairly successful in his chosen pursuit. Judge Broadhurst is comfortably situated. He has a good farm well stocked and well improved. On the 10th of October, 1844, he was married to Miss Melinda D. Faubion, a daughter of Rev. Jacob Faubion, an early settler of this county. The Judge and wife have had 11 children, eight of whom are living: James H., Sarah F., wife of A. F. Tetton; Martha A., wife of John A. Holt; Thomas H., John R., Ruth I., George W. and Mary H. Mary A., Cynthia E. and Franklin S. are deceased. The Judge and his family are members of the M. E. Church South. In 1860 Judge Broadhurst was elected to the office of justice of the peace, the duties of which he discharged for four years. Eight years afterwards he was elected a member of the county court, and held that office for six years. In 1882 he was re-elected to the county bench for a term of six years, and is now serving out his second term. He takes a commendable and public-spirited interest in the affairs of the county, and the fact that they are conducted on principles of business intelligence and economy, and are in an enviable

HISTORY OF CLAY COUNTY

condition, is due to the close attention, efficiency and good judgment which characterize the official conduct of the members of its county court. Judge Broadhurst is a man of good business qualifications and high character, and is one of the highly esteemed citizens of the county.

DAVID T. BRONAUGH

(Farmer and Stock-raiser, Post-office, Barry).

Among the prominent agriculturists of Gallatin township may very properly be mentioned the subject of the present sketch. Mr. Bronaugh has an excellent stock farm of 320 acres, which is largely run in grass, but enough being reserved for grain to answer his purposes as a stock-raiser. He is a man of industry and enterprise and although he has hardly yet more than reached middle age, he has succeeded, by his sterling qualities and good judgment as a business farmer, in coming to the front. Mr. Bronaugh was born in the county April 25, 1843. His parents were John and Hannah (Morton) Bronaugh, both from Kentucky. They came here in 1842. His father was a man of considerable business prominence. In Kentucky he was cashier of a bank for some years. He then went to Louisville, and for a time was connected with one of the leading wholesale grocery houses of that city. After coming to Missouri he gave his entire time and attention to farming and stock-raising. He died here in 1883. His wife is still living. He was a member of the Episcopal Church, as she still is. They have five children, but David T. is the only one living. He was reared on the farm in this county, and in 1861 enlisted in the Southern army under Gen. Price, continuing in the service until the close of the war. He was in nearly all the battles in which his command took part, including those of Springfield, Mo., and Corinth, Miss. After the war Mr. Bronaugh returned home and engaged in farming and raising stock, which he has continued ever since. In 1871 he was married to Miss Mary Newler, a daughter of E. M. and Jane Newler. Mr. and Mrs. B. are members of the Christian Church. They have two children, John and Newler.

CHARLES W. BUSTER

(Farmer, Post-office, Blue Eagle).

Mr. Buster has a good farm of 480 acres, well improved and well stocked. He is engaged in both general farming and raising stock, and is one of the enterprising farmers and highly respected citizens of Gallatin township. Like most of the older residents of this part of the county, he is of Kentucky parentage His parents, James J. and Lucy D. (Younger) Buster, came to Missouri from Kentucky away back in 1820. They first located in Howard county, but in a short time settled in Clay county. However, it should be said by way of correction of the above that the father, James J. Buster, came to this county in 1822. He married Miss Younger, who had previously come out with her parents, November 25, 1824, in Clay

HISTORY OF CLAY COUNTY

county. They had eleven children, three of whom are living. The father died in April, 1851; the mother in 1876. She was a member of the Primitive Baptist Church. Charles W. was born February 26, 1833, in Clay county. He was reared on his father's farm in this county, where he followed farming and handling stock until 1853, when he went to California. There he was engaged in mining for two years. Returning then to Clay county, he resumed farming and stock raising. For four years preceding 1863 he was merchandising at Kearney, but since then has given his undivided attention to farming. December 23, 1851, he was married to Miss Georgia A., a daughter of John and Harriet Minter. Mr. and Mrs. Buster have had ten children, eight of whom are living: Harriet E., Charles E., James R. (deceased), Helen, John, Lucy, Mattie, Emma, Bradley (deceased) and Lillie.

WILLIAM C. CAMPBELL

(Farmer, Post-office, Harlem).

Mr. Campbell is a native of Kentucky, born in Madison county, March 22, 1820. His father, also named William, was a Virginian by nativity, and came from Bedford county, that State, when a boy with his parents to Madison county, Ky., in 1789. He there grew up and was married to Miss Elizabeth Snoddy, and in 1834 they came to Missouri and settled in Clay county. He was an energetic farmer and was for a number of years magistrate of his township. He died here in 1859. His wife died in 1857. They had nine children. Six lived to be grown but only two are now living. William C. Campbell was 14 years of age when his parents came to this county. He was brought up to the occupation of farming and handling stock, which he has followed ever since. In 1851 he was married to Miss Amanda, a daughter of William and Amelia Evans. Mr. and Mrs. Campbell have had three children, but William C. is the only one living. The others were Ella and Emma. Mr. and Mrs. Campbell are members of the Christian Church. Mr. Campbell is still living on the homestead which his father improved on coming to this county. It is a good place of 560 acres, well improved, including a substantial brick house.

DAN CARPENTER

(Dealer in General Merchandise, Barry, Mo.).

Dan Carpenter was born at Hanging Rock, Lawrence county, Ohio, March 7, 1825, and received what education he could get in the common schools of his native and adopted State. At the age of 18 years he emigrated with his parents to Clinton county, Mo., in 1843. In 1845 he was established in merchandising at Randolph, Clay county, Mo., with his elder brother, Amos Carpenter. In 1847 he removed to Barry, in the same county, where he has continued in mercantile pursuits until the present. In 1850 he crossed the plains to California with an ox-train of merchandise. Selling most of his

515

goods in Salt Lake City, he arrived in Placerville, California, the 22d of September, just five months from his departure — as many months as it now requires days to make the same trip. Returning to Missouri in 1851, *via* Panama and New Orleans, he re-engaged in merchandising with a reasonable degree of success, and has won for himself a good reputation for fair, honest and honorable dealing. In merchandising, and buying and selling produce, he has had business frequently amounting to $50,000 per annum. In December, 1853, he was married to Miss Pauline Gash, daughter of Joseph D. and Eliza Gash, who was born in Buncombe county, N. C. While an infant her parents emigrated to Missouri, settling in Clay county in 1832, and by industry and economy, became of easy circumstances. Her father died in 1851, and mother in 1865, both being substantial and influential members of the Cumberland Presbyterian Church. Mrs. Carpenter is an estimable Christian lady, and prominent in every good work for the promotion of the interests of society, and especially for the good of the young, having been a prominent Sabbathschool teacher for thirty years, and an instructor of young ladies in music. In 1859 Mr. C. professed faith in Christ, united with, and was soon made an elder in the Cumberland Presbyterian Church, which office he still holds. In 1860 he was elected a superintendent of a Sabbath school, which position he still occupies, and has seen over 150 of his pupils united to the church. Has been postmaster at Barry, with two intermissions of about four years, since 1852, serving under every administration from Franklin Pierce to Chester A. Arthur, and hopes to be honored by a continuance under Mr. Cleveland, of whom he was an ardent admirer and earnest supporter — being thoroughly Democratic in every political sentiment, unless in being a prohibitionist in principle and practice for over thirty years, he differs with the principles of that party. Believing its principles to be misunderstood, he holds to the party that has ever advocated "the greatest good to the greatest number." In 1866 he began improving, and in 1869 moved upon a good farm of 160 acres, and engaged in fruit raising and general agriculture, having one of the largest orchards in the county.

His chief endeavor is to promote the glory of God and influence his friends to become Christians, and no weather hinders the attendance of himself and wife upon the means of grace or their work in the Sabbath school. For many years he has been an occasional correspondent of his county, church and agricultural papers, discussing with freedom all questions of public, religious and agricultural interest. His father, William Carpenter, was a native of Harrison county, Va., born in 1792, whose father was a Methodist minister, and his mother, Hannah Clark, daughter of Samuel Clark, was born in Spottsylvania county, same State, 1798. Wm. Carpenter was a merchant by occupation and surveyor by profession; was prominent in the affairs of Lawrence county, O., where he came at an early age with his parents; was colonel of a regiment of Ohio militia, at that time more honorable than now, and at one time represented his county in the Legislature, but declined re-election to the "muddy pool of politics." He

HISTORY OF CLAY COUNTY

belonged to the "minute men," and was called to the front in the War of 1812. After his death his widow received a pension on account of his services, he persistently refusingto apply for it during his lifetime, declaring the Government needed the money worse than he did. How isit at the present day? Every thing that can swear or prove the loss of a hair or toe-nail is clamoring to be hung on the pension list. During the late unpleasantness he moved from his elegant home in Chester county to Leavenworth City, Kas., on account of his attachment to the Union. After the "cruel war was over" he moved to Weston, Platte county, Mo., where he died in 1873 at the age of 82 years. At one time he had amassed a considerable fortune for that day, before millionaires had become thick as blackberries, but the ravages of war swept a large part of it away. He was a man of large experience, a logical mind, a close thinker and was thoroughly informed in history, science, mechanics, morals, politics and religion, and in his seventy-fifth year was admitted to the bar as a practitioner of law in the Platte County Circuit Court. Mrs. C., his wife, was a pious, Godly woman, who attended strictly to household duties and made home happy as only such mothers can do. She died in peace with God and man in 1882, in the eighty-fourth year of her age. The subject of this sketch enjoys the confidence of his friends and neighbors to an almost unlimited degree, and in the absence of ministers has held funeral services for about 100 of his neighbors, and their children who have gone the way of all the earth, offering them the consolations of the gospel of Christ, shedding the tear of sympathy with them over the "loved and lost" and assuring them of a "glorious resurrection," and a happy home beyond on the golden shore, where friends and loved ones meet to part no more. His prayer is that whether he lives long or dies soon, he may be found doing the Master's will and be ready for the call "Come up higher." With him and his good wife, their highest aspirations are

"To serve the present age
Their calling to fulfill.
Mav it all their powers engage
To do their Master's will."

SAMUEL DOOLEY

(Farmer and Stock-raiser, and Justice of the Peace, Post-office, Barry).

'Squire Dooley came to this county from Kentucky in 1866. He had been reared in Montgomery county, in that State, and made it his home until he left Kentucky, now nearly 20 years ago. However, during the war he was away in the Southern service about three years. He enlisted in 1862 and most of the time was under Gen. John Morgan, the great cavalry leader of the war. On coming to this county 'Squire Dooley resumed farming and stock-raising, which he had previously followed in Kentucky. He has a good farm of 120 acres, which is well improved. On the 9th of September, 1858, he was married to Miss Mary F. Wallen, a daughter of Isaac and America

HISTORY OF CLAY COUNTY

Wallen, both of early and respected families in Kentucky. The 'Squire and wife have three children: America B., Amelia J. and Georgia. Both parents are members of the Christian Church. He was elected to his present office, that of judicial magistrate, bailiwick of Gallatin, in 1882. He has made an efficient and upright magistrate and has administered justice to all whose causes have been heard in his court with an even, impartial hand. 'Squire D. was born in Clark county, Ky., February 14, 1837. His father, a farmer by occupation, died in Nicholas county, that State, in 1883. His mother, who was a Miss Rebecca Scohee before her marriage, is still living. It is a remarkable fact that all their ten children are also still living.

WASHINGTON W. DREW

(Farmer, Post-office, Barry).

Mr. Drew was born in Todd county, Ky., July 1, 1826. He was reared in his native county up to the age of 17 when his parents removed to Clay county, Mo. Here he grew to manhood and at the age of 20 enlisted for the Mexican War under Col. Doniphan. Young Drew was with Doniphan throughout his campaign across the plains through New Mexico and down beyond the further shore of the Rio Grande, to Old Mexico. After a service of something over a year he was honorably discharged and came home to Clay county, where he remained for about three years. But in 1850 he joined the general exodus of adventurous Argonauts from this part of the country to the Pacific coast and made the journey across the plains and through the devious canons of the Rocky Mountains. Mr. Drew did not rush back like a great many who hardly waited as long as a calf would from its mother before starting home again. He resolutely braved the perils and hardships of a miner's life in the wilderness for years and worked like a Trojan, as the seasons came and went, delving deep down into the bowels of the earth and beneath the rock-ribbed mountains of the Pacific slope for the treasures hid there for centuries before the ark reached a haven on the heights of Mount Ararat. He remained in California for about 15 years, principally engaged in mining, and then returned to his old home in Clay county. While there he passed the period of life when men usually take unto themselves a wife, and having safely escaped through the channel of matrimony up to middle age, he has ever since succeeded in continuing in a state of single blessedness. Mr. Drew is a farmer by occupation and has been engaged in farming ever since his return to Clay county. He has a well improved farm of about 200 acres. Mr. D. is a man well respected in the community, an energetic, good farmer and a worthy citizen.

LEWIS ELLIOTT

(Farmer, Post-office, Barry).

Mr. Elliott still resides in the county of his birth and where he was reared and received his education. The latter was obtained principally in the district schools of the neighborhood in which he was brought up. He was reared to a farm life, and thus acquired that taste for agricultural pursuits which subsequently influenced him to make farming his permanent calling. Among all the occupations he prefers the free and independent and manly pursuit of a farmer. He has a good home of 160 acres, which is well stocked and substantially improved. Mr. Elliott is an industrious farmer, and a man of good standing in the community. He was born on his father's homestead in this county in 1847. His parents, Zachary and Margaret (Endicot) Elliott, were both originally from Kentucky, and came here in an early day. His mother, however, was a descendant of the old Endicot family of Massachusetts, who came over in an early day to that colony. Representatives of the family subsequently settled in Pennsylvania, and thence in Kentucky. Mr. Elliott's father was a farmer and house carpenter, but in the latter years of his life followed farming pretty much altogether. He died in 1862, the mother preceding him to the grave in 1853. They had a family of four children, Lewis Elliott being now the only one living. During the war he served a short time in the Southern army, his service extending through the last year of the war, although he was but 16 years of age. In 1868, September 8, he was married to Miss Adeline A. Williams, a daughter of Edward and Frances Williams. The children, the fruits of their married life, are: Edward, James, Margaret, Hattie G. and Arthur. Mr. and Mrs. Elliott are members of the Christian Church.

JAMES C. EVANS

(Farmer, Post-office, Harlem).

Mr. Evans' grandfather, John Evans, was one of the first five householders who settled in Clay county with their families in 1820. He was from Madison county, Ky., and on first coming to this State resided for two years in Howard county. In 1829 he removed with his family to Clinton county, being one of the first settlers of that county. He died there in 1840. William B. Evans, the father of the subject of this sketch, was 12 years of age when his parents came to Howard county from Kentucky. Thence he went with them to Clay county, and with them from Clay to Clinton county in 1829. The following year, however, he crossed the river into Jackson county, where Kansas City now stands. There he met and was married to Miss Amelia McGee, a daughter of James H. and Eleanor McGee. That was in 1830, and the same year Mrs. Evans (his wife) had 80 acres of land set apart to her by her father from the family homestead, the same 80 now forming a part of Dundee place. Mr. Evans settled on this with his young wife, and made it their home for a number of years. The ownership of the land continued in Mrs. Evans' name until two years ago, when the title was transferred to the Dundee Company. Mr. Evans was one of the founders of Kansas City. He established the first ferry there. He helped to survey and

519

plat the place and bought the first lots sold. He early built a house of entertainment down at the ferry, and what is now the foot of Main street, where many and many a traveler stopped in those early days when on their way to and from the great West. He also had a large warehouse and storage buildings. He died at Kansas City in 1855. His wife, however, is still living, at the advanced age of 72. They had 10 children, five of whom are living, including the subject of this sketch. James C. Evans was born on the present site of Kansas City, April 25, 1833. He was reared in Jackson county, and given a good common school education. November 15, 1860, he was married in Clay county to Miss Elizabeth Campbell, a daughter of Samuel W. and Mary Campbell, early settlers of this county. The following year Mr. Evans removed to Clay county and settled on the farm where he now resides. He has been a resident of the county ever since. Mr. Evans has made himself one of the substantial citizens and successful farmers of the county. His home place is a fine farm of 250 acres, on which he has a handsome brick residence, built at a cost of $12,000. Mr. Evans is an active member of the Grange, and has been a member of that organization since it was first established in this county. He takes a warm interest in the welfare of the order. He is also one of the leading horticulturists of the West, and is now president of the State Horticultural Society. April 11, 1882, Mr. Evans had the misfortune to lose his wife. She left him eight children at her death. She was an earnest member of the Christian Church.

FRANK GARDNER

(Owner and Proprietor of the Capitol Mills, Moscow).

These mills, one of the leading flouring, grist and saw mills of the county, were erected by Mr. Gardner and John T. Ricketts, as partnership owners and proprietors, in 1870. Since then Mr. Gardner has become sole owner and the mills have been greatly enlarged and improved. Originally they included no saw-mill plant, but this has since been added. The entire mills were remodeled in 1882 and the new process was introduced. Altogether they now form a desirable and valuable piece of mill property. The flour capacity of the mills is 75 barrels every 24 hours. The flour manufactured at the Capitol Mills has made its way into popular favor by its own merits and is now in good demand wherever it has been used. Mr. Gardner is a thorough miller and as careful of the reputation of the mills, particularly of the class of work it does, both in the manufacture of breadstuff and of lumber, as he is of his own good name. Hence he never allows his trade-mark or brand to appear on any goods without he knows they are exactly what they are represented to be Mr. Gardner was primarially of Kentucky, born in Nelson county, May 2, 1835. His parents were John and Elizabeth (Brown) Gardner, his father originally from Virginia. He came out to Kentucky in an early day, and was an energetic farmer and trader in general produce in Nelson county. He

HISTORY OF CLAY COUNTY

died there in 1873. The mother died April 15, 1839. The father had been previously married, his first wife's maiden name being Annie Brown, a sister to his second wife. She died March 25, 1834. Three children by the second wife are living, including the subject of this sketch. He was reared on the farm up to the age of 20. He then began at the miller's trade, building and running mills, at which he has continued ever since. Mr. Gardner came to Missouri in 1866 and located in Clay county. He was married in Louisville, Ky., April 5, 1865. His wife was a Miss Kate Montgomery, a daughter of Raymond and Hettie Montgomery. Mr. and Mrs. G. have had seven children, five living: Fannie, Vernon, Benjamin, Katie and Lena. Ernest and Hubert, twins, are deceased. Mrs. Gardner is a member of the Catholic Church. She was born in Washington county, Ky., June 28, 1845.

M. LEE GASH

(Farmer, Post-office, Barry).

M. Lee Gash, son of Jos. D. and Eliza Gash, was born in Clay county, Mo., May 20, 1845. He received his education in the common schools of the county and attended one term at a well known college, in Jacksonville, Ill. His father and mother were natives of Buncombe county, N. C., and in 1832 emigrated west and settled in Gallatin township, Clay county, Mo., spending their days on the farm they first owned; they had a family of seven children, six of whom are still living. 'Squire Gash was an active, energetic business man, accumulating what was in that day considered quite a little fortune, mostly landed estate. Prominent in all objects of public good, he served as a justice of the peace for many years. He and his wife were faithful, earnest members of the Cumberland Presbyterian Church. He died in the vigor of manhood in 1851. His widow surviving him, continued all the business, especially farming, in which he was engaged, training her children for usefulness and in all Christian virtues, and died surrounded by them in June, 1865, trusting in a crucified Savior for resurrection and eternal life. M. Lee Gash was reared on the home farm, trained to agriculture and stock-raising, and has been successful as a rising man in his community. He has a warm heart and a home open to the needy, is an exemplary member of the Cumberland Presbyterian Church, and labors for the advancement of Christianity unfalteringly. November 6, 1876 he was married to Miss Mary A. Sparks, daughter of Henry and Sarah Sparks, formerly of Kentucky. Henry Sparks, after a life spent in the church, died December 31, 1884, leaving a widow in poor health, with a well founded hope of soon meeting him who has gone before, where partings never come. This marriage has been productive of two children: Dellie C. and Henry Hill. Mr. G. has a fine farm of 240 acres, well improved and stocked with fine cattle, sheep, hogs and horses, with a prospect of a long, happy and prosperous career, enjoying the respect and confidence of all who know him. His wife is an excellent lady, a cheerful and

HISTORY OF CLAY COUNTY

happy wife, a kind and faithful mother and consistent member of the church with her husband.

DAVID HORNER

(Farmer, Post-office, Acme).

Mr. Horner was born in the county Annagh, Ireland, January 11, 1829. His father was Joseph Horner and his mother's maiden name Barbara Blevins. When David was about 10 years of age the family came to America and settled in Clay county. The mother died here in 1876. There were eight children in the family, four of whom are living. Both parents were members of the M. E. Church. David completed his adolescence in this country and learned the practical details of farm life as he grew up. In 1864 he was married to Mrs. Martha ҏ. Musser, whose maiden name was Donaldson, daughter of James and Patsey Donaldson, formerly of Kentucky. Mr. and Mrs. Horner have lost two children in infancy and have none living. Mrs. H. is a member of the Presbyterian Church. He is a Methodist Episcopalian. Mr. Horner has a good farm and is pleasantly and comfortably situated at his home. He made his own start in life, having commenced a poor man, and all he possesses he has accumulated by honest industry and economy. He is one of the well respected citizens of Gallatin township.

JAMES HUGHES

(Farmer, Post-office, Blue Eagle).

Mr. Hughes' father, Patrick Hughes, was a native of Ireland and a molder of cast iron by trade. He came over to America in early manhood and located first in Rhode Island. He was married in that State to Miss Sarah McGarth. also formerly of Ireland, and three children were born to them, two of whom are living, one being the subject of this sketch. James Hughes was born in Rhode Island, March 10, 1837, and when in infancy was brought out by his parents to Missouri, who removed to Clay county, this State, in 1837. The mother died here in 1846. James was reared in this county and brought up to the occupation of a farmer. During the war he served for about eight months in the State militia. Mr. Hughes has a neat farm of 80 acres. He has never married, and is therefore living a life of single blessedness, a staid old bachelor, upon whom the smiles and wiles of all the maids have thus far made little or no effect.

SAMUEL N. JACKSON

(Dealer in Drugs and Groceries, Arnold Station).

A Kentuckian by nativity, Mr. Jackson was born in Monroe county, November 8, 1845. His father was James A. Jackson, a blacksmith by occupation, and who removed to Missouri with his family in 1852, settling at Independence. A year later he removed to Harrisonville,

Cass county, and in 1864 to Clay county, but seven years later to Texas, where he died January 23, 1883, aged 67 years. He was justice of the peace in Cass county for some years and postmaster at Austin. Mr. Jackson's mother (Samuel N.'s) was a Miss Mary S. Slaughter, formerly of Virginia. There were six children in the family, five of whom are living, including the subject of this sketch. The mother died December 24, 1882, aged 58. Samuel N. received a common school education as he grew up and engaged in his present business at Arnold Station in 1877. His business experience has been satisfactorily successful, and he has a good trade. December 31, 1868, he was married to Miss Missouri A. Foster, a daughter of John A. Foster, of Clay county. They have four children: Carrie Wesley, Lena May, Samuel N. and James A. His wife is a member of the Christian Church.

JACOB B. JOHNSON

(Farmer and Stock-Raiser, and of Johnson & Moore, Saw-millers, Post-office, Barry).

Mr. Johnson came to Missouri from Kentucky in 1863 and located in Clay county, near Barry, where he shortly bought a farm and engaged in farming and stock-raising. He continued that exclusively up to 1883, when he formed a partnership with Mr. John Moore in the saw mill, which they now run. Since then he has been carrying on his farm and assisting in the running of the saw mill. Mr. Johnson was born in Montgomery county, Ky., July 24, 1845, and was a son of Philip and Mary (Combes) Johnson. His mother died when he was about 13 years of age, and after that he went to live with his uncle, Thomas Johnson, of that county. His father was subsequently married twice, and removed to Fannin county, Tex., where he died in 1878, after a residence there of over twenty years. Jacob B. Johnson grew up in Montgomery county, Ky., and remained with his uncle until 1861, when he enlisted in the Southern service under Gen. Marshall. Subsequently he was transferred to Gen. Morgan's command and followed that doughty raider and gallant cavalry leader until the close of the war, or until a short time before the close. The last order received by Mr. J.'s command was a general order of surrender from Gen. Lee, in May, 1865. He then returned home to Montgomery county, Ky., and went to work. April 16, 1868, he was married to Miss Jennie Cooley, daughter of Jabez and Rebecca Cooley. From Kentucky Mr. Johnson came to Missouri in 1868, as stated above. He and wife have six children: Charles C., Losa L., James H., John T., Mary B. and Harry. Both parents are members of the Christian Church. Mr. J.'s farm contains 200 acres.

MARTIN A. KING

(Farmer, Post-Office, Liberty).

When the war broke out in 1861, or, rather, some months afterwards, in the fall of that year, Mr. King, who was born and reared in Clay county, enlisted in the Southern service and was out until well along in the following spring. While under Gen. Price he participated in the battles of Lexington, Pea Ridge and others. Returning home, with the view of taking no further part in the war, he soon found it would be impossible for him to remain without at least nominally joining the militia (Union) service, which he accordingly entered. He was in the militia, doing home service, during much of the remaining part of the war. His company was commanded by Capt. Garth, of Liberty. Since then Mr. King has been engaged in farming, as he had previously been. His homestead contains 330 acres, and is well improved. In other tracts he has 540 acres, which are also improved. Mr. King has made all he possesses by his own industry and energy. At the age of 11 years he was left an orphan and without a dollar. From boyhood, therefore, he has made his own way in the world and obtained what education he has, sufficient for all ordinary purposes, by his own application. He was born in this county September 22, 1842. His father, Daniel King, removed to Clay county with his family in 1827, and remained here for a period of twenty-five years, or until 1852. He then started on his way, moving to Arkansas, but died *en route* in Jackson county, this State. He had been justice of the peace of Clay county, and was a citizen well respected and of good standing. He was married three times; first, in Lawrence county, Ohio, and then twice in Clay county. His first wife died in this county in 1843. There were no children by either of his last two marriages. By his first wife there were five children, four of whom are living. Martin A., the subject of this sketch, was reared in this county, and about the time of the close of the war went to Kansas, but returned eighteen months afterwards. November 13, 1862, he was married to Miss Margaret R. Sutton, a daughter of James and Sarah Sutton. Mr. and Mrs. King have had ten children ; seven are living: Anna A., Mary J., Johanna, Hubert U., Maggie M., Ardena and Ardella. Sarah, and Fannie and Della, twins, all died at tender ages.

PHILIP KRAUS

(Dealer in General Merchandise, Harlem).

Mr. Kraus came to Harlem in 1866, and has been engaged in business at this place ever since. He is also postmaster. He has a good stock of general merchandise and an excellent trade. He was born in Germany April 26, 1831. He came to the United States in 1850, locating in Ohio, after which he engaged in peddling, which he followed for four years. In 1860 he engaged in merchandising at Shawneetown, Kas., and six years later he came to Harlem. He was married in Platte county in 1872 to Miss Mary K., a daughter of Peter Klaunn. They have had two children, one living, John P. The one deceased was Mary M. Mrs. Kraus is also deceased, having died in 1878. She was an exemplary member of the Lutheran Church. Mr. Kraus' parents were John and Catherine (Koomer) Kraus. They continue to make their home in Germany. There were eleven children in the family, three of whom are living.

J. N. LINDSEY

(Farmer, Post-office, Harlem).

Mr. Lindsey was born in Henry county, Ky., January 15, 1822, and was one in a family of eight children, four still living, of Thomas and Keziah (Jones) Lindsey, the father originally from Virginia. He died in 1860, and the mother in 1870, both in Henry county, Ky. J. N. Lindsey was reared in that county, and in 1857 came to Clay county, Mo., where he has ever since resided. Before coming here he was married, February 18, 1847, in Henry county, Ky., to Miss Elizabeth A. Myles, a daughter of Henry and Margaret Myles. Mr. and Mrs. Lindsey have had ten children, eight of whom are living: Mary N., John P., Sarah M., Anna K., Jemima J., Fannie E., Emma L. and George B. Thomas H. and William P. are deceased. Their mother, Mrs. Lindsey, died in 1870. She was an earnest, consistent member of the Presbyterian Church. Mr. Lindsey has a neat farm of 75 acres, where he resides.

JOHN NEAL,

(Farmer, Post-office, Blue Eagle).

Mr. Neal has a good farm of 490 acres, which is fairly improved. It is a comfortable homestead and his situation is one of comparatively easy circumstances. His occupation throughout life has been that of a farmer, and as the foregoing facts show, he has been satisfactorily successful. He was born in Mason county, Ky., January 19, 1826, and came to Clay county, Mo., with his parents in 1837. His father died here in 1844. He was a farmer by occupation and had been a soldier in the War of 1812. The mother died in 1873. She was a Miss Sidney L. Ellis. He was born in Kentucky in 1796. Of their family of three children, the subject of this sketch is the only one living. Mr. Neal, Jr., grew up in this county, and in 1846 enlisted under Col. Doniphan for the Mexican War. He accompanied Doniphan's command throughout its famous and romantic campaign to the West and on down the valley of the Rio Grande and across to the cathedral city of the Montezumas. After the war he returned to Clay county and resumed farming. In 1854 he was married to Miss Amanda Burnette of this county. She died in 1863, leaving one child, Edward. His second wife was Miss Virginia L. Woods, and they were married in 1868. She was a daughter of Thomas Woods of this county. They have one child, Thomas N. Mrs. Neal is a member of the Christian Church.

ROBERT REDDISH, M. D.

(Physician and Surgeon, Barry).

Dr. Reddish, born in Nelson county, Ky., April 11, 1835, was reared and educated in that county and in 1855 began the study of

HISTORY OF CLAY COUNTY

medicine at Mt. Washington, in Bullitt county, under Dr. S. M. Hobbs. After taking a course under Dr. Hobbs, he matriculated at the Kentucky School of Medicine of Louisville, Ky., in which he took a course of two terms, and graduated in the class of 1857. That fall his parents, Joseph E. and Jacyntha E. (King) Reddish, removed to Missouri but he preceded them in the spring, all locating at Barry, in Clay county. Here Dr. Reddish engaged in the practice of his profession and has ever since continued it with excellent success and without interruption, except for about a year, during the latter part of the war, which he spent at Nebraska City. His removal to that place was caused by the unsettled and dangerous condition of affairs in this county at that time. Indeed, the immediate cause of his removal was the murder of his father by a band of Jennison's Kansas Red Legs who gave out, however, that they were a company of Colorado troops under the command of Col. Ford. Dr. Reddish's father was an inoffensive old gentlemen who had taken no part in the war, either directly or indirectly, and was as highly respected as any man in the community. He was an industrious, hard working man who attended strictly to his own affairs. He was taken out unarmed, for he had never had any use for arms, and while a prisoner and utterly defenseless was shot down in cold blood, as foul and cruel a murder of a white-haired, harmless old man as was ever perpetrated, and as inexcusable as if he had been a helpless, sleeping infant. But such was one of the many outrages committed in this part of the country during the war. God only knows what the answer shall be for them hereafter. Dr. Reddish was married in this county, September 6, 1858. His wife was a Miss Annie E. Tillery, a daughter of Clayton and Annie Tillery, early settlers of this county. The Doctor and Mrs. R. have five children, three of whom are living: Frankie T., Anna B. and Joseph C. The deceased were William T. and Annie E. The Doctor and wife are members of the Christian Church. The Doctor has been fairly successful as a physician and has a good practice. He also has a good farm of 350 acres. He has been practicing medicine at Barry for the last 27 years.

CHRISTOPHER M. RUSSELL

(Farmer, Post-office, Harlem).

It was as early as 1817 that the Russell family came to Missouri. Mr. R.'s father, Andrew Russell, came from Tennessee when a young man. He located in Saline county. Two years later he was married there, in 1819, to a Miss Martin, of Clark county, Ky. In 1822 they removed to Clay county, and the father died here February 13, 1854. He served in the War of 1812 and in the Mormon War. The mother is still living, at the age of 83 years. They had a family of 14 children, six of whom are living. Christopher M. Russell, the subject of this sketch, was born in Clay county June 21, 1841. In 1861 he entered Price's army, and was in the service 12 months. He then returned home, and, November 7, 1865, was married to Miss Mary R.

526

HISTORY OF CLAY COUNTY

Baker, a daughter of Josiah and Sarah Baker, from Kentucky to this county. Mr. and Mrs. Russell have had 10 children, all daughters, and eight of whom are living, namely: Mattie, Ella, Bettie S., Ida, Annie E., Clara, Mary and Rosia. Maggie and Emma died at tender ages. Mr. Russell has always made farming his occupation. His homestead contains 160 acres. He also has 300 acres in other tracts.

CHRISTOPHER SCHRADER

(Post-office, Barry).

Mr. Christopher Schrader was born August 7, 1834, in Hasede, Hanover, Germany. His father was named Conrad Schrader, and his mother's maiden name was Elizabeth Ellechers. Both were born and reared in Hasede. They received but a common school education. At the age of 16 years Mr. Schrader's father volunteered to join the army under Napoleon the Great, and fought through the battle of Waterloo. After the defeat he served under the German empire for 15 years. The balance of his life he was strictly engaged in trading. He was known as a noble and generous man, blessed with many fond and tender friends. He died at the age of 83, in Hasede, Hanover, Germany, in 1875. His wife died in 1871. Their number of children were five: Joseph, Christopher, Daniel, Catherine and Gertrude. Catherine is deceased. Mr. Schrader's occupation was shoemaking, and, having learned his trade satisfactorily, he left his native country for America in the year of 1853, landing at New Orleans. Thence he came to Platte county, Mo. In 1855 he established a shoe shop at Barry, Mo., with the capital of $5. In the same year he was married to Miss Wilhelmine Mour, daughter of Wm. Mour, of Hanover, Germany, who died in the year 1835, leaving a wife and daughter to mourn his loss. His wife's name was Caroline Mour, who came to America in 1836, locating in St. Louis, Mo., for one year. Thence she came to Parkville, Platte county, Mo., where she married Christopher Diester, who became the father of seven children: Nina, Henry, Daniel, Thomas, Caroline, Magdalene and Christopher. Caroline, Christopher and Magdalene are deceased. Mrs. Schrader's mother's name was Caroline Biltamon, who was born and reared in Hanover, Germany. She was of a moral and religious family, members of the Lutheran Church. Her parents were well-to-do and highly respected by all. Mr. Schrader had a successful business for 15 years at Barry, Mo., endeavoring most earnestly to obtain an honorable position, which he has so far gained. He retired from business in 1869, engaging in farming and stock-raising, which also proved quite successful. He owns 253 acres of land and a vast herd of stock. He has one daughter married (Rosa) to a worthy young man of Kansas City, Mo., a distinguished druggist, well worthy of his position. His name is J. H. Wirthman.

527

SIDNEY SUMMERS

(Farmer, Post-office, Harlem).

Mr. Summers, as a farmer, has the benefit of a good education, which by no means is a small advantage. He took a course at the William Jewell College and acquired a good knowledge of the higher branches. Though a native of Kentucky, he was partly reared in this county, his parents having come here from Woodford county, that State, in 1858. He was born in Woodford county, March 14, 1842. His father, Adam H. Summers, was originally from Virginia, which he left at the age of 20. He was married in Woodford county to Miss Dolly Flemming. They had eight children, three of whom are living. He died here in 1865. Mr. Summers, Sr., was a farmer by occupation and a man in comfortable circumstances. He was a useful and well respected citizen. The mother is also deceased. Sidney Summers after he grew up was married in this county to Miss Bettie Russell, a daughter of Andrew Russell, whose sketch appears in this volume. They have one child, Lelia. He and wife are members of the Christian Church. Mr. Summers is a farmer by occupation and has a good place of 213 acres.

LLEWELLYN TILLERY

(Farmer and Stock-raiser, Post-office, Barry).

Mr. Tillery was a son of Capt. Clayton Tillery, one of the early settlers and well known and highly respected citizens of Clay county. He came here when a young man away back in 1821 and made his home in this county until his death, which occurred at an honored old age, in 1868. He was a farmer by occupation and was in comfortable circumstances. For thirty years he served as magistrate for Gallatin township and in old muster days he had command of a company of militia and was said to be a fine drill master, being a man of prepossessing military presence and a thorough disciplinarian. He was married soon after coming to Clay county but his wife only survived her marriage a short time, leaving two children at her death. Capt. Tillery was subsequently married to Mrs. Annie M. Vaughn. Three children were the fruits of Capt. Tillery's last union, one of whom was Llewellyn, the subject of this sketch. Capt. Tillery was an earnest and exemplary member of the Primitive Church. His last wife was also a member of that denomination, as was likewise his first wife. Llewellyn Tillery was born on the old family homestead in Gallatin township, November 3, 1843, and was reared on a farm, receiving as he grew up a common school education. On the outbreak of the Civil War, in 1861, although then only about 17 years of age, he enlisted in the Southern service, becoming a member of S. P. Daugherty's company, and remaining out until the close of the war. Young Tillery took part in thirteen principal engagements, and was twice wounded, being disabled by his wounds for a period, altogether, of

HISTORY OF CLAY COUNTY

five months. He made one of the bravest of the brave soldiers of the South and on more than one field of carnage and death attracted the attention and admiration of his comrades by his gallantry and intrepidity. Among the numerous great battles of the war the writer recalls the following mentioned by him: Pea Ridge, Vicksburg, Corinth, Big Blue, Baker's Creek, Atlanta, Ga., and Franklin, Tenn. After the war Mr. Tillery returned home and resumed farming and stock-raising and soon showed that a brave and faithful soldier could make equally as law-abiding and useful a citizen. Industry and good management soon began to bear their usual fruits, and as the years have come and gone, he has become comfortably situated. Several years after the war, in 1868, he was married in Augusta county, Va., to Miss Lou M. Conger, daughter of John S. Conger, of that county, and he now has an interesting family of children, and is doubtless one of the happiest and most contented of *pateres familias*, at least he has every appearance of being so.

ZATTU TODD

(Farmer, Post-office, Harlem).

Zattu Todd was born in Howard county, Mo., February 4, 1818. His father, Elisha Todd, was one of the first settlers of that county, coming there from Kentucky as early as 1809. He served in all the early Indian troubles in that part of the State. Subsequently, in 1822, he removed to Clay county. He was married in Estill county, Ky., in 1806, to Miss Sarah McMahon. She died in Clay county in 1849, and he also died here. They had five children, two of whom are living. Zattu Todd was principally reared in this county, and has made farming his life occupation. His place contains 330 acres, which is fairly improved. Mr. Todd has lived a peaceful home life, as had been his greatest desire. In 1845 he was married to Miss Margaret Rickets. She died 11 years afterwards, in 1856, having been the mother of five children, one of whom only, Mary E., now the widow of Roly Porter, is living. To his second wife Mr. Todd was married April 7, 1857. She was a Miss Mary A. Darby. She, too, was taken from him by death, dying August 24, 1872, without issue. Mr. Todd was married to his present wife, Miss Martha A. Morris, January 13, 1874, by Elder H. M. Richardson. She was the daughter of Darius and Maria Morris, of Mason county, Ky., and a member of the Missionary Baptist Church.

JOHN F. WHITAKER

(Farmer, Post-Office, Blue Eagle).

Mr. Whitaker was one of the early New England school teachers who came West from New Hampshire, away back in the "Forties." He was educated at Kimball's Union Academy, in New Hampshire, and came out to Kentucky in 1846. He taught school in that State two years, and then came to Clay county, Mo., where he continued teaching. Altogether he taught some fifteen years. A New Englander by nativity and education, he was very naturally a Union man during the war, and served in the militia of this State. Since retiring from the school-room, however, his principal occupation has been farming. He has a neat place of 80 acres, and is regarded as one of the industrious, intelligent farmers of the vicinity. Mr. Whitaker's first wife, who was a Miss Mary Chandler before her marriage, a daughter of Mack and Nancy Chandler, survived her marriage eighteen months, dying in 1850, and leaving one child: John W. His present wife was a Mrs. Dunsworth, relict of Jackson Dunsworth. They were married August 1, 1867. She was a native of Ohio, and a daughter of Elias and Ellen Reagen. She is a member of the Baptist Church. Mr. Whitaker was born in Sullivan county, N. H., May 9, 1825, and a son of Emery and Mary (Colston) Whitaker. His father, who was a farmer, died there in 1863, and his mother, originally from Vermont, died in Kentucky in 1878. They had a family of eight children, five of whom are living.

ADDENDUM.

In the first line of the first paragraph, on page 211, in the account of the battle of Blue Mills — it is stated that the Federals were "marching gaily along," etc., when a "galling fire was suddenly opened on them from both sides of the road." This would indicate that the Federals were marching in column along the road when fired on. Since the account was put in type, the compiler has been assured by Maj. L. M. James, of the Caldwell Home Guards, who was present, and now resides near Kingston, Caldwell county, that when fired on, the Federals were advancing in line of battle, extending from east to west on both sides of the road, the line having been so formed about five minutes, and an advance of 100 yards made before the Secession troops opened fire. Maj. James says that the locality and presence of the enemy had been discovered, but their exact position was not known, and that the Federal advance was conducted with reasonable prudence and caution.

HISTORY OF CLAY COUNTY

Adams, Araminta - 433
Adams, J.H. - 200
Adams, James and Sarah A. - 433
Adams, James F. - 428
Adams, Jas. H. - 273
Adams, Joshua - 377
Adams, Mattie - 423
Adams, Pleasant - 104, 377
Adams, Thos. - 509
Adams, Wm. - 383
Adkins, "Calhoun" - 291
Adkins, D.J. - 173, 177, 336
Adkins, Darwin - 289
Adler, Davie - 306
Adkins, Downing O. - 291
Adkins, Edward - 291
Adkins, Elizabeth - 512
Adkins, Emma - 226
Adkins, Leonidas - 291
Adkins, Lucinda - 360
Adkins, Robert - 289
Adkins, Wyatt - 113, 122, 282
Adkinson, James - 342
Adler, Bettie - 306
Agricultural Society, Clay County - 182
Aimmerman, Jos. - 450
Ainsworth, R. - 277
Aker, Bettie - 399
Aker, Preston - 399, 426, 427, 509
Akers, Preston - 383, 426, 452
Akers, Rev. - 379
Albright, M.M. - 454
Albright, Daniel - 464
Albright, Eliza - 464
Albright, Wm. - 454
Alexander, W.L. - 217
Allcorn, Andrew - 389
Allcorn, J.M. - 383
Allcorn, James - 389, 393
Allcorn, Sarah - 393
Allen, B. - 215
Allen, D.C. - 92, 97, 187, 222, 288
Allen, Dewitt C. - 292
Allen, Dinah A. - 157
Allen, James - 377
Allen, Dr. John - 295, 510
Allen's Landing - 118
Allen, Mary - 511
Allen, Nimrod D. - 511
Allen, O.D. - 509
Allen, Shuball - 94, 103, 107, 118, 125, 129, 292, 295, 377
Allen, Wm. - 106
Allison, Jane - 501
Allnut, Byron - 454
Almy, Helen - 455
Almy, Hiram and Rebecca - 455
American Fur Co. - 118
Ammons, Henry - 152
Anderson - 224
Anderson, Amos - 427
Anderson, Bill, - 252, 254, 267
Anderson, Henry - 427, 456, 468
Anderson, John - 427, 483
Anderson, Jos. and Mary - 456, 462, 483

Anderson, Kitty - 499
Anderson, Margaret - 462
Anderson, Mary - 468, 499
Anderson, Presley - 455
Anderson, Robert S. - 456
Anderson, Spencer - 455, 499
Anderson, Spencer and Catherine - 468
Anderson, T.L. - 275
Arbold, Arabella - 450
Archer, Martha - 405
Archer, Samuel - 412
Arnold, Alfred - 452
Arnold, Alvira - 450
Arnold, Franklin G. - 458
Arnold, H.W. - 458
Arnold, Harriet - 450
Arnold, J.B. - 463
Arnold, Lewis and Arabella - 458
Arnold, Mollie E. - 512
Arnold, Nettie - 463
Arnold, Thos. - 512
Arnold, Wm. - 458
Arhold, W.H. - 457
Arthur, Michael - 177, 285
Arthur, Turnham & Stephens - 119
Ashby, Daniel - 107
Askew, Daniel - 269
Atchison, Benj. A. - 459
Atchison, D.R. - 136, 209, 213, 215, 380
Atchison, David R. - 115, 126, 129, 156, 154, 169, 187
Atchison, Wm. - 459
Atkins, John - 450
Atkins, Jonathan - 404
Atkins, Robt - 141
Atkins, Wyatt - 98
Auhaha - 94
Aull, J. & R. - 119
Aull, Jas. - 100
Austin, Robt - 215
Austin, Wm. - 173
Averatt, Howard - 103, 106, 112, 377
Averett, Matthew - 106, 377
Averett, Wm. - 114, 377
Averett, Zachariah - 94, 106, 377

Babcock, Rev. - 383
Bacon, Thos. - 287, 288
Bailey, Bishop - 248, 422
Bailey, Geo. - 104
Bailey, O. George - 377
Baily, Christopher - 426
Bainbridge, D. - 281
Bainbridge, Darius - 423
Roker, Catherine - 459
Baker, Josiah - 527
Baldwin, Andrew - 298, 379
Baldwin, Caleb - 135
Baldwin, George - 298
Baldwin, Lucy A. - 501
Baldwin, Mary - 379
Ballard, J.B. - 390
Ballard, Thomas - 390
Barbour, John T. - 511
Barbout, Wm. H. - 512
Barger, Annie - 388

531

HISTORY OF CLAY COUNTY

Barnard, Landa - 434
Barnard, Mary - 434
Barnes, Richard S. - 512
Barnhart, Robert - 439
Barnhart, Minerva - 439
Barrett, Louisa - 499
Barrett, Nancy K. - 499
Barrett, Olivia - 499
Barrett, T.W. - 499
Barrett,/Wm. - 499
Barrett, Wm. M. - 160
Barlett, Angus - 256
Barthelette, Louis - 113
Barry, Patrick - 287
Bartleson, Andrew - 94
Bartleson, John - 94, 106, 114, 377
Barton, A. - 426
Basley, Charissa - 426
Bass, Eli - 273
Basset, S.T. - 386
Bassett, ST. - 388
Baster, John - 283
Baster, Stephen - 498, 499
Bates, Barton - 244
Bauer, C. - 450
Bauman, Maria - 473
Baxter, Jas. D. - 230
Baxter, John - 100
Bay, W.V.N. - 244
Beal, Wm. - 509
Beall, Wm. N.R. - 175
Beauchamp, John - 298
Beauchamp, Robbison - 298
Beaumont, Thomas - 288
Becker, Mary - 489
Becket, Margaret - 312
Beecher, Henry Ward - 181
Beierlein, Andreas - 450
Beierlein, An. H. - 450
Beil, Jsseph - 287
Begole, John - 298
Bell, Catherine - 392
Bell, E.D. - 383
Bell, Fielding - 397
Bell, George - 383
Bell, Geo. A. - 215
Bell, John M. - 107
Bell, Sanford - 153
Bell, Sarah - 397
Bellow, John - 511
Bellow, Wm. M. - 511
Belt, George - 288
Bennett, Lewis - 168
Benson, E.A. - 386
Benson, W.C. - 388
Benton, Mourning - 502
Benton, Thos. H. - 149
Bernard, John - 428
Bernard, Sarach - 428
Bernard, Sarah - 433
Berry, John - 328
Berry, John A. - 201
Berry, Katharine - 328
Berthold Mansion - 199
Best, Humphrey - 95
Bethel, Bluford - 500
Bethel, Chester - 500

Bevins, David - 107, 460
Bevins, James - 322
Bevins, R.E. - 482
Bevins, T.T. - 470
Bevins, Truman and Annie - 460
Bickery - 375
Big Shoal - 94
Bigelow Brothers - 267
Bigelow, John - 248
Bigelow, Simeon G. - 248
Bigelow, Solomon G. - 230
Biggers, Major - 231
Binswanger, Solomon - 164
Birch, Jas. H. - 137, 146
Birch, Thos. C. - 130
Bird, A.N. - 281
Bird, Asa - 389, 499
Bird, Benton - 427
Bird, Greenup - 260
Bird, William - 259
Bishop, Edw. and Eliza - 461
Bishop, George - 461
Bishop, John - 465
Bishop, Kezia - 465
Bissett, James - 247
Bivens, John - 382
Bivens. Missouri - 360
Black, G.L. - 281, 499
Black, Grandison - 278
Black Hawk War - 123
Blackstone, Lavena - 423
Blackwood, Gideon - 488
Blackwood, William - 429
Blake - 428
Bland, H.A. - 358
Bland, James - 333
Bland, Rebecca - 333
Blank, Wm. H. - 286
Blevins, Barbara - 522
Blink, Catherine - 489
Blue Lodge - 170
Blue Mills - 208
Blue Mills Landing - 205
Blue Mills Wounded - 218
Bluffton - 95
Bogan, James - 219
Bogard, Captain - 134
Boggess, Dennis - 429
Boggess, French - 328
Boggesss, James - 429
Bogess, Price - 328
Boggs, Jos - 101, 113
Bogle, D.K. - 342
Bohart, James - 324. 379
Bond, Mr. - 451
Bond, Bradley Y. - 247
Bone, E.F. - 383
Boone, Austin - 388
Boone, Melissa - 430
Boregard, Alpheus - 430
Boregard, John - 430
Boren, Malinda - 495
Bourgmont, M. de - 90, 91
Bouton, S.W. - 184
Bower, G.M. - 273
Bowlin, Delaney - 93
Bowls, S.D. - 308

532

HISTORY OF CLAY COUNTY

Bowman, Thos. J. - 230
Boyd, Colonel - 209
Boyles, John - 377
Bradford, Larkin 201, 288
Bradhurst, Jacob - 511
Bradhurst, Mary D. - 511
Bradley, J.W. - 379
Bradley, James - 281
Bradley, John - 278
Bradley, Samuel - 446
Bradley, T.K. - 288
Bradley, Terry - 277
Bradshaw, Mary - 370
Bradley, John 278
Brand, Jas. and Catherine - 489
Brand, Rachel - 488
Brasfield, Amanda - 393
Brasfield, Annie - 314
Brasfield, Eliza - 414
Brasfield, J.C. - 426
Brasfield, Jas. - 424
Brasfield, John - 288, 431, 432
Brasfield, Laura - 409
Brasfield, Leonard - 301, 324, 414
Brasfield, Thos. and Elizabeth - 431
Brasfield, Wiley - 432
Brasfield, Wm. - 300, 314
Brashear, Cyrus - 347
Brashear, Roxanna - 347
Bratten - 383
Bratton, Isabella - 373
Bratton, James - 373
Brawner, David and Sarah - 457
Brawner, Mary J. - 457
Breckinridge, Lynn and Eleanor - 431
Breckenridge, W.A. - 129, 371
Breckinridge, Mary J. - 371
Breckinridge, Eleanor - 426
Breden, Alice - 330
Bridge, First - 119
Bright, Jos. - 123
Brining, Wm. - 259
Brinkmeier, Elder - 378
Brinkmeier, H. - 450
Broadhurst, John - 257, 513
Brock, John - 153
Brock, Rebecca - 396
Brock, Winfield - 306
Bromson, Samuel - 511
Bronaugh, David T. - 514
Bronaugh, John - 514
Brooks, A.D. - 182
Brooks, Abijah - 423
Brooks, Abijah and Harriet - 436
Brooks, J.E. - 201
Brooks, James - 438
Brooks, Louisa - 409
Brooks, M.B. - 343
Brooks, Mary - 436
Brost, John J. - 509
Brost, Mary - 509
Brown, A.S. - 336
Brown, David - 182
Brown, Elizabeth - 520
Brown, H.D. - 412

Brown, Hugh - 95, 509
Brown, J.M. - 453
Brown, John - 180, 184, 202
Brown, Jos. - 95
Brown, Shelton - 452
Brown, Wm. - 378
Browner, David - 458
Browner, Mary J. - 458
Browning, Lucy - 435
Bruene, Henry - 450
Brummett - 96
Brunly, Elder - 378
Buchanan, Rachel - 426
Buchholtz, J.W. - 450
Buckingham, Elizabeth - 440
Buckgraye, James - 377
Burbank, John - 277
Burden, Robt - 123
Burdenk, R.H. - 452
Burgess, Anna - 466
Burgess, Charlton B. - 461
Burgess, Jos. - 462
Burkhead, S. - 333
Burnam, Joel - 129
Burnet, George - 123
Burnett, Geo. - 112
Burnett, Peter H. - 126
Burnette, Amanda - 525
Burnham, C.N. - 388
Burnham, Jas. A. - 215
Burns, James - 233, 287
Burns, Jane - 509
Burns, Jeremiah - 509
Burns, Lewis - 149
Burris - 280
Burris, David - 302
Burris, L.W. - 177, 186, 225, 233, 289, 381
Burris, Luke W. - 191, 255, 301
Buster, Chas. W. - 514
Buster, Jas. J. - 514
Buxton, Wm. - 390
Byrd, Greenup - 233
Byrd, M. - 432
Byrd, Wm. and Mary - 432

Cain, Robert - 115
Caffrey, John J. - 287
Caldwell Home Guards - 530
Caldwell, Mrs. Robert - 385
Calhoun, A.J. - 168, 204, 206, 222, 229, 237, 257.
Calhoun, Alexander - 303
Calhoun, Samuel -305
Calhoun, Thos. - 395
Call, James - 209
Callaway, John W. - 164
Callaway, Peter - 428
Callerman, Bass - 509
Callerman, John - 509
Calvert, Captain - 254
Cameron - 183
Campbell, Albert - 388
Campbell, Alexander - 286
Campbell, Elizabeth - 520
Camron, Elisha - 377

533

HISTORY OF CLAY COUNTY

Campbell, James – 133, 134
Campbell, Louisa – 330
Campbell, Nancy – 466
Campbell, Samuel W. – 520
Campbell, Thos. – 94
Campbell, Wm. – 94, 116, 383, 515
Camron, Elisha – 95, 103, 115, 123, 352, 376, 377,
Camron, Jonathan – 106, 377
Capitol Mills – 520
Capp, Captain – 219
Capps, John – 182
Caples, W.G. – 287
Carey, Anna – 218
Carey, Daniel – 318
Carpenter, Amos – 515
Carpenter, Benj. 153
Carpenter, Dan – 509, 515
Carpenter, Paley – 152
Carpenter, Wm. – 516
Carr, Dabney – 106
Carrell, John – 106
Carroll, James – 377
Carroll, John – 377
Carroll, Nancy – 403
Carter, Mr. – 457
Carter, Rev. – 383
Carter, Richard – 391
Carter, S.H. – 389
Carthage, Battle of – 205
Carthrae, Chas. – 119
Carson, Wm. – 273, 274
Casey, Eli – 283, 380
Case, Thos. – 288
Catherwood, Colonel – 224
Catheroood, E.C. – 223, 253
Cates, Richard – 205
Cave, Elizabeth – 494
Cave, Urial and Susan – 494
Cave, Uriel – 451
Celvinger – 388
Cerry, Jas. & Catherine – 509
Cever, J.C. – 453
Chancellor, Elizabeth – 413
Chancellor, James – 413
Chancellor, John – 323
Chandler, Mary – 530
Chaney, Nathan – 107
Chaney, Richard – 106
Chaney, Sallie – 472
Chanslor, Anderson – 152
Chapman, A.L. – 383
Chapman, John – 377
Chauncey, John – 282
Chevis, Thos. – 222, 286
Childs, Colonel – 208
Charlston, S. – 383
Chisis, Annie – 509
Chisis, Thos. – 509
Chorn, James – 144
Chouteau, F.P. – 100, 114
Chouteau, Pierre – 93
Christy, J.C. – 141
Chrisman, John – 259, 306
Chrisman, Joseph – 306
Christa, Ellen – 423
Christa, Wm. – 423
Churchill, Samuel – 187

Childs, Kit – 224
Clack, S.S. – 255
Clardy, G.C. – 423
Clardy, G.W. – 426
Clardy, Giles – 433
Clardy, J.B. – 433
Clardy, Wm. – 426
Clark, Benj. – 153
Clark, Uncle Dick – 496
Clark, Edw. – 449
Clark, Finis – 376
Clark, Giles – 423
Clark, Hannah – 516
Clark, James G. – 307
Clark, James H. – 307
Clark, Jesse – 271
Clark, John – 208, 454
Clark, Philip – 287
Clark, Richard – 499
Clark, Samuel – 516
Clark & Wilson – 141
Clark, Wm. – 92, 308, 324, 450
Clary, Norman – 433
Clause, Emma – 456
Clause, Geo. and Elizabeth – 456
Clay, H.B. – 423
Clay, Henry – 98
Clay, S.G. –509
Clay Co. Savings Assn. – 259
Clements, Arch – 247, 269
Clemson, James – 93
Clevenger, B.B. – 386
Clevinger, Jasper – 416
Clipper Newspaper – 452
Cloud, Martin – 142
Clover, H.H.A. – 244
Cobb, Jesse – 357
Cobb, Mary – 357
Cockrell, Francis M. – 309
Cockrell, Judson – 309
Cockerell, Vard – 228
Coffee, John T. – 228
Coffman, David – 248
Cole, Zerelda – 266
Coleman, Henry – 287, 288
Collett, Jos. – 115
Collier, John – 230, 377
Collins, Amelia – 226
Collins, Elizabeth – 458
Coolier, James – 328, 377
Collins, Jesse – 336
Coolins, Jno. W. – 152, 383
Collins, S.N. and Jane – 458
Collins, Wm. – 377
Colly, Patton – 253
Colly, Colston, Jas. – 250
Combs, J. – 388
Combes, Mary – 523
Compton, Gershom – 100
Confederates – 221
Conger, Lou M. – 529
Conington, Thos. – 152
Conley, Dr. – 376
Conn, John and Elizabeth
Conn, Mary – 470
Conway, Dr. – 283
Conrow, Aaron H. – 200
Cook, E.C. – 460

534

HISTORY OF CLAY COUNTY

Cook, Georgia - 493
Cook, James and Lucy - 493
Cooley, Frank - 380
Cooley, Jennie - 523
Cooper, Ben - 256, 257, 512
Cooper, Mary - 512
Copelin, Andrew - 106
Corbin, B.B. - 289
Corbin, Benjamin - 310
Corbin, Dr. - 356
Corbin, Lucy - 356
Corbin, Ovid - 310
Corbin, W.H. - 289
Corneulius, Absalom - 377
Cornelius, Benj. - 377
Cornelius, John - 377
Corum, Alfred - 257
Corum, Bersheba - 422
Corum, Eleanor - 423
Corum, James - 257
Corum, Nancy - 429
Corum, W.C. - 386
Corum, Wm. - 422
Costello, James - 462
"Cottage Home"- 385
Cotton, Caltha - 362
Cotts, Abram - 377
Couch, J.C. - 261
Courtney, Archilbald - 311
Courtney, A.C. - 173
Courtney, John - 311
Courtney, Jos. - 141
Courtney, Josephus - 463
Cox, Angeline - 252
Coryell, Lucy - 452
Crabster, Edward - 152
Cracker's Neck - 197
Crafton, Eli - 312
Craig, Benj. - 509
Craig, H.K. - 198
Craig, R.R. - 275, 276
Crasford - 383
Craven, Emily - 452
Cravens, C.L. - 386
Cravens, Dr. - 451
Crawford, A.B. - 427
Crawford, Alex B. - 434
Crawford, Captain - 129
Crawford, Mary - 96, 280, 476
Crawford, Nathan - 463
Crawford, Smith - 125, 463
Crawford, Vincent S. - 160
Creek, Abraham - 106, 107, 114, 421
Critchfield, Elliott - 218
Croach, W.A. - 388
Crockett, David - 377
Crockett, Jos. - 377
Cronin, Lucinda - 488
Crouse, C.M. - 510
Crow, Mattie - 423
Crow, Sarah - 423
Crowley, Captain - 204
Crowley, G.W. - 201
Crowley, Lide - 388
Crowley, Sam - 271
Croysdale, Abraham - 119
Crump & Thompsom - 183

Cruzat, Francisco - 91
Cullen, Peter - 287
Culver, H.C. - 267
Culver, Dr. Henry - 303
Cummons, Wm. - 296
Cunningham, - 284
Cunningham, Hannah O. - 144
Cunningham, Oliver H. - 144, 183
Curd, Mundy - 467
Curd, W.A. - 281
Curtis, Cyrus - 287
Cusick, Pat - 164
Cutler, A.P. - 453, 454
Cutler, S.L. - 453

Dagley - 271
Dagley, Bettie - 504
Dagley, Ellen - 413
Dagley, James - 377
Dailey, Alvis - 247
Dale, Mary - 146
Dale, R T.R. - 163, 255
Dale, Timothy - 449, 453
Dale, Weekley - 126, 449, 450
Dallis, George - 449
Damon, George - 313
Darby, Lon - 510
Darby, Mary A. - 529
Daugherty, S.P. - 528
Davenport, Mary E. - 435
Davenport, Wm. - 152, 201
Davidson, Martha - 404
Davis, Albert - 152, 408
Davis, Easter - 509
Davis, Edther - 509
Davis, Harmon - 114
Davis, Henry - 383
Davis, Herman - 458, 509
Davis, Hermon - 114
Davis, John - 93
Davis, Jos. - 452
Davis, Lucy - 408
Davis, Maggie - 356
Davis, Samuel and Eliza - 313
Davis, Sarah - 230
Davis, W.H.H. - 408
Davis, Wm. Sr. -377
Davis, William H.H. - 313
Davis, Wm. T. - 230
DeBerry, Alwilda - 432
DeBerry, J.D. - 426
DeBerry, J.D. and Mary - 426
DeBerry, John - 432
DeCourcey, Thos. W. - 139
Dean, Henry Clay -187
Dean, John - 94
Dearborn, J.A. - 286
Decier, Moses and Malinda - 495
Decker, Martha - 495
Denham, Silas - 479
Denny, George - 314
Denny, John - 314, 365
Denny, Mattie - 365
Denton, Jonathan - 377
Dever, Alexander - 257
Dever, Arthur - 257
Devlin, Joseph - 383

535

HISTORY OF CLAY COUNTY

Dibble, M. - 177
Dickerson, Elizabeth - 423
Dickey, J.C. - 386
Dicky, Sarah - 469
Diester, Christopher - 527
Dill, David H. - 212
Dillingham, Henry - 342
Dillingham, Elizabeth - 342
Dillon, Matthew - 287
Dillon, Wm. - 388
Diner, H. - 450
Ditto, Abraham - 464
Ditton, Eliza - 461
Ditto, Eliz. - 476
Ditto, J.P. - 476
Ditto, Jos. - 464
Ditto, Wm. - 464
Divine, Matthew - 437
Divine, E.A. - 437
Dobbins, Johanna - 494
Dockery, W.E. - 287, 383
Dodge, Wm. O. - 219
Doniphan, A.W. - 126, 129, 134, 136,
    160, 177, 182, 191, 192, 194, 195,
    200, 20', 225, 274, 275, 276
Doniphan, Alex. - 140, 293, 296, 345
Doniphan, Alex. W, - 142
Doniphan, John - 233
Donovan, Elza - 392
Doniphan, Gen. - 285
Donnelly, Bernard - 287
Donovan, E.P. - 383
Donovan, J.M. - 383.
Donovan, James - 392
Donovan, Park - 240, 247
Dolley, Samuel - 509, 517
Dougherty, Hannah - 316
Dougherty, John - 136, 172, 173, 317,
    319
Dougherty, L.B. - 207, 220
Dougherty, Lewis B. - 397
Dougherty, Major - 93
Dougherty, O'Fallon - 219
Dougherty, Robert - 316
Dougherty, Taylor - 152
Dougherty, W.W. - 286, 288
Dougherty, Wm. and Ellen - 316
Dougherty, Wm. W. - 315
Diuglas, Geo. and Jane - 427
Douglass, John W. - 164
Downing, Chas. - 323
Downing, Eliza - 371
Downing, Joseph -454
Downing, Sarah - 323
Draper, Benj. - 177
Drew, Washington W. - 518
Drohan, Wm . F. - 287
Drum, R.C. - 102
Drumhiller, Captain - 224
Dr7den, John D.S. - 244
Dryden, Milton - 257
Dryer, H. - 450
Duane, D.J. - 218
DuBois - 90
Ducker's Ferry - 133
Dudley, James W. - 412
Dudley, Katie - 412
Duggen Nancy - 477

Dulin, E.S. - 276, 277
Dunbar, James - 130
Dunbar, James - 128
Duncah, Alex - 116, 426, 482
Duncah, Annie - 438
Duncan, D.T. - 452, 494
Duncan, David - 451
Duncan, Helen - 426
Duncan, J.W. - 201
Duncan, Jas. - 120, 421
Duncan, Jennie - 482
Duncan, Mary - 325
Duncan, Stephen and Amelia - 438
Duncan, Stephen C. - 434
Duncan, Theo. - 201, 202, 203
Duncan, Wm. - 146, 421
Dundee Company - 519
Dunkerson, Cincinnati - 511
Dunkin, D.T. - 452
Dunn, Geo. W. - 222, 245
Dunn, J.C. - 204
Dunn, John - 168, 201
Dunn, John C. - 188
Dunn, John H. - 386
Dunn, Judge - 199
Dunsworth, Mrs. Jackson - 530
Dupuy, Bartholomew - 505
Duval, James - 281
Duvall, James - 378
Dyke, John - 123
Dykes, John - 450, 489
Dykes, John and Susan - 489

Earickson, Peregrine - 107
Early, Whitfield - 219
Easham, Elizabeth - 341
Eastin, James - 464
Eastin, John - 479
Eastin, R.J. and Nancy - 466
Easton, Bushwakker - 235
Eaton, James R. - 278, 319
Eaton, Madison - 494
Eby, Adam - 453
Ecton, Elizabeth - 426
Ecton, John - 256, 328, 422
Edwards, John - 450
Edwards, P.N. - 281
Edwards, Pres. N. - 380
Eichenberger, J.J. - 450
Elby, Adam - 454
Elgin, G.S. - 382
Elgin, S. - 383
Ellet, Jas. - 153
Ellington, "Pelig" - 116
Elliott, A.K. - 427
Elliott, Arthur - 519
Elliott, Edward - 519
Elliott, Geo. - 378
Elliott, Hattie G. - 519
Elliott, James - 341, 519
Elliott, Lewis - 518
Elliott, Margaret - 519
Elliott, Peter - 378
Elliott, R.B. - 452
Elliott, Zachary - 519
Ellis, A.C. - 187
Ellis (Died in California Gold Rush)
    -153

HISTORY OF CLAY COUNTY

Ellis, Sidney L. - 525
Ellison, Elizabeth - 442
Elmore, Rush - 175
Elston, B.F. - 501
Ely & Curtis - 100, 111
Ellis, John - 275
Ely, Lewis B. - 278
Elzea, G.W. - 510
Emerson, A.J. - 281, 454
Endicot, Margaret - 519
Endicott, Catherine - 509
Endicott, W.M. - 427
England, J.C. - 466
England, J.W. - 489
England, James and Nancy - 466
English, Chas. - 108
English, John - 509
English, Jonathan - 509
English, Polly - 509
Enlow, Rebecca - 438
Enlow, Thomas and Sarah - 438
Enterprise-Richfield - 173
Eorphage, H. - 450
Erastus, Wm. - 377
Essex & Hough - 100, 105
Estes, America - 313
Estes, Anderson - 153
Estes, Dinita - 488
Estes, Eliz. - 312
Estes, F.O. - 427
Estes, Geo. - 153
Estes, Henry - 94, 98, 115, 122, 173, 282, 312
Estes, Henry and Lucinda - 450, 488
Estes, Joel and Rachel - 450
Estes, Mill - 114
Estes, Peter - 94
Estes, Sarah - 201
Estes, Thos. - 94, 105, 106, 115, 152, 322
Estes, W.W. - 152, 313
Estes, Wm. & Joel Mill - 101
Estes, Wm. and Lainda - 301
Estes, Wm. W. - 322
Evans, Amanda - 515
Evans, James C. - 519, 520
Evans, John - 104, 106, 114, 115, 519, 520
Evans, R.P. - 204
Evans, Richard - 329
Evans, Wm. - 515
Evans, Wm. B. - 519
Everett - 286
Everett, T. - 383
Everts, Ben R. - 230
Ewing, Finis - 323
Ewing, J.B. - 323
Ewing, John D. - 140
Ewing, Robert C. - 323
Ewing, Thos. J. - 240

Falconer, Eliza U. - 342
Falconer, Nelson - 342
Far West Newspaper - 284
Farbis, J.F. - 191
Farr and Woolbridge - 164
Farrar, Benj. - 198
Faubion, Melinda D. - 513
Faubion, Jacob - 513

Faucett, Martha - 419
Feigat, Louis - 450
Ferguson, Lucinda - 441
Ferguson, Wm. - 389
Ferries - 101
Ferrill, Daniel - 119
Derrill, David - 449
Fetts, J.J. - 499
Field, J.T. - 237
Field, Jas. T. - 259
Field, Joseph - 308, 393
Field, Joseph Thornburg - 323
Field, Mary - 309
Field, Thos. - 393
Fields, Lina - 428
Fields, Newton - 383
Fields, Susan - 446
Fillery, E. - 450
Finley, John M. - 146
Finley, Travis - 98, 114, 498
Fish, H.C. - 386, 393
Fish, Hamilton - 394
Fish, Samuel - 394
Fisher, Merritt - 383
Fisher, R. - 168
Fitch, John and Sarah - 469
Fitch, Maggie - 469
Fitzgerald, Richard - 453
Fitzgerald, Theodoric - 426
Flack, J.V.B. - 384, 385, 386, 388, 395
Flack, M.S. - 388
Fleet, A.F. - 278
Fleming, R.W. - 182
Fleming, Samuel - 428
Fleming, Dolly - 528
Flemming, Lt. -232
Fleming, P. - 120, 507
Flemming, R.W. - 229
Flemming, Robt. - 243
Flemming, Robt. W. - 240
Fletcher, Jeffrey - 377
Foley, Elijah - 396
Foley, Henry C. - 396
Foley, James - 287
Follett, King - 135
Ford, Austin - 501
Ford, J.H. - 221, 251
Ford, Mrs. J.H. - 256
Ford, Jailer - 206
Ford, James D. - 324
Ford, James H. - 325
Ford, Robert A. - 500
Foree, A.T. - 173
Forre, Asa T. - 172
Foree, Jos. - 464
Foree, Martha - 464
Foreighner, Adam - 470
Fort Leavenworth - 102
Foster, Eleanor - 509
Foster, John - 509
Foster, John A. - 523
Foster, Missouri A. - 523
Foster, Susan - 509
Fowler, Chas. - 450
Fowler, John - 397
Fowler, Joseph and Mary - 397
Fowler, Robt. Y. - 106

537

HISTORY OF CLAY COUNTY

Fowler, William - 396
Frafenstein, Lieut. - 381
Fraher, James - 287, 325, 355
Fraher, Michael - 287
Fraher, Philip - 287, 325
Fraher, Thomas - 325, 326
Frame, Thos. - 452
Frampton, James and Elizabeth - 461
Frampton, Martha - 461
Francis, Pearle - 327
Francis, Sarah - 372
Francis, Wm. J. - 327
Franker, G.W. - 385
Frazer, J.F. - 383
Frazer, Mary Ann - 325
Frazer, Thos. - 325
Frazier, J.S. - 287
Frazier, John - 316
Frazier, Mary - 316
Free, Elizabeth - 378
Free Soil - 171
Frey, Margaret - 379
Frick, John H. - 471
Frick, Nicholas - 450
Fritzlen, Cynthia - 365
Froman, M.G. - 385
Frost, Elijah - 111
Frost's Ferry - 101
Frost, Thos. - 111
Fry, Abram - 380
Fry, Margaret - 416
Fry, Solomon - 95, 119, 123
Fugate, Hiram - 115
Funk, Chas. - 397
Funk, J.R. - 510
Funk, John and Nancy - 436
Funk, Jonathan - 435
Funk, Mary - 396
Funk, Richard - 379, 397
Futsle, Mary - 290

Gamble, Hamilton R. -106, 220, 228
Gano, Daniel - 381
Gardner, Benj. - 521
Gardner, Frank - 520
Gardner, John - 520
Gardner, Vernon - 521
Garlichs & Hale - 141
Garlichs, F. - 155
Garner, J.C. - 186
Garnett, W.C. - 278
Garret, Wm. P. and Angeline - 467
Garrett, A.S. - 454
Garrett, Ambrose - 467
Garrett, Berryman - 388
Garrett, Jackson- 499
Garrett, L.B. - 499
Garrett, L.P. - 386, 388, 454
Garrett, L.W. - 386
Garrett, Laban - 100, 111, 252
Garrett, W.P. - 454
Garrison, Flavel - 305
Garth's Militia - 250
Garth, Captain - 234, 235, 524
Garth, W.G. - 229
Garth, W.W. - 237
Garth, Wm. G. - 201, 230, 328
Garvey, W.S. - 229

Gash, O.P. - 383
Gash, Dellie C. - 521
Gash, Henry Hill - 521
Gash, Jos. D. - 516, 521
Gash, M. Lee - 521
Gash, Pauline - 516
Gash, T.K. - 205
Gashwiler, Susan - 366
Gasney, Thos. - 331, 455
Gates, John P. - 106
Gatewood, Julia - 299
Gaur, Margaret - 378
Gaw, Frances - 486
Geib, Christopher - 329
Geib, John - 329
Gentry, David and Lousa - 442
Gentry, Druggist - 440
Gentry, Jane - 496
Gentry, Martha - 442
Gentry, Richard - 124
George, Alwilda - 390
George, Bailey - 104
George, Baley and Jemima Withers- 398
George, George Washington - 397
George, Wm. - 390
Germans, St. Louis - 204
Gibbons, Dinah - 509
Gibbons, Thos. - 509
Gibbs, Luman - 135
Gilberth, Jane - 497
Gilberth, Jos. and Mary - 497
Gill, David P. - 509
Gill, E.G. - 400
Gill, Henry - 153
Gill, Julia - 378
Gill, T.Y. - 383
Gill, Thos. Y. - 380
Gillam, Robert 377
Gillespie, A. - 188
Gillespie, George - 330
Gillespie, J.W. - 201
Gillespie, James - 329
Gillespie, Jas. A. - 207
Gillespie, Jas. W. - 212, 215
Gilliam, Cornelius - 94, 121, 280, 376
Gilliam, Jesse - 103, 104, 105, 111
Gilliam, Letitia - 367
Gilmer, R.G. - 380, 381
Gilmer, Robert - 381
Gilmore, James - 103, 111
Gilmore, - 376
Gilmore, James- 95, 280
Gilmore, Robert - 95, 280, 289
Gilpin, Wm. - 143
Gittings, Darius - 255. 259
Giros, Armorer - 196
Givinner, F. - 257
Gladdin, Jas. - 106
Glasscock, Sampson - 388
Glover, Samuel - 275
Golmer, R.J. - 413
Goodson, John - 423
Goodwin, Joseph - 331
Goodwin, Wm. - 331
Gordon, B.T. - 423
Gordon, C.H. - 251
Gordon, John - 288

538

HISTORY OF CLAY COUNTY

Gordon, Judge - 358
Gordon, T.C. - 177, 225, 240
Gordon, Thos. - 332
Gordon, Thomas C. - 255
Gordon, Wm. F. - 331
Gorlich, Frederick - 288
Gosney, Bettie - 457
Gosney, Fielding - 468
Gosney, John - 427
Gosney, Richard - 467
Gosney, Susan - 468
Gosney, T.M. - 450
Gosney, Thos. - 457, 467
Gosney, Thos. M. - 173
Gosneyville - 427,
Gow, Elizabeth - 497
Grafenstein, Lt. - 266
Gragg, Samuel - 119
Gragg (Killed in California Gold Rush)
  - 153
Graham, F.M. - 427
Graham, J.D. - 386
Grant, John - 205
Grant, Nathaniel - 196, 198
Grant, P.B. - 286
Grant, Peter - 288
Grant, Samuel M. - 153
Gravenstein, Lt. - 235, 236
Graves, Franklin - 281
Graves, T.H. - 389
Gray, James - 107
Greason, Gideon - 469
Greason, W.O. - 454
Greason, Wm. O. - 468
Green, Duff - 109
Green, James S. - 187,
Green, John R. - 230, 237
Green, Major - 236
Green, Martin E. - 208
Greene, Henry - 377
Greene, Lewis - 377
Greenfield, Samuel G.T. - 436, 479
Gregg, David - 106
Gregg, Hannon - 336
Gregg, Josiah - 336
Greggy, Margaret - 336
Gregory, Jane - 307
Griffith, Annie - 393
Griffith, James - 393
Grigsby, Catherine - 359
Grigsby, Charlotte - 332
Grimes, Joel - 423
Grimes, John - 426
Grimes, Lizzie - 423
Grimes, Louis - 423
Grimes, Lucinda - 426
Grimes, Ruth - 423
Grimes, Sallie - 423
Grimshaw, Owen - 224
Grisby, Wm. - 286
Groom, A. - 281
Groom, Amos and Sallie - 472
Groom, Jacob - 93
Groom, Jane - 281
Groom, John - 452
Groom, John S. - 142, 207, 334
Groom, Joseph - 334, 336, 397

Groom, Mary J. - 472
Groom, Michael - 226
Groomer, Elizabeth - 450
Grooms, Captain - 231
Grooms, Isham - 377
Grooms, James - 306, 353
Grooms, John - 353
Grooms, Jos. - 95
Gromes, Pheoba - 402
Grooms, Wm. - 428
Groesbeck, John - 219
Grubbs, E.M. - 383
Grubbs, Hardin and Elizabeth - 399
Grubbs, Judson - 399
Guernsey, Otis - 426
Guitar, O. - 240
Gumm, John - 115
Gwinn, Berryman - 377

Hadley, Catherine - 334
Hadley, Samuel - 141, 146, 334
Haggerty, Thos. - 140
Hagner Bribe - 196
Hale, Jas. E. - 114
Halfacre, Geo. - 104
Halferty, J.D. - 386
Hall, Ailsey - 281
Hall, Anna - 338
Hall, Bill - 252
Hall, Edw. V. - 377
Hall, Elisha - 105, 106, 281
Hall, Eliza - 290, 430
Hall, G.D. - 452
Hall, James E. - 377
Hall, John - 105, 338
Hall, Sarah - 405
Hall, W.A. - 288
Hall, Willard P. - 137, 144, 222
Hall, Wm. - 103, 104, 452, 485
Halloway, Colonel - 203
Ham, Ann - 509
Hamilton, David - 107
Hamilton, Henry - 454
Hamilton, Robert - 428
Hamlin, Alive - 438
Hampton, Wade - 358
Hancock, Benj. - 101
Hancock, James - 177
Hand, G.R. - 509
Hand, S.R. - 423
Hanley, Thos. - 276
Hannibal & St. Louis - 183, 262
Hardin, Chas. - 221
Hardin, Chas. H. - 191
Harding, Chester - 267
Hardwick, Mrs. - 381
Hardwick, S.H. - 257,
Hardwick, Samuel - 187
Hardwicke, Alex - 377
Hardwicke, Eliz. - 380
Hardwicke, John - 107, 377
Hardwicke, Lewis - 377
Hardwicke, Philip - 336
Hardwicke, Sam - 288, 336, 355
Harlem - 508
Harmon, Jacob - 470
Harmon, John - 389, 470, 488

HISTORY OF CLAY COUNTY

Harmon, John T. - 469
Harmon, Margaret - 488
Harmon, Reese and Nancy - 470
Harpe, Big & Little - 127
Harper, John D. - 343
Harper, Thos. - 342
Harrel, Mr. - 284
Harrington, Susan - 407
Harrington, Thos. - 407
Harris, Alida - 452
Harris, George - 452
Harris, John - 95, 103, 106
Harris, O. - 388
Harris, Josephine - 485
Harris, Lura - 478
Harris, Marion - 378
Harris, Mary - 490
Harris, O.G. - 450
Harris, O.H. - 202
Harris, Solomon - 485
Harris, Susan - 378
Harris, Thos. A. - 208
Harris, Tyree - 274
Harris, Wm. - 478
Harrison, Henry - 206
Harrison, Lennie - 350
Harrison, Jason - 273
Harrison, M.C. - 350
Harsell, A. - 186
Harsell, Anthony - 116, 125, 202,
    229, 280, 299, 448
Harsel, Captain - 231
Hart, Joe - 234, 235
Harter, Abraham and Anna - 471
Hartel, Frederick - 450, 470
Hartel, Peter - 450
Haskill, Mrs. S.J. - 325
Hassel, John G. - 495
Hatcher, T.E. - 274
Hawkins, Alfred - 128, 130
Hawkins, B.F. - 182
Hawkins, John C. - 471
Hawkins, Nancy - 441
Hawkins, Wm. - 452, 471
Hayes, Benj. - 139
Hayes, Fannie - 437
Haynes, Milliner - 225, 259
Hays, G.H. - 427
Healy, Daniel - 287
Hedges, James - 286
Hedges, P. - 388
Hedges, James and Nancy - 450
Hehner, Peter - 450
Heinz, Christina - 474
Heisinger, Mr. - 267
Heisinger, Unionist - 267
Henderson, Geo. - 472
Henderson, Samuel - 202
Hendley, Judge - 283
Hendly, John - 120
Henry, James - 377
Hensely, Sam - 377
Hensley, Benjamin - 94
Herald of Freedom - 424
Herbert, Johannah - 325
Herndon, Eliza - 426
Herndon, Emeline - 426
Herndon, S.P. - 426

Herndon, Wiley - 380, 382
Hessel, Conrad - 450, 473
Heseel, Jacob - 473
Hessel, Jacob - 450
Hetherly, Ann - 127
Hetherly, George - 127
Hetherly, Jenny - 127
Hetherly, Thomas - 127, 128
Hetherly War - 127
Hezner, Alma - 433
Hezner, Dr. J.L. - 433
Hiatt, James - 280
Hickman & Lamme - 100, 111
Higgason, A.E. - 509
Hicks, Catherine - 455, 468
Higbee, Elias - 135
Hightower, James - 452
Hill, Elizabeth - 496
Hill, Henry - 281, 378, 418, 450
Hill, James - 378
Hill, Richard - 94, 106, 280
Hinkle, G.W. - 134, 135
Hinkston, Harlow - 499
Hinton, I.T. - 273
Hixon's Mill - 101
Hixon, Mr. - 283
Hixon, Thos. - 95
Hixson, Henry B. - 152
Hixson, J.H. - 152
Hixson, Jasper - 153
Hixson, Jasper M. - 152
Hobbs, Albert - 218
Hodge, Annie - 363
Hodge, Dr. John - 363
Hoff, Barbara - 471
Hogen, Louisana - 278
Hodges, Judge - 474
Hodges, W.V. - 406
Hoges, Wm. - 378
Hodges, John - 474
Hodges, Mary - 406
Hogrefe, H. - 450
Hogrefe, Henry - 378
Hogrefe, Heinrich - 450
Holdes, Thos. - 378
Hollenbeck, Miss - 476
Hollingsworth, Elias - 486
Hollingswoth, Eliza - 486
Hollingsworth, Geo. - 205
Hollingsworth, Samuel - 499
Holloway, Mary Ann - 506
Holloway, Spencer - 506
Holmes, David - 377
Holmes, S.H. - 260
Holt, Jerry - 454
Holt, John - 381
Holt, Captain - 204
Holt, Jerry - 453
Holt, John B. - 475
Holt, Mrs. - 388
Holt, P.G. - 385, 386, 388
Holt, Phil - 386
Holt, Rolla - 385
Holt, Wm. - 454
Holton, J.B. - 385
Holzbeirlein, Elder - 378
Holtzclaw, Archibald - 115, 427
Holtzclaw, Franklin - 427

HISTORY OF CLAY COUNTY

Holtzclaw, Peter - 134, 427
Homer, Wm. - 153
Hood, Robert - 100, 105, 111
Hope, Thos. - 386
Horner, David - 522
Horner, Joseph - 522
Hough, Harrison - 193
Houser, Christian - 107
Houston, John - 380
Howdeshell, Margaret - 96, 97, 280, 375
Hubbach, Mary - 348
Hubbard, James - 325
Hubbard, Moses - 493
Hubbard, R.G. - 224
Hubbell, W.D. - 274
Hubble, Wm. D. - 151
Huddleston, Susan - 306
Hudson, Belle - 341
Hudson, J.M. - 341
Hudtison, Nancy - 334
Huey, James - 388
Huff, Mary - 353
Huffaker, Catherine - 501
Huffaker, Geo. - 377
Huffaker, George - 112, 377
Huffaker, Geo. W. - 153
Huffaker, Jos. - 383, 475
Huffaker, Samuel - 383
Huffaker, Walter - 286
Huffaker, Washington - 153, 286, 475
Huffman, Ezekiel - 105, 106, 421
Hughes, A.S. - 120
Hughes, Allen - 364
Hughes, Andrew S. - 115, 116, 126
Hughes, Daniel - 115, 339, 340
Hughes, F.C. - 151
Hughes, G.L. - 287
Hughes, George - 272, 339
Hughes, Graham - 380
Hughes, Graham L. - 139
Hughes, J.M. - 288
Hughes, James - 522
Hughes, Jas. M. - 100, 141
Hughes, John - 486
Hughes, John T. - 200, 220, 228, 231
Hughes, Louisa - 364
Hughes, Patrick - 287, 522
Hughes, Roland - 273, 274, 276
Hugley, Jacob - 383
Hulin, Taylor - 230
Hull, Milton - 383
Hulott, Wm. - 509
Hulse, Mary and Polly - 427
Hume, Jennie - 208
Hume, Mary - 329
Hume, Thomas - 208
Humes, Henry - 446
Hunsaker, William - 277
Hunt, Ellen - 423
Hunt, M.O. - 388
Hunt, M.P. - 454
Hunt, Sallie - 423
Hunt, Samuel - 423
Hunter, John - 476
Hunter, R.M. - 476
Hurt, Cleopatra - 458
Hurt, Ellen - 491

Hurt, Joel and Sallie - 458, 491
Huston, J.S. - 186,
Hutchings, John - 103, 105, 111, 253
Hutchings, Moses - 399
Hutchings, Nancy - 378
Hutchings, Simon - 378
Hutchings, Smith - 253
Hutchins, John - 98, 282
Hutchins, Jos. - 377
Hutchins, Moses - 377
Hutchins, Robert - 377
Hutchins, Smith - 377
Hutchins, Wm. - 377
Hutchinson, Squire - 95,
Hutsell, Malinda - 435
Hyatt, Jas. - 94
Hyatt, Samuel - 94, 377
Hyder, Benj. - 428
Hymer, Wm. - 205

Imhoff, M. - 165
Indians - 87, 88, 89, 95, 106, 107, 116
Industrial Luminary - 172,
Irminger, Anna - 379
Irminger, Eliz. - 379
Irminger, Heinrich - 379
Irminger, John - 379
Irminger, Lizzie - 471
Irminger, Rudolph - 379
Irminger, Susanna - 379
Isley, Austin - 477
Isley, G.M. - 454
Isley, George - 476
Jack, Thos. - 107
Jackson, Claiborne F. - 106, 185, 190
Jackson, Congreve - 143
Jackson, Hancock - 186
Jackson, Jas. A. - 522, 523
Jackson, Samuel N. - 522
Jackson, W.M. - 274
Jackson, Wade - 273, 274, 276
Jacobs, Chas. - 400
Jacobs, Clayton - 400
Jacobs, Fannie - 370
Jacobs, Henry - 370
Jaggers, Benj. - 229
James, Alexander Franklin - 265, 266
James Boys - 265
James, Bushwacker - 235
James, Frank and Jesse - 153
James, Frank - 153, 226, 235, 236, 265, 266, 267, 268, 277, 381,
James, James - 377
James, Jesse - 250, 265, 267, 270, 276
James, Joel - 438
James, L.M. - 530
James, M.L. - 209, 230
James, Mary - 502
James, Moses L. - 209
James, Rev. Robert - 153, 265, 266, 267, 274, 276, 281
James, Susie - 266, 268
James, Widow - 266
Jartin, Andrew and Jane - 436
Jartin, Sallie - 436
Jenkins, Tilford - 402

541

HISTORY OF CLAY COUNTY

Jennett, James L. - 401
Jennison's Red Legs - 526
Jesse, Francis - 422
Jesse, Juliet - 422
Jesse, Richard - 422
Jesse, Woodford - 422
Jewell, William - 182, 273, 275, 276
Jewell, Wm., College - 212, 506
Job, Ibe - 134
Johnsey, J.W. - 287
Johnson, Alexander - 305
Johnson, Annie - 390
Johnson, Chas. C. - 523
Johnson, E.D. - 209, 219, 224
Johnson, Greenup - 329
Johnson, H.B. - 232
Johnson, Harry - 523
Johnson, J. - 383
Johnson, Jacob B. - 523
Johnson, James - 237
Johnson, Jas. H. - 523
Johnson, Jasper - 362
Johnson, Losa L. - 523
Johnson, Maria - 329
Johnson, Mary B. - 523
Johnson, Mary Robertson - 305
Johnson, Philip - 523
Johnson, Robert - 115
Johnson, Rachel - 433
Johnson, S.S. - 427
Johnson, Thos. - 523
Johnson, W.B. - 383
Jones, A.B. - 286, 423, 450
Jones, George - 340
Jones, H.M. - 139
Jones, J.M. - 255
Jones, Jas. - 206
Jones, Jas. M. - 259
Jones, Keziah - 525
Jones, Lewis - 93
Jones, M.R. - 383
Jones, R.H. - 426
Jones, Samuel - 237
Jones, Sheriff - 174
Jones, Wm. - 341
Judson, Docia - 446
Julius, John - 451
Jung, J.J. - 450
Justus, J.F. - 426
Justus, James - 251

Kaiestner, Maria - 493
Kaltenbach, F. - 450
Kaltenbach, Rev. - 378
Keas, L.B. - 489
Keatley, Catharine - 468 462
Keith, Perry - 152
Keller, J.M. - 151
Keller, Jacob - 341, 342
Keller, James - 342
Keller, James M. - 341
Kennedy, Jane - 315
Keller, John - 291, 341, 380
Keller, John R. - 141, 342
Keller, Martha - 291
Kelly, E.V. - 208
Kemper, B.W. - 250
Kemper, Captain - 249, 253
Kennedy, Dennis - 287

Kerr, Wm. H. - 172
Keyser, Benj. - 153
Kiley, Dennis J. - 287
Killer, John R. - 191
Killgrove - 388
Kimball, T.T. - 224
Kincaid, Wm. M. - 138
King, Abel - 153
King, Austin A. - 130, 135, 222, 255
King, Daniel - 524
King, Hubert U. - 524
King, Joel - 107
King, Martin A. - 523
King, Moses - 426
King, N.H. - 389
King, Randolph - 153
King, Richard - 389
Kipper, Jane - 413
Kirby, J.W. - 250
Klaunn, Mary K. - 524
Klauun, Peter - 524
Koehler, Maggie - 400
Koenig, Elder - 378
Koenig, Geo. - 450
Kolar, Catharine - 373
Knighton, E.F. - 510
Knights of Palermo - 245
Knous, Nathan - 132
Kraus, Jacob - 426
Kraus, John P. - 524
Kraus, Philip - 524
Krauss, James - 426
Krauss, Margaret - 426
Krekel, Arnold - 244

LaRue, Jesse and Jancy - 477
LaRue, Wm. - 477
Lackey, Jane - 467
Lafore, Sarah - 489
Lafore, Wm. - 489
Laffoon, Richard - 201
Lakin, Jas. F. - 217
Lamb, Joab - 453
Lambert, W. - 287
Lamborn, Wm. - 288
Lampkin, L.D. - 426
Lampson, J.F. - 453
Lampton, Louisa - 445
Lane, Flora - 368
Lane, Jim - 181
Lane, William H. - 368
Laney, Jane - 96
Laney, Patrick - 95, 96, 375, 377
Lankford, Elias - 223
Lard, Moses - 286, 426
Lard, Moses E. - 158, 167
Lawrence, A.J. - 427
Lawrence, John - 451, 452
Lawson, L.M. - 182
Lewright, Mattie - 321
Lawson, Leonidas - 277
Leach, Alworthy F. - 437
Leach, Daniel and Eliz. - 472
Leach, Dr. Wm. - 438
Leach, Nannie - 472
Leach, Wm. B. - 478
Leakey, Evaline - 404
Leard, John D. - 146

542

HISTORY OF CLAY COUNTY

Leath, Cotton - 437
Leavell, L.W. - 478
Lecompt, S.D. - 175
Ledgwood, John - 377
Ledwith, Z. - 287
Lee, Eliza - 352
Lee, John - 352
Lenhart, Wm. - 95, 377
Leonard, Abiel - 106
Leonard, Luther - 174
Leonard, Reeves, - 240
Lerty, John - 425
Leonard, T. - 288
Letton, "Ling" - 257
Letton, Neneon - 253
Levi, S. - 173
Lewis and Clark - 92
Lewis, J. - 237
Lewis, L.M. - 201, 287, 383
Lewis, Merriwether - 92
Lewis, Nancy - 378
Lewright, Wm. P. - 321
Leyba, Ferdinando - 91
Liberty - 100
Liberty, Bank 0f - 220
Liberty Arsenal - 174, 195
Liberty Blues - 129
Liberty Home Guards - 201
Liberty Landing - 118, 280
Liberty Tribune - 173, 188, 202, 220,
    225, 350
Lightburn, Alvin - 141, 343
Lightburne, A. 166 223, 287, 288
Lightburne, Richard - 344
Lightburne, Stafford - 344
Ligon, S.S. - 425
Ligon, W.C. - 274, 276
Ligon, Wm. C. - 275, 276
Liles, David - 96
Liles, Wm. - 96
Lincoln, Abraham - 114, 299
Lincoln, Ann - 299

Lincoln, C.J. - 229
Lincoln, Catherine -   322
Lincoln, Albert - 479, 450
Lincoln, Archibald - 230
Lincoln, David - 115, 322
Lincoln, Geo. - 114, 299
Lincoln, Julia - 299
Lincoln, Arch - 229
Lincoln, James E. - 481
Lincoln, John - 377
Lincoln, Thomas - 141, 299
Lindeman, Elizabeth - 509
Lindsey, Geo. B. - 525
Lindsey, J.N. - 525
Lindsey, John P. - 525
Lindsey, Sarah - 503
Lindsey, Thomas - 525
Ling, John R. - 454
Lingfelter, Louisana - 474
Linn, John - 383
Linn. L.F. - 383
Linville, Abraham - 94
Linville, John - 377
Linville, Richard - 101, 103, 106,
111,   113

Lionberger, Isaac - 274
Lisles, David and Wm. - 375
Litchfield, A.T. - 360
Litchworth, J.M. - 151
Litton, N.W. - 427
Litton, Nin. - 251
Lively, Elizabeth - 399
Livingston, John - 377
Livingston, Rev. - 426
Livingston, Wm. - 377, 558
Lloyd, John - 423
Lloyd, Nancy - 423
Lockett, Thos. - 277
Lockett, Thos. F. - 276
Logan, Larz - 482
Logan, Philip - 113
Lomax - 380
Long, F.R. - 233, 236, 255
Long, Garrard - 141
Long, Jas. - 142
Long, Peyton - 247, 251, 269
Long, Reuben - 119
Longs, The - 152
Lord, J.A. - 509

Love, Jas. - 182, 259, 261, 272
Loyd, Abner - 427
Loyd, John - 421
Lucas, W.P. - 306
Luke, J.W. - 499
Luminary - 173
Lynd, S.W. - 274
Lynn, Flora - 504
Lyon, Nathaniel - 201, 203

McAlester, B. - 277
McAlpine, Agnes - 298
McAlpine, Wm. R. - 298
McAtee, Belle - 438
McCafferty, Jas. P. - 218
McCall, Moses - 427
McCarty, Annie - 340
McCarty, Captan - 205
McCarty, Frank - 286
McCarty, Thomas - 142, 144, 163,
                204, 205, 340
McCarty, W.A. - 229
McCarty, Wm. - 340
McCarty, Wm. A. - 229
McClelland, Jas. - 104,
McClelland, Walker - 106
McClintock - 158
McClintock, A.K. - 142
McCord, J.S. - 230
McCorkle, Montgomery - 305
McCown, James - 448
McCown, John - 449
McCoy, Fielding - 119
McCoy, Jacob - 377
McCoy, Moses - 235, 306
McCoy, Robert - 377
McCracken, Francis - 427
McCracken, John - 389
McCray, D.O. - 385, 386
McCray, David - 402
McCray, Wm. and Nancy Carroll -
    403

543

HISTORY OF CLAY COUNTY

McCrorey, Thomas - 438
McCrory, John - 153
McCroskey, Isaac - 377
McDaniel, John - 140
McDaniel, R. E. - 273, 274, 275,
McDuff, Peter - 183
McElwee, David - 95, 280, 375, 376
McElwee, James - 96
McElwee, Sarah - 96
McElwee, Wm. - 96
McEwen, H. G. - 287
McEwing, Rev. - 383
McGarth, Sarah - 522
McGaugherty, Simpson - 163
McGaughey, S. - 141
McGee, Amelia - 519
McGee, B.L. - 454
McGee, Boston - 453, 454
McGee, Chas. - 94, 281, 282
McGee, James and Julia - 427,
McGee, James H. - 519
McGee, Mahala - 427
McGee, Samuel - 94, 427
McGee, Jane - 427
McGee, Thos. - 427
McGee, W.P. - 214
McGinnis, Cassie - 478
McGinnis, James - 478
McGowan, Hugh - 287
McGree, Zachariah - 106
McGregory, Matt - 426
McGrew Bros. - 281
McGuire, Isabella - 512
McIlvaine, Archibald - 498, 499
McIntyre, Wm. H. - - 453
McKee, David and Elizabeth - 402
McKee, Melvin - 402
McKissick, John - 104
McKneiss - 153
McKnight, Almyra - 491
McKoy, Jacob - 105
KcLain, Andrew - 288
McLain, John - 287
McMahan, Peter - 287
McMahon, Sarah - 529
McMurray, Blythe - 395
McMurray, Captain - 196
McNair, Alexander - 103
McNealy, Eliz. - 378
McNealy, Geo. - 378
McPherson, W.M. - 275
McQuiddy, Elizabeth - 418

Mackabell, A.E. - 428
Madden, Wm. L. - 196
Maddox, Mary - 395
Magee, Chas. - 111
Magill, Samuel - 106
Magill, David - 106, 421
Mahoney, Leonard - 287
Mailes, Henry - 95
Malott, South - 105
Manchester Mill, David 101, 507
Major, Dr. Herman - 482
Major, J.A.S. - 174
Major, John - 281

Major, John S. - 482
Major, Reuben - 483
Major, Sarah - 483
Major, Slaughter G. - 483
Majors, John - 452
Majors, John - 452, 501
Majors, Rufus M. - 501
Mallott, John S. - 115
Manchester, David - 105
Manchester's Mill - 101
Marcellus, Adeline - 484
Maret, Alvah - 222, 233, 259
Marquette, Father - 87
Marr, John - 427
Marsh, Benj. W. - 146
Marsh, Harriet - 315
Marsh, James - 315, 448
Marsh, James T. - 346
Marshall, A.W. - 205
Martin, Gill E. - 116
Martin, Isaac - 94
Martin, John - 437, 460
Martin, Lucinda - 311
Martin, Wesley - 256, 439
Martin, Wm. - 377
Martin, Zadock - 103, 114, 116
Martz, Rev. - 452
Marvin, E.M. - 287, 427
Mathews, Hiram - 388
Maughas, Dr. - 200
Maughas, G.M.B. - 184,
Maupin, N.C. - 390
Maxfield, A.H. - 277
May, Dr. - 376
Maye, Wm. - 378
Mayer, P. - 450
Mayhew, Rev. - 383
Means, Abijah - 106
Means, Andrew - 377, 404
Means, Sarah - 404
Means, Benj. - 124
Means, Foster - 403
Meek's Ferry - 121
Meffert, Frederick - 348
Meffert, Joseph - 347
Melon, B.F. - 383
Melone, H.C. - 288
Melone, Henry - 287, 288
Menger, H.M. - 450
Mereness, Martha - 309
Merritt, John - 312
Messick, John - 348, 350
Messick, Margaret - 350
Nessick, Thos. - 349
Methodists, Northern - 180
Mexican War Volunteers-142
Mezner, Dr. J.L. - 428
Milay, Michael - 287
Milbourn, Zenas - 484
Miller, Belle - 366
Miller, Clara - 354
Miller, D.S. - 197
Miller, David - 354
Miller, Edward - 488
Miller, Editor - 173, 188
Miller, James - 205

544

HISTORY OF CLAY COUNTY

Miller, John - 115, 124, 350
Miller, Linus - 219
Miller, Madison - 147, 275, 288
Miller, R.D. - 509
Miller, R.H. - 366
Miller, Robt. H. - 221, 225
Miller, Robert Hugh - 350
Miller, William - 114
Mills, Mahala P. - 511
Mille, Miss - 289
Mimms Hotel - 502
Mimms, John W. - 502
Mimms, Robt. W. - 502
Mindwiller, Fintan - 287
Minter, Georgia A. - 515
Minter, Jane - 505
Minter, John - 152, 515
Minter, Robert - 220, 388
Mirick, John L. - 231
Missouri City - 205
Missouri Depot - 195
Mitchell, Benj. - 485
Mitchell, Miss C.E. - 303
Mitchell, David - 236
Mitchell, Eliz,- 309
Mitchell, Fannie - 389
Mitchell, G.W. - 454
Mitchell, George - 309, 484
Mitchell, J.A. - 438
Mitchell, Mabry - 404
Mitchell, Mayberry - 107
Mitchell, Thos. - 303
Mitchell, W.B. - 389
Moad, G.L. - 288
Moberly, B.M. - 298
Moberly, Harriet - 298
Moberly, Jas. - 504
Moeller, Maria - 473
Monroe, A. - 281
Monroe, Elizabeth - 281
Monroe, Susan - 302
Monroe, Wm. - 281, 302
Montargee, Calisse - 101
Montgomery, Kate - 521
Montgomery, Raymond - 521
Montgomery, Thos. - 499
Moore, Abram - 379
Mooney, Alex - 450
Moore, David D. - 101
Moore, Edw. - 423
Moore, Elisah A. 352
Moore, J.J. - 221
Moore, James - 323, 351
Moore, Joel - 271
Moore, John - 523
Moore, John J. - 351
Moore, Jonah - 379
Moore, Jos. - 379
Moore, L.P. - 427
Moore, Lucy - 379
Moore, R.H. - 383
Moore, Richard - 164
Moore, Robert H. - 404
Moore, Ruth - 323
Moore, Samuel - 427
Moore, Samuels & Croysdale - 100
Moore, Wm. and Lucinda - 352

Morehead, Chas. R. - 293
Morfit, Henry - 208
Morfit, Kate - 308
Morgan, J.K. - 453
Morris, Charity - 462
Morris, Darius - 529
Morris, David - 173, 205
Morris, G.W. - 188
Morris, George - 288
Morris, Geo. W. - 173, 201
Morris, John - 146
Morris, Major - 206
Morris, Martha A. - 529
Morris, Robert - 452
Morrison, Arthur - 135
Morrison, Thos. - 287
Morrow, R.D. - 509
Morton, Hannah - 514
Morton, Joseph - 287
Morton, R.C. - 182, 240, 286
Morton, Richard - 237, 383, 509
Morton, W.A. - 151, 163, 191, 200,
    212, 229
Morton, Wm. - 153
Mosby, A.G. - 475
Mosby, Albert - 406
Mosby, Amanda - 278, 379
Mosby, Charles - 353
Mobby, Dewilton - 405
Mosby, James - 352
Mosby, John - 405
Mosby, Mary - 418
Mosby, Wade - 318, 352
Mosby, Wade and Rebecca - 405
Moseby, Daniel - 153
Moseby, John H. - 153
Moseby, Nicholas - 405
Moseby, Wade - 158
Mosley, Daniel - 152
Mosely, De Wilton - 230
Moss, J.H. - 187, 229, 240
Moss, Jas. H. - 142, 163, 191, 192,
            200, 201, 206, 229
Moss, O.P. - 129, 134, 137, 142,
            146, 173, 201, 202,
            204, 206, 229, 231
Moss, Woodson J. - 121
Motherhead, Nancy - 436
Motherhead, Nathaniel and Lucina 436
Mothershead, Captain - 204
Mothershead, G.W. - 201, 207
Mounted Rangers - 201, 202, 204
Mour, Caroline - 527
Mour, Wilhelmine - 527
Mudd, Henry - 406
Mudd, Wm. and Eliza - 407
Muehlenbrock, Elder - 378
Muehlenbrock, Henry - 450
Mueller, Conrad and Anna - 492
Mueller, Elizabeth - 493
Mueller, George - 494
Mulligan, Colonel - 207
Munday, Edmund - 95, 107
Munger, Wm. H. - 218
Munker, Jas. - 104, 106, 114
Munker, John - 114
Munkers, Agnes - 378

545

HISTORY OF CLAY COUNTY

Munkers, Berryman - 377
Munkers, James - 377, 378
Munkers, Jemima - 403
Munkers, Lafayette - 378
Munkers, Red - 449
Munkers, Richard - 377
Munkers, Wm. - 94, 377
Munson, Patsy - 511
Murphy, Jas. - 287
Murray, E.D. - 141, 259
Murray, Ephraim D. - 222, 237
Murray, M. - 173
Murray, Robt. - 94
Murray, Thos. D. - 237
Murray, Wm. - 113
Musser, Martha Donaldson - 522
Mustor. Mary - 443
Myall, Richard - 336
Myles, Elizabeth A. - 525

Nall, Fannie - 512
Nall, Henry - 512
Nancy, Polly - 423
Napton, W.B. - 149
Neal, Edward - 525
Neal, John - 201, 288, 525
Neal, Thos. N. - 525
Neally, R. - 141
Neeley, Clement - 407
Neeley, Elizabeth - 399
Neeley, Richard - 407
Neely, Nancy - 395
Neely, Richard - 399
Neeley, William - 399
Neely, R.A. - 186
Neidermeeimer, Elder - 378
Neidermeier, Rev. - 456
Neill, Annie - 356
Neill, Polly - 360
Neill, Rodman - 356
Nelkerson, Ernest - 428
Nelson, Nancy - 470
Netherton, A. -485
Netherton, Abraham - 452
Netherton. Eliza- 452
Netherton, John and Betsey - 485
Neulson, Henrich - 450
Newlee, C.A. - 353
Newlee, Wm. - 353
Newler, E.M. - 514
Newler, Mary - 514
Newlin, Jesse - 130
New Madrid Claim - 102
Newman, Alex - 377
Newman, L.W. - 288
Newman, Lance W. - 354
Newman, Payton, - 354
Newton, Elder - 379
Nichols, Amelia - 404
Nichols, Lydia - 407
Nolan, J.P. - 287
Noland, Patsy - 368
Norfleet, A.L. - 486
Norfleet, Lakkin and Frances - 486
Norman, J.H. - 509
Norris, John - 449
Norton. E.H. - 186, 255, 294

Norton, Elijah H. - 191, 192
Norton, John - 352
Norton, Judge - 352
Norton, Mary - 308
Norton, S.J. - 388, 389
Norton, W.A. - 225
Norvell, Dorotha - 392
Norvell, Robert - 392
Nowlin, B.W. - 226, 235, 246, 380
Nowlin, Bryan - 408
Nowlin, S.D. - 226
Nowlin, Samuel - 408
Nuelsen, Heinrich - 379, 450
Nutter, Darwin J. - 355
Nutter, James and Eliza - 319
Nutter, Sarah - 319

O'Brien, Jordan - 273, 274
O'Bryan, T.N. - 378
O'Bryant, T.N. - 229
O'Neal, O.H. - 182
O'Neil, D.J. - 218
Odell - 388
Odell, George - 253
Odell, J.M. - 386
Oder, Geo. and Louisa - 469
Odgen, Thomas - 142
Odle, Nehemiah - 377
Officer, James - 96, 377
Officer, Robt. - 95, 449, 450
Officer, Thos. - 95, 96, 104, 111, 114, 375, 377
Old Franklin - 95
Older, Sarah - 469
Oldham, James - 356
Oliver, Louisa - 334
Oliver, Mordecai - 147, 178, 222
Oliver, S.A. - 334
Oliver, Samuel - 376
Orleans, Fort - 90
Orr, Samuel - 185
Osage, Fort - 93,
Osborn, R.S. - 237
Osburn, Wm. - 135
Otey, John W. - 187
Overman, C. - 388
Overton, Aaron - 101, 118
Owen, E.G. - 288
Owen, Ed. - 288
Owen, Mary - 428
Owen, Nicholas - 428
Owens, B.C. - 454
Owens, Henry - 426, 435
Owens, John - 94, 103, 104, 105, 116, 122, 281, 282
Owens, Jonathan - 426
Owens, Missouri - 426
Owens, Sam - 133, 299
Owens, Margaret - 299
Owens, Sidney - 299
Owens, Wm. - 381

Page, James - 377
Page, Robert - 377
Pallen, Joshua - 100, 114
Palmer, Annie - 450

546

HISTORY OF CLAY COUNTY

Palmer, F.R. - 286, 383
Palmer, Isaac - 139
Palmer, Martin - 95, 105, 109, 376, 377
Paradise - 427,
Park, Cyrus - 357
Park, Geo. S. - 171
Park, J.W. - 279
Park, Marcus T. - 357
Parker, B.F. - 223
Parker, Captain - 224
Parker, G.E.T. - 428
Parker, Josiah - 287, 288
Parker, Josiah C. - 288
Parker, Mary J. - 426
Parmer, Martin - 96, 109
Parsons, Monroe M. - 186
Patcher, Rufus - 427
Pate, Robert - 177
Patrick, Chas. - 288
Patridge, Chas. - 491
Patridge, Fannie - 491
Patter, Eldridge - 95
Patterson, W.H. and Minerva - 439
Patterson, W.J. - 171
Patterson, Wm. H. - 438
Patton, Dr. - 221
Patton, Hattie - 402
Patton, Jeff. - 208, 210, 213
Patton, Nathaniel - 112
Paw-Paw Militia - 230, 240
Payne, A.H.F. - 139, 286, 422, 426, 450
Payne, Augusts H.F. - 450
Payne, Mayor - 174
Peebley, Thos. - 377
Peery, Sarah - 408
Peery, Thos. - 408
Pence, Adam and Annie - 487
Pence, Adam - 451
Pence, Capt. - 488
Pence, Edw. - 290
Pence, Elizabeth - 290
Pence, Emma - 292
Pence, Samuel - 455
Pence, Thos. - 153
Pence, W.H. - 292
Pence, Wm. H. - 487
Penick, W.R. - 224
Penick's Men - 231
Peper, Mary - 484
Peper, Wm. - 484
Perez, Manuel - 91
Perkins, C.N. - 388
Perkins, David - 273, 274, 276
Perkins, J.W. - 450, 452
Perkins, John - 379
Perkins, Rev. - 383
Perrin, Jasper - 428
Perry, Joab - 261
Perry, W.D.H. - 509
Peters, Anna F. - 351
Peters, John - 283, 351
Petterfield, Eliz. - 452
Pettigrew, W.J. - 286
Petty, Jesse - 310
Petty, Maria - 307
Petty, Sarah - 310

Petty, Wm. - 307
Pettz, L.T. - 389
Pevely, Thomas - 377
Phelps, A.J. - 450
Phelps, Captain - 224
Phelps, Maurice - 135
Piburn, Edward - 409
Piburn, John - 409
Pickerall, Bro. - 509
Pickrell, A.J. - 428
Piernas, Pedro - 91
Pierson, James - 385
Pile, Nancy, - 452
Piper, Margaret - 362
Pipes, A.W. - 488
Pipes, John - 488
Pipes, Nathaniel - 488
Pitt, J.E. - 200
Pitts, Fannie - 364
Pitts, Y.R. - 364
Pixlee, P.C. - 207, 220
Pixler, Wm. - 152
Pixley, Lillian - 414
Platte, Purchase - 125
Plitt, Geo. - 451, 452
Poage, John - 282
Poage, Mitchell - 105
Poage, Robert - 106
Poindexter, J.A. - 228
Pollock, Hannah - 422
Poole, Dave - 234
Poor, John - 98
Pope, Wm. - 212, 215
Porter, A.J. - 450
Porter, Abner J. - 489
Porter, Jo. - 228
Porter, Roly - 529
Porter, Samuel and Mary - 489
Porterfield, W.L. - 494
Posey, James - 410
Posey, Jane - 379
Posey, John - 410
Postlethwaite, Sarah - 430
Poteet, Mary - 280, 376
Powe, Wm. - 122, 282
Powell, Nathaniel - 377
Prather, J.A. - 388
Prather, J.S. - 386
Prather, John A. - 383
Prather, John S. - 411
Prather, Jos. - 378
Pratt, Ida M. - 372
Pratt, M.E. - 372
Pratt, Parley P. - 135
Prege, Elder - 378
Prentiss, Ben M. - 221
Prentiss, N.S. - 168
Preston, Sarah - 310
Price, America - 378
Price, Eben and Sarah - 412
Price, Ebenezer - 174, 375
Price, General - 208
Price, John - 378, 382
Price, John G. - 380
Price, M.F. - 275
Price, MR. - 276
Price, Martin - 389

547

HISTORY OF CLAY COUNTY

Price, Napoleon - 375
Price, R.M.G. - 177
Price, Mrs. Richard - 237
Price, Sterling - 137, 192
Price, Tom - 255
Price, W.E. - 173, 182
Price, Walter - 412
Price, Wm. - 1 378, 379
Price, W.I. - 504
Price, Wm. R. - 411
Price, Winfrey - 271
Price, Mrs. Winfrey E. - 256
Price, Winfrey E. - 155
Priegal, Rev. - 450
Prince, W.E. - 204
Pritt, Humphrey - 377
Proffit, John - 94
Provine, John - 305
Pryor, Jeff. - 248
Pyburne, Edward - 94, 377
Pyle, Alfred - 451

Quantrell, - 224, 234, 240
Quealey, J.A. - 184
Quick, Jane - 378

Rains, J.S. - 204
Rains, Jas.S. - 196
Ralbott, J.B. - 286
Rambaut, Thompson - 276
Ramey, W.S. - 509
Raney, Margaret - 416
Raney, Wm. -416
Ransom, R. - 176
Rarey, T.S. - 183
Raus, John - 450
Ray, John - 95
Ray, Ben B. - 107
Raymond, John - 358
Raymond, Richard - 358
Reagen, Elias - 530
Records, Dr. - 347
Redd, John F. - 193
Reddish, Anna B. - 526
Reddish, Frankie T. - 526
Reddish, Joseph C. - 526
Reddish, Jos. E. - 526
Reddish, Robert - 525
Reed, A.G. - 173
Reedd, Albert - 412
Reed, Allen G. - 358, 360
Reed, Catherine - 506
Reed, James - 160, 235, 413, 452
Reed, Emerine - 413
Reed, James F. - 360
Reed, Jane - 463
Reed, Jonathan - 111, 286, 377
Reed, Joseph - 286, 358
Reed, Missouri - 360
Reed, Nancy - 383
Reed, Robert and Sarah - 428
Reed, T.C. - 383
Reed, Thos. C. - 160
Rees, Amos - 130
Rees, L.N. - 223
Rees, Lewis N. - 130
Rees, Richard - 293

Reeves, Susan - 443
Reid, John - 422
Reed, Jonathan - 286
Reid, Johnny and Sally - 286
Reid, John W. - 143, 196
Reynolds, David - 454
Reynolds, W.T. - 229
Reynolds, Wm. T. - 229, 256
Rhea, Lt. - 254
Rhea, W.E. - 243
Rhea, Wm. E. - 232
Rhinehart, Peter - 452
Rhoads, W.H. - 426
Rice, Claiborne - 111
Rice, Cordies - 309
Rice, John J. - 441
Rice, N.L. - 386
Rice, Nancy - 546
Rice, Richard and Lucinda - 441
Rice, Wm. and Laura - 409
Rich, G.W. - 287
Rich, Rev. - 383
Rich, Hiram - 100
Richards, Lewis - 94
Richards, Noah - 100
Richardson, Mary - 397
Richardson, Samuel - 397
Richfield - 380
Richfield Monitor - 173
Richmond, R.F. - 275
Rickets, Margaret - 529
Rickets, Wm. -331
Ricketts, Benj. - 155
Ricketts, John T. - 520
Rigdon, Sidney - 134, 135
Riggins, B.L. - 326
Riggins, Rosa - 327
Riggs, Charlotte - 434
Riggs, Jonathan - 124
Riggs, Wm. - 386
Riley, A.M. - 225
Riley, Alfred - 449
Riley, Bennett - 120
Riley, Alfred - 353, 489
Riley, D.W. - 423
Riley, H.M. - 362
Riley, Hezekiah - 123, 448, 449, 450
Riley, Hulda - 460
Riley, J.G. - 440
Riley, J.T. - 490
Riley, James - 449, 460
Riley, James T. - 361
Riley, Lewis O. - 489
Riley, Locke - 450
Riley, Dr. S.A. - 440
Riley, Sarah - 475
Riley, Sue - 353
Riley, Wm. M. - 504
Ring, H.H. - 389
Ringo - 100
Ringo, J.W. - 139
Ringo, L.W. - 288
Ringo, S. & A.S. - 119
Ringo, Samuel - 283
Ritchie, John - 106
Rives, Col. - 296
Roane, Hugh - 305

548

HISTORY OF CLAY COUNTY

Robb, David and Joshua - 362
Robb, James S. - 362
Robb, Robert - 362
Robb, Wm. - 362
Roberts, A.J. - 379
Roberts, Aaron - 105, 386
Roberts, Boaz - 206, 231, 232
Roberts, David - 177
Roberts, Dennis, - 411
Roberts, Edw. - 377
Roberts, Jas. - 118
Foberts, John - 377
Roberts, Jonathan - 377
Roberts, Jonas - 377
Roberts, Lina - 207
Roberts, Luella - 411
Roberts, Nicholas - 377
Roberts, P. Smith - 214
Roberts, R. - 177
Robers, W.C. - 423
Roberts, Z. - 287
Robertson, A.W. - 414
Robertson, Andrew -94, 106, 290,
413
Robertson, Hugh - 413
Robertson, L.A. - 207
Robertson, Nellie - 305
Robertson, Ruth - 413
Robertson, Sarah - 459
Robidoux, John - 115
Robinson, Alex - 425
Robinson, Chas. - 178
Robinson, John - 275
Robinson, Minnie - 495
Robinson, Robett G. - 290
Robinson, Wm. H. - 426
Rock Island R.R. - 263
Rock Spring Skirmish - 203, 204
Rodgers, Mrs. A. - 452
Rodgers, Eliz. - 452
Rodgers, Wm. C. - 509
Roe, Robt. S. - 252
Rogers, G.W. - 479
Rogers, G. Mary - 350
Rogers, Thos. B. - 385
Rollins, B.G. - 427
Rollins, Ella - 441
Rollins, Emma - 441
Rollins, Jas. S. - 135
Rollins, John K. - 427
Roper, Benjamin and Nancy - 450
Rose, Jeremiah - 114
Ross, Andrew - 441
Ross, John - 212, 215
Ross, S.J. - 164
Ross, T.K. - 428
Ross, Wm. - 441
Rothwell, China - 363
Rothwell, Dr. - 389
Rothwell, John H. - 364
Rothwell, W.R. - 278
Rothwell, Wm. R. - 363
Rouse, Elder - 378
Rouse, Jas. - 509
Routt, H.L. - 151, 173, 188, 189,
191, 201, 204, 207

Routt, H.M. - 227
Routt, Henry - 365
Routt, Henry L. - 139, 172, 173, 196
Routt, Ice House - 197
Ruberson, John R. - 250
Ruff, C.F. - 143, 219
Ruffin, Edmond - 200
Runk, Richard - 383
Rupe, Mrs. - 256
Rush, Wilburn - 383
Russell, Andrew - 95, 105, 526, 528
Russell, Bettie - 528
Russell, Christopher M. - 526
Russell, Lelia - 528
Russell, Mary Ann - 328
Russell, Mrs. Wm. - 293
Russell, Wm. O. - 166
Rust, Wm. - 479
Ryder, R.P. - 278
Ryland, John F. - 130

St. Bernard bluff - 380
St. Cyr, Stephen A. - 122
St. Louis Republican - 173
Saeger, Wm. - 360
Sales, Annie - 394
Sales, Joel - 394
Sampson, Benj. - 101, 103, 106, 114
Samuel, Archie Peyton - 269
Samuel, Dr. - 266, 267, 268
Samuel, E.M. - 139, 155, 183, 184,
206, 226, 275, 285,
345
Samuel, Edw. - 276, 286
Samuel, Edward M. - 126
Samuel, Reuben - 266
Samuel, Wm. - 510
Samuels, M.M. - 141
Samuels, Reuben - 256
Samuels, Wm. - & Co. - 111
Samuels, Wm. - 100
Sanders, Major - 246
Sans, Daniel - 378
Saunders, J.D. - 490
Saunders, J.P. - 208, 215
Saunders, John and Nancy - 490
Savery, P.M. - 201
Sawyer, J.O. - 277
Scaggs, Carroll - 142
Schackelford, James and Mary - 497
Schenk, W. - 509
Schooe, Rebecca - 518
Schrader, Christopher - 526
Schrage, John - 218
Sconce, Captain - 119
Scott, Alex - 428
Scott, Fernando - 234, 266, 381
Scott, John - 186, 209, 217, 240
Scott, Lewis - 100, 115, 283, 287
Scott, R. - 220
Scruggs, M.D. - 201
Search, Leonard - 282
Searcy, Leonard - 116, 120, 283
Sebree, Uriah - 273
Seddons, J.S. - 224
Sell, Agnes - 471

549

HISTORY OF CLAY COUNTY

Semple, R.B. – 278
Sessions, Captain – 266, 381
Sessions, Darius – 177, 230, 235, 236
Settle, Emily – 293
Settle, Hirman – 293
Seymour, Calvin – 491
Seymour, Nancy – 500
Seymour, Wm. – 491

Shackelford, Agnes – 497
Shackelford, Bettie – 388
Shackelford, Hattie – 463
Shackelford, Ryland – 173
Shackelford, Ryland – 498
Shackelford, Samuel – 164
Shackleford, Sarah – 475
Shackelford, Wm. – 164
Shafer, J.R. – 427
Shafer, Joseph – 426
Shafer, Mary – 432
Shambaugh, Mr. – 221
Shannon, Lewis – 442
Shannon, Wm. H. – 427, 442
Shannon, Wilson – 174
Share, John D. – 317
Sharp, Conrad – 214
Shaver, Henry – 458
Shearin, Owen – 287
Sheets, J.L. – 386
Sheetz, James L. – 355
Shelby, Joe – 228, 254
Shelton, Lewis – 107
Shelton, Wm. – 377
Shepherd, Geo. – 248
Shepherd, Oll – 257
Sherley, Elijah – 349
Sherley, Margaret – 349
Sherman, John – 177
Shields, John – 103
Shipp, L. – 388
Shoffner, Daniel and Barbara – 477
Shoo-Fly – 388
Shores, F. – 383
Shouldis, E.J. – 495
Shouse, John – 309, 380, 504
Shouse, John W. – 503
Shouse, Mary – 405
Shouse, Matilda – 409
Shouse, Rebecca – 353
Shreck, Wm. – 450
Sibley, Geo. C. – 93
Sibley's Landing – 234
Sigel, Philip – 253
Silvey, James and Lucy – 433
Silvey, Phoebe – 433
Simmons, Wm. and Mourning – 415
Simmons, Willis – 414
Simms, Benj. –112
Simms, Zerelda James – 266
Simrall, H.F. – 315
Simrall, Horatio F. – 365
Simrall, James – 365
Simrall, Matilda – 509
Singleton, Julia – 410
Sirpan, J.S. = 452
Skillman, Harriet – 371
Skinner, Martha – 409

Skinner, Phineas – 446
Skinner, Robert – 409
Slack, General – 207
Slater, Wm. – 165
Slaughter, Catherine – 379
Slaughter, Eliz. – 379
Slaughter, Francis T. – 106
Slaughter, Mary S. – 523
Slaughter, Sarah – 504
Slaughter, Thos. – 375
Slaughter, Wm. – 375, 379, 427
Smith, A. – 377
Smith, Albetr – 511
Smith, Amanda – 467
Smith, America – 488
Smith, Annie – 373
Smith, Bennett – 423
Smith, Calvin – 166, 421, 424, 425
Smith, Chas. – 451
Smith, Christian – 373
Smith, David – 256, 258
Smith, E. – 386
Smith, Elijah – 105, 276, 280
Smith, Erastus – 427, 426
Smith, George – 450, 490
Smith, Mary – 490
Smith, Henry – 312
Smith, Hiram – 135
Smith, Humphrey – 420, 423, 425
Smith, Isabell – 490
Smith, J.M. – 488
Smith, Jacob – 467
Smith, "Raccoon" John – 219, 418
Smith, John P. – 499
Smith, Joe – 132, 135
Smith, Lt. – 254
Smith, Marrieta – 395
Smith, Mary F. – 511
Smith's Mill – 101
Smith, Nancy – 423
Smith, P.G. – 389
Smith, R.F. – 209
Smith, Samuel – 395, 415, 450
Smith, Terah – 377
Smith, Thos. – 107
Smith, W.B. – 386
Smith, Wm. B. – 415
Smtih, W.W. – 202
Smith, Wm. L. – 95, 103, 106, 115
125, 282, 380
Smith, Wm. W. – 233
Smith, "Yankee" – 424
Smithey, James – 286
Snaile, J.B. – 425
Snapp, J.W. – 385, 386
Sneed, Sebron G. – 101, 112, 113
Snell, Annie – 487
Snell, Mary – 289
Snethen, Mr. – 93
Snoddy, Elizabeth – 515
Snoddy, Miss M.E. – 496
Snow, Henry – 428
Sons of Malta – 245
Sons of Temperance – 139
Soper, Armilda – 481
Soper, Benj. – 236, 450, 481, 492

550

HISTORY OF CLAY COUNTY

Soper, Benjamin - 450
Soper, Eleanor - 306
Soper, Nancy - 492
Soper, P.T. - 450
Soper, P. Tapp - 492
Soper, Tapp - 202
South, S.D. - 274
South, Wheeler - 214
Sparks, Henry - 521
Sparks, Mary A. - 521
Sparks, Thos. D. - 427
Speares, Lee - 349
Speares, Nannie - 349
Spence, E.M. - 287, 288
Spencer, Barney - 451
Spencer, Thos. - 215
Spencer, Wilson - 377
Spicer - 375
Sprinkle, Laura - 312
Sprinkle, S.H. - 312
Srenck, Wm. - 378
Srite, Elizabeth - 429
Srite, John and America - 429
Stallings - 382
Stanley, D.S. - 203
Stanley, Page - 377
Stanton, Lizzie - 313
Stanton, Samuel - 313
Stapp, Abijah - 429
Stapp, Mary - 429
Stark, C.S. - 205
Starks, Roland - 114
State Guards - 203, 204, 205
Steamboating - 182
Steamer Majors - 212
Steamboat Missouri ; Mail - 144
Steamer New Sam Aaty - 234
Steamboat Tobacco Plant - 139
Steamboat Wakenda - 139
Steamer White Clloud - 205
Stein, A.E. - 203, 213
Stein, General - 206, (A.E.)
Stein, Gideon - 388
Stein, Wm. - 474
Steinmeier, Carl - 450
Stephens, B.C. - 452
Stephens, Richards C. - 123
Stephens, Sally - 281
Stephens, Wm. - 116
Stephenson, Wm. - 116
Stevens, Betsy - 509
Stevens, Carrie - 403
Stevens, Dr. E.W. - 403
Stevens, James - 509
Stevens, Lucinda - 509
Stevens, Thos. - 509
Stewart, Mary - 417
Stewart, O.C. - 288
Stewart, Bob- 188
Stewart, Robt M. - 190
Stifel, Captain - 204
Still, J.B. - 214
Stoffel, James - 449
Stogdale, J.J. - 324
Stogdale, John - 365
Stogdale, Wm. - 366
Stone, Ambrose - 249

Stone, Angeline - 467
Stone, Eleanor - 495
Stone, George - 362
Stone, Millie - 362
Stone, NR. - 182
Stone, R.J. - 362
Stone, Rockwell - 367
Stone, Wm. M. - 218
Story, Captain - 251
Story, Geo. S. - 225, 246
Story, J.S. - 381
Story, Joseph - 381
Story, Joseph - 437
Story, Mary E. - 501
Story, Smith - 114
Story, Thos. - 501
Storz, Mary - 379
Stothard - 380
Stout, Amos - 201, 205
Stout, Chas. D. - 119
Stout, Daniel - 281
Stout, Patsey - 281
Stout, Mrs. R.A. - 329
Stout, R.H. - 201
Stringfellow, B.F. - 173
Strode, Juda - 426
Stroeter, Emaneul and Maria - 493
Stroeter, John V. - 493
Strope, Daniel - 219
Strother, Thornton - 112
Sturgis, S.D. - 219
Sublette, L.B. - 142
Sublette, Linneus - 380
Sublette, Littleberry - 115, 119
Sullenger, John - 330
Sullivan, J.M. - 177
Sullivan, M.W. - 452
Summers, Adam H. - 428
Summers, David - 427
Summers, Mrs. (Farm) - 253
Summers, Lelia - 528
Summers, Mason - 286, 449
Summers, Sarah - 378
Summers, Sidney - 528
Sumner, E.V. - 175
Suter, John - 450
Sutton, Ellen - 346
Sutton, James - 524
Sutton, Margaret R. - 524
Sutton, Margaret R. - 524
Sutton, Temperance - 344
Sutton, Wm. - 346
Swartz, Casper - 443
Swartz, John - 426, 427, 443
Swearingen, Mary - 482
Swearingen, T.H. - 454
Swetnam, Caroline - 286
Swetnam, Chas. - 415
Swetnam, Thos. - 416
Swetnam, Thos. F. - 146
Swetnam, Thos. T. - 286

Talbott, Captain - 204
Talbott, J.B. - 163
Talbott, L.L. - 188
Talbott, L.S. - 201
Talbott, Lysander - 451

HISTORY OF CLAY COUNTY

Talbott, Richard - 205
Tapp, Lucy - 490
Tapp, Nancy - 492
Tapp, Z.M. - 484
Tarwater, W.A. - 287, 383
Tate, J.T. - 450
Tate, John - 426
Taylor, Chas. F. - 247, 249
Taylor, Fletch, - 235, 248, 267
Taylor, Daniel - 199
Taylor, Geo. - 94
Teamer, Mary - 513
Teaney, Samuel and Johanna - 494
Teaney, T.G. - 494
Thatcher, Daniel and Sarah - 431
Thatcher, E.B. - 433
Thatcher, Eleven L. - 444
Thatcher, John - 422
Thatcher, Minerva - 431
Thatcher, Wm. P. -445
Thomas, Robert - 274, 277
Thomason, Grafton - 369
Thomason, J.S. - 229
Thomason, John S. - 230, 250, 268
Thomason, Katie - 369
Thomason, Lt. - 232
Thomason, Martha A. - 503
Thomason, Oscar - 268
Thomason, Wm. - 155
Thompson, B.M. - 129
Thompson, G.W. - 510
Thompson, Gideon - 207, 220, 231
Thompson, J.T.V. - 122, 138, 141,
  177, 188, 225, 275, 276, 345
Thompson, Jas. T.V. - 173
Thompson, Jeff T. - 423
Thompson, John - 286, 377
Thompson, Keziah - 446
Thompson, L.B. - 205
Thompson, M. Jeff - 196, 202
Thompson, M.V. - 345
Thompson, Mary - 436, 443
Thompson, Mary A. - 323
Thompson, Robt - 140, 450
Thompson, Sally - 286.
Thompson, Sarah - 450
Thompson, T.N. - 274
Thompson, Wash. - 231
Thornton, C.C. - 205
Thornton, Colonel -121
Thornton's Ferry - 113
Thornton, J.C.C. "Coon" - 200, 253
Thornton, J.T. - 215
Thornton, John - 94, 95, 101, 103,
  104, 111, 122, 136
Thornton, Major - 206
Thorp, Chas. - 215
Thorp, James- 426
Thorp, Josiah - 107
Thorp, Wm. - 281, 423, 509
Thrail, John - 253
Thurney, Sarah - 378
Tiffin, Clayton - 254
Tigue, Nat. - 268
Tilford, Jane - 458
Tilford, Samuel - 94, 100, 103, 106,
  114

Tillery, Annie E. - 526
Tillery, B.F. - 233
Tillery, Clayton - 526, 528
Tillery, Clinton - 367
Tillery, Eppa - 95, 105, 106, 423
Tillery, Joel - 367
Tillery, Llewellyn - 528
Tillery, M.A. - 341
Tillery, Reuben - 114
Tillery, Samuel - 115
Tillman, Edw. - 445
Tillman, John - 445
Tilman, Edmund - 173
Timberlake, James R. - 368
Timberlake, John - 368
Tipton, John - 509
Tipton, Lucinda - 509
Titus, John - 382
Titus, Noah - 382
Todd, David - 105, 106
Todd, Elisha - 529
Todd, Geo. - 235, 253
Todd, T.W. - 423
Todd, Wm. - 114
Todd, Zattu - 529
Tooley, Victor - 383
Toplenure, John - 377
Torchlight newspaper - 326
Tose, Jere - 377
Town, of Atchison - 380
Town of Richfield - 380
Town of St. Bernard - 380
Towne, D.W.C. - 453, 454,
Towne, Hiram - 453
Townsend, Peyton - 281
Trabue, Samuel R. - 164
Tracey, A.W. - 229
Tracy, Captain - 234
Trader, J. - 379
Trader, J.W. - 450
Trader, Wm.S. - 45 2
Trail, Rachel - 390
Trent, Alexander - 107
Tribune - 283
Trigg, Dinah Ayres - 292
Trigg, Stephen - 292
Trimble, John - 416
Trimble, Wm. and Margaret Fry-416
Trotter, John - 377
Troxler, Wm. - 454
Trudeau, Zenon - 91
Trumbo, Adam and Hannah - 27
Trumbo, Ella - 459
Trumbo, Jacob - 369
Trumbo, John and Ora - 459
Tuley, Geo. C. - 164
Tunnel, Eliza J. - 500
Turner, Jefferson - 378
Turner, John - 94
Turner, Joseph - 378
Turner, Nancy - 296
Turner, Thos. - 423
Turner, W. - 120
Turner, Walker - 372
Turney, J.W. - 267
Turnham, Joel - 115, 118, 123, 172,
  173

HISTORY OF CLAY COUNTY

Turnum, Mary - 472,
Tutt, Amos - 427
Tutt, B.G. - 287

Unger, Wm. - 378
Uriel's Cave - 119
Uttinger, Sarah - 457

Vaghan, Eunis - 95
Vance, Barbara - 422
Vance, Wm. - 422
Vanderpools - 94
Vandivere, Bushwacker - 235
Van Horn R.T. - 255
Van Lear, G.W. - 215
Vaughan, Enos - 122, 282
Vaughan, Thos. - 116
Vaughn, Mrs. Annie M. - 582
Vaughn, Enos - 98, 106, 281
Vaughn, James L. - 427
Vaughn, John - 413
Vaughn, Joshua - 383
Vaughn, Josiah J. - 417
Vaughn, Patsy - 281
Vave, W.R. - 451
Venrick, Samuel - 427
Vertrees, J.C. - 204
Vertrees, Judge - 221
Vesser Family - 95
Vesser, John - 377
Veteto, John - 177
Vincent, Nathaniel - 163
Violett, Dent - 160
Volley, J.B. - 426

Wabash Railroad - 183, 262
Waddell, James - 273
Wade, John - 451
Wagner, David - 244
Wagy, Henry - 495
Wagy, Thos. - 494
Wakarusa War - 174
Welden, Benedict - 377
Walden, Mourning - 415
Walker, H.D. - 224
Walker, Jas. A. - 153
Walker, Katie - 263
Walker, Robt - 141
Walker, Sam - 263
Wall, Lydia - 306
Wallen, America - 518
Wallen, Isaac - 518
Wallen, Mary F. - 517
Waller, Bayard - 379, 383, 423,
  428, 509
Waller, Charles - 450
Waller, Fountain - 172, 173
Waller, G.B. - 426
Waller, J.G. - 327
Waller, J.W. - 383
Waller, James - 452
Waller, John - 152
Waller, Josiah - 286, 379, 427, 509
Waller, Margaret - 450
Waller, Martha - 327
Wallis, Captain - 129
Wallis, G.H. -173

Wallis, Geo. - 119, 125, 135
Wallis, Geo. H. - 142, 164, 417
Wallis, Geo. W. - 153
Wallis, Wm. - 142
Welton, Jane - 379
Ward, P.A. - 287
Warren, Wm. - 423, 458
Warren, Wolverton - 450
Washburn, Larian T. - 212
Washington Guards - 201
Watkins, A. Judson - 505
Watkins, Benj. - 505
Watkins, James - 336
Watkins, Joe B. - 505
Watkins, John & Co. - 505
Watkins, Kate - 499
Watkins, Mary - 499
Watkins Mills - 505
Watkins, Rebecca - 497
Watkins, Walter S. - 139
Watkins, Waltus - 499
Watkins, Waltus L. - 504
Watson, R.C. - 428
Watson, Rev. - 378, 423
Weaver, Elizabeth - 492
Weber, Henry - 379
Weber, Jacob - 378, 39   379
Weber, John - 378, 379
Weber, Katie - 474
Weber, Maria - 379
Weber, Samuel - 378, 379
Webster, Nancy - 490
Weeden, Henry J. - 509
Wells, Betsy - 485
Wells, Mary - 331
Weldon, Benedict - 107
Welton, Michael - 271
Welton, Sol. - 379
Wert, Joe -
West, Mrs. (Cole) - 267
West, Mary - 393
Wetzel, J.W. - 288
Whicher, J.W. - 269
Whitaker, Emery - 530
Whitaker, John F. - 529
Whitaker, John W. - 530
White, Amanda - 443
White, C.J. - 229, 230
White, Castle - 421
White Cloud - 120
White Cloud, Sally - 120
White, Mrs. J.C. - 290
White, James - 214
White, Jeremiah - 418
Whitlock, Columbus - 252, 422
Whitlock, Tarlton - 421
Whitmer, D.P. - 222, 245
Whitsell, Mrs. Emsley - 454
Whitsell, Hirman - 415
Whitsell, Mary A. - 415
Whorton, Martha - 504
Wierna, Michael - 212
Wight. Lyman - 134
Wiglesworth, Lillie - 447
Wiglesworth, Wm.T. and Mary - 447
Wild Bill - 256

553

HISTORY OF CLAY COUNTY

Wilfley, Colonel - 208
Wilhoit, Andrew - 496
Wilhoit, David - 454, 496
Wilhoit, Ella - 467
Wilhoit, James - 496
Wilhoit, Pleasant - 495
Wilhoit, S.B. - 458
Wilhoit, Sarah M. - 502
Wilhoit, Thos. - 467, 502,
Wilhoite, Fielding - 273
Wilkerson, Margaret 446
Wilkerson, W.W. - 426

Williams A.P. - 287
Williams, Adeline A. - 519
Williams, Edward - 519
Williams, I.N. - 388
Williams, I.T. - 281
Williams, J.G. - 426
Williams, James - 377, 446
Williams, Eliz. - 446
Williams, John F. - 240, 292, 379
Williams, Laura - 388
Williams, Mary - 352, 394
Williams, Shrewsbury - 119, 379, 380
Williams, Susie - 292
Williams, Thos. - 380
Williams, Wm. - 377
Williamson, Rev. - 450
Williamson, T.J. - 452
Williamson, Thos. - 428
Wills, James - 146, 173, 421
Wilmot, Canby - 288
Wilmot, J.D. - 452

Willmott, Wm. - 370

Wilson's Creek - 205
Wilson, Isaac - 94, 423
Wilson, Isabella - 423
Wilson, J.R. - 423
Wilson, John - 94, 351
Wilson, Lulu - 351
Wilson, Mattie - 358, 423
Wilson, Nancy - 390
Wilson, Rev. - 383
Wilson, Thomas - 358, 419
Wilson, Thos. W. - 389
Wilson, William - 419
Wilton, John - 377
Winn, Dolly - 299
Winn, George - 479
Winn, Harriet - 479
Winn, J.B. - 205
Winn, James and Malinda - 435
Winn, Jesse - 200
Winn, Maria - 435
Winn, Willis - 173
Winstead, J.T. - 454
Winstln, James - 160
Winston, Rev. - 427
Wirthman, J.H. - 527
Witcher, Wm. A. - 147
Withers, A. - 256
Withers, Abijah - 248, 367
Withers, Albert - 205
Withers, G.W. - 186, 200, 380
Withers, George - 271, 277
Withers, Geo. W. - 164, 172, 173

Withers, Jas. - 152, 378, 379
Withers, Julia - 367
Withers, Martha - 378
Withers, Sarah - 378
Withers, Minnie - 202
Withers, Susan - 378
Withers, Mrs. T.P. - 379
Withers, W.T. - 182
Witt, Emma - 500
Witt, Pryor - 500
Wollery, Jos. - 509
Wood, Gidson - 146
Woods, Isaac - 222, 259
Wood, Jesse T. - 124
Wood, Dr. Joseph - 295
Wood, Kemp M. - 256
Wood, L.F. - 173, 426, 427
Wood, Lewis -134
Wood, Lewis J. - 444
Wood, R.P. - 427
Wood, Wm. T. - 115, 126, 136
Woodruff, John C. - 218
Woods, Archibald - 509
Woods, B.F. - 182
Woods, Elizabeth - 339
Woods, J.C. - 510
Woods, John W. - 205
Woods, Kemp - 446
Woods, Kemp M. - 192. 438
Woods, Virginia L. - 525
Woodson, S.H. - 171, 196, 200
Woodward, Chesley - 111
Woodward, Lance - 354
Woodward, Susan - 354
Woolard, Alex. - 96, 375

Woolard, Jas. - 96, 315
Wooster, John - 177
Worthington, L. - 388
Worthington, L.H. - 388
Worthington, Mary 388
Wright, Elizabeth - 446, 496
Wright, John - 499
Wright, Lucius - 281
Wright, Wm. - 496
Wright, Wm. D. - 455
Writsman, Elizabeth - 504
Writesman, Peter - 114, 377, 504
Wyatt, Mary - 378
Wyman, A.W. - 385
Wymer, W.H. - 141
Wymore, Fannie - 361
Wymore, Geo. - 259, 371
Wymore, John - 372
Wymore, Margaret - 324
Wymore, Martin - 372
Wymore, Samuel - 324, 371
Wymore, Eliza - 371
Wymore, Wm. - 361
Wymore, Wm. H. - 260
Wysong, Amanda - 410
Wysong, L.G. - 410

Yarbrough, D.E. - 383
Yates, Arthur - 497
Yates, Eliza - 496
Yates, Elizabeth - 497

554

HISTORY OF CLAY COUNTY

Yates, Nancy - 450
Yates, Wm. - 118, 450, 497
Yocum, Jesse - 421
York, James - 152, 214
Young, Caroline - 416
Young, John - 331, 373
Young, Martitia - 286
Young, Mary -
Yound, Mattie - 412
Young, Peter - 373
Young, Rev. R.A. - 287
Young, Rosana - 331
Young, Thos. - 114
Young, Thos. J. - 173
Younger, Coleman - 234
Younger's Company - 250
Younger, J.W. - 267
Younger, John - 413
Younger, John W. - 229, 256
Younger, Lucy D. - 514
Youtsey, James C. - 427
Youtsey, John W. - 427
Youtsey, Mary - 443
Youtsey, Peter - 427

Zimmerman, Joseph - 450

Printed in Great Britain
by Amazon